SAFEGUARDING THE REPUBLIC

Essays and Documents in American Foreign Relations 1890-1991

Edited by Howard Jones
University of Alabama

McGRAW-HILL, INC.

New York St. Louis San Francisco Auckland Bogotá
Caracas Lisbon London Madrid Mexico
Milan Montreal New Delhi Paris San Juan
Singapore Sydney Tokyo Toronto

Safeguarding the Republic
Essays and Documents in American Foreign Relations, 1890-1991

2 3 4 5 6 7 8 9 0 DOC DOC 9 0 9 8 7 6 5 4 3 2

ISBN 0-07-033016-6

The editor was David C. Follmer;
the production supervisor was Richard A. Ausburn.
R. R. Donnelley & Sons Company was printer and binder.

Library of Congress Cataloging-in-Publication Data

Jones, Howard, (date).
Safeguarding the republic: essays and documents in American foreign relations, 1890-1991 / [edited by] Howard Jones.
p. cm.
Includes index.
ISBN 0-07-033016-6
1. United States—Foreign relations—20th century—Sources.
2. United States—Foreign relations—20th century.
E743.J64 1992
327.73–dc20 91-28687

Contributors

Wayne S. Cole has been a professor of history at the University of Maryland since 1965. He is the author of six books, including *Roosevelt and the Isolationists, 1932–45* (1983), and *Norway and the United States, 1905–1955* (1989).

Ralph F. de Bedts is Eminent Professor of History, Emeritus, of Old Dominion University. His honors include being named Fulbright Lecturer at the University of Hong Kong and winning a national contest for guest lectureship in American diplomatic history at the National University of Ireland. He is the author of four books, the latest of which is *Ambassador Joseph Kennedy, 1938–1940* (1987).

Robert A. Divine has taught since 1954 at the University of Texas at Austin, where he is the George W. Littlefield Professor in American History. His books include *The Illusion of Neutrality* (1962), *Roosevelt and World War II* (1969), *Blowing on the Wind: The Nuclear Test Ban Debate, 1954–1960* (1978), and *Eisenhower and the Cold War* (1981). In addition, he has edited two volumes of essays on the presidency of Lyndon B. Johnson and a collection of articles on the Cuban missile crisis.

Robert H. Ferrell has taught for many years at Indiana University, where he is now a professor emeritus. He is the author of *Peace in Their Time* (1952) and *American Diplomacy in the Great Depression* (1957), as well as of other books on World War I and the Truman and Eisenhower presidencies.

Joseph A. Fry is a professor of history at the University of Nevada, Las Vegas. He has published *Henry S. Sanford: Diplomacy and Business in Nineteenth Century America* (1989) and articles in various journals, including *Diplomatic History, Civil War History, South Atlantic Quarterly, Alabama Review,* and *Virginia Magazine of History and Biography.* He is currently completing a biography of John Tyler Morgan, the leading late nineteenth-century Southern expansionist.

George C. Herring is a professor of history at the University of Kentucky. A former editor of *Diplomatic History* and president of the Society for Historians of American Foreign Relations, he is the author of *America's Longest War: The United States and Vietnam, 1950–1975* (1985) and *The Secret Diplomacy of the Vietnam War* (1983).

Howard Jones is University Research Professor of History at the University of Alabama. He is the author of several books, including *Mutiny on the Amistad: The Saga of a Slave Revolt and Its Impact on American Abolition, Law, and Diplomacy* (1987), *The Course of American Diplomacy: From the Revolution to the Present* (1988), *"A New Kind of War": America's Global Strategy and the Truman Doctrine in Greece* (1989), with Randall B. Woods, *Dawning of the Cold War: The United States' Quest for Order* (1991), and the forthcoming *Union in Peril: The Anglo-American Recognition Crisis During the Civil War, 1861–1862.*

Burton I. Kaufman is a professor of history and department head at Virginia Polytechnic Institute and State University (Virginia Tech). He has written five books, the most recent of which is the *Korean War: Challenges in Crisis, Credibility and Command* (1986). He is presently completing a book titled *History of the Jimmy Carter Presidency.*

Bruce R. Kuniholm is director of the Institute of Policy Sciences and Public Affairs at Duke University and professor and chair of public policy studies and history. Among his publications are *The Origins of the Cold War in the Near East: Great Power Conflict and Diplomacy in Iran, Turkey, and Greece* (1980), *The Persian Gulf and United States Policy* (1984), and *The Palestinian Problem and United States Policy* (1986).

Lester D. Langley is Research Professor of History at the University of Georgia, where he teaches Latin American history. He has published ten books on U.S.-Latin American relations, including *The United States and the Caribbean in the Twentieth Century* (1980), *The Banana Wars: U.S. Intervention in the Caribbean, 1898–1934* (1983), *America and the Americas: The United States in the Western Hemisphere* (1989), and *Mexico and the United States: The Fragile Relationship* (1991).

James I. Matray is an associate professor of history at New Mexico State University. Author of several articles on U.S. policy toward Korea, his *The Reluctant Crusade: American Foreign Policy in Korea, 1941–1950* (1985) won the Phi Alpha Theta Best Book Prize in 1986. Currently, he is completing work on *A Historical Dictionary of the Korean War.*

Thomas J. McCormick is a professor of history at the University of Wisconsin—Madison. He is the author of *China Market: America's Quest for Informal Empire, 1893–1901* (1967), and *America's Half-Century: United States Foreign Policy in the Cold War* (1990).

Robert D. Schulzinger is a professor of history at the University of Colorado at Boulder. Among his recent publications are *Henry Kissinger: Doctor of Diplomacy* (1989) and *American Diplomacy in the Twentieth Century*, second edition (1990).

Nancy Bernkopf Tucker holds a joint appointment on the faculties of the Department of History and the School of Foreign Service at Georgetown University. She also served as a Council on Foreign Relations Fellow in the Office of Chinese Affairs of the U.S. Department of State (1986–87). The author of *Patterns in the Dust: Chinese-American Relations and the Recognition Controversy, 1949–1950* (1983), she has written numerous articles as well.

Betty Miller Unterberger is a professor of history at Texas A&M University. Among her publications are: *America's Siberian Expedition: A Study in National Policy* (1956, 1969), a prize-winning book of the American Historical Association; an edited study on *American Intervention in the Russian Civil War* (1969); numerous articles on Wilsonian diplomacy in scholarly journals; and most recently *The United States, Revolutionary Russia, and the Rise of Czechoslovakia* (1989). She has also won distinguished teaching awards from California State University and from Texas A&M University.

Randall B. Woods is the John A. Cooper, Sr., Professor of Diplomacy at the University of Arkansas. Among his books are *The Roosevelt Foreign Policy Establishment and the "Good Neighbor": Argentina and the United States, 1941–1945* (1979), *A Changing of the Guard: Anglo-America, 1941–1946* (1990), and, with Howard Jones, *Dawning of the Cold War: The United States' Quest for Order* (1991).

Contents

Preface

Safeguarding the republic has been the single most important stated objective of America's foreign policy since its inception in the late eighteenth century. This awesome responsibility became even more pronounced after the United States expanded its presence on the international scene during the 1890s. The efforts of American leaders to protect their nation from external danger provide the central thread holding together the essays and documents of *Safeguarding the Republic.*

The chief aim of this anthology is to enhance a student's interest in the history of America's foreign relations. It contains sixteen original essays and numerous supporting documents from American history. The essays are by specialists in each period studied and are intended to be both analytical and readable while highlighting the major issues confronting American policymakers and putting these issues in proper historical perspective. In an attempt to offer an intellectual balance that should prove challenging to the student, the contributors represent a wide range of interpretive approaches to history.

The excerpted documents following each essay were chosen by these historians based on personal experiences in the archives along with their own considerations about which primary sources would most likely prove interesting to students. The official documents include treaties, speeches, and diplomatic notes and cables. Many of these documents were culled from presidential libraries and the National Archives. Equally informative materials include selections from memoirs, press conferences, congressional hearings, newspaper editorials, and even a modernist poem criticizing Theodore Roosevelt's policies in Latin America. Further, there are both foreign and American documents, thereby emphasizing the international dimension in which recent American foreign policy has developed.

The essays and documents combine to illustrate a number of important themes in the nation's diplomacy: the primacy of realism in determining American actions intended to protect national security; the mosaic of explanations for America's peculiar brand of imperialism that sometimes revealed a missionary impulse fueled by the belief in American exceptionalism and other times demonstrated the desire to satisfy either strategic needs or commercial expansion; the frequent and inescapable transformation of perceptions into reality in shaping the nation's response to foreign and domestic troubles; the broad and complex interplay of domestic and foreign events; the inseparable roles of personalities, forces, and events in formulating policy; and the social, political, economic, strategic, and military interests that guided America's rise to world power status during the twentieth century. Most importantly, this book highlights the successes along with the frustrations and failures that often accompanied the nation's expanding global role, a process that forced its leaders to come to grips with the central paradox of recent American diplomacy—that increased power and broadened foreign commitments did not necessarily assure the international tranquility that was vital to America's own security.

Safeguarding the Republic is organized chronologically for the first eleven chapters in the belief that students will find this type of history easier to comprehend and in the hope that they will realize that decisions do not take place in a vacuum. If students understand that a decision on any issue occurs within the context of countless other ongoing and confusing events, they might recognize that casting judgments in retrospect is often unfair and that the historian's chief responsibility is to understand history as the participants themselves understood it. The book then departs from chronology with five topical chapters covering the past three decades. The topical organization will help students understand regional continuities in recent times, when most documents are not yet available for comprehensive historical treatment. Hopefully, *Safeguarding the Republic* can serve as a companion volume to a text on American diplomatic history, as a text itself along with supplementary readings, or as a text for political science classes dealing with the conduct of American foreign policy.

The United States continues to deal with dramatic events of recent times: the apparent end of the Cold War and the opening of Eastern Europe; the lowering of the Berlin Wall and the reunification of Germany; and, a prime illustration of the irony that success in the Cold War did not guarantee world peace, the war in the Persian Gulf that resulted in Kuwait's liberation from Iraqi occupation and yet did not resolve a series of both old and new international problems and tensions. The importance of understanding the documentary bases for Washington's decisions regarding both these recent developments and previous events becomes increasingly clear. Perhaps *Safeguarding the Republic* can promote that understanding.

A host of people helped to make this work possible. David C. Follmer first suggested this project and then saw it to completion. My appreciation goes also to those involved in the production of this work, particularly Anita Samen. As always, the inspiration provided by my family—ever broadening with its newest addition, my grandson Timothy—continues to prove indispensable. Finally, a special thanks goes to the historians who contributed to this volume. Not only have they been gracious, patient, and dependable throughout the entire process, but they have demonstrated a warm and sincere commitment to research and writing while confirming their resolve to show students that history can be the past come alive.

Tuscaloosa, Alabama
Autumn 1991

Howard Jones

SAFEGUARDING THE REPUBLIC

CHAPTER 1

The 1890s as a Watershed Decade

Thomas J. McCormick

The 1890s marked America's emergence as a great power. In a decade capped by the Spanish-American War of 1898, the United States largely transformed the Caribbean into "an American lake." It replaced Great Britain as the dominant foreign influence in Mexico. It made itself the paramount power in the North Pacific with an insular empire that stretched from Pearl Harbor to Manila Bay. It became a significant actor in the volatile saga of a Chinese empire that was politically unstable but economically attractive. Even Europe paid increasing attention to U.S. policy, for it seemed that American industrial supremacy presaged an economic "invasion of Europe" that threatened its domestic markets with "an American peril."

What made the 1890s a watershed decade? As is often the case with great transformations, it resulted from the reciprocal influence of rapid changes in both American domestic life and the international system. The most dramatic change in the latter was the decline of British hegemony. After the end of the Napoleonic Wars in 1815, Britain possessed such inordinate economic and military power that it could impose its international rules of behavior upon other nations and coalitions of nations. In particular, it sought to organize the world into a single, free-trade market. The consequent freeing of world commerce and the decline of political empires opened up vast opportunities for the British.

These changes in the international system were also of great value to the United States as it grew from its status of a newly industrializing country to that of a developed world power. British economic and military power helped to destroy the remnants of Spanish colonialism in the Western Hemisphere and prevent new empire building by other European states. In other words, Britain partially enforced the Monroe Doctrine in Latin America at a time when the United States' ability to enforce the doctrine's pledge to protect nations of the Western Hemisphere from colonization was largely limited to North America.

Similarly, Britain's Open Door policy with China—instituted after the Opium Wars in the early 1840s—provided the United States with an opportunity for "hitchhiking imperialism," the taking advantage of market opportunities in China opened by British might. In general, Britain's liberalization of world trade initiated a period of such prolonged global prosperity—especially after 1840—that the United States was able to finance its own rapid modernization via its export of cotton, food, and raw materials into the world market and via its import of foreign capital and technology into the domestic market.

The decline of British hegemony after 1870 dramatically changed America's international circumstances. No longer protected and served by British power, the United States had to be concerned more directly with the Monroe Doctrine in Latin America and the Open Door policy for free trade in Asia, neither of which was widely accepted by European continental powers. Once able to operate in a predictably stable international system under one nation's dominant control, the United States now had to function in a world marked by increasing imperial competition for regional power in Africa, Asia, Latin America, and the Near East. The demise of British preponderance brought with it diminished world trade as the global market fragmented into closed imperial economies and protected national markets that regulated and limited trade flows. As a consequence, the long economic boom between 1840 and 1870 gave way to the worldwide economic contraction of 1870 to 1900 sometimes known as the "long depression." In the United States, the contraction was felt in the depressions of 1873–78 and 1893–98 as well as several lesser recessions in the 1880s. In short, the predictable world environment of peace and prosperity had been replaced by an unpredictable milieu of conflict and contraction.

Interacting with these external changes were equally dramatic domestic transformations in American life. Some of the external changes required America to play a more global role; domestic changes made it possible to do so. Some of the domestic changes were economic, whereas others were political and ideological. The domestic economic changes flowed essentially from the maturation of the Industrial Revolution, which occurred a half century after its beginning. Small-scale, family-firm competition gave way to large-scale, corporate concentration, and fragmented regional markets broadened into a single, integrated national market linked by a continental railroad network. The "age of big business" had arrived. With it came new economic and social problems. The increase in real wages failed to keep pace with an enormous jump in productivity, stimulated by the increased use of power-driven machinery. The resulting overproduction tended to depress the rate of profit and prompted fear that the country faced permanent stagnation. At the same time, economic hard times fueled battles between capital and labor over how to divide the contracting economic pie in terms of profits and wages. The resulting class conflict took violent and frightening turns in what various writers have called the "year of violence'' (1877), ''the great upheaval'' (1886), and ''the terrible year'' (1894).

Paradoxically, the great productivity that partly caused these economic and social problems also offered a possible means for their solution. By the 1890s, the United States had replaced Great Britain as the dominant industrial power in the world. From cotton dresses to steel locomotives, American manufacturers could make comparable goods for less money than anyone else in the world economy—a fact demonstrating ''America's economic supremacy,'' as Brooks Adams, an American historian, termed it in 1900. That fact suggested the possibility of expanding U.S. market shares overseas, thus raising the rate of profit, restoring economic growth and prosperity, and reducing the social stress of class conflict. (doc. 1)

The United States' industrial maturation coincided with the completion of its political integration. It had taken a century of life under the Constitution to create a truly modern nation-state. Early American history had been marked by episodic threats of secession and disunion, by schisms in cultures and ethical values, and by competing wage and slavery labor systems. The terrible consequences had been a bloody, divisive civil war (1861–65) and a contentious period of Southern reconstruction (1865–77). Nonetheless, the Civil War effectively terminated all remaining possibilities of disunion, and the Reconstruction era came to an end in a manner that politically and economically reintegrated the South into the nation. As a result, the United States faced the world in the 1890s as a unified nation-state, ambitious to attain a status befitting its new power.

One powerful feature that bonded this new nation together was a ''civil religion,'' a secular body of values and beliefs that defined what it meant to be an American. At the core of this civil religion was the ideology of republicanism and the belief in the superiority of republican forms of government over all others. Corollary to that was the sense of American ''exceptionalism,'' the proud conviction that the American people and American nation were so exceptional, so unique, that no other nation could match the United States in making the practice of republicanism conform so nearly to its ideal. As such, the American republic became the model to which all others should aspire and the progressive goal toward which all modern history should move.

Historically, Americans had been divided over the proper means of expanding republicanism: promoting it by example (the United States as republican exemplar) vied with republican expansionism (manifest destiny) for the allegiance of Americans. Some wished to disdain territorial plunder, devote themselves to making America a better ethical and material model for the rest of the world, and have faith that others would voluntarily adopt the American model. Others doubted the ability or will of different peoples to copy the American model at a distance—especially those alleged to be inferior, such as Hispanics, Asians, and Africans. They argued that republicanism could only be exported by force. Indeed, it was argued that the United States had a providential mission as God's chosen nation—the second Israel—to extend its dominion over underutilized lands and underdeveloped peoples.

Those two contested visions of promoting republicanism deeply affected America's rise to world power in the 1890s. Americans disagreed on whether commercial and status considerations required the United States to create an overseas empire. In the "great debate" of the late 1890s, anti-imperialists said no to empire building. (doc. 2) Ruling alien lands and peoples seemed a moral contradiction to them: a free people ruling unfree peoples against their will. Moreover, empire building might even make Americans less free by necessitating a large standing army and navy, whose growing influence might threaten civilian democratic institutions. And finally, they argued that imperialism was unnecessary, since America's economic supremacy enabled the acquisition of larger overseas markets through free competition rather than through more limited colonial monopolies.

Imperialists such as Josiah Strong, the influential Protestant clergyman, argued that free market competition would not secure the necessary markets, since the other great powers were already using protective tariffs, trade quotas, imperial preference systems, and so on, to ensure that much of world trade was regulated rather than free. As such, the United States was better advised to create its own exclusive imperial trading spheres. (doc. 3) Moreover, the imperialists questioned the morality of exploiting underdeveloped lands for their trade and resources while giving nothing cultural or educational in return. Imperialism offered the opportunity to tutor indigenous peoples in the art of republicanism: how to write constitutions, hold elections, and administer local affairs. Such pro-imperialists were strongly influenced by social Darwinism (the notion that nations and races, like species, are involved in a natural selection process often called the "survival of the fittest") and believed that allegedly superior white societies would inevitably prevail over peoples of color. That triumph, however, brought with it a paternalistic responsibility to prepare colonial subjects for eventual self-government and self-determination—as soon as they were deemed "fit."

In the end, neither imperialists nor anti-imperialists prevailed. Ultimately, Americans chose a less dogmatic, more practical approach to world affairs. What worked at the least possible cost, where gain outweighed pain, became the major determinant for foreign policy. In concrete terms, formal empire building (acquiring colonies) was minimized because the costs of defending, stabilizing, and administering them often outweighed any material rewards. Moreover, imperialism pursued indiscriminately might seriously undermine popular support from Americans still committed to republicanism-by-example. Instead, the United States opted for "informal empire" by permitting a foreign country to retain its political independence while structuring its economic relations in ways that rendered it an American economic dependency. British commentators called it "imperialism-on-the-cheap."

Despite this preference for informal empire, there was also an awareness that political and strategic factors might occasionally make formal empire necessary. If a given country's political environment was either so inhospitable or unstable that American trade and investment could not flourish; if it occupied some strategic location at a key crossroad of world trade; or if other great powers were likely to take it if the United States did not preempt them, then more formal control might seem in order. Such instances, however, were to be kept at a minimum. ''Informal empire where possible, [more] formal empire where necessary,'' as two great British historians put it.

The American preference for informal empire was most evident in the Open Door policy toward China. The United States sought to keep the China market open to commercial penetration by American exporters by discouraging foreign partitioning of the Chinese empire and encouraging maintenance of Chinese political independence and territorial integrity. Toward these ends, the United States sought European and Japanese commitment to the Open Door policy, and later sought to prevent the great powers from exploiting the Boxer Rebellion crisis as an excuse to colonize parts of the Chinese empire. (doc. 4)

The drive for informal empire was also visible in Latin America, where an expanded Monroe Doctrine made the United States the hemisphere's protector against European interference. Pan-Americanism used both commerce and culture to bring the United States' southern neighbors into its orbit. (doc. 5) Consequently, the United States attempted to blunt perceived British designs on Nicaraguan and Venezuelan territory; to force the declining world leader to acknowledge the unilateral American right to build, operate, and fortify a Central American canal; to defuse a pro-British revolution in Brazil; and to replace the British as the dominant foreign economic power in Mexico.

While the United States pursued a policy of informal empire in China and Latin America, formal empire seemed more suited to immediate circumstances on numerous occasions. Consequently, the United States resorted to limited doses of ''insular imperialism,'' especially when it was necessary to protect strategically important shipping lanes and canal routes. In the Pacific, the need to secure trade routes to China led the United States to annex Hawaii, Wake, Guam, and the Philippines in 1898 as potential naval bases, coaling stations, and cable relay points on the way to Asia. Geography was the key determinant, but so too was the fear of German designs on the Philippines and Japanese interest in Hawaii.

Similarly, in the Caribbean the United States obtained formal or semiformal dominion over the island nations that stood as pickets guarding the sea lanes from Europe and the United States to the future Panama Canal zone. Puerto Rico became an American colony; the Virgin Islands became the object of a failed purchase attempt from Denmark; and Cuba became an American protectorate after the conclusion of the Spanish-American War.

Cuba was especially significant as a battleground in the great debate between republicanism-by-example (anti-imperialists) and republicanism-by-export (imperialists). The former sought to recognize the independence of Cuba *before* America went to war against Spain; the latter sought to use the war to make Cuba an American colony. In the end, the pragmatic William McKinley administration found a middle ground between the two with the Teller Amendment. (doc. 6) The amendment renounced any colonial designs on Cuba and promised *eventual* independence for the island—but not until "pacification" was achieved. The United States was left unilaterally free to define what constituted pacification and when it was achieved. The term was finally defined with the Platt Amendment of 1901, which, among other things, left the United States with a naval base and an open invitation to intervene in Cuba whenever it saw fit. (doc. 7)

The pragmatic resolution of the great debate provided the United States with a subtle blend of idealism and realism that was to facilitate the expansion of American influence in the twentieth century. Transformed from an anticolonial, underdeveloped society in its infancy to a maturing, industrial power in its young adulthood, the United States emerged from the 1890s as a possible successor to Britain's mantle of global hegemony. Forty years would pass and two world wars would be fought before the United States indeed became the dominant banker, policeman, and ideologue of the world order. Nonetheless, many of the historical preconditions were clearly present and widely recognized at this century's beginning: industrial supremacy as the world's most productive workshop; ideological assertiveness as the fountainhead of republican exceptionalism; and vast military potential as possible ally of Great Britain in imposing order on a disorderly world. The United States, as Henry Luce of Time, Inc., later put it, was poised to make the twentieth century "The American Century."

Document 1

Secretary of State William R. Day to Secretary of the Treasury Lyman J. Gage, U.S. Congress, 55th Cong., 2d sess., *House Documents*, no. 536, 1898, 1–5.

The export trade of the United States is undergoing a transformation which promises to profoundly influence the whole economic future of the country. As is well known, the United States has reached the foremost rank among the industrial nations. For a number of years its position as the greatest producer of manufactures as well as of raw products has been undisputed, but absorbed with its own internal development, and satisfied, for the time being, with the enormous home market of 70,000,000 of people, it has, until recently, devoted but little concerted effort to the sale of its manufactures outside of its own borders. Recently, however, the fact has become more and more apparent that the output of the United States manufacturers, developed by the remarkable inventive genius and industrial skill of our people with a rapidity which has excited attention throughout the great centers of manufacturing activity in Europe, has reached the point of large excess above the demands of home consumption. Under these circumstances it is not surprising that greater interest should be exhibited among our manufacturers, exporters, and economists in the enlargement of foreign markets for American goods.

The conditions of export trade, it may be assumed, are now being studied by every manufacturer who is confronted by the problem of finding new outlets for his products. The reports of the diplomatic and consular officers of the United States show that, as the result of individual effort, with but little concert of action among exporters, many lines of American manufacture—notably machinery, electrical apparatus, hardware, bicycles, and various other manufactures of iron and steel, leather, furniture, etc.—have already been introduced into European countries of long-established industrial preeminence and are finding ready sale in competition with their own home products. This apparent phenomenon is explained on various grounds, among the reasons given being the comparative cheapness of United States manufactures, notwithstanding the higher rates for labor, owing to the superior producing capacity of the American workman with the aid of improved labor-saving machinery.

The fact seems also to be well established that American goods have reached a point of excellence which commends them favorably to foreign consumers. This is unquestionably the fact as to our cotton goods in competition with British goods in Africa and the Far East. It has been demonstrated that even savages will pay more for American cotton goods than for the inferior article offered to them from European looms. In labor-saving machinery we seem to have no rival. In furniture it has been claimed that in Germany, where wood working has been developed to the highest point of artistic finish, American furniture easily undersells the German.

If the above results have been achieved with comparatively little effort, it must be apparent that, with intelligent and systematized action on the part of our manufacturers and exporters, aided, as far as practicable, by our diplomatic and consular representatives abroad, the United States has unfolded to it, in vast regions as yet unopened to the full activity of commerce, possibilities of commercial expansion limited only by the use we make of them. . . .

. . . [T]he sending abroad of commissions composed of commercial and industrial experts to study the actual conditions in promising markets seems to me to be a subject which should immediately engage the attention of Congress. Such commissions have been appointed from time to time with favorable results, but, in my opinion, the occasion has arisen for something more than sporadic effort. Government inquiry of this character has been directed mainly in the past to our sister republics of the Western Hemisphere. . . .

But besides the great commercial domain of the southern half of the Western Hemisphere there are vast undeveloped fields in Africa and the Far East. The value of these markets is sufficiently exemplified by the eager rivalry of the European powers in obtaining the largest possible spheres of influence in them, which has been one of the most striking features of diplomatic effort in recent years. Without reference to schemes of this character, it would seem to be obvious that the United States has important interests at stake in the partition of commercial facilities in regions which are likely to offer developing markets for its goods. Nowhere is this consideration of more interest than in its relation to the Chinese Empire. . . .

The Chinese Empire has an area about one-half that of the United States, exclusive of Alaska, with a population of over 400,000,000. Its foreign commerce amounts to about $200,000,000. In 1896 Great Britain had more than two-thirds of China's commerce, Japan ranking second with about one-eleventh, and the United States third with one-twelfth. In other words, the United States has already a larger share of Chinese trade than any European country other than Great Britain. China's industrial development is in its infancy, but within the last few years a number of cotton mills have been built and railroads projected, largely with the aid of American enterprise and industry. The Empire has numerous deposits of coal, iron, copper, and other mineral products, affording an unlimited field for development. . . .

In view of these considerations, I earnestly hope that Congress will make the modest provision asked for to enable the Department to give intelligent direction to future efforts to obtain a proper share for the United States in the development, which seems to be near at hand, of the vast resources of the Chinese Empire under modern conditions of industry and trade.

Document 2

William Graham Sumner, "The Fallacy of Territorial Extension," in *War and Other Essays by William Graham Sumner*, Albert G. Keller, ed., New Haven: Yale University Press, 1911, 285–86, 289–93.

The traditional belief is that a state aggrandizes itself by territorial extension, so that winning new land is gaining in wealth and prosperity, just as an individual would gain if he increased his land possessions. . . .

The notion that gain of territory is gain of wealth and strength for the state, after the expedient size has been won, is a delusion. . . .

What private individuals want is free access, under order and security, to any part of the earth's surface, in order that they may avail themselves of its natural resources for their use, either by investment or commerce. If, therefore, we could have free trade with Hawaii while somebody else had the jurisdiction, we should gain all the advantages and escape all of the burdens. . . .

If we could go to Canada and trade there our products for those of that country, we could win all for our private interests which that country is able to contribute to the welfare of mankind, and we should have nothing to do with the civil and political difficulties which harass the government. . . .

The case of Cuba is somewhat different. If we could go to the island and trade with the same freedom with which we can go to Louisiana, we could make all the gains, by investment and commerce, which the island offers to industry and enterprise, provided that either Spain or a local government would give the necessary security, and we should have no share in political struggles there. It may be that the proviso is not satisfied, or soon will not be. Here is a case, then, which illustrates the fact that states are often forced to extend their jurisdiction whether they want to do so or not. Civilized states are forced to supersede the local jurisdiction of uncivilized or half-civilized states, in order to police the territory and establish the necessary guarantees of industry and commerce. It is idle to set up absolute doctrines of national ownership in the soil which would justify a group of population in spoiling a part of the earth's surface for themselves and everybody else. The island of Cuba may fall into anarchy. If it does, the civilized world may look to the United States to take the jurisdiction and establish order and security there. We might be compelled to do it. It would, however, be a great burden, and possibly a fatal calamity to us. . . .

This confederated state of ours was never planned for indefinite expansion or for an imperial policy. We boast of it a great deal, but we must know that its advantages are won at the cost of limitations, as is the case with most things in this world. The fathers of the Republic planned a confederation of free and peaceful industrial commonwealths, shielded by their geographical position from the jealousies, rivalries, and traditional policies of the Old World and bringing all the resources of civilization to bear for the domestic happiness of the population only. They meant to have no grand statecraft or "high politics," no "balance of power" or "reasons of state," which had cost the human race so much. They meant to offer no field for what Benjamin Franklin called the "pest of glory." It is the limitation of this scheme of the state that the state created under it must forego a great number of the grand functions of European states; especially that it contains no methods and apparatus of conquest, extension, domination, and imperialism. The plan of the fathers would have no controlling authority for us if it had been proved by experience that that plan was narrow, inadequate, and mistaken. Are we prepared to vote that it has proved so? For our territorial extension has reached limits which are complete for all purposes and leave no necessity for "rectification of boundaries." Any extension will open questions, not close them. Any extension will not make us more secure where we are, but will force us to take new measures to secure our new acquisitions. The preservation of acquisitions will force us to reorganize our internal resources, so as to make it possible to prepare them in advance and to mobilize them with promptitude. This will lessen liberty and require discipline. It will increase taxation and all the pressure of government. It will divert the national energy from the provision of self-maintenance and comfort for the people, and will necessitate stronger and more elaborate governmental machinery. All this will be disastrous to republican institutions and to democracy. Moreover, all extension puts a new strain on the internal cohesion of the preexisting mass, threatening a new cleavage within. If we had never taken Texas and Northern Mexico we should never have had secession.

The sum of the matter is that colonization and territorial extension are burdens, not gains. Great civilized states cannot avoid these burdens. They are the penalty of greatness because they are the duties of it. . . . England, as a penalty of her greatness, finds herself in all parts of the world face to face with the necessity of maintaining her jurisdiction and of extending it in order to maintain it. When she does so she finds herself only extending law and order for the benefit of everybody. It is only in circumstances like hers that burdens have any compensation.

Document 3

Josiah Strong, *Expansion Under New World Conditions*, New York: Baker & Taylor, 1900, 247–302.

Admiral [George] Dewey's guns at Manila [May 1, 1898] did more than to sink the Spanish fleet; they battered down our Chinese wall of political isolation.

[President George] Washington in his Farewell Address laid down a rule touching our foreign relations, which was eminently wise for our national infancy. . . .

. . . When that advice was given, we were isolated from the remainder of the world, both geographically and economically; and political isolation was a logical corollary. Now all this is radically changed. The city of Washington is nearer to European capitals today than they were to each other a hundred years ago; and the nation which is the greatest producer and consumer in the world finds economic isolation doubly impossible. Of course political isolation was doomed to disappear with the geographic and economic foundations on which it rested. . . .

. . . This is a commercial age, and commercial considerations are the mainspring of national policies. It is the supreme interests of nations, or what appear to be, which shape their politics both at home and abroad; and in this day industrial and commercial interests are supreme. . . . It is idle to suppose that we can be a part, and a principal part, of the organized commercial and industrial life of the world and yet maintain a policy of political isolation. We might as well attempt to divorce cause and effect. Political questions are as inseparable from industrial and commercial interests in the great world life of which we are so large a part, as they are in national life. . . .

It is quite too late to ask whether we will expand. We are already expanded. American troops in China, marching shoulder to shoulder with those of the Great Powers, and doing their full share to rebuke barbarism and restore order, not to mention the fact that the American flag now floats over Hawaii, Porto Rico, and the Philippines, make it sufficiently obvious that we have already crossed the Rubicon which bounded our insularity. . . .

The only wise course for us is frankly to recognize the changed conditions of the world and intelligently to adapt to them a new world policy, the aim of which shall be not national aggrandizement, but the noblest ministry to the new world life.

In the realization of this aim we must be guided by an enlightened world conscience. . . .

. . . Jane Addams has wisely said: "We may make a mistake in politics as well as in morals by forgetting that new conditions are ever demanding the evolution of a new morality, along old lines but in larger measure. Unless the present situation extends our nationalism into internationalism, unless it has thrust forward our patriotism into humanitarianism, we cannot meet it." . . .

Adopting a world policy involves a world police and the acceptance of our proper share of the cost. This means an adequate standing army, which need not be large, . . . and a powerful navy. . . .

But as the world is gradually being civilized and civilization is gradually being Christianized, armies are finding new occupations. As *The Outlook* [July 29, 1899] says: "The army among Anglo-Saxon peoples is no longer a mere instrument of destruction. It is a great reconstructive organization. It is promoting law, order, civilization, and is fighting famine and pestilence in India. It is lightening taxes, building railroads, opening markets, laying the foundations of justice and liberty, in Egypt. It is reorganizing society on a basis of physical health, fairly paid industry, honest administration, popular rights, and public education, in Cuba." . . .

. . . Selfishness, hatred, and revenge are no more necessary to the soldier who is engaged in preserving the world's order than to the policeman who is quelling a riot, or to a parent who is correcting a child. . . .

We are now prepared to consider our relations to the Philippines. Our policy should be determined not by national ambition, nor by commercial considerations, but by our duty to the world in general and to the Filipinos in particular. By discharging these obligations we shall best fulfill our duty to ourselves. . . .

As a part of the great world life, these people cannot be permitted a lawless independence. If they are capable of being a law unto themselves, then neither the United States nor any other Power should extend authority over them. If they are incapable of self-government, then to give them independence would wrong the world in general and themselves in particular. The practical question then [is] this: Are the Filipinos capable of self-government? . . .

I know of no witness, who has had personal observation of the Filipinos, who declares them to be capable of self-government. . . . [T]he Philippine Commission . . . states that at present the basis of self-government does not exist among the Filipinos, and that if America should withdraw, "the government of the Philippines would speedily lapse into anarchy." The report continues: "Thus the welfare of the Filipinos coincides with the dictates of national honor in forbidding our abandonment of the archipelago. We cannot from any point of view escape the responsibility of the government which our sovereignty entails, and the Commission is strongly persuaded that the performance of our national duty will prove the greatest blessing to the people of the Philippine Islands." . . .

All this does not mean that the Anglo-Saxon race should become a Don Quixote, riding atilt at every windmill on the world's horizon, "but it does mean the consciousness in ourselves and the declaration to others that our national sympathies are everywhere on the side of justice, freedom, and education; it does mean the natural self-consciousness that in this respect our spirit and that of the people of Great Britain are one; and it does mean that the enemies of justice, freedom, and education the world over must hereafter reckon with America and Great Britain as the open, avowed, and courageous friends of these inalienable rights of humanity." [*The Outlook*, Aug. 27, 1898]

Such a world policy as is urged is not only justified, but required, by the new world life on which we have entered. True enough it is unprecedented, but so are the new world conditions which demand it. The wise words of [Ralph Waldo] Emerson, true when written, are peculiarly applicable today: "We live in a new and exceptional age. America is another word for opportunity. Our whole history appears like a last effort of Divine Providence in behalf of the human race; and a literal, slavish following of precedents, as by a justice of the peace, is not for those who at this hour lead the destinies of this people." Conservatism demands precedents; progress creates them. The first precedent is always unprecedented. The world moves.

It is time to dismiss "the craven fear of being great," to recognize the place in the world which God has given us, and to accept the responsibilities which it devolves upon us in behalf of Christian civilization.

Document 4

Secretary of State John Hay to U.S. Ambassador to Great Britain Joseph Choate, Sept. 6, 1899, U.S. Department of State, *Papers Relating to the Foreign Relations of the United States* (hereafter referred to as *FRUS*), *1899*, Washington, D.C.: Government Printing Office, 1902, 131–33.

The Government of Her Britannic Majesty has declared that its policy and its very traditions precluded it from using any privileges which might be granted it in China as a weapon for excluding commercial rivals, and that freedom of trade for Great Britain in that Empire meant freedom of trade for all the world alike. While conceding by formal agreements, first with Germany and then with Russia, the possession of "spheres of influence or interest" in China in which they are to enjoy special rights and privileges, more especially in respect of railroads and mining enterprises, Her Britannic Majesty's Government has therefore sought to maintain at the same time what is called the "open-door" policy, to insure to the commerce of the world in China equality of treatment within said "spheres" for commerce and navigation. This latter policy is alike urgently demanded by the British mercantile communities and by those of the United States, as it is justly held by them to be the only one which will improve existing conditions, enable them to maintain their positions in the markets of China, and extend their operations in the future. While the Government of the United States will in no way commit itself to a recognition of exclusive rights of any power within or control over any portion of the Chinese Empire under such agreements as have within the last year been made, it can not conceal its apprehension that under existing conditions there is a possibility, even a probability, of complications arising between the treaty powers which may imperil the rights insured to the United States under our treaties with China.

This Government is animated by a sincere desire that the interests of our citizens may not be prejudiced through exclusive treatment by any of the controlling powers within their so-called "spheres of interest" in China, and hopes also to retain there an open market for the commerce of the world, remove dangerous sources of international irritation, and hasten thereby united or concerted action of the powers at Pekin in favor of the administrative reforms so urgently needed for strengthening the Imperial Government and maintaining the integrity of China in which the whole western world is alike concerned. It believes that such a result may be greatly assisted by a declaration by the various powers claiming "spheres of interest" in China of their intentions as regards treatment of foreign trade therein. The present moment seems a particularly opportune one for informing her Britannic Majesty's Government of the desire of the United States to see it make a formal declaration and to lend its support in obtaining similar declarations from the various powers claiming "spheres of influence" in China. . . .

First. Will in no wise interfere with any treaty port or any vested interest within any so-called "sphere of interest" or leased territory it may have in China.

Second. That the Chinese treaty tariff of the time being shall apply to all merchandise landed or shipped to all such ports as are within said "sphere of interest" (unless they be "free ports"), no matter to what nationality it may belong, and that duties so leviable shall be collected by the Chinese Government.

Third. That it will levy no higher harbor dues on vessels of another nationality frequenting any port in such "sphere" than shall be levied on vessels of its own nationality, and no higher railroad charges over lines built, controlled, or operated within its "sphere" on merchandise belonging to citizens or subjects of other nationalities transported through such "sphere" than shall be levied on similar merchandise belonging to its own nationals transported over equal distances.

The recent ukase of His Majesty the Emperor of Russia, declaring the port of Ta-lien-wan open to the merchant ships of all nations during the whole of the lease under which it is to be held by Russia, removing as it does all uncertainty as to the liberal and conciliatory policy of that power, together with the assurances given this Government by Russia, justifies the expectation that His Majesty will cooperate in such an understanding as is here proposed, and our ambassador at the court of St. Petersburg has been instructed accordingly to submit the propositions above detailed to His Imperial Majesty, and ask their early consideration. Copy of my instruction to Mr. [Charlemagne] Tower is herewith inclosed for your confidential information.

The action of Germany in declaring the port of Kiaochao a "free port," and the aid the Imperial Government has given China in the establishment there of a Chinese custom-house, coupled with the oral assurance conveyed the United States by Germany that our interests within its "sphere" would in no wise be affected by its occupation of this portion of the province of Shang-tung, tend to show that little opposition may be anticipated from that power to the desired declaration.

The interests of Japan, the next most interested power in the trade of China, will be so clearly served by the proposed arrangement, and the declaration of its statesmen within the last year are so entirely in line with the views here expressed, that its hearty cooperation is confidently counted on.

You will, at as early date as practicable, submit the considerations to Her Britannic Majesty's principal secretary of state for foreign affairs and request their immediate consideration.

I inclose herewith a copy of the instruction sent to our ambassador at Berlin bearing on the above subject.

Document 5

Secretary of State Richard Olney to U.S. Ambassador to Great Britain Thomas F. Bayard, July 20, 1895, Department of State, *FRUS, 1895*, Part I, 1895, 1896, 552–62.

That there are circumstances under which a nation may justly interpose in a controversy to which two or more other nations are the direct and immediate parties is an admitted canon of international law. . . . We are concerned at this time, however, not so much with the general rule as with a form of it which is peculiarly and distinctively American. Washington, in the solemn admonitions of the Farewell Address, explicitly warned his countrymen against entanglements with the politics or the controversies of European powers.

Europe, [he said,] has a set of primary interests which to us have none or a very remote relation. Hence she must be engaged in frequent controversies the causes of which are essentially foreign to our concerns. Hence, therefore, it must be unwise in us to implicate ourselves by artificial ties in the ordinary vicissitudes of her politics or the ordinary combinations and collisions of her friendships or enmities. Our detached and distant situation invites and enables us to pursue a different course. . . .

Twenty years later, however, the . . . Monroe administration therefore did not hesitate to accept and apply the logic of the Farewell Address by declaring in effect that American non-intervention in European affairs necessarily implied and meant European non-intervention in American affairs. . . .

The Monroe administration, however, did not content itself with formulating a correct rule for the regulation of the relations between Europe and America. It aimed at also securing the practical benefits to result from the application of the rule. Hence the message just quoted declared that the American continents were fully occupied and were not the subjects for future colonization by European powers. To this spirit and this purpose, also, are to be attributed the passages of the same message which treat any infringement of the rule against interference in American affairs on the part of the powers of Europe as an act of unfriendliness to the United States. It was realized that it was futile to lay down such a rule unless its observance could be enforced. It was manifest that the United States was the only power in this hemisphere capable of enforcing it. It was therefore courageously declared not merely that Europe ought not to interfere in American affairs, but that any European power doing so would be regarded as antagonizing the interests and inviting the opposition of the United States.

That America is in no part open to colonization, though the proposition was not universally admitted at the time of its first enunciation, has long been universally conceded. We are now concerned, therefore, only with that other practical application of the Monroe doctrine the disregard of which by an European power is to be deemed an act of unfriendliness towards the United States. The precise scope and limitations of this rule cannot be too clearly apprehended. It does not establish any general protectorate by the United States over other American states. It does not relieve any American state from its obligations as fixed by international law nor prevent any European power directly interested from enforcing such obligations or from inflicting merited punishment for the breach of them. It does not contemplate any interference in the internal affairs of any American state or in the relations between it and other American states. It does not justify any attempt on our part to change the established form of government of any American state or to prevent the people of such state from altering that form according to their own will and pleasure. The rule in question has but a single purpose and object. It is that no European power or combination of European powers shall forcibly deprive an American state of the right and power of self-government and of shaping for itself its own political fortunes and destinies. . . .

. . . Today the United States is practically sovereign on this continent, and its fiat is law upon the subjects to which it confines its interposition. Why? It is not because of the pure friendship or good will felt for it. It is not simply by reason of its high character as a civilized state, nor because wisdom and justice and equity are the invariable characteristics of the dealings of the United States. It is because, in addition to all other grounds, its infinite resources [and] isolated position render it master of the situation and practically invulnerable as against any or all other powers.

All the advantages of this superiority are at once imperiled if the principle be admitted that European powers may convert American states into colonies or provinces of their own. The principle would be eagerly availed of, and every power doing so would immediately acquire a base of military operations against us. What one power was permitted to do could not be denied to another, and it is not inconceivable that the struggle now going on for the acquisition of Africa might be transferred to South America. If it were, the weaker countries would unquestionably be soon absorbed, while the ultimate result might be the partition of all South America between the various European powers. The disastrous consequences to the United States of such a condition of things are obvious. The loss of prestige, of authority, and of weight in the councils of the family of nations, would be among the least of them. Our only real rivals in peace as well as enemies in war would be found located at our very doors. Thus far in our history we have been spared the burdens and evils of immense standing armies and all the other accessories of huge warlike establishments, and the exemption has largely contributed to our national greatness and wealth as well as to the happiness of every citizen. But, with the powers of Europe permanently encamped on American soil, the ideal conditions we have thus far enjoyed can not be expected to continue. We too must be armed to the teeth, we too must convert the flower of our male population into soldiers and sailors, and by withdrawing them from the various pursuits of peaceful industry we too must practically annihilate a large share of the productive energy of the nation. . . .

There is, then, a doctrine of American public law, well founded in principle and abundantly sanctioned by precedent, which entitles and requires the United States to treat as an injury to itself the forcible assumption by an European power of political control over an American state. The application of the doctrine to the boundary dispute between Great Britain and Venezuela remains to be made and presents no real difficulty. Though the dispute relates to a boundary line, yet, as it is between states, it necessarily imports political control to be lost by one party and gained by the other. The political control at stake, too, is of no mean importance, but concerns a domain of great extent—the British claim, it will be remembered, apparently expanded in two years some 33,000 square miles—and, if it also directly involves the command of the mouth of the Orinoco, is of immense consequence in connection with the whole river navigation of the interior of South America. . . .

Thus, as already intimated, the British demand that her right to a portion of the disputed territory shall be acknowledged before she will consent to an arbitration as to the rest seems to stand upon nothing but her own *ipse dixit*. She says to Venezuela, in substance: "You can get none of the debatable land by force, because you are not strong enough; you can get none by treaty, because I will not agree; and you can take your chance of getting a portion by arbitration, only if you first agree to abandon to me such other portion as I may designate." It is not perceived how such an attitude can be defended nor how it is reconcilable with that love of justice and fair play so eminently characteristic of the English race. It in effect deprives Venezuela of her free agency and puts her under virtual duress. Territory acquired by reason of it will be as much wrested from her by the strong hand as if occupied by British troops or covered by British fleets. It seems therefore quite impossible that this position of Great Britain should be assented to by the United

States, or that, if such position be adhered to with the result of enlarging the bounds of British Guiana, it should not be regarded as amounting, in substance, to an invasion and conquest of Venezuelan territory.

In these circumstances, the duty of the President appears to him unmistakable and imperative. Great Britain's assertion of title to the disputed territory combined with her refusal to have that title investigated being a substantial appropriation of the territory to her own use, not to protest and give warning that the transaction will be regarded as injurious to the interests of the people of the United States as well as oppressive in itself would be to ignore an established policy with which honor and welfare of this country are closely identified. . . .

Document 6

Teller Amendment, Apr. 20, 1898, U.S. Congress, 55th Cong., 2d sess., *Senate Documents*, no. 24, 1898, 738–39.

Joint Resolution For the recognition of the independence of the people of Cuba, demanding that the Government of Spain relinquish its authority and government in the Island of Cuba, and to withdraw its land and naval forces from Cuba and Cuban waters, and directing the President of the United States to use the land and naval forces of the United States to carry these resolutions into effect.

Whereas the abhorrent conditions which have existed for more than three years in the Island of Cuba, so near our own borders, have shocked the moral sense of the people of the United States, have been a disgrace to Christian civilization, culminating, as they have, in the destruction of a United States battle ship, with two hundred and sixty-six of its officers and crew, while on a friendly visit in the harbor of Havana, and can not longer be endured, as has been set forth by the President of the United States in his message to Congress of April eleventh, eighteen hundred and ninety-eight, upon which the action of Congress was invited: Therefore,

Resolved by the Senate and the House of Representatives of the United States of America in Congress assembled, First. That the people of the Island of Cuba are, and of right ought to be, free and independent.

Second. That it is the duty of the United States to demand, and the Government of the United States does hereby demand, that the Government of Spain at once relinquish its authority and government in the Island of Cuba and withdraw its land and naval forces from Cuba and Cuban waters.

Third. That the President of the United States be, and he hereby is, directed and empowered to use the entire land and naval forces of the United States, and to call into the actual service of the United States the militia of the several States, to such extent as may be necessary to carry these resolutions into effect.

Fourth. That the United States hereby disclaims any disposition or intention to exercise sovereignty, jurisdiction, or control over said Island except for the pacification thereof, and asserts its determination, when that is accomplished, to leave the government and control of the Island to its people.

Document 7

Platt Amendment, Feb. 25, 1901, *Congressional Record*, 56th Cong., 2d sess., 1901, 2954.

The PRESIDING OFFICER (Mr. [Orville] Platt of Connecticut in the chair) laid before the Senate the following message from the President of the United States; which was read, referred to the Committee on Foreign Relations, and ordered to be printed:

To the Congress of the United States:

I commend to the Congress timely consideration of measures for maintaining diplomatic and consular representatives in Cuba and for carrying out the provisions of the act making appropriation for the support of the Army for the fiscal year ending June 30, 1902, approved March 2, 1901, reading as follows:

"*Provided further*, That in fulfillment of the declaration contained in the joint resolution approved April 20, 1898, entitled 'For the recognition of the independence of the people of Cuba, demanding that the Government of Spain relinquish its authority and government in the island of Cuba, and to withdraw its land and naval forces from Cuba and Cuban waters, and directing the President of the United States to use the land and naval forces of the United States to carry these resolutions into effect,' the President is hereby authorized to 'leave the government and control of the island of Cuba to its people' so soon as a government shall have been established in said island under a constitution which, either as a part thereof or in an ordinance appended thereto, shall define the future relations of the United States with Cuba substantially as follows:

"I.

"That the government of Cuba shall never enter into any treaty or other compact with any foreign power or powers which will impair or tend to impair the independence of Cuba, nor in any manner authorize or permit any foreign power or powers to obtain, by colonization or for military or naval purposes or otherwise, lodgment in or control over any portion of said island.

"II.

"That said government shall not assume or contract any public debt to pay the interest upon which, and to make reasonable sinking fund provision for the ultimate discharge of which, the ordinary revenues of the island, after defraying the current expenses of government, shall be inadequate.

"III.

"That the government of Cuba consents that the United States may exercise the right to intervene for the preservation of Cuban independence, the maintenance of a government adequate for the protection of life, property, and individual liberty, and for discharging the obligations with respect to Cuba imposed by the treaty of Paris on the United States, now to be assumed and undertaken by the government of Cuba.

"IV.

"That all acts of the United States in Cuba during its military occupancy thereof are ratified and validated, and all lawful rights acquired thereunder shall be maintained and protected.

"V.

"That the government of Cuba will execute, and as far as necessary extend, the plans already devised or other plans to be mutually agreed upon, for the sanitation of the cities of the island, to the end that a recurrence of epidemic and infectious diseases may be prevented, thereby assuring protection to the people and commerce of Cuba, as well as to the commerce of the southern ports of the United States and the people residing therein.

"VI.

"That the Isle of Pines shall be omitted from the proposed constitutional boundaries of Cuba, the title thereto being left to future adjustment by treaty.

"VII.

"That to enable the United States to maintain the independence of Cuba, and to protect the people thereof, as well as for its own defense, the government of Cuba will sell or lease to the United States lands necessary for coaling of naval stations at certain specified points, to be agreed upon with the President of the United States.

"VIII.

"That by way of further assurance the government of Cuba will embody the foregoing provisions in a permanent treaty with the United States."

The people of Cuba having framed a constitution embracing the foregoing requirements, and having elected a president who is soon to take office, the time is near for the fulfillment of the pledge of the United States to leave the government and control of the island of Cuba to its people. I am advised by the Secretary of War that it is now expected that the installation of the government of Cuba and the termination of the military occupation of that island by the United States will take place on the 20th of May next.

It is necessary and appropriate that the establishment of international relations with the government of Cuba should coincide with its inauguration, as well to provide a channel for the conduct of diplomatic relations with the new State as to open the path for the immediate negotiation of conventional agreements to carry out the provisions of the act above quoted.

It is also advisable that consular representation be established without delay at the principal Cuban ports in order that commerce with the island may be conducted with due regard to the formalities prescribed by the revenue and navigation statutes of the United States, and that American citizens in Cuba may have the customary local resorts open to them for their business needs and, the case arising, for the protection of their rights.

CHAPTER 2

Theodore Roosevelt and the Rise of America to World Power

Joseph A. Fry

From his ''bully pulpit'' in the White House, President Theodore Roosevelt repeatedly exhorted the United States toward greatness, making it hardly coincidental that the nation's status as a world power was confirmed during his presidency. To be sure, many of the prerequisites for national eminence were in place when TR assumed office in 1901. He presided over the world's leading producer of wheat, cotton, iron, coal, and steel. The worth of U.S. manufactured goods totaled three times that of England, the nearest competitor. Exports easily outdistanced imports, and American capitalists busily scanned the globe for investment opportunities. The United States' military capacity and potential were also manifest. Both the ease with which it had vanquished Spain in 1898 and the subsequent annexation of an island empire elicited grudging European respect. America's ongoing construction of a navy that by 1909 ranked second only to that of Great Britain decisively reinforced that respect. Still, it was Roosevelt's irrepressible personality, boundless energy, modern conception of the presidency, and activist foreign policy that transformed this potential for greatness into reality.

Roosevelt was the most popular president ever to lead the nation, and his toothy grin, bristling mustache, and wire-rimmed glasses seemed omnipresent between 1901 and 1909. This was not accidental. TR's pithy quotes, physical exploits, and sheer enjoyment of life made great copy. He relished being the center of attention. ''Father always wanted to be the bride at every wedding and the corpse at every funeral,'' his son once observed. The elder Roosevelt had been careful to have reporters in tow for his night patrols as New York City's police commissioner and for his charge up San Juan Hill against the Spanish in Cuba. Once in the White House, he continued to cultivate and manage the press with a deftness that made him, in the words of one historian, the first chief executive to exploit fully the ''modern, public side of the presidency.''

Roosevelt's understanding of the powers of the presidency was also distinctly modern. Here again, personality and public policy coincided. Congenitally incapable of inactivity or a policy of drift, TR was "pure act," as Henry Adams, an American historian, once observed. Regarding foreign policy, Roosevelt believed that it was the president's responsibility to act and to lead: Congress was too diffuse, the people too ill-informed. Aggressively utilizing his powers as commander-in-chief, TR unilaterally dispatched troops to quash revolutions in Latin America. Three times, when Congress objected to his policies, he circumvented the Senate by negotiating executive agreements that did not require congressional approval. Just before leaving office in 1909, Roosevelt noted that he had often consulted William Howard Taft or Elihu Root, an American lawyer and statesman, on important issues. "The biggest matters, however, such as the [Treaty of] Portsmouth peace, the acquisition of Panama, and sending the fleet around the world, I managed without consultation with anyone; for when a matter is of capital importance, it is well to have it handled by one man only." Acting on these assumptions, TR consciously and significantly expanded the president's foreign policy prerogatives and helped lay the foundations for what one writer has called the "imperial presidency."

Roosevelt's influence was derived from more than personality or aggressive use of the presidency. No president, save John Quincy Adams, had entered office so well prepared for foreign policy leadership. A voracious reader and acute student of history, TR had conferred frequently in the 1890s with experts and theorists such as Alfred Thayer Mahan, Brooks Adams, and John Hay, and he had served as President William McKinley's assistant secretary of the navy. Supplementing these experiences and studies with extensive European travel and personal contacts, Roosevelt had formulated a coherent theoretical basis for the nation's foreign policy.

Roosevelt's conception of the proper U.S. foreign policy was based on numerous cultural and historical assumptions combined with sophisticated strategic calculations and a clear understanding of the uses of power. He began with the conviction that the world was divided between superior, civilized races (particularly the Anglo-Saxons) and inferior, barbaric peoples. Distinguished by their accomplishments in government, intellectual pursuits, and technology, the superior races were both destined and obligated to dominate and nurture their barbarian neighbors. While extending "civilization" and "morality," such imperial domination imposed essential order and stability, regenerated the inferior races, and preserved the vitality of the colonial masters. Given these laudable results, TR had no reservations about the use of force; indeed, he judged that "all the great masterful races have been fighting races" and pronounced war against savages as "the most ultimately righteous of all wars." Roosevelt considered the United States' suppression of the American Indians the epitome of these historical processes, and he applauded the acquisition of an island empire following the Spanish-American War. This perspective permeated his well-known speech "The Strenuous Life," in which he prodded the United

States to accept its role as a great and civilized nation and "to play a great part in the world." (doc. 1) Only by assuming the mantle of empire could Americans show themselves "equal to one of the great tasks set modern civilization."

To this enthusiasm for shouldering the "white man's burden," TR added a clear understanding of the power necessary to accomplish great things. Roosevelt decried a policy of bluff because it destroyed both personal and national credibility. Instead, he advocated preparedness and the maxims "walk softly and carry a big stick" and "never draw unless you intend to shoot." He did not, however, define preparedness in purely military terms; the exploitation of natural resources, the development of industrial capacity, and the preservation of the national character also demanded attention. Still, when TR sought to wield the big stick, he thought first of a formidable navy. In his February 23, 1904, letter to Elijah Burton, Republican congressman from Ohio, Roosevelt forcefully asserted that national responsibilities must be balanced against the power to accomplish them, that weakness invites attack, and that only powerful nations exert decisive international influence—especially for peace. (doc. 2)

While urging the nation to play an active and influential role in world affairs, Roosevelt devoted relatively little attention to economic considerations. Indeed, he frequently cited the selfish, "stock-jobbing mentality" of businessmen as an impediment to a vigorous foreign policy. Despite such attacks on materialism, TR recognized that competing in the race for commercial supremacy was critical to achieving world power. Moreover, members of his cabinet kept the issue of economic expansion clearly in view. None was more attentive than Elihu Root, who served as secretary of war from 1899 to 1904 and as secretary of state from 1905 to 1909. One of the nation's leading corporation lawyers with close ties to the eastern business and social establishment, Root personified the influences that would exercise great sway in twentieth-century American foreign policy. In his 1906 speech to the Trans-Mississippi Commercial Congress (doc. 3), Root accentuated the crucial transformation of the United States from a debtor to a creditor nation. Although he significantly understated the extent to which previous generations of Americans had looked abroad economically, his emphasis on the efficient and aggressive search for export and investment markets was both timely and prophetic.

As Roosevelt confronted specific decisions, he added sophisticated strategic calculations to his historical, racial, and economic considerations. TR understood that the United States had satiated its "land hunger" in the Spanish-American War. By comparing his inclination to annex Santo Domingo to the desire of a "gorged boa constrictor . . . to swallow a porcupine wrong-end-to," he accurately captured the national sentiment. Also cognizant of the "increasing interdependence and complexity of international political and economic relations," Roosevelt sought to block European probing in the Caribbean. He perceived two threats to the enforcement of the Monroe Doctrine: the chronic insolvency and instability of the United States' southern neighbors and Germany's territorial ambitions. The first invited outside intervention to collect debts and protect foreign citizens or property; the second made Germany the European nation most anxious to exploit such opportunities. When Roosevelt combined these strategic imperatives with his conception of America's role as a superior, civilized nation, the result was the persistent pursuit of order and stability. Only a quiescent Caribbean precluded European intervention and provided the proper environment for U.S. commerce and Latin American progress.

The Platt Amendment to the Army Appropriations Bill of 1901 (see doc. 7, chap. 1) epitomized the United States' determination to impose order and stability on the Caribbean. Prompted by Secretary of War Root, Senator Orville Platt of Connecticut stipulated the conditions by which Cuba might end the military occupation imposed by the United States after the defeat of Spain in 1898. When Cuba reluctantly wrote the Platt Amendment into its 1901 constitution and into a treaty with the United States two years later, the island nation was left as an American protectorate. U.S. soldiers withdrew in 1903 but returned in 1906, 1912, and 1917, and over the subsequent fifty years no Cuban government survived without American approval.

Both TR's apprehension over German intentions and his willingness to wield the big stick were manifest in his response to a combined British-German-Italian blockade and occupation of Venezuela in December 1902. Although he dismissed the Venezuelan dictator, Cipriano Castro, as an "unspeakably villainous little monkey" and condemned Venezuela's refusal either to pay or arbitrate its debts, Roosevelt would tolerate no permanent German presence. He recounted his handling of this incident in an August 1916 letter to historian William Roscoe Thayer. (doc. 4)

Forcing the kaiser to back down did not remedy the ongoing problem of fiscal and political instability in the Caribbean. TR acknowledged that the Europeans were justified in collecting on their loans and protecting their citizens. Therefore, Roosevelt reasoned that if by enforcing the Monroe Doctrine "we intend to say 'Hands off' to the powers of Europe, sooner or later we must keep order ourselves." When Santo Domingo appeared to be "drifting into chaos" in 1904, Roosevelt moved to stifle the potential coup. In his annual message to Congress in December 1904, the president added the "Roosevelt Corollary" to the Monroe Doctrine. (doc. 5) Henceforth, the United States would exercise "international police power" in the Western Hemisphere. When the Senate rejected a treaty authorizing the United States to administer the Dominican customs houses, Roosevelt characteristically bypassed the chamber by negotiating an executive agreement with Carlos Morales, the president of Santo Domingo. In his fifth annual message the following year (doc. 6), TR asserted that this arrangement had avoided revolutionary chaos, blocked foreign intervention, and laid the basis for orderly progress.

Within the context of an orderly, well-policed Caribbean, Roosevelt most coveted a canal through Central America. Eager to make "the dirt fly," he was furious when the Colombian Senate rejected a 1903 treaty granting the United States a right-of-way through Panama. Although Colombia had acted entirely within its rights as an independent nation, TR castigated Colombian President José Marroquín for breaking his word. As he allegedly admitted in 1911, Roosevelt then "took" the canal. He extended implicit encouragement to Panamanian insurgents; dispatched naval vessels to Panama; and countenanced the use of American marines to ensure the successes of the November 3 revolution against Colombian authority. He then boldly justified this intervention through an 1846 treaty in which the United States had pledged to uphold, rather than destroy, Colombian sovereignty. Acting with unseemly haste, Roosevelt extended de facto recognition to the Panamanian government on November 6, 1903, and twelve days later concluded a treaty granting the United States liberal concessions for constructing the canal and extensive control over Panamanian affairs. TR's 1903 letters to Secretary of State John Hay, editor Albert Shaw, and Chicago lawyer Otto Gresham (docs. 7–10) revealed his contempt for the Colombians, his readiness to intervene, his tendency to inject concepts of individual honor into international affairs, and his identification of U.S. interests with progress and world civilization. In its editorial "Beyond the Domain of Law," the *New York Times* sharply and effectively critiqued the transparent expediency and probable illegality of Roosevelt's actions. (doc. 11)

"The American course had rested at bottom on bullying," one scholar noted, "and virtually all of Latin America saw it that way." Rubén Darío, one of the leading figures in the modernist school of Spanish poetry, eloquently voiced this Latin indignation. (doc. 12) In addition to expressing central modernist themes praising Latin culture and denouncing imperialism, he directed his fury toward Roosevelt. That focus, together with Darío's stature and talent, sets this poem apart from others of that genre.

Imposing order through force in the Philippines elicited similarly harsh criticism. In seizing the islands from Spain, the United States had acquired a determined guerrilla resistance to colonial rule. Not until 1902 were the Filipino insurgents suppressed, and then only after the loss of 4,200 American soldiers, the expenditure of $400 million, the killing of 18,000 guerrillas, and the deaths of at least 100,000 civilians from disease and starvation. Critics of the war were especially aghast at the conduct of some American soldiers. The "water cure," by which information was extracted from Filipino prisoners, was the most infamous of the atrocities. Testifying before a special Senate committee, former soldiers Grover Flint and Charles S. Riley provided vivid descriptions of this torture. (docs. 13 and 14) The committee also obtained a report by Major Cornelius Gardner, the U.S. governor of Tayabas Province. (doc. 15) In phrases later echoed in accounts of U.S. experience in Vietnam, Gardner detailed the difficulty in identifying the enemy, highlighted American racial attitudes toward

Asians, and noted the implications of taking the lives and destroying the property of noncombatants.

Although President Roosevelt favored the punishment of U.S. soldiers who "committed cruelties in the Philippines," he unflinchingly defended the American war effort. Comparing Emilio Aguinaldo, the Philippine leader, to Sitting Bull, Roosevelt declared that "as peace, order and prosperity followed our expansion over the lands of the Indians, so they will follow us in the Philippines." TR responded to critics of the war in his 1902 Memorial Day speech at Arlington National Cemetery. (doc. 16)

The nation's greatly expanded international presence under Roosevelt was not confined to rendering the Caribbean an American lake or to assuming the imperial mantle in the Pacific. TR also interjected the United States directly into the European balance of power by agreeing in 1905 to help resolve the Franco-German crisis over Morocco. Although he approved the use of force against less-developed peoples, Roosevelt promoted the peaceful settlement of disputes among "civilized" nations. In challenging French suzerainty over this small North African state, Germany had provoked a war scare and tested France's entente with Great Britain. At Germany's request, Roosevelt solicited a meeting of the interested European states at Algeciras, Spain. He suggested the terms of settlement and put pressure on Kaiser Wilhelm II to accept the resulting treaty. While preventing the partition of Morocco and preserving peace, this agreement left France and Spain in control of the Moroccan police force and reasserted open-door access to the nation's commerce. TR had acted primarily from a desire to bolster France and Great Britain and hence preserve the European balance of power and avoid war. In his letter to *New York Tribune* owner Whitelaw Reid, Roosevelt colorfully described his role in this principally European struggle. (doc. 17) Still, American interests extended well beyond the balance of power; prospects for foreign trade commanded significant attention. Secretary of State Root's instructions to the U.S. representatives to the Algeciras Conference explicitly outlined the preferred operation of the open door—an operation for which the United States contended worldwide. (doc. 18)

Roosevelt's avid participation in big-power politics also led him to help mediate the Russo-Japanese War of 1904–05. Here again, TR sought order and stability by preserving the balance of power. Upon entering office, he viewed Russia as the principal threat to Chinese territorial integrity, the Open Door policy, and the uneasy standoff among the imperial powers in Asia. Hence he concluded that the Japanese were "playing our game" in their surprise attack on Russia's Pacific fleet in 1904. However, as the war extended into 1905, he recognized the dangers of either Japanese exhaustion or a decisive Japanese victory. Japan deserved to benefit from its victory, but Russia needed to be left "face-to-face with Japan so that each may have a moderative action on the other." Therefore, TR responded eagerly when Japan requested that he call a peace conference. Demonstrating his capacity for subtle, secretive diplomacy, he worked for several months to arrange the conference at Portsmouth, New Hampshire, in August 1905, where he skillfully persuaded the participants to accept a settlement. Roosevelt clarified his role in his October 15, 1905, letter to historian George Kennan. (doc. 19)

Careful calculations of U.S. interests and power characterized TR's subsequent dealings with Japan. In contrast to the Caribbean, where American power was supreme and American interests vital, Roosevelt's Far Eastern policy was measured and restrained. When Japan began to consolidate power and close the commercial open door in Korea and southern Manchuria after 1905, TR refrained from directly challenging the rising Asian nation. In the 1905 Taft-Katsura Agreement, he acknowledged Japan's dominance in Korea in return for its pledge not to attack the Philippines. When conflict arose over the mistreatment of Japanese citizens in California, TR negotiated the "Gentlemen's Agreement" of 1907, which aimed at stopping the emigration of Japanese laborers in return for halting California's discriminatory practices. Roosevelt incisively explained his assessment of the U.S. position relative to Japan and China in his December 22, 1910, letter to William Howard Taft. (doc. 20) Neither U.S. power nor U.S. interests warranted a confrontation with Japan on the Asian mainland.

Still, TR worried in early 1907 that the Japanese were becoming "cocky and unreasonable." His response was dramatic and characteristic. In July 1907 he dispatched the entire fleet of 16 U.S. battleships on a world cruise. When key congressmen fretted over a possible Japanese attack and protested that the cruise lacked legitimate funding, Roosevelt replied that he had the funds to send the fleet halfway around the world—where it would have to stay without additional allocations. He got the money; the fleet's flawless performance, including a visit to Tokyo, helped clear the air with Japan. TR rendered his account of the "Great White Fleet's" voyage to British historian George Otto Trevelyn on October 1, 1911. (doc. 21)

Tangible results of TR's actions came the following year with the Root-Takahira Agreement. This exchange of diplomatic notes provided a concise summary of the state of U.S. relations with Japan as Roosevelt left office. (doc. 22) Both nations professed peaceful intentions; both agreed to respect each other's territorial possessions; both agreed to the principle (if not the operation) of the Open Door policy; and both agreed to the "independence and integrity of China." By not stipulating the "territorial integrity" of China, as Secretary of State John Hay's 1900 Open Door note had done, the agreement acknowledged Japan's exploitation of Manchuria.

The Root-Takahira Agreement also symbolized the United States' greatly expanded international involvement under Roosevelt, the first president "to act self-consciously as the leader of a great power," according to one writer. Like the man, TR's diplomacy was complex. His policies embodied the energy, the power, the racial assumptions, and the arrogance that led to the American suppression of Philippine independence, the domination of the Caribbean, and the alienation of Latin America. TR also demonstrated the realism, the perception, the discretion, and the subtlety that helped preserve peace and the balance of power at Algeciras and Portsmouth while producing a working relationship with Japan. Although Roosevelt did not convert all American people to his enthusiasm for international activism, his presidency remains synonymous with the rise of America to world power.

Document 1

President Theodore Roosevelt, "The Strenuous Life," speech before the Hamilton Club, Chicago, Apr. 10, 1899, *The Strenuous Life: Essays and Addresses,* New York: The Century Co., 1903, 4–10.

As it is with the individual, so it is with the nation. It is a base untruth to say that happy is the nation that has no history. Thrice happy is the nation that has a glorious history. Far better it is to dare mighty things, to win glorious triumphs, even though checkered by failure, than to take rank with those poor spirits who neither enjoy much nor suffer much, because they lie in the gray twilight that knows not victory nor defeat. . . .

We of this generation do not have to face a task such as that our fathers faced, but we have our tasks, and woe to us if we fail to perform them! We cannot, if we would, play the part of China, and be content to rot by inches in ignoble ease within our borders, taking no interest in what goes on beyond them, sunk in a scrambling commercialism; heedless of the higher life, the life of aspiration, of toil and risk, busying ourselves only with the wants of our bodies for the day, until suddenly we should find, beyond a shadow of question, what China has already found, that in this world the nation that has trained itself to a career of unwarlike and isolated ease is bound, in the end, to go down before other nations which have not lost the manly and adventurous qualities. If we are to be a really great people, we must strive in good faith to play a great part in the world. We cannot avoid meeting great issues. All that we can determine for ourselves is whether we shall meet them well or ill. In 1898 we could not help being brought face to face with the problem of war with Spain. All we could decide was whether we should shrink like cowards from the contest, or enter into it as beseemed a brave and high-spirited people; and, once in, whether failure or success should crown our banners. So it is now. We cannot avoid the responsibilities that confront us in Hawaii, Cuba, Porto Rico, and the Philippines. . . . To refuse to deal with them at all merely amounts to dealing with them badly. We have a given problem to solve. If we undertake the solution, there is, of course, always danger that we may not solve it aright; but to refuse to undertake the solution simply renders it certain that we cannot possibly solve it aright. The timid man, the lazy man, the man who distrusts his country, the overcivilized man, who has lost the great fighting, masterful virtues, the ignorant man, and the man of dull mind, whose soul is incapable of feeling the mighty lift that thrills "stern men with empires in their brains"—all these, of course, shrink from seeing the nation undertake its new duties; shrink from seeing us build a navy and an army adequate to our needs; shrink from seeing us do our share of the world's work, by bringing order out of chaos in the great, fair tropic islands from which the valor of our soldiers and sailors has driven the Spanish flag. These are the men who fear the strenuous life, who fear the only national life which is really worth leading. They believe in that cloistered life which saps the hardy virtues in a nation, as it saps them in the individual; or else they are wedded to that base spirit of gain and greed which recognizes in commercialism the be-all and end-all of national life, instead of realizing that, though an indispensable element, it is, after all, but one of the many elements that go to make up true national greatness. . . .

We cannot sit huddled within our own borders and avow ourselves merely an assemblage of well-to-do hucksters who care nothing for what happens beyond. Such a policy would defeat even its own end; for as the nations grow to have ever wider and wider interests, and are brought into closer and closer contact, if we are to hold our own in the struggle for naval and commercial supremacy, we must build up our power without our own borders. We must build the Isthmian Canal, and we must grasp the points of vantage which will enable us to have our say in deciding the destiny of the oceans of the East and the West.

So much for the commercial side. From the standpoint of international honor the argument is even stronger. The guns that thundered off Manila and Santiago left us echoes of glory, but they also left us a legacy of duty. If we drove out a mediaeval tyranny only to make room for savage anarchy, we had better not have begun the task at all. It is worse than idle to say that we have no duty to perform, and can leave to their fates the islands we have conquered. Such a course would be the course of infamy. It would be followed at once by utter chaos in the wretched islands themselves. Some stronger, manlier power would have to step in and do the work, and we would have shown ourselves weaklings, unable to carry to successful completion the labors that great and high-spirited nations are eager to undertake.

The work must be done; we cannot escape our responsibility; and if we are worth our salt, we shall be glad of the chance to do the work—glad of the chance to show ourselves equal to one of the great tasks set modern civilization.

Document 2

President Theodore Roosevelt to Theodore Elijah Burton (Republican congressman from Ohio), Feb. 23, 1904, *The Letters of Theodore Roosevelt* (hereafter referred to as *TRL*), Elting E. Morison, ed., Cambridge, Massachusetts: Harvard University Press, 1951–54, vol. 4, 736–37.

The one unforgivable crime is to put one's self in a position in which strength and courage are needed, and then to show lack of strength and courage. This is precisely the crime committed by those who advocate or have acquiesced in the acquisition of the Philippines, the establishment of naval stations in Cuba, the negotiation of the treaty for building the Panama Canal, the taking of Porto Rico and Hawaii, and the assertion of the Monroe Doctrine, and who nevertheless decline to advocate the building of a navy such as will alone warrant our attitude in any one, not to say all, of these matters. It is perfectly allowable, although I think rather ignoble, to take the attitude that this country is to occupy a position in the New World analogous to that of China in the Old World, to stay entirely within her borders, not to endeavor to assert the Monroe Doctrine, incidentally to leave the Philippines, to abandon the care of the Panama Canal, to give up Hawaii and Porto Rico, etc., etc., and therefore to refuse to build up any navy. It is also allowable, and as I think, in the highest degree farsighted and honorable, to insist that the attitude of the republican party in all these matters during the last eight years has been the wise and proper attitude, and to insist therefore that the navy shall be kept up and built up as required by the needs of such an attitude. But any attempt to combine the two attitudes is fraught with the certainty of hopeless and ignominious disaster to the Nation. To be rich, aggressive, and yet helpless in war, is to invite destruction. If everything that the republican party has done during the past eight years is all wrong; if we ought not to have annexed Hawaii, or taken the Philippines, or established a kind of protectorate over Cuba, or started to build the Panama Canal, then let us reverse these policies and give up building a navy; but to my mind it is to inflict a great wrong on the generations who come after us if we persevere in these policies and do not back them up by building a navy. . . .

. . . If we are to have a naval station in the Philippines; if we are to have a fleet in Asiatic waters, or to exert the slightest influence in eastern Asia where our people hope to find a market, then it is of the highest importance that we have a naval station at Subig Bay. If we are not to have that station, and are not to have a navy, then we should be manly enough to say that we intend to abandon the Philippines at once; not to try to keep a naval station there; and not to try to exercise that influence in foreign affairs which comes only to the just man armed who wishes to keep the peace. China is now the sport and plaything of stronger powers because she has constantly acted on her belief in despising and making little of military strength afloat or ashore, and is therefore powerless to keep order within or repel aggression from without. The little powers of Europe, although in many cases they lead honorable and self-respecting national lives, are powerless to accomplish any great good in foreign affairs, simply and solely because they lack the element of force behind their good wishes. We on the contrary have been able to do so much for The Hague Tribunal and for the cause of international arbitration; we have been able to keep the peace in the waters south of us; to put an end to bloody misrule and bloody civil strife in Cuba, in the Philippines, and at Panama; and we are able to exercise a pacific influence in China, because, and only because, together with the purpose to be just and to keep the peace we possess a navy which makes it evident that we will not tamely submit to injustice, or tamely acquiesce in breaking the peace.

Document 3

Secretary of State Elihu Root, "Address Before the Trans-Mississippi Commercial Congress," Nov. 20, 1906, *Papers Relating to the Foreign Relations of the United States* (hereafter referred to as *FRUS*), *1906*, Washington, D.C.: Government Printing Office, 1909, vol. 1, 1457–58.

A little less than three centuries of colonial and national life have brought the people inhabiting the United States, by a process of evolution, natural and with the existing forces inevitable, to a point of distinct and radical change in their economic relations to the rest of mankind.

During the period now past the energy of our people, directed by the formative power created in our early population by heredity, by environment, by the struggle for existence, by individual independence, and by free institutions, has been devoted to the internal development of our own country. The surplus wealth produced by our labors has been applied immediately to reproduction in our own land. . . . We have been always a debtor nation, borrowing from the rest of the world, drawing all possible energy toward us and concentrating it with our own energy upon our own enterprises. The engrossing pursuit of our own opportunities has excluded from our consideration and interest the enterprises and the possibilities of the outside world. Invention, discovery, the progress of science, capacity for organization, the enormous increase in the productive power of mankind, have accelerated our progress and have brought us to a result of development in every branch of internal industrial activity marvelous and unprecedented in the history of the world.

Since the first election of President [William] McKinley the people of the United States have for the first time accumulated a surplus of capital beyond the requirements of internal development. That surplus is increasing with extraordinary rapidity. We have paid our debts to Europe and have become a creditor instead of a debtor nation; we have faced about; we have left the ranks of the borrowing nations and have entered the ranks of the investing nations. Our surplus energy is beginning to look beyond our own borders, throughout the world, to find opportunity for the profitable use of our surplus capital, foreign markets for our manufactures, foreign mines to be developed, foreign bridges and railroads and public works to be built, foreign rivers to be turned into electric power and light. As in their several ways England and France and Germany have stood, so we in our own way are beginning to stand and must continue to stand toward the industrial enterprise of the world.

That we are not beginning our new role feebly is indicated by $1,518,561,666 of exports in the year 1905 as against $1,117,513,071 of imports and by $1,743,864,500 exports in the year 1906 as against $1,226,563,843 of imports. Our first steps in the new field indeed are somewhat clumsy and unskilled. In our own vast country, with oceans on either side, we have had too little contact with foreign peoples readily to understand their customs or learn their languages; yet no one can doubt that we shall learn and shall understand and shall do our business abroad, as we have done it at home, with force and efficiency.

Document 4

President Theodore Roosevelt to William Roscoe Thayer (biographer of John Hay), Aug. 21, 1916, *TRL*, vol. 8, 1101–03.

There is now no reason why I should not speak of the facts connected with the disagreement between the United States and Germany over the Venezuela matter, in the early part of my administration as President, and of the final amicable settlement of the disagreement.

At that time the Venezuelan Dictator-President [Cipriano] Castro had committed various offences against different European nations, including Germany and England. The English Government was then endeavoring to keep on good terms with Germany, and on this occasion acted jointly with her. Germany sent a squadron of war vessels to the Venezuelan coast, and they were accompanied by some English war vessels. I had no objection whatever to Castro's being punished, as long as the punishment did not take the form of seizure of territory and its more or less permanent occupation by some old-world power. At this particular point such seizure of territory would have been a direct menace to the United States because it would have threatened or partially controlled the approach to the projected Isthmian Canal.

I speedily became convinced that Germany was the leader, and the really formidable party, in the transaction; and that England was merely following Germany's lead in rather half hearted fashion. . . . I also became convinced that Germany intended to seize some Venezuela harbor and turn it into a strongly fortified place of arms, on the model of Kiauchau, with a view to exercising some measure of control over the future Isthmian Canal, and over South American affairs generally.

For some time the usual methods of diplomatic intercourse were tried. Germany declined to agree to arbitrate the question at issue between her and Venezuela, and declined to say that she would not take possession of Venezuelan territory, merely saying that such possession would be "temporary"—which might mean anything. I finally decided that no useful purpose would be served by further delay, and I took action accordingly. I assembled our battle fleet, under Admiral [George] Dewey, near Porto Rico, for "maneuvers," with instructions that the fleet should be kept in hand and in fighting trim and should be ready to sail at an hour's notice. . . . I told [Secretary of State] John Hay that I would now see the German Ambassador, Herr [Theodor] von Holleben, myself and that I intended to bring matters to an early conclusion. Our navy was in very efficient condition, being superior to the German navy.

I saw the Ambassador, and explained that in view of the presence of the German Squadron on the Venezuelan coast I could not permit longer delay in answering my request for an arbitration, and that I could not acquiesce in any seizure of Venezuelan territory. The Ambassador responded that his Government could not agree to arbitrate, and that there was no intention to take "permanent" possession of Venezuelan territory. I answered that Kiauchau was not a "permanent" possession of Germany's—that I understood that it was merely held by a ninety nine years lease; and that I did not intend to have another Kiauchau, held by similar tenure, on the approach to the Isthmian Canal. The Ambassador repeated that his Government would not agree to arbitrate. I then asked him to inform his government that if no notification for arbitration came during the next ten days I would be obliged to order Dewey to take his fleet to the Venezuelan coast and see that the German forces did not take possession of any territory. He expressed very grave concern, and asked me if I realized the serious consequences that would follow such action; . . . I answered that I had thoroughly counted the cost before I decided on the step, and asked him to look at the map, as a glance would show him that there was no spot in the world where Germany in the event of conflict with the United States would be at a greater disadvantage than in the Caribbean sea.

A week later the Ambassador came to see me, talked pleasantly on several subjects, and rose to go. I asked him if he had any answer to make from his Government to my request, and when he said no, I informed him that . . . Dewey would be ordered to sail twenty four hours in advance of the time I had set. He expressed deep apprehension, and said that his Government would not arbitrate. However, less than twenty four hours before the time I had appointed for cabling the order to Dewey, the Ambassador notified me that His Imperial Majesty the German Emperor had directed him to request me to undertake the arbitration myself. I felt, and publicly expressed, great gratification at this outcome, and great appreciation of the course the German Government had finally agreed to take. Later I secured the consent of the German Government to have the arbitration undertaken by the Hague Tribunal.

Document 5

''Roosevelt Corollary'' to the Monroe Doctrine, in President Theodore Roosevelt's fourth annual message to Congress, Dec. 6, 1904, *A Compilation of the Messages and Papers of the Presidents, 1789–1908,* James D. Richardson, comp., Washington, D.C.: Bureau of National Literature and Art, 1909, vol. 10, 831–32.

It is not true that the United States feels any land hunger or entertains any projects as regards the other nations of the Western Hemisphere save such as are for their welfare. All that this country desires is to see the neighboring countries stable, orderly, and prosperous. Any country whose people conduct themselves well can count upon our hearty friendship. If a nation shows that it knows how to act with reasonable efficiency and decency in social and political matters, if it keeps order and pays its obligations, it need fear no interference from the United States. Chronic wrongdoing, or an impotence which results in a general loosening of the ties of civilized society, may in America, as elsewhere, ultimately require intervention by some civilized nation, and in the Western Hemisphere the adherence of the United States to the Monroe Doctrine may force the United States, however reluctantly, in flagrant cases of such wrongdoing or impotence, to the exercise of an international police power. If every country washed by the Caribbean Sea would show the progress in stable and just civilization which with the aid of the Platt amendment Cuba has shown since our troops left the island, and which so many of the republics in both Americas are constantly and brilliantly showing, all question of interference by this Nation with their affairs would be at an end. Our interests and those of our southern neighbors are in reality identical. They have great natural riches, and if within their borders the reign of law and justice obtains, prosperity is sure to come to them. While they thus obey the primary laws of civilized society they may rest assured that they will be treated by us in a spirit of cordial and helpful sympathy. We would interfere with them only in the last resort, and then only if it became evident that their inability or unwillingness to do justice at home and abroad had violated the rights of the United States or had invited foreign aggression to the detriment of the entire body of American nations.

Document 6

President Theodore Roosevelt's fifth annual message to Congress, Dec. 5, 1905, *A Compilation of the Messages and Papers of the Presidents, 1789–1908,* James D. Richardson, comp., Washington, D.C.: Bureau of National Literature and Art, 1909, vol. 11, 1155–56.

Santo Domingo, in her turn, has now made an appeal to us to help her, and not only every principle of wisdom but every generous instinct within us bids us respond to the appeal. . . . There was imminent danger of foreign intervention. The previous rulers of Santo Domingo had recklessly incurred debts, and owing to her internal disorders she had ceased to be able to provide means of paying the debts. The patience of her foreign creditors had become exhausted, and at least two foreign nations were on the point of intervention, and were only prevented from intervening by the unofficial assurance of this Government that it would itself strive to help Santo Domingo in her hour of need. In the case of one of these nations, only the actual opening of negotiations to this end by our Government prevented the seizure of territory in Santo Domingo. . . .

Accordingly, the Executive Department of our Government negotiated a treaty under which we are to try to help the Dominican people to straighten out their finances. This treaty is pending before the Senate. In the meantime a temporary arrangement has been made which will last until the Senate has had time to take action upon the treaty. Under this arrangement the Dominican Government has appointed Americans to all the important positions in the customs service, and they are seeing to the honest collection of the revenues, turning over 45 per cent. to the Government for running expenses and putting the other 55 per cent. into a safe depository for equitable division in case the treaty shall be ratified, among the various creditors, whether European or American.

The Custom Houses offer well-nigh the only sources of revenue in Santo Domingo, and the different revolutions usually have as their real aim the obtaining of these Custom Houses. The mere fact that the Collectors of Customs are Americans, that they are performing their duties with efficiency and honesty, and that the treaty is pending in the Senate gives a certain moral power to the Government of Santo Domingo which it has not had before. This has completely discouraged all revolutionary movement, while it has already produced such an increase in the revenues that the Government is actually getting more from the 45 per cent. that the American Collectors turn over to it than it got formerly when it took the entire revenue. . . .

Under the course taken, stability and order and all the benefits of peace are at last coming to Santo Domingo, danger of foreign intervention has been suspended, and there is at last a prospect that all creditors will get justice. . . . If the arrangement is terminated by the failure of the treaty chaos will follow; and if chaos follows, sooner or later this Government may be involved in serious difficulties with foreign Governments over the island, or else may be forced itself to intervene in the island in some unpleasant fashion.

Document 7

President Theodore Roosevelt to Secretary of State John Hay, Aug. 19, 1903, *TRL*, vol. 3, 566–67.

On your way back cannot you stop here, and we will go over the canal situation? The one thing evident is to do nothing at present. If under the treaty of 1846 [between the United States and New Granada (later Colombia)] we have a color of right to start in and build the canal, my offhand judgment would favor such proceeding. It seems that the great bulk of the best engineers are agreed that that route is the best, and I do not think that the Bogota lot of jack rabbits should be allowed permanently to bar one of the future highways of civilization.

Document 8

President Theodore Roosevelt to Secretary of State John Hay, Sept. 15, 1903, *TRL*, vol. 3, 599.

I entirely approve of your idea. Let us do nothing in the Colombia matter at present. I shall be back in Washington by the 28th instant, and you a week or two afterwards. Then we will go over the matter very carefully and decide what to do. At present I feel that there are two alternatives. (1) To take up Nicaragua; (2) in some shape or way to interfere when it becomes necessary so as to secure the Panama route without further dealing with the foolish and homicidal corruptionists in Bogota. I am not inclined to have any further dealings whatever with those Bogota people.

Document 9

President Theodore Roosevelt to Albert Shaw (editor of *Review of Reviews*), Oct. 10, 1903, *TRL*, vol. 3, 628.

The alternatives were to go to Nicaragua, against the advice of the great majority of competent engineers . . . or else to take the territory by force without any attempt at getting a treaty. I cast aside the proposition made at this time to foment the secession of Panama. Whatever other governments can do, the United States cannot go into the securing by such underhand means, the secession. Privately, I freely say to you that I should be delighted if Panama were an independent State, or if it made itself so at this moment; but for me to say so publicly would amount to an instigation of a revolt, and therefore I cannot say it.

Document 10

President Theodore Roosevelt to Otto Gresham (Chicago lawyer and former member of Board of Education), Nov. 30, 1903, *TRL*, vol. 3, 662–63.

Panama revolted from Colombia because Colombia, for corrupt and evil purposes or else from complete governmental incompetency, declined to permit the building of the great work which meant everything to Panama. By every law, human and divine, Panama was right in her position.

Now, how anyone can conceive that Colombia has the slightest right in the matter I do not understand. We have been more than just, have been generous to a fault, in our dealings with Colombia. . . .

The case in a nutshell is this: The government of Colombia was solemnly pledged to give us the right to dig that canal. The government of Colombia now . . . asserts that it will instantly carry out that pledge and ratify the treaty we proposed[,] . . . yet last summer the government refused to ratify this treaty, and said that in view of the unanimous adverse action of the Colombian Congress it had no power to do what we desired. Of course this means that it was guilty of deliberate bad faith. The Colombians have not been badly treated; they have been well treated, and have themselves behaved badly; . . . the United States owes Colombia nothing in law or in morals. The Colombians need not come here to ask justice from me. They have received exact justice, after I had in vain endeavored to persuade them to accept generosity. In their silly efforts to damage us they cut their own throats. They tried to hold us up; and too late they have discovered their criminal error.

Document 11

"Beyond the Domain of Law," the *New York Times*, Nov. 11, 1903, 8.

We are maturing our plans for building this canal across the State of Panama. Before the world, in its relation to us even, that State is not yet severed from Colombia. We have at most acknowledged a de facto Government. Independence has not been established, and with all our haste, hurry, and recklessness we have not yet recognized it. But we have taken our measures with a firm mind and a sure hand to bring about its independence, and the prompt recognition and permanent protection of the new republic must follow as logical consequences. Nevertheless, at the present moment we are actually planning to construct a canal through the territory of a sovereign State without its consent. Protests are heard, of course. Everybody is not asleep. All consciences are not benumbed. . . .

In its essence, in fact and in law, the proceeding is one of conquest and spoliation, not one in which we are merely making good a treaty guarantee. The treaty of 1846 with New Granada was one for mutual advantage. In view of the weakness of New Granada and of our strength, we guaranteed that communication and commercial transit across the Isthmus should be open, safe, and convenient. The guarantee was given and accepted for mutual benefit. We now execute that guarantee in a manner and by measures which rob the Republic of Colombia of her richest State. We intervene between her and her revolted citizens by force and show of force sufficient to deter her from taking effective measures to suppress the insurrection. We go beyond the strictly limited object of the guarantee, the maintenance of open communication, and prevent the Bogota Government from taking the military measures necessary to preserve and enforce its authority. Who would have the hardihood to say that the treaty contemplated any such situation as this? That the Government of New Granada could have intended to confer upon us powers and rights in the exercise of which we should dismember it is simply unthinkable; it is absurd.

. . . Surely the most reckless defender of the Administration's policy of adventure on the Isthmus would not contend that New Granada ever intended to confer upon us, under the treaty, rights which we could in any contingency lawfully employ to protect insurgents against its authority, not merely along the lines of a railroad and canal, but throughout a whole State. . . .

It is, then, an act of conquest in which we are engaged, and conquest lies outside the domain of law. If we had gone to the Isthmus with troops and men-of-war, if we had openly and with force of arms attacked the Colombians and driven them out, we should have acquired the right to build the canal by the title of war. We acquire it now by the mixed title of intrigue and war—for intervention is war. There are a great many Americans who look upon the title as soiled and repugnant, who are ashamed of the means by which we get it.

Document 12

Rubén Darío, "To Roosevelt," 1905, in *Selected Poems of Rubén Darío*, Lysander Kemp, trans., Austin: University of Texas Press, 1965, 69–70. Reprinted by permission of the University of Texas Press.

The voice that would reach you, Hunter, must speak
in Biblical tones, or in the poetry of Walt Whitman.
You are primitive and modern, simple and complex;
you are one part George Washington and one part Nimrod.
You are the United States,
future invader of our naive America
with its Indian blood, an America
that still prays to Christ and still speaks Spanish.

You are a strong, proud model of your race;
you are cultured and able; you oppose Tolstoy.
You are an Alexander-Nebuchadnezzar,
breaking horses and murdering tigers.
(You are a Professor of Energy,
as the current lunatics say).

You think that life is a fire,
that progress is an irruption,
that the future is wherever
your bullet strikes.

No.

The United States is grand and powerful.
Whenever it trembles, a profound shudder
runs down the enormous backbone of the Andes.
If it shouts, the sound is like the roar of a lion.
And Hugo said to Grant: "The stars are yours."
(The dawning sun of the Argentine barely shines;
the star of Chile is rising . . .) A wealthy country,
joining the cult of Mammon to the cult of Hercules;

while Liberty, lighting the path
to easy conquest, raises her torch in New York.

But our own America, which has had poets
since the ancient times of Nezahualcóyotl;
which preserved the footprints of great Bacchus,
and learned the Panic alphabet once,
and consulted the stars; which also knew Atlantis
(whose name comes ringing down to us in Plato)
and has lived, since the earliest moments of its life,
in light, in fire, in fragrance, and in love—
the America of Moctezuma and Atahualpa,
the aromatic America of Columbus,
Catholic America, Spanish America,
the America where noble Cuauhtémoc said:
"I am not on a bed of roses"—our America,
trembling with hurricanes, trembling with Love:
O men with Saxon eyes and barbarous souls,
our America lives. And dreams. And loves.
And it is the daughter of the Sun. Be careful.
Long live Spanish America!
A thousand cubs of the Spanish lion are roaming free.
Roosevelt, you must become, by God's own will,
the deadly Rifleman and the dreadful Hunter
before you can clutch us in your iron claws.

And though you have everything, you are lacking one thing:
God!

Document 13

Grover Flint (former soldier), Apr. 21, 1902, testimony on affairs in the Philippine Islands, "Hearings before the Committee on the Philippines of the United States Senate," 57th Cong., 1st sess., *Senate Documents*, no. 33, vol. 2, 1767–68.

Q. Please tell the committee what you actually saw?

A. That is, you want me to describe one individual case of a man being put through the water cure?

Q. Yes; I would like you to do that, sir.

A. Very good, sir. A man is thrown down on his back and three or four men sit or stand on his arms and legs and hold him down, and either a gun barrel or a rifle barrel or a carbine barrel or a stick as big as a belaying pin—that is, with an inch circumference— . . . is simply thrust into his jaws and his jaws are thrust back, and, if possible, a wooden log or stone is put under his head— . . .

Q. His jaws are forced open, you say? How do you mean, crosswise?

A. Yes, sir; as a gag. In the case of very old men I have seen their teeth fall out—I mean when it was done a little roughly. He is simply held down, and then water is poured onto his face, down his throat and nose from a jar, and that is kept up until the man gives some sign of giving in or becomes unconscious, and when he becomes unconscious he is simply rolled aside and he is allowed to come to. That is as near a description as I think I can give. . . .

Q. Is the water allowed to remain in the man or is it in any way expelled from him, by any method?

A. Well, I know that in a great many cases, in almost every case, the men have been a little roughly handled; they were rolled aside rudely, so that water was expelled. A man suffers tremendously; there is no doubt about it. His suffering must be that of a man who is drowning, but who can not drown.

Q. Did you ever see a man place his foot on a man's stomach to force the water out?

A. Yes, sir.

Document 14

Charles S. Riley (former soldier), Jan. 14, 1902, testimony on affairs in the Philippine Islands, "Hearings before the Committee on the Philippines of the United States Senate," 57th Cong., 1st sess., *Senate Documents,* no. 33, vol. 2, 1529–30.

Q. Where did they take him [a Filipino prisoner]?

A. They took him downstairs outside the building, and he stood in front of the building, waiting for his horse. He was to guide the expedition up into the mountains.

Q. While standing on the sidewalk what took place?

A. More information was sought for; and as he refused to answer, a second treatment was ordered. . . .

Q. In front?

A. Yes; on the stone walk. They started to take him inside the building and Captain [Edwin F.] Glenn said, "Don't take him inside. Right here is good enough." One of the men of the Eighteenth Infantry went to his saddle and took a syringe from the saddlebag, and another man was sent for a can of water, what we call a kerosene can, holding about 5 gallons. He brought this can of water down from upstairs, and then a syringe was inserted, one end in the water and the other end in his mouth. This time he was not bound, but he was held by four or five men and the water was forced into his mouth from the can, through the syringe.

Q. Was this another party?

A. No; this was the same man. The syringe did not seem to have the desired effect, and the doctor ordered a second one. The man got a second syringe, and that was inserted in his nose. Then the doctor ordered some salt, and a handful of salt was procured and thrown into the water. Two syringes were then in operation. The interpreter stood over him in the meantime asking for this second information that was desired. Finally he gave in and gave the information that they sought, and then he was allowed to rise. . . .

Q. How long did the second infliction of this torture continue?

A. About the same as the first; from about five to fifteen minutes. I could not tell you the exact time.

Q. How many men held this Filipino down when the first torture was inflicted?

A. About four men; one to each arm and one to each leg.

Document 15

Major Cornelius Gardner, June 1902, report on the Philippines, in B. O. Flower, "Some Dead Sea Fruit of Our War of Subjugation," *The Arena*, vol. 27, 648–49.

"Of late by reason of the conduct of the troops such as the extensive burning of the barrios in trying to lay waste the country so that the insurgents cannot occupy it, the torturing of natives by so-called water-cure and other methods to obtain information, the harsh treatment of natives generally, and the failure of inexperienced lately-appointed lieutenants commanding posts to distinguish between those who are friendly and those unfriendly and to treat every native as if he were, whether or no, an *insurrecto* at heart, . . . and a deep hatred toward us engendered. If these things need be done, they had best be done by native troops, so that the people of the United States will not be credited therewith.

"Almost without exception, soldiers and also many officers refer to natives in their presence as 'Niggers,' and natives are beginning to understand what the word 'Nigger' means. The course now being pursued in this province and in the provinces of Batangas, Laguna, and Samar is in my opinion sowing the seeds for a perpetual revolution against us hereafter whenever a good opportunity offers. Under present conditions the political situation in this province is slowly retrograding, the American sentiment is decreasing, and we are daily making permanent enemies. In the course above referred to, troops make no distinction often between the property of those natives who are insurgent or insurgent sympathizers, and the property of those who heretofore have risked their lives by being loyal to the United States and giving us information against their countrymen in arms. Often every house in a barrio is burned. In my opinion the small number of irreconcilable insurgents still in arms, although admittedly difficult to catch, does not justify the means employed, and especially when taking into consideration the suffering that must be undergone by the innocent and its effects upon the relations with these people hereafter."

Document 16

President Theodore Roosevelt's address at Arlington National Cemetery, Memorial Day, 1902, in *Presidential Addresses and State Papers*, New York: The Review of Reviews Company, 1910, vol. 1, 59–65.

Just at this moment the Army of the United States . . . is carrying to completion a small but peculiarly trying and difficult war in which is involved not only the honor of the flag but the triumph of civilization over forces which stand for the black chaos of savagery and barbarism. . . .

The fact really is that our warfare in the Philippines has been carried on with singular humanity. For every act of cruelty by our men there have been innumerable acts of forbearance, magnanimity, and generous kindness. These are the qualities which have characterized the war as a whole. The cruelties on our part have been wholly exceptional. . . .

Peace and freedom—are there two better objects for which a soldier can fight? Well, these are precisely the objects for which our soldiers are fighting in the Philippines. When there is talk of the cruelties committed in the Philippines, remember always that by far the greater proportion of these cruelties have been committed by the insurgents against their own people—as well as against our soldiers—and that not only the surest but the only effectual way of stopping them is by the progress of the American arms. The victories of the American Army have been the really effective means of putting a stop to cruelty in the Philippines. . . .

Our soldiers conquer; and what is the object for which they conquer? To establish a military government? No. . . . The military power is used to secure peace, in order that it may itself be supplanted by the civil power. The progress of the American arms means the abolition of cruelty, the bringing of peace, and the rule of law and order under the civil government. Other nations have conquered to create irresponsible military rule. We conquer to bring just and responsible civil government to the conquered.

But our armies do more than bring peace, do more than bring order. They bring freedom. . . . Wherever in the Philippines the insurrection has been definitely and finally put down, there the individual Filipino already enjoys such freedom, such personal liberty under our rule, as he could never even have dreamed of under the rule of an "independent" Aguinaldian [Emilio Aguinaldo, leader of insurgents] oligarchy.

Document 17

President Theodore Roosevelt to Whitelaw Reid (owner of *New York Tribune*), June 27, 1906, *TRL*, vol. 5, 319.

In this Algeciras matter you will notice that while I was most suave and pleasant with the Emperor [Kaiser Wilhelm II] yet when it became necessary at the end I stood him on his head with great decision. Of course the vital feature of what I did was the verbal statement to [Hermann Speck von] Sternberg that in case the Emperor declined to submit to what was reasonable I should have to make public all of our correspondence in order to justify my position in entering into the negotiations. This last statement will in all probability never be made public.

Document 18

Secretary of State Elihu Root to Ambassador Henry White and Minister Samuel F. Gummeré, Nov. 28, 1905, *FRUS, 1905*, 678–79.

Our interest and right comprise and are limited to an equal share in whatever privileges of residence, trade, and protection are enjoyed by, or may be hereafter conceded by, the Shereefian Government [of Morocco] to aliens and their local agencies, and it follows that we have a like concern in the enlargement of those privileges in all appropriate ways. . . .

The organization, by means of an international agreement, of the Moroccan police outside of the border region is a measure whereby far-reaching reform may be accomplished to the benefit of all the powers having relations with Morocco. Intercourse with that country demands the existence of internal conditions favorable thereto. Security of life and property; equality of opportunities for trade with all natives; amelioration of those domestic conditions of religion and class which now weigh upon non-Mussulmans, and which impair the freedom of salutary foreign intercourse with the native population; improvement of the condition of the people that will enable them to profit by the opportunities of foreign traffic; orderly and certain administration of impartial justice; rigorous punishment of crimes against persons and property; exemption from erratic taxes and burdens; removal of class restrictions, and the power to repress subversive disorder and preserve the public peace—all these enter as important factors into the problems of effectively policing the interior and of removing the barriers which have heretofore opposed the foreigner at the threshold and the non-Mussulman in the interior. In short, while it is to the advantage of the powers to secure the "open door" it is equally vital to their interests and no less so to the advantage of Morocco that the door, being open, shall lead to something; that the outside world shall benefit by assured opportunities, and that the Moroccan people shall be made in a measure fit and able to profit by the advantages of the proposed reform.

Document 19

President Theodore Roosevelt to historian George Kennan, Oct. 15, 1905, *TRL*, vol. 5, 56–58.

I wish to write you as to your article called "The Sword of Peace in Japan." As far as I am concerned it is of exceedingly little importance what anyone says about the peace negotiations. My object in bringing them was not my own personal credit or even the advancement of this country, but the securing of peace. Peace was secured. Personally I believe that the credit of this country was greatly increased by it, and as far as I am personally affected I have received infinitely more praise for it than in my opinion I deserved. . . . But you are writing as a man supposed to know the facts at first hand. Your writings will be read here and read in Japan, and while you may not do much damage to America you may do some to Japan if you get your facts crooked. They are crooked in this article. You say that it seems to you that "it would have been much better both for Russia and Japan if President Roosevelt had waited until the close of this campaign before he had proposed a peace conference." What I am about to say is for your own information and not for the public. I acted at the time I did at the written request of Japan, and when Japan made the request I explained to the Japanese Government that in my judgment she would not get an indemnity, and she asked me to bring about the peace meeting with full knowledge of the fact that in my opinion she neither deserved nor would get an indemnity. . . . It is simply nonsense for anyone to talk of the Japanese being in a position to demand an indemnity. No nation that does not give up anything ever gets an indemnity in such circumstances or ever could get it unless the other nation was hopelessly frightened. In recent times no sensible nation has made such a request. . . . The prime motive influencing Japan to wish peace was not any one of those that you give, but her great personal interest in obtaining peace on the very terms that finally were obtained and at that very time. . . . The head men of many villages and country communities in Japan were notifying the government that they could not spare any more of their young men; that if more of their young men were drawn for the army the rice fields would have to be partially abandoned and a partial famine would ensue, and that moreover the little savings of their people had all been exhausted. I believe that Japan was partly influenced by proper motives of humanity and by the desire to have the respect of the nations as a whole, and that this feeling had its weight in influencing the Japanese statesmen who knew the facts to disregard the views held by the Tokyo mob and which are substantially the views set forth by you. But the main factor in influencing Japan was undoubtedly the fact that to go on with the war meant such an enormous loss, such an enormous cost to her, that she could not afford to incur it save from dire need. For example, you speak about her not having obtained the north half of Sakhalin Island. She had not reduced to possession this north half of Sakhalin, and there were Russian forces still there, a fact of which you do not seem to be aware. . . . Do what I could I was unable to get the Czar [Nicholas II] to yield more than the south half of Sakhalin. On the point of honor he insisted on keeping the comparatively valueless northern half. So far from advising the Japanese to give up on the question of Sakhalin, I explicitly told and wrote them that in my judgment they would be justified in fighting for Sakhalin. I did not appreciate quite how urgent their need of peace was. They, as I think with eminent propriety, went a little beyond what I advised and made peace without getting the northern half of Sakhalin. I had told them all along that to fight for an indemnity merely, would forfeit the respect of everybody whose respect was worth having, and would be an act of wicked folly, for it would mean at the very best at least another year of war, and mortgaging the future of Japan for a generation to come, while they would get nothing of any value to them. . . .

The above are the facts. They are for your private information. I do not intend to make public any of the details about this peace, because the Japanese have asked me not to make public those details which they think would in any way embarrass them, and I am anxious to do what they desire.

Document 20

Theodore Roosevelt to President William Howard Taft, Dec. 22, 1910, *TRL*, vol. 7, 189–90.

Our vital interest is to keep the Japanese out of our country, and at the same time to preserve the good will of Japan. The vital interest of the Japanese, on the other hand, is in Manchuria and Korea. It is therefore peculiarly our interest not to take any steps as regards Manchuria which will give the Japanese cause to feel, with or without reason, that we are hostile to them, or a menace—in however slight a degree—to their interests. Alliance with China, in view of China's absolute military helplessness, means of course not an additional strength to us, but an additional obligation which we assume; and as I utterly disbelieve in the policy of bluff, in national and international no less than in private affairs, or in any violation of the old frontier maxim, "Never draw unless you mean to shoot," I do not believe in our taking any position anywhere unless we can make good; and as regards Manchuria, if the Japanese choose to follow a course of conduct to which we are adverse, we cannot stop it unless we are prepared to go to war, and a successful war about Manchuria would require a fleet as good as that of England, plus an army as good as that of Germany. The "open-door" policy in China was an excellent thing, and will I hope be a good thing in the future, so far as it can be maintained by general diplomatic agreement; but as has been proved by the whole history of Manchuria, alike under Russia and under Japan, the "open-door" policy, as a matter of fact, completely disappears as soon as a powerful nation determines to disregard it, and is willing to run the risk of war rather than forego its intention.

Document 21

Theodore Roosevelt to British historian George Otto Trevelyan, Oct. 1, 1911, *TRL*, vol. 7, 393–94.

[Alfred] Von Tirpitz [German secretary of war] was particularly interested in the voyage of the battle fleet round the world, and he told me frankly that he had not believed we could do it successfully, and added that your (the English) Naval Office and Foreign Office had felt the same way—which I told him I knew. He then said that he expected that Japan would attack us while the fleet was on its way round, and asked me if I had not also expected this. I told him that I had not expected such an attack, but that I had thought it possible. . . .

My point of view at the time the fleet sailed, was that if the Japanese attacked it, it was a certain sign that they were intending to attack us at the first favorable opportunity. I had been doing my best to be polite to the Japanese, and had finally become uncomfortably conscious of a very, very slight undertone of veiled truculence in their communications in connection with things that happened on the Pacific Slope; and I finally made up my mind that they thought I was afraid of them. . . . I definitely came to the conclusion that . . . it was time for a showdown. I had great confidence in the fleet; I went over everything connected with it and found that the administrative officers on shore were calmly confident that they could keep everything in first-class shape, while the officers afloat, from the battleship commanders to the lieutenants in charge of the torpedo boats, were straining like hounds in a leash, and the enlisted men were at least as eager, all desertions stopping and the ships becoming for the first time overmanned as soon as there was a rumor that we might have trouble with Japan, and that the fleet might move round to the Pacific. I felt that, in any event, if the fleet was not able to get to the Pacific in first-class shape, we had better find it out; and if Japan intended to have war it was infinitely better that we should gain two or three months necessary to prepare our fleet to start to the Pacific, instead of having to take those two or three months after war began.

Accordingly, in answer to the question of Von Tirpitz, I told him that when the fleet had once started, it meant that we had gained three months anyhow and that the fleet was doing what it would have to do in any event if the Japanese went to war; and so that if they did make war it would be proof positive that I had followed exactly the right course; and that if they did not go to war, but became peaceful, it would also be proof positive that I had followed exactly the right course. The latter was what actually happened; and every particle of trouble with the Japanese Government and the Japanese press stopped like magic as soon as they found that our fleet had actually sailed, and was obviously in good trim.

Document 22

Secretary of State Elihu Root to Ambassador Kogoro Takahira, Nov. 30, 1908, *FRUS, 1908*, 511–12.

I am happy to be able to confirm to your excellency, on behalf of the United States, the declaration of the two Governments embodied in the following words:

1. It is the wish of the two Governments to encourage the free and peaceful development of their commerce on the Pacific Ocean.

2. The policy of both Governments, uninfluenced by any aggressive tendencies, is directed to the maintenance of the existing status quo in the region above mentioned, and to the defense of the principle of equal opportunity for commerce and industry in China.

3. They are accordingly firmly resolved reciprocally to respect the territorial possessions belonging to each other in said region.

4. They are also determined to preserve the common interests of all powers in China by supporting by all pacific means at their disposal the independence and integrity of China and the principle of equal opportunity for commerce and industry of all nations in that Empire.

5. Should any event occur threatening the status quo as above described or the principle of equal opportunity as above defined, it remains for the two Governments to communicate with each other in order to arrive at an understanding as to what measures they may consider it useful to take.

CHAPTER 3

Wilsonian Diplomacy

Betty Miller Unterberger

Woodrow Wilson guided his country through eight of the most crucial years of the modern epoch. For the world it was a period of revolutionary upheaval, cataclysmic world war, and shifts in the balance of power that threatened the very foundations of international order. Wilson's diplomacy rested upon principles and assumptions drawn from the beliefs and ethical values of the Christian tradition and from his deep commitment to democracy as the most advanced, humane, and effective form of government. Historians generally have regarded Wilson as an idealist, yet this popular view fails to focus on his true genius—his ability to manipulate abstract principles brilliantly to justify motives that were shaped by his appreciation of the country's political interests. Of all twentieth-century leaders, Wilson was the first effective—and certainly the most eloquent—champion of anti-imperialism, human rights, and self-determination. Wilson believed strongly in the free enterprise system and in a world united by trade. But he believed even more strongly that it was morally wrong for rich powers to exploit underdeveloped countries and colonies. Finally, Wilson was the most ardent champion of peace and world unity among all leaders of his time. Like Theodore Roosevelt, Wilson was an advocate of a strong presidential role in making foreign policy.

The acid test of Wilson's sincerity about promoting human rights abroad was the long, nagging problem of Mexico, where the first authentic sociopolitical revolution of the twentieth century broke out in 1911. The revolution took an ugly turn in February 1913 when Victoriano Huerta, a cruel but able general, murdered Francisco I. Madero, the popular new revolutionary president, and proclaimed himself president. Huerta promised to accord full protection to foreign property, and Japan and the major European powers hastened to recognize his government. Although under pressure from domestic business interests, President Wilson hesitated. He would not, he said privately, recognize a "government of butchers." However, he offered to mediate between Huerta and the followers of Madero, the Constitutionalists, who had begun the revolution anew under Venustiano Carranza. (docs. 1 and 2)

Encouraged by the British, whose subjects had large oil and other interests in Mexico, Huerta replied by establishing a military dictatorship. In response, Wilson virtually compelled the British to withdraw support from Huerta. (doc. 3) Emotionally committed to the cause of the Mexican Revolution, Wilson threw his support to the Constitutionalists and permitted them to purchase arms in the United States in early 1914.

When Huerta consolidated his power in the spring of 1914, Wilson sent marines and sailors into Veracruz and seized the port on April 22. He had ample reason to believe that he was forestalling outside intervention in support of Huerta, as reports from Mexico indicated that large arms shipments were heading toward the country from both Europe and Japan. Wilson successfully resisted strong pressure from military leaders to make the Veracruz landing the beginning of an all-out invasion of Mexico. When heavy casualties were incurred, particularly on the Mexican side, Wilson was appalled and quickly accepted an offer of mediation by the ambassadors to the United States of Argentina, Brazil, and Chile. Huerta fled to Spain in July 1914, but Wilson did not extend de facto recognition to the Carranza regime until October 1915. Wilson's experience in Mexico after the occupation of Veracruz had convinced him that it was futile, even foolish, to attempt to alter the course of a profound social and economic revolution. (doc. 4)

Wilson's ultimate belief in self-determination becomes clearer in a later episode involving Mexico. On March 9, 1916, Pancho Villa, who then was the main rival to President Carranza, attacked and burned the border town of Columbus, New Mexico; nineteen inhabitants were killed. Wilson sent a punitive expedition headed by General John J. Pershing into Mexican territory to apprehend Villa. Carranza, however, demanded the immediate withdrawal of Pershing's command from Mexican soil. Once again there was talk of war, but Wilson saw no glory in conquering a poor people who were struggling for liberty. Once Carranza had succeeded in decimating Villa's forces and the threat of a U.S. war with Germany loomed larger, Wilson withdrew Pershing in January 1917 and accorded formal recognition to Carranza's new constitutional regime on April 21.

At the outset of World War I in 1914, Wilson favored a policy of strict neutrality. On August 4 he issued a proclamation of neutrality and a few weeks later appealed to his fellow citizens to be neutral in thought as well as deed. On February 4, 1915, in "retaliation" against the British blockade, Berlin announced that all enemy vessels would be torpedoed without warning in a broad area around the British Isles and that even neutral vessels would not be safe. Wilson quickly responded (on February 10) that the United States would hold Germany to "strict accountability" for illegal destruction of American ships and lives.

After the May 7, 1915, sinking of the British liner *Lusitania* took 1,200 lives, including 128 Americans, Wilson sent a series of notes appealing to the German government to abandon its campaign of terror against unarmed passenger liners. (doc. 5) The Berlin government responded evasively or negatively. (doc. 6) On August 19 a German submarine sank another British liner, the *Arabic*, causing more American casualties. As a result, Berlin agreed reluctantly not to sink unarmed passenger ships without warning. Wilson then sought unsuccessfully to force the British to cease their illegal interferences with neutral ships and commerce. (doc. 7)

After these crises, Wilson moved more aggressively because the British foreign secretary, Sir Edward Grey, indicated that his government might be willing to discuss peace terms with certain guarantees from the United States. On February 22, 1916, Colonel Edward House, the president's confidant, joined Grey in initiating what later became known as the House–Grey Memorandum. When the Allies thought the moment appropriate, according to the paper, the United States would call a peace conference to end the war and, if the Germans refused to participate, would probably enter the war on the Allied side. (doc. 8)

The controversy with Germany came to a new and threatening head with the March 24 sinking and resulting heavy casualties of the unarmed French channel packet *Sussex*. Believing that the British were eager to implement the House–Grey Memorandum and hoping to serve as mediator in negotiating a righteous peace, an infuriated Wilson delivered an ultimatum to the German government. The German leaders capitulated reluctantly, but attached many qualifications to their *Sussex* pledge. Wilson then pressed the British government to give its consent to American mediation under the House–Grey Memorandum. The British, who never were prepared to accept Wilson's mediation so long as they thought they had a chance to win, responded negatively. Wilson was convinced that the British were fighting for unworthy objectives and set out upon a course of independent mediation.

On December 18 Wilson sent an appeal to all the belligerents, imploring them to state the terms upon which they would be willing to conclude a peace settlement. Although none returned satisfactory responses, Wilson opened secret negotiations with the British and German governments for a peace conference in the immediate future. While he waited for replies from Berlin and London, Wilson made one final futile attempt to mediate between the embattled belligerents. On January 22, 1917, he delivered one of his most moving addresses. Only a negotiated "peace without victory," he declared, would be permanent and only a "peace between equals" could last. Wilson proposed that "all nations henceforth avoid entangling alliances" but unite in a "concert of power." (doc. 9)

The Germans replied first by announcing that submarines would begin unrestricted operations on February 1. They would sink all ships in the war zone—neutral as well as Allied—without warning. Deeply distressed, Wilson two days later broke diplomatic relations with Germany but refused to move toward war unless the Germans undertook "overt" acts against American lives and property. On February 26, in a further effort to defend American interests short of war, Wilson asked Congress for authority to arm

American merchant ships. When Congress defeated the measure, Wilson on March 9 invoked the authority of an old piracy statute and instructed the navy to put guns and gun crews on merchant vessels.

By March 20, Wilson had concluded that armed neutrality could not protect American maritime rights against the German challenge. Besides, a near paralysis of American foreign trade had occurred when American shipowners refused to send their unarmed vessels into the blockaded area. Morever, an infamous telegram from Alfred Zimmermann, German secretary of state for foreign affairs, caused Wilson to lose all faith in the German government. (doc. 10) At the same time, Wilson was heartened by news of the Russian Revolution on March 15, which drove Czar Nicholas II from his throne and made Russia a fit partner for a "league of honor." After the long-dreaded "overt" acts in the Atlantic had occurred—German U-boats sank four unarmed merchant vessels in the first two weeks of March—the sentiment grew for war. Most importantly, Wilson knew that he would have much greater influence at the eventual peace conference as a leader of the belligerents than as a neutral outsider. On April 2, 1917, a subdued and solemn Wilson asked Congress to recognize that a state of war existed between the United States and the German Empire. (doc. 11)

Wilson announced his program to the world in his famed Fourteen Points Address to Congress on January 8, 1918. It was high time, he said, for peace-loving nations to avow their ideals and objectives. These Wilson summarized in a series of general points, which included open peace covenants, freedom of the seas, reduction of armaments, removal of artificial barriers to international trade, impartial settlement of colonial claims, and the establishment of a league of nations. Three points—the establishment of a league of nations, the restoration of Belgium, and the self-determination of Russia—were indispensable to a just settlement, according to Wilson. (doc. 12)

Meanwhile, the Bolshevik Revolution dashed Wilson's hopes of having Russia as a reliable ally and gravely impaired his ability to establish a new world order. Wilson strenuously opposed the Allied decision to intervene in the civil war raging between the Bolsheviks (the Reds) and various conservative groups (the Whites). Wilson strongly believed that the Russian people had the right to determine their own institutions and form of government and that military intervention in Russia was thus futile and wrong. In the sixth of his Fourteen Points he had demanded for Russia the free and unembarrassed opportunity to determine its own future without outside pressure or intervention. But, under heavy pressure from the Allies, he reluctantly consented to a limited American cooperation with Allied plans. (doc. 13) With the approval of the Bolshevik government, he sent some 5,000 men to northern Russia to prevent the Germans from seizing military supplies at the ports of Murmansk and Archangel. Wilson dispatched another 7,000 men to Siberia to guarantee a safe exit for a Czech army formed from Austro-Hungarian prisoners-of-war that had been fighting in Russia and later sought to go to France to fight on the Western Front.

More importantly, Wilson also wanted to keep a close watch on the Japanese, who had already landed a force in Vladivostok in April 1918 and were supporting several counterrevolutionary groups in return for political and economic concessions. Having witnessed the penetration of Japanese imperialism on the Asian mainland between 1914 and 1917, Wilson had no illusions concerning Tokyo's true intentions regarding Siberia. When it became evident that Japan was prepared to embark upon an independent expedition under the auspices of the Sino-Japanese Military Agreements of May 1918, the necessity of stopping the Japanese drive for empire became imperative. Thus by virtue of war and revolution, Soviet Russia became the scene of the battle, and the United States emerged as the defender of the Open Door policy and both Russian and Chinese sovereignty in northeastern Asia.

Both American expeditions to Russia carried strict presidential orders not to intervene in the Russian civil war. (docs. 14 and 15) Immediately upon the arrival of troops in North Russia and Siberia, however, the divergence of views concerning the purpose of intervention became clear. While Great Britain and France attempted to extend the scope of military and political action in Russia—and while Japan proceeded with its plans to occupy Manchuria and the Russian Far East—the United States tried to restrain the independent operations of its allies in the interests of the overall war effort. By the time the Armistice of November 11, 1918, was signed, Japan had sent three divisions to Russia (or some 70,000 men), all under the direct control of the general staff in Tokyo. (doc. 16)

Wilson had always believed that the proper policy for the Allied and Associated powers was "to clear out of Russia and leave it to the Russians to fight it out among themselves." Yet, American troops remained in Siberia for two reasons. First, American evacuation would have left Japan in virtual control of North Manchuria and East Siberia. Second, Britain, France, and Japan were opposed to any withdrawal, and Wilson did not wish to jeopardize his program at the Paris Peace Conference by independent action. Thus, to block Japan and to further his league, he followed a policy that appeared to contradict both the principles that he had enunciated concerning Russia and those of his proposed league.

Wilson went to Europe in late December 1918 determined to fight for a just peace. He was hailed as a messiah from the New World sent to redeem the Old. The situation was different when the peace conference opened in Paris on January 18, 1919. No representatives from the defeated powers or Russia were present. Wilson stood alone against the Allied heads of state, who now sought only revenge against Germany. These leaders, under pressure from nationalistic majorities within their own countries, resisted Wilson's ideals in the interests of dividing the territories of the vanquished and of making Germany pay the costs of the war. In addition, several unfortunate domestic events had resulted in a considerable diminution of

Wilson's position as spokesman for the American people. The repudiation of Wilson's October appeal to the American people to elect a Democratic Congress had seriously undermined his leadership. (doc. 17) Moreover, his decision to go to Paris in person infuriated Republicans, who saw it as flamboyant grandstanding. Wilson further ruffled Republican feathers when he failed to name a single prominent Republican in his official peace delegation. This had serious repercussions when a Republican-dominated Senate reviewed Wilson's handiwork in Paris.

Wilson fought heroically and doggedly throughout the conference for his Fourteen Points. (doc. 18) Although he made a number of significant compromises in the peace treaty, he won many more of his Fourteen Points than he lost. Wilson's greatest victory was the establishment of the League of Nations. (doc. 19)

When Wilson returned to the United States in late February 1919, he conferred with the House and Senate foreign relations committees and heard criticisms of the covenant. Critics noted that it contained no recognition of the Monroe Doctrine, did not exclude internal affairs from the jurisdiction of the League of Nations, and made no provision for the withdrawal of member nations. Consequently, Wilson set to work and obtained all the changes his critics demanded, even though the effort required him to make new compromises with the Allied leaders.

Immediately after his return to the United States in July 1919, Wilson presented the Versailles treaty to the Senate in an eloquent and confident address. (doc. 20) Wilson did not know it, but Republican Henry Cabot Lodge, the new chairman of the Senate Foreign Relations Committee, had decided to kill the treaty if at all possible. Lodge was a wily strategist. He did not dare openly oppose the treaty at first; instead, he effectively used delaying tactics to confuse and divide public opinion. He held long hearings and read aloud every word of the 264-page treaty to his committee.

With the treaty bogged down in the Senate and a deadlock imminent, Wilson embarked upon a barnstorming appeal to the country. He set out from Washington on September 3 and traveled more than 8,000 miles to deliver 37 major addresses to large and enthusiastic audiences all the way to the Pacific Coast and then back to Colorado. But the trip took a heavy toll on Wilson's limited physical reserves. He collapsed after an eloquent address at Pueblo, Colorado, on September 25. A few days later, on October 2, Wilson suffered a massive stroke that paralyzed his left side.

Meanwhile, on September 10 Lodge reported the treaty to the Senate with a number of reservations and amendments. The amendments were voted down, whereupon Lodge offered a list of fourteen reservations. (doc. 21) Most of them were unimportant. However, the senator's second reservation stated that upon ratifying the treaty, the United States assumed no obligations under Article X of the covenant to preserve the independence and territorial integrity of member nations; it also stated that the United States would not commit its armed forces to uphold the covenant unless Congress—by joint resolution in every instance—so provided. Wilson absolutely refused to accept Lodge's second reservation on the ground that it nullified, rather than ratified, the treaty. He would not allow compromise on Article X, the "heart of the covenant" and the key to collective security. (doc. 22) Hence, when the treaty came up for a vote in the Senate on November 19, 1919, most Democrats joined the isolationist "bitter enders" to defeat approval with the Lodge reservations. On a second vote, the Republicans and bitter enders combined to defeat approval without the Lodge reservations. When the treaty with the Lodge reservations came up for a vote for a second time on March 19, 1920, Wilson again instructed Democratic senators to vote it down. Enough of them heeded Wilson's command to defeat approval.

Some historians have accused Wilson of "infanticide"—of killing his own child, the League of Nations. It is certainly true that he prevented Senate approval on the final vote. The reasons for Wilson's decision to oppose approval of the Versailles treaty with the Lodge reservations were diverse. First, he believed that the question of the character of American participation in the League of Nations was so fundamental that it could not be compromised. As he had said repeatedly during his western tour, the United States should either enter the league without crippling reservations and provide leadership in building a new world order, or the country should stay out of the league. Second, although Wilson's illness had not weakened his ordinary mental processes, it had gravely affected his temperament and ability to make decisions. In normal health, he probably would have worked out a compromise acceptable to a large majority of senators. Finally, Wilson was so isolated in the White House that he was out of touch both with the situation on Capitol Hill and with public opinion. He may have refused to accept the Lodge reservations because he believed that the Senate would not dare reject the entire treaty merely because it did not approve of every provision of the league covenant. Whatever the reasons, the treaty was doomed.

For the rest of his life Wilsom remained confident of the rectitude of his own position and of the ultimate triumph of his cause. As he said in a speech on Armistice Day in 1923, "We shall inevitably be forced by the moral obligations of freedom and honor to retrieve that fatal error and assume once more the role of courage, self-respect, and helpfulness which every true American must wish to regard as our natural part in the affairs of the world." Regrettably, Wilson did not live long enough to know the great and commanding relevance that many of his ideas would acquire before the century had ended. In Wilson's vision of the future needs of world society, he was far ahead of any other statesman of his time.

Document 1

President Woodrow Wilson, an address on Mexican affairs to a joint session of Congress, Aug. 27, 1913, *The Papers of Woodrow Wilson* (hereafter referred to as *PWW*), Arthur S. Link, David W. Hirst, John E. Little et al., eds., vol. 28, Princeton, New Jersey: Princeton University Press, 1966, 227–30.

The deplorable posture of affairs in Mexico I need not describe, but I deem it my duty to speak very frankly of what this Government has done and should seek to do in fulfillment of its obligation to Mexico herself, as a friend and neighbor, and to American citizens whose lives and vital interests are daily affected by the distressing conditions which now obtain beyond our southern border.

Those conditions touch us very nearly. Not merely because they lie at our very doors. . . . The peace, prosperity, and contentment of Mexico mean more, much more, to us than merely an enlarged field for our commerce and enterprise. They mean an enlargement of the field of self-government and the realization of the hopes and rights of a nation with whose best aspirations, so long suppressed and disappointed, we deeply sympathize. We shall yet prove to the Mexican people that we know how to serve them without first thinking how we shall serve ourselves. . . .

The present circumstances of the Republic, I deeply regret to say, do not seem to promise even the foundations of such a peace. We have waited many months, months full of peril and anxiety, for the conditions there to improve, and they have not improved. They have grown worse, rather. The territory in some sort controlled by the provisional authorities at Mexico City has grown smaller, not larger. The prospect of the pacification of the country, even by arms, has seemed to grow more and more remote; and its pacification by the authorities at the capital is evidently impossible by any other means than force. Difficulties more and more entangle those who claim to constitute the legitimate government of the Republic. They have not made good their claim in fact. Their successes in the field have proved only temporary. War and disorder, devastation and confusion, seem to threaten to become the settled fortune of the distracted country. As friends we could wait no longer for a solution which every week seemed further away. It was our duty at least to volunteer our good offices—to offer to assist, if we might, in effecting some arrangement which would bring relief and peace and set up a universally acknowledged political authority there. . . .

Meanwhile, what is it our duty to do? Clearly, everything that we do must be rooted in patience and done with calm and disinterested deliberation. Impatience on our part would be childish, and would be fraught with every risk of wrong and folly. We can afford to exercise the self-restraint of a really great nation which realizes its own strength and scorns to misuse it. It was our duty to offer our active assistance. It is now our duty to show what true neutrality will do to enable the people of Mexico to set their affairs in order again and wait for a further opportunity to offer our friendly counsels.

Document 2

President Woodrow Wilson, an address on Latin American policy in Mobile, Alabama, Oct. 27, 1913, *PWW*, vol. 28, 451.

I want to take this occasion to say that the United States will never again seek one additional foot of territory by conquest. She will devote herself to showing that she knows how to make honorable and fruitful use of the territory she has; and she must regard it as one of the duties of friendship to see that from no quarter are material interests made superior to human liberty and national opportunity. I say this, not with a single thought that anyone will gainsay it, but merely to fix in our consciousness what our real relationship with the rest of America is. It is the relationship of a family of mankind devoted to the development of true constitutional liberty. We know that that is the soil out of which the best enterprise springs. We know that this is a cause which we are making in common with our neighbors, because we have had to make it for ourselves.

Document 3

John Reed to Joseph Patrick Tumulty, with enclosure, June 30, 1914, *PWW*, vol. 30, 231–38.

Here is the final draft of the article,—somewhat reconstructed, according to the plan you suggested,—which I hope can be authorized for publication.

I am extremely desirous of neither violating the President's confidence in any particular, nor of bothering him or you. But I thought what he said was so valuable, that it would do great good to get it out some way . . . .

Enclosure: I had always got the impression that the President was a trifle cold and a trifle pedantic. Well, he isn't. He doesn't even choose his words when he is talking to you, and yet everything he says is sharply, definitively said,—often with the easy simplicity of [Abraham] Lincoln's talk. He seems animated by extremely simple ideals,—Christianity, Liberty, and Fair Play. His seems, at first, a mind so simple as to be naive. Presently you discover that this simplicity is the result of passing through an enormous complexity. He has every appearance of frankness with you; he answers your questions straight. . . .

The startling thing about President [Woodrow] Wilson's Mexican policy is that it is so obvious. It is neither "sentimental" nor "narrowly Presbyterian." There is nothing particularly secret about it. He has expressed it scores of times, and the political diagnosticians have refused to accept his words at their face value. They have all missed the point.

It is quite in character that Mr. Wilson, in the Government's foreign policy, returns to the attitude that this nation once took toward the world. We boast still that the Revolution of 1775 gave impetus and encouragement to revolutionary democracy all over Europe. We are proud that this nation was dedicated as a refuge for the oppressed of the world; that American sympathy has always been on the side of a people in revolt,—the Poles, the French, the Russians. We like to remember that the United States government allied itself with the struggling French Republic, although it was born in blood, and that we went to war with Spain to set free the half-Indian population of a small island. At least, that is what the great mass of the people thought we went to war with Spain for. . . .

The dominant note of the President's words,—the point to which he returned again and again, was that as long as he was there the United States government would not give its support to tyrannies. That sounds harmless,—as harmless as any platitude spoken by any statesman. But if a platitude is translated literally into terms of action, it becomes a startling thing. I think it means simply this: that it is none of our concern what government the people of any country elect to set up; but it is of very grave concern to us, as citizens of a country founded on the principle of self-government, that the people of that country be allowed to set it up. If Mr. Wilson refused to recognize the [Victoriano] Huerta government primarily because it was a government founded upon assassination, that was a very inadequate reason indeed. But he did not. That it was a government founded upon assassination was secondary; the important thing was that it was not a government by the people.

I got a very clear impression that the President was emphatically opposed to interfering in the internal affairs of Mexico, and as he spoke I realized that he had not interfered, paradoxical as it may seem. That he has appeared to do so is due to the very interests that have tried to force upon us the conquest of Mexico. . . .

After Mr. Wilson's declaration of his interest in the land problem in Mexico, it seemed to be the general opinion that he intended to interfere in the distribution of the great estates to the peons. I have got an entirely different impression. His policy of non-interference still holds good. As far as this government is concerned the Mexicans can restore the land as they see fit. If they want to confiscate the great estates, that is their business; but it is in accordance with the President's belief in Law and Government, that he should prefer to see the Mexican government buy the lands back rather than take them,—pay their owners compensation with respect only to the fairness of their titles, and not to their political opinions at all. I do not believe, however, that the President will dictate any such course of action. . . .

It is clearly the President's purpose that no one shall take advantage of Mexico,—in any way; neither military dictators, citizens of this country, citizens of foreign countries, nor foreign governments. It is because of this that the United States has interposed itself between Mexico and the nations of the world in the present crisis, but the situation is full of dangerous possibilities. The President has already pointed out that even the Monroe doctrine does not give this country any more right to protect Mexico in her foreign relations, than it does to interfere in her internal affairs. That is why he earnestly hopes that the new Mexican government will not begin the wholesale confiscation of foreign concessions. Many concessions were given to foreigners in Mexico in strict accordance with Mexican law; and throughout the civilized world it has been shown that it is practically impossible under any circumstances to deprive a man of his lawful property, no matter what his political offences have been. Besides these, however, many of the great concessions granted by President [Porfirio] Díaz and his officers were illegal. But even they are now more or less valid,—under whatever Statute of Limitations is in force in Mexico. The principle of Quieting of Title is a very widespread one in law. Moreover, there are certain concessions,—such as Lord Cowdray's [S. Weetman Pearson] oil holdings, which are practically the British navy's only supply of oil,—that would be insisted upon by foreign governments without respect as to whether they were right or wrong. As to Huerta, however, shortly after his dissolution of Congress President Wilson served notice on the world that from that date no concessions or contracts would be recognized by this government.

This extraordinarily simple and direct policy toward Mexico, though it has not been recognized by the American people, has been pretty thoroughly accepted in the Chancelleries of Europe. It is a novelty in world politics, and its effect is bound to be tremendous in its effect on the dealing of nations with one another. . . .

According to the evidence of his words and acts, the President is fighting everywhere the small predatory minorities which balk the People's struggle for intelligence and life. But often the very conditions which gave rise to these minorities were established peaceably, with the consent of the people they oppress; and in that case if possible the conditions must be changed by the people peaceably, for upon the principle of government without coercion rests our civilization.

So the President seemed to fear that the Mexican Revolution might not be able to destroy by force the network of foreign exploitation that is choking the people.

Document 4

President Woodrow Wilson to Secretary of War Lindley Miller Garrison, Aug. 8, 1914, *PWW*, vol. 30, 362.

I have your letter of this morning and understand perfectly the motives and the sense of duty which led you to write it.

But my judgment remains unaltered and I want you to know why.

We shall have no right at any time to intervene in Mexico to determine the way in which the Mexicans are to settle their own affairs. I feel sufficiently assured that the property and lives of foreigners will not suffer in the process of the settlement. The rest is political and Mexican. Many things may happen of which we do not approve and which could not happen in the United States, but I say very solemnly that that is no affair of ours. Our responsibility will come after the settlement and in the determination of the question whether the new government is to receive the recognition of the Government of the United States or not. There are in my judgment no conceivable circumstances which would make it right for us to direct by force or by threat of force the internal processes of what is a profound revolution, a revolution as profound as that which occurred in France. All the world has been shocked ever since the time of the revolution in France that Europe should have undertaken to nullify what was done there, no matter what the excesses then committed.

I speak very solemnly but with clear judgment in the matter, which I hope God will give me strength to act upon.

Document 5

Secretary of State William Jennings Bryan to Ambassador to Germany James W. Gerard, May 13, 1915, U.S. Department of State, *Papers Relating to the Foreign Relations of the United States* (hereafter referred to as *FRUS*), *1915, Supplement*, Washington, D.C.: Government Printing Office, 1928, 393–96.

Please call on the Minister of Foreign Affairs and, after reading to him this communication, leave him with a copy:

In view of recent acts of the German authorities in violation of American rights on the high seas which culminated in the torpedoing and sinking of the British steamship *Lusitania* on May 7, 1915, by which over 100 American citizens lost their lives, it is clearly wise and desirable that the Government of the United States and the Imperial German Government should come to a clear and full understanding as to the grave situation which has resulted.

The sinking of the British passenger steamer *Falaba* by a German submarine on March 28, through which Leon C. Thrasher, an American citizen, was drowned; the attack on April 28 on the American vessel *Cushing* by a German aeroplane; the torpedoing on May 1 of the American vessel *Gulflight* by a German submarine, as a result of which two or more American citizens met their death; and, finally, the torpedoing and sinking of the steamship *Lusitania*, constitute a series of events which the Government of the United States has observed with growing concern, distress, and amazement. . . .

The Government of the United States has been apprised that the Imperial German Government considered themselves to be obliged by the extraordinary circumstances of the present war and the measures adopted by their adversaries in seeking to cut Germany off from all commerce, to adopt methods of retaliation which go much beyond the ordinary methods of warfare at sea, in the proclamation of a war zone from which they have warned neutral ships to keep away. This Government has already taken occasion to inform the Imperial German Government that it can not admit the adoption of such measures or such a warning of danger to operate as in any degree an abbreviation of the rights of American shipmasters or of American citizens bound on lawful errands as passengers on merchant ships of belligerent nationality; and that it must hold the Imperial German Government to a strict accountability for any infringement of those rights, intentional or incidental. It does not understand the Imperial German Government to question those rights. It assumes, on the contrary, that the Imperial Government accept, as of course, the rule that the lives of non-combatants, whether they be of neutral citizenship or citizens of one of the nations at war, can not lawfully or rightfully be put in jeopardy by the capture or destruction of an unarmed merchantman, and recognize also, as all other nations do, the obligation to take the usual precaution of visit and search to ascertain whether a suspected merchantman is in fact of belligerent nationality or is in fact carrying contraband of war under a neutral flag. . . .

American citizens act within their indisputable rights in taking their ships and in traveling wherever their legitimate business calls them upon the high seas, and exercise those rights in what should be the well-justified confidence that their lives will not be endangered by acts done in clear violation of universally acknowledged international obligations, and certainly in the confidence that their own Government will sustain them in the exercise of their rights.

Long acquainted as this Government has been with the character of the Imperial German Government and with the high principles of equity by which they have in the past been actuated and guided, the Government of the United States can not believe that the commanders of the vessels which committed these acts of lawlessness did so except under a misapprehension of the orders issued by the Imperial German naval authorities. . . . It confidently expects, therefore, that the Imperial German Government will disavow the acts of which the Government of the United States complains, that they will make reparation so far as reparation is possible for injuries which are without measure, and that they will take immediate steps to prevent the recurrence of anything so obviously subversive of the principles of warfare for which the Imperial German Government have in the past so wisely and so firmly contended. . . .

Expressions of regret and offers of reparation in case of the destruction of neutral ships sunk by mistake, while they may satisfy international obligations, if no loss of life results, can not justify or excuse a practice, the natural and necessary effect of which is to subject neutral nations and neutral persons to new and immeasurable risks.

Document 6

Ambassador to Germany James W. Gerard to Secretary of State William Jennings Bryan, May 15, 1915, *FRUS, 1915, Supplement*, 396.

Your . . . May 13, 11 a.m., did not arrive until 10 p.m. last night. It was sent from Rome 4 p.m. yesterday. I presented it at 10.30 this morning to [Minister of Foreign Affairs Gottlieb] Von Jagow personally; he asked that he might read it himself as he understands written better than spoken English. While reading it he laughed and said, "Right of free travel on the seas, why not right of free travel on land in war territory?"

In confidential conversation he said that there would have to be a sitting of the authorities and no answer should be expected before Monday or Tuesday, but that he was sure Germany would never give up this method of submarine warfare. I am myself positive that Germany will continue this method of war and that it is only a question of short time before other American ships or lives are destroyed, and if that happens you say that United States will not omit any act necessary to maintain the rights which you have claimed for the United States and its citizens.

Your cables require two days or more to reach Germany and therefore, in view of your note and what I take to be the inevitable consequences, I hope you will cable me full instructions now as to all possible contingencies.

Document 7

Secretary of State Robert Lansing to Ambassador to Great Britain Walter Hines Page, Oct. 21, 1915, *FRUS, 1915, Supplement*, 578, 582.

I desire that you present a note to Sir Edward Grey [the British foreign secretary] in the sense of the following:

The Government of the United States has given careful consideration to your excellency's notes . . . relating to restrictions upon American commerce by certain measures adopted by the British Government during the present war. This government has delayed answering in the hope that the announced purpose of His Majesty's Government "to exercise their belligerent rights with every possible consideration for the interest of neutrals" and their intention of "removing all causes of avoidable delay in dealing with American cargoes" and of causing "the least possible amount of inconvenience to persons engaged in legitimate trade," as well as their "assurances to the United States Government that they would make it their first aim to minimize the inconveniences" resulting from the "measures taken by the Allied Governments," would in practice not unjustifiably infringe upon the neutral rights of American citizens engaged in trade and commerce. It is, therefore, a matter of regret that this hope has not been realized, but that, on the contrary, interferences with American ships and cargoes destined in good faith to neutral ports and lawfully entitled to proceed have become increasingly vexatious, causing American shipowners and American merchants to complain to this Government of the failure to take steps to prevent an exercise of belligerent power in contravention of their just rights. As the measures complained of proceed directly from orders issued by the British Government, are executed by British authorities, and arouse a reasonable apprehension that, if not resisted, they may be carried to an extent even more injurious to American interests. . . .

The United States . . . has no other course but to contest seizures of vessels at sea upon conjectural suspicion and the practice of bringing them into port for the purpose, by search or otherwise, of obtaining evidence, for the purpose of justifying prize proceedings, of the carriage of contraband or of breaches of the order in council of March 11. Relying upon the regard of the British Government for the principles of justice so frequently and uniformly manifested prior to the present war, this Government anticipates that the British Government will instruct their officers to refrain from these vexatious and illegal practices.

Document 8

House-Grey Memorandum, Feb. 22, 1916, *PWW*, vol. 36, 180 note 2.

(Confidential) Colonel [Edward] House told me that President [Woodrow] Wilson was ready, on hearing from France and England that the moment was opportune, to propose that a Conference should be summoned to put an end to the war. Should the Allies accept this proposal and should Germany refuse it, the United States would probably enter the war against Germany.

Colonel House expressed the opinion that, if such a Conference met, it would secure peace on terms not unfavourable to the Allies; and, if it failed to secure peace, the United States would leave the Conference as a belligerent on the side of the Allies, if Germany was unreasonable. Colonel House expressed an opinion decidedly favourable to the restoration of Belgium, the transfer of Alsace and Lorraine to France, and the acquisition by Russia of an outlet to the sea, though he thought that the loss of territory incurred by Germany in one place would have to be compensated by concessions to her in other places outside Europe. If the Allies delayed accepting the offer of President Wilson, and if, later on, the course of the war was so unfavourable to them that the intervention of the United States would not be effective, the United States would probably disinterest themselves in Europe, and look to their own protection in their own way.

Document 9

President Woodrow Wilson, an address to the Senate, Jan. 22, 1917, *PWW*, vol. 40, 533–36.

On the eighteenth of December last I addressed an identic note to the governments of the nations now at war requesting them to state, more definitely than they had yet been stated by either group of belligerents, the terms upon which they would deem it possible to make peace. . . .

. . . The statesmen of both of the groups of nations now arrayed against one another have said, in terms that could not be misinterpreted, that it was no part of the purpose they had in mind to crush their antagonists. But the implications of these assurances may not be equally clear to all,—may not be the same on both sides of the water. I think it will be serviceable if I attempt to set forth what we understand them to be.

They imply, first of all, that it must be a peace without victory. It is not pleasant to say this. I beg that I may be permitted to put my own interpretation upon it and that it may be understood that no other interpretation was in my thought. I am seeking only to face realities and to face them without soft concealments. Victory would mean peace forced upon the loser, a victor's terms imposed upon the vanquished. It would be accepted in humiliation, under duress, at an intolerable sacrifice, and would leave a sting, a resentment, a bitter memory upon which terms of peace would rest, not permanently, but only as upon quicksand. Only a peace between equals can last. Only a peace the very principle of which is equality and a common participation in a common benefit. The right state of mind, the right feeling between nations, is as necessary for a lasting peace as is the just settlement of vexed questions of territory or of racial and national allegiance.

The equality of nations upon which peace must be founded if it is to last must be an equality of rights; the guarantees exchanged must neither recognize nor imply a difference between big nations and small, between those that are powerful and those that are weak. Right must be based upon the common strength, not upon the individual strength, of the nations upon whose concert peace will depend. Equality of territory or of resources there of course cannot be; nor any other sort of equality not gained in the ordinary peaceful and legitimate development of the peoples themselves. But no one asks or expects anything more than an equality of rights. Mankind is looking now for freedom of life, not for equipoises of power.

Document 10

Ambassador to Great Britain Walter Hines Page to President Woodrow Wilson and Secretary of State Robert Lansing, Feb. 24, 1917, *PWW*, vol. 41, 280–81.

[Arthur J.] Balfour [of Admiralty] has handed me the text of a cipher telegram from [Alfred] Zimmermann, German Secretary of State for Foreign Affairs, to the German Minister to Mexico [Heinrich von Eckhardt], which was sent via Washington and relayed by [Ambassador Johann von] Bernstorff on January nineteenth. . . .

"We intend to begin on the first of February unrestricted submarine warfare. We shall endeavor in spite of this to keep the United States of America neutral. In the event of this not succeeding, we make Mexico a proposal of alliance on the following basis: make war together, make peace together, generous financial support and an understanding on our part that Mexico is to reconquer the lost territory in Texas, New Mexico, and Arizona. The settlement in detail is left to you. You will inform the President of the above most secretly as soon as the outbreak of war with the United States of America is certain and add the suggestion that he should, on his own initiative, invite Japan to immediate adherence and at the same time mediate between Japan and ourselves. Please call the President's attention to the fact that the ruthless employment of our submarines now offers the prospect of compelling England in a few months to make peace. Signed, ZIMMERMANN."

Document 11

President Woodrow Wilson's address to a joint session of Congress, Apr. 2, 1917, *PWW*, vol. 41, 519–21.

Gentlemen of the Congress: I have called the Congress into extraordinary session because there are serious, very serious, choices of policy to be made, and made immediately, which it was neither right nor constitutionally permissible that I should assume the responsibility of making.

On the third of February last I officially laid before you the extraordinary announcement of the Imperial German Government that on and after the first day of February it was its purpose to put aside all restraints of law or of humanity and use its submarines to sink every vessel that sought to approach either the ports of Great Britain and Ireland or the western coasts of Europe or any of the ports controlled by the enemies of Germany within the Mediterranean. . . .

. . . The present German submarine warfare against commerce is a warfare against mankind.

It is a war against all nations. American ships have been sunk, American lives taken, in ways which it has stirred us very deeply to learn of, but the ships and people of other neutral and friendly nations have been sunk and overwhelmed in the waters in the same way. There has been no discrimination. The challenge is to all mankind. Each nation must decide for itself how it will meet it. The choice we make for ourselves must be made with a moderation of counsel and a temperateness of judgment befitting our character and our motives as a nation. We must put excited feeling away. Our motive will not be revenge or the victorious assertion of the physical might of the nation, but only the vindication of right, of human right, of which we are only a single champion. . . .

With a profound sense of the solemn and even tragical character of the step I am taking and of the grave responsibilities which it involves, but in unhesitating obedience to what I deem my constitutional duty, I advise that the Congress declare the recent course of the Imperial German Government to be in fact nothing less than war against the government and people of the United States; that it formally accept the status of belligerent which has thus been thrust upon it; and that it take immediate steps not only to put the country in a more thorough state of defense but also to exert all its power and employ its resources to bring the Government of the German Empire to terms and end the war.

Document 12

President Woodrow Wilson's Fourteen Points Address, Jan. 8, 1918, *PWW,* vol. 45, 537.

VI. The evacuation of all Russian territory and such a settlement of all questions affecting Russia as will secure the best and freest cooperation of the other nations of the world in obtaining for her an unhampered and unembarrassed opportunity for the independent determination of her own political development and national policy and assure her of a sincere welcome into the society of free nations under institutions of her own choosing; and, more than a welcome, assistance also of every kind that she may need and may herself desire. The treatment accorded Russia by her sister nations in the months to come will be the acid test of their good will, of their comprehension of her needs as distinguished from their own interests, and of their intelligent and unselfish sympathy.

Document 13

Secretary of State Robert Lansing to the Allied Ambassadors, Aide-Mémoire, July 17, 1918, *FRUS, 1918, Russia,* 1932, vol. 2, 287–90.

The whole heart of the people of the United States is in the winning of this war. The controlling purpose of the Government of the United States is to do everything that is necessary and effective to win it. It wishes to cooperate in every practicable way with the Allied Governments and to cooperate ungrudgingly; for it has no ends of its own to serve and believes that the war can be won only by common counsel and intimate concert of action. It has sought to study every proposed policy or action in which its cooperation has been asked in this spirit, and states the following conclusions in the confidence that, if it finds itself obliged to decline participation in any undertaking or course of action, it will be understood that it does so only because it deems itself precluded from participating by imperative considerations either of policy or of fact. . . .

It is the clear and fixed judgment of the Government of the United States, arrived at after repeated and very searching reconsiderations of the whole situation in Russia, that military intervention there would add to the present sad confusion in Russia rather than cure it, injure her rather than help her, and that it would be of no advantage in the prosecution of our main design, to win the war against Germany. It can not, therefore, take part in such intervention or sanction it in principle. Military intervention would, in its judgment, even supposing it to be efficacious in its immediate avowed object of delivering an attack upon Germany from the east, be merely a method of making use of Russia, not a method of serving her. Her people could not profit by it, if they profited by it all, in time to save them from their present distresses, and their substance would be used to maintain foreign armies, not to reconstitute their own. Military action is admissible in Russia, as the Government of the United States sees the circumstances, only to help the Czecho-Slovaks consolidate their forces and get into successful cooperation with their Slavic kinsmen and to steady any efforts at self-government or self-defense in which the Russians themselves may be willing to accept assistance. Whether from Vladivostok or from Murmansk and Archangel, the only legitimate object for which American or Allied troops can be employed, it submits, is to guard military stores which may subsequently be needed by Russian forces and to render such aid as may be acceptable to the Russians in the organization of their own self-defense. For helping the Czecho-Slovaks there is immediate necessity and sufficient justification. Recent developments have made it evident that there is in the interest of what the Russian people themselves desire, and the Government of the United States is glad to contribute the small force at its disposal for that purpose. It yields, also, to the judgment of the Supreme Command in the matter of establishing a small force at Murmansk, to guard the military stores at Kola, and to make it safe for Russian forces to come together in organized bodies in the north. But it owes it to frank counsel to say that it can go no further than these modest and experimental plans. It is not in a position, and has no expectation of being in a position, to take part in organized intervention in adequate force from either Vladivostok or Murmansk and Archangel. It feels that it ought to add, also, that it will feel at liberty to use the few troops it can spare only for the purposes here stated and shall feel obliged to withdraw those forces, in order to add them to the forces at the western front, if the plans in whose execution it is now intended that they should cooperate should develop into others inconsistent with the policy to which the Government of the United States feel constrained to restrict itself. . . .

It hopes to carry out the plans for safeguarding the rear of the Czecho-Slovaks operating from Vladivostok in a way that will place it and keep it in close cooperation with a small military force like its own from Japan, and if necessary from the other Allies, and that will assure it of the cordial accord of all the Allied powers; and it proposes to ask all associated in this course of action to unite in assuring the people of Russia in the most public and solemn manner that none of the governments uniting in action either in Siberia or in northern Russia contemplates any interference of any kind with the political sovereignty of Russia, any intervention in her internal affairs, or any impairment of her territorial integrity either now or hereafter, but that each of the associated powers has the single object of affording such aid as shall be acceptable, and only such aid as shall be acceptable, to the Russian people in their endeavor to regain control of their own affairs, their own territory, and their own destiny.

It is the hope and purpose of the Government of the United States to take advantage of the earliest opportunity to send to Siberia a commission of merchants, agricultural experts, labor advisers, Red Cross representatives, and agents of the Young Men's Christian Association accustomed to organizing the best methods of spreading useful information and rendering educational help of a modest sort, in order in some systematic manner to relieve the immediate economic necessities of the people there in every way for which opportunity may open. The execution of this plan will follow and will not be permitted to embarrass the military assistance rendered in the rear of the westward-moving forces of the Czecho-Slovaks.

Document 14

President Woodrow Wilson to Secretary of State Robert Lansing, Aug. 23, 1918, *The Lansing Papers, FRUS, 1914–1920*, vol. 2, 378–79.

I hope you will do just what you here suggest. The other governments are going much faster,—are, indeed, acting upon a plan which is altogether foreign from ours and inconsistent with it.

Please make it plain to the French Ambassador [Jules Jusserand] that we do not think cooperation in political action necessary or desirable in eastern Siberia because we contemplate no political action of any kind there, but only the action of friends who stand at hand and wait to see how they can help. The more plain and emphatic this is made the less danger will there be or [*of*?] subsequent misunderstandings and irritations.

Document 15

Secretary of State Robert Lansing to French Ambassador Jules Jusserand, Aug. 31, 1918, *FRUS, 1918, Russia*, vol. 2, 362.

I have the honor to acknowledge the receipt of your excellency's note of August 12, 1918, in regard to the coordination of the action of the Allies in Siberia and northern Russia. . . .

Since the beginning of the revolutionary movement this Government has maintained an attitude of strict impartiality as between contending political parties and, as it contemplates no change in this attitude, it deems cooperation in any political action impossible and believes it would be as unnecessary as it is undesirable. It prefers to occupy a position in eastern Siberia merely as a friend who stands at hand ready to help in the most practical and wholehearted manner.

While, therefore, this Government cannot see its way clear to concur in the suggestion that a representative of the United States should assume the chairmanship of such an inter-Allied board, I beg to express my appreciation of your excellency's courtesy and consideration.

Document 16

Secretary of State Robert Lansing to Ambassador to Japan Rowland Morris, Nov. 16, 1918, *FRUS, 1918, Russia*, vol. 2, 433–34.

1. The United States has viewed with surprise the presence of the very large number of Japanese troops now in north Manchuria and eastern Siberia. Reliable information shows the number of these troops to be so great as to constitute a definite departure from the express understanding for cooperation between Japan and the United States and quite unwarranted by any military necessity.

2. This Government believes that any undertaking in regard to the Siberian situation must be based on a spirit of frank and open cooperation. It is convinced that any monopoly of control such as that now exercised by Japan in north Manchuria and in the eastern part of the Trans-Baikal will arouse suspicion and prove open to the charges of exploitation. Such monopoly is certainly opposed not only to the purpose of this Government to assist Russia but also to its views regarding China. . . .

. . . This Government therefore deems

If only they could have peered into the future! Four major developments of American policy took place beginning with the Harding administration, and each in a different way ended in failure. In those failures, as we now can see, world peace was lost.

In 1921 the people of the United States had the power to move toward preserving peace and for varying reasons failed to do so. The first of the American opportunities to preserve peace was symbolized by the Washington Naval Conference of 1921–22, a large assemblage that included the United States, England, Japan, France, and Italy, and that gave every evidence of a triumphant conclusion to a serious international problem—that of disarmament—but in fact did little to solve it. (doc. 1) Disarmament, perhaps better described as the limitation of arms, had concerned statesmen since the late nineteenth century, when armaments started to become increasingly complex as a result of the industrial age. Naval armaments principally concerned the United States, for not only could they lead to war, but in the early 1920s the cost of great ships seemed unduly high, $60 million for a battleship. The world's three great navies—England's, the United States', Japan's—by that time had all been on the victorious side in 1918, and it appeared foolish for the victors to fight one another. Americans also were concerned with the need to do something for world peace, having refused membership in the League of Nations. The new Republican administration especially desired to do something, for its political party had rejected Wilson's proffered peace settlement.

Whatever the intentions, the principal result of the conference was a limitation of ships that were no longer useful, such as battleships. (The Battle of Jutland had demonstrated the insufficiency of battleships. In that fog-bound afternoon in early 1916, German gunners blew up British battleships.) In addition, the Americans and British attempted to force the Japanese to accept a much smaller ratio of ships, an effort assisted by the American breaking of the Japanese code used to communicate with Tokyo, but a tactic that further antagonized the Japanese. In a concession that reflected Japan's superior position in the Pacific, the Americans and British promised not to fortify further such possessions as the Philippines and Hong Kong and thus virtually consigned the far Pacific to their Japanese rivals. (doc. 2)

The Washington Naval Conference should have been a beginning, not an end. Although there were subsequent naval conferences at Geneva and London—and nominal triumphs at the London Naval Conference of 1930—they resulted in small gains compared even to Washington. The future also demanded limitation of land armaments, of tanks, artillery, and especially planes. Air war would upset battle strategy on both land and sea. Americans took almost no interest in land armaments and were constantly reminding Europeans that the American army was minuscule. The U.S. government passed the problem of land disarmament to the Europeans. Here a contention between the British and French governments over proper policy toward Germany allowed the secret violation of the Versailles limitations on German arms during the 1920s and eventually permitted open rearmament under Adolf Hitler in the 1930s. (The British believed that if they were friendly to the postwar German government, the Weimar Republic, it would cooperate, whereas the French believed that the best way to obtain cooperation was to hold the lid on the Germans.) It is true that disarmament was a frail basis for peace in any case, that arms were only a symptom of deeper international trouble. Such failure to disarm suggested a general unwillingness to move toward preserving peace. This one can see in retrospect. Even so, the United States did not really pursue a rigorous negotiation for disarmament.

A second effort to ensure peace during the 1920s was the Kellogg-Briand Pact of 1928, and again came failure. The pact, also known as the Pact of Paris, was proposed originally as a treaty between France and the United States but later was expanded to include all nations in an alliance for peace that rested on the outlawry of war. Here, however, the effort was lost from the outset: the treaty encapsulated the hopes of many ill-informed Americans and Europeans and contained the maneuverings of American diplomats who did not want to help the French government, which originally had proposed the alliance with the United States as part of an effort to isolate Germany. The French proposition was much too sly an effort, which angered officials in the State Department when Foreign Minister Aristide Briand offered it. (docs. 3 and 4) Thereafter they did their best to embarrass Briand, in part by proposing to include all nations in the pact, thus adhering to a well-known and much-respected rule: the more nations signing a pact, the more worthless the pact becomes. Secretary of State Frank B. Kellogg, a lawyer, then began to envision a grand peace pact—the culmination of his life's work with the law—making war illegal. The many diplomats who had worked with Kellogg to make the pact useless were astonished at his conversion. But Kellogg's essential legalism allowed the European nations to offer reservations to the pact, which weakened its effectiveness by guaranteeing no interference in a state's right of self-defense or in its decision as to when conditions justify a war for that objective. (doc. 5) By that time Briand had tired of what was becoming a charade and was happy to sign what almost immediately proved to be a worthless treaty: within months of the pact's signing in Paris an undeclared war broke out between Russia and China. (doc. 6)

To mention the fate of the "Multilateral Pact," as it was sometimes called, is of course to be critical of generations of Americans for their naive view of Europe and Europeans. From the beginning they had believed in an Old World and a New, a city upon a hill: God had sifted the wheat to send the choice grain to America. European political or military entanglements meant only trouble for the United States. It was popular to suspect European governments of dark behavior, especially after the First World War. That great conflict had lightly touched the United States, which suffered 50,000 battlefield deaths, compared to millions suffered by Europeans. But that price was too high to risk further involvement in a pact against war. The people of the United States had lived too long with their belief in the Old and New worlds.

A third area of international affairs in which Americans might well have helped Europeans (and for that matter people everywhere) preserve world peace lay in the financing of postwar reconstruction and the development of national economies. This portion of American postwar policy proved similarly erroneous. Here the lack of wisdom was remarkable, but it was a different kind of ignorance than that fueled by sheer dislike of European involvement. President Wilson had thought he could dictate to the Allies, but that required a willingness to forgo payment of war debts. The national and international customs of the time did not permit forsaking of debts. During the war, the United States had given Britain, France, and other nations access to the U.S. Treasury to finance war orders. In the first months after the war, the American government continued this largess. These loans should have been turned into gifts, as happened with lend-lease aid following World War II. The entire balance of payments of nations was out of kilter after the First World War. But leaders simply did not understand what had happened. At the beginning of the 1920s, the European debtor nations considered wartime and postwar loans to be obligations, not possible gifts, and tried to arrange repayment schedules with the United States. These schedules, which were largely drawn by the mid-1920s, could not be met if international balances of payments could not easily right themselves. The latter proved to be true once the Great Depression began with the crash of the New York stock market in 1929 and Britain and other governments had to go off the gold standard and block their currencies in other ways.

It is not surprising, then, that the United States' victorious European allies were bound to connect the repayment of war debts owed to Americans with their efforts to extract reparations from the defeated Central Powers, principally Germany. The French at first believed that the Germans would pay for everything, and both the French and British governments carefully kept open the total of German reparations until 1921 so as to measure the possibilities against the war debts. The American government refused to admit a connection, even after the British government announced it would pay no more to the United States than it collected from Germany. In the 1920s, two conferences rearranged reparations schedules, and on each occasion an American banker was put in charge of a formula for payment. Finally, in 1931, after the depression forced America's debtors to threaten to default, the administration of President Herbert Hoover admitted the inadmissible and announced the so-called Hoover Moratorium, a one-year recess on payment of both war debts and reparations. (doc. 7)

Unlike naval disarmament and the Kellogg-Briand Pact, the debts-reparations imbroglio probably would have been impossible to avoid because it was unprecedented and also too complicated. Previously there had been no international payments other than the $1 billion reparation the German government extracted from France after the Franco-Prussian War of 1870–71. In the 1920s, nations had little experience handling such payments. Moreover, the complexity of the situation was great: What was to be done about the war debts? What was the proper response toward a Germany that bore considerable responsibility for starting the war in 1914 and yet did not want to pay because of the war's human and material losses?

A payment plan for both war debts and reparations had been worked out by the mid-1920s, but by 1929 another reparations plan proved necessary. This plan called for dividing reparations into two categories: absolute and conditional (payments that might not be necessary). This flimsy formula did not work and Hoover offered the moratorium, which was no solution but rather a delay in seeking a solution. By the end of the moratorium, payments came due late in 1932, and the reality of the situation became clear: the European and other debtors neither collected from Germany nor paid the United States other than partially, conditionally, or in blocked accounts. The continued economic unrest, exacerbated by the debts-reparations problem, further impeded an international climate conducive to peace.

The fourth failure of American policy during this dismal international era was an attempt to deal with the Far Eastern crisis, as Secretary of State Henry L. Stimson described Japan's occupation of the Chinese province of Manchuria beginning in 1931. The invasion marked the first open break in the provisions of the Pact of Paris. Interestingly, it was not a European nation that broke the pact, a development that Americans had not anticipated.

Stimson, who served as Hoover's secretary of state, realized that in the midst of the Great Depression he could do nothing more than scold the Japanese government, although on occasion he gave the impression that a military move might be possible. Many years earlier, he had been a protégé of Theodore Roosevelt and tended to admire military solutions. But under Hoover, the government had its hands full trying to confront domestic economic uncertainties caused by the depression that eventually became international in scope and involved all industrial nations. The Great Depression lasted until American entrance in World War II in 1941 and was the worst domestic crisis in American history, save for the Civil War. Thus, Hoover refused any military solution to the Far Eastern crisis and left Stimson only with "swords of ice," as he described his measures of nonrecognition of Japan's new position in Manchuria. Among these measures that became known as the "Stimson Doctrine" (doc. 8), the secretary of state informed the chairman of the Senate Foreign Relations Committee of the possibility of abandoning the nonfortification agreement of the Washington Naval Conference and fortifying the Philippines against Japan. What Stimson and most Americans did not understand was that the Japanese civil government was weak and that the army was getting out of hand. It was the beginning of military rule in Japan, which would lead to Pearl Harbor.

The documents that follow are reflections of the confusions noted in preceding pages, and the present-day reader can fairly easily discern what was going on behind the words and even what the words might have encouraged—because words have consequences. It is clear that for the most part American words would not work, given the economic fragility of the peace and the Great Depression in the offing and then in reality. Moreover, neither Americans nor Europeans understood how fragile peace was after the huge economic, social, and intellectual dislocations of World War I. In 1921, Secretary of State Charles Evans Hughes only touched the surface of the disarmament problem when he asked for limitation of battleships. In 1927 to 1928, State Department officials rightly believed that the French government sought an alliance against Germany by trying to play a trick on what it presumed were innocent Americans, but once the Americans proposed a countertrick by making the treaty multilateral in nature, the Kellogg-Briand Pact took on a life of its own and became, at least in Kellogg's eyes, a great American contribution to world peace. The debts-reparations tangle led to Hoover's solution, the moratorium, which lasted a few months. Finally, the Stimson Doctrine with its ringing phrases did little to support Japan's civilians against army officers who felt they needed to regenerate Japan by securing what they described as a Greater East Asia Co-Prosperity Sphere, a place for trade and enterprise on the Asian mainland, even if they had to carve it from the territory of helpless China.

Document 1

Secretary of State Charles Evans Hughes, address to the Washington Naval Conference, Nov. 12, 1921, U.S. Congress, 67th Cong., 1st sess., *Senate Documents,* Washington, D.C.: Government Printing Office, 1921, vol. 9, 11–17.

Gentlemen: It is with a deep sense of privilege and responsibility that I accept the honor you have conferred.

Permit me to express the most cordial appreciation of the assurances of friendly cooperation, which have been generously expressed by the representatives of all the invited Governments. The earnest desire and purpose, manifested in every step in the approach to this meeting, that we should meet the reasonable expectation of a watching world by effective action suited to the opportunity is the best augury for the success of the Conference.

The President [Warren G. Harding] invited the Governments of the British Empire, France, Italy, and Japan to participate in a conference on the subject of limitation of armament, in connection with which Pacific and Far Eastern questions would also be discussed. It would have been most agreeable to the President to have invited all the Powers to take part in this Conference, but it was thought to be a time when other considerations should yield to the practical requirements of the existing exigency, and in this view the invitation was extended to the group known as the Principal Allied and Associated Powers, which, by reason of the conditions produced by the war, control in the main the armament of the world. The opportunity to limit armament lies within their grasp.

It was recognized, however, that the interests of other Powers in the Far East made it appropriate that they should be invited to participate in the discussion of Pacific and Far Eastern problems, and, with the approval of the five Powers, an invitation to take part in the discussion of those questions has been extended to Belgium, China, the Netherlands, and Portugal.

The inclusion of the proposal for the discussion of Pacific and Far Eastern questions was not for the purpose of embarrassing or delaying an agreement for limitation of armament, but rather to support that undertaking by availing ourselves of this meeting to endeavor to reach a common understanding as to the principles and policies to be followed in the Far East and thus greatly to diminish, and if possible wholly to remove, discernible sources of controversy. It is believed that by interchanges of views at this opportune time the Governments represented here may find a basis of accord and thus give expression to their desire to assure enduring friendship.

In the public discussions which have preceded the Conference, there have been apparently two competing views; one, that the consideration of armament should await the result of the discussion of Far Eastern questions, and, another, that the latter discussion should be postponed until an agreement for limitation of armament has been reached. I am unable to find sufficient reason for adopting either of these extreme views. I think that it would be most unfortunate if we should disappoint the hopes which have attached to this meeting by a postponement of the consideration of the first subject. The world looks to this Conference to relieve humanity of the crushing burden created by competition in armament, and it is the view of the American Government that we should meet that expectation without any unnecessary delay. It is therefore proposed that the Conference should proceed at once to consider the question of the limitation of armament.

This, however, does not mean that we must postpone the examination of Far Eastern questions. These questions of vast importance press for solution. It is hoped that immediate provision may be made to deal with them adequately, and it is suggested that it may be found to be entirely practicable through the distribution of the work among designated committees to make progress to the ends sought to be achieved without either subject being treated as a hindrance to the proper consideration and disposition of the other.

The proposal to limit armament by an agreement of the Powers is not a new one, and we are admonished by the futility of earlier efforts. It may be well to recall the noble aspirations which were voiced twenty-three years ago in the imperial rescript of His Majesty the Emperor of Russia [Nicholas II]. It was then pointed out with clarity and emphasis that "The intellectual and physical strength of the nations, labor, and capital are for the major part diverted from their natural application and unproductively consumed. Hundreds of millions are devoted to acquiring terrible engines of destruction, which, though today regarded as the last word of science, are destined tomorrow to lose all value in consequence of some fresh discovery in the same field. National culture, economic progress, and the production of wealth are either paralyzed or checked in their development. Moreover, in proportion as the armaments of each Power increase, so do they less and less fulfill the object which the governments have set before themselves. The economic crisis, due in great part to the system of armaments a l'outrance and the continual danger which lies in this massing of war materials, are transforming the armed peace of our days into a crushing burden, which the peoples have more and more difficulty in bearing. It appears evident, then, that if this state of things were prolonged it would inevitably lead to the calamity which it is desired to avert, and the horrors of which make every thinking man shudder in advance. To put an end to these incessant armaments and to seek the means of warding off the calamities which are threatening the whole world—such is the supreme duty which is today imposed on all States."

It was with this sense of obligation that His Majesty the Emperor of Russia proposed the Conference, which was "to occupy itself with this grave problem" and which met at The Hague in the year 1899. Important as were the deliberations and conclusions of that Conference, especially with respect to the pacific settlement of international disputes, its result in the specific matter of limitation of armament went no further than the adoption of a final resolution setting forth the opinion "that the restriction of military charges, which are at present a heavy burden on the world, is extremely desirable for the increase of the material and moral welfare of mankind," and the utterance of the wish that the Governments "may examine the possibility of an agreement as to the limitation of armed forces by land and sea, and of war budgets."

It was seven years later that the Secretary of State of the United States, Mr. Elihu Root, in answering a note of the Russian Ambassador suggesting in outline a program of the Second Peace Conference, said: "The Government of the United States, therefore, feels it to be its duty to reserve for itself the liberty to propose to the Second Peace Conference, as one of the subjects for consideration, the reduction or limitation of armaments, in the hope that, if nothing further can be accomplished, some slight advance may be made toward the realization of the lofty conception which actuated the Emperor of Russia in calling the First Conference." It is significant that the Imperial German Government expressed itself as "absolutely opposed to the question of disarmament" and that the Emperor of Germany [Kaiser Wilhelm II] threatened to decline to send delegates if the subject of disarmament was to be discussed. In view, however, of the resolution which had been adopted at the First Hague Conference the delegates of the United States were instructed that the subject of limitation of armament "should be regarded as unfinished business, and that the Second Conference should ascertain and give full consideration to the results of such examination as the Governments may have given to the possibility of an agreement pursuant to the wish expressed by the First Conference." But by reason of the obstacles which the subject had encountered, the Second Peace Conference at The Hague, although it made notable progress in provision for the peaceful settlement of controversies, was unable to deal with limitation of armament except by a resolution in the following general terms: "The Conference confirms the resolution adopted by the Conference in 1899 in regard to the limitation of military expenditure; and inasmuch as military expenditure has considerably increased in almost every country since that time, the Conference declares that it is eminently desirable that the Governments should resume the serious examination of this question."

This was the fruition of the efforts of eight years. Although the effect was clearly perceived, the race in preparation of armament, wholly unaffected by these futile suggestions, went on until it fittingly culminated in the greatest war of history; and we are now suffering from the unparalleled loss of life, the destruction of hopes, the economic dislocations and the widespread impoverishment which measure the cost of the victory over the brutal pretensions of military force.

But if we are warned by the inadequacy of earlier endeavors for limitation of armament, we can not fail to recognize the extraordinary opportunity now presented. We not only have the lessons of the past to guide us, not only do we have the reaction from the disillusioning experiences of war, but we must meet the challenge of imperative economic demands. What was convenient or highly desirable before is now a matter of vital necessity. If there is to be economic rehabilitation, if the longings for reasonable progress are not to be denied, if we are to be spared the uprisings of peoples made desperate in the desire to shake off burdens no longer endurable, competition in armament must stop. The present opportunity not only derives its advantage from a general appreciation of this fact, but the power to deal with the exigency now rests with a small group of nations, represented here, who have every reason to desire peace and to promote amity. The astounding ambition which lay athwart the promise of the Second Hague Conference no longer menaces the world, and the great opportunity of liberty-loving and peace-preserving democracies has come. Is it not plain that the time has passed for mere resolutions that the responsible Powers should examine the question of limitation of armament? We can no longer content ourselves with investigations, with statistics, with reports, with the circumlocution of inquiry. The essential facts are sufficiently known. The time has come, and this Conference has been called, not for general resolutions or mutual advice, but for action. We meet with full understanding that the aspirations of mankind are not to be defeated either by plausible suggestions of postponement or by impracticable counsels of perfection. Power and responsibility are here and the world awaits a practicable program which shall at once be put into execution.

I am confident that I shall have your approval in suggesting that in this matter, as well as in others before the Conference, it is desirable to follow the course of procedure which has the best promise of achievement rather than one which would facilitate division; and thus, constantly aiming to agree so far as possible, we shall, with each point of agreement, make it easier to proceed to others.

The question, in relation to armament, which may be regarded as of primary importance at this time, and with which we can deal most promptly and effectively, is the limitation of naval armament. There are certain general considerations which may be deemed pertinent to this subject.

The first is that the core of the difficulty is to be found in the competition in naval programs, and that, in order appropriately to limit naval armament, competition in its production must be abandoned. Competition will not be remedied by resolves with respect to the method of its continuance. One program inevitably leads to another, and if competition continues, its regulation is impracticable. There is only one adequate way out and that is to end it now.

It is apparent that this can not be accomplished without serious sacrifices. Enormous sums have been expended upon ships under construction and building programs which are now under way can not be given up without heavy loss. Yet if the present construction of capital ships goes forward other ships will inevitably be built to rival them and this will lead to still others. Thus the race will continue so long as ability to continue lasts. The effort to escape sacrifices is futile. We must face them or yield our purpose.

It is also clear that no one of the naval Powers should be expected to make these sacrifices alone. The only hope of limitation of naval armament is by agreement among the nations concerned, and this agreement should be entirely fair and reasonable in the extent of the sacrifices required of each of the Powers. In considering the basis of such an agreement, and the commensurate sacrifices to be required, it is necessary to have regard to the existing naval strength to the great naval Powers, including the extent of construction already effected in the case of ships in process. This follows from the fact that one nation is as free to compete as another, and each may find grounds for its action. What one may do another may demand the opportunity to rival, and we remain in the thrall of competitive effort. I may add that the American delegates are advised by their naval experts that the tonnage of capital ships may fairly be taken to measure the relative strength of navies, as the provision for auxiliary combatant craft should sustain a reasonable relation to the capital ship tonnage allowed.

It would also seem to be a vital part of a plan for the limitation of naval armament that there should be a naval holiday. It is proposed that for a period of not less than 10 years there should be no further construction of capital ships.

I am happy to say that I am at liberty to go beyond these general propositions and, on behalf of the American delegation acting under the instructions of the President of the United States, to submit to you a concrete proposition for an agreement for the limitation of naval armament.

It should be added that this proposal immediately concerns the British Empire, Japan, and the United States. In view of the extraordinary conditions due to the World War affecting the existing strength of the navies of France and Italy, it is not thought to be necessary to discuss at this stage of the proceedings the tonnage allowance of these nations, but the United States proposes that this matter be reserved for the later consideration of the Conference.

In making the present proposal the United States is most solicitous to deal with the question upon an entirely reasonable and practicable basis, to the end that the just interests of all shall be adequately guarded and that national security and defense shall be maintained. Four general principles have been applied:

(1) That all capital-ship building programs, either actual or projected, should be abandoned;

(2) That further reduction should be made through the scrapping of certain of the older ships;

(3) That in general regard should be had to the existing naval strength of the Powers concerned;

(4) That the capital ship tonnage should be used as the measurement of strength for navies and a proportionate allowance of auxiliary combatant craft prescribed. . . .

I have sketched the proposal only in outline, leaving the technical details to be supplied by the formal proposition which is ready for submission to the delegates.

The plan includes provision for the limitation of auxiliary combatant craft. This term embraces three classes, that is (1) auxiliary surface combatant craft, such as cruisers (exclusive of battle cruisers), flotilla leaders, destroyers, and various surface types; (2) submarines, and (3) airplane carriers.

I shall not attempt to review the proposals for these various classes, as they bear a definite relation to the provisions for capital fighting ships.

With the acceptance of this plan the burden of meeting the demands of competition in naval armament will be lifted. Enormous sums will be released to aid the progress of civilization. At the same time the proper demands of national defense will be adequately met and the nations will have ample opportunity during the naval holiday of 10 years to consider their future course. Preparation for offensive naval war will stop now.

I shall not attempt at this time to take up the other topics which have been listed upon the tentative agenda proposed in anticipation of the Conference.

Document 2

Five-Power Naval Treaty, Feb. 6, 1922, U.S. Department of State, *Papers Relating to the Foreign Relations of the United States* (hereafter referred to as *FRUS*), 1922, Washington, D.C.: Government Printing Office, 1938, vol. 1, 247–53, 264–65.

The United States of America, the British Empire, France, Italy and Japan;

Desiring to contribute to the maintenance of the general peace, and to reduce the burdens of competition in armament; Have resolved, with view to accomplishing these purposes, to conclude a treaty to limit their respective naval armament. . . .

Article I

The Contracting Powers agree to limit their respective naval armament as provided in the present Treaty. . . .

Article III

. . . [T]he Contracting Powers shall abandon their respective capital ship building programs, and no new capital ships shall be constructed or acquired by any of the Contracting Powers except replacement tonnage. . . .

Article IV

The total capital ship replacement tonnage of each of the Contracting Powers shall not exceed in standard displacement, for the United States 525,000 tons (533,400 metric tons); for the British Empire 525,000 tons (533,400 metric tons); for France 175,000 tons (177,800 metric tons); for Italy 175,000 tons (177,800 metric tons); for Japan 315,000 tons (320,040 metric tons).

Article V

No capital ship exceeding 35,000 tons (35,560 metric tons) standard displacement shall be acquired by, or constructed by, for, or within the jurisdiction of, any of the Contracting Powers.

Article VI

No capital ship of any of the Contracting Powers shall carry a gun with a calibre in excess of 16 inches (406 millimetres). . . .

Article XI

No vessel of war exceeding 10,000 tons (10,160 metric tons) standard displacement, other than a capital ship or aircraft carrier, shall be required by, or constructed by, for, or within the jurisdiction of, any of the Contracting Powers. Vessels not specifically built as fighting ships nor taken in time of peace under government control for fighting purposes, which are employed on fleet duties or as troop transports or in some other way for the purpose of assisting in the prosecution of hostilities otherwise than as fighting ships, shall not be within the limitations of this Article.

Article XII

No vessel of war or any of the Contracting Powers, hereafter laid down, other than a capital ship, shall carry a gun with a calibre in excess of 8 inches (203 millimetres).

Article XIII

. . . [N]o ship designated in the present Treaty to be scrapped may be reconverted into a vessel of war.

Article XIV

No preparations shall be made in merchant ships in time of peace for the installation of warlike armaments for the purpose of converting such ships into vessels of war, other than the necessary stiffening of decks for the mounting of guns not exceeding 6 inch (152 millimetres) calibre.

Article XV

No vessel of war constructed within the jurisdiction of any of the Contracting Powers for a non-Contracting Power shall exceed the limitations as to displacement and armament prescribed by the present Treaty for vessels of a similar type which may be constructed by or for any of the Contracting Powers. . . .

Article XVI

If the construction of any vessel of war for a non-Contracting Power is undertaken within the jurisdiction of any of the Contracting Powers, such Power shall promptly inform the other Contracting Powers of the date of the signing of the contract and the date on which the keel of the ship is laid; and shall also communicate to them the particulars relating to the ship. . . .

Article XVII

In the event of a Contracting Power being engaged in war, such Power shall not use as a vessel of war any vessel of war which may be under construction within its jurisdiction for any other Power, or which may have been constructed within its jurisdiction for another Power and not delivered.

Article XVIII

Each of the Contracting Powers undertakes not to dispose by gift, sale or any mode of transfer of any vessel of war in such a manner that such vessel may become a vessel of war in the Navy of any foreign Power.

Article XIX

The United States, the British Empire and Japan agree that the *status quo* at the time of the signing of the present Treaty, with regard to fortifications and naval bases, shall be maintained in their respective territories and possessions specified hereunder:

(1) The insular possessions which the United States now holds or may hereafter acquire in the Pacific Ocean, except (*a*) those adjacent to the coast of the United States, Alaska and the Panama Canal Zone, not including the Aleutian Islands, and (*b*) the Hawaiian Islands;

(2) Hong Kong and the insular possessions which the British Empire now holds or may hereafter acquire in the Pacific Ocean, east of the meridian of 110° east longitude, except (*a*) those adjacent to the coast of Canada, (*b*) the Commonwealth of Australia and its Territories, and (*c*) New Zealand;

(3) The following insular territories and possessions of Japan in the Pacific Ocean, to wit: the Kurile Islands, the Bonin Islands, Amami-Oshima, the Loochoo Islands, Formosa and the Pescadores, and any insular territories or possessions in the Pacific Ocean which Japan may hereafter acquire.

The maintenance of the *status quo* under the foregoing provisions implies that no new fortifications or naval bases shall be established in the territories and possessions specified; that no measures shall be taken to increase the existing naval facilities for the repair and maintenance of naval forces, and that no increase shall be made in the coast defences of the territories and possessions above specified. This restriction, however, does not preclude such repair and replacement of worn-out weapons and equipment as is customary in naval and military establishments in time of peace. . . .

Article XXI

If during the term of the present Treaty the requirements of the national security of any Contracting Power in respect of naval defence are, in the opinion of that Power, materially affected by any change of circumstances, the Contracting Powers will, at the request of such Power, meet in conference with a view to the reconsideration of the provisions of the Treaty and its amendment by mutual agreement.

In view of possible technical and scientific developments, the United States, after consultation with the other Contracting Powers, shall arrange for a conference of all the Contracting Powers which shall convene as soon as possible after the expiration of eight years from the coming into force of the present Treaty to consider what changes, if any, in the Treaty may be necessary to meet such developments. . . .

Article XXIII

The present Treaty shall remain in force until December 31st, 1936, and in case none of the Contracting Powers shall have given notice two years before that date of its intention to terminate the Treaty, it shall continue in force until the expiration of two years from the date on which notice of termination shall be given by one of the Contracting Powers, whereupon the Treaty shall terminate as regards all the Contracting Powers.

Document 3

Proposal by French Minister of Foreign Affairs Aristide Briand for a Franco-American treaty, Apr. 6, 1927, *FRUS, 1927*, 1942, vol. 2, 611–13.

At a time when the thought of the Western World is turning back to the solemn date of the entry of the United States into the War, I address to the American people the heartfelt expression of the very fraternal and trusting sentiments which will always be cherished for them by the French people. I have not forgotten that it fell to my lot to be the first to learn through an official communication from Mr. [William G.] Sharp, then Ambassador of the United States at Paris, that the Federal Government had come to a decision which would exert such considerable influence in the history of the World War.

Ten years have gone by since the American nation, with magnificent enthusiasm, associated itself with the Allied Nations for the defense of threatened liberties, and in the course of those years the same spirit of justice and humanity has not ceased to inspire our two countries, equally concerned to bring the war to an end and to prevent its return.

France wishes around her an atmosphere of confidence and peace, and her efforts for this are shown by the signing of agreements aimed to remove the threat of conflicts. The limitation of armaments, sought also sincerely by our two Governments, is in response to the ardent wishes of the whole French people, on whom have weighed for more than half a century heavy military charges and who sustained for four years in their territory devastations not yet repaired.

The discussions over disarmament have brought out all the complexity of the technical problem submitted to the examination of experts, but they have served at least to make clear, politically, the common inspiration and identity of aims which exist between France and the United States. Two great democratic nations, devoted to the same ideal of peace, are following the same path towards the same end. The divergencies of views which may appear between them bear only on questions of procedure or method. And even where the proposals of France cannot meet those of the United States, they at least make it clear to the American people how far France, with the one reservation of her security, is ready to go in the way of accomplishment.

Is it necessary to recall the French proposals at Geneva tending to limit the most dangerous threats of war in the future by the control of the industrial and chemical armaments of states? France went even further when she proposed the international establishment of a "General Staff of Peace". Finally, in the organization of her own national forces, she gives, at this very moment, evidence of her eminently peaceful motives by contemplating the reconstitution of her armament from a purely defensive standpoint. The new military law at the present moment submitted to the French Parliament has indeed been conceived by men most inimical to the danger of militarism. It aims for the first time to "abolish the idea of profitable war" and to place upon all, both men and women, the abominable burden of war, the whole nation thus being placed on guard against a common danger. Does not such organization exclude all aggressive tendency?

More than this or that question of procedure in the technical framing of a project of disarmament, this fundamental question of a policy of peace, that is to say a will for peace and mind for peace, is what truly matters. For disarmament, after all, can only result from the will for peace on the part of the nations of the civilized world. And it is on this point that American thought is always sure to agree with French thought.

For those who devote themselves to this living reality of a policy of peace, the United States and France are already appearing in the world as being morally bound together. If there were any need between these two great democracies to testify more convincingly in favor of peace and to present to the peoples a more solemn example, France would be ready publicly to subscribe, with the United States, to any mutual engagement tending, as between those two countries, to "outlaw war", to use an American expression. The renunciation of war as an instrument of national policy is a conception already familiar to the signatories of the Covenant of the League of Nations and of the Treaties of Locarno. Any engagement subscribed to in the same spirit by the United States with another nation such as France would greatly contribute in the eyes of the world to broaden and strengthen the foundation upon which the international policy of peace is being raised. Thus two great friendly nations, equally devoted to the cause of peace, would give the world the best illustrations of this truth, that the accomplishment most immediately to be attained is not so much disarmament as the practice of peace.

In memory of this tenth anniversary of the entrance of the United States into the war, the American Legion is preparing to make a pious pilgrimage to France where rest its dead and where it will hold its annual convention. I hope that the Legion will come here in as large numbers as possible. They will be welcome. From their too short stay among us they will carry away, I know, the memory of a France at work, as desirous of peace as she has been ardent in war, and widely open to all that is great and generous which makes her heart beat in unison with yours.

Document 4

The Department of State's private view of the Aristide Briand proposal, June 24, 1927, *FRUS, 1927*, 1942, vol. 2, 617–18.

The text of Mr. [Aristide] Briand's proposals for a Treaty to outlaw war, contained in telegram No. 260, of June 22, 1927, from the Embassy at Paris, a copy of which is attached, should be carefully considered from every point of view.

Mr. Briand's insistence that negotiations should begin at once without awaiting the arrival in this country of M. [Paul] Claudel would seem to indicate that he was most anxious to keep this topic in the public eye most prominently during the meeting of the Naval Conference at Geneva in order to draw attention away from the fact that France is not there represented in a constructive step towards World Peace.

The vague wording and lack of precision in the draft seems also intended to give the effect of a kind of perpetual alliance between the United States and France, which would certainly serve to disturb the other great European Powers,—England, Germany and Italy. This would be particularly true as it would make the neutral position of the United States during any European war in which France might be engaged extremely difficult, since France might deem it necessary to infringe upon our rights as a neutral under this guaranty of non-aggression. A further point which Mr. Briand has not touched on is the question of France's obligations under the Covenant of the League of Nations to aid the League in the punishment of an aggressor state. It might likewise be used internally in France to postpone the ratification of the Debt Settlement and to create a feeling that payment was unnecessary.

In order to avoid this interpretation, it would be incumbent on the United States at once to offer a treaty in the same terms to England and Japan, more especially as we are negotiating with them at the present moment and could hardly wish them to feel that we were entering into an alliance at the same time with another Power.

Certainly a single treaty of this nature, and, according to press despatches, France desires that it be an absolutely unique instrument, would raise the question of an alliance with a country outside the American hemisphere. A series of such agreements, unless it were absolutely world wide, would raise the same objections. All this tends to indicate that it would be best to keep the subject in abeyance at least until the conclusion of some agreement in Geneva. However, when the time comes actually to negotiate, it would seem that the only answer to the French proposition would be that, as far as our relations with France were concerned, adequate guarantees were contained in the [Secretary of State William Jennings] Bryan Treaty [1914] and that if any step further than this were required, it should be in the form of a universal undertaking not to resort to war, to which the United States would at any time be most happy to become a party. Before such a time, treaties of the nature which France suggests become practically negative military alliances.

Document 5

Foreign Secretary Sir Austen Chamberlain to American Chargé d'Affaires in London Ray Atherton, British reservations to the proposed Kellogg-Briand Pact, July 18, 1928, *FRUS, 1928*, 1942, vol. 1, 112–14.

I am happy to be able to inform you that after carefully studying the note which you left with me on the 23rd June, transmitting the revised text of the draft of the proposed treaty for the renunciation of war, His Majesty's Government in Great Britain accept the proposed treaty in the form transmitted by you and will be glad to sign it at such time and place as may be indicated for the purpose by the Government of the United States.

My Government have read with interest the explanations contained in your note as to the meaning of the draft treaty, and also the comments which it contains upon the considerations advanced by other Powers in the previous diplomatic correspondence.

You will remember that in my previous communication of the 19th of May I explained how important it was to my Government that the principle should be recognised that if one of the parties to this proposed treaty resorted to war in violation of its terms, the other parties should be released automatically from their obligations towards that party under the treaty. I also pointed out that respect for the obligations arising out of the Covenant of the League of Nations and the Locarno treaties [1925] was the foundation of the policy of the Government of this country, and that they could agree to any new treaty which would weaken or undermine these engagements.

The stipulation now inserted in the preamble under which any signatory Power hereafter seeking to promote its national interests by resort to war against another signatory is to be denied the benefits furnished by the treaty is satisfactory of my Government, and is sufficient to meet the first point mentioned in the preceding paragraph.

His Majesty's Government in Great Britain do not consider, after mature reflection, that the fulfilment of the obligations which they have undertaken in the Covenant of the League of Nations and in the Treaty of Locarno is precluded by their acceptance of the proposed treaty. They concur in the view enunciated by the German Government in their note of the 27th April that those obligations do not contain anything which could conflict with the treaty proposed by the United States Government.

My Government have noted with peculiar satisfaction that all the parties to the Locarno Treaty are now invited to become original signatories of the new treaty, and that it is clearly the wish of the United States Government that all members of the League should become parties either by signature or accession. In order that as many States as possible may participate in the new movement, I trust that a general invitation will be extended to them to do so.

As regards the passage in my note of the 19th May relating to certain regions of which the welfare and integrity constitute a special and vital interest for our peace and safety, I need only to repeat that His Majesty's Government in Great Britain accept the new treaty upon the understanding that it does not prejudice their freedom of action in this respect.

I am entirely in accord with the views expressed by Mr. [Frank B.] Kellogg in his speech of the 28th April that the proposed treaty does not restrict or impair in any way the right of self-defense, as also with his opinion that each State alone is competent to decide when circumstances necessitate recourse to war for that purpose.

In the light of the foregoing explanations, His Majesty's Government in Great Britain are glad to join with the United States and with all other Governments similarly disposed in signing a definitive treaty for the renunciation of war in the form transmitted in your note of the 23rd June. They rejoiced to be associated with the Government of the United States of America and the other parties to the proposed treaty in a further and signal advance in the outlawry of war.

Document 6

Kellogg-Briand Pact, Aug. 27, 1928, *FRUS, 1928*, 1942, vol. 1, 155.

Article I

The High Contracting Parties solemnly declare in the names of their respective peoples that they condemn recourse to war for the solution of international controversies, and renounce it as an instrument of national policy in their relations with one another.

Article II

The High Contracting Parties agree that the settlement or solution of all disputes of conflicts of whatever nature or of whatever origin they may be, which may arise among them, shall never be sought except by pacific means. . . .

Document 7

Hoover Moratorium, June 20, 1931, *FRUS, 1931*, 1946, vol. 1, 33–35.

The American Government proposes the postponement during one year of all payments on intergovernmental debts, reparations and relief debts, both principal and interest, of course, not including obligations of governments held by private parties. Subject to confirmation by Congress, the American Government will postpone all payments upon the debts of foreign governments to the American Government payable during the fiscal year beginning July 1 next, conditional on a like postponement for one year of all payments on intergovernmental debts owing the important creditor powers.

This course of action has been approved by the following Senators: Henry F. Ashurst, Hiram Bingham, Wm. E. Borah, James F. Byrnes, Arthur Capper, Simeon D. Fess, Duncan U. Fletcher, Carter Glass, William J. Harris, Pat Harrison, Cordell Hull, William H. King, Dwight W. Morrow, George H. Moses, David A. Reed, Claude A. Swanson, Arthur Vandenberg, Robert F. Wagner, David L. Walsh, Thomas J. Walsh, James E. Watson; and by the following Representatives: Isaac Bacharach, Joseph W. Byrns, Carl R. Chindbloom, Frank Crowther, James W. Collier, Charles R. Crisp, Thomas H. Cullen, George P. Darrow, Harry A. Estep, Willis C. Hawley, Carl E. Mapes, J. C. McLaughlin, Earl C. Michener, C. William Ramseyer, Bertrand H. Snell, John Q. Tilson, Allen T. Treadway and Will R. Wood. It has been approved by Ambassador Charles G. Dawes and by Mr. Owen D. Young.

The purpose of this action is to give the forthcoming year to the economic recovery of the world and to help free the recuperative forces already in motion in the United States from retarding influences from abroad.

The world-wide depression has affected the countries of Europe more severely than our own. Some of these countries are feeling to a serious extent the drain of this depression on national economy. The fabric of intergovernmental debts, supportable in normal times, weighs heavily in the midst of this depression.

From a variety of causes arising out of the depression such as the fall in the price of foreign commodities and the lack of confidence in economic and political stability abroad there is an abnormal movement of gold into the United States which is lowering the credit stability of many foreign countries. These and the other difficulties abroad diminish buying power for our exports and in a measure are the cause of our continued unemployment and continued lower prices to our farmers.

Wise and timely action should contribute to relieve the pressure of these adverse forces in foreign countries and should assist in the reestablishment of confidence, thus forwarding political peace and economic stability in the world.

Authority of the President to deal with this problem is limited as this action must be supported by the Congress. It has been assured the cordial support of leading members of both parties in the Senate and the House. The essence of this proposition is to give time to permit debtor governments to recover their national prosperity. I am suggesting to the American people that they be wise creditors in their own interest and be good neighbors.

I wish to take this occasion also to frankly state my views upon our relations to German reparations and the debts owed to us by the allied Governments of Europe. Our government has not been a party to, or exerted any voice in determination of reparation obligations. We purposely did not participate in either general reparations or the division of the colonies or property. The repayment of debts due to us from the Allies for the advance for war reconstruction were settled upon a basis not contingent upon German reparations or related thereto. Therefore, reparations is necessarily wholly a European problem with which we have no relation.

I do not approve in any remote sense of the cancellation of the debts to us. World confidence would not be enhanced by such action. None of our debtor nations has ever suggested it. But as the basis of settlement of these debts was the capacity under normal conditions of the debtor to pay, we should be consistent with our own policies and principles if we take into account the abnormal situation now existing in the world. I am sure the American people have no desire to pay and it is our view that broad vision requires that our government should recognize the situation as it exists.

This course of action is entirely consistent with the policy which we have hitherto pursued. We are not involved in the discussion of strictly European problems, of which the payment of German reparations is one. It represents our willingness to make a contribution to the early restoration of world prosperity in which our own people have so deep an interest.

I wish further to add that while this action had no bearing on the conference for limitation of land armaments to be held next February, inasmuch as the burden of competitive armaments has contributed to bring about this depression, we trust that by this evidence of our desire to assist we shall have contributed to the good will which is so necessary in the solution of this major question.

Document 8

Stimson Doctrine, Jan. 7, 1932, *FRUS, 1932*, 1948, vol. 3, 8.

With the recent military operations about Chinchow, the last remaining administrative authority of the Government of the Chinese Republic in South Manchuria, as it existed prior to September 18th, 1931, has been destroyed. The American Government continues confident that the work of the neutral commission recently authorized by the Council of the League of Nations will facilitate an ultimate solution of the difficulties now existing between Japan and China. But in view of the present situation and of its own rights and obligations therein, the American Government deems it to be its duty to notify both the Government of the Chinese Republic and the Imperial Japanese Government that it cannot admit the legality of any situation *de facto* nor does it intend to recognize any treaty or agreement entered into between those rights of the United States or its citizens in China, including those which relate to the sovereignty, the independence, or the territorial and administrative integrity of the Republic of China, or to the international policy relative to China, commonly known as the open door policy; and that it does not intend to recognize any situation, treaty or agreement which may be brought about by means contrary to the covenants and obligations of the Pact of Paris of August 27, 1928, to which Treaty both China and Japan, as well as the United States, are parties.

CHAPTER 5

From Isolation to Intervention in World War II: 1933–41

Wayne S. Cole

During the 1930s, millions of people all over the world suffered economic distress and feared approaching war. Those unsettled times produced political crises and even revolutions in dozens of countries. Governments initiated various forms of economic nationalism. Benito Mussolini's Fascists in Italy, Joseph Stalin's Communists in the Soviet Union, and a military clique in Japan all tightened their grips. In the midst of that turmoil, Adolf Hitler and his National Socialists (Nazis) came to power in Germany in 1933. Though victorious in World War I, Great Britain and France had acute difficulties of their own. And the shiny new League of Nations never commanded the power or effectiveness that U.S. President Woodrow Wilson had envisaged for it.

Americans, too, suffered from the Great Depression. Blaming hard times on President Herbert Hoover and other Republicans, voters in 1932 turned to the personable Democratic candidate, Franklin D. Roosevelt of New York. Though he was a big-navy advocate and had previously favored membership in the League of Nations, the tall and handsome patrician said little about foreign affairs in his 1932 campaign. He later came out against membership in the league. During his more than twelve years in the White House, FDR grappled with the most severe depression and the most destructive war in modern history.

During his first term (1933–37), Roosevelt focused most of his attention on domestic matters, particularly on his New Deal program to end the depression and restore prosperity. To win adoption of his New Deal, Roosevelt depended on a political alliance between liberals from the urban Northeast (many of whom were Democrats politically and internationalists on foreign affairs) and western agrarian progressives (most of whom were Republicans politically and isolationists on foreign affairs). Consequently, though Roosevelt took some foreign policy initiatives during his first term, they were carefully restrained so that they would not endanger the political alliance on which his New Deal depended.

Insofar as Americans considered foreign affairs during FDR's first term, the majority resolved that the United States should never again become embroiled in European wars. They did not want the United States cut off from the rest of the world nor trade and credit relations with other countries severed. But most Americans wanted the United States to stay out of "entangling alliances" and European wars. That was the meaning of U.S. "isolationism" in the twentieth century.

Roosevelt's Good Neighbor Policy, which favored cooperation with Latin America, in contrast to previous interventionist policies, and Secretary of State Cordell Hull's Reciprocal Trade Agreements Act had internationalist implications. But from 1934 to 1936, the administration cooperated with a Senate committee, chaired by Gerald P. Nye of North Dakota, when it investigated munitions industries, which seemed to have led the United States into World War I for their own profit. This demonstrated unmistakable isolationist tendencies. Roosevelt also signed neutrality legislation designed to prevent American involvement in future wars. As president, he never worked for U.S. membership in the League of Nations.

In the 1936 campaign, Roosevelt continued his focus on domestic and New Deal matters. Those who feared involvement in alliances or foreign wars had little reason to complain about his approach to foreign affairs during his first term. Americans reelected FDR by a landslide.

Roosevelt's second term showed substantial changes from his first term. Opposition mounted against expanded New Deal proposals. Despite its many accomplishments, the New Deal had not ended the depression for most Americans. Democratic majorities in Congress were cut sharply in the elections of 1938. FDR needed to revise his political priorities.

In addition, alarming developments abroad forced the American people and their leaders to pay attention. In 1935 and 1936, the League of Nations' collective security efforts failed to block Italian aggression against Ethiopia in East Africa. The bloody Spanish Civil War (1936–39) brought a Nationalist government to power under Generalissimo Francisco Franco. In 1937 Japan widened its long undeclared war against China.

Most alarming were developments in Hitler's Nazi Germany. Hitler quickly converted his government into a Nazi dictatorship and by 1935 was rapidly rearming Germany in violation of the Versailles treaty. He promised to restore German greatness by "righting the wrongs" of the Versailles settlement and by suppressing Jews. Hitler's demagogic appeals and Nazi ruthlessness combined with Allied timidity, the ineffectiveness of the League of Nations, and American isolationism to enable Nazi Germany to make huge strides toward the accomplishment of Hitler's announced goals—and more.

In 1936, Hitler remilitarized the Rhineland in violation of existing treaties. In the *Anschluss* (union) of March 1938, he incorporated Austria into "Greater Germany." In the autumn of 1938, after British Prime Minister

Neville Chamberlain and French Premier Édouard Daladier attempted to appease Hitler by signing the Munich Pact, Germany seized the Sudetenland of Czechoslovakia. In the spring of 1939, in violation of his Munich promises, Hitler dismembered the rest of Czechoslovakia. In August, Nazi Germany shocked the world by concluding a nonaggression pact with Stalin's Communist Russia, thus opening the door for Hitler's move into Poland.

On September 1, 1939, Hitler loosed his *blitzkrieg* (lightning war), led by the *Luftwaffe* (air force), against Poland. Refusing to yield any farther, Britain and France declared war on Germany on September 3, but they could not save Poland, which fell by the end of the month. During the winter of 1939–40, headlines focused on the "Winter War" in which Stalin's Soviet Union crushed Finnish resistance in northeast Europe.

In the spring of 1940, Hitler's military forces continued the assault. They first overran Denmark and Norway, and then, on May 10, the German *blitzkrieg* turned south and struck the Netherlands, Luxembourg, and Belgium. German advances quickly forced the British to evacuate their troops from the European continent at Dunkirk. Nazi Germany, with help from Mussolini's Fascist Italy, forced the surrender of France in June.

During the ensuing Battle of Britain, Royal Air Force fighter planes successfully denied the German *Luftwaffe* control of the skies over England. Consequently, Hitler first postponed and then canceled his plans to invade England. This was the first indication that the military forces of Nazi Germany were anything less than invincible.

It remained to be seen, however, whether Britain could survive over the longer term. Many doubted that Britain alone could ever conquer Hitler's Nazi Germany on the mainland of Europe. On June 22, 1941, Hitler broke the nonaggression pact and struck eastward against Stalin's Soviet Union. Most experts expected Germany to roll over its new enemy just as it had rolled over every other continental European country. If Japan triumphed in Asia, and if Germany and Italy triumphed on the European continent and in North Africa, Britain's survival could once again be brought into serious question. And if Britain fell, Latin America and the United States in the Western Hemisphere could be next. Neither the American people nor their leaders could ignore such alarming developments. They were forced to fundamentally reconsider U.S. policies and the nation's place in world affairs.

In the 1930s, the majority of American people had believed the United States was mistaken in entering World War I—that they had been "suckers" to get involved. Many were convinced that restrictions on trade and credit relations with belligerents, along with limits on presidential discretion in foreign affairs, might have prevented American involvement in that conflict. Through mandatory neutrality legislation, they hoped that Congress could restrain the war-making proclivities of both big business and big government, which later generations would call "the military-industrial complex" and "the imperial presidency." (doc. 1) By 1937 those neutrality laws, signed by President Roosevelt, included a mandatory arms embargo, a ban on foreign loans, a cash-and-carry policy on goods that was intended to keep American ships off the high seas in war, and a ban on travel by Americans on belligerent ships.

Nonetheless, President Roosevelt and a minority of the American people (particularly in the urban Northeast and in the Democratic South) drew quite different conclusions from World War I. They believed that the United States had outgrown its traditional policies of neutrality and noninvolvement and that it had been a tragic mistake for the United States to reject the Versailles treaty and membership in the League of Nations. They believed that the United States had a better chance of preventing war and avoiding involvement by cooperating actively with like-minded nations to preserve peace and, if necessary, to block aggressors. Roosevelt had cautiously explored such alternatives in his first term. During his second term he carefully stepped up such efforts.

In October 1937, President Roosevelt called for a ''quarantine'' of aggressor states. (doc. 2) Early in 1939, he advocated ''methods short of war, but stronger and more effective than mere words'' to deter aggressors. After war erupted in Europe in the autumn of 1939, he persuaded Congress to repeal the arms embargo. In September 1940 he worked out the ''destroyer deal'' with Great Britain, exchanging fifty overage American destroyers for bases on British possessions in the Western Hemisphere. He also increased military production and preparations. That same month he signed the first peacetime military conscription law in American history. Early in 1941, he persuaded Congress to adopt lend-lease legislation enabling him to transfer war goods to countries resisting the Axis powers. He ordered the American navy to patrol the western Atlantic and report German submarines to British planes and ships. In September he ordered American warships to fire on German submarines without warning—the ''shoot-on-sight'' policy. (doc. 3) In November he persuaded Congress to repeal what remained of the neutrality legislation, thereby allowing armed American merchant ships, escorted by American navy vessels, to carry products through belligerent waters to the ports of countries fighting the Axis. In the Pacific, President Roosevelt gradually tightened the economic screws on Japan by requiring American businesses to secure licenses before exporting vital raw materials and thus exerting moral pressure on them not to deal with Tokyo. After Japanese troops occupied French Indochina in July 1941, the president froze Japanese assets and stopped the flow of oil to Japan.

Until the summer of 1940 (when Nazi Germany swept over Western Europe and forced the surrender of France), the overwhelming majority of American people had believed it more important to stay out of the war than to assure the defeat of the Axis. Like the famous airman Colonel Charles A. Lindbergh, many believed that the United States could successfully defend itself in the Western Hemisphere. (doc. 4) However, from the autumn of 1940 onward (after the fall of France and the Battle of Britain), the majority of Americans believed it more important to assure defeat of the Axis than to stay out of the war. Each of President Roosevelt's "aid-short-of-war" proposals after the autumn of 1939 won the support of approximately two-thirds of the American people. Nonetheless, nearly 80 percent of Americans continued to oppose a declaration of war on the Axis powers.

These foreign affairs concerns were debated at both the highest decision-making level in Washington and at the grass-roots level all over the United States. Mass pressure groups organized to marshal public opinion for or against particular policies and actions. On the so-called interventionist side were the Committee to Defend America by Aiding the Allies (doc. 5), and the more militant Fight for Freedom Committee. On the isolationist or noninterventionist side was the America First Committee. (doc. 6) Much criticized at the time, these committees were agencies for the democratic processes in a spirited debate on American foreign policies.

Despite pro-Chinese and anti-Japanese sentiments, Americans were also reluctant to risk war in the Pacific. President Roosevelt shared that reluctance. He considered Hitler's Nazi Germany the most dangerous threat to peace and security; he did not want a war in Asia that would interfere with the main task of defeating Germany in Europe.

Nonetheless, under Roosevelt's leadership the United States gradually tightened economic pressures on Japan. By August 1941, the United States (along with Britain and the Netherlands) had stopped the flow of all goods to Japan—including scrap iron and oil. Through diplomatic negotiations in 1941, the Japanese tried to persuade the United States to relax its economic restrictions while leaving Japan free to press ahead with its military operations against China. (doc. 7) But the United States would not ease these restrictions unless Japan abandoned its aggression in China. (doc. 8) That diplomatic impasse could not be resolved through peaceful negotiations.

Americans had broken Japanese diplomatic codes and knew the negotiations were breaking down. They expected the Japanese to strike—and soon. But they did not know where or when. If the Japanese bypassed American installations and struck only at British, French, and Dutch forces, American leaders worried whether the American people would support a declaration of war on Japan. The United States sent war warnings to military commanders in Hawaii and the Philippines. President Roosevelt made a last-minute appeal to Japan's Emperor Hirohito. American leaders knew that Japanese forces were moving south. But they did not know the location and movement of Japan's main fleet and aircraft carriers—until the Japanese attacked Pearl Harbor on Sunday morning, December 7, 1941. Japan hoped to cripple American power in the Pacific long enough to enable Japanese forces to sweep over the Dutch East Indies and other strategic territories in the South Pacific and Southeast Asia. Japanese leaders hoped the United States either could not or would not undertake the massive military operations necessary to dislodge them.

The Japanese attack united the American people and ended the heated foreign policy debate. With only one dissenting vote in the House of Representatives, Congress quickly declared war against Japan. When Hitler proclaimed war against the United States on December 11, Congress unanimously voted for war against Germany and Italy that same day. World War II was a reality for the United States.

Critics of the administration's foreign policies charged President Roosevelt with provoking the Japanese attack and with withholding essential information from military commanders in the Pacific. There were various investigations, including a major joint congressional inquiry after the war. Though a minority continued to suspect Roosevelt and his top advisers of skulduggery, the majority placed primary blame on the military commanders at Pearl Harbor, Admiral Husband E. Kimmel and General Walter C. Short. Most historians, after years of careful research, are persuaded that Roosevelt and his advisers did not deliberately provoke the Japanese attack and did not know the Japanese were going to attack at Pearl Harbor.

The surprise attack violently projected the United States into World War II as a full belligerent. Despite terrible losses at Pearl Harbor and elsewhere, the attack helped assure Japan's ultimate defeat by uniting the American people behind the war effort. The attack also abruptly destroyed America's historic traditions of neutrality and noninvolvement in European wars; after Pearl Harbor neither the American people nor the U.S. government could ever return to isolationism.

Document 1

Senator Gerald P. Nye, radio address on "Neutrality for the U.S.," Jan. 6, 1936, Gerald P. Nye Papers, Herbert Hoover Library, West Branch, Iowa.

Neutrality is to be had if we are willing to pay the price of abandonment of expectation of profits from the blood of other nations at war. But it defies any man to write a neutrality program that would long endure and succeed in keeping us neutral if the policy contemplated a business boom or even "business as usual" in America while other nations are at war and wanting supplies from our mines, fields and factories. . . .

Twenty years ago we were as highly resolved to stay out of Europe's war as we are to stay out of the one that seems to be in the making over there right now. But experience reveals that resolve alone, without a settled and determined policy of neutrality, is not enough to keep us out. War 20 years ago in Europe created markets for and brought profits to some Americans totaling perhaps five billion dollars. But those same profits were, after all, what took us to war, with a consequent cost of thousands of American lives, broken homes and bodies, a debt of twenty billion dollars plus a depression that we haven't yet conquered. Who will contend that the profit from that war offsets the cost of it that was and is ours?

In the spirit of wanting to avoid repetition of that experience 20 years ago. . . I want to discuss the proposed neutrality policy which has been developed as a result of this thought and consideration.

Better understanding of that program is to be had if we will first briefly face experience of other days, experience which must be the guide in present neutrality consideration.

We saw the last European war until 1917 as one in no degree our business. . . . We rejoiced at the moment that leadership of our Government was showing greatest determination to keep America out of that war, a leadership affording a policy that was presumed to be a guarantee of our neutrality. That neutrality policy is now known as a permissive or a discretionary policy, with its administration in no degree mandatory upon the President. That the policy failed, and that miserably, is record.

The outbreak of war in Europe brought an immediate business pickup in America. Increasingly large orders for supplies for all kinds were being placed with us by participants which gave us a new prosperity. Little did we dream what continuation of that prosperity was going to cost us in the end.

The [Woodrow] Wilson permissive neutrality policy held that it was not an unneutral act for America to sell munitions to nations at war so long as it was our policy to sell to both sides alike, and free trade in munitions was the result. Suddenly we became enraged, discovering that this permissive policy of neutrality was based upon international law defining our rights as a neutral upon the high seas, that Great Britain was not recognizing or abiding by that law. Britain, by her blockade, was interfering with our American commerce with Germany, writing new contraband definitions, searching and seizing the cargoes of American ships destined for Germany or even neutral ports which Great Britain suspicioned might be for ultimate German use. By reason of these practices we were losing even our normal trade with the Central Powers. We didn't like this interference with our trade and profits. President Wilson wrote notes of protest to Britain—notes which when now compared with those of protest later dispatched to Germany, sound like an apology. We were placated, however, with larger orders from the allies which much more than offset our loss of trade with Germany. These allied orders were tremendous and caused us to quite overlook the fact that our neutral policy was no longer one finding us furnishing munitions to both sides. It was our increasing commerce with the Allies upon which our prosperity now depended. Who doesn't remember how bitterly severe were our notes of protest to Germany when Germany, in retaliation of the British blockade, used the submarine to destroy commerce upon which the allies were dependent. But, while this business with the Allies was maintaining a marvelous prosperity for us and while we were counting as a great thing so long as we kept out of it, we were nevertheless highly resolved to continue our neutrality "so called."

The Allies soon exhausted their own means of buying from us. They needed American credit. Our permissive neutrality policy of the hour forbade loans and credits, but it appears that such pressure was brought as caused the administrators of that policy to turn their back upon it. It was concluded, by that administration, that while loans should be prohibited to any nation at war, credits would be countenanced. Our own economic well-being was so dependent upon the continuing boom market of war that we would only cut our own throats by refusing the credit that would let the Allies continue buying from us! So, for a time, the Allies bought upon credit furnished by Americans. But the time comes when individual credit is exhausted and the Allies need large loans if they are to continue buying

American supplies. If these loans couldn't be had Europe couldn't continue buying from us! Somewhere the strings were pulled that caused our neutrality administrators to permit loans to the Allies contrary to our neutrality policy—a discretionary policy. To have insisted against loans would have ended the profits and the prosperity of Americans flowing from Europe's war!

Ah, business continues good; prosperity remains on every hand! War isn't such a bad thing when we don't have to be in it! "But," we said, "look at those Germans; they are destroying American cargoes going to England and France and sinking English passenger vessels with Americans on board! Maybe something ought to be done about it! But, whatever we do, let's not get into that war!" That was our reasoning at the hour. How childish it all was—this expectation of success in staying out of a war politically while economically we stayed in it; how childish this permissive flip-flop neutrality policy of ours and our belief that we could go on and on supplying the sinews of war to one or even both sides and avoid ourselves being ultimately drawn into the engagement with our lives and our fortunes at stake.

Well, to make a long story short, our prosperity, which at the moment was our commerce with the Allies, demanded a more and more warlike attitude on our part. Our rights on the high seas, our commerce is declared in jeopardy! And then, lo and behold, along comes our Ambassador at London, Mr. [Walter Hines] Page, with the alarming word by cablegram to President Wilson that "the approach crisis has gone beyond the ability of the [J. P.] Morgans' financial agency for the British and French governments. Perhaps our going to war is the only way in which our present pre-eminent trade position can be maintained and a panic averted."

Follow Mr. Page's reasoning. Europe's war had given us more than a normal commerce and a prosperity which we enjoyed! To lose or abandon this commerce would have brought us the panic that would ensue by going back to the normal state that existed before war came to Europe. So, declares Mr. Page, going to war against Germany is the only way to avoid a panic. . . .

Thirty days after this pronouncement by Page we were in the war, not for the cause which he had stated, not to maintain our trade position, mind you, but to make the world safe for democracy and to end war.

After we had started stretching our permissive American neutrality policy to accommodate our commercial interests the allied powers were never in doubt as to what America would ultimately do. They saw what we didn't seem to realize, namely, that where our pocketbook was there would we and our hearts ultimately be. . . .

Insistence now upon establishment of a mandatory policy of neutrality is no reflection upon any one man. It is only fair to say that the present [Franklin D.] Roosevelt determination to keep us out of war is no higher than was that expressed by Wilson. Yet . . . while the Wilson administration was declaring itself neutral, parts of that administration were actually contemplating the hour when we would ultimately get into the war without a doubt as to which side we would enter on.

. . . Robert Lansing, wartime Secretary of State and custodian of our neutrality in 1915 and 1916, set down in writing the history he saw made during those years. . . .

. . . [Edward M.] House and Page were moving definitely to take us into the war on Britain's side. "Having the settled conviction," this 'neutral' Secretary of State writes of the beginning of his service, "that eventually this country would enter the war on the side of the Allies, I prepared for my own guidance a memorandum as to our foreign policies based on the hypothesis that the United States would join in the conflict against the central powers.'' And then in his memorandum he wrote: ''Germany must not be permitted to win this war or to break even. American public opinion must be prepared for the time which may come when we will have to cast aside our neutrality and become one of the champions of democracy.''

First reaction upon reading these confessions is of anger over how America was actually played with and jobbed in the name of a discretionary neutrality policy by an administration that was enjoying the confidence of the people as one determined to keep us out of war. The reaction might better be, however, one of high resolve to permit no more of discretionary neutrality policy if we really desire to be neutral.

Based upon such facts and such experience Senator [Bennet Champ] Clark [D–Mo.] and I today introduced in the Senate a bill proposing a strict policy of neutrality, the enforcement of which shall at once be not permissive or at the discretion of the President, but mandatory upon him. The bill presents requirements and advantages roughly stated as follows:

First, at the outbreak of war between other nations the President shall by proclamation forbid the exportation of arms, ammunition and implements of war for the use of those nations, and that the President shall, not ''may'' but shall, extend this embargo to other nations if and when they may become engaged in such war.

Second, the bill proposes an embargo on other items of commerce which may be considered essential war materials, such as oil, and provides that the President shall forbid exportation to nations at war of these materials beyond what was the average annual exportation of these materials to those nations during the five-year period preceding the outbreak of war.

Third, the bill requires that the President shall upon the outbreak of war between foreign states proclaim that the buyer of any and all articles to or through the field of operations of belligerent states shall be at the risk solely of the buyer and the bill provides that the buyers shall be without redress in any court of the United States. Thus, it will be seen, there is provided a strict ''cash and carry'' basis with buyers taking their own risk in accomplishing delivery of supples they buy from us in time of war.

Fourth, the bill requires that the President shall require American passengers to refrain from traveling on the vessels of belligerent states, and provides that passengers who ignore this requirement at once forfeit their right to protection of the United States. Thus we can avoid a repetition of the Lusitania experience.

Fifth, the bill introduced today does with loans and credits to time of war precisely what it does with war materials—it embargoes and limits them. . . .

There are those who will insist that this measure is too severe. We, who sponsor it, feel that in the light of experience, nothing short of those provisions is deserving of the title of a neutrality policy and we beg the confidence of the people of the land in it not as an instrument that will completely prevent war, but as one that will make it extremely difficult for the United States to be drawn into another foreign war that becomes our war only because of selfish interests that profit from the blood spilled in the wars of other lands.

Document 2

President Franklin D. Roosevelt's "Quarantine Address," Chicago, Illinois, Oct. 5, 1937, U.S. Department of State, *Papers Relating to the Foreign Relations of the United States* (hereafter referred to as *FRUS*), *Japan, 1931–1941*, Washington, D.C.: Government Printing Office, 1943, vol. 1, 380–83.

The political situation in the world, which of late has been growing progressively worse, is such as to cause grave concern and anxiety to all the peoples and nations who wish to live in peace and amity with their neighbors. . . .

The present reign of terror and international lawlessness began a few years ago . . . through unjustified interference in the internal affairs of other nations or the invasion of alien territory in violation of treaties and has now reached a stage where the very foundations of civilization are seriously threatened. . . .

Without a declaration of war and without warning or justification of any kind, civilians, including women and children, are being ruthlessly murdered with bombs from the air. In times of so-called peace ships are being attacked and sunk by submarines without cause or notice. Nations are fomenting and taking sides in civil warfare in nations that have never done them any harm. Nations claiming freedom for themselves deny it to others.

Innocent people and nations are being cruelly sacrificed to a greed for power and supremacy which is devoid of all sense of justice and humane consideration. . . .

If those things come to pass in other parts of the world let no one imagine that America will escape, that it may expect mercy, that this Western Hemisphere will not be attacked, and that it will continue tranquilly and peacefully to carry on the ethics and the arts of civilization. . . .

The peace-loving nations must make a concerted effort in opposition to those violations of treaties and those ignorings of humane instincts which today are creating a state of international anarchy and instability from which there is no escape through mere isolation or neutrality.

Those who cherish their freedom and recognize and respect the equal right of their neighbors to be free and live in peace, must work together for the triumph of law and moral principles in order that peace, justice, and confidence may prevail in the world. There must be a return to a belief in the pledged word, in the value of a signed treaty. There must be recognition of the fact that national morality is as vital as private morality. . . .

There is a solidarity and interdependence about the modern world, both technically and morally, which makes it impossible for any nation completely to isolate itself from economic and political upheavals in the rest of the world, especially when such upheavals appear to be spreading and not declining. There can be no stability or peace either within nations or between nations except under laws and moral standards adhered to by all. International anarchy destroys every foundation for peace. It jeopardizes either the immediate or the future security of every nation, large or small. It is, therefore, a matter of vital interest and concern to the people of the United States that the sanctity of international treaties and the maintenance of international morality be restored.

The overwhelming majority of the peoples and nations of the world today want to live in peace. They seek the removal of barriers against trade. They want to exert themselves in industry, in agriculture, and in business, that they may increase their wealth through the production of wealth-producing goods rather than striving to produce military planes and bombs and machine guns and cannon for the destruction of human lives and useful property. . . .

I am compelled and you are compelled, nevertheless, to look ahead. The peace, the freedom, and the security of 90 percent of the population of the world is being jeopardized by the remaining 10 percent, who are threatening a breakdown of all international order and law. Surely the 90 percent who want to live in peace under law and in accordance with moral standards that have received almost universal acceptance through the centuries, can and must find some way to make their will prevail.

The situation is definitely of universal concern. . . .

It seems to be unfortunately true that the epidemic of world lawlessness is spreading.

When an epidemic of physical disease starts to spread, the community approves and joins in a quarantine of the patients in order to protect the health of the community against the spread of the disease.

It is my determination to pursue a policy of peace and to adopt every practicable measure to avoid involvement in war. It ought to be inconceivable that in this modern era, and in the face of experience, any nation could be so foolish and ruthless as to run the risk of plunging the whole world into war by invading and violating in contravention of solemn treaties the territory of other nations that have done them no real harm and which are too weak to protect themselves adequately. Yet the peace of the world and the welfare and security of every nation is today being threatened by that very thing.

No nation which refuses to exercise forbearance and to respect the freedom and rights of others can long remain strong and retain the confidence and respect of other nations. No nation ever loses its dignity or good standing by conciliating its differences and by exercising great patience with and consideration for the rights of other nations.

War is a contagion, whether it be declared or undeclared. It can engulf states and peoples remote from the original scene of hostilities. We are determined to keep out of war, yet we cannot insure ourselves against the disastrous effects of war and the dangers of involvement. We are adopting such measures as will minimize our risk of involvement, but we cannot have complete protection in a world of disorder in which confidence and security have broken down.

If civilization is to survive the principles of the Prince of Peace must be restored. Shattered trust between nations must be revived.

Most important of all, the will for peace on the part of peace-loving nations must express itself to the end that nations that may be tempted to violate their agreements and the rights of others will desist from such a cause. There must be positive endeavors to preserve peace.

America hates war. America hopes for peace. Therefore, America actively engages in the search for peace.

Document 3

President Franklin D. Roosevelt's "Shoot-on-Sight" speech, Sept. 11, 1941, in *Public Papers and Addresses of Franklin D. Roosevelt, 1941: The Call to Battle Stations*, New York: Harper & Brothers, 1950, 384–92.

The Navy Department of the United States has reported to me that on the morning of September fourth the United States destroyer *Greer*, proceeding in full daylight toward Iceland, had reached a point southeast of Greenland. She was carrying American mail to Iceland. She was flying the American flag. Her identity as an American ship was unmistakable.

She was then and there attacked by a submarine. Germany admits that it was a German submarine. The submarine deliberately fired a torpedo at the *Greer*, followed later by another torpedo attack. In spite of what Hitler's propaganda bureau has invented, and in spite of what any American obstructionist organization may prefer to believe, I tell you the blunt fact that the German submarine fired first upon this American destroyer without warning, and with deliberate design to sink her.

Our destroyer, at the time, was in waters which the Government of the United States had declared to be waters of self-defense—surrounding outposts of American protection in the Atlantic.

In the North of the Atlantic, outposts have been established by us in Iceland, in Greenland, in Labrador and in Newfoundland. Through these waters there pass many ships of many flags. They bear food and other supplies to civilians; and they bear matériel of war, for which the people of the United States are spending billions of dollars, and which, by Congressional action, they have declared to be essential for the defense of our own land.

The United States destroyer, when attacked, was proceeding on a legitimate mission. . . .

This was piracy—piracy legally and morally. It was not the first nor the last act of piracy which the Nazi Government has committed against the American flag in this war. For attack has followed attack.

A few months ago an American flag merchant ship, the *Robin Moor*, was sunk by a Nazi submarine in the middle of the South Atlantic, under circumstances violating long-established international law and violating every principle of humanity. The passengers and the crew were forced into open boats hundreds of miles from land, in direct violation of international agreements signed by nearly all Nations including the Government of Germany. No apology, no allegation of mistake, no offer of reparations has come from the Nazi Government. . . .

Five days ago a United States Navy ship on patrol picked up three survivors of an American-owned ship operating under the flag of our sister Republic of Panama—the *S.S. Sessa*. On August seventeenth, she had been first torpedoed without warning, and then shelled, near Greenland, while carrying civilian supplies to Iceland. It is feared that the other members of her crew have been drowned. In view of the established presence of German submarines in this vicinity, there can be no reasonable doubt as to the identity of the flag of the attacker.

Five days ago, another United States merchant ship, the *Steel Seafarer*, was sunk by a German aircraft in the Red Sea two hundred and twenty miles south of Suez. She was bound for an Egyptian port. . . .

In the face of all this, we Americans are keeping our feet on the ground. . . .

. . . But it would be inexcusable folly

to minimize such incidents in the face of evidence which makes it clear that the incident is not isolated, but is part of a general plan.

The important truth is that these acts of international lawlessness are a manifestation of a design which has been made clear to the American people for a long time. It is the Nazi design to abolish the freedom of the seas, and to acquire absolute control and domination of these seas for themselves.

For with control of the seas in their own hands, the way can obviously become clear for their next step—domination of the United States—domination of the Western Hemisphere by force of arms. Under Nazi control of the seas, no merchant ship of the United States or of any other American Republic would be free to carry on any peaceful commerce, except by the condescending grace of this foreign and tyrannical power. The Atlantic Ocean which has been, and which should always be, a free and friendly highway for us would then become a deadly menace to the commerce of the United States, to the coasts of the United States, and even to the inland cities of the United States.

The Hitler Government, in defiance of the laws of the sea, in defiance of the recognized rights of all other Nations, has presumed to declare, on paper, that the great areas of the seas—even including a vast expanse lying in the Western Hemisphere—are to be closed, and that no ships may enter them for any purpose, except at peril of being sunk. Actually they are sinking ships at will and without warning in widely separated areas both within and far outside of these far-flung pretended zones.

This Nazi attempt to seize control of the oceans is but a counterpart of the Nazi plots now being carried on throughout the Western Hemisphere—all designed toward the same end. For Hitler's advance guards—not only his avowed agents but also his dupes among us—have sought to make ready for him footholds and bridgeheads in the New World, to be used as soon as he has gained control of the oceans. . . .

To be ultimately successful in world mastery, Hitler knows that he must get control of the seas. He must first destroy the bridge of ships which we are building across the Atlantic and over which we shall continue to roll the implements of war to help destroy him, to destroy all his works in the end. He must wipe out our patrol on sea and in the air if he is to do it. He must silence the British Navy.

I think it must be explained over and over again to people who like to think of the United States Navy as an invincible protection, that this can be true only if the British Navy survives. And that, my friends, is simple arithmetic.

For if the world outside of the Americas falls under Axis domination, the shipbuilding facilities which the Axis powers would then possess in all of Europe, in the British Isles, and in the Far East would be much greater than all the shipbuilding facilities and potentialities of all of the Americas—not only greater, but two or three times greater—enough to win. Even if the United States threw all its resources into such a situation, seeking to double and even redouble the size of our Navy, the Axis powers, in control of the rest of the world, would have the manpower and the physical resources to outbuild us several times over.

It is time for all Americans, Americans of all the Americas to stop being deluded by the romantic notion that the Americas can go on living happily and peacefully in a Nazi-dominated world.

Generation after generation, America has battled for the general policy of the freedom of the seas. . . .

That has been our policy, proved time and time again, in all our history. . . .

Unrestricted submarine warfare in

1941 constitutes a defiance—an act of aggression—against that historic American policy.

It is now clear that Hitler has begun his campaign to control the seas by ruthless force and by wiping out every vestige of international law, every vestige of humanity.

His intention has been made clear. The American people can have no further illusions about it.

No tender whisperings of appeasers that Hitler is not interested in the Western Hemisphere, no soporific lullabies that a wide ocean protects us from him—can long have any effect on the hard-headed, far-sighted, and realistic American people.

Because of these episodes . . . we Americans are now face to face not with abstract theories but with cruel, relentless facts.

This attack on the *Greer* was no localized military operation in the North Atlantic. This was no mere episode in a struggle between two Nations. This was one determined step toward creating a permanent world system based on force, on terror, and on murder.

And I am sure that even now the Nazis are waiting to see whether the United States will by silence give them the green light to go ahead on this path of destruction.

The Nazi danger to our Western world has long ceased to be a mere possibility. The danger is here now—not only from a military enemy but from an enemy of all law, all liberty, all morality, all religion.

There has now come a time when you and I must see the cold, inexorable necessity of saying to these inhuman, unrestrained seekers of world conquest and permanent world domination by the sword: "You seek to throw our children and our children's children into your form of terrorism and slavery. You have now attacked our own safety. You shall go no further."

Normal practices of diplomacy—note writing—are of no possible use in dealing with international outlaws who sink our ships and kill our citizens.

One peaceful Nation after another has met disaster because each refused to look the Nazi danger squarely in the eye until it actually had them by the throat.

The United States will not make that fatal mistake.

No act of violence, no act of intimidation will keep us from maintaining intact two bulwarks of American defense: First, our line of supply of matériel to the enemies of Hitler; and second, the freedom of our shipping on the high seas.

No matter what it takes, no matter what it costs, we will keep open the line of legitimate commerce in these defensive waters.

We have sought no shooting war with Hitler. We do not seek it now. But neither do we want peace so much, that we are willing to pay for it by permitting him to attack our naval and merchant ships while they are on legitimate business.

I assume that the German leaders are not deeply concerned, tonight or any other time, by what we Americans or the American Government say or publish about them. We cannot bring about the downfall of Nazism by the use of long-range invective.

But when you see a rattlesnake poised to strike, you do not wait until he has struck before you crush him.

These Nazi submarines and raiders are the rattlesnakes of the Atlantic. They are a menace to the free pathways of the high seas. They are a challenge to our sovereignty. They hammer at our most precious rights when they attack ships of the American flag—symbols of our independence, our freedom, our very life.

It is clear to all Americans that the time has come when the Americas themselves must now be defended. A continuation of attacks in our own waters, or in waters that could be used for further and greater attacks on us, will inevitably weaken our American ability to repel Hitlerism. . . .

The time for active defense is now. . . .

In the waters which we deem necessary for defense, American naval vessels and American planes will no longer wait until Axis submarines lurking under the water, or Axis raiders on the surface of the sea, strike their deadly blow—first.

Upon our naval and air patrol—now operating in large number over a vast expanse of the Atlantic Ocean—falls the duty of maintaining the American policy of freedom of the seas—now. That means, very simply, very clearly, that our patrolling vessels and planes will protect all merchant ships—not only American ships but ships of any flag—engaged in commerce in our defensive waters. They will protect them from submarines; they will protect them from surface raiders. . . .

It is no act of war on our part when we decide to protect the seas that are vital to American defense. The aggression is not ours. Ours is solely defense.

But let this warning be clear. From now on, if German or Italian vessels of war enter the waters, the protection of which is necessary for American defense, they do so at their own peril.

The orders which I have given as Commander in Chief of the United States Army and Navy are to carry out that policy—at once.

The sole responsibility rests upon Germany. There will be no shooting unless Germany continues to seek it.

That is my obvious duty in this crisis. That is the clear right of this sovereign Nation. This is the only step possible, if we would keep tight the wall of defense which we are pledged to maintain around this Western Hemisphere.

I have no illusions about the gravity of this step. I have not taken it hurriedly or lightly. It is the result of months and months of constant thought and anxiety and prayer. In the protection of your Nation and mine it cannot be avoided.

The American people have faced other grave crises in their history—with American courage, and with American resolution. They will do no less today.

They know the actualities of the attacks upon us. They know the necessities of a bold defense against these attacks. They know that the times call for clear heads and fearless hearts.

And with that inner strength that comes to a free people conscious of their duty, and conscious of the righteousness of what they do, they will—with Divine help and guidance—stand their ground against this latest assault upon their democracy, their sovereignty, and their freedom.

Document 4

Charles A. Lindbergh's radio address, "The Air Defense of America," May 19, 1940, Charles A. Lindbergh Papers, Yale University Library, New Haven, Connecticut.

Let us re-examine the position of America in the air. New discoveries and developments affect nations in different ways. In Europe, aviation has affected England adversely and Germany advantageously. One nation may have a psychology and topography which promotes the development of aviation, while another finds itself entirely unadjusted to the tempo of the air.

Judged by aeronautical standards, we in the United States are in a singularly fortunate position. Our people have natural ability in the design, construction, and operation of aircraft. Our highly organized industry, our widely separated centers of population, our elimination of formalities in inter-state travel, all contribute to the development of American aviation. From the standpoint of defense, we still have two great oceans between us and the warring armies of Europe and Asia. In fact there is hardly a natural element contributing to air strength and impregnability that we do not now possess. Aviation is for us an asset. It adds to our national safety. With a firm and clear cut policy, we can build an air defense for America that will stand above these shifting sands of war. . . .

Let us not be confused by this talk of invasion by European aircraft. The air defense of America is as simple as the attack is difficult when the true facts are faced. We are in danger of war today not because European people have attempted to interfere with the internal affairs of America, but because American people have attempted to interfere with the internal affairs of Europe.

It is true that bombing planes can be built with sufficient range to cross the Atlantic and return. They can be built either in America or Europe. Aeronautical engineers have known this for many years. But the cost is high, the target large, and the military effectiveness small. Such planes do not exist today in any air force. A foreign power could not conquer us by dropping bombs in this country unless the bombing were accompanied by an invading army. And an invading army requires thousands of small bombers and pursuit planes; it would have little use for high trans-Atlantic aircraft.

No, the advantage lies with us, for great armies must still cross oceans by ship. Only relatively small forces can be transported by air today, and over distances of a few hundred miles at most. This has great significance in Europe, but it is not an element that we have to contend with in America. Such a danger can come, in any predictable future, only through division and war among our own peoples. As long as American nations work together [to] maintain reasonable defense forces, there will be no invasion by foreign aircraft. And no foreign navy will dare to approach within bombing range of our coasts.

Our danger in America is an internal danger. We need not fear a foreign invasion unless American peoples bring it on through their own quarreling and meddling with affairs abroad. Our eyes should not search beyond the horizon for problems which lie at our feet. The greatest lesson we can draw from Europe today is that national strength must be built within a nation itself and cannot be achieved by limiting the strength of others.

What of the unforeseen developments of science? Rocket propulsion? New forms of energy? New methods of destruction? No generation can entirely safeguard the future for those that follow. They must meet their own problems as those problems arise. The greatest inheritance we can pass on to our children is a reasonable solution of the problems that confront us in our own time—a strong nation, a lack of debt, a solid American character free from the entanglements of the Old World. Let us guard America today as our forefathers guarded it in the past. . . .

But the course we have been following in recent months leads to neither strength nor friendship nor peace. It will leave us hated by victor and vanquished alike, regardless of which way the tide of battle turns. One side will claim that we aided its enemies; the other, that we did not help enough. . . .

Let us turn again to America's traditional role—that of building and guarding our own destiny. We need a greater air force, a greater army, and a greater navy; they have been inadequate for many years.

Let us form with our neighboring nations a clear cut and definite policy of American defense. But above all, let us stop this hysterical chatter of calamity and invasion that has been running rife these last few days. It is not befitting the people who built this nation.

That the world is facing a new era is beyond question. Our mission is to make it a better era. But regardless of which side wins this war, there is no reason, aside from our own actions, to prevent a continuation of peaceful relationships between America and the countries of Europe. If we desire peace, we need only stop asking for war. No one wishes to attack us, and no one is in a position to do so.

The only reason that we are in danger of becoming involved in this war is because there are powerful elements in America [urging] us to take part. They represent a small minority of the people, but they control much of the machinery of influence and propaganda. They seize every opportunity to push us closer to the edge.

It is time for the underlying character of this country to rise and assert itself, to strike down these elements of personal profit and foreign interest. This underlying character of America is our true defense. Until it awakes and takes the reins in hand once more, the production of airplanes, cannon, and battleships is of secondary importance. Let us turn our eyes to our own nation. We cannot aid others until we have first placed our own country in a position of spiritual and material leadership and strength.

Document 5

Official statement of policy of the Committee to Defend America by Aiding the Allies, Nov. 20, 1940, Committee to Defend America Papers, Princeton University Library, Princeton, New Jersey, leaflet.

The American people must face squarely the realities of this day and hour. They must ask themselves if they can afford to permit the British Commonwealth of Nations to be defeated and the British fleet to be destroyed or added to the forces of despotism which seek to dominate the world. . . . Defeat of Britain and her allies would leave the United States alone, confronted with a totalitarian world which not only scorns our freedom and is greedy for our wealth but would not leave us free to maintain our way of life and our institutions. Sooner or later, with Britain defeated, war inevitably would come to this hemisphere.

The war which Britain is now waging looms larger than a national issue for empire advantage; it is a moral issue of world import to civilization itself. The fate of human freedom, freedom of thought, of religion, of individual initiative, is dependent upon victory of Britain and her allies.

To the appeasers who argue that Britain and the United States could make a peace with an aggressor in control of his conquests, we reply that this world cannot live four-fifths slave and one-fifth free.

Also we say regretfully that no one can guarantee that the United States can avoid active military involvement. But one thing is certain; the only chance of avoiding war is by giving all material assistance to Great Britain and her allies immediately. That is [our] policy. The aid must be sufficient and speedy. It is now insufficient and slow.

In addition to previous suggestions the committee urges the following steps to increase aid to the Allies:

1. Aid to the Allies and American defense, which are parts of the same problem, can only be accomplished by very greatly increased American arms production. The battle for civilization and democracy may be won or lost on the American assembly line. To this end we will support the President in the use of his full legal powers under a state of national emergency if necessary, to mobilize at once all the industrial resources of the nation for maximum production. . . .

2. The life line between Great Britain and the United States is the sea route to the Western Hemisphere. Under no circumstances must this line be cut and the United States must be prepared to maintain it. The United States should supply Great Britain with all possible merchant vessels to fly the British flag. The United States should produce boats as rapidly as in the World War days, for lease or rent to the British. . . .

3. The time has come when Congress should assume a larger share of responsibility, with the President, for the policy of aid to the Allies. Consequently, we favor . . . a repeal or modification of restrictive statutes which hamper this nation in its freedom of action when it would cooperate with nations defending themselves from attack by nations at war in violation of treaties with the United States. . . .

The Axis alliance has united the wars in the Atlantic and Pacific into a world war. For the first time in the history of the United States we are, as a nation, confronted with a hostile world alliance.

The Committee recommends a firm policy in the Pacific:

1. We should give all material and financial help to China that is possible without lessening our aid to Great Britain.

2. The United States should extend its embargoes upon exportation of all war materials to Japan.

3. The United States and Great Britain should announce that their naval bases in the Pacific are open to each other's fleets.

4. The United States should establish a clear naval understanding with Great Britain which will permit the two fleets to be placed in the most advantageous position to protect the Atlantic for the democracies and to stop the spread of war in the Pacific. The world's future is secure if the British and American fleets control the seas.

Nations which are still free must again proclaim their faith in the ability of democracy to organize the world for justice and security. . . .

On these fundamental issues, on which the future of civilization depends, the Committee will oppose appeasement in all its forms.

Document 6

America First Committee Principles, 1941, America First Committee Papers, Hoover Library on War, Revolution, and Peace, Stanford University, California, pamphlet.

1. Our first duty is to keep America out of foreign wars. Our entry would only destroy democracy, not save it. The path to war is a false path to freedom.

2. Not by acts of war abroad but by preserving and extending democracy at home can we aid democracy and freedom in other lands.

3. In 1917 we sent our American ships into the war zone and this led us

to war. In 1941 we must keep our naval convoys and merchant vessels on this side of the Atlantic.

4. We must build a defense for our own shores so strong that no foreign power or combination of powers can invade our country by sea, air or land.

5. Humanitarian aid is the duty of a strong, free country at peace. With proper safeguard for the distribution of supplies we should feed and clothe the needy people of England and other occupied countries and so keep alive their hope for the return of better days.

6. The America First Committee advocates a National Advisory Referendum on the Question of Peace or War.

(We exclude from our rolls Fascists, Nazis, Communists and members of subversive organizations.)

Document 7

Japan's final diplomatic proposals to the United States, Nov. 20, 1941, *FRUS, Japan, 1931–1941*, vol. 2, 755–56.

Draft Proposal Handed by the Japanese Ambassador (Kichisaburo Nomura) to the Secretary of State (Cordell Hull) on November 20, 1941.

1. Both the Governments of Japan and the United States undertake not to make any armed advancement into any of the regions in the South-eastern Asia and the Southern Pacific area excepting the part of French Indo-China where the Japanese troops are stationed at present.

2. The Japanese Government undertakes to withdraw its troops now stationed in French Indo-China upon either the restoration of peace between Japan and China or the establishment of an equitable peace in the Pacific area.

In the meantime the Government of Japan declares that it is prepared to remove its troops now stationed in the southern part of French Indo-China to the northern part of the said territory upon the conclusion of the present arrangement which shall later be embodied in the final agreement.

3. The Government of Japan and the United States shall cooperate with a view to securing the acquisition of those goods and commodities which the two countries need in Netherlands East Indies.

4. The Governments of Japan and the United States mutually undertake to restore their commercial relations to those prevailing prior to the freezing of the assets.

The Government of the United States shall supply Japan a required quantity of oil.

5. The Government of the United States undertakes to refrain from such measures and actions as will be prejudicial to the endeavors for the restoration of general peace between Japan and China.

Document 8

Final diplomatic proposals presented by the United States to Japan, Nov. 26, 1941, *FRUS, Japan, 1931–1941*, vol. 2, 768–70.

Document Handed by the Secretary of State to the Japanese Ambassador on November 26, 1941

Outline of Proposed Basis for Agreement Between the United States and Japan

Section I

Draft Mutual Declaration of Policy

The Government of the United States and the Government of Japan both being solicitous for the peace of the Pacific affirm that their national policies are directed toward lasting and extensive peace throughout the Pacific area, that they have no territorial designs in that area, that they have no intention of threatening other countries or of using military force aggressively against any neighboring nation, and that, accordingly, in their national policies they will actively support and give practical application to the following fundamental principles upon which their relations with each other and with all other governments are based:

(1) The principle of inviolability of territorial integrity and sovereignty of each and all nations.

(2) The principle of non-interference in the internal affairs of other countries.

(3) The principle of equality, including equality of commercial opportunity and treatment.

(4) The principle of reliance upon international cooperation and conciliation for the prevention and pacific settlement of controversies and for the improvement of international conditions by peaceful methods and processes. . . .

Section II

Steps To Be Taken by the Government of the United States and by the Government of Japan

The Government of the United States and the Government of Japan propose to take steps as follows:

1. The Government of the United States and the Government of Japan will endeavor to conclude a multilateral non-aggression pact among the British Empire, China, Japan, the Netherlands, the Soviet Union, Thailand and the United States.

2. Both Governments will endeavor to conclude among the American, British, Chinese, Japanese, the Netherland and Thai Governments an agreement whereunder each of the Governments would pledge itself to respect the territorial integrity of French Indochina. . . .

Such agreement would provide also that each of the Governments party to the agreement would not seek or accept preferential treatment in its trade or economic relations with Indochina and would use its influence to obtain for each of the signatories equality of treatment in trade and commerce with French Indochina.

3. The Government of Japan will withdraw all military, naval, air and police forces from China and from Indochina.

4. The Government of the United States and the Government of Japan will not support—militarily, politically, economically—any government or regime in China other than the National Government of the Republic of China with capital temporarily at Chungking.

5. Both Governments will give up all extraterritorial rights in China, including rights and interests in and with regard to international settlements and concessions, and rights under the Boxer Protocol of 1901. . . .

6. The Government of the United States and the Government of Japan will enter into negotiations for the conclusion between the United States and Japan of a trade agreement, based upon reciprocal most-favored-nation treatment and reduction of trade barriers by both countries, including an undertaking by the United States to bind raw silk on the free list.

7. The Government of the United States and the Government of Japan will, respectively, remove the freezing restrictions on Japanese funds in the United States and on American funds in Japan.

8. Both Governments will agree upon a plan for the stabilization of the dollar-yen rate, with the allocation of funds adequate for this purpose, half to be supplied by Japan and half by the United States.

9. Both Governments will agree that no agreement which either has concluded with any third power or powers shall be interpreted by it in such a way as to conflict with the fundamental purpose of this agreement, the establishment and preservation of peace throughout the Pacific area. . . .

CHAPTER 6

World War II and the Diplomacy of the Grand Alliance

Randall B. Woods

When the United States joined the struggle against the Axis powers following Japan's attack on Pearl Harbor on December 7, 1941, Allied victory was by no means certain. A jubilant Winston Churchill journeyed to Washington on New Year's Day, 1942, to meet with President Franklin D. Roosevelt and to sign the Declaration of the United Nations. (doc. 1) This declaration pledged the signatories to wage all-out warfare until the Axis powers were defeated. But despite the optimism of this first wartime Roosevelt-Churchill encounter, the Allies met defeat on virtually every front in 1942. In the Far East, Pearl Harbor was just a diversion from Japanese amphibious landings in Southeast Asia. By the late spring of 1942, Thailand, Shanghai, the Dutch East Indies, and the Philippines had all been overrun. From their outposts in New Guinea, Japanese forces threatened Australia; from their positions in Burma, they menaced India.

Germany controlled virtually the entire European continent. In the spring of 1940, Hitler executed an adroit end run around French defenses, drove through Belgium and the Netherlands, and forced the emergency evacuation of the entire British expeditionary force from Dunkirk. For the rest of the year, the Nazis harassed Britain with a barrage of bombs and rumors of amphibious landings across the English Channel. But on June 22, 1941, Hitler threw all caution to the wind and invaded the Soviet Union. Following the initial advances in the summer and fall of 1941, the Germans waited out the bitter winter and then drove north and south as the Russian snows melted in the spring. The German *Wehrmacht* (army) then occupied most of European Russia. Meanwhile, in North Africa Field Marshal Erwin Rommel and the Afrika Corps threatened the Suez Canal from the west.

By the close of the year, however, the Allies had halted the Axis advance. Royal Air Force night fighters inflicted heavy losses on the German *Luftwaffe* (air force) in the Battle of Britain, and the long-feared Nazi invasion never materialized. British Field Marshal Bernard Montgomery relieved pressure on Egypt and the Suez Canal by taking El Alamein. Then, in

November 1942, British and American troops waded ashore at Oman and Algiers in North Africa. After putting up token resistance, troops loyal to Vichy France (the puppet government established by the Germans to rule central and southern France) surrendered, and the Allies thus secured a foothold from which they would launch successful attacks on Sicily and Italy in 1943. In a herculean effort, Russian armies stopped the German advance at Stalingrad in late 1942 and early 1943. Meanwhile, in the Far East a makeshift American task force had surprised the Japanese navy, sinking four enemy carriers in the Battle of Midway.

Although fifty nations eventually signed the Declaration of the United Nations, this Grand Alliance was dominated by the Big Three: the United States, the Soviet Union, and the United Kingdom. As long as a common enemy threatened their existence, the partners displayed a modicum of cooperation. Nonetheless, from the very outset of the war, ideological differences, historical mistrust, and divergent strategic and economic objectives strained the alliance. Geographic, linguistic, historic, and cultural ties meant that contacts between Britain and the United States were closer and more frequent than those between the Soviet Union and either of the other partners. Nevertheless, differences over how to fight the war and how to order the postwar world meant that the relationship would be uneasy at best.

To hold down Allied casualties and to lay the basis for Anglo-American control of Central Europe after the war, Churchill pressed for massive strategic bombing of occupied Europe, followed by an Allied invasion through the Balkans—the "soft underbelly" of Europe. The Roosevelt administration and its principal military planners, Generals George C. Marshall and Dwight D. Eisenhower, rejected this approach as time-consuming and essentially diversionary. They won acceptance of a plan that called for massing troops in the British Isles and then launching a frontal assault on occupied Europe. Only after a series of bitter meetings did Churchill and his advisers reconcile themselves to "Operation Overlord," the code name assigned to the cross-channel invasion. And the proud Britons only succumbed then because America's superiority in manufacturing, agricultural output, and manpower placed it in the position to dictate strategy.

In fact, a substantial number of Englishmen believed that their former colonists were determined to use World War II to accelerate American replacement of Great Britain as the leader of the non-Communist world. Throughout the war, the Roosevelt administration wielded the leverage provided by lend-lease aid and Britain's need for postwar economic aid to force a dissolution of the sterling bloc, a trading bloc comprising Britain and the Commonwealth nations whose members gave one another preferential treatment in the form of lower rates. The Roosevelt administration insisted that Britain reduce imperial preferences and eliminate exchange controls. Churchill became so enraged at this assault on his country's trade and currency system that he drafted a bitter appeal to FDR on February 5, 1942.

(doc. 2) But, afraid of offending his English-speaking ally, the prime minister decided not to send his indignant telegram. For the rest of the war, Britain continued to fight a losing, rear-guard action against Washington's efforts to establish its preeminence within the capitalist world.

If the relationship between Britain and America was frequently strained, the Soviet-American alliance was at times downright rancorous. A number of factors contributed to mutual distrust. The Soviets had not forgotten American participation in the 1918–19 Allied intervention in Russia, nor the long years of diplomatic isolation from 1919 to 1933. Joseph Stalin and his colleagues were convinced that the overriding goal of Western diplomacy from 1936 to 1938 was to turn Germany's aggressions eastward by appeasing them with Czech and Polish territory. When the United States did not get desperately needed war matériel to the Soviets as quickly as the Kremlin believed it should following the German invasion of Russia in 1941, Stalin accused the West of deliberately holding back. Even more galling to the Russian leadership was its allies' failure to launch a frontal attack on Axis-occupied Europe in 1942 and 1943. In May 1942, Soviet Foreign Minister Vyacheslav Molotov journeyed to Washington and demanded the immediate establishment of a second front on the western side of the Continent to relieve beleaguered Soviet armies in the east. Prompted by sympathy for Russia's plight and a desire to boost his ally's morale, Roosevelt promised Molotov a second front before the year was out. (doc. 3) But 1942 and 1943 passed without a major assault in the west. With increasing bitterness, the Soviets charged that the administration was deliberately standing by while Germany and Russia bled each other to death. Not until June 1944 would British, American, and Canadian troops splash ashore at Normandy.

Roosevelt was a great believer in personal diplomacy, and throughout 1942 and 1943 he pressed his Soviet colleague to meet with him and Churchill to iron out strategic differences. Citing the precariousness of the military situation in Russia, Stalin demurred. Roosevelt and Churchill met several times during this period, however, and at the Casablanca Conference in January 1943, the two leaders issued a joint statement that some historians believe had a profound impact on both the course of the war and on the ensuing peace. During a postmeeting press conference, Roosevelt and Churchill pledged that their countries would fight on until the "unconditional surrender" of all the Axis powers had been secured. (doc. 4) According to Roosevelt's and Churchill's critics, this pledge could not be retracted once it was made. It spurred Hitler and Germany to fight to the bitter end, thus devastating Central Europe and rendering it vulnerable to communization. The British and American commitment to unconditional surrender also allegedly prevented a negotiated settlement with the Japanese, thus necessitating the use of the atomic bomb.

By the fall of 1943, the Red Army had won the Battle of Stalingrad, and Stalin indicated he was at long last ready to meet with his Western partners. The leaders of the anti-Axis coalition gathered at Teheran in November.

Although the Big Three discussed everything from postwar treatment of Germany and Italy to the mechanics of establishing a second front, they made no hard decisions at Teheran about occupation policies, the postwar boundaries of Europe, or any other specific economic or strategic question. Despite Churchill's protestations, Roosevelt insisted throughout the war that military and political decisions should be kept separate. He feared that discussions of reparations and spheres of interest would fracture an already fragile alliance. Churchill, however, wanted to define and limit Soviet power while the Red Army was still in Russia.

Though the foreign ministers of the Allied nations had met in Moscow the previous October and there endorsed the concept of a postwar collective security system (doc. 5), Roosevelt's plan to ensure permanent peace and stability was to continue the Grand Alliance (including a rehabilitated China) into the postwar period. At Teheran FDR outlined the ''Four Policemen'' concept, whereby the Big Three and China would supervise their respective regions, promote democracy and self-determination, and halt aggression. (doc. 6) Unfortunately, Roosevelt was unwilling or unable to see that the powers held differing views of their respective spheres of interest. Stalin wanted to annex the Baltic states and the eastern third of Poland and to spread Communism into as much of Eastern and Central Europe as possible. Churchill was determined to retard the growth of Soviet power on the Continent and to resurrect the prewar British Empire.

London's struggle to persuade Washington to recognize that war was merely an extension of politics and to perceive the Soviet Union as a threat to the postwar balance of power continued through 1944—but to no avail. On February 29 of that year, Roosevelt wrote Churchill and explained that the United States had no intention of stationing troops in Western Europe following the Axis surrender. (doc. 7) Though isolationism had gone underground following Pearl Harbor, it was still a force to be reckoned with. Nor was Roosevelt willing to divert troops from Operation Overlord to secure control of Central Europe. Following the successful invasion of Italy in 1943, British and American soldiers slowly and painfully inched their way up the peninsula. In mid–1944, as Operation Overlord was unfolding, Rome finally surrendered. Churchill and his military chieftains wanted to continue into northern Italy and penetrate the Ljubljana Gap in Yugoslavia, a principal corridor into Central Europe. Such a strategy would protect at least some of the central and southeastern portions of Europe from Soviet occupation. Roosevelt, Eisenhower, and Marshall, however, insisted on an amphibious landing in southern France. This enterprise, code-named ''Operation Anvil,'' would lead to the capture of the Rhône Valley and facilitate an attack on the heart of Germany. On July 1, Churchill wrote Roosevelt and explained his reasons for funding and supplying his approach, rather than Operation Anvil. (doc. 8) Roosevelt remained unmoved, however, and the assault on southern France proceeded apace.

In September 1944, the British and American leaders met alone once again in the Canadian fortress city of Quebec. Roosevelt's plans for a stable and peaceful postwar world in part called for allaying Soviet fears of the West. Above all, he believed, this strategy required a harsh policy toward Germany. At Quebec the Americans presented the British with the Morgenthau Plan, which was named after Secretary of the Treasury Henry Morgenthau and called for the dismemberment and deindustrialization of Germany. Churchill and Foreign Secretary Anthony Eden resisted. They looked forward to a de-Nazified and rehabilitated Germany that would serve as a bulwark against Soviet expansion. Confronted with Britain's continuing need for lend-lease aid and a large postwar loan from the United States, Churchill quickly reversed himself. Morgenthau recorded that turnabout in his diary. (doc. 9)

By the fall of 1944, the Red Army had already moved into Rumania and Bulgaria and was poised to sweep through Poland. In desperation, Churchill flew to Moscow in October to try to work out a spheres-of-interest agreement with Stalin that would retain a Western foothold in at least part of Eastern Europe. The Soviet leader was amenable, and the famous "percentages deal" was hammered out, whereby Britain and the Soviet Union were assigned varying degrees of influence in the Balkan nations and in Eastern Europe. (doc. 10) To Churchill's dismay, Roosevelt refused to endorse the agreement. The Red Army continued its advance unchecked.

As 1945 opened, it was clear that an Allied victory was just a matter of time. British, American, and Canadian forces were ready to invade Germany from the west while Russian forces entered from the east. In the Far East, General Douglas MacArthur had retaken the Philippines and was preparing for the final assault on the Japanese home islands. At long last, the Americans declared, it was time to discuss the postwar order. The Big Three gathered for that purpose at the Crimean resort town of Yalta in February. The Yalta accords established occupation zones for Germany, set out guidelines for reparations, and, in the Declaration on Liberated Europe, promised free elections as quickly as possible in areas under Allied control. In fact, the Soviet Union was in physical possession of most of Eastern Europe and eastern Germany. It would be as free to act unilaterally in its occupation zones as the Western powers were in theirs. Yalta did nothing to change that. In a separate accord, Stalin promised that the Soviet Union would enter the war against Japan as soon as Germany was defeated, in return for large chunks of Japanese and Chinese territory. (doc. 11)

From April through June, the soon-to-be-victorious Allied nations met in San Francisco to draft the charter of the United Nations, a collective security organization intended to promote democracy and national self-determination, raise living standards, and prevent armed aggression. The preamble to the charter, signed on June 26, 1945, is a paean to international cooperation. (doc. 12) From the outset, however, the writing of the charter was dominated by the principle of national sovereignty rather than internationalism. Provisions guaranteeing the permanent members of the Security

Council the right of veto, coupled with Article 51 permitting regional collective security arrangements, guaranteed that the fledgling organization would be more of a debating society than a peacekeeping organization.

In July 1945, the Allied leaders gathered in the Berlin suburb of Potsdam to work out the details of occupation policies for Europe and to discuss the final stages of the war against Japan. FDR had died on April 12, and America was represented by President Harry S. Truman. After the meeting began, Churchill learned that his Conservative party had lost the general election to Labour and that he had to give way to the new prime minister, Clement Attlee. Stalin did not have to stand for election and was present throughout the deliberations. By the time Truman arrived at Potsdam, he had been briefed on the top-secret Manhattan Project, whereby American scientists had labored frantically throughout the war to develop an atomic bomb. After the meeting began, the president was informed that the first atomic device had been exploded at Los Alamos, New Mexico. At this point, Truman faced a crucial choice of policies for ending the war against Japan. He could proceed with a conventional invasion, an option that would require a year and a half and perhaps 100,000 American casualties. He could try to negotiate a surrender from the Japanese, or he could use the bomb to bring Japan to its knees. A group of Truman's advisers informed him that if he would promise the Japanese that the person and institution of the emperor would remain inviolate, Tokyo would surrender. Recalling Roosevelt's pledge of unconditional surrender, and sensitive to an American public opinion hardened by wartime propaganda and news of Japanese atrocities, the new president rejected this course. In the Potsdam Declaration, Truman and Attlee called on the Japanese to surrender unconditionally, promising them only that their nation would not be dismembered nor its population enslaved. (doc. 13) Receiving no answer that he considered meaningful, Truman ordered the atomic bombing of Hiroshima and Nagasaki. Whether or not Truman could have avoided the onus of being the only national leader ever to have used an atomic weapon in war is still a question hotly debated by historians.

The Grand Alliance was purely a creation of World War II. That the United States, Great Britain, and the Soviet Union agreed to join forces, shed their blood, and expend their treasure in a common cause was itself a comment on the enormity of the threat posed to the status quo by the Axis powers. Ideologically, the three leading anti-Fascist nations had nothing in common. America was a maturing capitalist society. Britain was a postindustrial commonwealth that was simultaneously seeking to cling to an empire and to implement a program of liberal socialism. The Soviet Union was a nation ruled by a paranoid dictator and justified by Marxist rhetoric. In terms of pure economic and military power, World War II accelerated both the rise to international preeminence of the United States and the Soviet Union and the decline of Western Europe. Ironically, the very conflict that drew America and Russia together created a power vacuum that would form the basis of their rivalry in the postwar period. As has so often been the case in world history, military triumph contained within itself the seeds of future conflict.

Document 1

United Nations Declaration, Jan. 1, 1942, U.S. Department of State, *Papers Relating to the Foreign Relations of the United States* (hereafter referred to as *FRUS*), *General, 1942,* Washington, D.C.: Government Printing Office, 1960, vol. 1, 25–26.

Declaration by United Nations:

A Joint Declaration by the United States of America, the United Kingdom of Great Britain and Northern Ireland, the Union of Soviet Socialist Republics, China, Australia, Belgium, Canada, Costa Rica, Cuba, Czechoslovakia, Dominican Republic, El Salvador, Greece, Guatemala, Haiti, Honduras, India, Luxembourg, Netherlands, New Zealand, Nicaragua, Norway, Panama, Poland, South Africa, Yugoslavia

The Governments signatory hereto,

Having subscribed to a common program of purposes and principles embodied in the Joint Declaration of the President of the United States of America and the Prime Minister of the United Kingdom of Great Britain and Northern Ireland dated August 14, 1941, known as the Atlantic Charter.

Being convinced that complete victory over their enemies is essential to defend life, liberty, independence and religious freedom, and to preserve human rights and justice in their own lands as well as in other lands, and that they are now engaged in a common struggle against savage and brutal forces seeking to subjugate the world, Declare:

(1) Each Government pledges itself to employ its full resources, military or economic, against those members of the Tripartite Pact and its adherents with which such government is at war.

(2) Each Government pledges itself to cooperate with the Governments signatory hereto and not to make a separate armistice or peace with the enemies.

The foregoing declaration may be adhered to by other nations which are, or which may be, rendering material assistance and contributions in the struggle for victory over Hitlerism.

Done at Washington
January First, 1942.

Document 2

British Prime Minister Winston Churchill to President Franklin D. Roosevelt, Feb. 5, 1942, PREM 4/17/3, Records of the Prime Minister, Public Record Office, Kew, England.

1. Cabinet considered this matter on Monday when a very marked balance of opinion was expressed that it would not be wise for us to be forced to agree in its present form to Clause 7 with its reference to "no discrimination" before the discussions which we are willing to begin at once, have taken place. However

a reply has been prepared which will be considered in a few days.

2. As I told you I consider situation is completely altered by entry of the United States into the war. This makes us no longer a combatant receiving help from a generous sympathiser, but two comrades fighting for life side by side. In this connection it must be remembered that for a large part of 27 months we carried on the struggle single-handed, and that had we failed the full malice of the Axis Powers, whose real intentions can now be so clearly seen, would have fallen upon the United States. This would be all the more true if we were to fail now. In these circumstances, the Lend-Lease goods which have reached this country before the pooling arrangements were made ought not to be a cause of the prejudgment of our future co-operation in the economic rebuilding of the world.

3. Again as I told you, the question of Imperial Preference might easily fall into its place in a large settlement in which the United States became a low tariff country and it might well be that you would find us more forward even than Congress in pressing for the sweeping away of all obstructions on International trade. Here it must be remembered that for more than half a century we practised a most extreme system of free imports both into the United Kingdom and into all Colonies under our control. We were forced to abandon this policy only by the continued rise of Protective Tariffs in other countries.

4. It is not a question of division in this country upon the lines of Protection versus Free Trade, though there is danger of that, but of the inappropriateness in time and circumstance of our being forced to part with our freedom of honourable discussion with you upon an issue, which in certain aspects touches our sovereignty and independence. This might be represented by some as the acceptance by the British Government and by the British Empire as a condition of tutelage, which would I am sure be a great pity. The key-note of our relations must surely be equality, coupled with rivalry in sacrifice and effort against the common foe, and for the sake of the common cause of liberty and democracy.

5. Personally, as you know, I have been all my life an opponent of Imperial Preference, and even now I care little for it as such, but I feel very strongly that the natural manner in which to settle this manner is for the full discussion to take place without our hands being tied beforehand by a declaration which might be read as if any inter-Empire trade arrangements were to be regarded as "discrimination" and therefore banned.

I earnestly hope that you will consider this point of view and will not press upon us unduly a one-sided submission when all depends upon the most whole-hearted common action. However I will put the matter before the Cabinet again.

Document 3

Franklin D. Roosevelt's Promise of a Second Front, 1942, U.S. Department of State, *Papers Relating to the Foreign Relations of the United States* (hereafter referred to as FRUS), *1942*, vol. 3, Washington, D.C.: Government Printing Office, 1942, 575–77.

Opening the general discussion, the President remarked to Admiral [Ernest J.] King and General [George C.] Marshall that he first wished to place them *au courant* with the questions Mr. [Vyacheslav] Molotov had raised, and he hoped that Mr. Molotov himself would then put the situation before them in detail. Mr. Molotov, the President continued, had just come from London, where he had been discussing with the British authorities the problem of a second (invasion) front in Western Europe. He had, the President added, been politely received, but had as yet obtained no positive commitment from the British. There was no doubt that on the Russian front the Germans had enough superiority in aircraft and mechanized equipment to make the situation precarious. The Soviets wished the Anglo-American combination to land sufficient combat troops on the continent to draw off 40 German divisions from the Soviet front. We appreciated, he continued, the difficulties of the situation and viewed the outlook as serious. We regarded it as our obligation to help the Soviets to the best of our ability, even if the extent of this aid was for the moment doubtful. . . .

Mr. Molotov thereupon remarked that, though the problem of the second front was both military and political, it was predominantly political. There was an essential difference between the situation in 1942 and what it might be in 1943. In 1942 Hitler was the master of all Europe save a few minor countries. He was the chief enemy of everyone. To be sure, as was devoutly to be hoped, the Russians might hold and fight on all through 1942. But it was only right to look at the darker side of the picture. On the basis of his continental dominance, [Adolf] Hitler might throw in such reinforcements in manpower and material that the Red Army might *not* be able to hold out against the Nazis. Such a development would produce a serious situation which we must face. The Soviet front would become secondary, the Red Army would be weakened, and Hitler's strength would be correspondingly greater, since he would have at his disposal not only more troops, but also the foodstuffs and raw materials of the Ukraine and the oil-wells of the Caucasus. In such circumstances the outlook would be much less favorable for all hands, and he would not pretend that such developments were also outside the range of possibility. The war would thus become tougher and longer. The merit of a new front in 1942 depended on the prospects of Hitler's further advantage, hence the establishment of such a front should not be postponed. The decisive element in the whole problem lay in the question, when are the prospects better for the United Nations: in 1942 or 1943. . . .

. . . But the main danger lay in the probability that Hitler would try to deal the Soviet Union a mighty crushing blow. If, then, Great Britain and the United States, as allies, were to create a new front and to draw off 40 German divisions from the Soviet front, the ratio of strength would be so altered that the Soviets could either beat Hitler this year or insure beyond question his ultimate defeat.

Mr. Molotov therefore put this question frankly: could we undertake such offensive action as would draw off 40 German divisions which would be, to tell the truth, distinctly second-rate outfits? If the answer should be in the affirmative, the war would be decided in 1942. If negative, the Soviets would fight on alone, doing their best, and no man would expect more from them than that. He had not, Mr. Molotov added, received any positive answer in London. Mr. [Winston] Churchill had proposed that he should return through London on his homeward journey from Washington, and had promised Mr. Molotov a more concrete answer on his second visit. Mr. Molotov admitted he realized that the British would have to bear the brunt of the action if a second front were created, but he also was cognizant of the role the United States plays and what influence this country exerts in questions of major strategy. Without in any way minimizing the risks entailed by a second front action this summer, Mr. Molotov declared his government wanted to know in frank terms what position we take on the question of a second front, and whether we were prepared to establish one. He requested a straight answer. . . .

The President then put to General Marshall the query whether developments were clear enough so that we could say to Mr. [Joseph] Stalin that we are preparing a second front. "Yes," replied the General. The President then authorized Mr. Molotov to inform Mr. Stalin that we expect the formation of a second front this year.

Document 4

Unofficial report of remarks of President Franklin D. Roosevelt and British Prime Minister Winston Churchill to press correspondents at the conclusion of the Casablanca Conference, Jan. 26, 1943, *Christian Science Monitor*, Jan. 27, 1943, 10.

The President pointed out to correspondents that the successful landings in French North Africa which had changed the whole outlook of the war since November 8 were a realization of plans he and Mr. Churchill had formulated at Washington as far back as last June.

Now the time had come for a review of events in the light of progress made in various theaters of war, and for drawing up plans in regard to steps to be taken in 1943.

Premier [Joseph] Stalin was cordially invited to attend these talks which if he had accepted would necessarily have been held considerably farther eastward.

But the Russian leader replied that, although he greatly desired to come, he could not leave his country owing to his duties as Commander-in-Chief of the Soviet forces engaged in transforming the grim Russian defense into sweeping advances of the winter offensive. . . .

Now the staff chiefs are going their various ways to put 1943 plans into what the official communiqué described as "active and concerted execution."

President Roosevelt emphasized that the future plans of the Allies are keyed onto the necessity of lending the utmost possible aid to the Russian offensive.

This is being done by throwing a maximum strain on German manpower and going on with the process of inexorable attrition of German matériel now being carried out with notable success in Mediterranean regions.

At the same time within the scope of this policy all possible help is to be given to the Chinese.

The Axis is now finding itself with the disadvantages the democracies formerly had of having to meet heavy defense demands on a widening perimeter, so that the Axis has the utmost difficulty to obtain adequate concentration of military power in any one sector.

Peace is to come, Mr. Roosevelt said, by total elimination of German, Italian, and Japanese war power. This doesn't mean destruction of the people in those unhappy countries, but total and merciless destruction of the machinery they have built up for imposing totalitarian doctrines on the world.

In this connection the President reminded his listeners of the famous American General, Ulysses Simpson Grant, whose initials U.S. were adapted to express his resoluteness in the nickname "Unconditional Surrender" Grant. The democracies' war plans were to compel the "unconditional surrender" of the Axis.

Mr. Churchill, who didn't refer to typewritten notes as did Mr. Roosevelt, said he was in entire agreement with everything Mr. Roosevelt had said. The Prime Minister declared that nothing could come between the two of them who were now such firm friends, and he described the conference here as the happiest in his long experience of such meetings.

Document 5

Communiqué on Moscow Conference, Oct. 19–30, 1943, U.S. Department of State, *Bulletin*, Nov. 6, 1943, vol. 9, 307.

(1) *Anglo-Soviet-American Communiqué, Released Nov. 1, 1943*

The Conference of Foreign Secretaries of the United States of America, Mr. Cordell Hull, of the United Kingdom, Mr. Anthony Eden, and of the Soviet Union, Mr. V. M. Molotov, took place at Moscow from the 19th to 30th of October 1943. There were twelve meetings. . . .

The Governments of the United States, the United Kingdom and the Soviet Union have been in close cooperation in all matters concerning the common war effort. But this is the first time that the Foreign Secretaries of the three Governments have been able to meet together in conference.

In the first place there were frank and exhaustive discussions of measures to be taken to shorten the war against Germany and her satellites in Europe. Advantage was taken of the presence of military advisers, representing the respective Chiefs of Staff, in order to discuss definite military operations, with regard to which decisions had been taken and which are already being prepared, and in order to create a basis for the closest military cooperation in the future between the three countries.

Second only to the importance of hastening the end of the war was the unanimous recognition by the three Governments that it was essential in their own national interests and in the interest of all peace-loving nations to continue the present close collaboration and cooperation in the conduct of the war into the period following the end of hostilities, and that only in this way could peace be maintained and the political, economic and social welfare of their peoples fully promoted.

This conviction is expressed in a declaration in which the Chinese Government joined during the Conference and which was signed by the three Foreign Secretaries and the Chinese Ambassador at Moscow on behalf of their governments. This declaration, published today, provides for even closer collaboration in the prosecution of the war and in all matters pertaining to the surrender and disarmament of the enemies with which the four countries are respectively at war. It sets forth the principles upon which the four governments agree that a broad system of international cooperation and security should be based. Provision is made for the inclusion of all other peace-loving nations, great and small, in this system.

The Conference agreed to set up machinery for ensuring the closest cooperation between the three Governments in the examination of European questions arising as the war develops. For this purpose the Conference decided to establish in London a European Advisory Commission to study these questions and to make joint recommendations to the three Governments. . . .

(2) *Declaration of Four Nations on General Security, Oct. 30, 1943*

The Governments of the United States of America, the United Kingdom, The Soviet Union and China: united in their determination, in accordance with the Declaration by the United Nations of January 1, 1942, and subsequent declarations, to continue hostilities against those Axis powers with which they respectively are at war until such powers have laid down their arms on the basis of unconditional surrender;

conscious of their responsibility to secure the liberation of themselves and the peoples allied with them from the menace of aggression;

recognizing the necessity of ensuring a rapid and orderly transition from war to peace and of establishing and maintaining international peace and security with the least diversion of the world's human and economic resources for armaments;

jointly declare:

1. That their united action, pledged for the prosecution of the war against their respective enemies, will be continued for the organization and maintenance of peace and security.

2. That those of them at war with a common enemy will act together in all matters relating to the surrender and disarmament of that enemy.

3. That they will take all measures deemed by them to be necessary to provide against any violation of the terms imposed upon the enemy.

4. That they recognize the necessity of establishing at the earliest practicable date a general international organization, based on the principle of the sovereign equality of all peace-loving states, and open to membership by all such states, large and small, for the maintenance of international peace and security.

5. That for the purpose of maintaining international peace and security pending the reestablishment of law and order and the inauguration of a system of general security, they will consult with one another and as occasion requires with other members of the United Nations with a view to joint action on behalf of the community of nations.

Document 6

President Franklin D. Roosevelt and Soviet Premier Joseph Stalin on the "Four Policemen," at Teheran, *FRUS, 1943, Conferences at Cairo and Teheran,* 1943, 530–33.

The President then said the question of a post-war organization to preserve peace had not been fully explained and dealt with and he would like to discuss with the Marshal the prospect of some organization based on the United Nations.

The President then outlined the following general plan:

(1) There would be a large organization composed of some 35 members of the United Nations which would meet periodically at different places, discuss and make recommendations to a smaller body.

Marshal Stalin inquired whether this organization was to be world-wide or European, to which the President replied, world-wide.

The President continued that there would be set up an executive committee composed of the Soviet Union, the United States, United Kingdom and China, together with two additional European states, one South American, one Near East, one Far Eastern country, and one British Dominion. He mentioned that Mr. [Winston] Churchill did not like this proposal for the reason that the British Empire only had two votes. This

Executive Committee would deal with all non-military questions such as agriculture, food, health, and economic questions, as well as the setting up of an International Committee. This Committee would likewise meet in various places.

Marshal Stalin inquired whether this body would have the right to make decisions binding on the nations of the world.

The President replied, yes and no. It could make recommendations for settling disputes with the hope that the nations concerned would be guided thereby, but that, for example, he did not believe the Congress of the United States would accept as binding a decision of such a body. The President then turned to the third organization which he termed "The Four Policemen," namely, the Soviet Union, United States, Great Britain, and China. This organization would have the power to deal immediately with any threat to the peace and any sudden emergency which requires this action. He went on to say that in 1935, when Italy attacked Ethiopia, the only machinery in existence was the League of Nations. He personally had begged France to close the Suez Canal, but they instead referred it to the League which disputed the question and in the end did nothing. The result was that the Italian Armies went through the Suez Canal and destroyed Ethiopia. The President pointed out that had the machinery of the Four Policemen, which he had in mind, been in existence, it would have been possible to close the Suez Canal. The President then summarized . . . the idea that he had in mind.

Marshal Stalin said that he did not think that the small nations of Europe would like the organization composed of the Four Policemen. He said, for example, that a European state would probably resent China having the right to apply certain machinery to it. And in any event, he did not think China would be very powerful at the end of the war. He suggested as a possible alternative, the creation of a European or a Far Eastern Committee and a European or a Worldwide organization. He said that in the European Commission there would be the United States, Great Britain, the Soviet Union and possibly one other European state.

The President said that the idea just expressed by Marshal Stalin was somewhat similar to Mr. Churchill's idea of a Regional Committee, one for Europe, one for the Far East, and one for the Americas. Mr. Churchill had also suggested that the United States be a member of the European Commission, but he doubted if the United States Congress would agree to the United States' participation in an exclusively European Committee which might be able to force the dispatch of American troops to Europe.

The President added that it would take a terrible crisis such as at present before Congress would ever agree to that step.

Marshal Stalin pointed out that the world organization suggested by the President, and in particular the Four Policemen, might also require the sending of American troops to Europe.

Document 7

President Franklin D. Roosevelt to British Prime Minister Winston Churchill, Feb. 29, 1944, PREM 3/197/3, Records of the Prime Minister, Public Record Office, Kew, England.

Now comes this business of what to do when we get into Germany. I understand that your Staff presented a long and comprehensive document—with every known kind of terms—to the European Advisory Commission, and that the Russians have done somewhat the same.

My people over here believe that a short document of surrender terms should be adopted. This, of course, has nothing to do with the locality of the occupying forces after they get into Germany, but it is an instrument of surrender which is in conformity with the general principles.

I am enclosing (a) an argument—facts bearing on the problem and (b) a proposed acknowledgement of unconditional surrender by Germany.

I hope much that you will read the argument. I think it is very cogent.

I am trying as hard as I can to simplify things—and sometimes I shudder at the thought of appointing as many new Committees and Commissions in the future as we have in the past!

I note that in the British proposal the territory of Germany is divided up in accordance with the British plan. "Do please don't" ask me to keep any American forces in France. I just cannot do it! I would have to bring them all back home. As I suggested before, I denounce and protest the paternity of Belgium, France and Italy. You really ought to bring up and discipline your own children. In view of the fact that they may be your bulwark in future days, you should at least pay for their schooling now!

Document 8

British Prime Minister Winston Churchill to President Franklin D. Roosevelt, July 1, 1944, in Howard Ehrman, *Grand Strategy,* vol. 5, *History of the Second World War,* United Kingdom Military Series, London: His Majesty's Stationery Office, 1956, 575–77.

1. We are deeply grieved by your telegram. There are no differences whatever between my War Cabinet colleagues and the British Chiefs of Staff. The splitting up of the campaign in the Mediterranean into two operations neither of which can do anything decisive, is, in my humble and respectful opinion, the first major strategic and political error for which we two have to be responsible. . . .

6. I should not be frank if I did not assure you that I fear a costly stalemate for you unless far more American divisions, at the expense of [General Dwight D.] Eisenhower, are thrust into ANVIL [code name for the invasion of southern France] to make it good at all costs by the great power of the United States. Little account is to be taken of [Field Marshal Sir Harold] Alexander's operations. The last decision given by the British and American Chiefs of Staff here a fortnight ago was: "The destruction of the German armed forces in Italy south of the Pisa-Rimini line must be completed. There should be no withdrawal from the battle of any Allied forces that are necessary for this purpose" (telegram number 3116 dated June 14th from CCS [Combined Chiefs of Staff] to Generals [Sir Henry Maitland] Wilson and Eisenhower). However, I received from Alexander on June 28th a long distressing telegram in which the following passage occurs:

"The ghost of ANVIL hangs heavily over the battlefront. For example, the Americans have been ordered to send 517 RCT [Regimental Combat Team] and 117 Cav Recce [reconnaissance] Squadrons which are actually in contact with the enemy. They are also required to release now an engineer regiment and other service units required for the conduct of battle. The French do not appear to be putting their hearts into the present operations and reason is undoubtedly because they have their eyes turned in another direction.

The air effort will shortly be curtailed owing to moves of fighting units to Corsica. Eighth Army are not directly concerned with ANVIL, but as long as there is doubt and uncertainty about the future so long will there be a moral weakening. Armies have a very delicate sense and they are beginning to look over their shoulders. You will no doubt remember the Biblical quotation 'For if the trumpet give an uncertain sound, who shall prepare himself to the battle.' If the momentum of my offensive is to be kept to its maximum, I must receive confirmation that Italian campaign is to be backed. If on the other hand it is decided to go all out for ANVIL, then I must know so that I can recast my present plans. In the event of the latter decision I have proposed to General Wilson that I should fly home and table certain proposals aimed at producing best results my emasculated forces will be able to achieve in support of the war effort.''

7. I have considered your suggestion that we should lay our respective cases before [Joseph] Stalin. The passage in the very nice telegram I have received from him yesterday (which follows this immediately) seems to suggest that he does not underrate the Italian front. I do not know what he would say if the issue was put to him to decide. On military grounds he might be greatly interested in the eastward movement of Alexander's Army which, without entering the Balkans, would profoundly affect all the forces there and which, in conjunction with any attacks he may make upon Roumania or with Roumania against Hungarian Transylvania, might produce the most far-reaching results. On a long-term political view, he might prefer that the British and Americans should do their share in France in the very hard fighting that is to come, and that east, middle and southern Europe should fall naturally into his control. However it is better to settle the matter for ourselves and between ourselves.

8. What can I do, Mr. President, when your Chiefs of Staff insist on casting aside our Italian offensive campaign, with all its dazzling possibilities, relieving [Adolf] Hitler of all his anxieties in the Po Basin (vide BONIFACE), and when we are to see the integral life of this campaign drained off into the Rhone Valley in the belief that it will in several months carry effective help to Eisenhower so far away in the north?

9. If you still press upon us the directive of your Chiefs of Staff to withdraw so many of your forces from the Italian campaign and leave all our hopes there dashed to the ground, his Majesty's Government, on the advice of their Chiefs of Staff, must enter a solemn protest. I need scarcely say that we shall do our best to make a success of anything that is undertaken. We shall therefore forward your directive to General Wilson as soon as you let us know that there is no hope of reconsideration by your Chiefs of Staff or by yourself. Our Chiefs of Staff are letting yours know the corrections on points of detail which they think necessary in the previous draft.

10. It is with the greatest sorrow that I write to you in this sense. But I am sure that if we could have met, as I so frequently proposed, we should have reached a happy agreement. I send you every personal good wish. However we may differ on the conduct of the war, my personal gratitude to you for your kindness to me and for all you have done for the cause of freedom will never be diminished.

Document 9

Secretary of the Treasury Henry Morgenthau, Morgenthau Plan, 1944, Presidential Diary, Sept. 15, 1944 and Diary, vol. 772, 1–3, 153–63, 208–12, Papers of Henry Morgenthau, Roosevelt Library, Hyde Park, New York.

5. Octagon [code name for Quebec Conference of 1944]

His first evening in Quebec Morgenthau attended a state dinner where the President asked him to explain the Treasury's proposals for Germany. As the Secretary wrote in a reminiscing article several years later, "I had barely got under way before low mutters and baleful looks indicated that the Prime Minister [Churchill] was not the most enthusiastic member of my audience. . . . I have never seen him more irascible and vitriolic than he was that night. . . . After I finished my piece he turned loose on me the full flood of his rhetoric, sarcasm and violence. He looked on the Treasury Plan, he said, as he would on chaining himself to a dead German.

"He was slumped in his chair, his language biting, his flow incessant, his manner merciless. I have never had such a verbal lashing in my life.

"The President [Franklin D. Roosevelt] sat by, saying very little. This was part of his way of managing Churchill. He let the Prime Minister wear himself out attacking me; he used me, so to speak, to draw the venom. Then, when the time came, he could move in with his superb and infectious humor and compose the situation. But I went unhappily to bed just the same and spent a sleepless night."

The next morning Lord Cherwell cheered Morgenthau. Churchill's attitude the previous night, Cherwell said, had surprised him; the Prime Minister had not altogether understood what Morgenthau was driving at. Cherwell himself, in contrast, seemed to agree with the Morgenthau Plan, which he and the Secretary discussed prior to their meeting at noon that day with Roosevelt, Churchill, and [Sir Anthony] Eden. Morgenthau described that noon conference in his Diary only a few hours after it ended:

Churchill, turning to Lord Cherwell and myself, said, "Where are the minutes on this matter of the Ruhr?" Then according to our agreement we said that we didn't have them. The reason we didn't have them was because I felt, when I read the minutes which Lord Cherwell had written, that it presented much too weak a case, and I thought that we could get Churchill to go much further. He seemed quite put out that we didn't have the minutes of the previous meeting, and the President said the reason we didn't have them was because Henry interspersed the previous discussion with too many dirty jokes, and that sort of broke the ice. So Churchill broke in and said, "Well, I'll restate it," which he did, and he did it very forcefully and very clearly. Then he suggested that Lord Cherwell and I withdraw and try to do a job on dictating it, which we did. It only took us a few minutes, and we came back up to the room where they were meeting and just calmly walked in. When Churchill read our very short memorandum, he said, "No, this isn't what I want." Then he started to talk and dictate to us, and I said, "I don't know what the rules of the game are, but is there any reason why we can't have a stenographer present? Then you could dictate directly to her." He said, "By all means" and Cherwell went out and got Churchill's secretary and she came in and he began to dictate to her. He dictated the memorandum, which finally stood just the way he dictated it. He dictates extremely well because he is accustomed to doing it when he is writing his books.

While Churchill was dictating, he used the memorandum which I had dictated as a sort of a text.

Roosevelt's important contribution, while Churchill was dictating, was that when he got talking about the metallurgical, chemical and electrical industries, Roosevelt had him insert the very important words "in Germany." What Roosevelt meant—because it came up later—that he didn't have in mind just the Ruhr and the Saar, but he had in mind entire Germany and that the matter we were talking about, namely, the ease with which metallurgical, chemical and electrical industries in Germany can be converted from peace to war, does not only apply to the Ruhr and the Saar, but the whole of Germany, which of course is terribly important.

When Churchill got through, Eden seemed quite shocked at what he heard, and he turned to Churchill and said, "You can't do this. After all, you and I publicly have said the opposite. Furthermore, we have a lot of things in the works in London which are quite different." Then Churchill and Eden seemed to have quite a bit of argument about it. Roosevelt took no part in it, and I took a small part and kept throwing things in. Churchill's main argument was what this meant in the way of trade; they would get the export trade of Germany. So Eden said, "How do you know what it is or where it is?" and Churchill answered him quite testily, "Well, we will get it wherever it is." I was quite amazed and shocked at Eden's attitude; in fact, it was so different from the way he talked when we were in London. Finally Churchill said, "Now I hope, Anthony, you're not going to do anything about this with the War Cabinet if you see a chance to present it. . . . After all, the future of my people is at stake, and when I have to choose between my people and the German people, I am going to choose my people." Churchill got nasty with Eden and I understand from the President that all the rest of the day Eden was not at all helpful. The President was quite disappointed.

Of course the fact that Churchill has dictated this himself strengthens the whole matter tremendously. Naturally, I am terrifically happy over it as we got just what we started out to get.

Document 10

Winston Churchill-Joseph Stalin Percentage Deal, Oct. 1944, in Winston S. Churchill, *Triumph and Tragedy*, vol. 6, *The Second World War*, New York: Houghton Mifflin, 1962, 196–97.

The moment was apt for business, so I [Churchill] said, "Let us settle about our affairs in the Balkans. Your armies are in Rumania and Bulgaria. We have interests, missions, and agents there. Don't let us get at cross-purposes in small ways. So far as Britain and Russia are concerned, how would it do for you to have ninety per cent predominance in Rumania, for us to have ninety per cent of the say in Greece, and go fifty-fifty about Yugoslavia?" While this was being translated I wrote out on a half-sheet of paper:

Rumania	
Russia	90%
The others	10%
Greece	
Great Britain (in accord with U.S.A.)	90%
Russia	10%
Yugoslavia	50-50%
Hungary	50-50%
Bulgaria	
Russia	75%
The others	25%

I pushed this across to Stalin, who had by then heard the translation. There was a slight pause. Then he took his blue pencil and made a large tick upon it, and passed it back to us. It was all settled in no more time than it takes to set down.

Of course we had long and anxiously considered our point, and were only dealing with immediate war-time arrangements. All larger questions were reserved on both sides for what we then hoped would be a peace table when the war was won.

After this there was a long silence. The pencilled paper lay in the centre of the table. At length I said, "Might it not be thought rather cynical if it seemed we had disposed of these issues, so fateful to millions of people, in such an offhand manner? Let us burn the paper." "No, you keep it," said Stalin.

Document 11

Yalta Conference Protocol of Proceedings, 1945, *FRUS, 1945, The Conferences at Malta and Yalta,* 975–80.

The Crimea Conference of the Heads of the Governments of the United States of America [Roosevelt], the United Kingdom [Churchill], and the Union of Soviet Socialist Republics [Stalin] which took place from February 4th to 11th came to the following conclusions:

I. World Organization

It was decided:

1. that a United Nations Conference on the proposed world organization should be summoned for Wednesday, 25th April, 1945, and should be held in the United States of America.

2. the Nations to be invited to this Conference should be:

a. the United Nations as they existed on the 8th February, 1945; and

b. such of the Associated Nations as have declared war on the common enemy by 1st March, 1945. (For this purpose by the term "Associated Nations" was meant the eight Associated Nations and Turkey.) When the Conference on World Organization is held, the delegates of the United Kingdom and United States of America will support a proposal to admit to original membership two Soviet Socialist Republics, i.e. the Ukraine and White Russia.

3. that the United States Government on behalf of the Three Powers should consult the Government of China and the French Provisional Government in regard to decisions taken at the present Conference concerning the proposed World Organization. . . .

II. Declaration on Liberated Europe

The following declaration has been approved:

The Premier of the Union of Soviet Socialist Republics, the Prime Minister of the United Kingdom and the President of the United States of America have consulted with each other in the common interests of the peoples of their countries and those of liberated Europe. They jointly declare their mutual agreement to concert during the temporary period of instability in liberated Europe the policies of their three governments in assisting the peoples of the former Axis satellite states of Europe to solve by democratic means their pressing political and economic problems.

The establishment of order in Europe and the rebuilding of national economic life must be achieved by processes which will enable the liberated peoples to destroy the last vestiges of Nazism and Fascism and to create democratic institutions of their own choice. This is a principle of the Atlantic Charter—the right of all peoples to choose the form of government under which they will live—the restoration of sovereign rights and self-government to those peoples who have been forcibly deprived of them by the aggressor nations.

To foster the conditions in which the liberated peoples may exercise these rights, the three governments will jointly assist the people in any European liberated state or former Axis satellite state in Europe where in their judgment conditions require (a) to establish conditions of internal peace; (b) to carry out emergency measures for the relief of distressed peoples; (c) to form interim governmental authorities broadly representative of all democratic elements in the population and pledged to the earliest possible establishment through free elections of governments responsive to the will of the people; and (d) to facilitate where necessary the holding of such elections.

The three governments will consult the other United Nations and provisional authorities or other governments in Europe when matters of direct interest to them are under consideration.

When, in the opinion of the three governments, conditions in any European liberated state or any former Axis satellite state in Europe make such action necessary, they will immediately consult together on the measures necessary to discharge the joint responsibilities set forth in this declaration.

By this declaration we reaffirm our faith in the principles of the Atlantic Charter, our pledges in the Declaration by the United Nations, and our determination to build in cooperation with other peace-loving nations world order under law, dedicated to peace, security, freedom and general well-being of all mankind.

In issuing this declaration, the Three Powers express the hope that the Provisional Government of the French Republic may be associated with them in the procedure suggested.

III. Dismemberment of Germany

It was agreed that Article 12 (a) of the Surrender Terms for Germany should be amended to read as follows:

> The United Kingdom, the United States of America and the Union of Soviet Socialist Republics shall possess supreme authority with respect to Germany. In the exercise of such authority they will take such steps, including the complete disarmament, demilitarization and dismemberment of Germany as they deem requisite for future peace and security.

The study of the procedure for the dismemberment of Germany was referred to a Committee, consisting of Mr. [Anthony] Eden (Chairman), Mr. [John G.] Winant and Mr. [Fedor T.] Gousev. This body would consider the desirability of associating with it a French representative.

IV. Zone of Occupation for the French and Control Council for Germany

It was agreed that a zone in Germany, to be occupied by the French Forces, should be allocated to France. This zone would be formed out of the British and American zones and its extent would be settled by the British and Americans in consultation with the French Provisional Government.

It was also agreed that the French Provisional Government should be invited to become a member of the Allied Control Council of Germany.

V. Reparation

The heads of the three governments agreed as follows:

1. Germany must pay in kind for the losses caused by her to the Allied nations in the course of the war. Reparations are to be received in the first instance by those countries which have borne the main burden of the war, have suffered the heaviest losses and have organized victory over the enemy.

2. Reparation in kind to be exacted from Germany in three following forms:

a. Removals within 2 years from the surrender of Germany or the cessation of organized resistance from the national wealth of Germany located on the territory of Germany herself as well as outside her territory (equipment, machine-tools, ships, rolling stock, German investments abroad, shares of industrial, transport and other enterprises in Germany etc.), these removals to be carried out chiefly for purpose of destroying the war potential of Germany.

b. Annual deliveries of goods from current production for a period to be fixed.

c. Use of German labor.

3. For the working out on the above principles of a detailed plan for exaction of reparation from Germany an Allied Reparation Commission will be set up in Moscow. It will consist of three representatives—one from the Union of Soviet Socialist Republics, one from the United Kingdom and one from the United States of America.

4. With regard to the fixing of the total sum of the reparation as well as the distribution of it among the countries which suffered from the German aggression the Soviet and American delegations agreed as follows:

The Moscow Reparation Commission should take in its initial studies as a basis for discussion the suggestion of the Soviet Government that the total sum of the reparation in accordance with the points (a) and (b) of the paragraph 2 should be 20 billion dollars and that 50% of it should go to the Union of Soviet Socialist Republics.

The British delegation was of the opinion that pending consideration of the reparation question by the Moscow Reparation Commission no figures of reparation should be mentioned.

The above Soviet-American proposal has been passed to the Moscow Reparation Commission as one of the proposals to be considered by the Commission. . . .

VII. Poland

The following Declaration on Poland was agreed by the Conference:

A new situation has been created in Poland as a result of her complete liberation by the Red Army. This calls for the establishment of a Polish Provisional Government which can be more broadly based than was possible before the recent liberation of Western part of Poland. The Provisional Government which is now functioning in Poland should therefore be recognized on a broader democratic basis with the inclusion of democratic leaders from Poland itself and from Poles abroad. This new Government should then be called the Polish Provisional Government of National Unity.

Mr. [Vyacheslav] Molotov, Mr. [W. Averell] Harriman and Sir A. Clark Kerr are authorized as a commission to consult in the first instance in Moscow with members of the present Provisional Government and with other Polish democratic leaders from within Poland and from abroad, with a view to the reorganization of the present Government along the above lines. This Polish Provisional Government of National Unity shall be pledged to the holding of free and unfettered elections as soon as possible on the basis of universal suffrage and secret ballot. In these elections all democratic and anti-Nazi parties shall have the right to take part and to put forward candidates.

When a Polish Provisional Government of National Unity has been properly formed in conformity with the above, the Government of the U.S.S.R., which now maintains diplomatic relations with the present Provisional Government of Poland, and the Government of the United Kingdom and the Government of the United States of America will establish diplomatic relations with the new Polish Provisional Government of National Unity, and will exchange Ambassadors by whose reports the respective Governments will be kept informed about the situation in Poland.

The three Heads of Government consider that the Eastern frontier of Poland should follow the Curzon Line with digressions from it in some regions of five to eight kilometers in favor of Poland. They recognize that Poland must receive substantial accession of territory in the North and West. They feel that the opinion of the new Polish Provisional Government of National Unity should be sought in due course on the extent of these accessions and that the final delimitation of the Western frontier of Poland should therefore await the Peace Conference. . . .

Agreement on Soviet Entry into the War Against Japan, 1945

The leaders of the three Great Powers—the Soviet Union, the United States of America and Great Britain—have agreed that in two or three months after Germany has surrendered and the war in Europe has terminated the Soviet Union shall enter into the war against Japan on the side of the Allies on condition that:

1. The *status quo* in Outer-Mongolia (The Mongolian People's Republic) shall be preserved;

2. The former rights of Russia violated by the treacherous attack of Japan in 1904 shall be restored, viz:

a. the southern part of Sakhalin as well as all the islands adjacent to it shall be returned to the Soviet Union,

b. The commercial port of Dairen shall be internationalized, the preeminent interests of the Soviet Union in this port being safeguarded and the lease of Port Arthur as a naval base of the USSR restored,

c. The Chinese-Eastern Railroad and the South-Manchurian Railroad which provides an outlet to Dairen shall be jointly operated by the establishment of a joint Soviet-Chinese Company it being understood that the preeminent interests of the Soviet Union shall be safeguarded and that China shall retain full sovereignty in Manchuria;

3. The Kuril islands shall be handed over to the Soviet Union.

It is understood, that the agreement concerning Outer-Mongolia and the ports and railroads referred to above will require concurrence of Generalissimo Chiang Kai-Shek. The President will take measures in order to obtain this concurrence on advice from Marshal Stalin.

The Heads of the three Great Powers have agreed that these claims of the Soviet Union shall be unquestionably fulfilled after Japan has been defeated.

For its part the Soviet Union expresses its readiness to conclude with the National Government of China a pact of friendship and alliance between the USSR and China in order to render assistance to China with its armed forces for the purpose of liberating China from the Japanese yoke.

Document 12

Charter of the United Nations, signed in San Francisco on June 26, 1945, U.S. Department of State, *Bulletin*, July 24, 1945, vol. 12, 1119.

WE THE PEOPLES OF THE UNITED NATIONS DETERMINED

to save succeeding generations from the scourge of war, which twice in our lifetime has brought untold sorrow to mankind, and

to reaffirm faith in fundamental human rights, in the dignity and worth of the human person, in the equal rights of men and women and of nations large and small, and

to establish conditions under which justice and respect for the obligations arising from treaties and other sources of international law can be maintained, and

to promote social progress and better standards of life in larger freedom,

AND FOR THESE ENDS

to practice tolerance and live together in peace with one another as good neighbors, and

to unite our strength to maintain international peace and security, and

to ensure, by the acceptance of principles and the institution of methods, that armed force shall not be used, save in the common interest, and

to employ international machinery for the promotion of the economic and social advancement of all peoples,

HAVE RESOLVED TO COMBINE OUR EFFORTS TO ACCOMPLISH THESE AIMS.

Accordingly, our respective Governments, through representatives assembled in the city of San Francisco, who have exhibited their full powers found to be in good and due form, have agreed to the present Charter of the United Nations and do hereby establish an international organization to be known as the United Nations.

Document 13

British Prime Minister Winston Churchill to President Harry S. Truman, July 25, 1945, *FRUS, 1945, The Conference of Berlin (The Potsdam Conference)*, 1960, vol. 2, 1279–81.

My Dear Mr. President, I thank you for your letter of July 25, . . .

I return the copy of the Proclamation to Japan by the Heads of Governments of the United States, the United Kingdom, and the Republic of China, which I received from you yesterday. I am willing to sign it on behalf of His Majesty's Government in its present form, and I hope you will issue it as you propose whenever you choose and as soon as possible.

On a minor point, I suggest that the word "industries" might be added where shown in paragraph 11, otherwise the word "those" would seem at first sight to apply to Reparations.

Yours very sincerely,

Winston S. Churchill

[Attachment]

(1) We,—The President of the United States, the Prime Minister of Great Britain, and the President of the Republic of China [Chiang Kai-shek], representing the hundreds of millions of our countrymen, have conferred and agree that Japan shall be given an opportunity to end this war.

(2) The prodigious land, sea and air forces of the United States, the British Empire and of China, many times reinforced by their armies and air fleets from the west, are poised to strike the final blows upon Japan. This military power is sustained and inspired by the determination of all the Allied nations to prosecute the war against Japan until she ceases to resist.

(3) The result of the futile and senseless German resistance to the might of the aroused free peoples of the world stands forth in awful clarity as an example to the people of Japan. The might that now converges on Japan is immeasurably greater than that which, when applied to the resisting Nazis, necessarily laid waste to the lands, the industry and the method of life of the whole German people. The full application of our military power, backed by our resolve, *will* mean the inevitable and complete destruction of the Japanese armed forces and just as inevitably the utter devastation of the Japanese homeland.

(4) The time has come for Japan to decide whether she will continue to be controlled by those self-willed militaristic advisers whose unintelligent calculations have brought the Empire of Japan to the threshold of annihilation, or whether she will follow the path of reason.

(5) Following are our terms. We will not deviate from them. There are no alternatives. We shall brook no delay.

(6) There must be eliminated for all time the authority and influence of those who have deceived and misled the people of Japan into embarking on world conquest, for we insist that a new order of peace, security and justice will be impossible until irresponsible militarism is driven from the world.

(7) Until such a new order is established *and* until there is convincing proof that Japan's war-making power is destroyed, points in Japanese territory to be designated by the Allies shall be occupied to secure the achievement of the basic objectives we are here setting forth.

(8) The terms of the Cairo Declaration shall be carried out and Japanese sovereignty shall be limited to the islands of Honshu, Hokkaido, Kyushu, Shikoku and such minor islands as we determine.

(9) The Japanese military forces, after being completely disarmed, shall be permitted to return to their homes with the opportunity to lead peaceful and productive lives.

(10) We do not intend that the Japanese shall be enslaved as a race or destroyed as a nation, but stern justice shall be meted out to all war criminals, including those who have visited cruelties upon our prisoners. The Japanese Government shall remove all obstacles to the revival and strengthening of democratic tendencies among the Japanese people. Freedom of speech, of religion, and of thought, as well as respect for the fundamental human rights shall be established.

(11) Japan shall be permitted to maintain such industries as will sustain her economy and permit the exaction of just reparations in kind, but not those which would enable her to re-arm for war. To this end, access to, as distinguished from control of, raw materials shall be permitted. Eventual Japanese participation in world trade relations shall be permitted.

(12) The occupying forces of the Allies shall be withdrawn from Japan as soon as these objectives have been accomplished and there has been established in accordance with the freely expressed will of the Japanese people a peacefully inclined and responsible government.

(13) We call upon the Government of Japan to proclaim now the unconditional surrender of all the Japanese armed forces, and to provide proper and adequate assurances of their good faith in such action. The alternative for Japan is prompt and utter destruction.

CHAPTER 7

The Cold War in Europe and the Near East

Howard Jones

The last half of the 1940s was one of the most pivotal periods in the history of America's foreign affairs. Not only did the United States complete the Allied victory in World War II and thereby usher in the atomic age, but it also took the lead in restoring order and reestablishing a balance of power in Europe and the Near East that would bring economic and political stability and thereby reduce the threat of totalitarianism during the Cold War. The result, however, was heightened rivalry with the Soviet Union and the division of countries that were vulnerable to outside pressure into opposing spheres of interest. Crises occurred almost in staccato fashion, drawing the United States deeper and deeper into a highly charged international atmosphere characterized by threats and counterthreats. According to the White House, the Americans' sole possession of the atomic bomb had forced the Soviets into ''a new kind of war'' that included subversion, infiltration, and the use of propaganda to undermine pro-Western governments and encourage their capitulation to Communism. Soviet tactics required the United States to adopt a firm and yet flexible policy in containing the challenge on military as well as social, economic, and political fronts. Yet the United States did not make an automatic global commitment; its decision to extend assistance to besieged countries depended on whether the area in question was both vital to American interests and capable of being saved. The two chief Cold War adversaries entered first into indirect confrontations in Europe and the Near East and then, finally, into a direct encounter over Berlin during which the White House considered using the atomic bomb for the third time.

If the Cold War did not begin in the late 1940s, it certainly reached a highly dangerous level of intensity. The Grand Alliance of World War II had been both strange and strained, held together only by the fierce drive to defeat Hitler. But as soon as the Allies turned the corner in the war in late 1943, they focused on postwar objectives and, in so doing, exposed the bases for their certain rivalry. Another far-reaching development was crucial. The massive destruction sustained by Great Britain during two world wars in the twentieth century had reduced that once-proud empire to a secondary status in global politics and thereby left a bipolar power structure dominated by the United States and, although not yet on an equal plane, the Soviet Union.

Once the Third Reich collapsed in May 1945 and the Japanese surrendered the following September, the long-standing American-Soviet differences in culture, ideology, and political objectives became unmistakably clear. Capitalism and Communism provided the spiritual drive of their ensuing contest, while the American commitment to national self-determination, expressed in the Atlantic Charter announced by Britain and the United States in 1941 and in the Yalta Declaration on Liberated Europe in 1945, furnished the rationale for a nearly inevitable battle over the Soviets' insistence upon security. As the United States called for free and open elections in the postwar era, the Soviets reminded the West of two German invasions of their homeland in the twentieth century alone and demanded "friendly neighbors" in Eastern Europe—claims that were understandable though irreconcilable with America's wartime aims. Thus did perceptions become reality. From Washington's perspective, the Soviets appeared bent upon spreading Communism throughout the world. In Moscow, however, every countermove taken by the United States against what the Soviets considered legitimate claims was further proof of capitalist aggression and therefore a continuation of the West's longtime effort to encircle and isolate their country.

Whether or not the Soviets were involved in helping to foment the problems in Europe and the Near East, the Truman administration believed they were and acted accordingly. The U.S. chargé in Moscow, George F. Kennan, attempted to explain the bases for the Soviets' seemingly aggressive behavior in his "Long Telegram" to the State Department in February 1946. (doc. 1) The Kremlin, he insisted, harbored a deep-seated insecurity and almost neurotic distrust of the West that would never allow a warm, harmonious relationship. The United States must understand the Soviet menace and maintain a strong and united country from within while keeping a close relationship with its allies. The following month, the venerable Winston Churchill spoke before President Harry S. Truman and a college audience in Fulton, Missouri, and warned darkly that the Soviets were lowering an "iron curtain" across Eastern Europe. In autumn of that same year, presidential counsel Clark Clifford submitted a lengthy study of Soviet objectives that urged the United States to counter the Communist threat with a global policy that was multifaceted in approach but nonetheless rested on an extensive military buildup capable of engaging in atomic and biological warfare. (doc. 2)

By 1947 the eastern Mediterranean was the central area of East-West concern. After warding off the Soviets' attempt to expand into Iran, the Truman administration found itself involved in a series of near clashes with the Kremlin over Turkey and Greece. The Soviets, it appeared, were trying to gain control over the Turkish straits before turning to Greece, thereby hoping to break the British lifeline into the Mediterranean and permit Soviet entry into the Middle East. Once in that position, they could seize the region's vast oil reserves, deny them to Western Europe, and force its capitulation to Communism. A ''war of nerves'' had already ensued in the autumn of 1946 as Soviet soldiers marched menacingly along the common Soviet-Turkish border, and Soviet officials heightened longtime demands for at least partial control of the Bosporus and Dardanelles straits connecting the Black Sea with the Mediterranean. In the meantime, an insurgency in Greece, believed by Washington to be encouraged if not inspired by the Soviet Union and Greece's neighboring Communist regimes, erupted in a vicious civil war between royalists and Communist-led guerrillas. (docs. 3 and 4) When the British bowed out of the area in early 1947 because of financial difficulties, the administration in Washington reacted with the Truman Doctrine in March, a military and economic assistance program specifically limited to Greece and Turkey but nonetheless leaving the ominous impression that the United States would intervene wherever freedom was in danger. (doc. 5) As the Greek Civil War raged on until the Athens government's victory in October 1949, the Truman administration seriously considered sending American combat troops along with its operational advisers already in the field. (docs. 6 and 7)

East-West tensions continued to mount as the United States shored up its defenses for a long and bitter Cold War. In the summer of 1947, Kennan published his views on Soviet conduct in an article (signed ''X'') in the July issue of *Foreign Affairs* magazine. Communism, he eloquently and persuasively argued, was similar to the church in its determination to emerge triumphant over the long run, and could be stopped only by a patient and vigilant policy of containment. If the West could halt the spread of Communism, the result would be either a relaxation of Soviet aggression and a reform of the country's own internal structure, or a continued resistance to domestic change that would ultimately cause a revolution from within. Congress meanwhile showed its support for a firm foreign policy by passing the National Security Act. The far-reaching measure institutionalized the Joint Chiefs of Staff, established the National Security Council to advise the president, replaced the secretary of war with a secretary of defense, and created the Central Intelligence Agency, which soon moved from its original mandate of gathering and analyzing intelligence at home to engaging in covert operations outside the United States.

While Washington's attention was on the Near East, problems grew in Germany, which, despite tensions in other parts of the Continent, soon emerged as the flashpoint of great-power competition in the Cold War. Located at the crossroads of East and West, Germany remained rich in manpower and resources despite its defeat in the war and, to the Soviets, loomed as a continued threat to their national security. At the Potsdam

Conference in July–August 1945, the Big Three (Great Britain, the Soviet Union, and the United States) had divided Germany into four zones of occupation (one went to France) and then did the same with Berlin, which lay inside the Soviet zone. (doc. 8) But mutual differences between East and West caused the lines to harden and threaten to become permanent. Secretary of State James F. Byrnes declared in a stirring speech at Stuttgart in September 1946 that the Potsdam agreements were not working. Therefore, to guarantee the security of western Germany and western Berlin, the United States intended to maintain troops on the Continent indefinitely.

When in early 1948 the United States responded to Western Europe's ongoing economic needs with the Marshall Plan, the atmosphere became conducive to a crisis over Berlin. The assistance effort, as Secretary of State George C. Marshall made clear in his famous June 1947 commencement address at Harvard University, was both humanitarian and strategic in purpose. (doc. 9) Primarily a massive economic aid program, the Marshall Plan (passed by Congress in April 1948) also was intended to contain the spread of Communism by integrating Western Europe economically and by reintegrating Germany into the European economy. The Kremlin, however, feared that a June 1948 conference in London attended by the United States and several other Western countries would encourage the creation of a separate government in West Germany and hence constitute a severe threat to Soviet security. (doc. 10) Soviet Premier Joseph Stalin therefore ordered a surface blockade of Berlin that same June, probably intending to hold it hostage until the West agreed to return to wartime agreements that stipulated a divided city and country under four-power control. The ensuing crisis raised the specter of all-out war. Indeed, the Truman administration thought Stalin wanted all of Germany as well as the West's departure from Europe, and discussed a range of possible actions—including a preemptive strike and the use of the atomic bomb—before settling on an equivalent response in the form of an airlift.

Instead of forcing a return to the Potsdam agreements and dividing the Western alliance, the Soviets' blockade of Berlin tightened the West and alienated world opinion. In April 1949 twelve countries, including the United States, signed the North Atlantic Treaty (eventually forming the North Atlantic Treaty Organization, or NATO), a defensive military pact that had been under way for some time but received final impetus by the Berlin crisis. (doc. 11) The following May the airlift, with British cooperation, convinced the Soviets to lift the blockade in exchange for the assurance of renewed East-West talks regarding Germany.

By early 1950 the thrust of U.S. involvement in foreign matters had shifted dramatically to a hard-line, military orientation. The Truman Doctrine had become overwhelmingly military because of the bitter war in Greece; the Marshall Plan had become distinctly military by the time it gave way to the Mutual Security Program in 1952; two Germanies and two Berlins had become realities, all militarily occupied and promising to remain at the front of Cold War tensions; NATO had united much of the West in a collective security system; and, in September 1949, the Soviets exploded their own atomic device and President Truman responded by ordering the development of a hydrogen bomb that had a vastly expanded potential for destruction. In January 1950 the president instructed the Departments of State and Defense to review America's foreign and defense policies and present a set of recommendations intended to enhance its security. The result was a top-secret study that the National Security Council submitted to Truman in April. NSC–68, as the study was known, called for a vast increase in the nation's defense budget in preparation for meeting the Soviet challenge all over the world. (doc. 12) Although the containment policy in its beginnings was more flexible and restrained in distinguishing between vital and peripheral interests of the United States, it now defined any endangered area as vital to American security. Indeed, the security of the United States and that of the world had become synonymous. Then, as if scripted by some unseen hand, the focus of East-West rivalry turned suddenly from a fairly secure Europe and Near East to Asia, where war broke out in Korea in June and provided support for the Truman administration's far-reaching objectives contained in NSC–68.

During the perilous 1940s, the Truman administration reacted firmly and yet patiently to each crisis with a multifaceted strategy intended to prevent all-out war while convincing Moscow that it could not win a struggle of wills and endurance. By the opening of the new decade, however, the Cold War had taken new and more dangerous directions both in geography and intensity. Only today, in the late twentieth century, has Soviet *glasnost* (openness) justified the Truman administration's foreign policy.

Document 1

Chargé d'Affaires in the Soviet Union George F. Kennan to Secretary of State James F. Byrnes, Feb. 22, 1946, U.S. Department of State, *Foreign Relations of the United States* (hereafter referred to as *FRUS*), *1946, Eastern Europe; The Soviet Union*, Washington, D.C.: Government Printing Office, 1969, vol. 6, 697–709.

(a) USSR still lives in antagonistic "capitalistic encirclement" with which in the long run there can be no permanent peaceful coexistence. As stated by [Premier Joseph] Stalin in 1927 to a delegation of American workers:

"In course of further development of international revolution there will emerge two centers of world significance: a socialist center, drawing to itself the countries which tend toward socialism, and a capitalist center, drawing to itself the countries that incline toward capitalism. Battle between these two centers for command of world economy will decide fate of capitalism and of communism in entire world."

(b) Capitalist world is beset with internal conflicts, inherent in nature of capitalist society. These conflicts are insoluble by means of peaceful promise. Greatest of them is that between England and US.

(c) Internal conflicts of capitalism

inevitably generate wars. . . .

(d) Intervention against USSR, while it would be disastrous to those who undertook it, would cause renewed delay in progress of Soviet socialism and must therefore be forestalled at all costs.

(e) Conflicts between capitalist states, though likewise fraught with danger for USSR, nevertheless hold out great possibilities for advancement of socialist cause, particularly if USSR remains militarily powerful, ideologically monolithic and faithful to its present brilliant leadership. . . .

So much for premises. To what deductions do they lead from standpoint of Soviet policy? To following:

(a) Everything must be done to advance relative strength of USSR as factor in international society. Conversely, no opportunity must be missed to reduce strength and influence, collectively as well as individually of capitalist powers.

(b) Soviet efforts, and those of Russia's friends abroad, must be directed toward deepening and exploiting of differences and conflicts between capitalist powers. If these eventually deepen into an "imperialist" war, this war must be turned into revolutionary upheavals within the various capitalist countries.

(c) "Democratic-progressive" elements abroad are to be utilized to maximum to bring pressure to bear on capitalistic governments along lines agreeable to Soviet interests.

(d) Relentless battle must be waged against socialist and social democratic leaders abroad. . . .

Nevertheless, all these theses, however baseless and disproven, are being boldly put forward again today. What does this indicate? It indicates that Soviet party line is not based on any objective analysis of situation beyond Russa's borders; that it has, indeed, little to do with conditions outside of Russia; that it arises mainly from basic inner-Russian necessities which existed before recent war and exist today.

At bottom of Kremlin's neurotic view of world affairs is traditional and instinctive Russian sense of insecurity. Originally, this was insecurity of a peaceful agricultural people trying to live on vast exposed plain in neighborhood of fierce nomadic peoples. To this was added, as Russia came into contact with economically advanced West, fear of more competent, more powerful, more highly organized societies in that area. But this latter type of insecurity was one which afflicted rather Russian rulers than Russian people; for Russian rulers have invariably sensed that their rule was relatively archaic in form, fragile and artificial in its psychological foundation, unable to stand comparison or contact with political systems of Western countries. For this reason they have always feared foreign penetration, feared direct contact between Western world and their own, feared what would happen if Russians learned truth about world without or if foreigners learned truth about world within. And they have learned to seek security only in patient but deadly struggle for total destruction of rival power, never in compacts and compromises with it.

It was no coincidence that Marxism, which had smouldered ineffectively for half a century in Western Europe, caught hold and blazed for first time in Russia. Only in this land which had never known a friendly neighbor or indeed any tolerant equilibrium of separate powers, either internal or international, could a doctrine thrive which viewed economic conflicts of society as insoluble by peaceful means. After establishment of Bolshevist regime, Marxist dogma, rendered even more truculent and intolerant by Lenin's interpretation, became a perfect vehicle for sense of insecurity with which Bolsheviks, even more than previous Russian rulers, were afflicted. In this dogma, with its basic altruism of purpose, they found justification for their instinctive fear of outside world, for the dictatorship without which they did not know how to rule, for cruelties they did not dare not to inflict, for sacrifices they felt bound to demand. In the name of Marxism they sacrificed every single ethical value in their methods and tactics. Today they cannot dispense with it. It is the fig leaf of their moral and intellectual respectability. Without it they would stand before history, at best, as only the last of that long succession of cruel and wasteful Russian rulers who have relentlessly forced country on to ever new heights of military power in order to guarantee external security of their internally weak regimes. This is why Soviet purposes must always be solemnly clothed in trappings of Marxism, and why no one should underrate importance of dogma in Soviet affairs. Thus Soviet leaders are driven [by?] necessities of their own past and present position to put forward a dogma which [apparent omission] outside world as evil, hostile and menacing, but as bearing within itself germs of creeping disease and destined to be wracked with growing internal convulsions until it is given final *coup de grace* by rising power of socialism and yields to new and better world. This thesis provides justification for that increase of military and police power of Russian state, for that isolation of Russian population from outside world, and for that fluid and constant pressure to extend limits of Russian police power which are together the natural and instinctive urges of Russian rulers. Basically this is only the steady advance of uneasy Russian nationalism, a centuries old movement in which conceptions of offense and defense are inextricably confused. But in new guise of international Marxism, with its honeyed promises to a desperate and war torn outside world, it is more dangerous and insidious than ever before.

It should not be thought from above that Soviet party line is necessarily disingenuous and insincere on part of all those who put it forward. Many of them are too ignorant of outside world and mentally too dependent to question [apparent omission] self-hypnotism, and who have no difficulty making themselves believe what they find it comforting and convenient to believe. Finally we have the unsolved mystery as to who, if anyone, in this great land actually receives accurate and unbiased information about the outside world. In atmosphere of oriental secretiveness and conspiracy which pervades this government, possibilities for distorting or poisoning sources and currents of information are infinite. The very disrespect of Russians for objective truth—indeed, their disbelief in its existence—leads them to view all stated facts as instruments for furtherance of one ulterior purpose or another. There is good reason to suspect that this Government is actually a conspiracy within a conspiracy; and I for one am reluctant to believe that Stalin himself receives anything like an objective picture of outside world. Here there is ample scope for the type of subtle intrigue at which Russians are past masters. Inability of foreign governments to place their case squarely before Russian policy makers—extent to which they are delivered up in their relations with Russia to good graces of obscure and unknown advisers whom they never see and cannot influence—this to my mind is most disquieting feature of diplomacy in Moscow, and one which Western statesmen would do well to keep in mind if they would understand nature of difficulties encountered here. . . .

Soviet policy, as Department implies in its query under reference, is conducted on two planes: (1) official plane represented by actions undertaken officially in name of Soviet Government; and (2) subterranean plane of actions undertaken by agencies for which Soviet Government does not admit responsibility.

. . . On official plane we must look for following:

(a) Internal policy devoted to increasing in every way strength and prestige of Soviet state: intensive military-industrialization; maximum development of armed forces; great displays to impress outsiders; continued secretiveness about internal matters, designed to conceal weakness and to keep opponents in dark.

(b) Wherever it is considered timely and promising, efforts will be made to advance official limits of Soviet power. For the moment, these efforts are restricted to certain neighboring points conceived of here as being of immediate strategic necessity, such as Northern Iran, Turkey, possibly Bornholm. However, other points may at any time come into question, if and as concealed Soviet political power is extended to new areas. Thus a "friendly" Persian Government might be asked to grant Russia a port on the Persian Gulf. Should Spain fall under Communist control, question of Soviet base at Gibraltar Strait might be activated. But such claims will appear on official level only when unofficial preparation is complete.

(c) Russians will participate officially in international organizations where they see opportunity of extending Soviet power or of inhibiting or diluting power of others. Moscow sees in UNO [United Nations Organization] not the mechanism for a permanent and stable world society founded on mutual interest and aims of all nations, but an area in which aims just mentioned can be favorably pursued. As long as UNO is considered here to serve this purpose, Soviets will remain with it. But if at any time they come to conclusion that it is serving to embarrass or frustrate their aims for power expansion and if they see better prospects for pursuit of these aims along other lines, they will not hesitate to abandon UNO. . . . I reiterate, Moscow has no abstract devotion to UNO ideals. Its attitude to that organization will remain essentially pragmatic and tactical.

(d) Toward colonial areas and backward or dependent peoples, Soviet policy, even on official plane, will be directed toward weakening of power and influence and contacts of advanced Western nations, on theory that in so far as this policy is successful, there will be created a vacuum which will favor Communist-Soviet penetration. Soviet pressure for participation in trusteeship arrangements thus represents, in my opinion, a desire to be in a position to complicate and inhibit exertion of Western influence at such points rather than to provide major channel for exerting of Soviet power. . . .

(e) Russians will strive energetically to develop Soviet representation in, and official ties with, countries in which they sense strong possibilities of opposition to Western centers of power. . . .

(f) In international economic matters, Soviet policy will really be dominated by pursuit of autarchy for Soviet Union and Soviet-dominated adjacent areas taken together. . . .

(g) With respect to cultural collaboration, lip service will likewise be rendered to desirability of deepening cultural contacts between peoples, but this will not in practice be interpreted in any way which could weaken security position of Soviet peoples. . . .

(h) Beyond this, Soviet official relations will take what might be called "correct" course with individual foreign governments, with great stress being laid on prestige of Soviet Union and its representatives and with punctilious attention to protocol, as distinct from good manners. . . .

Agencies utilized for promulgation of policies on this plane are following:

1. Inner central core of Communist Parties in other countries. While many of persons who compose this category may also appear and act in unrelated public capacities, they are in reality working closely together as an underground operating directorate of world communism, a concealed Comintern [Communist International] tightly coordinated and directed by Moscow. It is important to remember that this inner core is actually working on underground lines, despite legality of parties with which it is associated.

2. Rank and file of Communist Parties. . . . Whereas formerly foreign Communist Parties represented a curious (and from Moscow's standpoint often inconvenient) mixture of conspiracy and legitimate activity, now the conspiratorial element has been neatly concentrated in inner circle and ordered underground, while rank and file—no longer even taken into confidence about realities of movement—are thrust forward as bona fide internal partisans of certain political tendencies within their respective countries, genuinely innocent of conspiratorial connection with foreign states. Only in certain countries where communists are numerically strong do they now regularly appear and act as a body. As a rule they are used to penetrate, and to influence or dominate, as case may be, other organizations less likely to be suspected of being tools of Soviet Government. . . .

3. A wide variety of national associations or bodies which can be dominated or influenced by such penetration. These include: labor unions, youth leagues, women's organizations, racial societies, religious societies, social organizations, cultural groups, liberal magazines, publishing houses, etc.

4. International organizations which can be similarly penetrated through influence over various national components. Labor, youth and women's organizations are prominent among them. Particular, almost vital, importance is attached in this connection to international labor movement. In this, Moscow sees possibility of sidetracking western governments in world affairs and building up international lobby capable of compelling governments to take actions favorable to Soviet interests in various countries and of paralyzing actions disagreeable to USSR.

5. Russian Orthodox Church, with its foreign branches, and through it the Eastern Orthodox Church in general.

6. Pan-Slav movement and other movements (Azerbaijan, Armenian, Turcoman, etc.) based on racial groups within Soviet Union.

7. Governments or governing groups willing to lend themselves to Soviet purposes in one degree or another, such as present Bulgarian and Yugoslav Governments, North Persian regime, Chinese Communists, etc. Not only propaganda machines but actual policies of these regimes can be placed extensively at disposal of USSR.

It may be expected that component parts of this far-flung apparatus will be utilized, in accordance with their individual suitability, as follows:

(a) To undermine general political and strategic potential of major western powers. Efforts will be made in such countries to disrupt national self confidence, to hamstring measures of national defense, to increase social and industrial unrest, to stimulate all forms of disunity. All persons with grievances, whether economic or racial, will be urged to seek redress not in mediation and compromise, but in defiant violent struggle for destruction of other elements of society. Here poor will be set against rich, black against white, young against old, newcomers against established residents, etc.

(b) On unofficial plane particularly violent efforts will be made to weaken power and influence of Western Powers of [on] colonial backward, or dependent peoples. On this level, no holds will be barred. Mistakes and weaknesses of western colonial administration will be mercilessly exposed and exploited. Liberal opinion in Western countries will be mobilized to weaken colonial policies. Resentment among dependent peoples will be stimulated. And while latter are being encouraged to seek independence of Western Powers, Soviet-dominated puppet political machines will be undergoing preparation to take over domestic power in respective colonial areas when independence is achieved.

(c) Where individual governments stand in path of Soviet purposes pressure will be brought for their removal from office. . . .

(d) In foreign countries Communists will, as a rule, work toward destruction of all forms of personal independence, economic, political or moral. Their system can handle only individuals who have been brought into complete dependence on higher power. Thus, persons who are financially independent—such as individual businessmen, estate owners, successful farmers, artisans and all those who exercise local leadership or have local prestige, such as popular local clergymen or political figures, are anathema. It is not by chance that even in USSR local officials are kept constantly on move from one job to another, to prevent their taking root.

(e) Everything possible will be done to set major Western Powers against each other. Anti-British talk will be plugged among Americans, anti-American talk among the British. Continentals, including Germans, will be taught to abhor both Anglo-Saxon powers. Where suspicions exist, they will be fanned; where not, ignited. . . .

(f) In general, all Soviet efforts on unofficial international plane will be negative and destructive in character, designed to tear down sources of strength beyond reach of Soviet control. This is only in line with basic Soviet instinct that there can be no compromise with rival power and that constructive work can start only when Communist power is dominant. But behind all this will be applied insistent, unceasing pressure for penetration and command of key positions in administration and especially in police apparatus of foreign countries. The Soviet regime is a police regime par excellence, reared in the dim half world of Tsarist police intrigue, accustomed to think primarily in terms of police power. This should never be lost sight of in gauging Soviet motives. . . .

In summary, we have here a political force committed fanatically to the belief that with US there can be no permanent *modus vivendi*, that it is desirable and necessary that the internal harmony of our society be disrupted, our traditional way of life be destroyed, the international authority of our state be broken, if Soviet power is to be secure. . . .

. . . I would like to record my conviction that problem is within our power to solve—and that without recourse to any general military conflict. And in support of this conviction there are certain observations of a more encouraging nature I should like to make:

(1) Soviet power, unlike that of Hitlerite Germany, is neither schematic nor adventuristic. It does not work by fixed plans. It does not take unnecessary risks. Impervious to logic of reason, and it is highly sensitive to logic of force. For this reason it can easily withdraw—and usually does—when strong resistance is encountered at any point. Thus, if the adversary has sufficient force and makes clear his readiness to use it, he rarely has to do so. If situations are properly handled there need be no

prestige-engaging showdowns.

(2) Gauged against Western World as a whole, Soviets are still by far the weaker force. Thus, their success will really depend on degree of cohesion, firmness and vigor which Western World can muster. And this is factor which it is within our power to influence.

(3) Success of Soviet system, as form of internal power, is not yet finally proven. It has yet to be demonstrated that it can survive supreme test of successive transfer of power from one individual or group to another. . . . Soviet internal system will now be subjected, by virtue of recent territorial expansions, to series of additional strains which once proved severe tax on Tsardom. We here are convinced that never since termination of civil war have mass of Russian people been emotionally farther removed from doctrines of Communist Party than they are today. In Russia, party has now become a great and—for the moment—highly successful apparatus of dictatorial administration, but it has ceased to be a source of emotional inspiration. Thus, internal soundness and permanence of movement need not yet be regarded as assured.

(4) All Soviet propaganda beyond Soviet security sphere is basically negative and destructive. It should therefore be relatively easy to combat it by any intelligent and really constructive program.

For these reasons I think we may approach calmly and with good heart problem of how to deal with Russia. As to how this approach should be made, I only wish to advance, by way of conclusion, following comments:

(1) Our first step must be to apprehend, and recognize for what it is, the nature of the movement with which we are dealing. We must study it with same courage, detachment, objectivity, and same determination not to be emotionally provoked or unseated by it, with which doctor studies unruly and unreasonable individual.

(2) We must see that our public is educated to realities of Russian situation. I cannot over-emphasize importance of this. Press cannot do this alone. It must be done mainly by Government, which is necessarily more experienced and better informed on practical problems involved. In this we need not be deterred by [ugliness?] of picture. I am convinced that there would be far less hysterical anti-Sovietism in our country today if realities of this situation were better understood by our people. . . .

(3) Much depends on health and vigor of our own society. World communism is like malignant parasite which feeds only on diseased tissue. This is point at which domestic and foreign policies meet. Every courageous and incisive measure to solve internal problems of our own society, to improve self-confidence, discipline, morale, and community service of our own people, is a diplomatic victory over Moscow worth a thousand diplomatic notes and joint communiqués. . . .

(4) We must formulate and put forward for other nations a much more positive and constructive picture of sort of world we would like to see than we have put forward in past. It is not enough to urge people to develop political process similar to our own. Many foreign peoples, in Europe at least, are tired and frightened by experiences of past, and are less interested in abstract freedom than in security. They are seeking guidance rather than responsibilities. We should be better able than Russians to give them this. And unless we do, Russians certainly will.

(5) Finally we must have courage and self-confidence to cling to our own methods and conceptions of human society. After all, the greatest danger that can befall us in coping with this problem of Soviet communism, is that we shall allow ourselves to become like those with whom we are coping.

Document 2

Clark M. Clifford, "American Relations with the Soviet Union," Sept. 24, 1946, Conway File, Truman Library, Independence, Missouri, 1–79.

Their basic policies, domestic and foreign, are designed to strengthen the Soviet Union and to insure its victory in the predicted coming struggle between Communism and Capitalism.

Generalissimo [Joseph] Stalin and his associates are preparing for the clash by many means, all of them designed to increase the power of the Soviet Union. They are assuring its internal stability through the isolation of its citizens from foreign influences and by maintaining strict police controls. They are supporting armed forces stronger than those of any potential combination of foreign powers and they are developing as rapidly as possible a powerful and self-sufficient economy. They are seizing every opportunity to expand the area, directly or indirectly, under Soviet control in order to provide additional protection for the vital areas of the Soviet Union. The Kremlin seeks to prevent the formation of any combination of foreign powers possibly hostile to the Soviet Union by insisting [on] Soviet participation, with veto power, in any international organization affecting Soviet interest, and by discouraging through intimidation or otherwise the formation of regional blocs or other international associations which do not include the U.S.S.R. Every opportunity to foment antagonisms among foreign powers is exploited, and the unity and strength of other nations is undermined by discrediting their leadership, stirring up domestic discord, and inciting colonial unrest. . . .

The Soviet Government, in developing the theme of "encirclement," maintains continuous propaganda for domestic consumption regarding the dangerously aggressive intentions of American "atom diplomacy" and British imperialism, designed to arouse in the Soviet people fear and suspicion of all capitalistic nations.

Despite the fact that the Soviet Government believes in the inevitability of a conflict with the capitalist world and prepares for that conflict by building up its own strength and undermining that of other nations, its leaders want to postpone the conflict for many years. The western powers are still too strong, the U.S.S.R. is still too weak. Soviet officials must therefore not provoke, by their policies of expansion and aggression, too strong a reaction by other powers. . . .

The key to an understanding of current Soviet foreign policy, in summary, is the realization that Soviet leaders adhere to the Marxian theory of ultimate destruction of capitalist states to postpone the inevitable conflict in order to strengthen and prepare the Soviet Union for its clash with the western democracies. . . .

The Soviet Union regards control of Europe east of the general line from Stettin to Trieste as essential to its preset security. It will tolerate no revival influence in that region and it will insist on the maintenance there of "friendly" governments, that is, governments willing to accept Soviet domination. . . .

The Soviet Union's main concern regarding the other nations of western Europe is to prevent the formation of a Western Bloc. It will also, of course, encourage the growth of local communist parties.

The Near East is an area of great strategic interest to the Soviet Union because of the shift of Soviet industry to southeastern Russia, within range of air attack from much of the Near East, and because of the resources of the area. The Soviet Union is interested in obtaining the withdrawal of British troops from Greece and the establishment of a "friendly" government there. It hopes to make Turkey a puppet state which could serve as a springboard for the domination of the eastern Mediterranean. It is trying by diplomatic means to establish itself in the Dodecanese and Tripolitania and it already has a foothold in the Mediterranean through its close alliances with Albania and Yugoslavia.

The U.S.S.R. is attempting to form along its Middle Eastern frontier a protective zone of politically subordinate states incapable of hostile action against it and it is seeking, at the same time, to acquire for its own use in those states ports and waterways, pipelines and oilfields. It wishes to ensure continued indirect control of Azerbaijan and northern Iran, and the withdrawal, or reduction, of British military strength and influence in Arab states. The U.S.S.R. is playing both sides of the Jewish situation by encouraging and abetting the emigration of Jews from Europe into Palestine, by denouncing British and American Jewish policies, and by inflaming the Arabs against these policies. The long-range Soviet aim is the economic, military and political domination of the entire Middle East. . . .

The most obvious Soviet threat to American security is the growing ability of the U.S.S.R. to wage an offensive war against the United States. This has not hitherto been possible, in the absence of Soviet long-range strategic air power and an almost total lack of sea power. Now, however, the U.S.S.R. is rapidly developing elements of her military strength which she hitherto lacked and which will give the Soviet Union great offensive capabilities. Stalin has declared his intention of sparing no effort to build up the military strength of the Soviet Union. Development of atomic weapons, guided missiles, materials for biological warfare, a strategic air force, submarines of great cruising range, naval mines and minecraft, to name the most important, are extending the effective range of Soviet military power well into areas which the United States regards as vital to its security. . . .

Although the Soviet Union at the present moment is precluded from military aggression beyond the land mass of Eurasia, the acquisition of a strategic air force, naval forces and atomic bombs in quantity would give the U.S.S.R. the capability of striking anywhere on the globe. Ability to wage aggressive warfare in any area of the world is the ultimate goal of Soviet military policy. . . .

As long as the Soviet Government maintains its present foreign policy, based upon the theory of an ultimate struggle between Communism and Capitalism, the United States must assume that the U.S.S.R. might fight at any time for the twofold purpose of expanding the territory under communist control and weakening its potential capitalist opponents. The Soviet Union was able to flow into the political vacuum of the Balkans, Eastern Europe, the Near East, Manchuria and Korea because no other nation was both willing and able to prevent it. Soviet leaders were encouraged by easy success and they are now preparing "for any eventuality.". . .

The main deterrent to Soviet attack on the United States, or to attack on areas of the world which are vital to our security, will be the military power of this country. It must be made apparent to the Soviet Government that our strength will be sufficient to repel any attack and sufficient to defeat the U.S.S.R. decisively if a war should start. The prospect of defeat is the only sure means of deterring the Soviet Union.

The Soviet Union's vulnerability is limited due to the vast area over which its key industries and natural resources are widely dispersed, but it is vulnerable to atomic weapons, biological warfare, and long-range air power. Therefore, in order to maintain our strength at a level which will be effective in restraining the Soviet Union, the United States must be prepared to wage atomic and biological warfare. A highly mechanized army, which can be moved either by sea or by air, capable of seizing and holding strategic areas, must be supported by powerful naval and air forces. A war with the U.S.S.R. would be "total" in a more horrible sense than any previous war and there must be constant research for both offensive and defensive weapons. . . .

. . .The mere fact of preparedness may be the only powerful deterrent to Soviet aggressive action and in this sense the only sure guaranty of peace. . . .

Our policies must also be global in scope. . . .

In conclusion, as long as the Soviet Government adheres to its present policy, the United States should maintain military forces powerful enough to restrain the Soviet Union and to confine Soviet influence to its present area. All nations not now within the Soviet sphere should be given generous economic assistance and political support in their opposition to Soviet penetration. Economic aid may also be given to the Soviet Government and private trade with the U.S.S.R. permitted provided the results are beneficial to our interests and do not simply strengthen the Soviet program. We should continue to work for cultural and intellectual understanding between the United States and the Soviet Union but that does not mean that, under the guise of an exchange program, communist subversion and infiltration in the United States will be tolerated. In order to carry out an effective policy toward the Soviet Union, the United States Government should coordinate its own activities, inform and instruct the American people about the Soviet Union, and enlist their support based upon knowledge and confidence. These actions by the United States are necessary before we shall be able to achieve understanding and accord with the Soviet Government on any terms other than its own.

Document 3

Lieutenant General Stylianos Kitrilakis, Greek General Staff, "A Survey of the War Against the Bandits in Greece," Mar. 8, 1948, Plans and Operations 091 Greece, section IX, case 129, Record Group 319, Army Staff Records, Modern Military Division, National Archives, Washington, D.C., 1–9.

I. General Characteristics of the Anti-Bandit Campaign

The war which Greece has been fighting for the last two years is unconventional, many-sided and simultaneously civil and international.

1. From a military point-of-view it is an *unconventional* war, because it is carried out by the unorthodox methods of guerilla warfare. Such methods were successfully employed against the invading armies during the occupation of the Country, being particularly adapted to the Greek terrain. It is true that during the enemy occupation the partisans were greatly assisted, both morally and materially, by the civil population. But it is unfortunately equally true that the bandits of today are also assisted by a significant part of the population. This may be explained by the following facts:

a. If one were to assume that about

ten percent of the voting population is made up of political sympathizers of communism, and, further, that about one fifth of this number is made up of persons who follow the KKE [Greek Communist Party] line consciously and actively, one is bound to reach the conclusion that there must be about 150,000 persons in Greece (including the women and minor males who are impressed into the guerilla ranks) who may be regarded as forming the reserve and potential army of the bandits in Greece.

b. In addition, there is a considerable number of people who, though not deliberate communists themselves, are nevertheless so confused in their ideological thinking as to be regarded, for all practical purposes, as actual supporters of the bandits. They are the so-called fellow-travellers of Greece.

c. Because of fear, a great part of the rural population maintains a passive attitude towards the bandits and not only fails to join the struggle against them, but even refuses to supply the Greek Army with intelligence.

d. No serious attempt has yet been made officially to rouse the population wholeheartedly against the enemy; the present war has not yet been described as a *real* war and as one waged, not against a few co-nationals, but against an alien enemy.

2. This war is also peculiarly *many-sided*, being carried out simultaneously in several fields.

a. In the political and economic fields an attempt is made by the enemy to create confusion in the minds of the people by means of a great variety of slogans and to present its campaign as a struggle of democracy against fascism and imperialism and as a popular crusade for social justice.

b. In the economic field, a systematic effort is made by the enemy to increase the misery of the people and to bring about economic chaos through material destruction of all sorts and by compelling large masses of people to abandon their homes in order to swell the numbers of government-supported refugees.

c. In the moral field, the enemy conducts, both at home and abroad, a well-organized propaganda campaign against this country through various organizations and agencies which are, as a rule, carefully camouflaged and which are in fact protected by the laws of the Greek State.

d. Finally, the enemy seeks to corrode the very foundations of the State itself through infiltration into its administrative machinery. Communists, fellow-travellers and individuals who act to this end through levity of character or political ambition constitute the secret army of the enemy's agents and informers who, from official positions, do untold damage to the national effort in various underground ways.

3. This war is also *both civil and international.*

a. It is waged by foreign powers without a formal declaration of war with the result that the instigating powers do not have to bear any of the responsibilities of belligerency.

b. The small but ruthless minority of the population which is actually carrying on this war can use the entire territory of Greece as a theatre of operations; owing to the peculiar character of the campaign, it can maintain the initiative and refuse to accept battle; it can launch raids against any vulnerable point in the country; and, being unrestricted by obedience to law or moral principle, can terrorize the population into providing information.

c. The enemy is greatly assisted morally not only by a well-organized campaign that aims at defaming any measure of defence of the State against its enemies, but, what is more, by the very laws of the State itself. The production of legal and legalistic evidence against the evil-doers is extremely difficult under the circumstances, while their persecution without adequate legal proof is trumpeted at home and abroad as arbitrary and undemocratic. In times of war, it is customary for those who are known to sympathize with the foreign enemy to be arrested and interned; it is usually considered unnecessary to the authorities to establish guilt of active participation on behalf of the enemy. But in Greece at present the law requires that a person should be legally proved guilty of actually taking part in subversive activities against the State before law proceedings can be instituted against him. The enemy may in fact now use at his ease and convenience all the protection offered by the peace-time laws of a democracy that were enacted for an entirely different type of transgressor. . . .

II. Methods and Means Used by the Guerillas

The agencies used by the communists for the purpose of subjugating Greece are (1) the guerilla army, which is daily becoming better organized and which operates *overtly* in the mountainous districts, and (2) the secret army of communists in the cities, towns and villages of Greece, which operates *covertly*.

1. The overt armed forces of communism; Its Agencies, Task, Methods and Tactics.

In spite of the heavy losses which the guerillas suffered in the course of the year 1947, it is estimated that their army numbers about 25,000 men today as compared with 15,000 which it numbered last spring. This increase is to be explained chiefly by their method of forcibly impressing individuals into their ranks in the districts they control. The brutal methods of coercion used by the bandits render the morale of such forcibly recruited personnel of no account.

The food necessary to the bandits is secured by them through the pillaging of villages.

Military equipment is supplied from abroad in steadily increasing quantities, as is provided by the fact that the bandits are using artillery and other heavy weapons on a constantly increasing scale. It is to be expected that this external source of supply will remain inexhaustible as long as Greece's northern neighbors wish the activities of the guerillas to continue in Greece; it is also to be expected that the numerical strength of the guerillas will increase in the future.

The guerillas know only too well that they would be crushed were they to attempt to face the Greek army and to give a decisive battle. Consequently, their aim is not to defeat the Greek Army in organized battle array. Their aim is to maintain anarchy in the country and to aggravate the misery of the people by constantly making such raids and attacks as would be of the maximum damage to the country and of a minimum wastage to themselves. . . .

a. The guerillas have concentrated the main part of their forces along Greece's northern frontiers. This enables them (1) to secure hospitalization and supplies in the neighbouring territories; (2) to retreat safely into the neighbouring countries, whenever pursued by the Greek Army, and to get reorganized and reinforced there, and (3) acting through the neighbouring territories in absolute security, to undertake wide surprise manoeuvres against the Greek Army; the latter lacks any such freedom of movements as it is constantly cautioned against even approaching the border for more general reasons.

b. In addition, the guerillas have established armed bands in the interior of the country. . . . These bands are distributed in localities naturally favored by the configuration of the terrain. Through these bands, the communists seek (1) to maintain disorder within the country by pillaging, sabotage, demolition of plants and technical works, attacks against lines of communication and raids against towns, and (2) forcibly to recruit new guerillas for the purpose of replacing casualties or of forming new bands. The methods applied by these bands are those employed by highway brigands. Small mobile bands operating on the Greek mountains, almost all parts of which are accessible, act by surprise and avoid clashes with the Army by taking refuge in hidden lairs on the steep summits.

c. The bandit army can operate in this manner only because it can rely for its activities on the communist organization operating within the country. More specifically, it relies on the so-called "self-defence" units as well as on the various other supplying agencies which camouflage their activities under respectable sounding titles. As is well known, there is no inhabited locality, no matter how small, which does not have a "self-defence" unit. Such a unit (1) provides the bands with the necessary intelligence with regard to movements of troops, order of battle, identification of loyalist citizens, activities of local authorities, etc. (informers); (2) supplies the bands with food (provisioners); (3) is in charge of laying mines at the appropriate place and time (saboteurs); and (4) has the responsibility of recruiting new guerillas, of dispatching them to the bands and of making arrangements for forcible recruiting (recruiting officers). It would hardly be an exaggeration to state that without these "self-defence" units, not merely the activities, but the very subsistence of the bands would become extremely problematical, if not wholly impossible. Accordingly, these units must be mercilessly exterminated by any possible means first and foremost before the bandits can be effectively crushed. Their annihilation is an essential prerequisite to victory.

2. The covert forces of communism.

Around these self-defence units a whole secret army, infinitely more numerous than the total of bands operating on the mountains, is active in the rear of the regular Greek forces and especially in the large urban centres.

a. The following agencies exist in such urban centres: (1) Important centres comprising the political and military leadership of the bands as well as centres of intelligence which supply the bands with information of all kinds, (2) centres for the collection of funds and supplies of all sorts for the benefit of the guerillas as well as recruiting centres, both types following the methods employed by the E.A.M. [Greek Communist resistance] during the occupation, (3) centres of propaganda of an insidiously deceitful and diabolically artful sort that aims at undermining the confidence of the loyalist population, at suggesting that the struggle is futile, and at presenting the rebellion as a democratic movement, (4) centres of communist instruction and "enlightenment" employed for the purpose of neutralizing any measure taken by the State that might impede the aims of communism.

b. As agents employed for the aforesaid tasks are used (1) individuals from all social classes and professionals who follow the K.K.E. line blindly, (2) persons in the pay of the communists, and (3) fellow-travellers who support the bandits either because they have misinterpreted socialism or because they have chosen to play a double game for reasons of political opportunism or of personal interest or security.

c. Such individuals of all three categories unfortunately exist even within the state machinery and sometimes occupy positions of vital importance, both in the capital and in the provinces. They constitute that mysterious force so often responsible for certain characteristic administrative lapses, and unexplainable cases of inertness, procrastination and irregularity. Thus, (1) secret documents reach the bandit command before they reach their own addressees, (2) draft measures against the bandits and mere intentions of the administration come to the bandits' knowledge not merely before their implementation but even before they are formulated into decisions, and (3) important information regarding impending secret moves or intentions of the communists is somewhere drowned mysteriously without ever reaching its destination.

III. Ways of Overcoming the Guerillas

It is obvious that just as communism is attacking the Greek State on all sides and in manifold ways, in the same manner must the State react if it is to crush militant communism both in the mountains and in the rear of the Army.

1. The campaign against the armed guerillas of the mountains.

Since the guerillas are divided into two distinct groups, each group having its own objectives, methods and tactics, it follows that the methods to be employed by the Army in facing them must also be of two general types. As was stated above, one of the two groups controls a strip of territory along the northern frontier. Being organized in a military manner and being effectively equipped and regularly supplied, this group is in a position to put up an effective defence, especially along the Greek-Albanian frontier, to any move on the part of the Army. What is more, it is in a position to assume the initiative and to act offensively, as was demonstrated by the attack on Konitsa, its chief objective being to put under its control an inhabited locality of some size to be used as the "capital" of Marco's [General Markos Vafiadis] hunta. It would be an error to assume that the bandits would not attempt a similar move in the future; if anything at all, the attempt should be expected to be stronger than any previous one.

In other words, this first group acts as a regular army on terrain that has been previously well organized. It is considerably well equipped, having recently been supplied with artillery as well. It is to be expected that this group will keep getting gradually stronger in material unless, of course, Greece's northern neighbors were to decide to stop supporting it. Consequently, the Army facing this group must adapt their methods to those of the enemy, especially as concerns fieldcraft, mobility, manoeuvring ability and aggressive spirit, the objective being the complete cleaning up of all such territory along the frontier as is now under bandit control. To this end, an adequate number of troops, equipped with heavy weapons and artillery, will be required. In particularly wooded and ravined areas relatively larger forces will be needed. Moreover, for a district to be regarded as having been actually cleaned up, the purely operational movements, even when successful, would not suffice. If would be essential for all or part of the troops undertaking the operation to remain in occupation of the district for some time for the purpose of completely combing the area in order to clean it up of any bandit remnants and to discover stores and dumps which the guerillas are known carefully to camouflage in all areas which they have held for some time. Furthermore, measures must be taken by the Army to prevent the recontamination of the area before the responsibility for order is turned over to the public security forces.

The second group consists of guerillas in the interior of the country operating by bands in the manner of highway brigands. Some of the regular forces dealing with them will have to assume the responsibility of guarding certain vulnerable points, such as plants and urban centres, while other forces will have to undertake the task of exterminating these bands by using more or less the same methods now used by the guerillas. Acting as speed columns, they will have to move rapidly and by surprise; to go in search of the bandits instead of waiting for the bandits to come to them; to move by night; to pursue the bandit mercilessly wherever he may decide to flee until they manage to inspire him with terror and with the feeling that there is no place in the country where he may stay in safety by night or by day.

2. The campaign against the enemy in the "rear" of the Army.

The campaign against the corrosive effects of communists in the inhabited areas in the rear of the Army must be vigorous, courageous, and effective. No half-measures are adequate. Attempts at camouflaging urban banditry should not be tolerated. Ideas and principles should be respected in a democratic society but it would be suicidal on the part of a democratic state to allow its enemies to take advantage of the civic liberties it offers in order to destroy these very liberties. The campaign in the rear of the Army must be conducted as part of a war against a foreign enemy. The fact that the bandits and their fellow-travellers were born in Greece and speak the Greek language does not make them Greeks. What distinguishes a person as belonging to a nationality is his way of thinking, feeling and acting. Whoever, for any reason whatsoever, acts against his Nation in order to further foreign designs is a traitor and must be treated as such regardless of his ideology. In this sense, the bandit war in Greece is not a civil war; it is a foreign war since foreigners are fomenting it.

From a purely military point-of-view, the organization of the country's defence against its internal enemies is of primary importance. To prevent a possible collapse of the internal front, it is necessary to organize the internal front effectively, now, for the effect of such a collapse on the Army would be fatal. It should not escape our notice that the troops at the front are already experiencing a painful anxiety, wondering why the fifth column inside the country is allowed to pursue its activities at the expense of the fighting army. Such wonderings are not conducive to the keeping up of an army's morale. Countries that were much stronger than Greece have been known to collapse because of such unforgivable tolerance and ineffective organization in the rear.

Consequently, it is essential to the life of Greece as a nation that the internal front be completely and immediately cleared of any communist danger. Were the internal front to collapse, the country's armed resistance would also automatically collapse with the result that Greece's territorial integrity and political independence would be faced with a hideous fait accompli. Conversely it is to be hoped that a safe rear would permit the army to keep up its resistance until world public opinion is finally formed.

That it is vitally necessary for the internal front to be urgently organized is further shown by the following considerations:

a. There is no coordination among the various state services which are directly concerned with internal security.

b. It has not been fully realized yet that Greece is at war and that in times of war every other consideration should give way to the war effort and to the exigency of victory at any cost. The ordinary citizen has not been made to realize yet that his attitude towards those who for any reason are in sympathy with the bandits or who fail to participate in the fight against communism should be the attitude of a citizen towards enemy agents inside his country in time of war.

c. The press has not been encouraged to cooperate fully in the effort to enlighten the people. For lack of such encouragement the leading classes have likewise failed to take a firm stand. This abstinence is regarded by some people as indifference in the face of an unprecedented national emergency while others look upon it as overcautious in a desire to play safe.

d. As compared with the enemy's voluminous and highly organized propaganda against Greece at home and abroad, no systematic effort has been made to inform public opinion in Greece and abroad of the justice of Greece's cause, of her sacrifices in the interests of world democracy and of the complex elements that enter into a war against guerillas in the mountains and communists in the towns. The "sensational" news that some foreign correspondents delight in selling to their newspapers sometimes show no regard for truth.

Document 4

Memorandum for President Harry S. Truman from Rear Admiral in the U.S. Navy and Director of Central Intelligence R. H. Hillenkoetter, Jan. 2, 1948, Central Intelligence Group, President's Secretary's File, Truman Papers, Truman Library, Independence, Missouri.

The formation on 24 December [1947] of the "Provisional Democratic Government of Free Greece" is the first of several successive steps which the USSR could take to gain control in Greece. The announcement of the new Government could be followed in turn by (1) maximum propaganda exploitation of the Markos [Vafiadis] regime with the aim of increasing Greek Communist morale and effectiveness and weakening the resistance of the Greek people and their confidence in the ability of the US-supported Greek Government to achieve victory in the Civil War; (2) recognition of the regime by one or more of the Satellites and increased overt assistance to the guerillas by the Satellites; and (3) Soviet recognition and overt Soviet assistance. Each of these steps would improve Communist capabilities for assuming power in Greece, but they would proportionately involve the Satellites and/or the USSR in increasing risk of US or UN counter-action. . . .

Recognition by one or more of the Satellites would provide a convenient means for increasing reinforcement of the guerrillas both in arms and in personnel. Such aid could be represented by Soviet propaganda as comparable to US aid under the Truman Doctrine. The opportunity afforded for quibbling over which of the two governments is truly representative of the Greek people would enable the USSR to veto application of the UN Charter provisions regarding acts of aggression or threats to peace. Moreover, as a preliminary step, recognition could be accorded by Albania which is neither a member of the UN nor included in the Balkan Peace Treaties and is technically still at war with Greece. Such steps, however, would involve definite risks. A collapse of the Markos regime after it had been recognized would be a damaging blow to international Communist prestige. Recognition by Yugoslavia or Bulgaria might provoke US or UN censure or action. Increased overt Satellite support could conceivably result in such strong Western reaction as to precipitate a general war.

Soviet recognition and direct Soviet military assistance would give the Markos regime its maximum capability for success but such a step would create even graver risks of involving the USSR in war with the West.

It is still not believed that the USSR is prepared to engage in a world war. Therefore it seems probable that the Soviet Union will move cautiously in directing recognition and reinforcement of the guerrilla government. The Kremlin will not place itself in a position from which it cannot easily extricate itself. The Kremlin will move step by step, increasing the Soviet/Satellite commitment as long as (a) it is convinced of the eventual success of the Markos regime; and (b) its estimate of developing Western reaction leads it to believe that further action would not provoke a general war. Under such conditions, this progressive commitment will presumably continue until the USSR is convinced that the next overt step would result in the support of the Greek Government by US troops.

Indication of this cautious approach is to found in the failure to specify the location of the new government, the comparatively scant attention given to its formation by the Moscow press, and the fact that the Satellites have withheld immediate recognition. On the other hand, strong indications that the USSR will order some definite action in support of the new regime are to be noted in the current guerrilla offensive, in increased evidence of military concentrations in Yugoslavia and Albania, and in the tone of Soviet propaganda outside the USSR.

It therefore appears probable that, subject to its estimate of Western reaction, the Kremlin will direct the following steps:

(1) Recognition of the Markos regime by Albania. Albania would then be used as the medium for supplying the guerrillas with arms and personnel from Yugoslavia and Bulgaria. . . .

(2) Increased military aid to the guerrillas including aircraft, heavy artillery, and tanks together with personnel trained to use such technical equipment. The present fighting in Epirus indicates that, while the guerrillas already possess sufficient strength to mount a dangerous local offensive, they will not be able to hold territory in Greece without such equipment and personnel. There is evidence that these reinforcements are already being assembled in southern Yugoslavia and Albania.

(3) Granting of belligerent rights to, or recognition of the Markos regime by Rumania, Yugoslavia, and Bulgaria as a preliminary to direct overt assistance to the guerrillas.

(4) Withhold[ing of] Soviet recognition of the regime until the latter has gained complete control of Greece.

Document 5

The Truman Doctrine, President Harry S. Truman's special message to the Congress on Greece and Turkey, Mar. 12, 1947, *Public Papers of the Presidents of the United States, Harry S. Truman, 1947*, Washington, D.C.: Government Printing Office, 1963, 176–80.

Mr. President, Mr. Speaker, Members of the Congress of the United States. The gravity of the situation which confronts the world today necessitates my appearance before a joint session of the Congress.

The foreign policy and the national security of this country are involved.

One aspect of the present situation, which I wish to present to you at this time for your consideration and decision concerns Greece and Turkey.

The United States has received from the Greek Government an urgent appeal for financial and economic assistance. Preliminary reports from the American Economic Mission now in Greece and reports from the American Ambassador in Greece [Lincoln MacVeagh] corroborate the statement of the Greek

Government that assistance is imperative if Greece is to survive as a free nation.

I do not believe that the American people and the Congress wish to turn a deaf ear to the appeal of the Greek Government.

Greece is not a rich country. Lack of sufficient natural resources has always forced the Greek people to work hard to make both ends meet. Since 1940, this industrious and peace-loving country has suffered invasion, four years of cruel enemy occupation, and bitter internal strife.

When forces of liberation entered Greece they found that the retreating Germans had destroyed virtually all the railways, roads, port facilities, communications, and merchant marine. More than a thousand villages had been burned. Eighty-five percent of the children were tubercular. Livestock, poultry, and draft animals had almost disappeared. Inflation wiped out practically all savings.

As a result of these tragic conditions, a militant minority, exploiting human want and misery, was able to create political chaos which, until now, has made economic recovery impossible.

Greece is today without funds to finance the importation of those goods which are essential to bare existence. Under these circumstances, the people of Greece cannot make progress in solving their problems of reconstruction. Greece is in desperate need of financial and economic assistance to enable it to resume purchases of food, clothing, fuel, and seeds. These are indispensable for the subsistence of its people and are obtainable only from abroad. Greece must have help to import the goods necessary to restore internal order and security so essential for economic and political recovery.

The Greek Government also asked for the assistance of experienced American administrators, economists, and technicians to insure that the financial and other aid given to Greece shall be used effectively in creating a stable self-sustaining economy and in improving its public administration.

The very existence of the Greek state is today threatened by the terrorist activities of several thousand armed men, led by communists, who defy the Government's authority at a number of points, particularly along the northern boundaries. A commission appointed by the United Nations Security Council is at present investigating disturbed conditions in northern Greece, and alleged border violations along the frontier between Greece on the one hand and Albania, Bulgaria, and Yugoslavia on the other.

Meanwhile, the Greek Government is unable to cope with the situation. The Greek Army is small and poorly equipped. It needs supplies and equipment if it is to restore the authority of the Government throughout Greek territory.

Greece must have assistance if it is to become a self-supporting and self-respecting democracy.

The United States must supply that assistance. We already extended to Greece certain types of relief and economic aid, but these are inadequate.

There is no other country to which democratic Greece can turn.

No other nation is willing and able to provide the necessary support for a democratic Greek Government.

The British Government, which has been helping Greece, can give no further financial or economic aid after March 31. Great Britain finds itself under the necessity of reducing or liquidating its commitments in several parts of the world, including Greece.

We considered how the United Nations might assist in this crisis. But the situation is an urgent one requiring immediate action, and the United Nations and its related organizations are not in a position to extend help of the kind that is required.

It is important to note that the Greek Government has asked for our aid in utilizing effectively the financial and other assistance we may give to Greece, and in improving its public administration. It is of the utmost importance that we supervise the use of any funds made available to Greece, in such a manner that each dollar spent will count toward making Greece self-supporting, and will help to build an economy in which a healthy democracy can flourish.

No government is perfect. One of the chief virtues of democracy, however, is that its defects are always visible and under democratic processes can be pointed out and corrected. The government of Greece is not perfect. Nevertheless it represents 85 percent of the members of the Greek Parliament who were chosen in an election last year. Foreign observers, including 692 Americans, considered this election to be a fair expression of the views of the Greek people.

The Greek Government has been operating in an atmosphere of chaos and extremism. It has made mistakes. The extension of aid by this country does not mean that the United States condones everything that the Greek Government has done or will do. We have condemned in the past, and we condemn now, extremist measures of the right or left. We have in the past advised tolerance, and we advise tolerance now.

Greece's neighbor, Turkey, also deserves our attention.

The future of Turkey as an independent and economically sound state is clearly no less important to the freedom-loving peoples of the world than the future of Greece. The circumstances in which Turkey finds itself today are considerably different from those of Greece. Turkey has been spared the disasters that have beset Greece; and during the war, the United States and Great Britain furnished Turkey with material aid. Nevertheless, Turkey now needs our support.

Since the war Turkey has sought financial assistance from Great Britain and the United States for the purpose of effecting that modernization necessary for the maintenance of its national integrity.

That integrity is essential to the preservation of order in the Middle East.

The British Government has informed us that, owing to its own difficulties, it can no longer extend financial or economic aid to Turkey.

As in the case of Greece, if Turkey is to have the assistance it needs, the United States must supply it. We are the only country able to provide that help.

I am fully aware of the broad implications involved if the United States extends assistance to Greece and Turkey, and I shall discuss these implications with you at this time.

One of the primary objectives of the foreign policy of the United States is the creation of conditions in which we and other nations will be able to work out a way of life free from coercion. This was a fundamental issue in the war with Germany and Japan. Our victory was won over countries which sought to impose their will, and their way of life, upon other nations.

To insure the peaceful development of nations, free from coercion, the United States has taken a leading part in establishing the United Nations. The United Nations is designed to make possible lasting freedom and independence for all its members. We shall not realize our objectives, however, unless we are willing to help free peoples to maintain their free institutions and their national integrity against aggressive movements that seek to impose upon them totalitarian regimes. This is no more than a frank recognition that totalitarian regimes imposed on free peoples, by direct or indirect aggression, undermine the foundations of international peace and hence the security of the United States.

The peoples of a number of countries of the world have recently had totalitarian regimes forced upon them against their will. The Government of the United States has made frequent protests against coercion and intimidation, in violation of the Yalta agreement, in Poland, Rumania, and Bulgaria. I must also state that in a number of other countries there have been similar developments.

At the present moment in the world history nearly every nation must choose between alternative ways of life. The choice is too often not a free one.

One way of life is based upon the will of the majority and is distinguished by free institutions, representing government, free elections, guarantees of individual liberty, freedom of speech and religion, and freedom from political oppression.

The second way of life is based upon the will of the minority forcibly imposed upon the majority. It relies on terror and oppression, a controlled press and radio, fixed elections, and the suppression of personal freedoms.

I believe that it must be the policy of the United States to support free peoples who are resisting attempted subjugation by armed minorities or by outside pressures.

I believe that we must assist peoples to work out their own destinies in their own way.

I believe that our help should be primarily through economic and financial aid which is essential to economic stability and orderly political processes.

The world is not static, and the status quo is not sacred. But we cannot allow changes in the status quo in violation of the Charter of the United Nations by such methods as coercion, or by such subterfuges as political infiltration. In helping free and independent nations to maintain their freedom, the United States will be giving effect to the principles of the Charter of the United Nations.

It is necessary only to glance at a map to realize that the survival and integrity of the Greek nation are of grave importance in a much wider situation. If Greece should fall under the control of an armed minority, the effect upon its neighbor Turkey, would be immediate and serious. Confusion and disorder might well spread throughout the entire Middle East.

Moreover, the disappearance of Greece as an independent state would have a profound effect upon those countries in Europe whose peoples are struggling against great difficulties to maintain their freedoms and their independence while they repair the damages of war.

It would be an unspeakable tragedy if these countries, which have struggled so long against overwhelming odds, should lose that victory for which they sacrificed so much. Collapse of free institutions and loss of independence would be disastrous not only for them but for the world. Discouragement and possibly failure would quickly be the lot of neighboring peoples striving to maintain their freedom and independence.

Should we fail to aid Greece and Turkey in this fateful hour, the effect will be far reaching to the West as well as to the East.

We must take immediate and resolute action.

I, therefore, ask the Congress to provide authority for assistance to Greece and Turkey, in the amount of $400,000,000 for the period ending June 30, 1948. In requesting these funds,

I have taken into consideration the maximum amount of relief assistance which would be furnished to Greece out of the $350,000,000 which I recently requested that the Congress authorize for the prevention of starvation and suffering in countries devastated by the war.

In addition to funds, I ask the Congress to authorize the detail of American civilian and military personnel to Greece, and Turkey, at the request of those countries, to assist in the tasks of reconstruction, and for the purpose of supervising the use of such financial and material assistance as may be furnished. I recommend that authority also be provided for the instruction and training of selected Greek and Turkish personnel.

Finally, I ask that the Congress provide authority which will permit the speediest and most effective use, in terms of needed commodities, supplies, and equipment, of such funds as may be authorized.

If further funds, or further authority, should be needed for purposes indicated in this message, I shall not hesitate to bring the situation before the Congress. On this subject the executive and legislative branches . . . must work together.

This is a serious course upon which we embark.

I would not recommend it except that the alternative is much more serious.

The United States contributed $341,000,000,000 toward winning World War II. This is an investment in world freedom and world peace.

The assistance that I am recommending for Greece and Turkey amounts to little more than one-tenth of 1 percent of this investment. It is only common sense that we should safeguard that investment and make sure that it was not in vain.

The seeds of totalitarian regimes are nurtured by misery and want. They spread and grow in the evil soil of poverty and strife. They reach their full growth when the hope of a people for a better life has died.

We must keep that hope alive.

The free peoples of the world look to us for support in maintaining their freedoms.

If we falter in our leadership, we may endanger the peace of the world—and we shall surely endanger the welfare of our own Nation.

Great responsibilities have been placed upon us by the swift movement of events.

I am confident that the Congress will face these responsibilities squarely.

Document 6

General William L. Livesay, director of Joint U.S. Military Advisory Group in Greece, address to U.S. advisers to Greek army, Jan. 16, 1948, Livesay Papers, U.S. Army Military History Institute, Carlisle Military Barracks, Pennsylvania.

The job here in Greece is to quell the riots and establish a stable Greece. This is fundamentally a job for the Greeks; we are not taking over their responsibility; it is still their responsibility; they have the entire responsibility for it. We are to advise them and assist them in every way that we can. It is my belief that the Greek Army reinforced by NDC [National Defense Corps] battalions with equipment we are now giving them and certain increases that they are getting, have that capability if they will get out and do it. It is up to us to assist them, advise them and instill aggressive spirit necessary to accomplish that mission. We are here as representatives of the American Government and no action on our part must be such that it will lower the prestige of the American Government or British Government or, incidentally, the Greek Government. In one sense of the word, in addition to being technical Army officers, we are diplomats and the manner in which we go at our work and present the advice will determine to a large extent the success that we have. Endeavor to develop a technique in giving your advice that the individual Greek officer will think it was his idea in the first place. Not only give advice on how but instill confidence that is necessary for him to have to complete his job. If our manner of giving advice is such that it gives him an inferiority complex, then he will not efficiently command his unit. Your success or failure in your job is going to be determined by what you get the Greek commanders to do. You are not building up a reputation as a unit commander yourself and any success of the Greek commander does not detract from your ability. In other words, if you have an idea, you advise the Greek commander of this idea; he immediately thinks it is his idea—that is fine. If you feel that that was my idea and the way he's taking it and carrying the ball detracts from my prestige, that is the wrong idea. Build up his prestige and the amount and extent to which you do it and his success is a determination of your success as adviser to him. . . .

Give advice freely and firmly but remember that we accept no duty that makes you responsible to the Greek Government and when you give advice, the decision rests with the Greek commander. If you advise a commander to go around the right flank and he says we will go around the left flank, give him your reasons and if you are convinced make a suggestion but make it clear that the decision is his and the results are his responsibility. If he takes your advice all good and well, and if it does not work, it is still his responsibility and in a polite way we must make that clear to him. If he fails consistently to take your advice, let me know. Again remember to handle the thing diplomatically.

You must insist on aggressive action. At the same time almost the entire Greek army is on the defensive; they think in defensive terms. We must instill aggressiveness in them; they must carry the fight to the bandits and not accept wherever the bandits want to fight. . . .

We must remember we are not in a position to demand and it would be futile to try to conform their thinking to our thinking. We are not trying to make an American Army out of the Greek Army; we will do the job with the tools which we have. . . .

The present directive that I have is that in general the advice of the American Group will have to do with logistics and operations leaving to the British Mission their present mission of organization and training. As you know the only purpose of supplying an army with equipment is to let it carry out operations. The only purpose of organizing and training an army is to accomplish successfully its operations so there is no distinct dividing line between logistics, training, organization and operation. It is one integrated unit, and as just as General [Stuart] Rawlins and I are working right together here in Athens, that is the way I visualize our operation in the field. We have certain responsibilities like one man charged with operation but there is no compartmentation. One man carries the ball but I want members of the American Group going up to consult freely and accept advice and suggestions from the British Mission that are there. I am sure that under those conditions we will function as one team carrying on the teamwork that is necessary to accomplish our objective. . . .

In order to give proper advice you will have to go out among the troops and see what is going on. Don't go to Army Headquarters and spend your time but get out among the troops. Go down to battalions and see what they are doing. That is what I have been wanting to do since I have been here but I have been tied up getting supplies in here. In addition to information about your own work, I want to know more about the Greek Army than I do.

The Greek Army is responsible for your protection so when you go out on a trip, let the Greek Commander or his staff know where you are going and why so he will have time to make the necessary arrangements for you to go and arrange your protection. It is a Greek custom that they want to know where everybody is going so always let them know before you make a trip. When you go someplace in a vehicle do not transport any Greek people except your driver and an interpreter. The purpose of that is this. If you are riding a Greek vehicle and taking several Greeks and are ambushed by bandits they have a good talking point if you are riding soldiers. Vehicles will be marked with distinctive markings—tin American Flags—7 x 10—to put on front and back and you will get a written memorandum from me with details and be sure you always ride in these vehicles. Transporting Greeks only applies to trips.

You carry no arms. Your conduct, if you are caught in an operation, is more or less entirely up to you. The thing for you to do is to take cover. You are not armed and you take the best cover you can and see what you can but don't get involved in combat. That is rather a large order but it has a lot for careful consideration. If you get ambushed without arms and take off down the road you will lose prestige among the Greeks so don't give the Greeks the idea you are afraid when you take cover. You are not armed and that is your protection. (He gave an example.) If I were lying in a hole and there was a Greek rifle close to me and I knew a bandit was coming to shoot me, there is not much doubt what I would do. You can be judged in the same way. In the final analysis observe combat but don't get involved in it.

Document 7

Secretary of Defense James V. Forrestal's Memorandum to the National Security Council, Apr. 19, 1948, "Comments on Certain Courses of Action Proposed with Respect to Greece and Answers to Specified Questions Contained in the Memorandum by the Secretary of the National Security Council dated 24 February 1948," Record Group 218, Joint Chiefs of Staff File List 092 Greece (12-30-47), section 2, Modern Military Division, National Archives, Washington, D.C.

In the implementation of the United States policy to assist in maintaining the territorial integrity and political independence of Greece, what should be the assigned missions, estimated strengths and types of forces . . . and to what locations would they be dispatched? What would be the probable effectiveness of such forces? If it should be determined that a United States token armed force . . . is to be dispatched to Greece, it would consist of either a Marine brigade or division or an Army regimental combat team or division, the Marines to be accompanied by supporting Marine aviation and the Army to be accompanied by Air Force support. Token forces, if dispatched, should be assigned the mission of assisting by their presence to stabilize conditions and encourage

Greek resistance to communist efforts while avoiding combat involvement. They should occupy such locations as to make avoidance of combat involvement reasonably practicable. . . .

Ground forces at present available for meeting any or all requirements additional to present commitments are limited to a numerical strength of about four divisions, consisting of three under-strength Army divisions and about two Marine divisions. The Air Force has available air units sufficient in number and strength to gain and maintain air supremacy over the combined air forces of Albania, Yugoslavia and Bulgaria, but insufficient to gain and maintain air supremacy if opposed by available Soviet air units. Due to limitations of suitable airfields, only a small portion of available Air Force units could be deployed in Greece or on other airfields sufficiently near to Greece to make their operations effective in supporting United States ground forces deployed in Greece proper.

There is no prospect, even with prompt and favorable action regarding the measures for preparedness recommended herein by the Joint Chiefs of Staff, of early appreciable augmentation of these ground and air forces. Furthermore, their employment in Greece would make them unavailable for other and quite possibly more critical emergency use.

If they were dispatched to Greece, their assigned mission should be . . . to assist actively, by operations involving actual combat, in the military objectives of the Greek National Government. Their locations would depend initially on the military situation at the time of their arrival and would be adjusted thereafter to meet changing conditions. They might, for example, assist in preventing entrance or exit of guerrilla bands across the Greek frontier. Since this frontier is approximately 550 miles long, it is estimated that this form of assistance would require from three to five divisions.

If there should be overt action against Greece by Albania, Yugoslavia and Bulgaria, successful defense of Greece against an active attack, even if not overtly supported by the USSR, would require, because of geographic factors, a preponderance of defensive forces and equipment, with well-prepared defensive positions. Available ground forces of the United States and Greece together are numerically far inferior, however, to those of the adjacent Soviet satellite states.

In summary, the effectiveness and advisability of dispatching available United States forces to Greece are open to serious question in that . . . such forces will probably be unnecessary if Soviet satellites do not initiate open warfare and will be insufficient if the Soviet satellites do attack.

Document 8

Protocol of Proceedings, Berlin Conference (Potsdam), Aug. 1, 1945, *FRUS*, 1945, *The Conference of Berlin (The Potsdam Conference)*, vol. 2, 1960, 1481–86.

II. THE PRINCIPLES TO GOVERN THE TREATMENT OF GERMANY IN THE INITIAL CONTROL PERIOD

A. *Political Principles*

1. In accordance with the Agreement on Control Machinery in Germany, supreme authority in Germany is exercised, on instructions from their respective Governments, by the Commanders-in-Chief of the armed forces of the United States of America, the United Kingdom, the Union of Soviet Socialist Republics, and the French Republic, each in his own zone of occupation, and also jointly, in matters affecting Germany as a whole, in their capacity as members of the Control Council.

2. So far as practicable, there shall be uniformity of treatment of the German population throughout Germany.

3. The purposes of the occupation of Germany by which the Control Council shall be guided are:

(1) The complete disarmament and demilitarization of Germany and the elimination or control of all German industry that could be used for military production. . . .

14. During the period of occupation Germany shall be treated as a single economic unit. To this end common policies shall be established in regard to:

(a) mining and industrial production and allocation;

(b) agriculture, forestry and fishing;

(c) wages, prices and rationing;

(d) import and export programs for Germany as a whole;

(e) currency and banking, central taxation and customs;

(f) reparation and removal of industrial war potential;

(g) transportation and communications. . . .

III. GERMAN REPARATION

1. Reparation claims of U.S.S.R. shall be met by removals from the zone of Germany occupied by the U.S.S.R., and from appropriate German external assets.

2. The U.S.S.R. undertakes to settle the reparation claims of Poland from its own share of reparations.

3. The reparations claims of the United States, the United Kingdom and other countries entitled to reparations shall be met from the Western Zones and from appropriate German external assets.

4. In addition to the reparations to be taken by the U.S.S.R. from its own zone of occupation, the U.S.S.R. shall receive additionally from the Western Zones:

(a) 15 per cent of such usable and complete industrial capital equipment, in the first place from the metallurgical, chemical and machine manufacturing industries as is unnecessary for the German peace economy and should be removed from the Western Zones of Germany, in exchange for an equivalent value of food, coal, potash, zinc, timber, clay products, petroleum products, and such other commodities as may be agreed upon.

(b) 10 per cent of such industrial capital equipment as is unnecessary for the German peace economy and should be removed from the Western Zones, to be transferred to the Soviet Government on reparations account without payment or exchange of any kind in return. . . .

Document 9

Remarks by Secretary of State George C. Marshall at Harvard University, June 5, 1947, *FRUS, 1947, The British Commonwealth; Europe*, vol. 3, 1972, 237–39.

I need not tell you gentlemen that the world situation is very serious. That must be apparent to all intelligent people. I think one difficulty is that the problem is one of such enormous complexity that the very mass of facts presented to the public by press and radio make it exceedingly difficult for the man in the street to reach a clear appraisement of the situation. Furthermore, the people of this country are distant from the troubled areas of the earth and it is hard for them to comprehend the plight and consequent reactions of the long-suffering peoples, and the effect of those reactions on their governments in connection with our efforts to promote peace in the world.

In considering the requirements for the rehabilitation of Europe the physical loss of life, the visible destruction of cities, factories, mines and railroads was correctly estimated, but it has become obvious during recent months that this visible destruction was probably less serious than the dislocation of the entire fabric of European economy. For the past ten years conditions have been highly abnormal. The feverish preparation for war and the more feverish maintenance of the war effort engulfed all aspects of national economies. Machinery has fallen into disrepair or is entirely obsolete. Under the arbitrary and destructive Nazi rule, virtually every possible enterprise was geared into the German war machine. Long-standing commercial ties, private institutions, banks, insurance companies and shipping companies disappeared, through the loss of capital, absorption through nationalization or by simple destruction. In many countries, confidence in the local currency has been severely shaken. The breakdown of the business structure of Europe during the war was complete. Recovery has been seriously retarded by the fact that two years after the close of hostilities a peace settlement with Germany and Austria has not been agreed upon. But even given a more prompt solution of these difficult problems, the rehabilitation of the economic structure of Europe quite evidently will require a much longer and greater effort than had been foreseen.

There is a phase of this matter which is both interesting and serious. The farmer has always produced the foodstuffs to exchange with the city dweller for the other necessities of life. This division of labor is the basis of modern civilization. At the present time it is threatened with breakdown. The town and city industries are not producing adequate goods to exchange with the food-producing farmer. Raw materials and fuel are in short supply. Machinery is lacking or worn out. The farmer or the peasant cannot find the goods for sale which he desires to purchase. So the sale of his farm produce for money which he cannot use seems to him an unprofitable transaction. He, therefore, has withdrawn many fields from crop cultivation and is using them for grazing. He feeds more grain to stock and finds for himself and his family an ample supply of food, however short he may be on clothing and the other ordinary gadgets of civilization. Meanwhile people in the cities are short on food and fuel. So the governments are forced to use their money and credits to procure these necessities abroad. This process exhausts funds which are urgently needed for reconstruction. Thus a very serious situation is rapidly developing which bodes no good for the world. The modern system of the division of labor upon which the exchange of products is based is in danger of breaking down.

The truth of the matter is that Europe's requirements for the next three or four years of foreign food and other essential products—principally from America—are so much greater than her present ability to pay that she must have substantial additional help, or face economic, social and political deterioration of a grave character.

The remedy lies in breaking the vicious circle and restoring the confidence of the European people in the economic future of their own countries and of Europe as a whole. The manufacturer and the farmer throughout wide areas must be able and willing to exchange their products for currencies the continuing value of which is not open to question.

Aside from the demoralizing effect on the world at large and the possibilities of disturbances arising as a result of the desperation of the people concerned, the consequences to the economy of the United States should be apparent to all. It is logical that the United States should do whatever it is able to do to assist in the return of normal economic health to the world, without which there can be no political stability and no assured peace. Our policy is directed not against any country or doctrine but against hunger, poverty, desperation, and chaos. Its purpose should be the revival of a working economy in the world so as to permit the emergence of political and social conditions in which free institutions can exist. Such assistance, I am convinced, must not be on a piece-meal basis as various crises develop. Any assistance that this Government may render in the future should provide a cure rather than a mere palliative. Any government that is willing to assist in the task of recovery will find full cooperation, I am sure, on the part of the United States Government. Any government which maneuvers to block the recovery of other countries cannot expect help from us. Furthermore, governments, political parties or groups which seek to perpetuate human misery in order to profit therefrom politically or otherwise will encounter the opposition of the United States.

It is already evident that, before the United States Government can proceed much further in its efforts to alleviate the situation and help start the European world on its way to recovery, there must be some agreement among the countries of Europe as to the requirements of the situation and the part those countries themselves will take in order to give proper effect to whatever action might be undertaken by this Government. It would be neither fitting nor efficacious for this Government to undertake to draw up unilaterally a program designed to place Europe on its feet economically. This is the business of the Europeans. The initiative, I think, must come from Europe. The role of this country should consist of friendly aid in the drafting of a European program and of later support of such a program so far as it may be practical for us to do so. The program should be a joint one, agreed to by a number, if not all European nations.

An essential part of any successful action on the part of the United States is an understanding on the part of the people of America of the character of the problem and the remedies to be applied. Political passion and prejudice should have no part. With foresight, and a willingness on the part of our people to face up to the vast responsibility which history has clearly placed upon our country, the difficulties I have outlined can and will be overcome.

Document 10

Communiqué of the London Conference on Germany, June 7, 1948, *FRUS, 1948, Germany and Austria*, 1973, vol. 2, 313–17.

In accordance with an announcement issued on June 2 at the conclusion of informal discussions on Germany between representatives of United States, United Kingdom, France and three Benelux countries a report containing agreed recommendations on all items discussed was submitted as a whole since their main provisions are mutually dependent and form an indivisible program. Principal features of this report are the following:

I. ASSOCIATION OF BENELUX COUNTRIES IN POLICY REGARDING GERMANY

The recommendations include specific provisions for a close association between military governments and Benelux representatives in Germany on matters affecting Benelux interests. Moreover full opportunities will be given the Benelux representatives to be kept informed of developments in the western zones.

II. ROLE OF THE GERMAN ECONOMY IN THE EUROPEAN ECONOMY AND CONTROL OF THE RUHR

(A) As stated in the communiqué of March 6 it had been agreed that for the political and economic well-being of the countries of Western Europe and of a democratic Germany, there must be a close association of their economic life. This close association, which will enable Germany to contribute to and participate in European recovery, has been ensured by the inclusion on April 16 of the combined zone and French zone in the organization for European economic cooperation as full members.

(B) It was agreed to recommend the establishment of an international authority for the control of the Ruhr in which United States, United Kingdom, France, Benelux countries and Germany would participate, and which does not involve the political separation of the Ruhr area from Germany. It does, however, contemplate control of distribution of coal, coke and steel of Ruhr in order that on the one hand industrial concentration in that area shall not become an instrument of aggression, and on the other will be able to make its contribution to all countries participating in a European cooperative economic program, including, of course, Germany itself. A draft agreement containing the provisions for its establishment is attached as Annex I. This agreement is to be concluded by the United States, United Kingdom and France as occupying powers. Moreover the Benelux countries are to be fully associated with the preparation of the more detailed agreement provided for in Article 12, and are to be consulted as to the time when the authority begins to exercise its functions.

(C) Arising out of the discussions on the Ruhr it has been recommended that the principle of non-discrimination against foreign interests in Germany be reaffirmed, and that each government should promptly study the problem of safeguarding foreign interests in order that there may be subsequently established . . . an intergovernmental group to review the question and make recommendations to their governments.

III. EVOLUTION OF POLITICAL AND ECONOMIC ORGANIZATION OF GERMANY

(A) Further consideration has been given by all delegates to the problem of the evolution of the political and economic organization of Germany. They recognize, taking into account the present situation, that it is necessary to give the German people the opportunity to achieve on the basis of a free and democratic form of government the eventual reestablishment of German unity at present disrupted. In these circumstances they have reached the conclusion that it would be desirable that the German people in the different states should now be free to establish for themselves the political organization and institutions which will enable them to assume those governmental responsibilities which are compatible with the minimum requirements of occupation and control and which ultimately will enable them to assume full governmental responsibility. The delegates consider that the people in the States will wish to establish a constitution with provisions which will allow all the German states to subscribe as soon as circumstances permit.

Therefore the delegates have agreed to recommend to their governments that the military governors should hold a joint meeting with the Ministers-President of the western zone in Germany. At that meeting the Ministers-President will be authorized to convene a Constituent Assembly in order to prepare a constitution for the approval of the participating states.

Delegates to this Constituent Assembly will be chosen in each of the states in accordance with procedure and regulations to be determined by the legislative bodies of the individual states.

The constitution should be such as to enable the Germans to play their part in bringing to an end the present division of Germany not by the reconstitution of a centralized Reich but by means of a federal form of government which adequately protects the rights of the respective states, and which at the same time provides for adequate central authority and which guarantees the rights and freedoms of the individual.

If the constitution as prepared by the Constituent Assembly does not conflict with these general principles the military governors will authorize its submissions for ratification by the people in the respective states.

At the meeting with the military governors the Ministers-President will also be authorized to examine the boundaries of the several states in order to determine what modifications might be proposed to the military governors for the purpose of creating a definitive system which is satisfactory to the peoples concerned.

(B) Further discussions have taken place between the United States, United Kingdom and French delegations on measures for coordinating economic policies and practices in the combined zone. Agreed recommendations have been reached on the joint conduct and control of the external trade of the whole area. It has been recognized that a complete economic merger of the two areas cannot effectively take place until further progress has been made in establishing the necessary German institutions common to the entire area.

IV. PROVISIONAL TERRITORIAL ARRANGEMENTS

The delegations have agreed to submit for the consideration of their governments proposals for dealing with certain minor provisional territorial adjustments in connection with the western frontiers of Germany.

This problem was considered in three aspects: (A) General Provisions. (B) Measures during the period in which the occupying powers retain supreme authority in Germany. (C) Measures after the period in which the occupying powers retain supreme authority in Germany.

General Provision.

The United States, United Kingdom, and French Delegates reiterated the firm views of their governments that there could not be any general withdrawal of their forces from Germany until the peace of Europe is secured and without prior consultation. During this period there should be no general withdrawal of the forces of occupation of the United States, France or the United Kingdom without prior consultation. It was further recommended that the governments concerned should consult if any of them should consider that there was a danger of resurgence of German military power or of the adoption by Germany of a policy of aggression.

Measures during the period in which the occupying powers retain supreme authority in Germany.

The provisions on the German Armed Forces and the German General Staff as contained in 4-power agreements were reaffirmed, as well as the exercise of controls by the military governors with respect to disarmament and demilitarization, level of industry and certain aspects of scientific research. To ensure the maintenance of disarmament and demilitarization in the interests of security, the three military governors should set up a military security board in the western zones of Germany to carry out the proper inspections and make the necessary recommendations to the military governors, who decide the action to be taken.

Measures after the period in which the occupying powers retain supreme authority in Germany.

It was affirmed that Germany must not again be permitted to become an aggressive power and that prior to the general withdrawal of the forces of occupation agreement will be reached among the governments concerned with respect to necessary measures of demilitarization, disarmament and control of industry and with respect to occupation of key areas. Also there should be a system of inspection to ensure the maintenance of the agreed provisions of German disarmament and demilitarization.

The present recommendations, which in no way preclude and on the contrary should facilitate eventual 4-power agreement on the German problem, are designed to solve the urgent political and economic problems arising out of the present situation in Germany. Because of the previous failure to reach comprehensive 4-power decisions on Germany, the measures recommended mark a step forward in the policy which the powers represented at these talks are determined to follow with respect to the economic reconstruction of Western Europe, including Germany, and with respect to the establishment of a basis for the participation of a democratic Germany in the community of free peoples.

Document 11

North Atlantic Treaty, Apr. 4, 1949, *FRUS*, *1949, Western Europe*, 1975, vol. 4, 281–84.

The Parties of this Treaty reaffirm their faith in the purposes and principles of the Charter of the United Nations and their desire to live in peace with all peoples and all governments.

They are determined to safeguard the freedom, common heritage and civilization of their peoples, founded on the principles of democracy, individual liberty and the rule of law.

They seek to promote stability and well-being in the North Atlantic area.

They are resolved to unite their efforts for collective defense and for the preservation of peace and security.

They therefore agree to this North Atlantic Treaty:

ARTICLE 1

The Parties undertake, as set forth in the Charter of the United Nations, to settle any international disputes in which they may be involved by peaceful means in such a manner that international peace and security, and justice, are not endangered, and to refrain in their international relations from the threat or use of force in any manner inconsistent with the purposes of the United Nations.

ARTICLE 2

The Parties will contribute toward the further development of peaceful and friendly international relations by strengthening their free institutions, by bringing about a better understanding of the principles upon which these institutions are founded, and by promoting conditions of stability and well-being. They will seek to eliminate conflict in their international economic policies and will encourage economic collaboration between any or all of them.

ARTICLE 3

In order more effectively to achieve the objectives of this Treaty, the Parties, separately and jointly, by means of continuous and effective self-help and mutual aid, will maintain and develop their individual and collective capacity to resist armed attack.

ARTICLE 4

The Parties will consult together whenever, in the opinion of any of them, the territorial integrity, political independence or security of any of the Parties is threatened.

ARTICLE 5

The Parties agree that an armed attack against one or more of them in Europe or North America shall be considered an attack against them all; and consequently they agree that, if such an armed attack occurs, each of them, in exercise of the right of individual or collective self-defense recognized by Article 51 of the Charter of the United Nations, will assist the Party or Parties so attacked by taking forthwith, individually and in concert with the other Parties, such action as it deems necessary, including the use of armed force, to restore and maintain the security of the North Atlantic area.

Any such armed attack and all measures taken as a result thereof shall immediately be reported to the Security Council. Such measures shall be terminated when the Security Council has taken the measures necessary to restore and maintain international peace and security.

ARTICLE 6

For the purpose of Article 5 an armed attack on one or more of the Parties is deemed to include an armed attack on the territory of any of the Parties in Europe or North America, on the Algerian departments of France, on the occupation forces of any Party in Europe, on the islands under the jurisdiction of any Party in the North Atlantic area north of the Tropic of Cancer or on the vessels or aircraft in this area of any of the Parties.

ARTICLE 7

This Treaty does not affect, and shall not be interpeted as affecting, in any way the rights and obligations under the

Charter of the Parties which are members of the United Nations, or the primary responsibility of the Security Council for the maintenance of international peace and security.

ARTICLE 8

Each Party declares that none of the international engagements now in force between it and any other of the Parties or any third state is in conflict with the provisions of this Treaty, and undertakes not to enter into any international engagement in conflict with this Treaty.

ARTICLE 9

The Parties hereby establish a council, on which each of them shall be represented, to consider matters concerning the implementation of this Treaty. The council shall be so organized as to be able to meet promptly at any time. The council shall set up such subsidiary bodies as may be necessary; in particular it shall establish immediately a defense committee which shall recommend measures for the implementation of Articles 3 and 5.

ARTICLE 10

The Parties may, by unanimous agreement, invite any other European state in a position to further the principles of this Treaty and to contribute to the security of the North Atlantic area to accede to this Treaty. Any state so invited may become a party to the Treaty by depositing its instrument of accession with the Government of the United States of America. The Government of the United States of America will inform each of the Parties of the deposit of each such instrument of accession.

ARTICLE 11

This Treaty shall be ratified and its provisions carried out by the Parties in accordance with their respective constitutional processes. The instruments of ratification shall be deposited as soon as possible with the Government of the United States of America, which will notify all the other signatories of each deposit. The Treaty shall enter into force between the states which have ratified it as soon as the ratifications of the majority of the signatories, including the ratifications of Belgium, Canada, France, Luxembourg, the Netherlands, the United Kingdom and the United States, have been deposited and shall come into effect with respect to other states on the date of the deposit of their ratifications.

ARTICLE 12

After the Treaty has been in force for ten years, or at any time thereafter, the Parties shall, if any of them so requests, consult together for the purpose of reviewing the Treaty, having regard for the factors then affecting peace and security in the North Atlantic area, including the development of universal as well as regional arrangements under the Charter of the United Nations for the maintenance of international peace and security.

ARTICLE 13

After the Treaty has been in force for twenty years, any Party may cease to be a party one year after its notice of denunciation has been given to the Government of the United States of America, which will inform the governments of the other Parties of the deposit of each notice of denunciation.

ARTICLE 14

This Treaty, of which the English and French texts are equally authentic, shall be deposited in the archives of the Government of the United States of America. Duly certified copies thereof will be transmitted by that Government to the Governments of the other signatories.

Document 12

NSC–68 [National Security Council Study no. 68], Apr. 14, 1950, *FRUS, 1950, National Security Affairs; Foreign Economic Policy,* 1977, vol. 1, 252–92.

As for the policy of "containment," it is one which seeks by all means short of war to (1) block further expansion of Soviet power, (2) expose the falsities of Soviet pretensions, (3) induce a retraction of the Kremlin's control and influence and (4) in general, so foster the seeds of destruction within the Soviet system that the Kremlin is brought at least to the point of modifying its behavior to conform to generally accepted international standards.

It was and continues to be cardinal in this policy that we possess superior overall power in ourselves or in dependable combination with other like-minded nations. One of the most important ingredients of power is military strength. In the concept of "containment," the maintenance of a strong military posture is deemed to be essential for two reasons: (1) as an ultimate guarantee of our national security and (2) as an indispensable backdrop to the conduct of the policy of "containment." Without superior aggregate military strength, in being and readily mobilizable, a policy of "containment"—which is in effect a policy of calculated and gradual coercion—is no more than a policy of bluff.

At the same time, it is essential to the successful conduct of a policy of "containment" that we always leave open the possibility of negotiation with the U.S.S.R. . . .

If war should begin in 1950, the United States and its allies will have the military capability of conducting defensive operations to provide a reasonable measure of protection to the Western Hemisphere, bases in the Western Pacific, and essential military bases in the United Kingdom and in the Near and Middle East. We will have the capability of conducting powerful offensive air operations against vital elements of the Soviet war-making capacity. . . .

If the potential military capabilities of the United States and its allies were rapidly and effectively developed, sufficient forces could be produced probably to deter war, or if the Soviet Union chooses war, to withstand the initial Soviet attacks, to stabilize supporting attacks, and to retaliate in turn with even greater impact on the Soviet capabilities. From the military point of view alone, however, this would require not only the generation of the necessary military forces but also the development and stockpiling of improved weapons of all types. . . .

A more rapid build-up of political, economic, and military strength and thereby of confidence in the free world than is now contemplated is the only course which is consistent with progress toward achieving our fundamental purpose. The frustration of the Kremlin design requires the free world to develop a successfully functioning political and economic system and a vigorous political offensive against the Soviet Union. These, in turn, require an adequate military shield under which they can develop . . . a firm policy intended to check and to roll back the Kremlin's drive for world domination. . . .

A comprehensive and decisive program to win the peace and frustrate the Kremlin design should be so designed that it can be sustained for as long as necessary to achieve our national objectives. It would probably involve:

(1) The development of an adequate political and economic framework for the achievement of our long-range objectives.

(2) A substantial increase in

expenditures for military purposes. . . .

(3) A substantial increase in military assistance programs, designed to foster cooperative efforts, which will adequately and efficiently meet the requirements of our allies. . . .

(4) Some increase in economic assistance programs and recognition of the need to continue these programs until their purposes have been accomplished.

(5) A concerted attack on the problem of the United States balance of payments, along the lines already approved by the President.

(6) Development of programs designed to build and maintain confidence among other peoples in our strength and resolution, and to wage overt psychological warfare calculated to encourage mass defections from Soviet allegiance and to frustrate the Kremlin design in other ways.

(7) Intensification of affirmative and timely measures and operations by covert means in the field of economic warfare and political and psychological warfare with a view to fomenting and supporting unrest and revolt in selected strategic satellite countries.

(8) Development of internal security and civilian defense programs.

(9) Improvement and intensification of intelligence activities.

(10) Reduction of Federal expenditures for purposes other than defense and foreign assistance, if necessary by the deferment of certain desirable programs.

(11) Increased taxes. . . .

The threat to the free world involved in the development of the Soviet Union's atomic and other capabilities will rise steadily and rather rapidly. For the time being, the United States possesses a marked atomic superiority over the Soviet Union which, together with the potential capabilities of the United States and other free countries in other forces and weapons, inhibits aggressive Soviet action. This provides an opportunity for the United States, in cooperation with other free countries, to launch a build-up of strength which will support a firm policy directed to the frustration of the Kremlin design. The immediate goal of our efforts to build a successfully functioning political and economic system in the free world backed by adequate military strength is to postpone and avert the disastrous situation which, in light of the Soviet Union's probable fission bomb capability and possible thermonuclear bomb capability, might arise in 1954 on a continuation of our present programs. By acting promptly and vigorously in such a way that this date is, so to speak, pushed into the future, we would permit time for the process of accommodation, withdrawal and frustration to produce the necessary changes in the Soviet system. Time is short, however, and the risks of war attendant upon a decision to build up strength will steadily increase the longer we defer it. . . .

. . . In particular, the United States now faces the contingency that within the next four or five years the Soviet Union will possess the military capability of delivering a surprise atomic attack of such weight that the United States must have substantially increased general air, ground, and sea strength, atomic capabilities, and air and civilian defenses to deter war and to provide reasonable assurance, in the event of war, that it could survive the initial blow and go on to the eventual attainment of its objectives. In return, this contingency requires the intensification of our efforts in the fields of intelligence and research and development.

The whole success of the proposed program hangs ultimately on recognition by this Government, the American people, and all free peoples, that the cold war is in fact a real war in which the survival of the free world is at stake.

CHAPTER 8

The Korean War

James I. Matray

For many years, the Korean War attracted little attention from either American diplomatic historians or the general public. Clay Blair even titled his detailed study of the Korean conflict *The Forgotten War*. But Blair's account is only one of a swelling stream of new books that have appeared since 1981 focusing not only on the war itself, but on U.S. policy toward Korea before the fighting started. This revival of interest has been a direct response to the disastrous American experience in the Vietnam War. Because the United States also fought a "limited war" in Korea to halt Communist expansion, writers naturally have turned to that conflict in hopes of explaining how and why the United States intervened in Vietnam. More importantly, an increasing number of scholars have concluded that the Korean War was a turning point in American foreign policy during the Cold War. Reacting to the outbreak of hostilities in Korea, the United States not only expanded its commitment to block Communist seizures of power elsewhere in Asia, most notably Vietnam, but it also vastly increased defense spending, strengthened the North Atlantic Treaty Organization (NATO), and pressed for German rearmament. The Korean War therefore persuaded American leaders that only the direct application of military power could contain what they then perceived as a far more dangerous Soviet threat menacing the entire world.

Early accounts of the Korean War almost without exception focused on events beginning with the North Korean invasion of South Korea. However, a more recent consensus establishes the origins of the war in World War II. Prior to 1941, the United States had been the first Western nation to sign a treaty with Korea (in 1882), even though it had no vital interests in this remote Asian country and was largely indifferent to its fate. But after the Japanese attack on Pearl Harbor, President Franklin D. Roosevelt and his advisers immediately acknowledged the importance of this strategic peninsula for the maintenance of postwar peace in Asia. Realistically, the administration advocated the creation of a trusteeship for the achievement of Korea's independence, and Roosevelt publicly committed the United States to this wartime policy at the first Cairo Conference in 1943. There he joined

British Prime Minister Winston Churchill and the leader of the Chinese Nationalist government, Chiang Kai-shek, in signing the Cairo Declaration, stating that the Allies, "mindful of the enslavement of the people of Korea, are determined that in due course Korea shall become free and independent." Given past Sino-Russian competition for control over Korea, Roosevelt knew it was imperative to obtain Soviet endorsement for the Cairo Declaration, or Korea once again would become the victim of great-power rivalry. At the Yalta Conference in 1945, Soviet Premier Joseph Stalin accepted a four-power trusteeship plan that would provide protection for Korea until it developed the political experience necessary to maintain its own independence.

When Harry S. Truman became president following Roosevelt's death in April 1945, however, Soviet expansion into Eastern Europe had begun to alarm American leaders. Almost from the outset, Truman expected Soviet actions in Korea to parallel Stalin's policies in Poland. Within a week after taking office, Truman began to search for some alternative to a trusteeship in Korea that would eliminate any chance for a repetition of Soviet expansion. No one will ever know whether a trusteeship would have brought Korean unity and independence because the atomic bomb seemed to offer Truman a better solution. Japan's prompt surrender after an atomic attack would preempt Soviet entry into the Pacific war, thereby permitting the United States to occupy Korea unilaterally and remove any possibility for "sovietization." But Truman's gamble failed. When Stalin declared war on Japan and sent the Red Army into Korea prematurely on August 12, 1945, the United States proposed Korea's division into Soviet and American zones of military occupation at the 38th degree of latitude, or parallel. Only Stalin's acceptance of this desperate eleventh-hour plan saved the peninsula from unification under Communist rule. Accepting Korea's division into suitable spheres of influence, the Soviet leader probably also hoped to trade this concession for an equal voice in determining Japan's future development.

Korea soon found itself a captive of the Cold War. As Soviet-American relations in Europe deteriorated, neither side was willing to acquiesce in any agreement that would appreciably strengthen its adversary. This became clear when the United States and the Soviet Union tried to implement a revived trusteeship scheme following the Moscow Conference in late 1945, which created a Joint U.S.-U.S.S.R. Commission to consider Korean unification. Eighteen months of intermittent negotiations by the commission failed to produce agreement on a representative group of Koreans to form a provisional government. Meanwhile, political and economic conditions in southern Korea deteriorated, causing American occupation officials to urge military withdrawal as soon as possible. As the United States demobilized, reductions in defense spending intensified pressure for disengagement and ultimately forced the administration to develop a new policy. In response to a State Department request, the U.S. Joint Chiefs of Staff submitted an assessment of Korea's strategic significance in September 1947 (doc. 1) that added weight to the argument for prompt withdrawal. With Communist power growing in China, however, the Truman administration was unwilling to abandon southern Korea precipitously, fearing criticism from Republican opponents at home and damage to U.S. credibility abroad. Seeking an answer to its dilemma, the United States referred the Korean issue to the United Nations, which passed a resolution calling for reunification after internationally supervised nationwide elections.

American leaders knew that the Soviet Union would not cooperate with the UN resolution. Discarding any hope for early reunification, the administration's policy had shifted to the creation of a separate government south of the 38th parallel that was ultimately capable of defending itself. While the United States provided military and economic aid, a stamp of legitimacy from the United Nations would further enhance southern Korea's chances of survival. Bowing to American pressure, the UN supervised and certified as valid the elections in the south during May 1948, resulting in the formation of South Korea (Republic of Korea) the following summer. The Soviet Union responded in kind, sponsoring in September the formation of North Korea (Democratic People's Republic of Korea). And so there were two Koreas, with President Syngman Rhee establishing a repressive, dictatorial, anti-Communist regime in the south and Premier Kim Il-sung following the Soviet model for political, economic, and social development in the north. These events magnified the need for the United States to withdraw, because Stalin, acting on a North Korean request, announced that Soviet troops would pull out of the country by the end of 1948. Although the administration had planned to leave South Korea before 1949, a major uprising against the Rhee government in October 1948 persuaded Truman to postpone military withdrawal until June 29, 1949.

Truman believed that South Korea could survive and prosper without protection from American troops, despite the existence of a powerful army in North Korea; prior to withdrawal the administration had undertaken a commitment to train, equip, and supply a security force in South Korea capable of maintaining internal order and deterring a North Korean attack. It had also submitted to Congress a three-year program of technical and economic aid for recovery and self-sufficient growth. To build political support for the Korean assistance package, Secretary of State Dean Acheson delivered a speech before the National Press Club on January 12, 1950 (doc. 2), offering an optimistic appraisal of South Korea's future. Later, critics would charge that Acheson's exclusion of South Korea from the U.S. "defensive perimeter" gave the Communists a "green light" to launch an invasion. But the administration was acting on the key assumption that Moscow would not permit the North Koreans to practice open aggression. By June 1950, Truman's policy of containment through economic means seemed to have marked success in the region. South Korea had acted vigorously to control spiraling inflation, while elections in May had given Rhee's opponents control over the legislature. Finally, the South Korean army had virtually eliminated guerrilla threats to internal order, prompting the United States to consider a sizable increase in military aid.

However, on the morning of June 25, 1950, North Korea invaded South Korea. Revisionist historians have charged that South Korea started the war, but they have provided only circumstantial evidence of its guilt. Not only do the size and speed of the Communist army's advance point to North Korean responsibility for initiating hostilities, but Kim Il-sung's later purge of top officials, who erroneously predicted popular uprisings in support of South Korea's "liberation," constitutes an indirect confession that such a calculation had been part of a planned attack. Most early histories of the Korean War accepted Truman's judgment that Stalin ordered the North Korean attack as part of a Soviet blueprint for world conquest. At the time, State Department adviser George F. Kennan disagreed. Stressing interests over ideology, he argued that the Kremlin expected its conquest of Korea to weaken the U.S. position in Japan. Soviet leader Nikita Khrushchev claimed in his memoirs that the invasion was Kim Il-sung's plan and Stalin only approved it. (doc. 3) Regardless of Soviet involvement, one conclusion seems clear: If North Korea had not been bent on reunification, there would have been no war. Rhee was just as determined to end the artificial division of Korea, but Washington purposely limited his military capabilities to prevent an assault northward. Reflecting this drive for reunification was a rising number of violent clashes at the 38th parallel after 1948, suggesting that the Korean conflict was the climax of an ongoing civil war.

Truman administration officials never doubted that North Korea had attacked on orders from Moscow. "Communism," Truman argued in his memoirs, "was acting in Korea just as Hitler, Mussolini, and the Japanese had acted ten, fifteen, and twenty years earlier." If North Korea's aggression went unchallenged, he concluded, "the world was certain to be plunged into another world war." Rejecting appeasement, Truman announced on June 27, 1950, that the United States was providing assistance to South Korea in its efforts to repel the invasion and also was strengthening local defenses against Communist expansion elsewhere in Asia. (doc. 4) Yet the administration was reluctant to commit ground troops to Korea, referring the matter instead to the United Nations and banking on South Korea's ability to defend itself. After North Korea ignored a UN resolution calling for a cease-fire and withdrawal of North Korean troops, the Security Council passed a second resolution urging its members to help defend South Korea. Moscow was unable to veto these measures because it was boycotting the Security Council in protest over the UN refusal to seat the People's Republic of China, providing evidence that North Korea may have attacked earlier than Stalin expected. The Truman administration therefore was able to portray American intervention as an act of collective security, although the United States and South Korea contributed far more in every way than did the other fifteen nations who fought on the UN side.

Truman finally committed ground combat forces on June 30 after General Douglas MacArthur advised that without them, Communist conquest of South Korea was certain. The president never asked Congress to declare war, agreeing with a newsman's description of the fighting in Korea as a ''police action.'' As Washington sent in more troops and supplies, North Korea's advance continued until the UN Command, created under a UN resolution of July 7, had retreated to the Pusan Perimeter, a rectangular area in the southeast corner of the Korean peninsula. Despite this seemingly desperate situation, MacArthur already had developed plans for a counteroffensive in coordination with an amphibious landing behind enemy lines that would permit him to ''compose and unite'' Korea. Truman's advisers, certain that battlefield victory was inevitable, debated throughout July whether to seek forcible reunification once the Communist army had been thrown out of South Korea. Initially, Secretary of State Acheson opposed crossing the 38th parallel, stating publicly on June 29 that U.S. military action ''is solely for the purpose of restoring [South Korea] to its status prior to the invasion.'' However, State Department official John M. Allison worked to change Acheson's mind, arguing persuasively that the United States should destroy the North Korean army and then sponsor free elections for a government to rule a united Korea. (doc. 5) American military leaders were reluctant to endorse this drastic change in war aims until UN defensive lines finally stabilized in late July. Significantly, the Joint Chiefs of Staff advised Truman on July 31 that occupying North Korea would be desirable if the Soviet Union did not intervene.

MacArthur launched the first UN counterattack on August 7, 1950. By then, Truman had decided to authorize an attempt at forcible reunification. On August 17, Ambassador Warren Austin divulged this decision in a speech at the United Nations. ''Shall only a part of the country be assured this freedom? I think not,'' he declared. MacArthur's planned counteroffensive thus assumed added importance, for it would not only reverse the course of the war but would also permit the United States to reunite Korea. The Joint Chiefs of Staff had serious reservations about MacArthur's intention to land at the port of Inchon, forty miles west of Seoul, because of its narrow access and high tides. But on September 15, the Inchon landing succeeded brilliantly, and two weeks later, after liberating Seoul, UN forces were poised for an advance across the 38th parallel. American leaders realized that extending hostilities northward risked Soviet or Chinese intervention and possibly a global war. Therefore, Truman's plan for conquering North Korea, which he approved on September 1, included precautions. First, the joint chiefs would instruct MacArthur to permit only Korean forces in the most northern provinces. Second, the United States would obtain explicit UN support for reunification. After North Korea refused to surrender, the UN passed a resolution on October 7 instructing MacArthur to ''ensure conditions of stability throughout Korea.''

To the Chinese, MacArthur's advance into North Korea constituted a grave threat to their national security. Chinese Communist leaders may have been aware of Kim Il-sung's invasion plans, but they could not have welcomed the Korean War because it prevented the elimination of the Chinese Nationalist redoubt on Taiwan. In late July, MacArthur had visited the island and announced plans to strengthen the military capabilities of Chiang Kai-shek's regime. Then, much to Truman's chagrin, the militantly anti-Communist MacArthur sent a message to the Veterans of Foreign Wars that seemed to threaten China. (doc. 6) Nevertheless, Chinese Foreign Minister Chou En-lai hoped to restrain the United States by assuring the Indian ambassador on October 2 that China would intervene if American forces crossed the parallel. Administration officials thought the Chinese were bluffing. MacArthur, during a personal meeting with Truman at Wake Island on October 15, predicted that ''if the Chinese tried to get down to Pyongyang [North Korea's capital] there would be the greatest slaughter.'' Even after the first clash between UN troops and Chinese ''volunteers'' later that month, the general remained supremely confident, despite Washington's refusal on November 8 to authorize bombing in Manchuria because of British objections. On November 24, MacArthur launched his ''Home-by-Christmas Offensive,'' with American troops as the vanguard. Two days later, however, the Chinese counterattacked in force, sending UN troops into a massive retreat. An atmosphere of crisis soon gripped Washington as Truman declared a state of national emergency.

Following Chinese military intervention, Truman decided to fight a ''limited war'' in Korea to achieve the original goal of restoring the prewar status quo. MacArthur opposed this strategy, arguing that escalation or evacuation were the only options. By March 1951, however, General Matthew B. Ridgway, the newly appointed U.S. Eighth Army commander, had proved that the administration's ''limited war'' strategy was feasible by driving Chinese Communist forces back into North Korea. Truman then planned to propose a cease-fire, laying the basis for his final clash with MacArthur. In the first of two acts of insubordination, MacArthur scuttled the president's peace initiative by issuing a humiliating public ultimatum to the Chinese Communists demanding immediate surrender. Then, Republican Congressman Joseph W. Martin read on the floor of the U.S. House of Representatives a letter from MacArthur essentially accusing the administration of appeasement in Korea. This directly violated a Joint Chiefs of Staff directive of December 6, 1950, requiring all government officials to obtain clearance for public comments on the war. On April 11, Truman recalled MacArthur, which ignited a fire storm of criticism. Returning home to ticker-tape parades, MacArthur delivered a televised address to a joint session of Congress in which he declared that there was ''no substitute for victory.'' (doc. 7) During subsequent Senate hearings on MacArthur's firing, the testimony of General Omar N. Bradley, chairman of the Joint Chiefs of Staff, was an effective rebuttal to MacArthur's arguments. (doc. 8)

Nevertheless, most Americans by now doubted the wisdom of continuing to fight "Mr. Truman's War."

Meanwhile, UN forces had repulsed two Chinese Communist offensives and had established a defensive position just north of the 38th parallel. Stalemate on the battlefield apparently persuaded the belligerents to seek an armistice. After Soviet UN Ambassador Jacob Malik publicly advocated a cease-fire, truce negotiations opened in July at Kaesong, located near the 38th parallel. Washington was determined to confine the discussions to military matters, thus preventing China from using the talks to gain admission to the United Nations or control over Taiwan. But the administration's desire for a political victory motivated its proposal for a demilitarized zone above the 38th parallel and thus deep in North Korea. The nasty initial exchange on this issue established an acrimonious tone that guaranteed protracted negotiations. (doc. 9) After the Communists suspended talks for two months—protesting an alleged UN violation of the neutral zone—General Ridgway took advantage of his improved military position to secure a concession from the Communists: the negotiating site would be moved from the tense area of Kaesong to nearby Panmunjom. In November, the delegates agreed that the demilitarized zone would follow the line of battle but then haggled over inspection procedures to enforce the truce. There was rapid approval of a postwar political conference to discuss withdrawal of foreign troops and reunification, but then the talks became hopelessly deadlocked on the issue of prisoner-of-war (POW) repatriation. Truman adopted an inflexible stance on the principle of nonforcible repatriation (doc. 10), while the Communists demanded return of all POWs, as the Geneva Convention of 1949 required. This issue led the United Nations to suspend the talks in October 1952, although it was clear that Chinese Nationalist guards at UN camps had used terrorist "reeducation" tactics to persuade POWs to refuse repatriation.

In November 1952, angry American voters elected Dwight D. Eisenhower as president in large part because they expected him to end what had become a very unpopular war in Korea. Fulfilling a campaign pledge, the general visited the Korean battlefront in December, where he concluded that further ground assaults would be futile. According to his memoirs (doc. 11), Eisenhower decided instead to convince the Communists that the alternative to a truce was an expanded war that included the possible employment of atomic weapons. These threats, if received and understood, may have influenced China, but some writers argue that the Chinese, facing major internal economic problems and wanting peaceful coexistence with the West, already had decided to make peace once Truman left office. Stalin's death on March 5 only added to China's sense of political vulnerability and caused the Communist delegation to break the logjam at Panmunjom later that month. After accepting a UN proposal for exchanging sick and wounded POWs, the two sides agreed in June to turn over those POWs resisting repatriation to a committee of neutral nations. At this juncture,

Rhee, who opposed any armistice that left Korea divided, almost torpedoed the pending cease-fire when he released 27,000 North Korean POWs. Eisenhower eventually bought Rhee's acceptance of the truce with promises of financial assistance and a mutual security pact. Fortunately, the incident only delayed the armistice until July 27, 1953.

From 1941 to 1953, the goal of U.S. policy in Korea was remarkably consistent, as three administrations sought to build a Korean nation that at least appeared to reflect the American model of political, economic, and social development. In pursuit of this objective, the United States paid a steadily increasing price, as it would later in Vietnam. At first, Washington relied primarily on economic means to create a prosperous South Korea, anticipating that the North Korean people would eventually overthrow their Communist rulers and seek peaceful amalgamation. After North Korea attacked, the Truman administration's decision to ensure South Korea's survival was predictable, as was its foolish stab at military conquest. Once China intervened, American involvement in Korea became very costly. In addition to 33,000 dead and 105,000 wounded, Congress implemented the expensive rearmament program outlined in NSC-68, a secret study completed by the State and Defense Departments and submitted to the president by the National Security Council in April 1950. Relations with China were poisoned for twenty years, especially after Washington persuaded the UN to condemn the Chinese for aggression in Korea. American officials spoke about collective security, but the Korean War in fact severely strained relations between the United States and its allies. MacArthur only made alliance politics worse, and Truman, after acting to protect both the nation's interests and its Constitution, ended his tenure as the most unpopular president in American history. His efforts did nothing to weaken the Soviet Union, while leaving the United States more closely wedded to the odious regimes of Chiang Kai-shek and Syngman Rhee. American experiences in Korea after 1945 were extremely unpleasant, begging the question of whether the United States understood the real lessons of this war before Vietnam.

Document 1

Joint Chiefs of Staff assessment of Korea's strategic significance, Sept. 29, 1947, *Public Papers of the Presidents of the United States: Harry S. Truman, 1952–53*, Washington, D.C.: Government Printing Office, 1965, vol. 8, 1046.

The Joint Chiefs of Staff consider that, from the standpoint of military security, the United States has little strategic interest in maintaining the present troops and bases in Korea for the reasons hereafter stated.

In the event of hostilities in the Far East, our present forces in Korea would be a military liability and could not be maintained there without substantial reinforcement prior to the initiation of hostilities. Moreover, any offensive operation the United States might wish to conduct on the Asiatic continent most probably would by-pass the Korean peninsula.

If, on the other hand, an enemy were able to establish and maintain strong air and naval bases in the Korean peninsula, he might be able to interfere with United States communications and operations in East China, Manchuria, the Yellow Sea, Sea of Japan and adjacent islands. Such interference would require an enemy to maintain substantial air and naval forces in an area where they would be subject to neutralization by air action. Neutralization by air action would be more feasible and less costly than large scale ground operations.

In light of the present severe shortage of military manpower, the corps of two divisions, totaling some 45,000 men now maintained in South Korea, could well be used elsewhere, the withdrawal of these forces from Korea would not impair the military position of the Far East Command unless in consequence, the Soviets establish military strength in South Korea capable of mounting an assault in Japan.

At the present time, the occupation of Korea is requiring very large expenditures for the primary purpose of preventing disease and disorder which might endanger our occupation forces with little, if any, lasting benefit to the security of the United States.

Authoritative reports from Korea indicate that continued lack of progress toward a free and independent Korea, unless offset by an elaborate program of economic, political and cultural rehabilitation, in all probability will result in such conditions, including violent disorder, as to make the position of United States occupation forces untenable. A precipitate withdrawal of our forces under such circumstances would lower the military prestige of the United States, quite possibly to the extent of adversely affecting cooperation in other areas more vital to the security of the United States.

Document 2

Secretary of State Dean Acheson's speech to the National Press Club, Jan. 12, 1950, U.S. Department of State, *Bulletin*, Jan. 23, 1950, vol. 12, 111–19.

I am frequently asked: Has the State Department got an Asian policy? . . .

There is in this vast area what we might call a developing Asian consciousness, and a developing pattern, and this, I think, is based upon two factors. . . .

One of these factors is a revulsion against the acceptance of misery and poverty as the normal condition of life. . . . The other common aspect that they have is the revulsion against foreign domination. Whether that foreign domination takes the form of colonialism or whether it takes the form of imperialism, they are through with it. They have had enough of it, and they want no more. . . .

Now, let me come to another underlying and important factor which determines our relations and, in turn, our policy with the peoples of Asia. That is the attitude of the Soviet Union toward Asia, and particularly towards those parts of Asia which are contiguous to the Soviet Union. . . .

The attitude and interest of the Russians in north China, and in these other areas as well, long antedates communism. . . . But the Communist regime has added new methods, new skills, and new concepts to the thrust of Russian imperialism. This Communistic concept and techniques have armed Russian imperialism with a new and most insidious weapon of penetration. Armed with these new powers, what is happening in China is that the Soviet Union is detaching the northern provinces of China from China and is attaching them to the Soviet Union. This process is complete in outer Mongolia. It is nearly complete in Manchuria, and I am sure that in inner Mongolia and in Sinkiang there are very happy reports coming from Soviet agents to Moscow. . . .

. . . This fact that the Soviet Union is taking the four northern provinces of China is the single most significant, most important fact, in the relation of any foreign power with Asia.

What does that mean for us? . . . It means that nothing that we do and nothing that we say must be allowed to obscure the reality of this fact. All the efforts of propaganda will not be able to obscure it. The only thing that can obscure it is the folly of ill-conceived adventures on our part which easily could do so, and I urge all who are thinking about these foolish adventures to remember that we must not seize the unenviable position which the Russians have carved out for themselves. We must not undertake to deflect from the Russians to ourselves the righteous anger, and the wrath, and the hatred of the Chinese people which must develop. . . . That, I suggest to you this afternoon, is the first and the greatest rule in regard to the formulation of American policy toward Asia.

I suggest that the second rule is very like the first. That is to keep our own purposes perfectly straight, perfectly pure, and perfectly aboveboard and do not get them mixed-up with legal quibbles or the attempt to do one thing and really achieve another. . . .

What is the situation in regard to the military security of the Pacific area, and what is our policy in regard to it? . . .

The defensive perimeter runs along the Aleutians to Japan and then goes to the Ryukyus. We hold important defense positions in the Ryukyu Islands, and those we will continue to hold. . . .

The defensive perimeter runs from the Ryukyus to the Philippine Islands. . . . It is hardly necessary for me to say an attack on the Philippines could not and would not be tolerated by the United States. But I hasten to add that no one perceives the imminence of any such attack.

So far as the military security of other areas in the Pacific is concerned, it must be clear that no person can guarantee these areas against military attack. But it must also be clear that such a guarantee is hardly sensible or necessary within the realm of practical relationship.

Should such an attack occur—one hesitates to say where such an armed attack could come from—the initial reliance must be on the people attacked to resist it and then upon the commitments of the entire civilized world under the Charter of the United Nations which so far has not proved a weak reed to lean on by any people who are determined to protect their independence against outside aggression. But it is a mistake, I think, in considering Pacific and Far Eastern problems to become obsessed with military considerations. Important as they are, there are other problems that press, and these other problems are not capable of solution through military means. These other problems arise out of the susceptibility of many areas, and many countries in the Pacific area, to subversion and penetration. That cannot be stopped by military means. . . .

. . . I should like to point out two facts to you and then discuss in more detail some of these areas.

The first fact is the great difference between our responsibility and our opportunities in the northern part of the

Pacific area and in the southern part of the Pacific area. In the north, we have direct responsibility in Japan and we have direct opportunity to act. The same thing to a lesser degree is true in Korea. There we had direct responsibility, and there we did act, and there we have a greater opportunity to be effective than we have in the more southerly part. . . .

. . . American assistance can be effective when it is the missing component in a situation which might otherwise be solved. The United States can not furnish all these components to solve the question. It can not furnish determination, it can not furnish the will, and it can not furnish the loyalty of a people to its government. But if the will and if the determination exists and if the people are behind their government, then, . . . is there a very good chance. In that situation, American help can be effective. . . .

. . . In Korea, we have taken great steps which have ended our military occupation, and in cooperation with the United Nations, have established an independent and sovereign country recognized by nearly all the rest of the world. We have given that nation great help in getting itself established. We are asking the Congress to continue that help until it is firmly established, and that legislation is now pending before the Congress. The idea that we should scrap all of that, that we should stop half way through the achievement of the establishment of this country, seems to me to be the most utter defeatism and utter madness in our interests in Asia. But there our responsibilities are more direct and our opportunities more clear. When you move to the south, you find that our opportunity is much slighter and that our responsibilities, except in the Philippines and there indirectly, are very small. . . .

So after this survey, what we conclude, I believe, is that there is a new day which has dawned in Asia. It is a day in which the Asian people are on their own, and know it, and intend to continue on their own. It is a day in which the old relationships between east and west are gone, relationships which at their worst were exploitation, and which at their best were paternalism. That relationship is over, and the relationship of east and west must now be in the Far East one of mutual respect and mutual helpfulness. . . . We and those others are willing to help, but we can help only where we are wanted and only where the conditions of help are really sensible and possible.

Document 3

Soviet Premier Nikita Khrushchev's account of the origins of the Korean War; in *Khrushchev Remembers*, Strobe Talbott, ed., Boston: Little, Brown, 1970, 367–69. Reprinted with permission.

About the time I was transferred from the Ukraine to Moscow at the end of 1949, Kim Il-sung arrived with his delegation to hold consultations with [Joseph] Stalin. The North Koreans wanted to prod South Korea with the point of a bayonet. Kim Il-sung said that the first poke would touch off an internal explosion in South Korea and that the power of the people would prevail—that is, the power which ruled in North Korea. Naturally Stalin couldn't oppose this idea. It appealed to his convictions as a Communist all the more because the struggle would be an internal matter which the Koreans would be settling among themselves. The North Koreans wanted to give a helping hand to their brethren who were under the heel of Syngman Rhee. Stalin persuaded Kim Il-sung that he should think it over, make some calculations, and then come back with a concrete plan. Kim went home and then returned to Moscow when he had worked everything out. He told Stalin he was absolutely certain of success. I remember Stalin had his doubts. He was worried that the Americans would jump in, but we were inclined to think that if the war were fought swiftly—and Kim Il-sung was sure that it could be won swiftly—then intervention by the USA could be avoided.

Nevertheless, Stalin decided to ask [Chinese Communist party leader] Mao Tse-tung's opinion about Kim Il-sung's suggestion. I must stress that the war wasn't Stalin's idea, but Kim Il-sung's. Kim was the initiator. Stalin, of course, didn't try to dissuade him. In my opinion, no real Communist would have tried to dissuade Kim Il-sung from his compelling desire to liberate South Korea from Syngman Rhee and from reactionary American influence. To have done so would have contradicted the Communist view of the world. I don't condemn Stalin for encouraging Kim. On the contrary, I would have made the same decision myself if I had been in his place.

Mao Tse-tung also answered affirmatively. He approved Kim Il-sung's suggestion and put forward the opinion that the USA would not intervene since the war would be an internal matter which the Korean people would decide for themselves.

I remember a high-spirited dinner at Stalin's dacha. Kim Il-sung told us about the conditions of life in Korea, and he stressed the many attractive things about South Korea—the good soil and excellent climate for growing rice, the prosperous fishing industry, and so on. He said that after the reunification of South and North Korea, Korea as a whole would benefit. Korea would be able to ensure the supply of raw materials for her industry from the north and to meet the food requirements to feed her people from the fish, rice, and other agricultural products which flourished in the south. We wished every success to Kim Il-sung and toasted the whole North Korean leadership, looking forward to the day when their struggle would be won.

We had already been giving arms to North Korea for some time. It was obvious that they would receive the requisite quantity of tanks, artillery, rifles, machine guns, engineering equipment, and antiaircraft weapons. Our air force planes were being used to shield Pyongyang and were therefore stationed in North Korea.

The designated hour arrived and the war began. The attack was launched successfully. The North Koreans swept south swiftly. But what Kim Il-sung had predicted—an internal uprising after the first shots were fired and Syngman Rhee was overthrown—unfortunately failed to materialize. The elimination of Syngman Rhee and his clique was supposed to be accomplished with the advance of the North Korean troops. At first it looked as though Kim Il-sung had been right. The South Korean regime was unstable and wasn't able to defend itself. The resistance was weak. Syngman Rhee indeed didn't have much support within South Korea, but there still weren't enough internal forces for a Communist insurrection in South Korea. Apparently the Party's preparatory organizational work had been inadequate. Kim had believed that South Korea was blanketed with Party organizations and that the people would rise up in revolt when the Party gave the signal. But this never happened.

The North Koreans occupied Seoul. We were all delighted and again wished Kim Il-sung every success because this was a war of national liberation. It was not a war of one people against another, but a class war. Workers, peasants, and intelligentsia under the leadership of the Labor Party of North Korea, which then stood and today still stands on Socialist principles, were united in battle against the capitalists. This in itself was a progressive development.

However, just as Kim Il-sung's army got as far as Pusan, its strength gave out. This was the last port city in the south. It would have to be seized before the war could end. If it had been seized, Korea would have been united. It would no longer have been divided. It would have been a single powerful Socialist country, rich in raw materials, industry, and agriculture.

But that didn't happen. . . .

Stalin was partly to blame for the precarious situation which the North Koreans were in. It's absolutely incomprehensible to me why he did it, but when Kim Il-sung was preparing for his march, Stalin called back all our advisors who were with the North Korean divisions and regiments, as well as all the advisors who were serving as consultants and helping to build up the army. I asked Stalin about this, and he snapped back at me, "It's too dangerous to keep our advisors there. They might be taken prisoner. We don't want there to be evidence for accusing us of taking part in this business. It's Kim Il-sung's affair." So our advisors were recalled. As a result, the North Korean army was in trouble from the very start. . . .

Document 4

President Harry S. Truman's statement on the Korean War, June 27, 1950, U.S. Department of State, *Bulletin,* July 3, 1950, vol. 23, 5.

In Korea the government forces, which were armed to prevent border raids and to preserve internal security, were attacked by invading forces from North Korea. The Security Council of the United Nations called upon the invading troops to cease hostilities and to withdraw to the 38th Parallel. This they have not done, but on the contrary have pressed the attack. The Security Council called upon all members of the United Nations to render every assistance to the United Nations in the execution of this resolution. In these circumstances I have ordered United States air and sea forces to give the Korean Government troops cover and support.

The attack upon Korea makes it plain beyond all doubt that communism has passed beyond the use of subversion to conquer independent nations and will now use armed invasion and war. It has defied the orders of the Security Council of the United Nations issued to preserve peace and security. In these circumstances the occupation of Formosa by Communist forces would be a direct threat to the security of the Pacific area and to United States forces performing their lawful and necessary functions in that area.

Accordingly I have ordered the Seventh Fleet to prevent any attack on Formosa. As a corollary of this action I am calling upon the Chinese Government on Formosa to cease all air and sea operations against the mainland. The Seventh Fleet will see that this is done. The determination of the future status of Formosa must await the restoration of security in the Pacific, a peace settlement with Japan, or consideration by the United Nations.

I have also directed that United States forces in the Philippines be strengthened and that military assistance to the

Philippine Government be accelerated.

I have similarly directed acceleration in the furnishing of military assistance to the forces of France and the associated states in Indochina and the dispatch of a military mission to provide close working relations with those forces.

I know that all members of the United Nations will consider carefully the consequences of this latest aggression in Korea in defiance of the Charter of the United Nations. A return to the rule of force in international affairs would have far-reaching effects. The United States will continue to uphold the rule of law.

Document 5

State Department official John M. Allison's memorandum on crossing the 38th parallel, July 24, 1950, U.S. Department of State, *Foreign Relations of the United States* (hereafter referred to as *FRUS*), *1950, Korea*, Washington, D.C.: Government Printing Office, 1976, vol. 7, 459–61.

I have read and studied carefully the Policy Planning Staff paper on the above subject, and I regret to state that I must enter an emphatic dissent from its philosophy and conclusions. As I understand it, the paper proposes in effect that we make known at once to General [Douglas] MacArthur and the US Delegation to the UN the fact that US objectives in Korea are limited to repelling the aggression of the North Koreans and bringing about the cessation of hostilities and the withdrawal of the attacking forces to the 38th parallel, after which a final solution of the Korean problem would be a matter for UN consideration. In other words we would go back to the *status quo ante bellum* and then ask the UN to start all over again doing what has been its attempt at three General Assemblies since 1947. The aggressor would apparently be consulted on equal or nearly equal terms and the real aggressor, the Soviet Union, would presumably go unpunished in any way whatsoever. The aggressor would be informed that all he had to fear from aggression was being compelled to start over again. . . .

The whole tone of the present paper implies that the North Korean regime has a legal status and that the area north of the 38th parallel is, in fact, a separate nation. This has no foundation in fact or morality. The North Korean regime is a creature of the Soviet Union set up in defiance of the will of the majority of the Korean people, and in deliberate violation of three Resolutions passed in the General Assembly.

The paper makes a false division between what it terms (a) the long term effort to bring about unity and independence in Korea and (b) the present enforcement action to repel North Korean aggression. It assumes the latter phase of the problem can be solved without regard for the former. This is a fundamental error. If a correct solution of the immediate problem is not reached, a correct long term solution will be impossible. . . .

While the paper rightly stresses the importance of the attitude of our UN Allies toward what is done in Korea, it gives only cursory attention to the attitude of the 20 million people of South Korea who have been wantonly attacked, and the more than 2 million Koreans who fled from Soviet oppression in the North and sought refuge in the South. There can be no sound solution which does not take fully into account the hopes of these millions. Any action which implied that the aggressors would suffer but mildly if at all and that the artificial division of Korea was to be perpetuated would cause the people and army of South Korea to lose what little morale they have left and would run the grave danger of turning them actively against American forces now in Korea. . . . The Korean people and Government are already insisting that the 38th parallel division must go and that the present opportunity to unify the country must be seized. American diplomats in Korea have expressed agreement. If this is not done the people of Korea will lose all faith in the courage, intelligence and morality of the United States. And I, for one, would not blame them.

The nub of the problem confronting the United States is correctly stated in the paper—namely whether the disadvantages of a failure to attain complete independence and unity for Korea outweigh the risk of a major conflict with the USSR or Communist China that such a settlement might involve. But the answer given or at least implied is, in my opinion, the wrong one.

While rightly pointing out the strategic importance of Korea to the USSR, one of the main reasons for this importance, that possession of Korea makes easier the ultimate conquest of Japan—the real prize in Asia is neither Korea nor even China—is ignored. And while accepting the fact that the USSR would not permit a regime hostile to it to exist in North Korea, there is no apparent realization of the fact that Japan is of critical importance to the United States and that we cannot afford to allow a regime hostile to American interests in Japan to dominate Korea.

The paper assumes we can buy more time by a policy of appeasement—for that is what this paper recommends—a timid, half-hearted policy designed not to provoke the Soviets to war. We should recognize that there is a grave danger of conflict with the USSR and the Chinese Communists whatever we do from now on—but I fail to see what advantage we gain by a compromise with clear moral principles and a shirking of our duty to make clear once and for all that aggression does not pay—that he who violates the decent opinions of mankind must take the consequences and that he who takes the sword will perish by the sword.

That this may mean war on a global scale is true—the American people should be told and told why and what it will mean to them.

Document 6

General Douglas MacArthur's message to Veterans of Foreign Wars, Aug. 17, 1950, U.S. Congress, Senate, Joint Committee on Armed Services and Foreign Relations, *Military Situation in the Far East,* 81st Cong., 1st sess., Washington, D.C.: Government Printing Office, 1951, 3477–80.

I trust that you will convey to all of my comrades-in-arms of the Veterans of Foreign Wars assembled on the occasion of our Fifty-first Annual National Encampment my assurance that their confidence and support will give this command much added strength to meet the tests of battle which lie immediately ahead.

Tell them that I am happy to report that their successors in arms now engaging the enemy along our battle lines in South Korea are exemplifying that same high standard of devotion, fortitude, and valor which characterized their own march to victory when they themselves engaged in combat in the field. . . .

In view of misconceptions currently being voiced concerning the relationship of Formosa to our strategic potential in the Pacific, I believe it in the public interest to avail myself of this opportunity to state my views thereon to you, all of whom, having fought overseas, understand broad strategic concepts.

To begin with, any appraisal of that strategic potential requires an appreciation of the changes wrought in the course of the past war. Prior thereto the western strategic frontier of the United States lay on the littoral line of the Americas with an exposed island salient extending out through Hawaii, Midway, and Guam to the Philippines.

That salient was not an outpost of enemy strength but an avenue of weakness along which the enemy could and did attack us. The Pacific was a potential area of advancement for any predatory force intent upon striking at the bordering land areas.

All of this was changed by our Pacific victory. Our strategic frontier then shifted to embrace the entire Pacific Ocean, which has become a vast moat to protect us as long as we hold it.

Indeed, it acts as a protective shield to all of the Americas and all free lands of the Pacific Ocean area we control to the shores of Asia by a chain of islands extending in an arc from the Aleutians to the Marianas held by us and our free Allies. From this island chain we can dominate with air power every Asiatic port from Vladivostok to Singapore and prevent any hostile movement into the Pacific.

Any predatory attack from Asia must be an amphibious effort. No amphibious force can be successful with our control of the sea lanes and the air over these lanes in its avenue of advance. . . .

Under such conditions the Pacific no longer represents menacing avenues of approach for a prospective invader—it assumes instead the friendly aspect of a peaceful lake. Our line of defense is a natural one and can be maintained with a minimum of military effort and expense.

It envisions no attack against anyone nor does it provide the bastions essential for offensive operations, but properly maintained would be an invincible defense against aggression. If we hold this line we may have peace—lose it and war is inevitable.

The geographic location of Formosa is such that in the hand of a power unfriendly to the United States it constitutes an enemy salient in the very center of this defensive perimeter, 100 to 150 miles closer to the adjacent friendly segments—Okinawa and the Philippines—than any point in continental Asia. . . .

Formosa in the hands of such a hostile power could be compared to an unsinkable aircraft carrier and submarine tender ideally located to accomplish offensive strategy and at the same time checkmate defensive or counteroffensive operations by friendly forces based on Okinawa and the Philippines.

This unsinkable carrier-tender has the capacity to operate from ten to twenty air groups of types ranging from jet fighters to B-29 type bombers as well as to provide forward operating facilities for short-range coastal submarines.

In acquiring this forward submarine base, the efficacy of the short-range submarine would be so enormously increased by the additional radius of activity as to threaten completely sea traffic from the south and interdict all sea lanes in the Western Pacific. Submarine blockade by the enemy with all its destructive ramifications would thereby become a virtual certainty.

Should Formosa fall and bases thereafter come into the hands of a potential enemy of the United States, the latter will have acquired an additional "fleet" which will have been obtained and can be maintained at an incomparably lower cost than could its equivalent in aircraft carriers and submarine tenders. . . .

Nothing could be more fallacious than the threadbare argument by those who advocate appeasement and defeatism in the Pacific that if we defend Formosa we alienate continental Asia.

Those who speak thus do not understand the Orient. They do not grant that it is in the pattern of the Oriental psychology to respect and follow aggressive, resolute and dynamic leadership—to quickly turn on a leadership characterized by timidity or vacillation—and they underestimate the Oriental mentality. Nothing in the last five years has so inspired the Far East as the American determination to preserve the bulwarks of our Pacific Ocean strategic position from future encroachment, for few of its people fail accurately to appraise the safeguard such determination brings to their free institutions.

To pursue any other course would be to turn over the fruits of our Pacific victory to a potential enemy. It would shift any future battle area 5,000 miles eastward to the coasts of the American continents, our own home coast; it would completely expose our friends in the Philippines, our friends in Australia and New Zealand, our friends in Indonesia, our friends in Japan, and other areas, to the lustful thrusts of those who stand for slavery against liberty, for atheism as against God.

The decision of President [Harry S.] Truman on June 27 lighted into flame a lamp of hope throughout Asia that was burning dimly toward extinction. It marked for the Far East the focal and turning point in this area's struggle for freedom. It swept aside in one great monumental stroke all of the hypocrisy and the sophistry which has confused and deluded so many people distant from the actual scene.

Document 7

General Douglas MacArthur's address to Congress, Apr. 19, 1951, U.S. Congress, Senate, Joint Committee on Armed Services and Foreign Relations, *Military Situation in the Far East,* 81st Cong., 1st sess., Washington, D.C.: Government Printing Office, 1951, 3553–58.

I do not stand here as advocate for any partisan cause, for the issues are fundamental and reach quite beyond the realm of partisan consideration. They must be resolved on the highest plane of national interest if our course is to prove sound and our future protected. I trust, therefore, that you will do me the justice of receiving that which I have to say as solely expressing the considered viewpoint of a fellow American. I address you with neither rancor nor bitterness in the fading twilight of life with but one purpose in mind, to serve my country. . . .

While Asia is commonly referred to as the gateway to Europe, it is no less true that Europe is the gateway to Asia, and the broad influence of the one cannot fail to have its impact upon the other.

There are those who claim our strength is inadequate to protect on both fronts, that we cannot divide our effort. I can think of no greater expression of defeatism. If a potential enemy can divide his strength on two fronts, it is for us to counter his effort.

The Communist threat is a global one. Its successful advance in one sector threatens the destruction of every other sector. You cannot appease or otherwise surrender to communism in Asia without simultaneously undermining our efforts to halt its advance in Europe. . . .

With this brief insight into the surrounding areas I now turn to the Korean conflict. While I was not consulted prior to the President's decision to intervene in the support of the Republic of Korea, that decision from a military standpoint proved a sound one. As I say, a brief and sound one as we hurled back the invaders and decimated his forces. Our victory was complete and our objectives within reach when Red China intervened with numerically superior ground forces. This created a new war and an entirely new situation, a situation not contemplated when our forces were committed against the North Korean invaders, a situation which called for new decisions in the diplomatic sphere to permit the realistic adjustment of military strategy. Such decisions have not been forthcoming.

While no man in his right mind would advocate sending our ground forces into continental China—and such was never given a thought—the new situation did urgently demand a drastic revision of strategic planning if our political aim was to defeat this new enemy as we had defeated the old.

Apart from the military need as I saw it to neutralize sanctuary, protection given to the enemy north of the Yalu, I felt that military necessity in the conduct of the war made necessary:

First, the intensification of our economic blockade against China.

Second, the imposition of a naval blockade against the China coast.

Third, removal of restrictions on air reconnaissance of China's coastal areas and of Manchuria.

Fourth, removal of restrictions on the forces of the Republic of China on Formosa with logistical support to contribute to their effective operation against the Chinese mainland.

For entertaining these views all professionally designed to support our forces committed to Korea and bring hostilities to an end with the least possible delay and at a saving of countless American and Allied lives, I have been severely criticized in lay circles, principally abroad, despite my understanding that from a military standpoint the above views have been fully shared in the past by practically every military leader concerned with the Korean campaign, including our own Joint Chiefs of Staff.

I called for reinforcements, but was informed that reinforcements were not available. I made clear that if not permitted to utilize the friendly Chinese force of some 600,000 men on Formosa; if not permitted to blockade the China coast to prevent the Chinese Reds from getting succor from without; and if there were to be no hope of major reinforcements, the position of the command from the military standpoint forbade victory. We could hold in Korea by constant maneuver and at an approximate area where our supply advantages were in balance with the supply line disadvantages of the enemy, but we could hope at best for only an indecisive campaign, with its terrible and constant attrition upon our forces if the enemy utilized his full military potential. I have constantly called for the new political decisions essential to a solution. Efforts have been made to distort my position. It has been said in effect that I was a warmonger. Nothing could be further from the truth. I know war as few other men now living know it, and nothing to me is more revolting. . . .

But once war is forced upon us, there is no other alternative than to apply every available means to bring it to a swift end. War's very object is victory—not prolonged indecision. In war, indeed, there can be no substitute for victory.

There are some who for varying reasons would appease Red China. They are blind to history's clear lesson. For history teaches with unmistakable emphasis that appeasement but begets new and bloodier war. It points to no single instance where the end has justified the means—where appeasement has led to more than a sham peace. Like blackmail, it lays the basis for new and successively greater demands, until, as in blackmail, violence becomes the only other alternative. Why, my soldiers asked of me, surrender military advantages to an enemy in the field? I could not answer. Some may say to avoid spread of the conflict into an all-out war with China; others, to avoid Soviet intervention. Neither explanation seems valid. For China is already engaging with the maximum power it can commit and the Soviet [Union] will not necessarily mesh its actions with our moves. Like a cobra, any new enemy will more likely strike whenever it feels that the relativity in military or other potential is in its favor on a world-wide basis.

The tragedy of Korea is further heightened by the fact that as military action is confined to its territorial limits, it condemns that nation, which it is our purpose to save, to suffer the devastating impact of full naval and air bombardment, while the enemy's sanctuaries are fully protected from such attack and devastation. Of the nations of the world, Korea alone, up to now, is the sole one which has risked its all against communism. The magnificence of the courage and fortitude of the Korean people defies description. They have chosen to risk death rather than slavery. Their last words to me were ''Don't scuttle the Pacific.''

I have just left your fighting sons in Korea. They have met all tests there and I can report to you without reservation they are splendid in every way. It was my constant effort to preserve them and end this savage conflict honorably and with the least loss of time and a minimum sacrifice of life. Its growing bloodshed has caused me the deepest anguish and anxiety. Those gallant men will remain often in my thoughts and in my prayers always.

I am closing my 52 years of military service. When I joined the Army even before the turn of the century, it was the fulfillment of all my boyish hopes and dreams. The world has turned over many times since I took the oath on the plain at West Point, and the hopes and dreams have long since vanished. But I since remember the refrain of one of the most popular barrack ballads of that day which proclaimed most proudly that—

''Old soldiers never die; they just fade away.'' And like the old soldier of that ballad, I now close my military career and just fade away—an old soldier who tried to do his duty as God gave him the light to see that duty.

Good-by.

Document 8

Testimony of General Omar N. Bradley, Chairman of the Joint Chiefs of Staff, at the MacArthur hearings, May 15, 1951, U.S. Senate, *Military Situation in the Far East*, 729–33.

What is the great issue at stake in this hearing?

Principally I would say that you are trying to determine the course we should follow as the best road to peace. There are military factors which must be evaluated before a sound decision can be made. At present the issue is obscured in the public mind by many details which do not relate to the task of keeping the peace and making America secure.

The fundamental military issue that has arisen is whether to increase the risk of a global war by taking additional measures that are open to the United States and its allies. We now have a localized conflict in Korea. Some of the military measures under discussion might well place the United States in the position of responsibility for broadening the war and at the same time losing most if not all of our allies.

General MacArthur has stated that there are certain additional measures which can and should be taken, and that by so doing no unacceptable increased risk of global war will result.

The Joint Chiefs of Staff believe that these same measures do increase the risk of global war and that such a risk should not be taken unnecessarily. . . . The Joint Chiefs of Staff, in view of their global responsibilities and their perspective with respect to the worldwide strategic situation, are in a better position than is any single theater commander to assess the risk of general war. Moreover, the Joint Chiefs of Staff are best able to judge our own military resources with which to meet this risk. . . .

We must understand—as we conduct our foreign affairs and our military affairs—that while power and nationalism prevail, it is up to us to gain strength through cooperative efforts with other nations which have common ideals and objectives with our own. At the same time, we must create and maintain the power essential to persuasion, and to our own security in such a world. . . .

One of the great power potentials of this world is the United States of America and her allies. The other great power in this world is Soviet Russia and her satellites. As much as we desire peace, we must realize that we have two centers of power supporting opposing ideologies.

From a global viewpoint—and with the security of our nation of prime importance—our military mission is to support a policy of preventing communism from gaining the manpower, the resources, the raw materials, and the industrial capacity essential to world domination. If Soviet Russia ever controls the entire Eurasian land mass, then the Soviet-satellite imperialism may have the broad base upon which to build the military power to rule the world.

Three times in the past five years the Kremlin-inspired imperialism has been thwarted by direct action.

In Berlin, Greece, and Korea, the free nations have opposed Communist aggression with a different type of action. But each time the power of the United States has been called upon and we have become involved. Each incident has cost us money, resources, and some lives.

But in each instance we have prevented the domination of one more area, and the absorption of another source of manpower, raw materials, and resources.

Korea, in spite of the importance of the engagement, must be looked upon with proper perspective. It is just one engagement, just one phase of this battle that we are having with the other power center in the world which opposes us and all we stand for. For five years this "guerrilla diplomacy" has been going on. In each of the actions in which we have participated to oppose this gangster conduct, we have risked World War III. But each time we have used methods short of total war. As costly as Berlin and Greece and Korea may be, they are less expensive than the vast destruction which would be inflicted upon all sides if a total war were to be precipitated.

I am under no illusion that our present strategy of using means short of total war to achieve our ends and oppose communism is a guarantee that a world war will not be thrust upon us. But a policy of patience and determination without provoking a world war, while we improve our military power, is one which we believe we must continue to follow.

As long as we keep the conflict within its present scope, we are holding to a minimum the forces we must commit and tie down.

The strategic alternative, enlargement of the war in Korea to include Red China, would probably delight the Kremlin more than anything else we could do. It would necessarily tie down additional forces, especially our sea power and our air power, while the Soviet Union would not be obliged to put a single man into the conflict.

Under present circumstances, we have recommended against enlarging the war. The course of action often described as a "limited war" with Red China would increase the risk we are taking by engaging too much of our power in an area that is not the critical strategic prize.

Red China is not the powerful nation seeking to dominate the world. Frankly, in the opinion of the Joint Chiefs of Staff, this strategy would involve us in the wrong war, at the wrong place, at the wrong time, and with the wrong enemy. . . .

Some critics have not hesitated to state that the policy our government is following, and its included strategy, is not that which has been recommended by the Joint Chiefs of Staff. . . .

This is just not so. The Joint Chiefs of Staff have continually given their considered opinion—always from a military viewpoint—concerning our global capabilities and responsibilities and have recommended our present strategy in and for Korea. This has been the course of action which the Secretary of Defense and the Commander in Chief have adopted as far as practicable. . . .

There are . . . those who deplore the present military situation in Korea and urge us to engage Red China in a larger war to solve this problem. Taking on Red China is not a decisive move, does not guarantee the end of the war in Korea, and may not bring China to her knees. . . . I would say that . . . victory over Red China would be many years away. We believe that every effort should be made to settle the present conflict without extending it outside Korea. If this proves to be impossible, then other measures may have to be taken. . . .

In my consideration of this viewpoint, I am going back to the basic objective of the American people—as much peace as we can gain without appeasement. . . .

From a military viewpoint, appeasement occurs when you give up something, which is rightfully free, to an aggressor without putting up a struggle, or making him pay a price. Forsaking Korea—withdrawing from the fight unless we are forced out—would be an appeasement to aggression. Refusing to enlarge the quarrel to the point where our global capabilities are diminished, is certainly not appeasement but is a militarily sound course of action under the present circumstances.

Document 9

Statement of North Korean People's Army General Nam Il on UN demilitarized zone proposal and Admiral C. Turner Joy's response, July 28, 1951, *FRUS, 1951, Korea and China*, 1983, vol. 15, 748–52.

Yesterday I heard with surprise your incredible statement and had a glance at that map of yours on which were 3 lines. . . . One of the 3 lines was apparently advocated by you to be fixed as the military demarcation line. . . . Such lines drawn at random were not worthy of attention . . . because your arguments were naive and illogical. . . . You maintained that the fixing of this military demarcation line and the delineation of a demilitarized zone must start from the consideration of the existing military realities and be free from the influence of any political or territorial considerations. Now among the so-called military considerations, you advocated the doctrine of military effectiveness. You contended that you held Air and Naval superiority and that therefore, the demarcation line drawn across the land must enable the area occupied by your ground forces to be pushed forward a great step into our area so as to reflect the present military situation. We consider that this theory of yours is based on a one-sided, simple and incorrect military point of view. We consider that in fixing a military demarcation line, due attention should indeed be paid to the military realities on the battlefront. Yet the armistice we seek is the first step toward the peaceful settlement of the Korean question. . . . Judging by this criterion, the entire tenor of your statement was to boast about the so-called military power and effectiveness on your side in an attempt to intimidate. You should be aware that such a gesture can intimidate nobody but, what is more important, such a gesture can only have a harmful effect on the armistice negotiations as the first step towards the peaceful settlement of the Korean question. You asserted that the advantages we would gain by the cessation of Air and Naval attacks by the United Nations Forces would be greater than the advantages given up by us in the withdrawal by our ground forces to the line running through Pyongyang and Wonsan. I would like to know, since the situation is so preponderantly favorable on your side, why did you not hold your ground in the Pyongyang-Wonsan line you had reached instead of withdrawing . . . under the cover and support of your Naval and Air Forces? May I advise you sincerely that these naive remarks you have made can have no good purpose for our negotiations. . . .

The factors constituting war power in fact are much more complicated than the effectiveness of the various arms of the forces. We have repeatedly stressed other factors as manpower, morale, political conditions, etc. Of course, I have not sufficient time to discuss military theories at present. I will only make a few remarks about the ridiculous theory about the 3 zones: land, air and sea.

It mentions in any military manual worthy of its name that military power is the sum total of the power of all arms of the forces. The position gained by any one of the arms is dependent upon the coordination of the other arms. . . . In other words, your battle lines on the ground are the concentrated expression of the military effectiveness of your land, air and sea forces.

I must further point out that the indiscriminate bombing and bombardment by your Naval and Air Forces have in the past year only destroyed a large number of peaceful towns and villages, killed and wounded innocent civilians of our country without being able to intimidate the Korean Peoples Army and the Chinese Peoples Volunteers. In fact, we are steadily overcoming the difficulties caused by your bombing and bombardment and are progressing in large strides. . . . You maintain that once all hostilities cease, you will be at a disadvantage and hence you propose that the military demarcation line must be deep in our side so that it will be no loss to you. Such logic of yours can only deceive those who are neurotic and muddle headed. Therefore the military demarcation line which you have proposed on such a fallacious theory is completely groundless and hence unworthy of consideration and cannot be considered. On the other hand, our proposal of fixing the 38 parallel as the military demarcation line between both sides reflects from the viewpoint of military consideration the relative war power of both sides at the present state. . . . What are the characteristics of the battlefront at the present stage? Since this year the situation of the battlefront has been changing all the time. . . .

This kind of situation will continue until agreement is reached through our negotiations and implemented. Therefore . . . all attempts to take the present military situation as the basis of the military demarcation line cannot reflect the military realities and consequently cannot be subject for consideration. . . .

Secondly, another characteristic of the battlefront is that the battlelines are changing all the time, while on the whole, remaining within the sphere of the region of the 38 parallel. Obviously any clear-headed military observer or military commander has to admit this powerful fact. . . . Therefore, proceeding purely from the military viewpoint alone, we deem that the 38 parallel as a military demarcation line is reasonable, realistic, and practicable. . . .

After giving you my deliberating criticism of your statement of yesterday, I would like to put to you a question. Seeing that you make such a completely absurd and arrogant statement for what actually have you come here? Have you come here to negotiate for peace or just to look for an excuse for extending the war? I formally ask you to give us your answer to this question. . . .

[Admiral Joy:] You closed your statement this morning with a rhetorical question so inappropriate, so irrelevant and so discourteous as to be unworthy of a reply. But you compounded this rude and graceless act by a formal request for a formal reply. It is for that reason that I dignify your question with an answer. In making that reply I need only cite the presence of the United Nations Command Delegation in this Armistice Conference as evidence of our sincere intent to seek an honorable and equitable basis for the termination of hostilities. If it were, as you imply, our objective to prolong hostilities, we should not need to come to an armistice conference in search of an excuse.

I wish to comment briefly on the tone of your remarks this morning. In your statement this morning you expressed yourself in rude terms applied to the United Nations Command Delegation, including many discourteous adjectives. In your discourtesy, you have resorted to bluster directed at this delegation. All here are presumed to be military men. Those peoples whose military organizations are respected throughout the world are proud of the reputation for courtesy and for objective mental attitudes towards serious questions unfailingly demonstrated by the personnel of their armed services. Military men are expected to be sufficiently mature to realize that bluster and bombast phrased in intemperate language do not and cannot affect the facts of any military situation. No amount of such vituperation as was indulged in by you this morning will sway the concentration of the United Nations Command Delegation on the serious problems before this conference. No am[oun]t of discourtesy will tempt the United Nations Command Delegation to utilize similar tactics.

You should understand, however, that rudeness such as you have displayed will lead to only one end if continued. That is, the United Nations Command Delegation will be compelled to conclude you have no serious or sincere purpose at this conference, and the prospect of peace in Korea will be greatly dimmed. With all the earnestness at my command I urge you to consider most seriously where your recent attitude may lead. I hope to note in your further remarks, tangible evidence that this conference will resume the high level of traditional courtesy between military men, which until this morning, it had enjoyed, so that progress in an atmosphere of logic and reason may go rapidly forward.

Document 10

President Harry S. Truman's defense of the nonforcible repatriation of POWs, Harry S. Truman, *Memoirs: Years of Trial and Hope, 1946–1952*, Garden City, New York: Doubleday, 1956, 460–63. Reprinted by permission of Margaret Truman Daniel.

We were most anxious, of course, to bring our prisoners back home. There had been many stories and much evidence of inhuman treatment of prisoners taken by the Communists. The Communists, however, refused Red Cross inspection of prison camps, although they finally furnished our side with a list of prisoners' names. Still, this accounted for only about one sixth of the number of prisoners they themselves claimed to have captured. . . .

On January 1, 1952, our side proposed that all prisoners of war who wished to be returned should be exchanged. It was here that the most serious wrangling began; it was here, also, that I insisted that we could not give ground.

Communism is a system that has no regard for human dignity or human freedom, and no right-thinking government can give its consent to the forcible return to such a system of men or women who would rather remain free. Just as I had always insisted that we could not abandon the South Koreans . . . so I now refused to agree to any solution that provided for the return against their will of prisoners of war to Communist domination. A public statement I made on May 7, 1952, expressed my thoughts in official language, but there is one sentence in it that says exactly what was in my mind in words that mean what they say:

"We will not buy an armistice by turning over human beings for slaughter or slavery." . . .

Here is . . . that statement: . . .

"After many trying months of negotiation, in which each issue has been dealt with individually, tentative agreement has been reached on all but three issues. It is now apparent that the three remaining issues cannot be resolved separately. The U.N. Command proposal offers a just and a real opportunity to resolve these three issues together and simultaneously. The three-point proposal is:

"a. That there shall not be a forced repatriation of prisoners of war—as the Communists have insisted. To agree to forced repatriation would be unthinkable. It would be repugnant to the fundamental moral and humanitarian principles which underlie our action in Korea. To return these prisoners of war in our hands by force would result in misery and bloodshed to the eternal dishonor of the United States and of the U.N.

"We will not buy an armistice by turning over human beings for slaughter or slavery. The U.N. Command has observed the most extreme care in separating those prisoners who have said they would forcibly oppose return to Communist control. We have offered to submit to an impartial re-screening—after an armistice—of those persons we would hold in our custody. Nothing could be fairer. For the Communists to insist upon the forcible return to them of persons who wish to remain out of their control, is an amazing disclosure before the whole world of the operation of their system.

"b. That the U.N. Command will not insist on prohibiting reconstruction or rehabilitation of airfields.

"c. That the neutral nations supervisory commission should comprise representatives of our countries: Poland and Czechoslovakia, chosen by the Communists; Sweden and Switzerland, chosen by the U.N. Command.

". . . The three parts of General [Matthew B.] Ridgway's proposal are all parts of a whole. They must be considered as an entity—not piecemeal. Our agreement is contingent upon acceptance of the whole proposal. This is our position. The Communists thus far have indicated only a willingness to withdraw their proposal that the U.S.S.R. be a member of the neutral inspection commission. This spurious issue was raised by them late in negotiations and its withdrawal is no real concession. . . .

". . . General Ridgway's proposal offers a sound and sensible way to settle the remaining issues all at once. It will have compelling appeal to those sincerely desiring peace." . . .

The Communists, however, still refused to make any concessions on the prisoner-exchange issue. They wanted to swap all the prisoners they held for all the prisoners held by our side. I had made it very clear that I would not agree to any trade of prisoners that might result in forcibly returning non-Communists to Communist control. To have agreed would have been not only inhumane and tragic but dishonorable as well, for our checks in the PW camps showed that the vast majority of the Chinese and North Koreans taken by our side preferred not to be returned under such conditions. We proposed, however, to exchange all who wanted to be exchanged.

Document 11

President Dwight D. Eisenhower's explanation for the armistice in the Korean War, Dwight D. Eisenhower, *Mandate for Change, 1953–1956,* Garden City, New York: Doubleday, 1963, 179–83. Reprinted by permission.

But now, in the spring of 1953, I was President and I considered several possible lines of action. First of all would be to let the war drag on, without a change in policy. If a satisfactory armistice could not be quickly achieved, continuing this way seemed to me intolerable. We were sustaining heavy casualties for little, if any, gain.

Another plan might be to attack to the north to gain an all-out military victory by conventional means. This was the least attractive of all plans. The Chinese and North Korean Communists had sat on the same defensive line for a solid year and a half. Being diligent workers, they had done a remarkable job of digging interlaced and underground entrenchments across the entire peninsula, with positions organized in depth. They had partially overcome former logistical deficiencies by bringing in large quantities of artillery and stores of ammunition during quiet periods, and had a force in Korea superior in numbers to that of the ROK [Republic of Korea] and United Nations forces combined.

These facts would not in themselves necessarily preclude an attack. The UN enjoyed air superiority, and, with the superior weapons and equipment and highly developed logistical system of the UN forces, an attack might well have been successful, particularly if accompanied by an amphibious landing in the enemy's rear. Nevertheless, any such attack would be costly, whether the objective was local or unlimited. . . . Moreover, if the purpose were to occupy the major part of the peninsula of Korea, success would put us in an extremely awkward position, with a substantial occupation of territory but no ability to use our weapons to complete the victory—that is, unless the "sanctuary" concept were discarded and attack on airfields and targets in Manchuria were allowed. Such a change would increase the danger of spreading the war.

An attack launched merely to move the line of contact to the narrow waist of the peninsula . . . would not in itself prove decisive and would never merit the cost in lives.

Clearly, then, a course of action other than a conventional ground attack in Korea was necessary.

In the light of my unwillingess to accept the status quo, several other moves were considered in the event that the Chinese Communists refused to accede to an armistice in a reasonable time. These possibilities differed in detail, but in order to back up any of them, we had to face several facts.

First, it was obvious that if we were to go over to a major offensive, the war would have to be expanded outside of Korea—with strikes against the supporting Chinese airfields in Manchuria, a blockade of the Chinese coast, and similar measures. Second, a build-up of both United States and ROK forces would be necessary. I had already authorized the raising of military aid to the ROK Army to permit an increase from 460,000 to 525,000 troops and the organization of two new divisions. This would bring the ROK Army up to fourteen divisions, as a step toward a total of twenty. In addition, there were more United States units available. . . . Build-up of Korean ammunition stocks would also be required, which would cut, undesirably but not fatally, into ammunition already committed to NATO.

Finally, to keep the attack from becoming overly costly, it was clear that we would have to use atomic weapons.

This necessity was suggested to me by General [Douglas] MacArthur while I, as President-elect, was still living in New York. The Joint Chiefs of Staff were pessimistic about the feasibility of using tactical atomic weapons on front-line positions, in view of the extensive underground fortifications which the Chinese Communists had been able to construct; but such weapons would obviously be effective for strategic targets in North Korea, Manchuria, and on the Chinese coast.

If we decided upon a major, new type of offensive, the present policies would have to be changed and the new ones agreed to by our allies. Foremost would be the proposed use of atomic weapons. In this respect American views have always differed somewhat from those of some of our allies. For the British, for example, the use of atomic weapons in war at that time would have been a decision of the gravest kind. My feeling was then, and still remains, that it would be impossible for the United States to maintain the military commitments which it now sustains around the world . . . did we not possess atomic weapons and the will to use them when necessary. But an American decision to use them at that time would have created strong disrupting feelings between ourselves and our allies. However, if an all-out offensive should be highly successful, I feel that the rifts so caused could, in time, be repaired.

Of course, there were other problems, not the least of which would be the possibility of the Soviet Union entering the war. In nuclear warfare the Chinese Communists would have been able to do little. But we knew that the Soviets had atomic weapons in quantity. . . . Of all the Asian targets which might be subjected to Soviet bombing, I was most concerned about the unprotected cities of Japan. . . .

The lack of progress in the long-stalemated talks—they were then recessed—and the nearly stalemated war both demanded, in my opinion, definite measures on our part to put an end to these intolerable conditions. One possibility was to let the Communist authorities understand that, in the absence of satisfactory progress, we intended to move decisively without inhibition in our use of weapons, and would no longer be responsible for confining hostilities to the Korean Peninsula. We would not be limited by any world-wide gentleman's agreement. In India and in the Formosa Straits area, and at the truce negotiations at Panmunjom, we dropped the word, discreetly, of our intention. We felt quite sure it would reach Soviet and Chinese Communist ears.

Soon the prospects for armistice negotiations seemed to improve. On the 22nd of February, General [Mark] Clark wrote a routine letter to the Communist high command to ask whether they would be willing to repatriate seriously sick and wounded prisoners of war in accordance with the Geneva Convention. The sending of this kind of letter was almost a common practice, but this time the Communists expressed willingness to repatriate and to resume truce negotiations. This exchange of letters resulted in a dramatic operation called "Little Switch," in which all sick and wounded prisoners . . . were returned from the hands of their captors to their own lines. . . .

One of the issues [in the armistice negotiations] was our insistence on settling the prisoners-of-war question before proceeding with the rest of the truce negotiations. This issue, of repatriation, we believed should serve as a test of the good faith of the Chinese Communists. All the time, however, there was the danger that the resumed truce negotiations would serve simply as a platform for further propaganda. In one White House meeting early in May there was considerable discussion about the current Red Chinese propaganda in favor of substituting a political conference—which, because of its extended nature, would probably hold us indefinitely to the status quo—for the armistice conference on the prisoners-of-war issue. All present at the meeting concurred in my conclusion that this was another stalling action and should be flatly rejected.

On the 4th of June the Communists submitted a prisoners-of-war proposal which seemed highly favorable. . . . When the Communist offer was received, . . . its terms accorded substantially with ours of May 25. The Communists were willing to go further than we could have expected on the question of release to civilian status of prisoners electing not to be returned to their homelands. We knew that many soldiers captured by United Nations forces would want to stay in South Korea. It now appeared . . . that the prisoners-of-war issue had been solved and there should be little hindrance to our reaching a full agreement. . . . It would be difficult to agree on a truce line, in the light of the ebb and flow of battle, which had been severe during recent weeks, in which period the Communists had made numerous gains against ROK units. . . .

On June 8 the Communists agreed to voluntary repatriation of prisoners of war, for months the biggest thorn in the side of the negotiators. The next day the negotiators at Panmunjom began dealing with the question of a final cease-fire line.

CHAPTER 9

Eisenhower's Foreign Policy

Burton I. Kaufman

When Dwight D. Eisenhower assumed the Oval Office on January 23, 1953, the major problem confronting his new administration was the Korean War (covered in the preceding chapter). But the new president also faced a series of other foreign policy dilemmas that encompassed the entire globe. Indeed, a widespread sense of crisis and despair pervaded the country as Americans sought to comprehend a chain of developments that challenged the United States' moral authority and world leadership.

To end the Korean War, Eisenhower resorted to "brinkmanship" diplomacy in raising the possibility of using nuclear weapons against the Chinese Communists if they did not agree to a truce. In a 1956 article in *Life* magazine, his secretary of state, John Foster Dulles, explained that the threat of nuclear war (or "massive retaliation") was sometimes necessary to prevent or—in the case of Korea—end war. In the same article, Dulles cited two other instances besides Korea in which the Eisenhower administration had resorted to brinkmanship in Asia.

The first of these came in Vietnam (then Indochina), where the French were fighting a losing war against Communist guerrillas known as the Viet Minh, named after their chieftain, Ho Chi Minh. By 1954, the United States was paying for almost 80 percent of the war. Still, the Viet Minh controlled more than half of the country. In a last desperate effort to salvage victory, the French sent their best troops into an isolated garrison north of Hanoi called Dien Bien Phu and, convinced that in a conventional battle they could defeat the guerrillas, dared the Viet Minh to come after them. Instead, the Viet Minh brought heavy artillery into the mountains surrounding Dien Bien Phu and inflicted heavy losses on the garrison. It was clear that the French, already tired of the war, would withdraw their troops from Vietnam if Dien Bien Phu fell.

In the end, the Eisenhower administration did nothing to save the beleaguered outpost. The president, however, believed that the loss of Vietnam might have a domino effect throughout the rest of Southeast Asia (doc. 1) and gave serious consideration to American military intervention in the war, including a conventional air strike against the Viet Minh surrounding

Dien Bien Phu. He was even prepared to use nuclear weapons against Chinese targets if the Chinese Communists intervened in the war. But he was not prepared to use tactical nuclear weapons to relieve the garrison, as Admiral Arthur Radford, chairman of the Joint Chiefs of Staff, and Vice President Richard M. Nixon wanted. Because Eisenhower was determined to avoid a second Korea, he also resisted unilateral intervention, insisting first on the support of Great Britain and the Congress, which was not forthcoming. (doc. 2) Without American intervention, Dien Bien Phu fell on May 8. Two months later, the French signed the Geneva Accords, which divided Vietnam at the 17th degree of latitude, or parallel, pending national elections.

The Eisenhower administration refused to sign the Geneva Accords. Instead, it led the way in forming the Southeast Asia Treaty Organization (SEATO) and in extending its protective umbrella to include southern Vietnam. The United States also gave its backing to the anti-Communist government of Ngo Dinh Diem in the south and supported his decision in 1956 not to hold nationwide elections, which he almost certainly would have lost to Ho Chi Minh in the north. Finally, it lent increasing economic and military aid, including military advisers, to Diem's government. In effect, the United States replaced France as the principal guardian of Southeast Asia against Communist expansion.

No sooner had the armistice in Vietnam been arranged than the administration faced another crisis, which involved a threat by the Chinese Communists to ''liberate'' the small islands of Quemoy and Matsu from the Chinese Nationalists. The crisis began in September 1954 when the Communists started shelling the islands. They also talked about an early liberation of Formosa (Taiwan). In response, Congress approved the Formosa Resolution, which gave Eisenhower virtually unlimited authority to take whatever steps were necessary to protect Formosa and neighboring islands against attack. (doc. 3)

A major threat of war between the United States and the People's Republic of China ensued as intermittent bombardment of Quemoy and Matsu continued. Once more the administration seriously considered using nuclear weapons against mainland China and might have done so had the Chinese actually launched an invasion of the islands. On March 12, Dulles made public his threat of atomic reprisal. The warning was evidently effective, for the next month the Chinese proposed a conference to discuss Far Eastern matters. Although the conference settled none of the differences between the countries, Chinese pressure on the islands lessened and the crisis subsided.

A similar crisis developed in 1958 after the Chinese Nationalists reinforced Quemoy and Matsu with 100,000 troops and the Communists began shelling the islands once more. This time Eisenhower came under heavy pressure at home and abroad to make a pledge to defend islands whose strategic value did not seem worth the risk of war. The administration found a solution. It compelled Chinese Nationalist leader Chiang Kai-shek to renounce publicly the use of force to regain control of mainland China. In return, the Beijing government agreed to a de facto cease-fire.

Despite the policy of brinkmanship the administration had followed in the Korean War, Vietnam, and the Quemoy and Matsu crisis, Eisenhower hesitated to continue along this path because he feared a nuclear war with the Soviet Union. The president was also alarmed at the high cost of the Cold War. He agreed, therefore, to meet with the Soviet leaders in Geneva in July 1955 after Moscow made a series of conciliatory gestures, including an agreement to end its military occupation of Austria. In this first post–World War II summit meeting, delegations from the United States, the Soviet Union, Great Britain, and France discussed German reunification, European security, disarmament, and East-West trade. Although none of these issues was resolved, reporters talked of a "spirit of Geneva." The meeting did seem to represent a thaw in the Cold War, at least until October, when another meeting at Geneva, this one of the nations' foreign ministers, grappled with these issues and broke down in deadlock.

Indeed, relations between Moscow and Washington reached another low point in the autumn of 1956 as a result of a new crisis in the Middle East and a revolution against Soviet control in Hungary. The Middle East crisis developed in July 1956, when Premier Gamal Abdel Nasser of Egypt nationalized the privately held Suez Canal following the cancellation of American, British, and French pledges of aid to Egypt for an enlargement of the Aswan Dam on the Nile River. Nasser seized the canal partly to pay for the dam. About the same time, however, he made threats against Israel. Great Britain and France, both large stockholders in the canal company, plotted with Israel, which wanted to launch a preemptive strike. On October 29, Israel attacked across the Sinai Desert and moved toward the canal. As prearranged, Great Britain and France demanded that Egypt and Israel stop fighting and withdraw from the area of the canal. When Nasser refused, they occupied the northern third of the waterway.

Eisenhower was furious because the allies had not consulted him and because he feared that the attack might draw the Egyptians (and other Arabs) closer to the Soviet Union. At the United Nations, Ambassador Henry Cabot Lodge called for an urgent meeting of the Security Council, where he presented the United States' position on the Suez crisis. (doc. 4) Eisenhower also put great economic pressure on Great Britain and France to end the war. Although humiliated and resentful toward the United States, they had little choice except to withdraw their forces. This outcome allowed Egypt to maintain control of the canal and made Nasser a hero throughout the Arab world.

In Hungary, meanwhile, the Soviet Union in 1956 was putting down a student-led revolution against its control. Following a liberalization of Stalinist restrictions by the new Soviet leader, Nikita Khrushchev, another Eastern European country, Poland, had successfully transferred leadership from the ruling politburo to Wladyslaw Gomulka, an independent Communist. News of Gomulka's success had led students and workers in Hungary to take to the streets, demanding that longtime Stalinist leader Erno Gero be replaced by Imre Nagy, whom the Soviets had deposed in 1955. At first, the Soviets gave in to these demands. But when Nagy announced that Hungary was withdrawing from the Warsaw Pact, Khrushchev sent tanks into Budapest and brutally crushed the revolution.

Frequent talk by Dulles and others about ''liberating'' Eastern Europe and ''rolling back'' Communism had led leaders of the Hungarian revolution to believe that the United States would come to their aid. Yet there was never a chance that Eisenhower would risk World War III by giving military support to the Hungarians, even if the United States had been militarily able to do so—which it was not. All the United States could do was to protest the action taken by the Soviet Union. (doc. 5) Talk about liberation was nothing more than that—talk. Taken together, the disarray of the Western allies caused by the Suez crisis and the failure of the United States to come to the aid of the Hungarians made the autumn of 1956 one of the bleakest for the United States in the history of the Cold War.

The Suez crisis also revealed the potency of Third World nationalism and the danger of growing Soviet influence among Third World nations. For the remainder of his administration, therefore, Eisenhower made the containment of Communism in the Third World one of his highest priorities. This approach meant continuing attention to developments in the Middle East and a new emphasis on relations with Latin America.

In 1957, Congress approved the Eisenhower Doctrine, which allowed the president to use military force to defend Middle Eastern nations that requested aid against Communist-inspired aggression. (doc. 6) The next year, Eisenhower sent 5,000 troops into Lebanon, arguing that they were needed to forestall a threatened Communist coup. Actually, the unrest involved nationalism, not Communism, and when the coup failed to materialize, the administration was subject to criticism at home and, to further complications, in the Middle East.

After 1958, President Eisenhower also showed increased concern about developments in Latin America. In Guatemala in 1954 (doc. 7), exiles led by the U.S. Central Intelligence Agency had overthrown the legitimately elected government of Jacobo Arbenz Guzmán after he threatened to expropriate the massive land holdings of United Fruit Company, placed Communists and leftists in government positions, and accepted a shipment of Soviet arms. (A year earlier, a similar CIA-led coup in Iran had toppled the leftist-leaning government of Muhammad Musaddiq and restored the shah as ruler.) Except for Guatemala, however, Eisenhower had focused on other areas of the world and largely ignored Latin America during his first term in office. Then, after a series of developments culminated in a riot during Vice President Nixon's visit to Venezuela in 1958, the administration began to show more concern about its Latin American policy.

Eisenhower's new interest in the region, however, came too late to prevent a Cuban revolution, led in 1959 by Fidel Castro, from turning bitterly anti-American. Although Washington promptly recognized the new Cuban government, Castro would not forgive the United States for supporting the repressive regime of former President Fulgencio Batista. Relations between Havana and Washington deteriorated after Castro seized American-owned property and conducted mass executions of former Batista officials. By 1960, Eisenhower had determined that Castro was a Communist and gave the CIA permission to plan for an invasion of Cuba by anti-Castro exiles. In early 1961, the administration severed diplomatic relations with Cuba.

Eisenhower's administration ended on a somber note in another important way. Fearing the rearmament of West Germany, in November 1958 Khrushchev precipitated a crisis over Berlin by threatening to conclude a separate peace treaty with East Germany, which would turn over access to West Berlin to the East German government if negotiations on European security, a nuclear-free Germany, and the end of four-power occupation of Berlin did not begin within six months. Although Eisenhower resisted pressure to mobilize for war, he held firm against the Soviet ultimatum. Fearful of provoking a nuclear war, Khrushchev backed down, and the crisis ended. He even visited the United States in 1959 and arranged with Eisenhower for a summit meeting in Paris, scheduled for May 1960.

The summit meeting never took place. On the eve of the conference, an American U-2 spy plane was shot down over Soviet territory. At first, the United States denied that the plane was on a spy mission, but when the Soviets released details of the flight and displayed the captured pilot, the lie was revealed. Although Khrushchev, who wanted the Paris summit to take place, gave Eisenhower every opportunity to dismiss the U-2 incident, the president made full disclosure of the spy flights and implied that they would continue. Furious, Khrushchev canceled the meeting. (doc. 8)

It is perhaps not surprising, therefore, that the Democratic candidate for president in 1960, John F. Kennedy, made the accusation that the United States had lost much of its prestige and influence under Eisenhower. But Eisenhower's overall foreign policy record was mixed. Consummate Cold Warriors, both the president and his secretary of state, John Foster Dulles, had allowed their perception of world events to be overly influenced by their strident anti-Communism. They had even engaged in covert operations to overthrow legitimately established governments. They had also heightened the pitch of Cold War rhetoric and pursued a policy of diplomatic confrontation with the Soviet Union.

At the same time, however, Eisenhower had followed Truman's lead in adhering to an internationalist foreign policy that sought to contain the spread of Communism. Moreover, if relations with the Soviet Union were not much better when Eisenhower left office than when he assumed the presidency in 1953, neither were they worse. It is also to his credit that he ended one war (Korea) and prevented the United States from becoming militarily involved in another (Vietnam) when many of his advisers were urging such a course. Finally, the Eisenhower administration gave the United States almost eight years of relative peace, more than that provided by both his predecessor and successor.

Document 1

President Dwight D. Eisenhower, news conference, Apr. 7, 1954, *Public Papers of the Presidents of the United States* (hereafter referred to as *PPP*): *Dwight D. Eisenhower*, Washington, D.C.: Government Printing Office, 1960, 381–90.

Question. Robert Richards, *Copley Press:* Mr. President, would you mind commenting on the strategic importance of Indochina to the free world? I think there has been, across the country, some lack of understanding on just what it means to us.

The President: You have, of course, both the specific and the general when you talk about such things.

First of all, you have the specific value of a locality in its production of materials that the world needs.

Then you have the possibility that many human beings pass under a dictatorship that is inimical to the free world.

Finally, you have broader considerations that might follow what you would call the "falling domino" principle. You have a row of dominoes set up, you knock over the first one, and what will happen to the last one is the certainty that it will go over very quickly. So you could have a beginning of a disintegration that would have the most profound influences.

Now, with respect to the first one, two of the items from this particular area that the world uses are tin and tungsten. They are very important. There are others, of course, the rubber plantations and so on.

Then with respect to more people passing under this domination, Asia, after all, has already lost some 450 million of its peoples to the Communist dictatorship, and we simply can't afford greater losses.

But when we come to the possible sequence of events, the loss of Indochina, of Burma, of Thailand, of the Peninsula, and Indonesia following, now you begin to talk about areas that not only multiply the disadvantages that you would suffer through loss of materials, sources of materials, but now you are talking really about millions and millions and millions of people.

Finally, the geographical position achieved thereby does many things. It turns the so-called island defensive chain of Japan, Formosa, of the Philippines and to the southward; it moves in to threaten Australia and New Zealand.

It takes away, in its economic aspects, that region that Japan must have as a trading area or Japan, in turn, will have only one place in the world to go—that is, toward the Communist areas in order to live.

So, the possible consequences of the loss are just incalculable to the free world.

Question. Raymond Brandt, *St. Louis Post-Dispatch:* Mr. President, what response has Secretary [of State John Foster] Dulles and the administration got to the requests for united action in Indochina?

The President: So far as I know there are no positive reactions as yet, because the time element would almost forbid.

The suggestions we have, have been communicated; and we will have communications on them in due course, I should say.

Question. Robert G. Spivack, *New York Post*: Mr. President, do you agree with Senator [John F.] Kennedy that independence must be guaranteed the people of Indochina in order to justify an all-out effort there?

The President: Well, I don't know, of course, exactly in what way the Senator was talking about this thing.

I will say this: for many years, in talking to different countries, different governments, I have tried to insist on this principle: no outside country can come in and be really helpful unless it is doing what the local people want.

Now, let me call your attention to this independence theory. Senator [Henry Cabot] Lodge, on my instructions, stood up in the United Nations and offered one country independence if they would just simply pass a resolution saying they wanted it, or at least said, "I would work for it." They didn't accept it. So I can't say that the associated states want independence in the sense that the United States is independent. I do not know what they want.

I do say this: the aspirations of those people must be met, otherwise there is in the long run no final answer to the problem.

Question. Joseph Dear, Madison *Capital Times*: Do you favor bringing this Indochina situation before the United Nations?

The President: I really can't say. I wouldn't want to comment at too great a length at this moment, but I do believe this: this is the kind of thing that must not be handled by one nation trying to act alone. We must have a concert of opinion, and a concert of readiness to react in whatever way is necessary.

Of course, the hope is always that it is peaceful conciliation and accommodation of these problems.

Question. James Patterson, *New York Daily News*: Mr. President, as the last resort in Indochina, are we prepared to go it alone?

The President: Again you are bringing up questions that I have explained in a very definite sense several times this morning.

I am not saying what we are prepared to do because there is a Congress, and there are a number of our friends all over this world that are vitally engaged.

I know what my own convictions on this matter are: but until the thing has been settled and properly worked out with the people who also bear responsibilities, I cannot afford to be airing them everywhere, because it sort of stultifies negotiation which is often necessary.

Document 2

Cablegram from Secretary of State John Foster Dulles to Ambassador to France Douglas Dillon, Apr. 5, 1954, in *The Eisenhower Administration, 1953–1961*, Robert L. Branyan and Laurence H. Larson, eds., New York: Random House, 1971, vol. 1, 329–31.

As I personally explained to [French Chief of Staff General Paul] Ely in presence of [Admiral Arthur] Radford [chairman of Joint Chiefs of Staff], it is not (rpt not) possible for US to commit belligerent acts in Indochina without full political understanding with France and other countries. In addition, Congressional action would be required. After conference at highest level, I must confirm this position. US is doing everything possible as indicated by 5175 to prepare public, Congressional and Constitutional basis for united action in Indochina. However, such action is impossible except on coalition basis with active British Commonwealth participation. Meanwhile US prepared, as has been demonstrated, to do everything short of belligerency.

FYI US cannot and will not be put in position of alone salvaging British Commonwealth interests in Malaya, Australia and New Zealand. This matter now under discussion with UK at highest level.

Document 3

Joint congressional resolution authorizing President Dwight D. Eisenhower to use U.S. forces to protect Formosa, Jan. 29, 1955, *The Eisenhower Administration, 1953–61*, Robert L. Branyan and Laurence H. Larson, eds., New York: Random House, 1971, vol. 2, 752.

Whereas the primary purpose of the United States, in its relations with all other nations, is to develop and sustain a just and enduring peace for all; and

Whereas certain territories in the West Pacific under the jurisdiction of the Republic of China are now under armed attack, and threats and declarations have been and are being made by the Chinese Communists that such armed attack is in aid of and in preparation for armed attack on Formosa and the Pescadores,

Whereas, such armed attack if continued would gravely endanger the peace and security of the West Pacific Area and particularly of Formosa and the Pescadores; and

Whereas the secure possession by friendly governments of the Western Pacific Island chain, of which Formosa is a part, is essential to the vital interests of the United States and all friendly nations in or bordering upon the Pacific Ocean; and

Whereas the President of the United States on January 6, 1955, submitted to the Senate for its advice and consent to ratification a Mutual Defense Treaty between the United States of America and the Republic of China, which recognizes that an armed attack in the West Pacific area directed against territories, therein described, in the region of Formosa and the Pescadores, would be dangerous to the peace and safety of the parties to the treaty: Therefore be it

Resolved by the Senate and House of Representatives of the United States of America in Congress assembled, That the President of the United States be and he hereby is authorized to employ the Armed Forces of the United States as he deems necessary for the specific purpose of securing and protecting Formosa and the Pescadores against armed attack, this authority to include the securing and protection of such related positions and territories of that area now in friendly hands and the taking of such other measures as he judges to be required or appropriate in assuring the defense of Formosa and the Pescadores.

This resolution shall expire when the President shall determine that the peace and security of the area is reasonably assured by international conditions created by action of the United Nations or otherwise, and shall so report to the Congress.

Document 4

Statement on the Middle East crisis by Ambassador Henry Cabot Lodge, Oct. 30, 1956, U.S. Department of State, *Bulletin*, Nov. 12, 1956, vol. 35, 748–50.

The United States has requested this urgent meeting of the Security Council to consider steps to be taken to bring about the immediate cessation of military action by Israel against Egypt.

The Security Council has been meeting on the Palestine question within the last few days and repeatedly in recent months to consider actions which the Council unanimously believed constituted a grave danger, and I am sure therefore that there can be no question about the adoption of the agenda.

I request, therefore, Mr. President, that you put to the vote the question of the adoption of the agenda, which I am certain each member of the Council will consider appropriate in these grave circumstances, and that the Council will act with the same unanimity now as it has on the Palestine question in numerous recent meetings.

After the adoption of the agenda, Mr. President, I would appreciate the opportunity to speak immediately on the substance of the question.

(The agenda was adopted unanimously, and Ambassador Lodge then made the following statement:)

We have asked for this urgent meeting of the Security Council to consider the critical developments which have occurred and are unfortunately still continuing in the Sinai Peninsula as a result of Israel's invasion of that area yesterday. It comes as a shock to the United States Government that this action should have occurred less than 24 hours after President [Dwight D.] Eisenhower had sent a second earnest, personal appeal to the Prime Minister of Israel [David Ben Gurion] urging Israel not to undertake any action against her Arab neighbors and pointing out that we had no reason to believe that these neighbors had taken steps justifying Israel's action of mobilization.

Certain things are clear.

The first is that, by their own admission, Israeli armed forces moved into Sinai in force "to eliminate Egyptian Fedayeen bases in the Sinai Peninsula." They have admitted the capture of Queseima and Ras el Naqb.

Secondly, reliable reports have placed Israeli armed forces near the Suez Canal.

Thirdly, Israel has announced that both the Egyptian and Israeli armed forces were in action in the desert battle.

An official announcement in Tel Aviv said that Egyptian fighter planes strafed Israeli troops. We have a report that President [Gamal Abdel] Nasser has called for full mobilization in Egypt today and that the Egyptian Army claims that it has halted the advance of major Israeli forces driving across the Sinai Peninsula.

The [UN] Secretary-General [Dag Hammarskjold] may receive more information from General [E. L. M.] Burns and the Truce Supervision Organization, and I am sure that we shall continue to be fully informed as we proceed with our deliberations here.

These events make the necessity for the urgent consideration of this item all too plain. Failure by the Council to react at this time would be a clear avoidance of its responsibility for the maintenance of international peace and security. The United Nations has a clear and unchallengeable responsibility for the maintenance of the armistice agreements.

The Government of the United States feels that it is imperative that the Council act in the promptest manner to determine that a breach of the peace has occurred, to order that the military actions undertaken by Israel cease immediately, and to make clear its view that the Israeli armed forces be immediately withdrawn behind the established armistice lines. Nothing less will suffice.

It is also to be noted that the Chief of Staff of the United Nations Truce Supervision Organization has already issued a cease-fire order on his own authority, which Israel has so far ignored. Information has reached us also that military observers of the United Nations Truce Supervision Organization have been prevented by Israeli authorities from performing their duties.

We as members of the Council accordingly should call upon all members of the United Nations to render prompt assistance in achieving a withdrawal of Israeli forces. All members specifically should refrain from giving any assistance which might continue or prolong the hostilities. No one nation certainly should take advantage of this situation for any selfish interest.

Each of us here, and all members of the United Nations, have a clear-cut responsibility to see that the peace and stability of the Palestine area is restored forthwith. Anything less is an invitation to disaster in this part of the world.

This is an immediate responsibility, Mr. President, which derives from the Council's obligations under its cease-fire orders and the armistice agreements between the Israelis and the Arab States and endorsed by this Security Council. It derives, of course, also from the larger responsibility under the [UN] Charter.

On behalf of the United States Government I give notice that I intend at the afternoon session to introduce a resolution whereby the Council will call upon Israel for a withdrawal and indicate such steps as will assure that she does. . . .

Now, Mr. President, in the interests of bringing the Council up to date so that the Council will be possessed of all the facts that we have, let me give this added information which has just been sent to me from Washington. As soon as President Eisenhower received his first knowledge obtained through press reports of the ultimatum delivered by the French and United Kingdom Governments to Egypt and Israel, planning temporary occupation within 12 hours of the Suez Canal Zone, he sent an urgent personal message to the Prime Minister of Great Britain [Anthony Eden] and to the Prime Minister of France [Guy Mollet]. President Eisenhower expressed his earnest hope that the United Nations organization would be given full opportunity to settle the issues in the controversy by peaceful means instead of by forceful ones.

Mr. President, the United States continues to believe that it is possible by such means to secure a solution which would restore the armistice conditions between Egypt and Israel as well as bring about a just settlement of the Suez Canal controversy.

Document 5

President Dwight D. Eisenhower to Soviet Premier Nikolai Bulganin, Nov. 5, 1956, *PPP: Dwight D. Eisenhower, 1956*, Washington, D.C.: Government Printing Office, 1958, 1080–81.

I have noted with profound distress the reports which have reached me today from Hungary.

The Declaration of the Soviet Government of October 30, 1956, which restated the policy of non-intervention in internal affairs of other states, was generally understood as promising the early withdrawal of Soviet forces from Hungary. Indeed, in that statement, the Soviet Union said that "the further presence of Soviet Army units in Hungary can serve as a cause for an even greater deterioration of the situation." This pronouncement was regarded by the United States Government and myself as an act of high statesmanship. It was followed by the express request of the Hungarian Government for the withdrawal of Soviet forces.

Consequently, we have been inexpressibly shocked by the apparent reversal of this policy. It is especially shocking that this renewed application of force against the Hungarian Government and people took place while negotiations were going on between your representatives and those of the Hungarian Government for the withdrawal of Soviet forces.

As you know, the Security Council of the United Nations has been engaged in an emergency examination of this problem. As late as yesterday afternoon the Council was led to believe by your representative that the negotiations then in progress in Budapest were leading to agreement which would result in the withdrawal of Soviet forces from Hungary as requested by the government of that country. It was on that basis that the Security Council recessed its consideration of this matter.

I urge in the name of humanity and in the cause of peace that the Soviet Union take action to withdraw Soviet forces from Hungary immediately and to permit the Hungarian people to enjoy and exercise the human rights and fundamental freedoms affirmed for all peoples in the United Nations Charter.

The General Assembly of the United Nations is meeting in emergency session this afternoon in New York to consider this tragic situation. It is my hope that your representative will be in a position to announce at the Session today that the Soviet Union is preparing to withdraw its forces from that country and to allow the Hungarian people to enjoy the right to a government of their own choice.

Document 6

The Eisenhower Doctrine, Mar. 9, 1957, U.S. Department of State, *Bulletin*, Mar. 25, 1957, vol. 36, 481.

Resolved by the Senate and House of Representatives of the United States of America in Congress assembled.

Sec. 1. That the President be and hereby is authorized to cooperate with and assist any nation or group of nations in the general area of the Middle East desiring such assistance in the development of economic strength dedicated to the maintenance of national independence.

Sec. 2. The President is authorized to undertake, in the general area of the Middle East, military assistance programs with any nation or group of nations of that area desiring such assistance. Furthermore, the United States regards as vital to the national interest and world peace the preservation of the independence and integrity of the nations of the Middle East. To this end, if the President determines the necessity thereof, the United States is prepared to use armed force to assist any such nation or group of nations requesting assistance against armed aggression from any country controlled by international communism:

Provided, that such employment shall be constant with the treaty obligations of the United States and the Constitution of the United States.

Sec. 3. The President is hereby authorized to use during the balance of this fiscal year 1957 for economic and military assistance under this joint resolution not to exceed $200,000,000 from any appropriation now available for carrying out the provisions of the Mutual Security Act of 1954. . . .

Sec. 4. The President should continue to furnish facilities and military assistance, within the provisions of the applicable law and established policies, to the United Nations Emergency Force in the Middle East, with a view to maintaining the truce in that region.

Sec. 5. The President shall within the months of January and July of each year report to the Congress his actions hereunder.

Sec. 6. This joint resolution shall expire when the President shall determine that the peace and security of the nations in the general area of the Middle East are reasonably assured by international conditions created by action of the United Nations or otherwise except that it may be terminated earlier by a concurrent resolution of the two Houses of Congress.

Document 7

State Department press release, June 30, 1954, U. S. Department of State, *Bulletin*, July 12, 1954, vol. 33, 43–45.

In Guatemala, international Communism had an initial success. It began ten years ago, when a revolution occurred in Guatemala. The revolution was not without justification. But the Communists seized on it, not as an opportunity for real reforms, but as a chance to gain political power.

Communist agitators devoted themselves to infiltrating the public and private organizations of Guatemala. They sent recruits to Russia and other Communist countries for revolutionary training and indoctrination in such institutions as the Lenin School in Moscow. Operating in the guise of "reformers" they organized the workers and peasants under Communist leadership. Having gained control of what they call "mass organizations" they moved on to take over the official press and radio of the Guatemalan Government. They dominated the Social Security organization and ran the agrarian reform program. Through the technique of the "popular front" they dictated to the Congress and the President.

The judiciary made one valiant attempt to protect its integrity and independence. But the Communists, using their control of the legislative body, caused the Supreme Court to be dissolved when it refused to give its approval to a Communist-contrived law. [Jacobo] Arbenz [Guzmán], who until this week was President of Guatemala, was openly manipulated by the leaders of Communism.

Guatemala is a small country. But its power, standing alone, is not a measure of the threat. The master plan of international Communism is to gain a solid political base in this hemisphere, a base that can be used to extend Communist penetration to the other peoples of the other American Governments. It was not the power of the Arbenz Government that concerned us but the power behind it.

If world Communism captures any American State, however small, a new and perilous front is established which will increase the danger to the entire free world and require even greater sacrifices from the American people.

The situation in Guatemala has

become so dangerous that the American States could not ignore it. At Caracas last March the American States held their Tenth Inter-American Conference. They then adopted a momentous statement. They declared that "the domination or control of the political institutions of any American State by the international communist movement . . . would constitute a threat to the sovereignty and political independence of the American States, endangering the peace of America."

There was only one American State that voted against this Declaration. That State was Guatemala.

The Caracas Declaration precipitated a dramatic chain of events. From their European base the Communist leaders moved rapidly to build up the military power of their agents in Guatemala. In May a large shipment of arms moved from behind the Iron Curtain into Guatemala. The shipment was thought to be secreted by false manifests and false clearances. Its ostensible destination was changed three times while en route.

At the same time, the agents of international Communism in Guatemala intensified efforts to penetrate and subvert the neighboring Central American States. They attempted political assassinations and political strikes. They used consular agents for political warfare.

Many Guatemalan people protested against their being used by a Communist dictatorship to serve the Communists' lust for power. The response was mass arrests, the suppression of constitutional guarantees, the killing of opposition leaders and other brutal tactics normally employed by Communism to secure the consolidation of its power.

In the face of these events and in accordance with the spirit of the Caracas Declaration, the nations of this hemisphere laid further plans to grapple with the danger. The Arbenz Government responded with an effort to disrupt the inter-American system. Because it enjoyed the full support of Soviet Russia, which is on the Security Council, it tried to bring the matter before the Security Council. It did so without first referring the matter to the American regional organization as is called for both by the United Nations Charter itself and by the treaty creating the American Organization.

The Foreign Minister of Guatemala openly connived in this matter with the Foreign Minister of the Soviet Union. The two were in open correspondence and ill-concealed privity. The Security Council at first voted overwhelmingly to refer the Guatemala matter to the Organization of American States. The vote was ten to one. But that one negative vote was a Soviet veto.

Then the Guatemalan Government, with a Soviet backing, redoubled its efforts to supplant the American States system by Security Council jurisdiction.

However, last Friday, the United Nations Security Council decided not to take up the Guatemalan matter, but to leave it in the first instance to the American States themselves. That was a triumph for the system and world organization, which the American States had fought for when the Charter was drawn up at San Francisco.

The American States then moved promptly to deal with the situation. Their "peace commission" left yesterday for Guatemala. Earlier the Organization of American States had voted overwhelmingly to call a meeting of their Foreign Ministers to consider the penetration of international Communism in Guatemala and the measures required to eliminate it. Never before has there been so clear a call uttered with such a sense of urgency and strong resolve.

Throughout the period I have outlined, the Guatemalan Government and Communist agents throughout the world have persistently attempted to obscure the real issue—that of Communist imperialism—by claiming that the United States is only interested in protecting American business. We regret that there have been disputes between the Guatemalan Government and the United Fruit Company. We have urged repeatedly that these disputes be submitted for settlement to an international tribunal or to international arbitration. That is the way to dispose of problems of this sort. But this issue is relatively unimportant. All who know the temper of the U.S. people and Government must realize that our overriding concern is that which, with others, we recorded at Caracas, namely the endangering by international Communism of the peace and and security of this hemisphere.

The people of Guatemala have now been heard from. Despite the armaments piled up by the Arbenz Government, it was unable to enlist the spiritual cooperation of the people.

Led by Colonel Castillo Armas, patriots arose in Guatemala to challenge the Communist leadership—and to change it. Thus, the situation is being cured by the Guatemalans themselves.

Last Sunday, President Arbenz of Guatemala resigned and seeks asylum. Others are following his example.

Tonight, just as I speak, Colonel Castillo Armas is in conference in El Salvador with Colonel [Elfegio] Monzón, the head of the Council which has taken over the power in Guatemala City. It was this power that the just wrath of the Guatemalan people wrested from President Arbenz who then took flight.

Now the future of Guatemala lies also at the disposal of the Guatemalan people themselves. It lies also at the disposal of leaders loyal to Guatemala who have not treasonably become the agents of an alien despotism which sought to use Guatemala for its own evil ends.

Document 8

Statement by President Dwight D. Eisenhower concerning the position taken by Soviet Chairman Nikita Khrushchev at the opening of the Paris Summit Conference, May 16, 1960, *PPP: Dwight D. Eisenhower, 1960–61*, 1961, 427–29.

Having been informed yesterday by General [Charles] de Gaulle and Prime Minister [Harold] Macmillan of the position which Mr. Khrushchev has taken in regard to this conference during his calls yesterday morning on them, I gave most careful thought as to how this matter should best be handled. Having in mind the great importance of this conference and the hopes that the peoples of all the world have reposed in this meeting, I concluded that in the circumstances it was best to see if at today's private meeting any possibility existed through the exercise of reason and restraint to dispose of this matter of the overflights, which would have permitted the conference to go forward.

I was under no illusion as to the probability of success of any such approach but I felt that in view of the great responsibility resting on me as President of the United States this effort should be made.

In this I received the strongest support of my colleagues President de Gaulle and Prime Minister Macmillan. Accordingly, at this morning's private session, despite the violence and inaccuracy of Mr. Khrushchev's statements, I replied to him on the following terms:

I had previously been informed of the sense of the statement just read by Premier Khrushchev.

In my statement of May 11th and in the statement of Secretary [of State Christian] Herter of May 9th, the position of the United States was made clear with respect to the distasteful necessity of espionage activities in a world where nations distrust each other's intentions. We pointed out that these activities had no aggressive intent but rather were to assure the safety of the United States and the free world against surprise attack by a power which boasts of its ability to devastate the United States and other countries by missiles armed with atomic warheads. As is well known, not only the United States but most other countries are constantly the targets of elaborate and persistent espionage of the Soviet Union.

There is in the Soviet statement an evident misapprehension on one key point. It alleges that the United States has, through official statements, threatened continued overflights. The importance of this alleged threat was emphasized and repeated by Mr. Khrushchev. The United States has made no such threat. Neither I nor my government has intended any. The actual statements go no further than to say that the United States will not shirk its responsibility to safeguard against surprise attack.

In point of fact, these flights were suspended after the recent incident and are not to be resumed. Accordingly, this cannot be the issue.

I have come to Paris to seek agreements with the Soviet Union which would eliminate the necessity for all forms of espionage, including overflights. I see no reason to use this incident to disrupt the conference.

Should it prove impossible, because of the Soviet attitude, to come to grips here in Paris with this problem and the other vital issues threatening world peace, I am planning in the near future to submit to the United Nations aerial surveillance to detect preparations for attack. This plan I had intended to place before this conference. This surveillance system would operate in the territories of all nations prepared to accept such inspection. For its part, the United States is prepared not only to accept United Nations aerial surveillance, but to do everything in its power to contribute to the rapid organization and successful operation of such international surveillance.

We of the United States are here to consider in good faith the important problems before this conference. We are prepared either to carry this point no further, or to undertake bilateral conversations between the United States and the U.S.S.R. while the main conference proceeds.

My words were seconded and supported by my Western colleagues who also urged Mr. Khrushchev to pursue the path of reason and common sense, and to forget propaganda. Such an attitude would have permitted the conference to proceed. Mr. Khrushchev was left in no doubt by me that his ultimatum would never be acceptable to the United States.

Mr. Khrushchev brushed aside all arguments of reason, and not only insisted upon this ultimatum, but also insisted that he was going to publish his statement in full at the time of his choosing.

It was thus made apparent that he was determined to wreck the Paris conference.

In fact, the only conclusion that can be drawn from his behavior this morning was that he came all the way from Moscow to Paris with the sole intention of sabotaging this meeting on which so much of the hopes of the world have rested.

In spite of this serious and adverse development, I have no intention whatsoever to diminish my continuing efforts to promote progress toward a peace with justice. This applies to the remainder of my stay in Paris as well as thereafter.

CHAPTER 10

Kennedy and the Cold War

Robert A. Divine

The Cold War was at its height when John F. Kennedy entered the White House on January 20, 1961. Two developments in the 1950s had evolved in the aftermath of World War II and had intensified the rivalry between the United States and the Soviet Union. The first was the revolution in weaponry brought about by the advent of the hydrogen bomb and the production of reliable intercontinental ballistic missiles (ICBMs). Although the United States had the lead in thermonuclear warheads, which were large enough to wipe out entire cities, the Soviet Union appeared to have opened up a lead in ICBMs. The second development was the emergence in the 1950s of Third World nations, some newly created out of former colonial areas and others gaining new, assertive leaders. Under Premier Nikita Khrushchev, the Soviets had made impressive gains in extending their influence over such nonaligned countries as Egypt, India, and Cuba, the last of which came under Fidel Castro's control in 1959.

During the 1960 presidential campaign against Richard M. Nixon, Kennedy had accused the Republicans under Dwight D. Eisenhower of falling behind the Soviets in the Cold War. In particular, JFK pointed to the Soviet-launched *Sputnik*, the first artificial satellite, to assert that the Russians were capable of opening up a missile gap over the United States by the early 1960s that would endanger American security. He also accused the Republicans of allowing the Communists to gain a foothold in Cuba, only ninety miles from Florida, with Castro's pro-Soviet dictatorship. Despite the narrowness of his margin of victory, Kennedy claimed he had a mandate to get the nation moving again and to regain world leadership from the Soviet Union. Thus, in his inaugural address (doc. 1) he focused exclusively on foreign policy as he called on the American people to "bear any burden, meet any hardship, support any friend, oppose any foe to assure the survival and the success of liberty."

In his first year in office, the new president concentrated on building up America's military strength. Unlike Eisenhower, who had tried to keep a ceiling on defense spending lest it bankrupt the economy, Kennedy got Congress to appropriate an additional $6 billion for national defense.

Critical of former Secretary of State John Foster Dulles's strategy of massive retaliation, Kennedy and Defense Secretary Robert McNamara implemented a new policy of flexible response designed to give the United States the ability to meet any Communist challenge from a brushfire war to a nuclear confrontation.

Under McNamara's guidance, this meant increases at all levels. The Kennedy administration more than doubled the number of ICBMs to be built (it had 63 in 1961), raising the goal from 450 to just over 1,000 Minuteman solid-fuel missiles that could be placed in hardened silos. In addition, Kennedy and McNamara doubled the projected number of submarines carrying Polaris missiles to create a total of 41, each carrying 16 missiles aimed at targets within Russia. At the same time, they added 300,000 men to the American army, enlarging it from 11 to 16 divisions, and added some 70 ships to the navy. Aware of the Communist tendency to avoid direct challenges by backing insurgency abroad, Kennedy authorized the development of special forces trained to counter guerrilla warfare; he took a personal interest in the Green Berets, the special troops being trained in North Carolina for counterinsurgency.

There was a major difficulty with this massive defense buildup—it made it very tempting to use force or the threat of force to resolve the problems of the Cold War. Eisenhower had been restrained by the relatively limited nature of the military force at his disposal, as well as by his own prudence; Kennedy not only was more inclined to challenge what he perceived as Soviet threats, but he would also have the military capability to do so. The result would be a series of crises that brought the Cold War to its most dangerous level yet.

The first grave crisis came over the divided city of Berlin. It followed two setbacks that Kennedy suffered in his early months in office. In April, the American-backed plan to land exiles at the Bay of Pigs in Cuba to fight Castro had been a disaster. (doc. 2) Two months later, JFK had fared badly in his first summit conference with Khrushchev at Vienna. Visibly shaken by the bluster of the Soviet leader, Kennedy had allowed the Russians to view him, in the words of veteran diplomat George F. Kennan, as a "tongue-tied young man who's not forceful and who doesn't have ideas of his own." When the Soviets proceeded with plans to turn over their zone of Berlin, located more than a hundred miles from West Germany, to the East Germans, the young president felt he had to take a firm stand.

On July 25, 1961, Kennedy escalated the Berlin situation into a major crisis. He announced plans for an additional buildup of the American army, the mobilization of reserve and national guard units, and, most ominous of all, a proposal for nationwide construction of fallout shelters to signal to the Soviets his willingness to run the risk of nuclear war. (doc. 3) The possibility of a nuclear showdown suddenly loomed large in the late summer of 1961, but in August Khrushchev decided to resolve the Berlin issue unilaterally by having the East German government build a wall to halt the flow of refugees to the West. The Berlin Wall became a symbol of the brutality of the Communist world, and Kennedy could present it as a victory, because Khrushchev was forced to give up his designs on the city of Berlin.

In time Kennedy came to view Berlin as the place where he had been tested and found not to be wanting. In late June 1963, during a trip to Europe, the president expressed his admiration for the courage of the citizens of Berlin in a speech on the steps of West Berlin's city hall. (doc. 4) He praised the people of Berlin for their devotion to liberty and for demonstrating the gulf between the freedom of the West and the enslavement of the East. ''All free men,'' he concluded, ''wherever they may live, are citizens of Berlin, and, therefore, as a free man, I take pride in the words, *Ich bin ein Berliner* [I am a Berliner].''

Fidel Castro posed an even greater challenge to Kennedy. Still smarting from the setback at the Bay of Pigs and fearful that Castro would spread Communism thoughout the hemisphere, JFK was determined to do all he could to unseat the Cuban dictator. Aware of this American threat, Castro turned to the Soviet Union for help. In the summer and fall of 1962, large quantities of Soviet arms, technicians, and even troops poured into Cuba quite openly, while at the same time Khrushchev secretly sent in 42 intermediate range ballistic missiles (IRBMs). He would later claim that the sole purpose of these potentially nuclear weapons was to deter an American invasion of the island, but his real motivation seems to have been to close the strategic gap that Kennedy was opening up with the increase in Minuteman and submarine-launched Polaris missiles. Indeed, the United States had 284 missiles aimed at Soviet targets, compared to only 44 Russian ICBMs capable of reaching the United States.

When a U-2 plane belatedly discovered the presence of the Soviet IRBMs in Cuba in mid-October, Kennedy decided he had to respond firmly. He quickly ruled out an immediate aerial strike against the missile sites, but he was equally opposed to a suggestion to pull out American Jupiter IRBMs from bases in Turkey in return for a Soviet missile withdrawal from Cuba. The president felt that the real issue that must determine his stance was not the actual military balance but rather the perception of power. He could not appear to be backing down in the face of the Communist threat; instead, he had to force Khrushchev to retreat by taking the missiles out of Cuba.

Kennedy finally settled on a two-stage policy. First, the United States would use its overwhelming naval advantage to blockade Cuba and thus prevent any additional missiles from arriving. At the same time, he would inform the American people and the world of the secret Russian move and create a nuclear confrontation to force Khrushchev to remove the IRBMs from Cuba. On Monday, October 22, he told a nationwide television audience of the missiles and of his response (doc. 5), stating that he would regard any missile fired from Cuba ''as an attack by the Soviet Union on the United States, requiring a full retaliatory response upon the Soviet Union.'' To make sure that the Soviets understood how high the stakes had become,

Kennedy called upon Khrushchev to abandon his course of "world domination" and "to move the world back from the abyss of destruction."

For the next week, the world trembled on the brink of nuclear war. (doc. 6) The first positive break came three days later, when Soviet ships in the Atlantic that were bound for Cuba (with one possibly carrying nuclear warheads for the missiles already there) changed course to avoid challenging the American blockade and returned to the Soviet Union. But work continued on the missile bases, which were nearing completion. On Friday, October 26, Khrushchev sent a long, rambling letter in which he seemed to offer a way out—he would remove the missiles in return for Kennedy's pledge never to invade Cuba. Kennedy was ready to accept when a second message arrived the following day. Much firmer in tone, it insisted on a swap of the American Jupiter missiles in Turkey as the price for Soviet withdrawal from Cuba—a price Kennedy had already ruled out as too high, saying that it would be bargaining at the point of a gun.

When a Russian surface-to-air missile brought down a U-2 overflying Cuba that same Saturday, the military pressured the president to proceed with plans for an invasion of the island on Monday. Kennedy approved plans for military action, but at the urging of his brother, Attorney General Robert Kennedy, he made one final effort at a peaceful resolution. Ignoring the second Soviet message, he responded to Khrushchev's personal appeal and agreed to make a public commitment never to invade Cuba in return for the removal of the Russian missiles. That same evening Robert Kennedy met with the Soviet ambassador to make it clear that this was the last chance for peace. "He should understand," Robert Kennedy later recalled telling Ambassador Anatoly Dobrynin, "that if they did not remove those bases, we would remove them. President Kennedy had great respect for the Ambassador's country and the courage of its people. Perhaps his country might feel it necessary to take retaliatory action; but before that was over, there would be not only dead Americans but dead Russians as well."

We now know that this was not President Kennedy's final offer; he had instructed Secretary of State Dean Rusk to propose through the United Nations a swap of the American missiles in Turkey for the Russian ones in Cuba. But this last concession proved unnecessary. On Sunday morning, Khrushchev agreed to take the missiles out of Cuba in return for Kennedy's no-invasion pledge.

Ever since, Kennedy's admirers have hailed the Cuban missile crisis as the young president's finest hour—the time when he proved his mettle by facing down the Soviet leader. But others have wondered how wise it was for the United States to use its clear nuclear superiority. By forcing the Soviets to accept a humiliating defeat, even one that they had brought on themselves, Kennedy ensured a further escalation in the nuclear arms race. Vowing never again to be on the short end of the strategic balance in a crisis, Soviet leaders began an all-out effort to increase their nuclear striking power, which would eventually lead them to surpass the United States in ICBMs by the 1970s. Thus short-run success had only increased the nation's long-term danger.

The immediate effect of the Cuban missile crisis was to lessen Cold War tensions. With both sides shaken by the nuclear confrontation, they quickly agreed to set up a special telephone "hot line" to speed communication between the White House and the Kremlin in a future crisis. The following spring, Kennedy showed a new willingness to seek accommodation with the Soviet leadership in a speech at American University. (doc. 7) Playing down the differences between the United States and the Soviet Union, he stressed their common goal in avoiding nuclear war. "We all breathe the same air," he pointed out. "We all cherish our children's future. And we are all mortal."

This new effort at accommodation reached fruition with the signing of the partial Nuclear Test-Ban Treaty in Moscow in late July 1963. (doc. 8) For years American and Soviet negotiations seeking an end to all nuclear tests had foundered on the difficulty in detecting small underground blasts. The new treaty allowed underground tests to continue (which would work to the benefit of the United States by enabling the American military to stay in front of the Soviets in warheads), but outlawed nuclear blasts in the atmosphere, underwater, and in outer space, where they could easily be detected. Though only a small step toward meaningful arms control, the Nuclear Test-Ban Treaty marked a major change in direction for Kennedy, who now seemed to place a new importance on limiting Cold War tensions with the Soviet Union.

There was one final crisis that Kennedy proved unable to put on the way to resolution. When he took office in 1961, he inherited an American commitment to support an independent regime in South Vietnam under Ngo Dinh Diem. Under attack from the Viet Cong insurgents in the south, who were backed by Communist North Vietnam, Saigon looked to Washington for help. The new president responded by increasing American military and financial aid to Saigon, especially by raising the number of American military advisers in South Vietnam from less than 1,000 to more than 16,000 by 1963.

For a time the American military assistance, particularly the introduction of large numbers of helicopters, helped Saigon limit the insurgency, but by the spring of 1963 widespread opposition to Diem's dictatorial rule, especially by Buddhists who resented control by a Catholic leader, had led to grave political instability in South Vietnam. In August, South Vietnamese generals who wanted to overthrow Diem asked for American support; Kennedy was sympathetic to their request, but refused to allow Americans to play too active a role in the overthrow of Diem. (docs. 9 and 10) The coup finally took place on November 1, 1963, and despite American efforts to spare Diem's life, he was killed in Saigon.

With Diem's passing, there was a vacuum of power in Saigon that only the United States could fill. In television interviews in the fall of 1963,

Kennedy gave contradictory signals, saying at one point that the future of South Vietnam had to be decided by the Vietnamese themselves, then adding that he believed the United States had to prevent the country from falling into Communist hands. (doc. 11) After Kennedy's own tragic death in November (doc. 12), his admirers would claim that the president intended to end the American involvement and would have done so if he had lived to serve a second term. But the fact remains that his policies had taken the United States deeper into the quagmire in Southeast Asia and had created a situation that led his successor to believe that escalation was the only way to honor the American commitment in Vietnam.

Any final judgment on Kennedy's foreign policy record must be tempered with the knowledge that he did not have the chance to serve long enough to achieve all of his objectives. He might eventually have found ways to limit the Cold War with the Soviet Union, to live in peace with Castro, and to arrange a strategic retreat from Vietnam. But his actions in office, notably his emphasis on building up superior military force and his penchant for confrontation with his opponents, had served only to intensify the Cold War. Convinced that the United States was losing the global struggle with the Soviet Union, he felt he had to take heroic measures to reverse the tide. In the process, his premature death left behind a tragic legacy—a vendetta with Castro's Cuba, an upward spiral in the deadly nuclear arms race, and almost certain escalation of the Vietnam War.

Document 1

President John F. Kennedy, inaugural address, Jan. 20, 1961, *Public Papers of the Presidents of the United States* (hereafter referred to as *PPP*): *John F. Kennedy, 1961*, Washington, D.C.: Government Printing Office, 1962, 1–3.

Vice President Johnson, Mr. Speaker, Mr. Chief Justice, President Eisenhower, Vice President Nixon, President Truman, Reverend Clergy, fellow citizens:

We observe today not a victory of party but a celebration of freedom—symbolizing an end as well as a beginning—signifying renewal as well as change. For I have sworn before you and Almighty God the same solemn oath our forebears prescribed nearly a century and three quarters ago.

The world is very different now. For man holds in his mortal hands the power to abolish all forms of human poverty and all forms of human life. And yet the same revolutionary beliefs for which our forebears fought are still at issue around the globe—the belief that the rights of man come not from the generosity of the state but from the hand of God.

We dare not forget today that we are the heirs of that first revolution. Let the word go forth from this time and place, to friend and foe alike, that the torch has been passed to a new generation of Americans—born in this century, tempered by war, disciplined by a hard and bitter peace, proud of our ancient heritage—and unwilling to witness or permit the slow undoing of those human rights to which this nation has always been committed, and to which we are committed today at home and around the world.

Let every nation know, whether it wishes us well or ill, that we shall pay any price, bear any burden, meet any hardship, support any friend, oppose any foe to assure the survival and the success of liberty.

This much we pledge—and more.

To those old allies whose cultural and spiritual origins we share, we pledge the loyalty of faithful friends. United, there is little we cannot do in a host of cooperative ventures. Divided, there is little we can do—for we dare not meet a powerful challenge at odds and split asunder.

To those new states whom we welcome to the ranks of the free, we pledge our word that one form of colonial control shall not have passed away merely to be replaced by a far more iron tyranny. We shall not always expect to find them supporting our view. But we shall always hope to find them strongly supporting their own freedom—and to remember that, in the past, those who foolishly sought power by riding the back of the tiger ended up inside.

To those peoples in the huts and villages of half the globe struggling to break the bonds of mass misery, we pledge our best efforts to help them help themselves, for whatever period is required—not because the communists may be doing it, not because we seek their votes, but because it is right. If a free society cannot help the many who are poor, it cannot save the few who are rich.

To our sister republics south of our border, we offer a special pledge—to convert our good words into good deeds—in a new alliance for progress—to assist free men and free governments in casting off the chains of poverty. But this peaceful revolution of hope cannot become the prey of hostile powers. Let all our neighbors know that we shall join with them to oppose aggression or subversion anywhere in the Americas. And let every other power know that this Hemisphere intends to remain the master of its own house.

To that world assembly of sovereign states, the United Nations, our last best hope in an age where the instruments of war have far outpaced the instruments of peace, we renew our pledge of support—to prevent it from becoming merely a forum for invective—to strengthen its shield of the new and the weak—and to enlarge the area in which its writ may run.

Finally, to those nations who would make themselves our adversary, we offer not a pledge but a request: that both sides begin anew the quest for peace, before the dark powers of destruction unleashed by science engulf all humanity in planned or accidental self-destruction.

We dare not tempt them with weakness. For only when our arms are sufficient beyond doubt can we be [sure] that they will never be employed.

But neither can two great and powerful groups of nations take comfort from our present course—both sides overburdened by the cost of modern weapons, both rightly alarmed by the steady spread of the deadly atom, yet both racing to alter that uncertain balance of terror that stays the hand of mankind's final war.

So let us begin anew—remembering on both sides that civility is not a sign of weakness, and sincerity is always subject to proof. Let us never negotiate out of fear. But let us never fear to negotiate.

Let both sides explore what problems unite us instead of belaboring those problems which divide us.

Let both sides, for the first time, formulate serious and precise proposals for the inspection and control of arms—and bring the absolute power to destroy other nations under the absolute control of all nations.

Let both sides seek to invoke the wonders of science instead of its terrors. Together let us explore the stars, conquer the deserts, eradicate disease, tap the ocean depths and encourage the arts and commerce.

Let both sides unite to heed in all corners of the earth the command of Isaiah—to "undo the heavy burdens . . . (and) let the oppressed go free."

And if a beach-head of cooperation may push back the jungle of suspicion, let both sides join in creating a new endeavor, not a new balance of power, but a new world of law, where the strong are just and the weak secure and the peace preserved.

All this will not be finished in the first one hundred days. Nor will it be finished in the first one thousand days, nor in the life of this Administration, nor even perhaps in our lifetime on this planet. But let us begin.

In your hands, my fellow citizens, more than mine, will rest the final success or failure of our course. Since this country was founded, each generation of Americans has been summoned to give testimony to its national loyalty. The graves of young Americans who answered the call to service surround the globe.

Now the trumpet summons us again—not as a call to bear arms, though arms we need—not as a call to battle, though embattled we are—but a call to bear the burden of a long twilight struggle, year in and year out, "rejoicing in hope, patient in tribulation"—a struggle against the common enemies of man: tyranny, poverty, disease and war itself.

Can we forge against these enemies a grand and global alliance, North and South, East and West, that can assure a more fruitful life for all mankind? Will you join in that historic effort?

In the long history of the world, only a few generations have been granted the role of defending freedom in its hour of maximum danger. I do not shrink from this responsibility—I welcome it. I do not believe that any of us would exchange places with any other people or any other generation. The energy, the faith, the devotion which we bring to this endeavor will light our country and all who serve it—and the glow from that fire can truly light the world.

And so, my fellow Americans: ask not what your country can do for you—ask what you can do for your country.

My fellow citizens of the world: ask not what America will do for you, but what together we can do for the freedom of man.

Finally, whether you are citizens of America or citizens of the world, ask of us here the same high standards of strength and sacrifice which we ask of you. With a good conscience our only sure reward, with history the final judge of our deeds, let us go forth to lead the land we love, asking His blessing and His help, but knowing that here on earth God's work must truly be our own.

Document 2

President John F. Kennedy, Bay of Pigs speech to the American Society of Newspaper Editors, Apr. 20, 1961, *PPP: John F. Kennedy, 1961*, 1962, 304–6.

The President of a great democracy such as ours, and the editors of great newspapers such as yours, owe a common obligation to the people: an obligation to present the facts, to present them with candor, and to present them in perspective. It is with that obligation in mind that I have decided in the last 24 hours to discuss briefly at this time the recent events in Cuba.

On that unhappy island, as in so many other arenas of the contest for freedom, the news has grown worse instead of better. I have emphasized before that this was a struggle of Cuban patriots against a Cuban dictator. While we could not be expected to hide our sympathies, we made it repeatedly clear that the armed forces of this country would not intervene in any way.

Any unilateral American intervention, in the absence of an external attack upon ourselves or an ally, would have been contrary to our traditions and to our international obligations. But let the record show that our restraint is not inexhaustible. Should it ever appear that the inter-American doctrine of noninterference merely conceals or excuses a policy of nonaction—if the nations of this Hemisphere should fail to meet their commitments against outside Communist penetration—then I want it clearly understood that this Government will not hesitate in meeting its primary obligations which are to the security of our Nation!

Should that time ever come, we do not intend to be lectured on "intervention" by those whose character was stamped for all time on the bloody streets of Budapest! Nor would we expect or accept the same outcome which this small band of gallant Cuban refugees must have known that they were chancing, determined as they were against heavy odds to pursue their courageous attempts to regain their Island's freedom.

But Cuba is not an island unto itself; and our concern is not ended by mere expressions of nonintervention or regret. This is not the first time in either ancient or recent history that a small band of freedom fighters has engaged the armor of totalitarianism.

It is not the first time that Communist tanks have rolled over gallant men and women fighting to redeem the independence of their homeland. Nor is it by any means the final episode in the eternal struggle of liberty against tyranny, anywhere on the face of the globe, including Cuba itself.

Mr. [Fidel] Castro has said that these were mercenaries. According to press reports, the final message to be relayed from the refugee forces on the beach came from the rebel commander when asked if he wished to be evacuated. His answer was: "I will never leave this country." That is not the reply of a mercenary. He has gone now to join in the mountains countless other guerrilla fighters, who are equally determined that the dedication of those who gave their lives shall not be forgotten, and that Cuba must not be abandoned to the Communists. And we do not intend to abandon it either!

The Cuban people have not yet spoken their final piece. And I have no doubt that they and their Revolutionary Council, led by Dr. [José Miró] Cardona [president of council]—and members of the families of the Revolutionary Council, I am informed by the Doctor yesterday, are involved themselves in the Islands—will continue to speak up for a free and independent Cuba.

Meanwhile we will not accept Mr. Castro's attempts to blame this nation for the hatred which his onetime supporters now regard his repression. But there are from this sobering episode useful lessons for us all to learn. Some may be still obscure, and await further information. Some are clear today.

First, it is clear that the forces of communism are not to be underestimated, in Cuba or anywhere else in the world. The advantages of a police state—its use of mass terror and arrests to prevent the spread of free dissent—cannot be overlooked by those who expect the fall of every fanatic tyrant. If the self-discipline of the free cannot match the iron discipline of the mailed fist—in economic, political, scientific and all the other kinds of struggles as well as the military—then the peril to freedom will continue to rise.

Secondly, it is clear that this Nation, in concert with all the free nations of this hemisphere, must take an ever closer and more realistic look at the menace of external Communist intervention and domination in Cuba. The American people are not complacent about Iron Curtain tanks and planes less than 90 miles from their shore. But a nation of Cuba's size is less a threat to our survival than it is a base for subverting the survival of other free nations throughout the hemisphere. It is not primarily our interest or our security but theirs which is now, today, in the greater peril. It is for their sake as well as our own that we must show our will.

The evidence is clear—and the hour is late. We and our Latin friends will have to face the fact that we cannot postpone any longer the real issue of survival of freedom in this hemisphere itself. On that issue, unlike perhaps some others, there can be no middle ground. Together we must build a hemisphere where freedom can flourish; and where any free nation under outside attack of any kind can be assured that all of our resources stand ready to respond to any request for assistance.

Third, and finally, it is clearer than ever that we face a relentless struggle in every corner of the globe that goes far beyond the clash of armies or even nuclear armaments. The armies are there, and in large number. The nuclear armaments are there. But they serve primarily as the shield behind which subversion, infiltration, and a host of other tactics steadily advance, picking off vulnerable areas one by one in situations which do not permit our own armed intervention.

Power is the hallmark of this offensive—power and discipline and deceit. The legitimate discontent of yearning people is exploited. The legitimate trappings of self-determination are employed. But once in power, all talk of discontent is repressed, all self-determination disappears, and the promise of a revolution of hope is betrayed, as in Cuba, into a reign of terror. Those who on instruction staged automatic "riots" in the streets of free nations over the efforts of a small group of young Cubans to regain their freedom should recall the long roll call of refugees who cannot now go back—to Hungary, to North Korea, to North Viet-Nam, to East Germany, or to Poland, or to any of the other lands from which a steady stream of refugees pours forth, in eloquent testimony to the cruel oppression now holding sway in their homeland.

We dare not fail to see the insidious nature of this new and deeper struggle. We dare not fail to grasp the new concepts, the new tools, the new sense of urgency we will need to combat it—whether in Cuba or South Viet-Nam. And we dare not fail to realize that this struggle is taking place every day, without fanfare, in thousands of villages and markets—day and night—and in classrooms all over the globe.

The message of Cuba, of Laos, of the rising din of Communist voices in Asia and Latin America—these messages are all the same. The complacent, the self-indulgent, the soft societies are about to be swept away with the debris of history. Only the strong, only the industrious, only the determined, only the courageous, only the visionary who determine the real nature of our struggle can possibly survive.

No greater task faces this country or this administration. No other challenge is more deserving of our every effort and energy. Too long we have fixed our eyes on traditional military needs, on armies prepared to cross borders, on missiles poised for flight. Now it should be clear that this is no longer enough—that our security may be lost piece by piece, country by country, without the firing of a single missile or the crossing of a single border.

We intend to profit from this lesson. We intend to reexamine and reorient our forces of all kinds—our tactics and our institutions here in this community. We intend to intensify our efforts for a struggle in many ways more difficult than war, where disappointment will often accompany us.

For I am convinced that we in this country and in the free world possess the necessary resource, and the skill, and the added strength that comes from a belief in the freedom of man. And I am equally convinced that history will record the fact that this bitter struggle reached its climax in the late 1950's and the early 1960's. Let me then make clear as the President of the United States that I am determined upon our system's survival and success, regardless of the cost and regardless of the peril!

Document 3

President John F. Kennedy, radio and television address on Berlin crisis, July 25, 1961, *PPP: John F. Kennedy, 1961*, 1962, 533–37.

Good evening:

Seven weeks ago tonight I returned from Europe to report on my meeting with Premier [Nikita] Khrushchev and the others. His grim warnings about the future of the world, his aide mémoire on Berlin, his subsequent speeches and threats which he and his agents have launched, and the increase in the Soviet military budget that he has announced, have all prompted a series of decisions by the Administration and a series of consultations with the members of the NATO organization. In Berlin, as you recall, he intends to bring to an end, through a stroke of the pen, *first* our legal rights to be in West Berlin—and *secondly* our ability to make good on our commitment to the two million free people of that city. That we cannot permit.

We are clear about what must be done—and we intend to do it. I want to talk frankly with you tonight about the first steps that we shall take. These actions will require sacrifice on the part of many of our citizens. More will be required in the future. They will require, from all of us, courage and perseverance in the years to come. But if we and our allies act out of strength and unity of purpose—with calm determination and steady nerves—using restraint in our words as well as our weapons—I am hopeful that both peace and freedom will be sustained.

The immediate threat to free men is in West Berlin. But that isolated outpost is not an isolated problem. The threat is worldwide. Our effort must be equally wide and strong, and not be obsessed by any single manufactured crisis. We face a challenge in Berlin, but there is also a challenge in Southeast Asia, where the borders are less guarded, the enemy harder to find, and the dangers of communism less apparent to those who have so little. We face a challenge in our own hemisphere, and indeed wherever else the freedom of human beings is at stake.

Let me remind you that the fortunes of war and diplomacy left the free people of West Berlin, in 1945, 110 miles behind the Iron Curtain.

This map makes very clear the problem that we face. The white is West Germany—the East is the area controlled by the Soviet Union, and as you can see from the chart, West Berlin is 110 miles within the area which the Soviets now dominate—which is immediately controlled by the so-called East German regime.

We are there as a result of our victory over Nazi Germany—and our basic rights to be there, deriving from that victory, include both our presence in West Berlin and the enjoyment of access across East Germany. These rights have been repeatedly confirmed and recognized in special agreements with the Soviet Union. Berlin is not a part of East Germany, but a separate territory under the control of the allied powers. Thus our rights there are clear and deep-rooted. But in addition to those rights is our commitment to sustain—and defend, if need be—the opportunity for more than two million people to determine their own future and choose their own way of life.

II.

Thus, our presence in West Berlin, and our access thereto, cannot be ended by any act of the Soviet government. The NATO shield was long ago extended to cover West Berlin—and we have given our word that an attack upon that city will be regarded as an attack upon us all.

For West Berlin—lying exposed 110 miles inside East Germany, surrounded by Soviet troops and close to Soviet supply lines, has many roles. It is more than a showcase of liberty, a symbol, an island of freedom in a Communist sea. It is even more than a link with the Free World, a beacon of hope behind the Iron Curtain, an escape hatch for refugees.

West Berlin is all of that. But above all it has now become—as never before—the great testing place of Western courage and will, a focal point where our solemn commitments stretching back over the years since 1945, and Soviet ambitions now meet in basic confrontation.

It would be a mistake for others to look upon Berlin, because of its location, as a tempting target. The United States is there; the United Kingdom and France are there; the pledge of NATO is there—and the people of Berlin are there. It is as secure, in that sense, as the rest of us—for we cannot separate its safety from our own.

I hear it said that West Berlin is militarily untenable. And so was Bastogne. And so, in fact, was Stalingrad. Any dangerous spot is tenable if men—brave men—will make it so.

We do not want to fight—but we have fought before. And others in earlier times have made the same dangerous mistake of assuming that the West was too selfish and too soft and too divided to resist invasions of freedom in other lands. Those who threaten to unleash the forces of war on a dispute over West Berlin should recall the words of the ancient philosopher: "A man who causes fear cannot be free from fear."

We cannot and will not permit the Communists to drive us out of Berlin, either gradually or by force. For the fulfillment of our pledge to that city is essential to the morale and security of Western Germany, to the unity of Western Europe, and to the faith of the entire Free World. Soviet strategy has long been aimed, not merely at Berlin, but at dividing and neutralizing all of Europe, forcing us back on our own shores. We must meet our oft-stated pledge to the free peoples of West Berlin—and maintain our rights and their safety, even in the face of force—in order to maintain the confidence of other free peoples in our word and our resolve. The strength of the alliance on which our security depends is dependent in turn on our willingness to meet our commitments to them.

III.

So long as the Communists insist that they are preparing to end by themselves unilaterally our rights in West Berlin and our commitments to its people, we must be prepared to defend those rights and those commitments. We will at all times be ready to talk, if talk will help. But we must also be ready to resist with force, if force is used upon us. Either alone would fail. Together, they can serve the cause of freedom and peace.

The new preparations that we shall make to defend the peace are part of the long-term build-up in our strength which has been underway since January. They are based on our needs to meet a world-wide threat, on a basis which stretches far beyond the present Berlin crisis. Our primary purpose is neither propaganda nor provocation—but preparation.

A first need is to hasten progress toward the military goals which the North Atlantic allies have set for themselves. In Europe today nothing less will suffice. We will put even greater resources into fulfilling those goals, and we look to our allies to do the same.

The supplementary defense build-ups that I asked from the Congress in March and May have already started moving us toward these and our other defense goals. They included an increase in the size of the Marine Corps, improved readiness of our reserves, expansion of our air and sea lift, and stepped-up procurement of needed weapons, ammunition, and other items. To insure a continuing invulnerable capacity to deter or destroy any aggressor, they provided for the strengthening of our missile power and for putting 50% of our B-52 and B-47 bombers on a ground alert which would send them on their way with 15 minutes' warning.

These measures must be speeded up, and still others must now be taken. We must have sea and air lift capable of moving our forces quickly and in large numbers to any part of the world.

But even more importantly, we need the capability of placing in any critical area at the appropriate time a force which, combined with those of our allies, is large enough to make clear our determination and our ability to defend our rights at all costs—and to meet all levels of aggressor pressure with whatever levels of force are required. We intend to have a wider choice than humiliation or all-out nuclear action.

While it is unwise at this time either to call up or send abroad excessive numbers of these troops before they are needed, let me make it clear that I intend to take, as time goes on, whatever steps are necessary to make certain that such forces can be deployed at the appropriate time without lessening our ability to meet our commitments elsewhere.

Thus, in the days and months ahead, I shall not hesitate to ask the Congress for additional measures, or exercise any of the executive powers that I possess to meet this threat to peace. Everything essential to the security of freedom must be done; and if that should require more men, or more taxes, or more controls, or other new powers, I shall not hesitate to ask them. The measures proposed today will be constantly studied, and altered as necessary. But while we will not let panic shape our policy, neither will we permit timidity to direct our program.

Accordingly, I am now taking the following steps:

(1) I am tomorrow requesting the Congress for the current fiscal year an additional $3,247,000,000 of appropriations for the Armed Forces.*

(2) To fill out our present Army Divisions, and to make more men available for prompt deployment, I am requesting an increase in the Army's total

*A letter to the President of the Senate transmitting amendments to the Department of Defense budget was released by the White House on July 26. On August 17 the President approved the Department of Defense Appropriation Act, 1962 (Public Law 87-144; 75 Stat. 365).

authorized strength from 875,000 to approximately 1 million men.

(3) I am requesting an increase of 29,000 and 63,000 men respectively in the active duty strength of the Navy and the Air Force.

(4) To fulfill these manpower needs, I am ordering that our draft calls be doubled and tripled in the coming months; I am asking the Congress for authority to order to active duty certain ready reserve units and individual reservists, and to extend tours of duty; and, under that authority, I am planning to order to active duty a number of air transport squadrons and Air National Guard tactical air squadrons, to give us the airlift capacity and protection that we need. Other reserve forces will be called up when needed.

(5) Many ships and planes once headed for retirement are to be retained or reactivated, increasing our airpower tactically and our sealift, airlift, and anti-submarine warfare capability. In addition, our strategic air power will be increased by delaying the deactivation of B-47 bombers.

(6) Finally, some $1.8 billion—about half of the total sum—is needed for the procurement of non-nuclear weapons, ammunition and equipment.

The details on all these requests will be presented to the Congress tomorrow. Subsequent steps will be taken to suit subsequent needs. Comparable efforts for the common defense are being discussed with our NATO allies. For their commitment and interest are as precise as our own.

And let me add that I am well aware of the fact that many American families will bear the burden of these requests. Studies or careers will be interrupted; husbands and sons will be called away; incomes in some cases will be reduced. But these are burdens which must be borne if freedom is to be defended—Americans have willingly borne them before—and they will not flinch from the task now.

IV.

We have another sober responsibility. To recognize the possibilities of nuclear war in the missile age, without our citizens knowing what they should do and where they should go if bombs begin to fall, would be a failure of responsibility. In May, I pledged a new start on Civil Defense. Last week, I assigned, on the recommendation of the Civil Defense Director, basic responsibility for this program to the Secretary of Defense, to make certain it is administered and coordinated with our continental defense efforts at the highest civilian level. Tomorrow, I am requesting of the Congress new funds for the following immediate objectives: to identify and mark space in existing structures—public and private—that could be used for fall-out shelters in case of attack; to stock those shelters with food, water, first-aid kits and other minimum essentials for survival; to increase their capacity; to improve our air raid warning and fall-out detection systems, including a new household warning system which is now under development; and to take other measures that will be effective at an early date to save millions of lives if needed.

In the event of an attack, the lives of those families which are not hit in a nuclear blast and fire can still be saved—*if* they can be warned to take shelter and *if* that shelter is available. We owe that kind of insurance to our families—and to our country. In contrast to our friends in Europe, the need for this kind of protection is new to our shores. But the time to start is now. In the coming months, I hope to let every citizen know what steps he can take without delay to protect his family in case of attack. I know that you will want to do no less.

Document 4

President John F. Kennedy, remarks in Berlin, June 26, 1963, *PPP: John F. Kennedy, 1963*, 1964, 524–25.

I am proud to come to this city as the guest of your distinguished Mayor [Willy Brandt], who has symbolized throughout the world the fighting spirit of West Berlin. And I am proud to visit the Federal Republic with your distinguished Chancellor [Konrad Adenauer], who for so many years has committed Germany to democracy and freedom and progress, and to come here in the company of my fellow American, General [Lucius D.] Clay [U.S. military governor during Berlin crisis of 1948–49], who has been in this city during its great moments of crisis and will come again if ever needed.

Two thousand years ago the proudest boast was "*civis Romanus sum.*" Today, in the world of freedom, the proudest boast is "*Ich bin ein Berliner.*"

I appreciate my interpreter translating my German!

There are many people in the world who really don't understand, or say they don't, what is the great issue between the free world and the Communist world. Let them come to Berlin. There are some who say that communism is the wave of the future. Let them come to Berlin. And there are some who say in Europe and elsewhere we can work with the Communists. Let them come to Berlin. And there are even a few who say that it is true that communism is an evil system, but it permits us to make economic progress. *Lass' sie nach Berlin kommen.* Let them come to Berlin.

Freedom has many difficulties and democracy is not perfect, but we have never had to put a wall up to keep our people in, to prevent them from leaving us. I want to say, on behalf of my countrymen, who live many miles away on the other side of the Atlantic, who are far distant from you, that they take the greatest pride that they have been able to share with you, even from a distance, the story of the last 18 years. I know of no town, no city, that has been besieged for 18 years that still lives with the vitality and the force, and the hope and the determination of the city of West Berlin. While the wall is the most obvious and vivid demonstration of the failures of the Communist system, for all the world to see, we take no satisfaction in it, for it is, as your Mayor has said, an offense not only against history but an offense against humanity, separating families, dividing husbands and wives and brothers and sisters, and dividing a people who wish to be joined together.

What is true of this city is true of Germany—real, lasting peace in Europe can never be assured as long as one German out of four is denied the elementary right of free men, and that is to make a free choice. In 18 years of peace and good faith, this generation of Germans has earned the right to be free, including the right to unite their families and their nation in lasting peace, with good will to all people. You live in a defended island of freedom, but your life is part of the main. So let me ask you, as I close, to lift your eyes beyond the dangers of today, to the hopes of tomorrow, beyond the freedom merely of this city of Berlin, or your country of Germany, to the advance of freedom everywhere, beyond the wall to the day of peace with justice, beyond yourselves and ourselves to all mankind.

Freedom is indivisible, and when one man is enslaved, all are not free. When all are free, then we can look forward to that day when this city will be joined as one and this country and this great Continent of Europe in a peaceful and hopeful globe. When that day finally comes, as it will, the people of West Berlin can take sober satisfaction in the fact that they were in the front lines for almost two decades.

All free men, wherever they may live, are citizens of Berlin, and, therefore, as a free man, I take pride in the words "*Ich bin ein Berliner.*"

Document 5

President John F. Kennedy, radio and television address on Cuban missile crisis, Oct. 22, 1962, *PPP: John F. Kennedy, 1962*, 1963, 806–9.

Good evening, my fellow citizens:

This Government, as promised, has maintained the closest surveillance of the Soviet military buildup on the island of Cuba. Within the past week, unmistakable evidence has established the fact that a series of offensive missile sites is now in preparation on that imprisoned island. The purpose of these bases can be none other than to provide a nuclear strike capability against the Western Hemisphere.

Upon receiving the first preliminary hard information of this nature last Tuesday morning at 9 a.m., I directed that our surveillance be stepped up. And having now confirmed and completed our evaluation of the evidence and our decision on a course of action, this Government feels obliged to report this new crisis to you in fullest detail.

The characteristics of these new missile sites indicate two distinct types of installations. Several of them include medium range ballistic missiles, capable of carrying a nuclear warhead for a distance of more than 1,000 nautical miles. Each of these missiles, in short, is capable of striking Washington, D.C., the Panama Canal, Cape Canaveral, Mexico City, or any other city in the southeastern part of the United States, in Central America, or in the Caribbean area.

Additional sites not yet completed appear to be designed for intermediate range ballistic missiles—capable of traveling more than twice as far—and thus capable of striking most of the major cities in the Western Hemisphere, ranging as far north as Hudson Bay, Canada, and as far south as Lima, Peru. In addition, jet bombers, capable of carrying nuclear weapons, are now being uncrated and assembled in Cuba, while the necessary air bases are being prepared.

This urgent transformation of Cuba into an important strategic base—by the presence of these large, long-range, and clearly offensive weapons of sudden mass destruction—constitutes an explicit threat to the peace and security of all the Americas, in flagrant and deliberate defiance of the Rio Pact of 1947 [Inter-American Treaty of Mutual Assistance], the traditions of this Nation and hemisphere, the joint resolution of the 87th Congress, the Charter of the United Nations, and my own public warnings to the Soviets on September 4 and 13. This action also contradicts the repeated assurances of Soviet spokesmen, both publicly and privately delivered, that the arms buildup in Cuba would retain its original defensive character, and that the Soviet Union had no need or desire to station strategic missiles on the territory of any other nation.

The size of this undertaking makes clear that it has been planned for some months. Yet only last month, after I had made clear the distinction between any introduction of ground-to-ground missiles and the existence of defensive antiaircraft missiles, the Soviet Government publicly stated on September 11 that, and I quote, "the armaments and military equipment sent to Cuba are designed exclusively for defensive purposes,'' that, and I quote the Soviet Government, ''there is no need for the Soviet Government to shift its weapons . . . for a retaliatory blow to any other country, for instance Cuba,'' and that, and I quote their government, ''the Soviet Union has so powerful rockets to carry these nuclear warheads that there is no need to search for sites for them beyond the boundaries of the Soviet Union.'' That statement was false.

Only last Thursday, as evidence of this rapid offensive buildup was already in my hand, Soviet Foreign Minister [Andrei] Gromyko told me in my office that he was instructed to make it clear once again, as he said his government had already done, that Soviet assistance to Cuba, and I quote, ''pursued solely the purpose of contributing to the defense capabilities of Cuba,'' that, and I quote him, ''training by Soviet specialists of Cuban nationals in handling defensive armaments was by no means offensive, and if it were otherwise,'' Mr. Gromyko went on, ''the Soviet Government would never become involved in rendering such assistance.'' That statement also was false.

Neither the United States of America nor the world community of nations can tolerate deliberate deception and offensive threats on the part of any nation, large or small. We no longer live in a world where only the actual firing of weapons represents a sufficient challenge to a nation's security to constitute maximum peril. Nuclear weapons are so destructive and ballistic missiles are so swift, that any substantially increased possibility of their use or any sudden change in their deployment may well be regarded as a definite threat to peace.

For many years, both the Soviet Union and the United States, recognizing this fact, have deployed strategic nuclear weapons with great care, never upsetting the precarious status quo which insured that these weapons would not be used in the absence of some vital challenge. Our own strategic missiles have never been transferred to the territory of any other nation under a cloak of secrecy and deception; and our history—unlike that of the Soviets since the end of World War II—demonstrates that we have no desire to dominate or conquer any other nation or impose our system upon its people. Nevertheless, American citizens have become adjusted to living daily on the bull's-eye of Soviet missiles located inside the U.S.S.R. or in submarines.

In that sense, missiles in Cuba add to an already clear and present danger—although it should be noted the nations of Latin America have never previously been subjected to a potential nuclear threat.

But this secret, swift, and extraordinary buildup of Communist missiles—in an area well known to have a special and historical relationship to the United States and the nations of the Western Hemisphere, in violation of Soviet assurances, and in defiance of American and hemispheric policy—this sudden, clandestine decision to station strategic weapons for the first time outside of Soviet soil—is a deliberately provocative and unjustified change in the status quo which cannot be accepted by this country, if our courage and our commitments are ever to be trusted again by either friend or foe.

The 1930's taught us a clear lesson: aggressive conduct, if allowed to go unchecked and unchallenged, ultimately leads to war. This nation is opposed to war. We are also true to our word. Our unswerving objective, therefore, must be to prevent the use of these missiles against this or any other country, and to secure their withdrawal or elimination from the Western Hemisphere.

Our policy has been one of patience and restraint, as befits a peaceful and powerful nation, which leads a worldwide alliance. We have been determined not to be diverted from our central concerns by mere irritants and fanatics. But now further action is required—and it is under way; and these actions may only be the beginning. We will not prematurely or unnecessarily risk the costs of worldwide nuclear war in which even the fruits of victory would be ashes in our mouth—but neither will we shrink from that risk at any time it must be faced.

Acting, therefore, in the defense of our own security and of the entire Western Hemisphere, and under the authority entrusted to me by the Constitution as endorsed by the resolution of the Congress, I have directed that the following *initial* steps be taken immediately:

First: To halt this offensive buildup, a strict quarantine on all offensive military equipment under shipment to Cuba is being initiated. All ships of any kind bound for Cuba from whatever nation or port will, if found to contain cargoes of offensive weapons, be turned back. This quarantine will be extended, if needed, to other types of cargo and carriers. We are not at this time, however, denying the necessities of life as the Soviets attempted to do in their Berlin blockade of 1948.

Second: I have directed the continued and increased close surveillance of Cuba and its military buildup. The foreign ministers of the OAS [Organization of American States], in their communiqué of October 6, rejected secrecy on such matters in this hemisphere. Should these offensive military preparations continue, thus increasing the threat to the hemisphere, further action will be justified. I have directed the Armed Forces to prepare for any eventualities; and I trust that in the interest of both the Cuban people and the Soviet technicians at the sites, the hazards . . . of continuing this threat will be recognized.

Third: It shall be the policy of this Nation to regard any nuclear missile launched from Cuba against any nation in the Western Hemisphere as an attack by the Soviet Union on the United States, requiring a full retaliatory response upon the Soviet Union.

Fourth: As a necessary military precaution, I have reinforced our base at Guantanamo, evacuated today the dependents of our personnel there, and ordered additional military units to be on a standby alert basis.

Fifth: We are calling tonight for an immediate meeting of the Organ of Consultation under the Organization of American States, to consider this threat to hemispheric security and to invoke articles 6 and 8 of the Rio Treaty in support of all necessary action. The United Nations Charter allows for regional security arrangements—and the nations of this hemisphere decided long ago against the military presence of outside powers. Our other allies around the world have also been alerted.

Sixth: Under the Charter of the United Nations, we are asking tonight that an emergency meeting of the Security Council be convoked without delay to take action against this latest Soviet threat to world peace. Our resolution will call for the prompt dismantling and withdrawal of all offensive weapons in Cuba, under the supervision of U.N. observers, before the quarantine can be lifted.

Seventh and finally: I call upon Chairman [Nikita] Khrushchev to halt and eliminate this clandestine, reckless, and provocative threat to world peace and to stable relations between our two nations. I call upon him further to abandon this course of world domination, and to join in an historic effort to end the perilous arms race and to transform the history of man. He has an opportunity now to move the world back from the abyss of destruction—by returning to his government's own words that it had no need to station missiles outside its own territory, and withdrawing these weapons from Cuba—by refraining from any action which will widen or deepen the present crisis—and then by participating in a search for peaceful and permanent solutions.

This Nation is prepared to present its case against the Soviet threat to peace, and our own proposals for a peaceful world, at any time and in any forum—in the OAS, in the United Nations, or in any other meeting that could be useful—without limiting our freedom of action. We have in the past made strenuous efforts to limit the spread of nuclear weapons. We have proposed the elimination of all arms and military bases in a fair and effective disarmament treaty. We are prepared to discuss new proposals for the removal of tensions on both sides—including the possibilities of a genuinely independent Cuba, free to determine its own destiny. We have no wish to war with the Soviet Union—for we are a peaceful people who desire to live in peace with all other peoples.

But it is difficult to settle or even discuss these problems in an atmosphere of intimidation. That is why this latest Soviet threat—or any other threat which is made either independently or in response to our actions this week—must and will be met with determination. Any hostile move anywhere in the world against the safety and freedom of peoples to whom we are committed—including in particular the brave people of West Berlin—will be met by whatever action is needed.

Finally, I want to say a few words to the captive people of Cuba, to whom this speech is being directly carried by special radio facilities. I speak to you as a friend, as one who knows of your deep attachment to your fatherland, as one who shares your aspirations for liberty and justice for all. And I have watched and the American people have watched with deep sorrow how your nationalist revolution was betrayed—and how your fatherland fell under foreign domination. Now your leaders are no longer Cuban leaders inspired by Cuban ideals. They are puppets and agents of an international conspiracy which has turned Cuba against your friends and neighbors in the Americas—and turned it into the first Latin American country to become a target for nuclear war—the first Latin American country to have these weapons on its soil.

These new weapons are not in your interest. They contribute nothing to your peace and well-being. They can only undermine it. But this country has no wish to cause you to suffer or to impose any system upon you. We know that your lives and land are being used as pawns by those who deny your freedom.

Many times in the past, the Cuban people have risen to throw out tyrants who destroyed their liberty. And I have no doubt that most Cubans today look forward to the time when they will be truly free—free from foreign domination, free to choose their own leaders, free to select their own system, free to own their own land, free to speak and write and worship without fear or degradation. And then shall Cuba be welcomed back to the society of free nations and to the associations of this hemisphere.

My fellow citizens: let no one doubt that this is a difficult and dangerous effort on which we have set out. No one can foresee precisely what course it will take or what costs or casualties will be incurred. Many months of sacrifice and self-discipline lie ahead—months in which both our patience and our will will be tested—months in which many threats and denunciations will keep us aware of our dangers. But the greatest danger of all would be to do nothing.

The path we have chosen for the present is full of hazards, as all paths are—but it is the one most consistent with our character and courage as a nation and our commitments around the world. The cost of freedom is always high—but Americans have always paid it. And one path we shall never choose, and that is the path of surrender or submission.

Our goal is not the victory of might, but the vindication of right—not peace at the expense of freedom, but both peace *and* freedom, here in this hemisphere, and, we hope, around the world. God willing, that goal will be achieved.

Thank you and good night.

Document 6

Soviet Premier Nikita Khrushchev's view of the missile crisis, in *Khrushchev Remembers*, Strobe Talbott, ed., Boston: Little, Brown, 1970, 493–500. Reprinted with permission.

The fate of Cuba and the maintenance of Soviet prestige in that part of the world preoccupied me even when I was busy conducting the affairs of state in Moscow and traveling to the other fraternal countries. While I was on an official visit to Bulgaria, for instance, one thought kept hammering away at my brain: what will happen if we lose Cuba? I knew it would have been a terrible blow to Marxism-Leninism. It would gravely diminish our stature throughout the world, but especially in Latin America. If Cuba fell, other Latin American countries would reject us, claiming that for all our might the Soviet Union hadn't been able to do anything for Cuba except to make empty protests to the United Nations. We had to think up some way of confronting America with more than words. We had to establish a tangible and effective deterrent to American interference in the Caribbean. But what exactly? The logical answer was missiles. The United States had already surrounded the Soviet Union with its own bomber bases and missiles. We knew that American missiles were aimed against us in Turkey and Italy, to say nothing of West Germany. Our vital industrial centers were directly threatened by planes armed with atomic bombs and guided missiles tipped with nuclear warheads. As Chairman of the Council of Ministers, I found myself in the difficult position of having to decide on a course of action which would answer the American threat but which would also avoid war. Any fool can start a war, and once he's done so, even the wisest of men are helpless to stop it—especially if it's a nuclear war.

It was during my visit to Bulgaria that I had the idea of installing missiles with nuclear warheads in Cuba without letting the United States find out they were there until it was too late to do anything about them. I knew that first we'd have to talk to [Fidel] Castro and explain our strategy to him in order to get the agreement of the Cuban government. My thinking went like this: if we installed the missiles secretly and then if the United States discovered the missiles were there after they were already poised and ready to strike, the Americans would think twice before trying to liquidate our installations by military means. I knew that the United States could knock out some of our installations, but not all of them. If a quarter or even a tenth of our missiles survived—even if only one or two big ones were left—we could still hit New York, and there wouldn't be much of New York left. I don't mean to say that everyone in New York would be killed—not everyone, of course, but an awful lot of people would be wiped out. I don't know how many: that's a matter for our scientists and military personnel to work out. They specialize in nuclear warfare and know how to calculate the consequences of a missile strike against a city the size of New York. But that's all beside the point. The main thing was that the installation of our missiles in Cuba would, I thought, restrain the United States from precipitous military action against Castro's government. In addition to protecting Cuba, our missiles would have equalized what the West likes to call "the balance of power." The Americans had surrounded our country with military bases and threatened us with nuclear weapons, and now they would learn just what it feels like to have enemy missiles pointing at you; we'd be doing nothing more than giving them a little of their own medicine. And it was high time America learned what it feels like to have her own land and her own people threatened. We Russians have suffered three wars over the last half century: World War I, the Civil War, and World War II. America has never had to fight a war on her own soil, at least not in the past fifty years. She's sent troops abroad to fight in the two World Wars—and made a fortune as a result. America has shed a few drops of her own blood while making billions by bleeding the rest of the world dry. . . .

I want to make one thing absolutely clear: when we put our ballistic missiles in Cuba, we had no desire to start a war. On the contrary, our principal aim was only to deter America from starting a war. We were well aware that a war which started over Cuba would quickly expand into a world war. Any idiot could have started a war between America and Cuba. Cuba was eleven thousand kilometers away from us. Only a fool would think that we wanted to invade the American continent from Cuba. Our goal was precisely the opposite: we wanted to keep the Americans from invading Cuba, and, to that end, we wanted to make them think twice by confronting them with our missiles. This goal we achieved—but not without undergoing a period of perilous tension.

When the Americans figured out what we were up to in Cuba, they mounted a huge press campaign against us, claiming that we were threatening the security of the United States and so on and so forth. In short, hostility began to build up, and the American press fanned the flames. Then one day in October President [John F.] Kennedy came out with a statement warning that the United States would take whatever measures were necessary to remove what he called the "threat" of Russian missiles on Cuba. The Americans began to make a belligerent show of their strength. They concentrated their forces against Cuba, completely surrounding the island with their navy. Things started churning. In our estimation the Americans were trying to frighten us, but they were no less scared than we were of atomic war. We hadn't had time to deliver all our shipments to Cuba, but we had installed enough missiles already to destroy New York, Chicago, and the other huge industrial cities, not to mention a little village like Washington. I don't think America had ever faced such a real threat of destruction as at that moment.

Meanwhile we went about our own business. We didn't let ourselves be intimidated. Our ships, with the remainder of our deliveries to Cuba, headed straight through an armada of the American navy, but the Americans didn't try to stop our ships or even check them. We kept in mind that as long as the

United States limited itself to threatening gestures and didn't actually touch us, we could afford to pretend to ignore the harassment. After all, the United States had no moral or legal quarrel with us. We hadn't given the Cubans anything more than the Americans were giving to their allies. We had the same rights and opportunities as the Americans. Our conduct in the international arena was governed by the same rules and limits as the Americans'.

We had almost completed our shipments. As the crisis approached the boiling point, the Western press began to seethe with anger and alarm. We replied accordingly, although not so hysterically. Our people were fully informed of the dangerous situation that had developed, although we took care not to cause panic by the way we presented the facts.

I remember a period of six or seven days when the danger was particularly acute. Seeking to take the heat off the situation somehow, I suggested to the other members of the government: "Comrades, let's go to the Bolshoi Theater this evening. Our own people as well as foreign eyes will notice, and perhaps it will calm them down. They'll say to themselves, 'If Khrushchev and our other leaders are able to go to the opera at a time like this, then at least tonight we can sleep peacefully.' " We were trying to disguise our own anxiety, which was intense.*

Then the exchange of notes began. I dictated the messages and conducted the exchange from our side. I spent one of the most dangerous nights at the Council of Ministers office in the Kremlin. I slept on a couch in my office—and I kept my clothes on. I didn't want to be like that Western minister who was caught literally with his pants down by the Suez events of 1956 and who had to run around in his shorts until the emergency was over. I was ready for alarming news to come any moment, and I wanted to be ready to react immediately.

President Kennedy issued an ultimatum, demanding that we remove our missiles and bombers from Cuba. I remember those days vividly. I remember the exchange with President Kennedy especially well because I initiated it and was at the center of the action on our end of the correspondence. I take complete responsibility for the fact that the President and I entered into direct contact at the most crucial and dangerous stage of the crisis.

The climax came after five or six days, when our ambassador to Washington, Anatoly Dobrynin, reported that the President's brother, [Attorney General] Robert Kennedy, had come to see him on an unofficial visit. Dobrynin's report went something like this:

"Robert Kennedy looked exhausted. One could see from his eyes that he had not slept for days. He himself said that he had not been home for six days and nights. 'The President is in a grave situation,' Robert Kennedy said, 'and he does not know how to get out of it. We are under very severe stress. In fact we are under pressure from our military to use force against Cuba. Probably at this very moment the President is sitting down to write a message to Chairman Khrushchev. We want to ask you, Mr. Dobrynin, to pass President Kennedy's message to Chairman Khrushchev through unofficial channels. President Kennedy implores Chairman Khrushchev to accept his offer and to take into consideration the peculiarities of the American system. Even though the President himself is very much against starting a war over Cuba, an irreversible chain of events could occur against his

*When the top men in the Kremlin turn up at the Bolshoi Theater in a body, all smiles, it frequently (though not infallibly) means that a crisis of some kind is brewing. One of the best remembered of such occasions was the evening before [L. P.] Beria's arrest. Beria himself, of course, was included in the party.

will. That is why the President is appealing directly to Chairman Khrushchev for his help in liquidating this conflict. If the situation continues much longer, the President is not sure that the military will not overthrow him and seize power. The American army could get out of control.' ''

I hadn't overlooked this possibility. We knew that Kennedy was a young President and that the security of the United States was indeed threatened. For some time we had felt there was a danger that the President would lose control of his military, and now he was admitting this to us himself. Kennedy's message urgently repeated the Americans' demand that we remove the missiles and bombers from Cuba. We could sense from the tone of the message that tension in the United States was indeed reaching a critical point.

We wrote a reply to Kennedy in which we said that we had installed the missiles with the goal of defending Cuba and that we were not pursuing any other aims except to deter an invasion of Cuba and to guarantee that Cuba could follow a course determined by its own people rather than one dictated by some third party.

While we conducted some of this exchange through official diplomatic channels, the more confidential letters were relayed to us through the President's brother. He gave Dobrynin his telephone number and asked him to call at any time. Once, when Robert Kennedy talked with Dobrynin, he was almost crying. ''I haven't seen my children for days now,'' Robert Kennedy said, ''and the President hasn't seen his either. We're spending all day and night at the White House; I don't know how much longer we can hold out against our generals.''

We could see that we had to reorient our position swiftly. ''Comrades,'' I said, ''we have to look for a dignified way out of this conflict. At the same time, of course, we must make sure that we do not compromise Cuba.'' We sent the Americans a note saying that we agreed to remove our missiles and bombers on the condition that the President give us his assurance that there would be no invasion of Cuba by the forces of the United States or anybody else. Finally Kennedy gave in and agreed to make a statement giving us such an assurance. . . .

In our negotiations with the Americans during the crisis, they had, on the whole, been open and candid with us, especially Robert Kennedy. The Americans knew that if Russian blood were shed in Cuba, American blood would surely be shed in Germany. The American government was anxious to avoid such a development. It had been, to say the least, an interesting and challenging situation. The two most powerful nations of the world had been squared off against each other, each with its finger on the button. You'd have thought that war was inevitable. But both sides showed that if the desire to avoid war is strong enough, even the most pressing dispute can be solved by compromise. And a compromise over Cuba was indeed found. The episode ended in a triumph of common sense. I'll always remember the late President with deep respect because, in the final analysis, he showed himself to be sober-minded and determined to avoid war. He didn't let himself become frightened, nor did he become reckless. He didn't overestimate America's might, and he left himself a way out of the crisis. He showed real wisdom and statesmanship when he turned his back on right-wing forces in the United States who were trying to goad him into taking military action against Cuba. It was a great victory for us, though, that we had been able to extract from Kennedy a promise that neither America nor any of her allies would invade Cuba.

Document 7

President John F. Kennedy, American University commencement address, June 10, 1963, *PPP: John F. Kennedy, 1963*, 1964, 460–64.

I have . . . chosen this time and this place to discuss a topic on which ignorance too often abounds and the truth is too rarely perceived—yet it is the most important topic on earth: world peace.

What kind of peace do I mean? What kind of peace do we seek? Not a Pax Americana enforced on the world by American weapons of war. Not the peace of the grave or the security of the slave. I am talking about genuine peace, the kind of peace that makes life on earth worth living, the kind that enables men and nations to grow and to hope and to build a better life for their children—not merely peace for Americans but peace for all men and women—not merely peace in our time but peace for all time.

I speak of peace because of the new face of war. Total war makes no sense in an age when great powers can maintain large and relatively invulnerable nuclear forces and refuse to surrender without resort to those forces. It makes no sense in an age when a single nuclear weapon contains almost ten times the explosive force delivered by all of the allied air forces in the Second World War. It makes no sense in an age when the deadly poisons produced by a nuclear exchange would be carried by wind and water and soil and seed to the far corners of the globe and to generations yet unborn.

Today the expenditure of billions of dollars every year on weapons acquired for the purpose of making sure we never need to use them is essential to keeping the peace. But surely the acquisition of such idle stockpiles—which can only destroy and never create—is not the only, much less the most efficient, means of assuring peace.

I speak of peace, therefore, as the necessary rational end of rational men. I realize that the pursuit of peace is not as dramatic as the pursuit of war—and frequently the words of the pursuer fall on deaf ears. But we have no more urgent task.

Some say that it is useless to speak of world peace or world law or world disarmament—and that it will be useless until the leaders of the Soviet Union adopt a more enlightened attitude. I hope they do. I believe we can help them do it. But I also believe that we must reexamine our own attitude—as individuals and as a Nation—for our attitude is as essential as theirs. And every graduate of this school, every thoughtful citizen who despairs of war and wishes to bring peace, should begin by looking inward—by examining his own attitude toward the possibilities of peace, toward the Soviet Union, toward the course of the cold war and toward freedom and peace here at home.

First: Let us examine our attitude toward peace itself. Too many of us think it is impossible. Too many think it unreal. But that is a dangerous, defeatist belief. It leads to the conclusion that war is inevitable—that mankind is doomed—that we are gripped by forces we cannot control.

We need not accept that view. Our problems are manmade—therefore, they can be solved by man. And man can be as big as he wants. No problem of human destiny is beyond human beings. Man's reason and spirit have often solved the seemingly unsolvable—and we believe they can do it again.

I am not referring to the absolute, infinite concept of universal peace and good will of which some fantasies and fanatics dream. I do not deny the value of hopes and dreams but we merely invite discouragement and incredulity by making that our only and immediate goal.

Let us focus instead on a more practical, more attainable peace—based not on a sudden revolution in human nature but on a gradual evolution in human institutions—on a series of concrete actions and effective agreements which are in the interest of all concerned. There is no single, simple key to this peace—no grand or magic formula to be adopted by one or two powers. Genuine peace must be the product of many nations, the sum of many acts. It must be dynamic, not static, changing to meet the challenge of each new generation. For peace is a process—a way of solving problems.

With such a peace, there will still be quarrels and conflicting interests, as there are within families and nations. World peace, like community peace, does not require that each man love his neighbor—it requires only that they live together in mutual tolerance, submitting their disputes to a just and peaceful settlement. And history teaches us that enmities between nations, as between individuals, do not last forever. However fixed our likes and dislikes may seem, the tide of time and events will often bring surprising changes in the relations between nations and neighbors.

So let us persevere. Peace need not be impracticable, and war need not be inevitable. By defining our goal more clearly, by making it seem more manageable and less remote, we can help all peoples to see it, to draw hope from it, and to move irresistibly toward it.

Second: Let us reexamine our attitude toward the Soviet Union. It is discouraging to think that their leaders may actually believe what their propagandists write. It is discouraging to read a recent authoritative Soviet text on *Military Strategy* and find, on page after page, wholly baseless and incredible claims—such as the allegation that "American imperialist circles are preparing to unleash different types of wars . . . that there is a very real threat of a preventive war being unleashed by American imperialists against the Soviet Union . . . [and that] the political aims of the American imperialists are to enslave economically and politically the European and other capitalist countries . . . [and] to achieve world domination . . . by means of aggressive wars."

Truly, as it was written long ago: "The wicked flee when no man pursueth." Yet it is sad to read these Soviet statements—to realize the extent of the gulf between us. But it is also a warning—a warning to the American people not to fall into the same trap as the Soviets, not to see only a distorted and desperate view of the other side, not to see conflict as inevitable, accommodation as impossible, and communication as nothing more than an exchange of threats.

No government or social system is so evil that its people must be considered as lacking in virtue. As Americans, we find communism profoundly repugnant as a negation of personal freedom and dignity. But we can still hail the Russian people for their many achievements—in science and space, in economic and industrial growth, in culture and in acts of courage.

Among the many traits the peoples of our two countries have in common, none is stronger than our mutual abhorrence of war. Almost unique, among the major world powers, we have never been at war with each other. And no nation in the history of battle ever suffered more than the Soviet Union suffered in the course of the Second World War. At least 20 million lost their lives. Countless millions of homes and farms were burned or sacked. A third of the nation's territory, including nearly two thirds of its industrial base, was turned into a wasteland—a loss equivalent to the devastation of this country east of Chicago.

Today, should total war ever break out

again—no matter how—our two countries would become the primary targets. It is an ironic but accurate fact that the two strongest powers are the two in the most danger of devastation. All we have built, all we have worked for, would be destroyed in the first 24 hours. And even in the cold war, which brings burdens and dangers to so many countries, including this Nation's closest allies—our two countries bear the heaviest burdens. For we are both devoting massive sums of money to weapons that could be better devoted to combating ignorance, poverty, and disease. We are both caught up in a vicious and dangerous cycle in which suspicion on one side breeds suspicion on the other, and new weapons beget counterweapons.

In short, both the United States and its allies, and the Soviet Union and its allies, have a mutually deep interest in a just and genuine peace and in halting the arms race. Agreements to this end are in the interests of the Soviet Union as well as ours—and even the most hostile nations can be relied upon to accept and keep those treaty obligations, and only those treaty obligations, which are in their own interest.

So, let us not be blind to our differences—but let us also direct attention to our common interests and to the means by which those differences can be resolved. And if we cannot end now our differences, at least we can help make the world safe for diversity. For, in the final analysis, our most basic common link is that we all inhabit this small planet. We all breathe the same air. We all cherish our children's future. And we are all mortal.

Third: Let us reexamine our attitude toward the cold war, remembering that we are not engaged in a debate, seeking to pile up debating points. We are not here distributing blame or pointing the finger of judgment. We must deal with the world as it is, and not as it might have been had the history of the last 18 years been different.

We must, therefore, persevere in the search for peace in the hope that constructive changes within the Communist bloc might bring within reach solutions which now seem beyond us. We must conduct our affairs in such a way that it becomes in the Communists' interest to agree on a genuine peace. Above all, while defending our own vital interests, nuclear powers must avert those confrontations which bring an adversary to a choice of either a humiliating retreat or a nuclear war. To adopt that kind of course in the nuclear age would be evidence only of the bankruptcy of our policy—or of a collective death-wish for the world.

To secure these ends, America's weapons are nonprovocative, carefully controlled, designed to deter, and capable of selective use. Our military forces are committed to peace and disciplined in self-restraint. Our diplomats are instructed to avoid unnecessary irritants and purely rhetorical hostility.

For we can seek a relaxation of tensions without relaxing our guard. And, for our part, we do not need to use threats to prove that we are resolute. We do not need to jam foreign broadcasts out of fear our faith will be eroded. We are unwilling to impose our system on any unwilling people—but we are willing and able to engage in peaceful competition with any people on earth.

Meanwhile, we seek to strengthen the United Nations, to help solve its financial problems, to make it a more effective instrument for peace, to develop it into a genuine world security system—a system capable of resolving disputes on the basis of law, of insuring the security of the large and the small, and of creating conditions under which arms can finally be abolished.

At the same time we seek to keep peace inside the non-Communist world, where many nations, all of them our friends, are divided over issues which weaken Western unity, which invite Communist intervention or which threaten to erupt into war. Our efforts in West New Guinea, in the Congo, in the Middle East, and in the Indian subcontinent, have been persistent and patient despite criticism from both sides. We have also tried to set an example for others—by seeking to adjust small but significant differences with our own closest neighbors in Mexico and in Canada.

Speaking of other nations, I wish to make one point clear. We are bound to many nations by alliances. Those alliances exist because our concern and theirs substantially overlap. Our commitment to defend Western Europe and West Berlin, for example, stands undiminished because of the identity of our vital interests. The United States will make no deal with the Soviet Union at the expense of other nations and other peoples, not merely because they are our partners, but also because their interests and ours converge.

Our interests converge, however, not only in defending the frontiers of freedom, but in pursuing the paths of peace. It is our hope—and the purpose of allied policies—to convince the Soviet Union that she, too, should let each nation choose its own future, so long as that choice does not interfere with the choices of others. The Communist drive to impose their political and economic system on others is the primary cause of world tension today. For there can be no doubt that, if all nations could refrain from interfering in the self-determination of others, the peace would be much more assured.

This will require a new effort to achieve world law—a new context for world discussions. It will require increased understanding between the Soviets and ourselves. And increased understanding will require increased contact and communication. One step in this direction is the proposed arrangement for a direct line between Moscow and Washington, to avoid on each side the dangerous delays, misunderstandings, and misreadings of the other's actions which might occur at a time of crisis.

We have also been talking in Geneva about other first-step measures of arms control, designed to limit the intensity of the arms race and to reduce the risks of accidental war. Our primary long-range interest in Geneva, however, is general and complete disarmament—designed to take place by stages, permitting parallel political developments to build the new institutions of peace which would take the place of arms. The pursuit of disarmament has been an effort of this Government since the 1920's. It has been urgently sought by the past three administrations. And however dim the prospects may be today, we intend to continue this effort—to continue it in order that all countries, including our own, can better grasp what the problems and possibilities of disarmament are.

The one major area of these negotiations where the end is in sight, yet where a fresh start is badly needed, is in a treaty to outlaw nuclear tests. The conclusion of such a treaty, so near and yet so far, would check the spiraling arms race in one of its most dangerous areas. It would place the nuclear powers in a position to deal more effectively with one of the greatest hazards which man faces in 1963, the further spread of nuclear arms. It would increase our security—it would decrease the prospects of war. Surely this goal is sufficiently important to require our steady pursuit, yielding neither to the temptation to give up the whole effort nor the temptation to give up our insistence on vital and responsible safeguards.

I am taking this opportunity, therefore, to announce two important decisions in this regard.

First: Chairman [Nikita] Khrushchev, [British] Prime Minister [Harold] Macmillan, and I have agreed that high-level discussions will shortly begin in Moscow looking toward early agreement on a comprehensive test ban treaty. Our hopes must be tempered with the caution of history—but with our hopes go the hopes of all mankind.

Second: To make clear our good faith and solemn convictions on the matter, I now declare that the United States does not propose to conduct nuclear tests in the atmosphere so long as other states do not do so. We will not be the first to resume. Such a declaration is no substitute for a formal binding treaty, but I hope it will help us achieve one. Nor would such a treaty be a substitute for disarmament, but I hope it will help us achieve it.

Finally, my fellow Americans, let us examine our attitude toward peace and freedom here at home. The quality and spirit of our own society must justify and support our efforts abroad. We must show it in the dedication of our own lives—as many of you who are graduating today will have a unique opportunity to do, by serving without pay in the Peace Corps abroad or in the proposed National Service Corps here at home.

But wherever we are, we must all, in our daily lives, live up to the age-old faith that peace and freedom walk together. In too many of our cities today, the peace is not secure because freedom is incomplete.

It is the responsibility of the executive branch at all levels of government—local, State, and National—to provide and protect that freedom for all of our citizens by all means within their authority. It is the responsibility of the legislative branch at all levels, wherever that authority is not now adequate, to make it adequate, And it is the responsibility of all citizens in all sections of this country to respect the rights of all others and to respect the law of the land.

All this is not unrelated to world peace. "When a man's ways please the Lord," the Scriptures tell us, "he maketh even his enemies to be at peace with him." And is not peace, in the last analysis, basically a matter of human rights—the right to live out our lives without fear of devastation—the right to breathe air as nature provided it—the right of future generations to a healthy existence?

While we proceed to safeguard our national interests, let us also safeguard human interests. And the elimination of war and arms is clearly in the interest of both. No treaty, however much it may be to the advantage of all, however tightly it may be worded, can provide absolute security against the risks of deception and evasion. But it can—if it is sufficiently effective in its enforcement and if it is sufficiently in the interests of its signers—offer far more security and far fewer risks than an unabated, uncontrolled, unpredictable arms race.

The United States, as the world knows, will never start a war. We do not want a war. We do not now expect a war. This generation of Americans has already had enough—more than enough—of war and hate and oppression. We shall be prepared if others wish it. We shall be alert to try to stop it. But we shall also do our part to build a world of peace where the weak are safe and the strong are just. We are not helpless before that task or hopeless of its success. Confident and unafraid, we labor on—not toward a strategy of annihilation but toward a strategy of peace.

Document 8

Communiqué and text of partial Nuclear Test-Ban Treaty, in Moscow, July 25, 1963, U.S. Department of State, *Bulletin,* July 1, 1963, vol. 49, 239–40.

COMMUNIQUÉ

The special representatives of the President of the U.S.A. and of the Prime Minister of the U.K., W. A. Harriman, Under Secretary of State for Political Affairs of the United States, and Lord Hailsham, Lord President of the Council and Minister for Science for the United Kingdom, visited Moscow together with their advisers on July 14. Mr. Harriman and Lord Hailsham were received by the Chairman of the Council of Ministers of the U.S.S.R., N. S. Khrushchev, who presided on July 15 at the first of a series of meetings to discuss questions relating to the discontinuance of nuclear tests, and other questions of mutual interest. The discussions were continued from July 16 to July 25 with A. A. Gromyko, Minister of Foreign Affairs of the U.S.S.R. During these discussions each principal was assisted by his advisers.

The discussions took place in a businesslike, cordial atmosphere. Agreement was reached on the text of a treaty banning nuclear weapons tests in the atmosphere, in outer space and under water. This text is being published separately and simultaneously with this communiqué. It was initialed on July 25 by A. A. Gromyko, Mr. Harriman and Lord Hailsham. Mr. Harriman and Lord Hailsham together with their advisers will leave Moscow shortly to report and bring back the initialed texts to their respective Governments. Signature of the Treaty is expected to take place in the near future in Moscow.

The heads of the three delegations agreed that the test ban treaty constituted an important first step toward the reduction of international tension and the strengthening of peace, and they look forward to further progress . . .

The heads of the three delegations discussed the Soviet proposal relating to a pact of nonaggression between the participants in the North Atlantic Treaty Organisation and the participants in the Warsaw Treaty [military pact of 1955 among Soviet Union, East Germany, and loyal Eastern European Communist states]. The three Governments have agreed fully to inform their respective allies in the two organisations concerning these talks and to consult with them about continuing discussion on this question with the purpose of achieving agreement satisfactory to all participants. A brief exchange of views also took place with regard to other measures, directed at a relaxation of tension.

TEXT OF TREATY

TREATY

banning nuclear weapon tests in the atmosphere, in outer space and under water

The Governments of the United States of America, the United Kingdom of Great Britain and Northern Ireland, and the Union of Soviet Socialist Republics, hereinafter referred to as the "Original Parties",

Proclaiming as their principal aim the speediest possible achievement of an agreement on general and complete disarmament under strict international control in accordance with the objectives of the United Nations which would put an end to the armaments race and eliminate the incentive to the production and testing of all kinds of weapons, including nuclear weapons,

Seeking to achieve the discontinuance of all test explosions of nuclear weapons for all time, determined to continue negotiations to this end, and desiring to put an end to the contamination of man's environment by radioactive substances,

Have agreed as follows:

Article I

1. Each of the Parties to this Treaty undertakes to prohibit, to prevent, and not to carry out any nuclear weapon test explosion, or any other nuclear explosion, at any place under its jurisdiction or control:

(a) in the atmosphere; beyond its limits, including outer space; or underwater, including territorial waters or high seas; or

(b) in any other environment if such explosion causes radioactive debris to be present outside the territorial limits of the State under whose jurisdiction or control such explosion is conducted. It is understood in this connection that the provisions of this subparagraph are without prejudice to the conclusion of a treaty resulting in the permanent banning of all nuclear test explosions, including all such explosions underground, the conclusion of which, as the Parties have stated in the Preamble to this Treaty, they seek to achieve.

2. Each of the Parties to this Treaty undertakes furthermore to refrain from causing, encouraging, or in any way participating in, the carrying out of any nuclear weapon test explosion, or any other nuclear explosion, anywhere which would take place in any of the environments described, or have the effect referred to, in paragraph 1 of this Article.

Article II

1. Any Party may propose amendments to this Treaty. The text of any proposed amendment shall be submitted to the Depositary [entrusted] Governments which shall circulate it to all Parties to this Treaty. Thereafter, if requested to do so by one-third or more of the Parties, the Depositary Governments shall convene a conference, to which they shall invite all the Parties, to consider such amendment.

2. Any amendment to this Treaty must be approved by a majority of the votes of all the Parties to this Treaty, including the votes of all of the Original Parties. The amendment shall enter into force for all by a majority of all the Parties, including the instruments of ratification of all of the Original Parties.

Article III

1. This Treaty shall be open to all States for signature. Any State which does not sign this Treaty before its entry into force in accordance with paragraph 3 of this Article may accede to it at any time.

2. This Treaty shall be subject to ratification by signatory States. Instruments of ratification and instruments of accession shall be deposited with the Governments of the Original Parties—the United States of America, the United Kingdom of Great Britain and Northern Ireland, and the Union of Soviet Socialist Republics—which are hereby designated the Depositary Governments.

3. This Treaty shall enter into force after its ratification by all the Original Parties and the deposit of their instruments of ratification.

4. For States whose instruments of ratification or accession are deposited subsequent to the entry into force of this Treaty, it shall enter into force on the date of the deposit of their instruments of ratification or accession.

5. The Depositary Governments shall promptly inform all signatory and acceding States of the date of each signature, the date of deposit of each in-

strument of ratification of and accession to this Treaty, the date of its entry into force, and the date of receipt of any requests for conferences or other notices.

6. This Treaty shall be registered by the Depositary Governments pursuant to Article 102 of the Charter of the United Nations.

Article IV

This Treaty shall be of unlimited duration.

Each Party shall in exercising its national sovereignty have the right to withdraw from the Treaty if it decides that extraordinary events, related to the subject matter of this Treaty, have jeopardized the supreme interests of its country. It shall give notice of such withdrawal to all other Parties to the Treaty three months in advance.

Article V

This Treaty, of which the English and Russian texts are equally authentic, shall be deposited in the archives of the Depositary Governments. Duly certified copies of this Treaty shall be transmitted by the Depositary Governments to the Governments of the signatory and acceding States.

Document 9

Telegram from State Department to Ambassador to Vietnam Henry Cabot Lodge, Aug. 24, 1963, *The Pentagon Papers: The Senator Gravel Edition*, Boston: Beacon Press, 1971, vol. 2, 734–35.

It is now clear that whether military proposed martial law or whether [Ngo Dinh] Nhu [Diem's brother] tricked them into it, Nhu took advantage of its imposition to smash pagodas with police and [Colonel Le Quang] Tung's Special Forces loyal to him, thus placing onus on military in eyes of world and Vietnamese people. Also clear that Nhu has maneuvered himself into commanding position.

US Government cannot tolerate situation in which power lies in Nhu's hands. [South Vietnamese Premier Ngo Dinh] Diem must be given chance to rid himself of Nhu and his coterie and replace them with best military and political personalities available.

If, in spite of all of your efforts, Diem remains obdurate and refuses, then we must face the possibility that Diem himself cannot be preserved.

We now believe immediate action must be taken to prevent Nhu from consolidating his position further. Therefore, unless you in consultation with [General Paul D.] Harkins [head of Military Assistance Command, Vietnam] perceive overriding objections you are authorized to proceed along following lines:

(1) First, we must press on appropriate levels of GVN [Government of Vietnam] following line:

(a) USG [U.S. Government] cannot accept actions against Buddhists taken by Nhu and his collaborators under cover martial law.

(b) Prompt dramatic actions redress situation must be taken, including repeal of decree 10, release of arrested monks, nuns, etc.

(2) We must at same time also tell key military leaders that US would find it impossible to continue support GVN militarily and economically unless above steps are taken immediately which we recognize requires removal of Nhus from the scene. We wish give Diem reasonable opportunity to remove

Nhus, but if he remains obdurate, then we are prepared to accept the obvious implication that we can no longer support Diem. You may also tell appropriate military commanders we will give them direct support in any interim period of breakdown central government mechanism.

(3) We recognize the necessity of removing taint on military for pagoda raids and placing blame squarely on Nhu. You are authorized to have such statements made in Saigon as you consider desirable to achieve this objective. We are prepared to take same line here and to have Voice of America make statement along lines contained in next numbered telegram whenever you give the word, preferably as soon as possible.

Concurrently, with above, Ambassador and country team should urgently examine all possible alternative leadership and make detailed plans as to how we might bring about Diem's replacement if this should become necessary.

Assume you will consult with General Harkins re any precautions necessary protect American personnel during crisis period.

You will understand that we cannot from Washington give you detailed instructions as to how this operation should proceed, but you will also know we will back you to the hilt on actions you take to achieve our objectives.

Needless to say we have held knowledge of this telegram to minimum essential people and assume you will take similar precautions to prevent premature leaks.

Document 10

Telegram from Ambassador to Vietnam Henry Cabot Lodge, to Secretary of State Dean Rusk, Aug. 29, 1963, *The Pentagon Papers: The Senator Gravel Edition*, Boston: Beacon Press, 1971, vol. 2, 738–39.

We are launched on a course from which there is no respectable turning back: the overthrow of the [South Vietnamese Premier Ngo Dinh] Diem government. There is no turning back in part because U.S. prestige is already publicly committed to this end in large measure and will become more so as the facts leak out. In a more fundamental sense, there is no turning back because there is no possibility, in my view, that the war can be won under a Diem administration, still less that Diem or any member of the family can govern the country in a way to gain the support of the people who count, i.e., the educated class in and out of government service, civil and military—not to mention the American people. In the last few months (and especially days) they have in fact positively alienated these people to an incalculable degree. So that I am personally in full agreement with the policy which I was instructed to carry out by last Sunday's telegram.

2. The chance of bringing off a Generals' coup depends on them to some extent; but it depends at least as much on us.

3. We should proceed to make all-out effort to get Generals to move promptly. To do so we should have authority to do following:

(a) That Gen. [Paul D.] Harkins [head of Military Assistance Command, Vietnam] repeat to Generals personally message previously transmitted by CAS [code name for CIA] officers. This should establish their authenticity. Gen. Harkins should have order on this.

(b) If nevertheless Generals insist on public statement that all U.S. aid to VN [Vietnam] through Diem regime has been stopped, we would agree, on express understanding that Generals will have started at same time. (We would seek persuade Generals that it would be better to hold this card for use in event of stalemate. We hope it will not be necessary to do this at all.)

(c) VNese Generals doubt that we have the will power, courage, and determination to see this thing through. They are haunted by the idea that we will run out on them even though we have told them pursuant to instructions, that the game had started.

5. We must press on for many reasons. Some of these are:

(a) Explosiveness of the present situation which may well lead to riots and violence if issue of discontent with regime is not met. Out of this could come a pro-Communist or at best a neutralist set of politicians.

(b) The fact that war cannot be won with the present regime.

(c) Our own reputation for steadfastness and our unwillingness to stultify ourselves.

(d) If proposed action is suspended, I believe a body blow will be dealt to respect for us by VNese Generals. Also, all those who expect U.S. to straighten out this situation will feel let down. Our help to the regime in past years inescapably gives a responsibility which we cannot avoid.

6. I realize that this course involves a very substantial risk of losing VN. It also involves some additional risk to American lives. I would never propose it if I felt there was a reasonable chance of holding VN with Diem. . . .

Document 11

President John F. Kennedy, NBC Television interview, Sept. 9, 1963, "[Chet] Huntley–[David] Brinkley Report," *PPP: John F. Kennedy, 1963,* 1964, 658–60.

Mr. Huntley: Mr. President, in respect to our difficulties in South Viet-Nam, could it be that our Government tends occasionally to get locked into a policy or an attitude and then finds it difficult to alter or shift that policy?

The President: Yes, that is true. I think in the case of South Viet-Nam we have been dealing with a government which is in control, has been in control for 10 years. In addition, we have felt for the last 2 years that the struggle against the Communists was going better. Since June, however, the difficulties with the Buddhists, we have been concerned about a deterioration, particularly in the Saigon area, which hasn't been felt greatly in the outlying areas but may spread. So we are faced with the problem of wanting to protect the area against the Communists. On the other hand, we have to deal with the government there. That produces a kind of ambivalence in our efforts which exposes us to some criticism. We are using our influence to persuade the government there to take those steps which will win back support. That takes some time and we must be patient, we must persist.

Mr. Huntley: Are we likely to reduce our aid to South Viet-Nam now?

The President: I don't think we think that would be helpful at this time. If you reduce your aid, it is possible you could have some effect upon the government structure there. On the other hand, you might have a situation which could bring about a collapse. Strongly in our mind is what happened in the case of China at the end of World War II, where China was lost, a weak government became increasingly unable to control events. We don't want that.

Mr. Brinkley: Mr. President, have you had any reason to doubt this so-called "domino theory," that if South Viet-Nam falls, the rest of southeast Asia will go behind it?

The President: No, I believe it. I believe it. I think that the struggle is close enough. China is so large, looms so high just beyond the frontiers, that if South Viet-Nam went, it would not only give them an improved geographic position for a guerrilla assault on Malaya, but would also give the impression that the wave of the future in southeast Asia was China and the Communists. So I believe it.

Mr. Brinkley: In the last 48 hours there have been a great many conflicting reports from there about what the CIA was up to. Can you give us any enlightenment on it?

The President: No.

Mr. Huntley: Does the CIA tend to make its own policy? That seems to be the debate here.

The President: No, that is the frequent charge, but that isn't so. Mr. [John] McCone, head of the CIA, sits in the National Security Council. We have had a number of meetings in the past few days about events in South Viet-Nam. Mr. McCone participated in every one, and the CIA coordinates its efforts with the State Department and the Defense Department.

Mr. Brinkley: With so much of our prestige, money, so on, committed in South Viet-Nam, why can't we exercise a little more influence there, Mr. President?

The President: We have some influence. We have some influence, and we are attempting to carry it out. I think we don't—we can't expect these countries to do every thing the way we want to do them. They have their own interest, their own personalities, their own tradition. We can't make everyone in our image and there are a good many people who don't want to go in our image. In addition, we have ancient struggles between countries. In the case of India and Pakistan, we would like to have them settle Kashmir. That is our view of the best way to defend the subcontinent against communism. But that struggle between India and Pakistan is more important to a good many people in that area than the struggle against the Communists. We would like to have Cambodia, Thailand, and South Viet-Nam all in harmony, but there are ancient differences there. We can't make the world over, but we can influence the world. The fact of the matter is that with the assistance of the United States, SEATO [Southeast Asia Treaty Organization], southeast Asia and indeed all of Asia has been maintained independent against a powerful force, the Chinese Communists. What I am concerned about is that Americans will get impatient and say because they don't like events in southeast Asia or they don't like the government in Siagon, that we should withdraw. That only makes it easy for the Communists. I think we should stay. We should use our influence in as effective a way as we can, but we should not withdraw.

Document 12

President John F. Kennedy, speech prepared for Dallas (at Trade Mart), Nov. 22, 1963, *PPP: John F. Kennedy, 1963,* 1964, 891–92.

I want to discuss with you today the status of our strength and our security because this question clearly calls for the most responsible qualities of leadership and the most enlightened products of scholarship. For this Nation's strength and security are not easily or cheaply obtained, nor are they quickly and simply explained. There are many kinds of strength and no one kind will suffice. Overwhelming nuclear strength cannot stop a guerrilla war. Formal pacts of alliance cannot stop internal subversion. Displays of material wealth cannot stop the disillusionment of diplomats subjected to discrimination.

Above all, words alone are not enough. The United States is a peaceful nation. And where our strength and determination are clear, our words need merely to convey conviction, not belligerence. If we are strong, our strength will speak for itself. If we are weak, words will be of no help.

I realize that this Nation often tends to identify turning-points in world affairs with the major addresses which preceded them. But it was not the Monroe Doctrine that kept all Europe away from this hemisphere—it was the strength of the British fleet and the width of the Atlantic Ocean. It was not General [George C.] Marshall's speech [calling for aid program to Europe that became the Marshall Plan] at Harvard which kept communism out of Western Europe—it was the strength and stability made possible by our military and economic assistance.

In this administration also it has been necessary at times to issue specific warnings—warnings that we could not stand by and watch the Communists conquer Laos by force, or intervene in the Congo, or swallow West Berlin, or maintain offensive missiles on Cuba. But while our goals were at least temporarily obtained in these and other instances, our successful defense of freedom was due not to the words we used, but to the strength we stood ready to use on behalf of the principles we stand ready to defend.

This strength is composed of many different elements, ranging from the most massive deterrents to the most subtle influences. And all types of strength are needed—no one kind could do the job alone. Let us take a moment, therefore, to review this Nation's progress in each major area of strength.

I.

First, as Secretary [of Defense Robert] McNamara made clear in his address last Monday, the strategic nuclear power of the United States has been so greatly modernized and expanded in the last 1,000 days, by the rapid production and deployment of the most modern missile systems, that any and all potential aggressors are clearly confronted now with the impossibility of strategic victory—and the certainty of total destruction—if by reckless attack they should ever force upon us the necessity of a strategic reply.

In less than 3 years, we have increased by 50 percent the number of Polaris submarines scheduled to be in force by the next fiscal year, increased by more than 70 percent our total Polaris purchase program, increased by more than 75 percent our Minuteman purchase program, increased by 50 percent the portion of our strategic bombers on 15-minute alert, and increased by 100 percent the total number of nuclear weapons available in our strategic alert forces. Our security is further enhanced by the steps we have taken regarding these weapons to improve the speed and certainty of their response, their readiness at all times to respond, their ability to survive an attack, and their ability to be carefully controlled and directed through secure command operations.

II.

But the lessons of the last decade have taught us that freedom cannot be defended by strategic nuclear power alone. We have, therefore, in the last 3 years accelerated the development and deployment of tactical nuclear weapons, and increased by 60 percent the tactical nuclear forces deployed in Western Europe.

Nor can Europe or any other continent rely on nuclear forces alone, whether they are strategic or tactical. We have radically improved the readiness of our conventional forces—increased by 45 percent the number of combat ready Army divisions, increased by 100 percent the procurement of modern Army weapons and equipment, increased by 100 percent our ship construction, conversion, and modernization program, increased by 100 percent our procurement of tactical aircraft, increased by 30 percent the number of tactical air squadrons, and increased the strength of the Marines. As last month's "Operation Big Lift"—which originated here in Texas—showed so clearly, this Nation is prepared as never before to move substantial numbers of men in surprisingly little time to advanced positions anywhere in the world. We have increased by 175 percent the procurement of airlift aircraft, and we have already achieved a 75 percent increase in our existing strategic airlift capability. Finally, moving beyond the traditional roles of our military forces, we have achieved an increase of nearly 600 percent in our special forces—those forces that are prepared to work with our allies and friends against the guerrillas, saboteurs, insurgents and assassins who threaten freedom in a less direct but equally dangerous manner.

CHAPTER 11

Vietnam War: 1963–75

George C. Herring

The Vietnam War had profound consequences for the United States. The American phase lasted twelve years, longer than any previous U.S. involvement in a war. It took the lives of more than 58,000 Americans and cost billions of dollars. The war set off a runaway inflation that devastated the U.S. economy in the 1970s. It divided Americans as no other event had since their own Civil War a century earlier. It brought fundamental changes in American foreign policy, discrediting the policy of containment, undermining the consensus that supported it, and leaving U.S. foreign policy temporarily in disarray.

Understanding Vietnam requires addressing two fundamental questions: Why did the United States commit billions of dollars, thousands of lives, and a vast military arsenal to an area so remote and seemingly so insignificant? Why, despite this huge commitment, did the world's richest and most powerful nation fail to achieve its objective, the preservation of an independent, non-Communist South Vietnam?

When President Lyndon B. Johnson dispatched combat troops to Vietnam in July 1965, thereby launching the American phase of the thirty-year post-colonial struggle over Indochina, he acted on assumptions that had guided U.S. policy for more than fifteen years and had gone virtually unquestioned inside and outside of government. Like Truman, Eisenhower, and Kennedy before him, Johnson was certain that the struggle in Vietnam was part of the larger Cold War conflict with the Soviet Union.

The war in fact began in September 1945 as a nationalist, anticolonial struggle when Ho Chi Minh's Viet Minh forces, in words borrowed from Thomas Jefferson, declared Vietnam independent from French rule. (doc. 1) Ho initiated the revolution without explicit direction from Moscow and sustained the subsequent war with France until 1949 without any external support. His revolution drew strength from its ability to identify with Vietnamese nationalism, and it had a momentum and drive of its own, quite apart from international Communism. In the supercharged atmosphere of the Cold War, however, Americans were not inclined to make fine distinctions. That Ho and some of his top lieutenants were Moscow-trained

Communists and that the Viet Minh received support from the Soviet Union and Communist China after 1949 gave credence to a view that became gospel among Americans: Ho Chi Minh was a stooge of the larger Communist conspiracy, his revolution an offshoot of Moscow's relentless drive for world domination.

Americans also generally agreed after 1950 that the fall of Vietnam to Communism would threaten their nation's vital interests. (doc. 2) Before 1941, Vietnam had seemed remote and insignificant. Policymakers first began to note its importance when Japan's intrusion into French Indochina in 1940 threatened the oil- and rubber-rich Dutch East Indies and endangered America's own colony in the Philippines. In 1950, Vietnam took on new importance. The Cold War with the Soviet Union had acquired international dimensions and had intensified to dangerous levels. In the context of a world divided into two hostile power blocs, a fragile global balance of power, and a zero-sum game in which any gain for Communism was automatically a loss for the "free world," areas such as Vietnam that had been of no more than marginal significance suddenly took on great importance.

There were more specific reasons why the United States attached growing significance to Vietnam after 1950. The domino theory proclaimed that the fall of Vietnam to Communism could lead quickly to the loss of the rest of Indochina and then all Southeast Asia; the loss would cost the Western nations and Japan access to crucial markets and raw materials and would deprive them of vital naval bases and sea routes, with implications possibly extending across the world. (doc. 1, chap. 14) The domino theory was reinforced by the so-called Munich analogy, the idea generally accepted in the 1950s that the failure of free nations to stand up to Germany and Japan in the 1930s had led inexorably to World War II. The apparently obvious lesson was that to avoid all-out war, aggression must be thwarted at the outset.

U.S. policymakers also agreed that the loss of Vietnam could have disastrous political consequences at home. This assumption derived from other perceived lessons of history, especially the rancorous and divisive debate that had followed the fall of China to Communism in 1949 and Republican use of this issue to discredit the Democrats in the 1952 elections. The conclusion, again apparently obvious, was that no administration, especially a Democratic administration, could survive the loss of Vietnam.

For these reasons, the United States gradually enlarged its role in Vietnam. It supported the French war effort after 1950, and by 1954 was absorbing nearly 80 percent of its cost. When the French were compelled to negotiate a settlement at Geneva in July 1954 and then began to withdraw from Vietnam, the United States moved in to replace them, attempting through nationalist leader Ngo Dinh Diem to establish an independent, non-Communist government in the southern half of the temporarily partitioned country. (doc. 3)

In was not a long step from the political intervention of 1954 to Johnson's 1965 decisions for full-scale war. Despite massive U.S. aid and unqualified U.S. support, Diem could not stabilize his government. (doc. 4) Reclusive and lacking in charisma, he could not rally the people to his side. His oppressiveness alienated much of the rural population and important political groups in the cities. Outraged that Diem, with U.S. backing, had ignored the provisions of the Geneva Accords calling for national elections to unify the country, former Viet Minh who had stayed in South Vietnam launched a rebellion against his government and created the National Liberation Front as the instrument of that rebellion. (doc. 5) In 1959, North Vietnam began to send men and supplies into the south to support the insurgency. By 1961, the Diem regime appeared doomed.

Both Kennedy and Johnson sharply escalated U.S. involvement. They agreed that failure to stand firm in Vietnam could damage U.S. credibility in the world and therefore did what they thought was necessary to preserve an independent, non-Communist South Vietnam. Kennedy expanded U.S. military and economic aid, and increased the number of U.S. military advisers to over 16,000. When Diem and his sinister brother Ngo Dinh Nhu (as head of the repressive Vietnam Bureau of Investigation) began to appear as much the problem as the solution, the Kennedy administration in late 1963 authorized a coup against them.

As necessary as it may have been, the overthrow of Diem left a huge vacuum that the United States quickly felt compelled to fill. In the aftermath of the coup, the military and political situation in South Vietnam deteriorated drastically. When North Vietnamese gunboats in August 1964 allegedly attacked U.S. ships in the Gulf of Tonkin, Johnson rammed through a compliant Congress a "blank check" authorization to take "all necessary measures to repel any armed attacks against the forces of the United States and to prevent further aggression." (docs. 6 and 7) Certain by early 1965 that without U.S. intervention South Vietnam would collapse, the Johnson administration initiated regular air attacks against North Vietnam. Six months later, the president authorized the dispatch of U.S. ground combat troops to prevent the fall of the embattled South Vietnamese government. (doc. 8)

Despite the vast commitment subsequently made in Vietnam, the United States was unable to achieve its major objective. Its strategy was badly flawed. Policymakers assumed that if the United States slowly increased the level of military pain, North Vietnam would see that the costs of the war were greater than the potential gain and would abandon the insurgency in the south. U.S. goals would thereby be achieved without risking a larger war with the Soviet Union and China.

The United States thus gradually escalated the war between 1965 and 1967. (doc. 9) The tonnage of bombs dropped on North Vietnam increased from 63,000 in 1965 to 226,000 in 1967, and the total eventually exceeded the tonnage dropped in all theaters in World War II. The United States expanded its ground forces to more than 500,000 men by late 1967, and the U.S. commander, General William C. Westmoreland, launched aggressive search-and-destroy operations throughout South Vietnam to attain victory by ridding it of all National Liberation Front and North Vietnamese main forces.

The bombing inflicted extensive damage, but it did not destroy North Vietnam's will to endure or decisively affect its ability to fight. The manner in which the United States applied the bombing virtually ensured its ineffectiveness. Gradual escalation gave the North Vietnamese time to construct a highly effective air defense system and to shelter key resources. Indeed, it probably encouraged them to hold out. The North Vietnamese also demonstrated dogged perseverance and great ingenuity in coping with the effects of the bombing. Some of their major losses were made up by sharply increased aid from the Soviet Union and China.

Westmoreland's strategy of attrition also failed. The North Vietnamese matched each American escalation with an escalation of their own. They fought when and where they chose, and if losses reached unacceptable levels, they melted into the countryside or retreated into sanctuaries in Laos, Cambodia, or North Vietnam. The enemy was hurt, in some cases badly, but its main forces were not destroyed. In addition, the firepower the United States deployed in South Vietnam devastated the country it was trying to save and alienated the population. Thus, despite impressive body count figures, by 1967 it was clear to many that the hopes of a quick and relatively inexpensive military victory were unfounded. The best the United States could attain was a stalemate. (doc. 10)

While the war dragged on with no end in sight, powerful opposition developed at home. Opposition to war was a long-standing American tradition, of course, and in the case of Vietnam it assumed formidable proportions. Pacifists who opposed all wars found in Vietnam confirmation of their views. The radical movement that had grown out of domestic strife in the 1960s saw the war as a clear example of the way the American ruling class exploited the masses to sustain a decadent capitalistic system. (docs. 11 and 12) Antiwar liberals, by far the largest group in the unwieldy coalition, increasingly questioned the war on both moral and practical grounds. By backing a corrupt, authoritarian government, they argued, the United States was betraying its own principles. Liberals also increasingly viewed the struggle in Vietnam as an internal conflict with at best an indirect relation to the Cold War, and they questioned its importance to American national security.

The antiwar movement significantly influenced the outcome of the war. It probably encouraged North Vietnam's determination to hold out. It did not turn the American people against the war, as some critics have argued. The cost in terms of lives lost and taxes paid was far more important in that regard. But the movement forced Vietnam into the public consciousness. It challenged the rationale of the war and indeed of an entire generation of Cold War policies. It limited the military options of both Johnson and Nixon and may have headed off any tendency toward more drastic escalation.

Perhaps most important, the disturbances and internal divisions caused by the antiwar movement caused fatigue and anxiety among the policymakers and the public and thus eventually encouraged efforts to find a way out. (doc. 13)

The Communist Tet Offensive of early 1968 marked a major turning point in the war. By directly attacking the cities, the North Vietnamese hoped to topple the South Vietnamese government, thus forcing the United States to withdraw. The offensive worked, but not as intended. The Americans and South Vietnamese repulsed the enemy attacks and inflicted huge losses on the North Vietnamese, especially on the Viet Cong. But the Tet fighting wreaked huge destruction in South Vietnam. It also exacerbated growing divisions between the United States and South Vietnam. Most important, it severely tried the patience of the American public and convinced some top officials that the United States could not accomplish its goals at acceptable cost. President Johnson reluctantly bent to these pressures on March 31, 1968, by putting a lid on further escalation of the war, stopping the bombing north of the 20th parallel, agreeing to negotiations, and by withdrawing from the presidential race.

Johnson's successor, Richard M. Nixon, quickly became ensnared by Vietnam. Nixon perceived that the divisions within the United States compelled him to end the war. But he was certain that unless he did so on terms that were "honorable" he would undermine America's position in the world, leaving the nation, in his words, a "pitiful, helpless giant." After his attempts to use slightly veiled threats of nuclear obliteration to intimidate the North Vietnamese into surrendering were unsuccessful, Nixon settled on a policy of "Vietnamization." (doc. 14) To appease public impatience, he began withdrawing U.S. troops from Vietnam and he increasingly shifted the responsibility for military operations to South Vietnamese forces. To keep pressure on the North Vietnamese, he secretly bombed military sanctuaries in Cambodia for nearly a year, and in 1970 and 1971 he launched military "incursions" into Cambodia and Laos.

Vietnamization was no more successful than the policies pursued by Johnson. Whatever time it bought for Nixon at home was more than offset by the huge public uproar over the Cambodian and Laotian incursions. The North Vietnamese accurately perceived that the United States could not remain in Vietnam indefinitely, and they saw no reason to compromise. Most important, the South Vietnamese were simply not ready to take up the burden Nixon thrust upon them, and without American support they could not do the job. Thus after an especially bloody period of warfare in 1972, Nixon agreed to terms the United States had earlier rejected, leaving 150,000 North Vietnamese troops in South Vietnam and accepting a coalition government.

The peace agreement of 1973 merely set the stage for another phase of the war. (doc. 15) U.S. troops were withdrawn by March 1973, leaving the South Vietnamese to face the enemy alone. Increasingly preoccupied with the Watergate scandal, Nixon was unable to uphold the agreement that had been wrought at such heavy cost, and a war-weary Congress slashed aid to South Vietnam. Recognizing that the United States was unlikely to reenter the war in any form, North Vietnam in early 1975 launched its final offensive. It achieved stunning success, and in April 1975, Saigon fell to the advancing forces, marking the end of a thirty-year struggle over Vietnam.

The effects of the war lingered long past April 1975. For Vietnam, the legacy was one of destruction, deprivation, and human misery, and the heavy-handed efforts of the victorious Hanoi regime to consolidate the nation and communize the economy made a bad situation worse. Fifteen years after the end of the war, Vietnam still wallowed in poverty and economic backwardness. For the United States, the effects were more subtle but nonetheless profound. The war helped set off the inflation that undermined the U.S. economy in the 1970s. It aroused popular suspicion of government that has not entirely dissipated. It brought an inglorious end to the policy of global interventionism pursued by the United States in the 1950s and 1960s. And the efforts of the Reagan administration in the 1980s to expunge the "Vietnam syndrome" and restore a policy of global containment were only partly successful. Indeed, as late as 1990, it seemed likely that the specter of Vietnam would continue to exert a significant influence on American foreign policy for years into the future.

Document 1

The Vietnamese Declaration of Independence, 1945, Information Service, Viet-Nam Delegation in France, *The Democratic Republic of Viet-Nam*, Paris, Imprimerie Centrale Commerciale, 1948, 3–5.

All men are created equal; they are endowed by their Creator with certain unalienable Rights; among these are Life, Liberty, and the pursuit of Happiness.

This immortal statement was made in the Declaration of Independence of the United States of America in 1776. In a broader sense, this means: All the peoples on the earth are equal from birth, all the peoples have a right to live, to be happy and free.

The Declaration of the French Revolution made in 1791 on the Rights of Man and the Citizen also states: "All men are born free and with equal rights, and must always remain free and have equal rights."

Those are undeniable truths.

Nevertheless, for more than eighty years, the French imperialists, abusing the standard of Liberty, Equality, and Fraternity, have violated our Fatherland and oppressed our fellow citizens. They have acted contrary to the ideals of humanity and justice.

In the field of politics, they have deprived our people of every democratic liberty.

They have enforced inhuman laws; they have set up three distinct political regimes in the North, the Center, and the South of Viet-Nam in order to wreck our national unity and prevent our people from being united.

They have built more prisons than schools. They have mercilessly slain our patriots; they have drowned our uprisings in rivers of blood.

They have fettered public opinion; they have practiced obscurantism against our people.

To weaken our race they have forced us to use opium and alcohol.

In the field of economics, they have fleeced us to the backbone, impoverished our people and devastated our land.

They have robbed us of our rice fields, our mines, our forests, and our raw materials. They have monopolized the issuing of bank notes and the export trade.

They have invented numerous unjustifiable taxes and reduced our people, especially our peasantry, to a state of extreme poverty.

They have hampered the prospering of our national bourgeoisie; they have mercilessly exploited our workers.

In the autumn of 1940, when the Japanese fascists violated Indochina's territory to establish new bases in their fight against the Allies, the French imperialists went down on their bended knees and handed over our country to them.

Thus, from that date, our people were subjected to the double yoke of the French and the Japanese. Their sufferings and miseries increased. The result was that, from the end of last year to the beginning of this year, from Quang Tri Province to the North of Viet-Nam, more than two million of our fellow citizens died from starvation. On March 9 [1945], the French troops were disarmed by the Japanese. The French colonialists either fled or surrendered, showing that not only were they incapable of "protecting" us, but that, in the span of five years, they had twice sold our country to the Japanese.

On several occasions before March 9, the Viet Minh League urged the French to ally themselves with it against the Japanese. Instead of agreeing to this proposal, the French colonialists so intensified their terrorist activities against the Viet Minh members that before fleeing they massacred a great number of our political prisoners detained at Yen Bay and Cao Bang.

Notwithstanding all this, our fellow citizens have always manifested toward the French a tolerant and humane attitude. Even after the Japanese *Putsch* of March, 1945, the Viet Minh League helped many Frenchmen to cross the frontier, rescued some of them from Japanese jails, and protected French lives and property.

From the autumn of 1940, our country had in fact ceased to be a French colony and had become a Japanese possession.

After the Japanese had surrendered to the Allies, our whole people rose to regain our national sovereignty and to found the Democratic Republic of Viet-Nam.

The truth is that we have wrested our independence from the Japanese and not from the French.

The French have fled, the Japanese have capitulated, Emperor Bao Dai has abdicated. Our people have broken the chains which for nearly a century have fettered them and have won independence for the Fatherland. Our people at the same time have overthrown the monarchic regime that has reigned supreme for dozens of centuries. In its place has been established the present Democratic Republic.

For these reasons, we, members of the Provisional Government, representing the whole Vietnamese people, declare that from now on we break off all relations of a colonial character with France; we repeal all the international obligation that France has so far subscribed to on behalf of Viet-Nam, and we abolish all the special rights the French have unlawfully acquired in our Fatherland.

The whole Vietnamese people, animated by a common purpose, are determined to fight to the bitter end against any attempt by the French colonialists to reconquer their country.

We are convinced that the Allied nations, which at Teheran and San Francisco have acknowledged the principles of self-determination and equality of nations, will not refuse to acknowledge the independence of Viet-Nam.

A people who have courageously opposed French domination for more than eighty years, a people who have fought side by side with the Allies against the fascists during these last years, such a people must be free and independent.

For these reasons, we, members of the Provisional Government of the Democratic Republic of Viet-Nam, solemnly declare to the world that Viet-Nam has the right to be a free and independent country—and in fact it is so already. The entire Vietnamese people are determined to mobilize all their physical and mental strength, to sacrifice their lives and property in order to safeguard their independence and liberty.

Document 2

Draft report by the National Security Council, "The Position of the United States with Respect to Indochina," Feb. 27, 1950, U.S. Department of State, *Foreign Relations of the United States* (hereafter referred to as *FRUS*), *1950*, Washington, D.C.: Government Printing Office, 1976, vol. 6, 745–47.

The Problem

1. To undertake a determination of all practicable United States measures to protect its security in Indochina and to prevent the expansion of communist aggression in that area.

Analysis

2. It is recognized that the threat of communist aggression against Indochina is only one phase of anticipated communist plans to seize all of Southeast Asia. It is understood that Burma is weak internally and could be invaded without strong opposition or even that the Government of Burma could be subverted. However, Indochina is the area most immediately threatened. It is also the only area adjacent to communist China which contains a large European army, which along with native troops is now in armed conflict with the forces of communist aggression. A decision to contain communist expansion at the border of Indochina must be considered as a part of a wider study to prevent communist aggression into other parts of Southeast Asia.

3. A large segment of the Indochinese nationalist movement was seized in 1945 by Ho Chi Minh, a Vietnamese who under various aliases has served as a communist agent for thirty years. He has attracted non-communist as well as communist elements to his support. In 1946, he attempted, but failed to secure French agreement to his recognition as the head of a government of Vietnam. Since then he has directed a guerrilla army in raids against French installations and lines of communication. French forces which have been attempting to restore law and order found themselves pitted against a determined adversary who manufactures effective arms locally, who received supplies of arms from outside sources, who maintained no capital or permanent headquarters and who was, and is able, to disrupt and harass almost any area within Vietnam (Tonkin, Annam and Cochinchina) at will.

4. The United States has, since the Japanese surrender, pointed out to the

French Government that the legitimate nationalist aspirations of the people of Indochina must be satisfied, and that a return to the prewar colonial rule is not possible. The Department of State has pointed out to the French Government that it was and is necessary to establish and support governments in Indochina particularly in Vietnam, under leaders who are capable of attracting to their causes the non-communist nationalist followers who had drifted to the Ho Chi Minh communist movement in the absence of any non-communist movement around which to plan their aspirations.

5. In an effort to establish stability by political means, where military measures had been unsuccessful, i.e., by attracting non-communist nationalists, now followers of Ho Chi Minh, to the support of anti-communist nationalist leaders, the French Government entered into agreements with the governments of the Kingdoms of Laos and Cambodia to elevate their status from protectorates to that of independent states within the French Union. The State of Vietnam was formed, with similar status, out of the former French protectorates of Tonkin, Annam and the former French Colony of Cochinchina. Each state received an increased degree of autonomy and sovereignty. Further steps towards independence were indicated by the French. The agreements were ratified by the French Government on 2 February 1950.

6. The Governments of Vietnam, Laos and Cambodia were officially recognized by the United States and the United Kingdom on February 7, 1950. Other Western powers have, or are committed to do likewise. The United States has consistently brought to the attention of non-communist Asian countries the danger of communist aggression which threatens them if communist expansion in Indochina is unchecked. As this danger becomes more evident it is expected to overcome the reluctance that they have had to recognize and support the three new states. We are therefore continuing to press those countries to recognize the new states. On January 18, 1950, the Chinese Communist Government announced its recognition of the Ho Chi Minh movement as the legal Government of Vietnam, while on January 30, 1950, the Soviet Government, while maintaining diplomatic relations with France, similarly announced its recognition.

7. The newly formed States of Vietnam, Laos and Cambodia do not as yet have sufficient political stability nor military power to prevent the infiltration into their areas of Ho Chi Minh's forces. The French Armed Forces, while apparently effectively utilized at the present time, can do little more than to maintain the *status quo*. Their strength of some 140,000 does, however, represent an army in being and the only military bulwark in that area against the further expansion of communist aggression from either internal or external forces.

8. The presence of Chinese Communist troops along the border of Indochina makes it possible for arms, material and troops to move freely from Communist China to the northern Tonkin area now controlled by Ho Chi Minh. There is already evidence of movement of arms.

9. In the present state of affairs, it is doubtful that the combined native Indochinese and French troops can successfully contain Ho's forces should they be strengthened by either Chinese Communist troops crossing the border, or Communist-supplied arms and material in quantity from outside Indochina strengthening Ho's forces.

Conclusions

10. It is important to United States security interests that all practicable measures be taken to prevent further

communist expansion in Southeast Asia. Indochina is a key area of Southeast Asia and is under immediate threat.

11. The neighboring countries of Thailand and Burma could be expected to fall under Communist domination if Indochina were controlled by a Communist-dominated government. The balance of Southeast Asia would then be in grave hazard.

12. Accordingly, the Departments of State and Defense should prepare as a matter of priority a program of all practicable measures designed to protect United States security interests in Indochina.

Document 3

Final declaration of the Geneva Conference on the problem of restoring peace in Indochina, July 1954, U.S. Department of State, *Bulletin*, Aug. 2, 1954, 164.

1. The Conference takes note of the Agreements ending hostilities in Cambodia, Laos and Viet-Nam and organizing international control and the supervision of the execution of the provisions of these agreements.

2. The Conference expresses satisfaction at the ending of hostilities in Cambodia, Laos and Viet-Nam; the Conference expresses its conviction that the execution of the provisions set out in the present Declaration and in the Agreements on the cessation of hostilities will permit Cambodia, Laos and Viet-Nam henceforth to play their part, in full independence and sovereignty, in the peaceful community of nations.

3. The Conference takes note of the declarations made by the Governments of Cambodia and of Laos of their intention to adopt measures permitting all citizens to take their place in the national community, in particular by participating in the next general elections, which, in conformity with the constitution of each of these countries, shall take place in the course of the year 1955, by secret ballot and in conditions of respect for fundamental freedoms.

4. The Conference takes note of the clauses in the Agreement on the cessation of hostilities in Viet-Nam prohibiting the introduction into Viet-Nam of foreign troops and military personnel as well as all kinds of arms and munitions. The Conference also takes note of the declarations made by the Governments of Cambodia and Laos of their resolution not to request foreign aid, whether in war material, in personnel or in instructors except for the purpose of the effective defence of their territory and, in the case of Laos, to the extent defined by the Agreements on the cessation of hostilities in Laos.

5. The Conference takes note of the clauses in the Agreement on the cessation of hostilities in Viet-Nam to the effect that no military base under the control of a foreign State may be established in the regrouping zones of the two parties, the latter having the obligation to see that the zones allotted to them shall not constitute part of any military alliance and shall not be utilized for the resumption of hostilities or in the service of an aggressive policy. The Conference also takes note of the declarations of the Governments of Cambodia and Laos to the effect that they will not join in any agreement with other States if this agreement includes the obligation to participate in a military alliance not in conformity with the principles of the Charter of the United Nations or, in the case of Laos, with the principles of the Agreement on the cessation of hostilities in Laos or, so long as their security is not threatened, the obligation to establish bases on Cambodian or Laotian territory

for the military forces of foreign powers.

6. The Conference recognizes that the essential purpose of the Agreement relating to Viet-Nam is to settle military questions with a view to ending hostilities and that the military demarcation line is provisional and should not in any way be interpreted as constituting a political or territorial boundary. The Conference expresses its conviction that the execution of the provisions set out in the present Declaration and in the Agreement on the cessation of hostilities creates the necessary basis for the achievement in the near future of a political settlement in Viet-Nam.

7. The Conference declares that, so far as Viet-Nam is concerned, the settlement of political problems, effected on the basis of respect for principles of independence, unity and territorial integrity, shall permit the Vietnamese people to enjoy the fundamental freedoms, guaranteed by democratic institutions established as a result of free general elections by secret ballot. In order to ensure that sufficient progress in the restoration of peace has been made and that all the necessary conditions obtain for free expression of the national will, general elections shall be held in July 1956, under the supervision of an international commission composed of representatives of the Member States of the International Supervisory Commission, referred to in the Agreement on the cessation of hostilities. Consultations will be held on this subject between the competent representative authorities of the two zones from 20 July 1955 onwards.

8. The provisions of the Agreements on the cessation of hostilities intended to ensure the protection of individuals and of property must be most strictly applied and must, in particular, allow everyone in Viet-Nam to decide freely in which zone he wishes to live.

9. The competent representative authorities of the Northern and Southern zones of Viet-Nam, as well as the authorities of Laos and Cambodia, must not permit any individual or collective reprisals against persons who have collaborated in any way with one of the parties during the war, or against members of such persons' families.

10. The Conference takes note of the declaration of the Government of the French Republic to the effect that it is ready to withdraw its troops from the territory of Cambodia, Laos and Viet-Nam, at the request of the governments concerned and within periods which shall be fixed by agreement between the parties except in the cases where, by agreement between the two parties, a certain number of French troops shall remain at specified points and for a specified time.

11. The Conference takes note of the declaration of the French Government to the effect that for the settlement of all the problems connected with the re-establishment and consolidation of peace in Cambodia, Laos and Viet-Nam, the French Government will proceed from the principle of respect for the independence and sovereignty, unity and territorial integrity of Cambodia, Laos and Viet-Nam.

12. In their relations with Cambodia, Laos and Viet-Nam, each member of the Geneva Conference undertakes to respect the sovereignty, the independence, the unity and the territorial integrity of the above-mentioned States, and to refrain from any interference in their internal affairs.

13. The members of the Conference agree to consult one another on any question which may be referred to them by the International Supervisory Commission, in order to study such measures as may prove necessary to ensure that the Agreements on the cessation of hostilities in Cambodia, Laos and Viet-Nam are respected.

Declaration by Walter Bedell Smith, Representing the U.S. Delegation to the Geneva Conference, July 21, 1954

The Government of the United States being resolved to devote its efforts to the strengthening of peace in accordance with the principles and purposes of the United Nations.

Takes note of the Agreements concluded at Geneva on July 20 and 21, 1954 between the (*a*) Franco-Laotian Command and the Command of the People's Army of Viet-Nam; (*b*) The Royal Khmer Army Command and the Command of the People's Army of Viet-Nam; (*c*) Franco-Viet-Namese Command and the Command of the People's Army of Viet-Nam, and of paragraphs 1 to 12 inclusive of the Declaration presented to the Geneva Conference on July 21, 1954.

Declares with regard to the aforesaid Agreements and paragraphs (i) it will refrain from the threat or the use of force to disturb them, in accordance with Article 2 (4) of the Charter of the United Nations dealing with the obligation of Members to refrain in their international relations from the threat or use of force; and (ii) it would view any renewal of the aggression in violation of the aforesaid agreements with grave concern and as seriously threatening international peace and security.

In connection with this statement in the Declaration concerning free elections in Viet-Nam, my Government wishes to make clear its position which it has expressed in a Declaration made in Washington on June 29, 1954, as follows:

"In the case of nations now divided against their will, we shall continue to seek to achieve unity through free elections, supervised by the United Nations to ensure that they are conducted fairly."

With respect to the statement made by the Representative of the State of Viet-Nam, the United States reiterates its traditional position that peoples are entitled to determine their own future and that it will not join in any arrangement which would hinder this. Nothing in its declaration just made is intended to or does indicate any departure from this traditional position.

We share the hope that the agreement will permit Cambodia, Laos and Viet-Nam to play their part in full independence and sovereignty, in the peaceful community of nations, and will enable the peoples of that area to determine their own future.

Document 4

Ambassador to South Vietnam Elbridge Durbrow, "Evaluation of Situation in Viet Nam, December 1957," Dec. 5, 1957, *FRUS, 1955–1957*, 1985, vol. 1, 872–73.

Certain problems now discernible have given us a warning which, if disregarded, might lead to a deteriorating situation in Viet Nam within a few years.

[South Vietnamese Premier Ngo Dinh] Diem achieved notable successes in the first two years of his regime and remains the only man of stature so far in evidence to guide this country. He has unified free Viet Nam, brought it relative security and stability, and firmly maintains a pro-West, anti-communist position.

In the last year, however, Diem has avoided making decisions required to build the economic and social foundations necessary to secure Viet Nam's future independence and strength. He has made it clear that he would give first priority to the build-up of his armed forces regardless of the country's requirements for economic and social development. Events abroad which increase the danger of communist infiltration and subversion, and which threaten Viet Nam with possible isolation in this area have contributed to his concern and to his determination to strengthen his armed forces.

Certain characteristics of Diem—his suspiciousness and authoritarianism—have also reduced the Government's limited administrative capabilities. He assumes responsibility for the smallest details of Government and grants his Ministers little real authority.

At the same time, discontent is felt in different segments of the population for varied reasons. The base of the regime's popular support remains narrow. The regime might overcome such discontent and finally win over the loyalty of a majority of Vietnamese both in the North and South if it could show its ability to give the country stronger protection and create sound economic and social bases for progress. Progress, which is demanded in Viet Nam as throughout Asia, is perhaps the touchstone of the regime's enduring viability. Yet precisely because Diem is now procrastinating in making decisions affecting fundamental problems of his country's development, the lag between the people's expectations and the Government's ability to show results will grow.

We consider it therefore of importance that we bring strong pressure on the President to reach certain decisions basically in the economic and social fields which have been before him for some months but on which he has not acted. He has resented this and may resent it more, but in ours and his long range interests we must do our utmost to cause him to move forward in these fields.

The purpose of this evaluation of the present situation in Viet Nam is to examine the elements giving rise to some concern regarding certain developments in Viet Nam, to provide the Department [of State] and interested agencies salient background and to set forth conclusions and recommend certain broad courses of action. We feel that a frank discussion of the solution as we see it may be helpful to all concerned.

Document 5

Manifesto of the South Vietnam National Front for Liberation, December 1960, *Vietnamese Studies* (Hanoi) no. 23, "South Vietnam from the N.F.L. to the Provisional Revolutionary Government," 247–54.

Over the past hundred years the Vietnamese people repeatedly rose up to fight against foreign aggression for the independence and freedom of their fatherland. In 1945, the people throughout the country surged up in an armed uprising, overthrew the Japanese and French domination and seized power. When the French colonialists invaded our country for the second time, our compatriots, determined not to be enslaved again, shed much blood and laid down many lives to defend their national sovereignty and independence. Their solidarity and heroic struggle during nine years led the resistance war to victory. The 1954 Geneva Agreements restored peace in our country and recognized "the sovereignty, independence, unity and territorial integrity of Viet Nam."

Our compatriots in South Viet Nam would have been able to live in peace, to earn their livelihood in security and to build a decent and happy life.

However, the American imperialists, who had in the past helped the French colonialists to massacre our people, have now replaced the French in enslaving the southern part of our country through a disguised colonial regime. They have been using their stooge—the Ngo Dinh Diem administration—in their downright repression and exploitation of our compatriots, in the manoeuvres to permanently divide our country and to turn its southern part into a military base in preparation for war in Southeast Asia.

The aggressors and traitors, working hand in glove with each other, have set up an extremely cruel dictatorial rule. They persecute and massacre democratic and patriotic people, and abolish all human liberties. They ruthlessly exploit the workers, peasants and other labouring people, strangle the local industry and trade, poison the minds of our people with a depraved foreign culture, thus degrading our national culture, traditions and ethics. They feverishly increase their military forces, build military bases, use the army as an instrument for repressing the people and serving the US imperialists' scheme to prepare an aggressive war.

Never, over the past six years, have gun shots massacring our compatriots ceased to resound throughout South Viet Nam. Tens of thousands of patriots here have been murdered and hundreds of thousands thrown into jail. All sections of the people have been living in a stifling atmosphere under the iron heel of the US-Diem clique. Countless families have been torn away and scenes of mourning are seen everywhere as a result of unemployment, poverty, exacting taxes, terror, massacre, drafting of manpower and pressganging, usurpation of land, forcible house removal, and herding of the people into "prosperity zones," "resettlement centres" and other forms of concentration camps.

High anger with the present tyrannical regime is boiling among all strata of the people. Undaunted in the face of barbarous persecution, our compatriots are determined to unite and struggle unflaggingly against the US imperialists' policy of aggression and the dictatorial and nepotic regime of the Ngo Dinh Diem clique. Among workers, peasants and other toiling people, among intellectuals, students and pupils, industrialists and traders, religious sects and national minorities, patriotic activities are gaining in scope and strength, seriously shaking the US-Diem dictatorial regime. . . .

At present, our people are urgently demanding an end to the cruel dictatorial rule; they are demanding independence and democracy, enough food and clothing, and peaceful reunification of the country.

To meet the aspirations of our compatriots, the *South Viet Nam National Front for Liberation* came into being, pledging itself to shoulder the historic task of liberating our people from the present yoke of slavery.

The *South Viet Nam National Front for Liberation* undertakes to unite all sections of the people, all social classes, nationalities, political parties, organizations, religious communities and patriotic personalities, without distinction of their political tendencies, in order to struggle for the overthrow of the rule of the US imperialists and their stooges—the Ngo Dinh Diem clique—and for the realization of independence, democracy, peace and neutrality pending the peaceful reunification of the fatherland.

Document 6

Telephone conversation between Secretary of Defense Robert S. McNamara and Admiral U. S. Grant Sharp, Aug. 4, 1964, Lyndon B. Johnson Papers, National Security File, Country File, Vietnam, Box 228, Lyndon B. Johnson Library, Austin, Texas.

McNamara: Hello, Ollie, this is Bob McNamara. What's the latest information on the action?

Sharp: The latest dope we have, Sir, is a sort of summation [that] . . . indicates a little doubt on just exactly what went on and we are trying to get a recap of it right now to—apparently the thing started by a sort of ambush attempt by the PTs [torpedo boats].

McNamara: In what respect? Describe that.

Sharp: I can't, Sir, because I haven't got it. That's all it said.

McNamara: OK.

Sharp: It said initial ambush attempt was definite. And that they were bothered by freak radar echoes and the sonar men giving these torpedo contacts, and, of course, in that sort of thing, these young fellows are apt to say any noise is a torpedo, so that, undoubtedly, there were not as many torpedos—you know, at one place there they had 21. There undoubtedly weren't that many. And we had the—the reports are a little confusing on what happened. Neither ship saw a ship or a wake. The *Turner Joy* tracked two contacts and fired on—that is, tracked them for a considerable period, and fired on, I think, something like 13 contacts. They—she claims three boats hit and one sunk, for sure—the *Turner Joy.* The *Maddox,* let me see, she doesn't claim a boat—oh yes, she does, too—she claims one or two, as I recall it, now. So that is the general picture, Sir.

McNamara: There isn't any possibility there was no attack, is there?

Sharp: Yes, I would say that there is a slight possibility, and that is what I am trying to find out right now, and about 20 minutes ago I told [Admiral] Tom Moore[r] [commander in chief of the Pacific Fleet] to get in touch with these people and get a definite report on it.

McNamara: OK. How soon do you think it will come in?

Sharp: Well, it should come in within an hour, but I have a slight doubt now, I must admit, and we are trying to get it nailed down because the Task Group Commander, that is, of the destroyer, says we need a daylight recce [reconnaissance] of the whole situation and the situation's in doubt, he says. Now I don't—I am in my office right now, which is just about half a block from the Command Center, as you know.

McNamara: Yes.

Sharp: And that particular piece of paper is down in the Command Center and I don't have it right here. I gave the Date Time Group to [Vice Admiral] Lloyd Mustin [from Defense Department] when I talked to him.

McNamara: We've got problems on timing here, of course, we don't want to release news of what happened without saying what we are going to do; we don't want to say what we are going to do before we do it.

Sharp: Right.

McNamara: We obviously don't want to do it until we are damn sure what happened.

Sharp: That's right.

McNamara: Now how do we reconcile all this?

Sharp: Well, I would recommend this, Sir. I would recommend that we hold this execute until we have a definite indication that this happened.

McNamara: Well, how do we get that?

Sharp: I think I can—I think I will have it in a couple of hours.

McNamara: OK. Well, the execute is scheduled for 7 PM our time which is three hours from now, right?

Sharp: Yes, Sir.

McNamara: All right, so if you have it in two hours, we still have an hour.

Sharp: It's 7 o'clock local out there.

McNamara: That's right, and that is three hours from now.

Sharp: Yes, Sir.

McNamara: If you get your definite information in two hours, we can still proceed with the execute and it seems to me we ought to go ahead on that basis: get the pilots briefed, get the planes armed, get everything lined up to go.

Sharp: Yes, Sir.

McNamara: Continue the execute order in effect, but between now and 6 o'clock get a definite fix and you call me directly.

Sharp: I agree, yes Sir, I will do that.

McNamara: OK, very good.

Sharp: Right, Sir. Bye.

Document 7

The Gulf of Tonkin Resolution, Aug. 7, 1964, U.S. Department of State, *Bulletin*, Aug. 29, 1964, 268.

To Promote the Maintenance of International Peace and Security in Southeast Asia.

Whereas naval units of the Communist regime in Vietnam, in violation of the principles of the Charter of the United Nations and of international law, have deliberately and repeatedly attacked United States naval vessels lawfully present in international waters, and have thereby created a serious threat to international peace; and

Whereas these attacks are part of a deliberate and systematic campaign of aggression that the Communist regime in North Vietnam has been waging against its neighbors and the nations joined with them in the collective defense of their freedom; and

Whereas the United States is assisting the peoples of southeast Asia to protect their freedom and has no territorial, military or political ambitions in that area, but desires only that these peoples should be left in peace to work out their own destinies in their own way: Now, therefore, be it

Resolved by the Senate and House of Representatives of the United States of America in Congress assembled,

That the Congress approves and supports the determination of the President, as Commander in Chief, to take all necessary measures to repel any armed attack against the forces of the United States and to prevent further aggression.

SEC. 2. The United States regards as vital to its national interest and to world peace the maintenance of international peace and security in southeast Asia. Consonant with the Constitution of the United States and the Charter of the United Nations and in accordance with its obligations under the Southeast Asia Collective Defense Treaty, the United States is, therefore, prepared, as the President determines, to take all necessary steps, including the use of armed force, to assist any member or protocol state of the Southeast Asia Collective Defense Treaty requesting assistance in defense of its freedom.

SEC. 3. This resolution shall expire when the President shall determine that the peace and security of the area is reasonably assured by international conditions created by action of the United Nations or otherwise, except that it may be terminated earlier by concurrent resolution of the Congress.

Document 8

John T. McNaughton for Robert S. McNamara, Mar. 24, 1965, draft memorandum on "Proposed Course of Action," *The Pentagon Papers as Published by The New York Times*, Neil Sheehan et al., eds., New York: Quadrangle, 1971, 432–40.

1. U.S. aims:

70%—To avoid a humiliating U.S. defeat (to our reputation as a guarantor).

20%—To keep SVN [South Vietnam] (and the adjacent) territory from Chinese hands.

10%—To permit the people of SVN to enjoy a better, freer way of life.

ALSO—To emerge from crisis without unacceptable taint from methods used.

NOT—to "help a friend," although it would be hard to stay in if asked out.

2. The situation: The situation in general is bad and deteriorating. The VC [Viet Cong] have the initiative. Defeatism is gaining among the rural population, somewhat in the cities, and even among the soldiers—especially those with relatives in rural areas. The Hop Tac area around Saigon is making little progress; the Delta stays bad; the country has been severed in the north. GVN [Government of Vietnam] control is shrinking to the enclaves, some burdened with refugees. In Saigon we have a remission: [Pham Huy] Quat is giving hope on the civilian side, the Buddhists have calmed, and the split generals are in uneasy equilibrium. . . .

Evaluation: It is essential—however badly SEA [Southeast Asia] may go over the next 1–3 years—that U.S. emerge as a "good doctor." We must have kept promises, been tough, taken risks, gotten bloodied, and hurt the enemy very badly. We must avoid harmful appearances which will affect judgments by, and provide pretexts to, other nations regarding how the U.S. will behave in future cases of particular interest to those nations—regarding U.S. policy, power, resolve and competence to deal with their problems. In this connection, the relevant audiences are the Communists (who must feel strong pressures), the South Vietnamese (whose morale must be buoyed), our allies (who must trust us as "underwriters") and the U.S. public (which must support our risk-taking with U.S. lives and prestige).

Document 9

Summary notes of 553rd National Security Council meeting, July 27, 1965, Lyndon B. Johnson Papers, Meeting Notes File, Box 1, Lyndon B. Johnson Library, Austin, Texas.

The President [Lyndon B. Johnson]: The situation in Vietnam is deteriorating. Even though we now have 80 to 90,000 men there, the situation is not very safe. We have these choices:

a. Use our massive power, including SAC [Strategic Air Command], to bring the enemy to his knees. Less than 10% of our people urge this course of action.

b. We could get out, on the grounds that we don't belong there. Not very many people feel this way about Vietnam. Most feel that our national honor is at stake and that we must keep our commitments there.

c. We could keep our forces at the present level, approximately 80,000 men, but suffer the consequences of losing additional territory and of accepting increased casualties. We could "hunker up." No one is recommending this course.

d. We could ask for everything we might desire from Congress—money, authority to call up the reserves, acceptance of the deployment of more combat battalions. This dramatic course of action would involve declaring a state of emergency and a request for several billion dollars. Many favor this course. However, if we do go all out in this fashion, Hanoi would be able to ask the Chinese Communists and the Soviets to increase aid and add to their existing commitments.

e. We have chosen to do what is necessary to meet the present situation, but not to be unnecessarily provocative to either the Russians or the Communist Chinese. We will give the commanders the men they say they need and, out of existing materiel in the U.S., we will give them the materiel they say they need. We will get the necessary money in the new budget and will use our transfer authority until January. We will neither brag about what we are doing or thunder at the Chinese Communists and the Russians.

This course of action will keep us there during the critical monsoon season and possibly result in some gains. Meanwhile, we will push on the diplomatic side. This means that we will use up our manpower reserves. We will not deplete them, but there will be a substantial reduction. Quietly, we will push up the level of our reserve force. We will let Congress push us but, if necessary, we will call the legislators back.

We will hold until January. The alternatives are to put in our big stack now or hold back until Ambassadors [Henry Cabot] Lodge [to South Vietnam] and [Arthur] Goldberg [to the United Nations] and the diplomats can work.

Document 10

Statement of Hon. George F. Kennan (then at Harvard U.), Feb. 10, 1966, U.S. Congress, Senate, *Hearings Before the Committee on Foreign Relations on S. 2793*, 89th Cong., 2d sess., Washington, D.C.: Government Printing Office, 1966, 331–36.

WISDOM OF U.S. MILITARY INVOLVEMENT IN VIETNAM

The first point I would like to make is that if we were not already involved as we are today in Vietnam, I would know of no reason why we should wish to become so involved, and I could think of several reasons why we should wish not to.

Vietnam is not a region of major military and industrial importance. It is difficult to believe that any decisive developments of the world situation would be determined in normal circumstances by what happens on that territory. If it were not for the considerations of prestige that arise precisely out of our present involvement, even a situation in which South Vietnam was controlled exclusively by the Vietcong, while regrettable, and no doubt morally unwarranted, would not, in my opinion, present dangers great enough to justify our direct military intervention.

Given the situation that exists today in the relations among the leading Communist powers, and by that I have, of course, in mind primarily the Soviet-Chinese conflict, there is every likelihood that a Communist regime in South Vietnam would follow a fairly independent course.

There is no reason to suspect that such a regime would find it either necessary or desirable in present circumstances to function simply as a passive puppet and instrument of Chinese power. And as for the danger that its establishment there would unleash similar tendencies in neighboring countries, this, I think, would depend largely on the manner in which it came into power. In the light of what has recently happened in Indonesia, and on the Indian subcontinent, the danger of the so-called domino effect, that is the effect that would be produced by a limited Communist success in South Vietnam, seems to me to be considerably less than it was when the main decisions were taken that have led to our present involvement. . . .

From the long-term standpoint, therefore, and on principle, I think our military involvement in Vietnam has to be recognized as unfortunate, as something we would not choose deliberately, if the choice were ours to make all over again today, and by the same token, I think it should be our Government's aim to liquidate this involvement just as soon as this can be done without inordinate damage to our own prestige or to the stability of conditions in that area. . . .

EXPANSION OF HOSTILITIES IS DANGEROUS

. . . I have great misgivings about any deliberate expansion of hostilities on our part directed to the achievement of something called victory—if by the use of that term we envisage the complete disappearance of the recalcitrance with which we are now faced, the formal submission by the adversary to our will, and the complete realization of our present stated political aims.

I doubt that these things can be achieved even by the most formidable military successes. . . .

The North Vietnamese and the Vietcong have between them a great deal of space and manpower to give up if they have to, and the Chinese can give them more if they need it. Fidelity to the Communist tradition would dictate that if really pressed to extremity on the military level these people should disappear entirely from the open scene and fall back exclusively on an underground political and military existence rather than to accept terms that would be openly humiliating and would represent in their eyes the betrayal of the future political prospects of the cause to which they are dedicated.

Any total rooting out of the Vietcong from the territory of South Vietnam could be achieved, if it could be achieved at all, only at the cost of a degree of damage to civilian life and of civilian suffering generally for which I would not like to see this country responsible.

And to attempt to crush North Vietnamese strength to a point where Hanoi could no longer give any support for Vietcong political activity in the South, would almost certainly, it seems to me, have the effect of bringing in Chinese forces at some point, whether formally or in the guise of volunteers, thus involving us in a military conflict with Communist China on one of the most unfavorable theaters of hostility that we could possibly choose.

EFFECT OF CONFLICT ON OTHER INTERESTS AND POLICIES

This is not the only reason why I think we should do everything possible to avoid the escalation of this conflict. There is another one which is no less weighty, and this is the effect the conflict is already having on our policies and interests further afield. This involvement seems to me to represent a grievous misplacement of emphasis in our foreign policies as a whole.

EFFECT ON CONFIDENCE OF OTHER COUNTRIES

Not only are great and potentially more important questions of world affairs not receiving, as a consequence of our involvement in Vietnam, the attention they should be receiving, but in some instances assets we already enjoy and hopefully possibilities we should be developing are being sacrificed to this unpromising involvement in a remote and secondary theater. Our relations with the Soviet Union have suffered grievously as was to be expected, and this at a time when far more important things were involved in those relations than what is ultimately involved in Vietnam and when we had special reason, I think, to cultivate those relations. And more unfortunate still, in my opinion, is the damage being done to the feelings entertained for us by the Japanese people. . . .

It is clear that however justified our action may be in our own eyes, it has failed to win either enthusiasm or confidence even among peoples normally friendly to us.

U.S. MOTIVES ARE MISINTERPRETED

Our motives are widely misinterpreted, and the spectacle emphasized and reproduced in thousands of press photographs and stories that appear in the press of the world, the spectacle of Americans inflicting grievous injury on the lives of a poor and helpless people, and particularly a people of different race and color, no matter how warranted by military necessity or by the excesses of the adversary, produces reactions among millions of people throughout the world profoundly detrimental to the image we would like them to hold of this country. . . .

U.S. RETREAT WOULD NOT CAUSE LOSS OF CONFIDENCE OF FREE WORLD

I also find it difficult, for reasons that I won't take time to go into here, to believe that our allies, and particularly our Western European allies, most of whom themselves have given up great territories within recent years, and sometimes in a very statesmanlike way, I find it hard to believe that we would be subject to great reproach or loss of confidence at their hands simply because we followed a defensive rather than an offensive strategy in Vietnam at this time. . . .

UNITED STATES SHOULD NOT SHOULDER POLITICAL BURDEN OF OTHER COUNTRIES

. . . I would like to say I am trying to look at this whole problem not from the moral standpoint but from the practical one. I see in the Vietcong a band of ruthless fanatics, many of them misled, no doubt, by the propaganda that has been drummed into them, but cruel in their methods, dictatorial, and oppressive in their aims, I am not conscious of having any sympathy for them. I think their claim to represent the people of South Vietnam is unfounded. A country which fell under this exclusive power would have my deepest sympathy; and I would hope that this eventuality at any rate would be avoided by a restrained and moderate policy on our part in South Vietnam.

But our country should not be asked, and should not ask of itself, to shoulder the main burden of determining the political realities in any other country, and particularly not in one remote from our shores, from our culture, and from the experience of our people. This is not only not our business, but I don't think we can do it successfully.

Document 11

Paul Booth, national secretary, SDS, press conference, "Build, Not Burn," Oct. 25, 1965, National Press Club, Washington, D.C.

Students for a Democratic Society wishes to reiterate emphatically its intention to pursue its opposition to the war in Vietnam, undeterred by the diversionary tactics of the administration.

We feel that the war is immoral at its root, that it is fought alongside a regime with no claim to represent its people, and that *it is foreclosing the hope of making America a decent and truly democratic society.*

The commitment of SDS, and of the whole generation we represent, is clear: we are anxious to build villages; we refuse to burn them. We are anxious to help and to change our country; we refuse to destroy someone else's country. We are anxious to advance the cause of democracy; we do not believe that cause can be advanced by torture and terror.

We are fully prepared to volunteer for service to our country and to democracy. We volunteer to go into Watts to work with the people of Watts to rebuild that neighborhood to be the kind of place that the people of Watts want it to be—and when we say "rebuild," we mean socially as well as physically. We volunteer to help the Peace Corps learn, as we have been learning in the slums and in Mississippi, how to energize the hungry and desperate and defeated of the world to make the big decisions. We volunteer to serve in hospitals and schools in the slums, in the Job Corps and VISTA [Volunteers in Service to America], in the new Teachers Corps—and to do so in such a way as to strengthen democracy at its grass-roots. And in order to make our volunteering possible, we propose to the President that all those Americans who seek so vigorously to build instead of burn be given their chance to do so. We propose that he test the young people of America: if they had a free choice, would they want to burn and torture in Vietnam or to build a democracy at home and overseas? There is only one way to make the choice real: let us see what happens if service to democracy is made grounds for exemption from the military draft. I predict that almost every member of my generation would choose to build, not to burn; to teach, not to torture; to help, not to kill. And I am sure that the overwhelming majority of our brothers and cousins in the army in Vietnam, would make the same choice if they could—to serve and build, not kill and destroy. . . .

Until the President agrees to our proposal, we have only one choice: we do in conscience object, utterly and wholeheartedly, to this war; and we will encourage every member of our generation to object, and to file his objection through the Form 150 provided by the law for conscientious objection.

Document 12

Resist (a draft resistance group), "A Call to Resist Illegitimate Authority," *The New York Review*, Oct. 12, 1967, 7.

To the young men of America, to the whole of the American people, and to all men of goodwill everywhere:

1. An ever growing number of young American men are finding that the American war in Vietnam so outrages their deepest moral and religious sense that they cannot contribute to it in any way. We share their moral outrage.

2. We further believe that the war is

unconstitutional and illegal. Congress has not declared a war as required by the Constitution. Moreover, under the Constitution, treaties signed by the President and ratified by the Senate have the same force as the Constitution itself. The Charter of the United Nations is such a treaty. The Charter specifically obligates the United States to refrain from force or the threat of force in international relations. It requires member states to exhaust every peaceful means of settling disputes and to submit disputes which cannot be settled peacefully to the Security Council. The United States has systematically violated all of these Charter provisions for thirteen years.

3. Moreover, this war violates international agreements, treaties and principles of law which the United States Government has solemnly endorsed. The combat role of the United States troops in Vietnam violates the Geneva Accords of 1954 which our government pledged to support but has since subverted. The destruction of rice, crops and livestock; the burning and bulldozing of entire villages consisting exclusively of civilian structures; the interning of civilian non-combatants in concentration camps; the summary executions of civilians in captured villages who could not produce satisfactory evidence of their loyalties or did not wish to be removed to concentration camps; the slaughter of peasants who dared to stand up in their fields and shake their fists at American helicopters;—these are all actions of the kind which the United States and the other victorious powers of World War II declared to be crimes against humanity for which individuals were to be held personally responsible even when acting under the orders of their governments and for which Germans were sentenced at Nuremberg to long prison terms and death. The prohibition of such acts as war crimes was incorporated in treaty law by the Geneva Conventions of 1949, ratified by the United States. These are commitments to other countries and to Mankind, and they would claim our allegiance even if Congress should declare war.

4. We also believe it is an unconstitutional denial of religious liberty and equal protection of the laws to withhold draft exemption from men whose religious or profound philosophical beliefs are opposed to what in the Western religious tradition have been long known as unjust wars.

5. Therefore, we believe on all these grounds that every free man has a legal right and a moral duty to exert every effort to end this war, to avoid collusion with it, and to encourage others to do the same. Young men in the armed forces or threatened with the draft face the most excruciating choices. For them various forms of resistance risk separation from their families and their country, destruction of their careers, loss of their freedom and loss of their lives. Each must choose the course of resistance dictated by his conscience and circumstances. Among those already in the armed forces some are refusing to obey specific illegal and immoral orders, some are attempting to educate their fellow servicemen on the murderous and barbarous nature of the war, some are absenting themselves without official leave. Among those not in the armed forces some are applying for status as conscientious objectors to American aggression in Vietnam, some are refusing to be inducted. Among both groups some are resisting openly and paying a heavy penalty, some are organizing more resistance within the United States and some have sought sanctuary in other countries.

6. We believe that each of these forms of resistance against illegitimate authority is courageous and justified. Many of us believe that open resistance to the war and the draft is the course of action

most likely to strengthen the moral resolve with which all of us can oppose the war and most likely to bring an end to the war.

7. We will continue to lend our support to those who undertake resistance to this war. We will raise funds to organize draft resistance unions, to supply legal defense and bail, to support families and otherwise aid resistance to the war in whatever ways may seem appropriate.

8. We firmly believe that our statement is the sort of speech that under the First Amendment must be free, and that the actions we will undertake are as legal as is the war resistance of the young men themselves. But we recognize that the courts may find otherwise, and that if so we might all be liable to prosecution and severe punishment. In any case, we feel that we cannot shrink from fulfilling our responsibilities to the youth whom many of us teach, to the country whose freedom we cherish, and to the ancient traditions of religion and philosophy which we strive to preserve in this generation.

9. We call upon all men of good will to join us in this confrontation with immoral authority. Especially we call upon the universities to fulfill their mission of enlightenment and religious organizations to honor their heritage of brotherhood. Now is the time to resist.

Document 13

Memorandum by Robert S. McNamara for President Lyndon B. Johnson, Nov. 1, 1967, Lyndon B. Johnson Papers, National Security File, Country File, Vietnam, Box 75, Lyndon B. Johnson Library, Austin, Texas.

SUBJECT: A Fifteen Month Program for Military Operations in Southeast Asia

Probable Results of Present Course of Action

In South Vietnam, I believe that following the present course of action will bring continued but slow progress. However, I do not anticipate that this progress will be readily visible to the general public either in the United States or abroad.

In North Vietnam, the bombing attacks have been unable to interrupt the flow of supplies and men needed to maintain the present level of enemy military action in the South. . . .

Nor is there any reason to believe that the steady progress we are likely to make, the continued infliction of grievous casualties, or the heavy punishment of air bombardment will suffice to break the will of the North Vietnamese and the Viet Cong to continue to fight. Nothing can be expected to break this will other than the conviction that they cannot succeed. This conviction will not be created unless and until they come to the conclusion that the US is prepared to remain in Vietnam for whatever period of time is necessary to assure the independent choice of the South Vietnamese people. The enemy cannot be expected to arrive at that conclusion in advance of the American public. And the American public, frustrated by the slow rate of progress, fearing continued escalation, and doubting that all approaches to peace have been sincerely probed, does not give the appearance of having the will to persist. As the months go by, there will be both increasing pressure for widening the war and continued loss of support for American participation in the struggle. There will be increasing calls for American withdrawal.

There is, in my opinion, a very real

question whether under these circumstances it will be possible to maintain our efforts in South Vietnam for the time necessary to accomplish our objectives there.

The alternative possibilities lie in the stabilization of our military operations in the South (possibly with fewer US casualties) and of our air operations in the North, along with a demonstration that our air attacks on the North are not blocking negotiations leading to a peaceful settlement. . . .

Complete Cessation of Bombing in the North

A decision to stop the bombing is a logical alternative to our present course in Vietnam. The bombing halt would have dual objectives. We would hope for a response from Hanoi, by some parallel reduction in its offensive activity, by a movement toward talks, or both. At a minimum, the lack of any response from Hanoi would demonstrate that it is North Vietnam and not the United States that is blocking a peaceful settlement.

If a halt is to be called in the bombing, we should be prepared to continue it indefinitely. During this time, however, we would plan to continue to bomb the infiltration trails in Laos. . . .

Stabilization of Our Military Effort

With or without a bombing halt, we could state clearly for both internal and public guidance our decision to stabilize our level of military effort in the absence of any major change in the enemy threat. The following elements would be involved in a decision to stabilize military operations:

In announcing this stabilization policy, we would have two objectives. First, we would hope to attract greater support by allaying apprehensions that the conflict would be expanded by our actions beyond Vietnam. Second, we would hope to increase pressure on Hanoi to enter into negotiations and/or to reduce their military efforts in the South. . . .

Recommendations

I recommend that we:

1. Decide on, and announce, the policy of stabilization outlined above, that we assert that we are making slow but steady progress and expect to move ahead without expanding our operations against the North, and without increasing the size of our forces in the South beyond those already planned.

2. Plan a halt in the bombing for some time before the end of the year. This halt seems advisable, if not mandatory, entirely apart from its actual effect in bringing about negotiations and a settlement of the Vietnamese conflict. The argument of many who oppose the American effort in Vietnam comes down to the proposition that American air attacks on North Vietnam are what keeps the war going and prevents political settlement. A cessation would thus clear the atmosphere and should minimize further loss of domestic and international support for our efforts. Moreover, I believe there is a strong possibility that a bombing halt would lead to suspension of overt enemy operations across the DMZ [Demilitarized Zone]. And a bombing halt is likely to lead to talks with Hanoi. It is possible that such talks would lead to productive negotiations on at least some issues. No other course affords any hope of these results in the next 15 months.

3. Review intensively the conduct of military operations in the South and consider programs which involve (a) reduced US casualties, (b) procedures for the progressive turn-over to the GVN [Government of Vietnam] of greater responsibility for security in the South, and (c) lesser destruction of the people and wealth of South Vietnam.

Document 14

President Richard M. Nixon, address to the nation on the war in Vietnam, Nov. 3, 1969, *Public Papers of the Presidents of the United States: Richard M. Nixon, 1969*, Washington, D.C.: Government Printing Office, 1971, 901–9.

Fifteen years ago North Vietnam, with the logistical support of Communist China and the Soviet Union, launched a campaign to impose a Communist government on South Vietnam by instigating and supporting a revolution.

In response to the request of the government of South Vietnam, President [Dwight D.] Eisenhower sent economic aid and military equipment to assist the people of South Vietnam in their efforts to prevent a Communist takeover. Seven years ago, President [John F.] Kennedy sent 16,000 military personnel to Vietnam as combat advisors. Four years ago, President [Lyndon B.] Johnson sent American combat forces to South Vietnam. . . .

For these reasons, I rejected the recommendation that I should end the war by immediately withdrawing all our forces. I chose instead to change American policy on both the negotiating front and the battlefront. . . .

Vietnamization

The defense of freedom is everybody's business—not just America's business. And it is particularly the responsibility of the people whose freedom is threatened. In the previous Administration, we Americanized the war in Vietnam. In this Administration, we are Vietnamizing the search for peace. . . .

Significant Results

After five years of Americans going into Vietnam, we are finally bringing American men home. By December 15, over 60,000 men will have been withdrawn from South Vietnam—including 20 percent of all of our combat forces. The South Vietnamese have continued to gain in strength. As a result they have been able to take over combat responsibilities from our American troops. . . .

Let me now turn to our program for the future.

We have adopted a plan which we have worked out in cooperation with the South Vietnamese for the complete withdrawal of all U.S. combat ground forces, and their replacement by South Vietnamese forces on an orderly scheduled timetable. This withdrawal will be made from strength and not from weakness. As South Vietnamese forces become stronger, the rate of American withdrawal can become greater. . . .

Only Two Choices

My fellow Americans, I am sure you recognize from what I have said that we really only have two choices open to us if we want to end this war.

I can order an immediate, precipitate withdrawal of all Americans from Vietnam without regard to the effects of that action.

Or we can persist in our search for a just peace through a negotiated settlement if possible, or through continued implementation of our plan for Vietnamization if necessary—a plan in which we will withdraw all our forces from Vietnam on a schedule in accordance with our program, as the South Vietnamese become strong enough to defend their own freedom.

I have chosen the second course.

It is not the easy way.

It is the right way.

It is a plan which will end the war and serve the cause of peace—not just in Vietnam but in the Pacific and in the world.

In speaking of the consequences of a precipitate withdrawal, I mentioned that our allies would lose confidence in America.

Far more dangerous, we would lose confidence in ourselves. The immediate reaction would be a sense of relief that our men were coming home. But as we saw the consequences of what we had done, inevitable remorse and divisive recrimination would scar our spirit as a people.

We have faced other crises in our history and have become stronger by rejecting the easy way out and taking the right way in meeting our challenges. Our greatness as a nation has been our capacity to do what had to be done when we knew our course was right.

Document 15

The Paris Peace Accords, 1973, U.S. Department of State, *Bulletin* 68, Feb. 12, 1973, 168–88.

The Parties participating in the Paris Conference on Viet-Nam,

With a view to ending the war and restoring peace in Viet-Nam on the basis of respect for the Vietnamese people's fundamental national rights and the South Vietnamese people's right to self-determination, and to contributing to the consolidation of peace in Asia and the world,

Have agreed on the following provisions and undertake to respect and to implement them:

Chapter I The Vietnamese People's Fundamental National Rights

Article 1. The United States and all other countries respect the independence, sovereignty, unity, and territorial integrity of Viet-Nam as recognized by the 1954 Geneva Agreements on Viet-Nam.

Chapter II Cessation of Hostilities—Withdrawal of Troops

Article 2. A cease-fire shall be observed throughout South Viet-Nam as of 2400 hours G.M.T., on January 27, 1973.

At the same hour, the United States will stop all its military activities against the territory of the Democratic Republic of Viet-Nam by ground, air and naval forces, wherever they may be based, and end the mining of the territorial waters, ports, harbors, and waterways of the Democratic Republic of Viet-Nam. The United States will remove, permanently deactivate or destroy all the mines in the territorial waters, ports, harbors, and waterways of North Viet-Nam as soon as this Agreement goes into effect.

The complete cessation of hostilities mentioned in this Article shall be durable and without limit of time.

Article 3. The parties undertake to maintain the cease-fire and to ensure a lasting and stable peace.

As soon as the cease-fire goes into effect:

a. The United States forces and those of the other foreign countries allied with the United States and the Republic of Viet-Nam shall remain in-place pending the implementation of the plan of troop withdrawal. The Four-Party Joint Military Commission described in Article 16 shall determine the modalities.

b. The armed forces of the two South Vietnamese parties shall remain in-place. The Two-Party Joint Military Commission described in Article 17 [not included here] shall determine the areas controlled by each party and the modalities of stationing.

c. The regular forces of all services and arms and the irregular forces of the parties in South Viet-Nam shall stop all offensive activities against each other and shall strictly abide by the following stipulations:

- All acts of force on the ground, in the air, and on the sea shall be prohibited;
- All hostile acts, terrorism and reprisals by both sides will be banned.

Article 4. The United States will not continue its military involvement or intervene in the internal affairs of South Viet-Nam.

Article 5. Within sixty days of the signing of this Agreement, there will be a total withdrawal from South Viet-Nam of troops, military advisers, and military personnel, including technical military personnel and military personnel associated with the pacification program, armaments, munitions, and war material of the United States and those of the other foreign countries mentioned in Article 3 (a). Advisers from the above-mentioned countries to all paramilitary organizations and the police force will also be withdrawn within the same period of time.

Article 6. The dismantlement of all military bases in South Viet-Nam of the United States and of the other foreign countries mentioned in Article 3 (a) shall be completed within sixty days of the signing of this Agreement.

Article 7. From the enforcement of the cease-fire to the formation of the government provided for in Article 9 (b) and 14 of this Agreement, the two South Vietnamese parties shall not accept the introduction of troops, military advisers, and military personnel including technical military personnel, armaments, munitions, and war material into South Viet-Nam.

The two South Vietnamese parties shall be permitted to make periodic replacement of armaments, munitions and war material which have been destroyed, damaged, worn out or used up after the cease-fire, on the basis of piece-for-piece, of the same characteristics and properties, under the supervision of the Joint Military Commission of the two South Vietnamese parties and of the International Commission of Control and Supervision.

Chapter III The Return of Captured Military Personnel and Foreign Civilians, and Captured and Detained Vietnamese Civilian Personnel

Article 8

a. The return of captured military personnel and foreign civilians of the parties shall be carried out simultaneously with and completed not later than the same day as the troop withdrawal mentioned in Article 5. The parties shall exchange complete lists of the above-mentioned captured military personnel and foreign civilians on the day of the signing of this Agreement.

b. The Parties shall help each other to get information about those military personnel and foreign civilians of the parties missing in action, to determine the location and take care of the graves of the dead so as to facilitate the exhumation and repatriation of the remains, and to take any such other measures as may be required to get information about those still considered missing in action.

c. The question of the return of Vietnamese civilian personnel captured and detailed in South Viet-Nam will be resolved by the two South Vietnamese parties on the basis of the principles of Article 21 (b) of the Agreement on the Cessation of Hostilities in Viet-Nam of July 20, 1954. The two South Vietnamese parties will do so in a spirit of national reconciliation and concord, with a view to ending hatred and enmity, in order to ease suffering and to reunite families. The two South Vietnamese parties will do their utmost to resolve this question within ninety days after the cease-fire comes into effect.

Chapter IV The Exercise of the South Vietnamese People's Right to Self-Determination

Article 9. The Government of the United States of America and the Government of the Democratic Republic of Viet-Nam undertake to respect the following principles for the exercise of the South Vietnamese people's right to self-determination:

a. The South Vietnamese people's right to self-determination is sacred, inalienable, and shall be respected by all countries.

b. The South Vietnamese people shall decide themselves the political future of South Viet-Nam through genuinely free and democratic general elections under international supervision.

c. Foreign countries shall not impose any political tendency or personality on the South Vietnamese people.

Article 10. The two South Vietnamese parties undertake to respect the cease-fire and maintain peace in South Viet-Nam, settle all matters of contention through negotiations, and avoid all armed conflict.

Article 11. Immediately after the cease-fire, the two South Vietnamese parties will:

• achieve national reconciliation and concord, end hatred and enmity, prohibit all acts of reprisal and discrimination against individuals or organizations that have collaborated with one side or the other;

• ensure the democratic liberties of the people: personal freedom, freedom of speech, freedom of the press, freedom of meeting, freedom of organization, freedom of political activities, freedom of belief, freedom of movement, freedom of residence, freedom of work, right to property ownership, and right to free enterprise.

Article 12

a. Immediately after the cease-fire, the two South Vietnamese parties shall hold consultations in a spirit of national reconciliation and concord, mutual respect, and mutual non-elimination to set up a National Council of National Reconciliation and Concord of three equal segments. The Council shall operate on the principle of unanimity. After the National Council of National Reconciliation and Concord has assumed its functions, the two South Vietnamese parties will consult about the formation of councils at lower levels. The two South Vietnamese parties shall sign an agreement on the internal matters of South Viet-Nam as soon as possible and do their utmost to accomplish this within ninety days after the cease-fire comes into effect, in keeping with the South Vietnamese people's aspirations for peace, independence and democracy.

b. The National Council of National Reconciliation and Concord shall have the task of promoting the two South Vietnamese parties' implementation of this Agreement, achievement of national reconciliation and concord and ensurance of democratic liberties. The National Council of National Reconciliation and Concord will organize the free and democratic general elections provided for in Article 9 (b) and decide the procedures and modalities of these general elections. The institutions for which the general elections are to be held will be agreed upon through consultations between the two South Vietnamese parties. The National Council of National Reconciliation and Concord will also decide the procedures and modalities of such local elections as the two South Vietnamese parties agree upon.

Article 13. The question of Vietnamese armed forces in South Viet-Nam shall be settled by the two South Vietnamese parties in a spirit of national reconciliation and concord, equality and mutual respect, without foreign interference, in accordance with the postwar situation. Among the questions to be discussed by the two South Vietnamese parties are steps to reduce their military effectives and to demobilize the troops being reduced. The two South Vietnamese parties will accomplish this as soon as possible.

Article 14. South Viet-Nam will pursue a foreign policy of peace and independence. It will be prepared to establish relations with all countries irrespective of their political and social systems on the basis of mutual respect for independence and sovereignty and accept economic and technical aid from any country with no political conditions attached. The acceptance of military aid by South Viet-Nam in the future shall come under the authority of the government set up after the general elections in South Viet-Nam provided for in Article 9 (b).

Chapter V The Reunification of Viet-Nam and the Relationship Between North and South Viet-Nam

Article 15. The reunification of Viet-Nam shall be carried out step by step through peaceful means on the basis of discussions and agreements between North and South Viet-Nam, without coercion or annexation by either party, and without foreign interference. The time for reunification will be agreed upon by North and South Viet-Nam.

Pending reunification:

a. The military demarcation line between the two zones at the 17th parallel is only provisional and not a political or territorial boundary, as provided for in paragraph 6 of the Final Declaration of the 1954 Geneva Conference.

b. North and South Viet-Nam shall respect the Demilitarized Zone on either side of the Provisional Military Demarcation Line.

c. North and South Viet-Nam shall promptly start negotiations with a view to reestablishing normal relations in various fields. Among the questions to be negotiated are the modalities of civilian movement across the Provisional Military Demarcation Line.

d. North and South Viet-Nam shall not join any military alliance or military bloc and shall not allow foreign powers to maintain military bases, troops, military advisers, and military personnel on their respective territories, as stipulated in the 1954 Geneva Agreements on Viet-Nam.

CHAPTER 12

U.S.-Soviet Relations: 1963 to the Present

Robert D. Schulzinger

In the generation after the Cuban missile crisis of October 1962, U.S.-Soviet relations alternated between periods of détente, or a relaxation of tension that sometimes approached genuine warmth, and episodes of intense confrontation that were among the chilliest of the Cold War era. Throughout this quarter of a century, Washington and Moscow competed for preeminence in world politics. At the same time, they tried to establish rules for their own relationship that would avoid a horrible war between two "superpowers" armed with enough thermonuclear weapons to destroy civilization and, possibly, humanity itself.

Barely thirteen months remained in the presidency of John F. Kennedy after his fateful confrontation with Soviet Premier Nikita Khrushchev over the installation of Soviet intermediate range ballistic missiles (IRBMs) in Cuba. During that year Kennedy took tentative but important steps toward reducing tension with the Soviet Union. In June 1963 he encouraged Americans to "reexamine their attitudes toward the Cold War." Indeed, he elevated both arms control and the effort to avoid accidental nuclear war between the United States and the Soviet Union to major foreign policy goals. Later that summer the two powers signed the limited Nuclear Test-Ban Treaty, in which they agreed to halt further nuclear explosions in the atmosphere, in outer space, or under water. (see chap. 10, doc. 8) The Senate quickly approved the treaty amid hopes that it represented a first step toward a total ban on nuclear tests and progress toward the mutual reduction of nuclear arsenals.

Such optimism proved premature, however, as relations between the United States and the Soviet Union cooled during the Lyndon B. Johnson administration. In October 1964 the Soviet Politburo ousted Khrushchev, whose foreign policy adventures had often seemed reckless. Replacing him at the top were Leonid Brezhnev and Aleksei Kosygin, who shared power for about four years. By 1968, however, Brezhnev established preeminence, which he maintained until his death in 1982. Brezhnev and Kosygin commenced a massive Soviet arms buildup designed to eliminate the nuclear inferiority that had compelled Khrushchev to retreat during the Cuban missile crisis. At the same time, American foreign policy became bogged down in Vietnam. After 1965 the Johnson administration had neither time nor ideas to fulfill Kennedy's promise to reexamine the Cold War.

Johnson met Kosygin once in a hastily arranged summit conference at Glassboro State College in southern New Jersey in late June 1967. The Soviet prime minister had come to New York to attend a special session of the United Nations General Assembly called to discuss the Arab-Israeli Six-Day War. As Johnson reported (doc. 1), the two men promised to continue arms control discussions between Secretary of State Dean Rusk and Soviet Foreign Minister Andrei Gromyko. The president acknowledged, however, that differences over Vietnam made agreements in other areas harder to reach.

The year 1968 provided a series of shocks at home, in Vietnam, and in Europe. In March, Johnson announced that he would not run for reelection, promising to devote his time to achieving peace in Vietnam by the end of the year. Hopes rose that he might visit the Soviet Union to continue the dialogue on arms control with Kosygin and to meet Brezhnev. But the Soviets dashed such hopes in August by sending tanks and troops to Czechoslovakia to crush that country's efforts, begun in the spring, to create "socialism with a human face." Johnson denounced the "patently contrived" justifications offered by the Soviets in support of their invasion—they claimed that the government of Czechoslovakia had invited them in to save the Communist system from "counterrevolutionaries"—and called on them to withdraw. (doc. 2) No further talk was heard about a summit meeting between LBJ and the Soviet leadership.

During the presidential election campaign of 1968, Richard M. Nixon, the Republican nominee, pointed to the Soviet invasion of Czechoslovakia as proof that the Soviets posed a serious threat to the United States. Upon hearing the news of the invasion, one of Nixon's supporters remarked that it "makes it kind of hard to be a dove [pacifist], doesn't it?"

It was all the more surprising, therefore, that as president, Nixon presided over one of the most prolonged periods of détente in Soviet-American relations since the end of World War II. The new president recognized, however, the need to end the stalemate in Vietnam and return the focus of U.S. foreign policy to managing and improving relations with the Soviet Union. At his first press conference, Nixon agreed that the United States needed "sufficiency" and not "superiority" in nuclear weapons, a formula popularized by Henry Kissinger, his new national security adviser. (doc. 3)

Over the next three years, Kissinger opened a "backchannel," or secret line of communication, between the White House and the Kremlin. Keeping the rest of the diplomatic machinery in the dark, Kissinger laid the basis for improved relations between the superpowers. Indeed, progress occurred on arms control. The two sides agreed to limit research and deployment of antiballistic missile systems and promised to slow the installation of more accurate intercontinental ballistic missiles (ICBMs), submarine-launched ballistic missiles (SLBMs), and air-to-ground ballistic missiles (AGBMs).

As the backchannel discussions went forward, President Nixon was keenly aware of the domestic political gains to be derived from a successful foreign policy that showed him reducing old enmities. He explained to Kissinger in March 1972 (doc. 4), as the national security adviser embarked on a visit to Moscow to lay the groundwork for a summit conference, the important "news value" of delaying the signing of arms control agreements until Nixon went to Moscow in May. Kissinger faithfully carried out these instructions, and dramatic late-night negotiations took place at the May summit between Nixon and Kissinger on one side and Soviet Communist Party General Secretary Brezhnev on the other.

The conversation bore fruit with what became known as the SALT I (Strategic Arms Limitation Talks or Treaty) agreements, the most significant of which were the Treaty on Anti-Ballistic Missile Systems, or ABM treaty (doc. 5), the Interim Agreement and Protocol on Limitation of Strategic Offensive Weapons (doc. 6), and the Basic Principles of Relations Between the U.S. and the U.S.S.R. (doc. 7) The ABM treaty limited each side to no more than two antiballistic missile sites, one protecting the capital and the other shielding a missile base. SALT I attempted to slow the arms race by limiting each side to the number of missiles presently deployed or under construction. Not a full-scale treaty, SALT I constituted more of an "agreement to agree" than a successful effort to cap the arms race. The Basic Principles meant more to the Soviets than to Nixon and Kissinger. Brezhnev presented it as a formal acknowledgment by the United States that the Soviet Union was a legitimate state, not the revolutionary outcast derided by the United States at the beginning of the Cold War.

Kissinger expressed euphoria over the agreements signed at Moscow when he briefed congressional committees on June 15, 1972. (doc. 8) He claimed that the SALT I agreements were "without precedent in the nuclear age; indeed in all relevant modern history." He hoped that the concrete results of the Moscow summit would soon translate into permanent détente between the superpowers.

They did not, as once more the spirit of cooperation between the United States and the Soviet Union ebbed after 1972. The "Yom Kippur War" of October 1973 in the Middle East and the Watergate scandal strained détente. During the former, the Soviet Union insisted that the Basic Principles entitled it to an equal say along with the United States in arranging a cease-fire between Israel, supported by Washington, and Egypt, its own ally. Some Americans worried that these Soviet moves competed with the United States in an area of primary American concern. Détente seemed to have unanticipated liabilities. Watergate further weakened American backing for détente by undermining the position of President Nixon, the foremost advocate of improved ties with the Soviet Union.

Nixon met twice with Brezhnev, in June 1973 in Washington and June

1974 in Moscow and the Crimea. At neither summit, however, did the leaders fulfill the promise of SALT I for a fully developed arms control treaty. At the second Moscow summit, Kissinger, now secretary of state as well as national security adviser, had to defend his emphasis on nuclear sufficiency rather than the "superiority" pressed by domestic skeptics of détente. "What in the name of God is strategic superiority?" he complained. "What do you do with it?"

Three months after Nixon resigned (in the aftermath of the Watergate scandal) in August 1974, Kissinger accompanied Gerald R. Ford, the new president, to the Siberian seaport of Vladivostok for another summit with Brezhnev. Once more they promised to "conclude a new agreement on the limitation of strategic offensive arms, to last through 1985." (doc. 9) Kissinger tried but failed to implement this pledge during the remainder of Ford's term. The victory of the Communist forces in Vietnam in April 1975 convinced some Americans that the Soviet Union had gained the upper hand in the global competition between the superpowers. Secretary of Defense James Schlesinger publicly disputed the value of détente and called for superiority over the Soviets. By the time Ford went to Helsinki for the Conference on Security and Cooperation in Europe in late July and early August 1975 (doc. 10), détente was seriously weakened. The Final Act of the conference (the Helsinki Accords) fixed the borders in Central Europe and certified the primacy of human rights. Such achievements, unthinkable five years earlier, did not, however, preserve a spirit of East-West cooperation.

Feuding between Schlesinger and Kissinger reached such a peak that Ford had to choose between them. In late October he fired Schlesinger and stripped Kissinger of his position as national security adviser, though leaving him as secretary of state. At the same time, Ford asserted that officials no longer would use the term "détente" to describe relations between the United States and the Soviet Union. "Peace through strength" would be the new slogan to characterize Washington's approach to the Soviets.

Ford's adoption of a harder line did not save him in the 1976 presidential campaign. Ronald Reagan, the former governor of California, challenged Ford for the Republican nomination. During the spring primary, Reagan, who lost the nomination by a small margin, charged that Kissinger's policy of détente with the Soviets offered "the peace of the grave." Jimmy Carter, the Democratic candidate and eventual winner of the general election, also campaigned against Kissinger's détente. Carter objected that Kissinger had overlooked human rights abuses in the Soviet Union and had not done enough to reduce nuclear arms.

In office Carter tried to go beyond Kissinger's efforts and nail down an arms control treaty with the Soviet Union. It took much longer than he or his advisers had anticipated, but by June 1979 the president was able to fly to Vienna and sign the SALT II treaty with Brezhnev. (doc. 11) Carter praised the SALT II treaty as "the most detailed, far-reaching, comprehensive treaty in the history of arms control. . . . It will make the world a safer place for both sides.'' Unfortunately for the future of arms control and for his own standing with the public, Carter was unable to persuade the Senate to approve SALT II. The administration had lost much of its initial public popularity by the summer of 1979, when the treaty went before the Senate. In November Iranian militants seized the U.S. Embassy in Teheran, Iran, beginning 444 days of captivity for 53 Americans. Six weeks after the hostage crisis began, the Soviet Union invaded Afghanistan with 70,000 troops to help an unpopular Communist government wage a war against nationalist guerrillas.

The invasion of Afghanistan shocked and infuriated Carter, who complained that Brezhnev had lied to him. When on January 4, 1980, Carter announced to the nation a series of retaliatory measures against Moscow, he proclaimed, in effect, that détente was dead and the Cold War had revived. (doc. 12) Later that month the president went farther and ordered young men to register with the Selective Service system for a possible call-up for the draft, which had been dropped in 1973. He also submitted a defense budget calling for an increase of 5 percent in real dollars.

While the Carter administration adopted a harsh anti-Soviet tone, Reagan won the Republican nomination and the November election by sounding even more anti-Communist themes. For the first three years of the Reagan administration, the United States and the Soviet Union appeared on a collision course. Indeed, some of the harshest rhetorical confrontations of the Cold War occurred during this period. For example, at his first news conference (doc. 13), Reagan went out of his way to denounce détente and the Soviet Union. A year later, while addressing the British Parliament (doc. 14), Reagan proclaimed that the Communist system in the Soviet Union and Eastern Europe was doomed.

Progress on arms control stalled during these years. In March 1983 Reagan announced that the United States would embark on a multiyear, multibillion-dollar research and development project to create a ''defensive shield'' against incoming ballistic missiles. Supporters of this plan labeled it the Strategic Defense Initiative (SDI), while opponents derided it as a ''Star Wars'' fantasy. The Soviets objected that it violated the terms of the ABM treaty and walked out of arms control discussions in Geneva.

The Soviet Union underwent a leadership crisis in the early 1980s that further complicated relations with the United States. Two aging caretakers took over after Brezhnev's death in 1982; each lasted a year or less. Then in March 1985, the Politburo selected Mikhail Gorbachev, young, well-educated, and dynamic, as the new general secretary. Promising *glasnost*, or greater openness, and *perestroika*, a restructuring of the economy, Gorbachev vowed to reduce the defense spending that was crushing the Soviet economy. To do so required an accommodation with the United States. For its part, the Reagan administration recognized that Gorbachev represented a new kind of Soviet leader whose charisma and command of details would force the United States to adopt more sophisticated policies.

In the last four years of the Reagan administration, the leaders of the two superpowers met five times—far more summits than any other American president or Soviet leader. The first, a get-acquainted session in Geneva in November 1985, was a frosty affair. At the second, in Reykjavik, Iceland, in October 1986, Gorbachev stunned Reagan by offering cuts of 50 percent in strategic missiles in return for dropping SDI. Reagan refused, and Secretary of State George P. Shultz looked glum as he announced at a news conference that no deal had been arranged. (doc. 15)

The next three meetings between Gorbachev and Reagan were much friendlier. When Gorbachev visited Washington in December 1987, the two leaders signed an Intermediate Nuclear Forces (INF) Treaty in which they agreed to remove all their IRBMs from Europe. (doc. 16) Six months later Reagan went to Moscow and received a rousing reception by students at Moscow State University. He praised *glasnost,* which he hoped would lead to a "new world of reconciliation, friendship, and peace." At the end of 1988, Gorbachev traveled once more to the United States, this time to New York to address the United Nations. He promised to withdraw 10,000 troops from Eastern Europe, a move that encouraged Reagan to say, "I heartily agree." The two men had their picture taken, along with President-elect George Bush, in New York Harbor under the Statue of Liberty. In one of his last speeches as president (doc. 17), Reagan described "a dramatic change in the Soviet system, a long-awaited break with the past, and the opening of a new era in international affairs."

The détente of the period after 1985 rested on firmer foundations than the earlier, short-lived eras of improvements in Soviet-American relations. Gorbachev ended the Communist party's monopoly on power in the Soviet Union, and Communist regimes in Eastern Europe fell in 1989 and 1990. Non-Communist parties won elections and formed governments in Poland, Czechoslovakia, Hungary, Rumania, and Bulgaria. A Christian Democratic government took power in East Germany in March 1990, and in October East Germany ceased to exist as it merged into the Federal Republic of Germany. These astonishing changes, most observers have argued, ended the Cold War. Bush and Gorbachev recognized that a safer but more unpredictable era had begun in world politics when they met for their first summit in Malta in December 1989. (doc. 18) Their meetings almost seemed routine as they met again three times in 1990. At their talks, held in conjunction with the Conference on Security and Cooperation in Europe, the two leaders signed a treaty sharply reducing conventional arms in Europe. (doc. 19) In March 1991, the Warsaw Pact ceased operating as a military alliance. That August, an attempted coup by hard-liners failed, leaving Gorbachev in office with a heightened interest in reform. The likelihood of direct military confrontation between East and West had nearly disappeared, and the promise of President Kennedy's American University speech had apparently been fulfilled.

Document 1

President Lyndon B. Johnson's remarks upon arriving at the White House following the Glassboro meeting with Soviet Chairman Aleksei Kosygin, June 25, 1967, *Public Papers of the Presidents* (hereafter referred to as *PPP*): *Lyndon B. Johnson, 1967*, Washington, D.C.: Government Printing Office, 1968, 652.

You will not be surprised to know that these two meetings have not solved all of our problems. On some we have made progress—great progress in reducing misunderstanding, I think, and in reaffirming our common commitment to seek agreement.

I think we made that kind of progress, for example, on the question of arms limitation. We have agreed this afternoon that Secretary of State [Dean] Rusk and Mr. [Andrei] Gromyko will pursue this subject further in New York in the days ahead. . . .

When nations have deeply different positions, as we do on these issues, they do not come to agreement merely by improving their understanding of each other's views. But such improvement helps. Sometimes in such discussions you can find elements—beginnings—hopeful fractions of common ground even within a general disagreement. It was so in the Middle East 2 weeks ago when we agreed on the need for a prompt cease-fire. And it is so today in respect to such simple propositions as that every state has a right to live; that there should be an end to the war in the Middle East; and that in the right circumstances there should be withdrawal of troops.

This is a long way from agreement, but it is a long way, also, from total difference.

On Vietnam, the area of agreement is smaller. It is defined by the fact that the dangers and the difficulties of any one area must never be allowed to become a cause of wider conflict. Yet even in Vietnam I was able to make it very clear, with no third party between us, that we will match and we will outmatch every step to peace that others may be ready to take.

As I warned on Friday, and as I just must warn again on this Sunday afternoon, meetings like these do not themselves make peace in the world. We must all remember that there have been many meetings before and they have not ended all of our troubles or all of our dangers.

But I can also repeat on this Sunday afternoon another thing that I said on last Friday: that it does help a lot to sit down and look at a man right in the eye and try to reason with him, particularly if he is trying to reason with you. . . .

I said on Friday that the world is very small and very dangerous. Tonight I believe that it is fair to say that these days at Hollybush have made it a little smaller still, but also a little less dangerous.

Document 2

Statement by President Lyndon B. Johnson calling on the Warsaw Pact allies to withdraw from Czechoslovakia, Aug. 21, 1968, *PPP: Lyndon B. Johnson, 1968*, 1969, 905.

The tragic news from Czechoslovakia shocks the conscience of the world. The Soviet Union and its allies have invaded a defenseless country to stamp out a resurgence of ordinary human freedom. It is a sad commentary on the Communist mind that a sign of liberty in Czechoslovakia is deemed a fundamental threat to the security of the Soviet system.

The excuses offered by the Soviet Union are patently contrived. The Czechoslovakian Government did not request its allies to intervene in its internal affairs. No external aggression threatened Czechoslovakia.

The action of the Warsaw Pact allies is in flat violation of the United Nations Charter. We are consulting urgently with others to consider what steps should be undertaken in the United Nations. Ambassador George Ball has been instructed to join with other nations in the Security Council to insist upon the Charter rights of Czechoslovakia and its people.

Meanwhile, in the name of mankind's hope for peace, I call on the Soviet Union and its associates to withdraw their troops from Czechoslovakia. I hope responsible spokesmen for governments and people throughout the world will support this appeal. It is never too late for reason too prevail.

Document 3

President Richard M. Nixon, news conference, Jan. 27, 1969, *PPP: Richard M. Nixon, 1969*, 1969, 18–19.

Q. Mr. President, back to nuclear weapons. Both you and Secretary [of Defense Melvin] Laird have stressed, quite hard, the need for superiority over the Soviet Union. But what is the real meaning of that in view of the fact that both sides have more than enough already to destroy each other, and how do you distinguish between the validity of that stance and the argument of Dr. [Henry A.] Kissinger [assistant to the president for national security affairs] for what he calls "sufficiency"?

The President. Here, again, I think the semantics may offer an inappropriate approach to the problem. I would say, with regard to Dr. Kissinger's suggestion of sufficiency, that that would meet, certainly, my guideline and, I think, Secretary Laird's guideline, with regard to superiority.

Let me put it this way: When we talk about parity, I think we should recognize that wars occur, usually, when each side believes it has a chance to win. Therefore, parity does not necessarily assure that a war may not occur.

By the same token, when we talk about superiority, that may have a detrimental effect on the other side in putting it in an inferior position and, therefore, giving great impetus to its own arms race.

Our objective in this administration, and this is a matter that we are going to discuss at the Pentagon this afternoon, and that will be the subject of a major discussion in the National Security Council within the month—our objective is to be sure that the United States has sufficient military power to defend our interests and to maintain the commitments which this administration determines are in the interest of the United States around the world.

I think "sufficiency" is a better term, actually, than either "superiority" or "parity."

Document 4

Memorandum from President Richard M. Nixon to Assistant to the President for National Security Affairs Henry A. Kissinger, Mar. 11, 1972, Staff Members' Office Files, Files of Harry R. Haldeman, Box 44, Nixon Presidential Materials Project, National Archives, Alexandria, Virginia.

I believe that the expectations for the Moscow trip are being built up too much. What I am concerned about is not that we will fail to achieve the various goals about which there has been speculation but that when we do make the formal agreements there will be no real news value to them because of their having been discounted by an enormous amount of discussion prior to the Summit.

There are two ways to attack this problem. First, as I have already indicated to you, it is vitally important that no final agreements be entered into until we arrive in Moscow and it is also important that speculation with regard to negotiation of such agreements be limited. I realize that the latter objective is very hard to achieve due to the fact that so many people will be talking to [Soviet Ambassador Anatoly] Dobrynin but we should make every possible effort to put a lid on speculation with regard to matters we expect to reach agreement on at the Summit with the Russians.

Another line of attack which should be used to the fullest extent possible is to begin a line of pessimism with regard to what may be accomplished in certain fields. This is particularly important insofar as SALT [Strategic Arms Limitation Talks or Treaty] is concerned. When I see a news story to the effect that we are asking Congress for funds to implement our SALT agreement as if it were an accomplished fact, I realize how difficult it is going to be for us to make the agreement seem like an achievement at the Summit. We know that there would be no possibility of the SALT agreement had we not done the work we have participated in up to this time. On the other hand, there will be an attempt to make it appear that all of this could have been achieved without any Summit whatever, and that all we did was to go to Moscow for a grandstand play.

Document 5

Treaty on the Limitation of Anti-Ballistic Missile Systems, May 26, 1972, in Moscow, U.S. Department of State, *Bulletin*, June 26, 1972, 918–19.

Article I

1. Each Party undertakes to limit anti-ballistic missile (ABM) systems and to adopt other measures in accordance with the provisions of this Treaty.

2. Each Party undertakes not to deploy ABM systems for a defense of the territory of its country and not to provide a base for such a defense, and not to deploy ABM systems for defense of an individual region except as provided for in Article III of this Treaty. . . .

Article III

Each Party undertakes not to deploy ABM systems or their components except that:

(a) within one ABM system deployment area having a radius of one hundred and fifty kilometers and centered on the Party's national capital, a Party may deploy: (1) no more than one hundred ABM launchers and no more than one hundred ABM interceptor missiles at launch sites, and (2) ABM radars within no more than six ABM radar complexes, the area of each complex being circular and having a diameter of no more than three kilometers; and

(b) within one ABM system deployment area having a radius of one hundred and fifty kilometers and containing ICBM [intercontinental ballistic missile] silo launchers, a Party may deploy: (1) no more than one hundred ABM launchers and no more than one hundred ABM interceptor missiles at launch sites, (2) two large phased-array ABM radars comparable in potential to corresponding ABM radars operational or under construction on the date of signature of the Treaty in an ABM system deployment area containing ICBM silo launchers, and (3) no more than eighteen ABM radars each having a potential less than the potential of the smaller of the above-mentioned two large phased-array ABM radars. . . .

Article V

1. Each Party undertakes not to develop, test, or deploy ABM systems or components which are sea-based, air-based, space-based, or mobile land-based.

2. Each Party undertakes not to develop, test, or deploy ABM launchers for launching more than one ABM interceptor missile at a time from each launcher, nor to modify deployed launchers to provide them with such a capability, nor to develop, test, or deploy automatic or semi-automatic or other similar systems for rapid reload of ABM launchers. . . .

Article XI

The Parties undertake to continue active negotiations for limitations on strategic offensive arms. . . .

Document 6

Interim Agreement (and Protocol) between the United States of America and the Union of Soviet Socialist Republics on certain measures with respect to the Limitation of Strategic Offensive Arms (SALT I), in Moscow, May 26, 1972, U.S. Department of State, *Bulletin,* June 26, 1972, 920–21.

Article I

The Parties undertake not to start construction of additional fixed land-based intercontinental ballistic missile (ICBM) launchers after July 1, 1972.

Article II

The Parties undertake not to convert land-based launchers for light ICBMs, or for ICBMs of older types deployed prior to 1964, into land-based launchers for heavy ICBMs of types deployed after that time.

Article III

The Parties undertake to limit submarine-launched ballistic missile (SLBM) launchers and modern ballistic missile submarines to the numbers operational and under construction on the date of signature of this Interim Agreement, and in addition to launchers and submarines constructed under procedures established by the Parties as replacements for an equal number of ICBM launchers of older types deployed prior to 1964 or for launchers on older submarines.

Article IV

Subject to the provisions of this Interim Agreement, modernization and replacement of strategic offensive ballistic missiles and launchers covered by this Interim Agreement may be undertaken. . . .

Article VII

The Parties undertake to continue active negotiations for limitations on strategic offensive arms. The obligations provided for in this Interim Agreement shall not prejudice the scope or terms of the limitations on strategic offensive arms which may be worked out in the course of further negotiations. . . .

[Protocol]

The Parties understand that, under Article III of the Interim Agreement, for the period during which that Agreement remains in force:

The U.S. may have no more than 710 ballistic missile launchers on submarines (SLBMs) and no more than 44 modern ballistic missile submarines. The Soviet Union may have no more than 950 ballistic missile launchers on submarines and no more than 62 modern ballistic missile submarines.

Additional ballistic missile launchers on submarines up to the above-mentioned levels, in the U.S.—over 656 ballistic missile launchers on nuclear-powered submarines, and in the U.S.S.R.—over 740 ballistic missile launchers on nuclear-powered submarines, operational and under construction, may become operational as replacements for equal numbers of ballistic missile launchers of older types deployed prior to 1964 or of ballistic missile launchers on older submarines.

The deployment of modern SLBMs on any submarine, regardless of type, will be counted against the total level of SLBMs permitted for the U.S. and the U.S.S.R.

This Protocol shall be considered an integral part of the Interim Agreement.

Document 7

Basic Principles of Relations Between the United States of America and the Union of Soviet Socialist Republics, May 29, 1972, *PPP: Richard M. Nixon, 1972*, 1973, 633–34.

The United States of America and the Union of Soviet Socialist Republics, . . .

Have agreed as follows:

First. They will proceed from the common determination that in the nuclear age there is no alternative to conducting their mutual relations on the basis of peaceful coexistence. Differences in ideology and in the social systems of the USA and the USSR are not obstacles to the bilateral development of normal relations based on the principles of sovereignty, equality, non-interference in internal affairs and mutual advantage.

Second. The USA and the USSR attach major importance to preventing the development of situations capable of causing a dangerous exacerbation of their relations. Therefore, they will do their utmost to avoid military confrontations and to prevent the outbreak of nuclear war. They will always exercise restraint in their mutual relations, and will be prepared to negotiate and settle differences by peaceful means. Discussions and negotiations on outstanding issues will be conducted in a spirit of reciprocity, mutual accommodation and mutual benefit.

Both sides recognize that efforts to

obtain unilateral advantage at the expense of the other, directly or indirectly, are inconsistent with these objectives. The prerequisites for maintaining and strengthening peaceful relations between the USA and the USSR are the recognition of the security interests of the Parties based on the principle of equality and the renunciation of the use or threat of force.

Third. The USA and the USSR have a special responsibility, as do other countries which are permanent members of the United Nations Security Council, to do everything in their power so that conflicts or situations will not arise which would serve to increase international tensions. Accordingly, they will seek to promote conditions in which all countries will live in peace and security and will not be subject to outside interference in their internal affairs. . . .

Seventh. The USA and the USSR regard commercial and economic ties as an important and necessary element in the strengthening of their bilateral relations and thus will actively promote the growth of such ties. They will facilitate cooperation between the relevant organizations and enterprises of the two countries and the conclusion of appropriate agreements and contracts, including long-term ones.

The two countries will contribute to the improvement of maritime and air communications between them. . . .

Eleventh. The USA and the USSR make no claim for themselves and would not recognize the claims of anyone else to any special rights or advantages in world affairs. They recognize the sovereign equality of all states.

The development of U.S.-Soviet relations is not directed against third countries and their interests. . . .

Document 8

Congressional briefing on U.S.-Soviet relations in the 1970s by Assistant to the President for National Security Affairs Henry A. Kissinger, June 15, 1972, Frank Church Papers, Box 134, Boise State University Library, Boise, Idaho.

The agreement which was signed 46 minutes before midnight in Moscow on the evening of May 26th by President [Richard M.] Nixon and General Secretary [Leonid] Brezhnev is without precedent in the nuclear age; indeed, in all relevant modern history.

Never before have the world's two most powerful nations, divided by ideology, history and conflicting interests, placed their central armaments under formally agreed limitation and restraint. It is fair to ask: What new conditions now prevail to have made this step commend itself to the calculated self-interests of both of the so-called superpowers, as it so clearly must have done for both willingly to undertake it? . . .

The international situation has been undergoing a profound structural change since at least the mid-1960s. The post-World War II pattern of relations among the great powers had been altered to the point that when this Administration took office, a major reassessment was clearly in order. . . .

Perhaps most important for the United States, our undisputed strategic predominance was declining just at a time when there was rising domestic resistance to military programs, and impatience for redistribution of resources from national defense to social demands.

Amidst all of this profound change, however, there was one important constant—the continuing dependence of most of the world's hopes for stability and peace upon the ability to reduce the tensions between the United States and the Soviet Union. . . .

Each of us has thus come into possession of power singlehandedly capable of exterminating the human race. Paradoxically, this very fact, and the global interests of both sides, create a certain commonality of outlook, a sort of interdependence for survival between the two of us.

Although we compete, the conflict will not admit of resolution by victory in the classical sense. We are compelled to coexist. We have an inescapable obligation to build jointly a structure for peace. Recognition of this reality is the beginning of wisdom for a sane and effective foreign policy today. . . .

The President, therefore, decided that the United States should work to create a set of circumstances which would offer the Soviet leaders an opportunity to move away from confrontation through carefully prepared negotiations. From the first, we rejected the notion that what was lacking was a cordial climate for conducting negotiations.

Past experience has amply shown that much heralded changes in atmospherics, but not buttressed by concrete progress, will revert to previous patterns, at the first subsequent clash of interests.

We have, instead, sought to move forward across a broad range of issues so that progress in one area would add momentum to the progress of other areas.

We hoped that the Soviet Union would acquire a stake in a wide spectrum of negotiations and that it would become convinced that its interests would be best served if the entire process unfolded. We have sought, in short, to create a vested interest in mutual restraint.

Document 9

Joint U.S.-Soviet Statement on the Limitation of Strategic Offensive Arms, Nov. 24, 1974, *PPP: Gerald R. Ford, 1974,* 1975, 657.

During their working meeting in the area of Vladivostok on November 23–24, 1974, the President of the USA Gerald R. Ford and General Secretary of the Central Committee of the CPSU [Communist Party of the Soviet Union] L. [Leonid] I. Brezhnev discussed in detail the question of further limitations of strategic offensive arms.

They reaffirmed the great significance that both the United States and the USSR attach to the limitation of strategic offensive arms. They are convinced that a long-term agreement on this question would be a significant contribution to improving relations between the US and the USSR, to reducing the danger of war and to enhancing world peace. Having noted the value of previous agreements on this question, including the Interim Agreement of May 26, 1972, they reaffirm the intention to conclude a new agreement on the limitation of strategic offensive arms, to last through 1985.

As a result of the exchange of views on the substance of such a new agreement the President of the United States of America and the General Secretary of the Central Committee of the CPSU concluded that favorable prospects exist for completing the work on this agreement in 1975.

Agreement was reached that further negotiations will be based on the following provisions.

1. The new agreement will incorporate the relevant provisions of the Interim Agreement of May 26, 1972, which will remain in force until October 1977.

2. The new agreement will cover the period from October 1977 through December 31, 1985.

3. Based on the principle of equality and equal security, the new agreement will include the following limitations:

a. Both sides will be entitled to have a certain agreed aggregate number of strategic delivery vehicles;

b. Both sides will be entitled to have a certain agreed aggregate number of ICBMs [intercontinental ballistic missiles] and SLBMs [submarine-launched ballistic missiles] equipped with multiple independently targetable warheads (MIRVs).

Document 10

Conference on Security and Cooperation in Europe: Final Act, Aug. 1, 1975, U.S. Department of State, *Bulletin*, Sept. 1, 1975, 324–25.

I. *Sovereign equality, respect for the rights inherent in sovereignty*

The participating States will respect each other's sovereign equality and individuality as well as all the rights inherent in and encompassed by its sovereignty, including in particular the right of every State to juridical equality, to territorial integrity and to freedom and political independence. They will also respect each other's right freely to choose and develop its political, social, economic and cultural systems as well as its right to determine its laws and regulations.

Within the framework of international law, all the participating States have equal rights and duties. They will respect each other's right to define and conduct as it wishes its relations with other States in accordance with international law and in the spirit of the present Declaration. They consider that their frontiers can be changed, in accordance with international law, by peaceful means and by agreement. They also have the right to belong or not to belong to international organizations, to be or not to be a party to bilateral or multilateral treaties including the right to be or not to be a party to treaties of alliance; they also have the right to neutrality.

II. *Refraining from the threat or use of force*

The participating States will refrain in their mutual relations, as well as in their international relations in general, from the threat or use of force against the territorial integrity or political independence of any State, or in any other manner inconsistent with the purposes of the United Nations and with the present Declaration. No consideration may be invoked to serve to warrant resort to the threat or use of force in contravention of this principle.

Accordingly, the participating States will refrain from any acts constituting a threat of force or direct or indirect use of force against another participating State. Likewise they will refrain from any manifestation of force for the purpose of inducing another participating State to renounce the full exercise of its sovereign rights. Likewise they will also refrain in their mutual relations from any act of reprisal by force.

No such threat or use of force will be employed as a means of settling disputes, or questions likely to give rise to disputes, between them.

III. *Inviolability of frontiers*

The participating States regard as inviolable all one another's frontiers as well as the frontiers of all States in Europe. . . .

VI. *Non-intervention in internal affairs*

The participating States will refrain from any intervention, direct or indirect, individual or collective, in the internal or external affairs falling within the domestic jurisdiction of another participating State. . . .

They will accordingly refrain from any form of armed intervention or threat of such intervention against another participating State.

They will likewise in all circumstances refrain from any other act of military, or of political, economic or other coercion designed to subordinate to their own interest the exercise by another participating State of the rights inherent in its sovereignty and thus to secure advantages of any kind.

Accordingly, they will, inter alia, refrain from direct or indirect assistance to terrorist activities, or to subversive or other activities directed towards the violent overthrow of the regime of another participating State.

VII. *Respect for human rights and fundamental freedoms, including the freedom of thought, conscience, religion or belief*

The participating States will respect human rights and fundamental freedoms, including the freedom of thought, conscience, religion or belief, for all without distinction as to race, sex, language or religion.

They will promote and encourage the effective exercise of civil, political, economic, social, cultural and other rights and freedoms of all which derive from the inherent dignity of the human person and are essential for his free and full development.

Within this framework the participating States will recognize and respect the freedom of the individual to profess and practise, alone or in community with others, religion or belief acting in accordance with the dictates of his own conscience.

The participating States on whose territory national minorities exist will respect the right of persons belonging to such minorities to equality before the law, will afford them the full opportunity for the actual enjoyment of human rights and fundamental freedoms and will, in this manner, protect their legitimate interests in this sphere.

The participating States recognize the universal significance of human rights and fundamental freedoms, respect for which is an essential factor for the peace, justice and well-being necessary to ensure the development of friendly relations and co-operation among themselves as among all States.

They will constantly respect these rights and freedoms in their mutual relations and will endeavour jointly and separately, including in co-operation with the United Nations, to promote universal and effective respect for them.

They confirm the right of the individual to know and act upon his rights and duties in this field.

In the field of human rights and fundamental freedoms, the participating States will act in conformity with the purposes and principles of the Charter of the United Nations and with the Universal Declaration of Human Rights. They will also fulfill their obligations as set forth in the international declarations and agreements in this field, including inter alia the International Covenants on Human Rights, by which they may be bound.

Document 11

Treaty Between the United States of America and the Union of Soviet Socialist Republics on the Limitation of Strategic Offensive Arms (SALT II), in Vienna, June 18, 1979, *PPP: Administration of Jimmy Carter, 1979*, 1980, 1051–58.

Article I

Each Party undertakes, in accordance with the provisions of this Treaty, to limit strategic offensive arms quantitatively and qualitatively, to exercise restraint in the development of new types of strategic offensive arms, and to adopt other measures provided for in this Treaty. . . .

Article III

1. Upon entry into force of this Treaty, each Party undertakes to limit ICBM [Intercontinental Ballistic Missile] launchers, SLBM [Submarine-Launched Ballistic Missile] launchers, heavy bombers, and ASBMs [Air-to-Surface Ballistic Missiles] to an aggregate number not to exceed 2,400.

2. Each Party undertakes to limit, from January 1, 1981, strategic offensive arms referred to in paragraph 1 of this Article to an aggregate number not to exceed 2,250, and to initiate reductions of those arms which as of that date would be in excess of this aggregate number.

3. Within the aggregate numbers provided for in paragraphs 1 and 2 of this Article and subject to the provisions of this Treaty, each Party has the right to determine the composition of these aggregates. . . .

Article IV

1. Each Party undertakes not to start construction of additional fixed ICBM launchers.

2. Each Party undertakes not to relocate fixed ICBM launchers. . . .

8. Each Party undertakes not to convert land-based launchers of ballistic missiles which are not ICBMs into launchers for launching ICBMs, and not to test them for this purpose. . . .

14. Each Party undertakes not to deploy at any one time on heavy bombers equipped for cruise missiles capable of a range in excess of 600 kilometers a number of such cruise missiles which exceeds the product of 28 and the number of such heavy bombers. . . .

Article VIII

1. Each Party undertakes not to flight-test cruise missiles capable of a range in excess of 600 kilometers or ASBMs from aircraft other than bombers or to convert such aircraft into aircraft equipped for such missiles.

2. Each Party undertakes not to convert aircraft other than bombers into aircraft which can carry out the mission of a heavy bomber as referred to in subparagraph 3(b) of Article II. . . .

Article XIX

1. This Treaty shall be subject to ratification in accordance with the constitutional procedures of each Party. This Treaty shall enter into force on the day of the exchange of instruments of ratification and shall remain in force through December 31, 1985, unless replaced earlier by an agreement further limiting strategic offensive arms. . . .

3. Each Party shall, in exercising its national sovereignty, have the right to withdraw from this Treaty if it decides that extraordinary events related to the subject matter of this Treaty have jeopardized its supreme interests. It shall give notice of its decision to the other Party six months prior to withdrawal from the Treaty. Such notice shall include a statement of the extraordinary events the notifying party regards as having jeopardized its supreme interests. . . .

Document 12

President Jimmy Carter's address to the nation, Jan. 4, 1980, *PPP: Administration of Jimmy Carter, 1980,* 1981, 21–24.

I come to you this evening to discuss the extremely important and rapidly changing circumstances in Southwest Asia. . . .

Recently, there has been another very serious development which threatens the maintenance of peace in Southwest Asia. Massive Soviet military forces have invaded the small, nonaligned, sovereign nation of Afghanistan, which had hitherto not been an occupied satellite of the Soviet Union.

Fifty thousand heavily armed Soviet troops have crossed the border and are now dispersed throughout Afghanistan, attempting to conquer the fiercely independent Muslim people of that country.

The Soviets claim, falsely, that they were invited into Afghanistan to help protect that country from some unnamed outside threat. But the President, who had been the leader of Afghanistan before the Soviet invasion, was assassinated—along with several members of his family—after the Soviets gained control of the capital city of Kabul. Only several days later was the new puppet leader even brought into Afghanistan by the Soviets.

This invasion is an extremely serious threat to peace because of the threat of further Soviet expansion into neighboring countries in Southwest Asia and also because such an aggressive military policy is unsettling to other peoples throughout the world.

This is a callous violation of international law and the United Nations Charter. It is a deliberate effort of a powerful atheistic government to subjugate an independent Islamic people.

We must recognize the strategic importance of Afghanistan to stability and peace. A Soviet-occupied Afghanistan threatens both Iran and Pakistan and is a steppingstone to possible control over much of the world's oil supplies. . . .

. . . Neither the United States nor any other nation which is committed to world peace and stability can continue to do business as usual with the Soviet Union.

I have already recalled the United States Ambassador from Moscow back to Washington. He's working with me and with my other senior advisers in an immediate and comprehensive evaluation of the whole range of our relations with the Soviet Union.

The successful negotiation of the SALT [Strategic Arms Limitation Talks or Treaty] II treaty has been a major goal and a major achievement of this administration, and we Americans, the people of the Soviet Union, and indeed the entire world will benefit from the successful control of strategic nuclear weapons through the implementation of this carefully negotiated treaty.

However, because of the Soviet aggression, I have asked the United States Senate to defer further consideration of the SALT II treaty so that the Congress and I can assess Soviet actions and intentions and devote our primary attention to the legislative and other measures required to respond to this crisis. As circumstances change in the future, we will, of course, keep the ratification of SALT II under active review in consultation with the leaders of the Senate.

The Soviets must understand our deep concern. We will delay opening of any new American or Soviet consular facilities, and most of the cultural and economic exchanges currently under consideration will be deferred. Trade with the Soviet Union will be severely restricted.

I have decided to halt or reduce exports to the Soviet Union in three areas that are particularly important to them. These new policies are being and will be coordinated with those of our allies.

I've directed that no high technology or other strategic items will be licensed for sale to the Soviet Union until further notice, while we revise our licensing policy.

Fishing privileges for the Soviet Union in United States waters will be severely curtailed.

The 17 million tons of grain ordered by the Soviet Union in excess of that amount which we are committed to sell will not be delivered. This grain was not intended for human consumption but was to be used for building up Soviet livestock herds. . . .

Although the United States would prefer not to withdraw from the Olympic games scheduled in Moscow this summer, the Soviet Union must realize that its continued aggressive actions will endanger both the participation of athletes and the travel to Moscow by spectators who would normally wish to attend the Olympic games. . . .

History teaches, perhaps, very few clear lessons. But surely one such lesson learned by the world at great cost is that aggression, unopposed, becomes a contagious disease.

The response of the international community to the Soviet attempt to crush Afghanistan must match the gravity of the Soviet action.

With the support of the American people and working with other nations, we will deter aggression, we will protect our Nation's security, and we will preserve the peace. The United States will meet its responsibilities.

Thank you very much.

Document 13

President Ronald Reagan, news conference, Jan. 29, 1981, *PPP: Administration of Ronald Reagan, 1981*, 1982, 57.

[Sam Donaldson, ABC News]

Goals of the Soviet Union

Q. Mr. President, what do you see as the long-range intentions of the Soviet Union? Do you think, for instance, the Kremlin is bent on world domination that might lead to a continuation of the cold war, or do you think that under other circumstances détente is possible?

The President. Well, so far détente's been a one-way street that the Soviet Union has used to pursue its own aims. I don't have to think of an answer as to what I think their intentions are; they have repeated it. I know of no leader of the Soviet Union since the revolution, and including the present leadership, that has not more than once repeated in the various Communist congresses they hold their determination that their goal must be the promotion of world revolution and a one-world Socialist or Communist state, whichever word you want to use.

Now, as long as they do that and as long as they, at the same time, have openly and publicly declared that the only morality they recognize is what will further their cause, meaning they reserve unto themselves the right to commit any crime, to lie, to cheat, in order to attain that, and that is moral, not immoral, and we operate on a different set of standards, I think when you do business with them, even at a détente, you keep that in mind.

Document 14

President Ronald Reagan, address to members of the British Parliament, June 8, 1982, *PPP: Administration of Ronald Reagan, 1982*, 1983, 744–47.

In an ironic sense Karl Marx was right. We are witnessing today a great revolutionary crisis, a crisis where the demands of the economic order are conflicting directly with those of the political order. But the crisis is happening not in the free, non-Marxist West, but in the home of Marxist-Leninism, the Soviet Union. It is the Soviet Union that runs against the tide of history by denying human freedom and human dignity to its citizens. It also is in deep economic difficulty. The rate of growth in the national product has been steadily declining since the fifties and is less than half of what it was then.

The dimensions of this failure are astounding: a country which employs one-fifth of its population in agriculture is unable to feed its own people. Were it not for the private sector, the tiny private sector tolerated in Soviet agriculture, the country might be on the brink of famine. These private plots occupy a bare 3 percent of the arable land but account for nearly one-quarter of Soviet farm output and nearly one-third of meat products and vegetables. Overcentralized, with little or no incentives, year after year the Soviet system pours its best resource into the making of instruments of destruction. The constant shrinkage of economic growth combined with the growth of military production is putting a heavy strain on the Soviet people. What we see here is a political structure that no longer corresponds to its economic base, a society where productive forces are hampered by political ones.

The decay of the Soviet experiment should come as no surprise to us. Wherever the comparisons have been made between free and closed societies—West Germany and East Germany, Austria and Czechoslovakia, Malaysia and Vietnam—it is the democratic countries that are prosperous and responsive to the needs of their people. And one of the simple but overwhelming facts of our time is this: Of all the millions of refugees we've seen in the modern world, their flight is always away from, not toward the Communist world. Today on the NATO line, our military forces face east to prevent a possible invasion. On the other side of the line, the Soviet forces also face east to prevent their people from leaving. . . .

As for the Soviet view, Chairman [Leonid] Brezhnev repeatedly has stressed that the competition of ideas and systems must continue and that this is entirely consistent with relaxation of tensions and peace.

Well, we ask only that these systems begin by living up to their own constitutions, abiding by their own laws, and complying with the international obligations they have undertaken. We ask only for a process, a direction, a basic code of decency, not for an instant transformation. . . .

While we must be cautious about forcing the pace of change, we must not hesitate to declare our ultimate objectives and to take concrete actions to move toward them. We must be staunch in our conviction that freedom is not the sole prerogative of a lucky few, but the inalienable and universal right of all human beings. So states the United Nations Universal Declaration of Human Rights, which, among other things, guarantees free elections. . . .

At the same time, we invite the Soviet Union to consider with us how the competition of ideas and values—which it is committed to support—can be conducted on a peaceful and reciprocal basis. For example, I am prepared to offer President Brezhnev an opportunity to speak to the American people on our television if he will allow me the same opportunity with the Soviet people. We also suggest that panels of our newsmen periodically appear on each other's television to discuss major events.

Now, I don't wish to sound overly optimistic, yet the Soviet Union is not immune from the reality of what is going on in the world. It has happened in the past—a small ruling elite either mistakenly attempts to ease domestic unrest through greater repression and foreign adventure, or it chooses a wiser course. It begins to allow its people a voice in their own destiny. Even if this latter process is not realized soon, I believe the renewed strength of the democratic movement, complemented by a global campaign for freedom, will strengthen the prospects for arms control and a world at peace. . . .

Document 15

Secretary of State George P. Shultz, news conference, Reykjavik, Iceland, Oct. 12, 1986, U.S. Department of State, *Bulletin*, December 1986, 9–10.

I have just spent 2 full, intensive days watching the President [Ronald Reagan] engage with the General Secretary of the Soviet Union [Mikhail Gorbachev] over the full range of issues that we are concerned about together. The President's performance was magnificent; and, I have never been so proud of my President as I have been in these sessions, and particularly this afternoon.

During the course of these 2 days, extremely important potential agreements were reached to reduce, in the first instance, strategic arms in half; to deal effectively with intermediate-range missiles; although, we didn't finally have the opportunity to come to grips with it probably to work out something satisfactory about nuclear testing; a satisfactory manner of addressing regional issues; humanitarian concerns; a variety of bilateral matters; and a tremendous amount of headway in the issues in space and defense involving the ABM [antiballistic missile] Treaty.

Throughout all of this, the President was constructive in reaching out and using his creativity and ingenuity to find these very sweeping and substantial and important agreements. It has been clear for a long time—and it was certainly clear today, and particularly this afternoon—the importance the Soviet leader attaches to the Strategic Defense Initiative (SDI), and I think it was quite apparent that at least a key reason why it was possible to reach such sweeping potential agreements was the very fact of SDI's vigorous presence.

In seeking to deal with these issues, the President was ready to agree to a 10-year period of nonwithdrawal from the ABM Treaty, a period during which the United States would do research, development, and testing which is permitted by the ABM Treaty and, of course, after which we would be permitted to deploy if we chose. However, as the agreement that might have been said, during this 10-year period, in effect, all offensive strategic arms and ballistic missiles would be eliminated so that at the end of the period the deployment of strategic defense would be substantially altered in what was needed and would be in the nature of an insurance policy—insurance against cheating, insurance against somebody getting hold of these weapons—so it would maintain an effective shield for the United States, for our allies, for the free world.

As we came more and more down to

the final stages, it became more and more clear that the Soviet Union's objective was effectively to kill off the SDI program and to do so by seeking a change described by them as "strengthening," but a change in the ABM Treaty that would so constrain research permitted under it that the program would not be able to proceed at all forcefully.

The President, hard as he had worked for this extraordinary range and importance of agreements, simply would not turn away from the basic security interests of the United States, our allies, and the free world by abandoning this essential defensive program. He had to bear in mind—and did bear in mind—that not only is the existence of the strategic defense program a key reason why we were able potentially to reach these agreements, but undoubtedly its continued existence and potential would be the kind of program you need in the picture to ensure yourself that the agreements reached would be effectively carried out. And so in the end, with great reluctance, the President, having worked so hard creatively and constructively for these potentially tremendous achievements, simply had to refuse to compromise the security of the United States, of our allies, and freedom by abandoning the shield that has held in front of freedom.

So in the end we are deeply disappointed at this outcome; although, I think it is important to recognize how effectively and constructively and hard the President worked and how much he achieved potentially, how ready he was to go absolutely the last—not just the last mile, but as you can see from what I've told you, quite a long distance to try to bring into being these potentially very significant agreements. But he could not allow the essential ingredient to be destroyed in the process—and would not do so.

Document 16

Departure remarks of President Ronald Reagan and Soviet Leader Mikhail Gorbachev at the conclusion of the Washington Summit, Dec. 10, 1987, U.S. Department of State, *Bulletin*, February 1988, 16–18.

President Reagan

I believe both the General Secretary and I can walk away from our meetings with a sense of accomplishment. We have proven that adversaries, even with the most basic philosophical differences, can talk candidly and respectfully with one another and, with perseverance, find common ground. We did not hide from the weighty differences that separate us; many of them, of course, remain. One of my predecessors, President Franklin Roosevelt, once said, "History cannot be rewritten by wishful thinking." Our discussions, in that spirit, were straightforward and designed to open a thoughtful communication between our governments on the critical issues that confront us. . . .

Of course, the greatest accomplishment of these 3 days was the signing of a treaty to eliminate a whole class of U.S. and Soviet nuclear weapons. Another one of my predecessors, a President I have admired since my youth, Calvin Coolidge, once said, "History is only made by action." Well, it took enormous effort and almost superhuman tenacity on the part of the negotiators on both sides, but the end-product is a treaty that does indeed make history. It is in the interest of both our peoples, yet I cannot help but believe that mankind is the biggest winner. At long last, we have begun the task of actually reducing these deadly weapons, rather than simply putting limits on their growth.

The INF [Intermediate-Range Nuclear Forces] Treaty, as proud of it as we are, should be viewed as a beginning, not an end. Further arms reduction is now possible. I am pleased some progress has been made toward a strategic arms reduction treaty over the last 3 days.

Individual agreements will not, in and of themselves, result in sustained progress. We need a realistic understanding of each other's intentions and objectives, a process for dealing with differences in a practical and straightforward manner, and we need patience, creativity, and persistence in achieving what we set out to do. As a result of this summit, the framework for building such a relationship has been strengthened.

I am determined to use this framework. My goal—which I believe you share, Mr. General Secretary—is a more constructive relationship between our governments—long-lasting rather than transitory improvements. Together, we can bring about a more secure and prosperous future for our peoples and a more peaceful world. Both of us are aware of the difficult challenges and special responsibilities inherent in this task. . . .

General Secretary Gorbachev

In these last hours before our departure for home, we note with satisfaction that the visit to Washington has, on the whole, justified our hopes. We have had 3 days of hard work, of business-like and frank discussions on the pivotal problems of Soviet-American relations and on important aspects of the current world situation.

A good deal has been accomplished. I would like to emphasize in particular an unprecedented step in the history of the nuclear age: the signing of the treaty under which the two militarily and strategically greatest powers have assumed an obligation to actually destroy a portion of their nuclear weapons, thus, we hope, setting in motion the process of nuclear disarmament.

In our talks with President Ronald Reagan, some headway has been made on the central issue of that process, achieving substantial reductions of strategic offensive arms which are the most potent weapons in the world, although we still have a lot of work to do. We have had a useful exchange of views which has clarified each other's positions concerning regional conflicts, the development of our bilateral ties, and human rights. On some of these aspects, it seems likely that we can soon identify specific solutions satisfactory both to us and to other countries. A useful result of the Washington talks is that we have been able to formulate a kind of agenda for joint efforts in the future. This puts the dialogue between our two countries on a more predictable footing and is undoubtedly constructive. . . .

I believe that what we have accomplished during the meeting and the discussions will, with time, help considerably to improve the atmosphere in the world at large and in America itself in terms of its more correct and tolerant perception of my country, the Soviet Union.

Today, the Soviet Union and the United States are closer to the common goal of strengthening international security. But this goal is yet to be reached. There is still much work to be done, and we must get down to it without delay.

Mr. President, esteemed citizens of the United States, we are grateful for your hospitality and we wish success, well-being, and peace to all Americans. Thank you and goodbye.

Document 17

President Ronald Reagan, radio address to the nation on Soviet-U.S. relations, Dec. 10, 1988, *Weekly Compilation of Presidential Documents*, October–December 1988, vol. 24, 1613–14.

My fellow Americans:

On Wednesday, this week, I met with Soviet President [Mikhail] Gorbachev for the fifth time. Together we stood under the gaze of Lady Liberty, speaking for the prospects of peace for the peoples of our two nations and for all the world. Yes, since our first summit in Geneva 3 years ago, we've traveled a great journey that has seen remarkable progress, a journey we continue to travel together. I am pleased that the Soviet Union has accepted our offer of humanitarian aid in the wake of their devastating earthquake tragedy.

This has also been a period of important change inside the Soviet Union. The greater openness permitted by Moscow can be found in films, art, and literature. There is greater tolerance for those seeking to peacefully assemble, and the official press carries more independent opinions and factual reporting.

And just a few years ago, who would have anticipated seeing a Soviet leader stand before the world community, heralding a plan for economic restructuring and military redeployments, and promising to meet the world community's highest standards of human rights? If this vision is realized and these promises are turned into deeds, we would be witnessing a dramatic change in the Soviet system, a long-awaited break with the past, and the opening of a new era in international affairs.

Certainly the Soviet reforms have their limits, and brave dissenters within that country who have sought a fuller measure of openness continue to be dealt with harshly. But I was encouraged by the new promises of reform that Mr. Gorbachev made before the United Nations and hope to see these and past promises translated into permanent institutional changes that will signal to the peoples of the Soviet Union and the world a courageous commitment to a new path of democratization. We already see unprecedented diversity in Eastern Europe, with some countries pursuing reforms that go even beyond the Soviet example, while other countries continue to lag behind. We hope to see the day when all countries of Eastern Europe enjoy the freedom, democracy, and self-determination that their peoples have long awaited.

Just a decade ago, some intellectuals widely predicted what they called convergence: the idea that the democratic world and the Communist world would merge into one hybrid system. The main question amounted to how much freedom would democratic nations have to give up in the bargain. But instead, the free world held firm to its democratic values, cleaving to truths deeply rooted in Western culture and our Judeo-Christian tradition. Moreover, we spoke openly of the moral superiority of our ideal of freedom. We candidly criticized the violations of human rights occurring behind the Iron Curtain. We rebuilt our defenses and with our allies worked to counter international aggression by our totalitarian adversaries. And we exhibited that scarcest of commodities: patience. And our steadfastness, our policies, our whole approach has borne fruit. Perhaps the most dramatic achievement came 1 year ago, when Mr. Gorbachev and I signed the historic INF [Intermediate-Range Nuclear Forces] treaty to eliminate an entire class of U.S. and Soviet nuclear missiles. . . .

Well, in these brightest of times, let us recall that in the darkest days of World War II, when hopes for the free world seemed most bleak, Winston Churchill rallied us to carry on, saying that "We have not journeyed all this way because we are made of sugar candy." By summoning all their strength and courage, and by pulling together, the Allies prevailed. The war was won. The decades following World War II were filled with political tensions and threats to world freedom. But in recent years, we've seen hopes for a free and peaceful future restored and the chance for a new U.S.-Soviet relationship emerge. To the American people and to our allies, I would echo Churchill and say we have not come this far through lack of strength or any weakness in our resolve, nor has there been anything inevitable about what we've achieved. The unity, confidence, power, and firmness of the democracies has brought us forward, and maintaining a strong alliance will keep us moving forward.

Document 18

Remarks of President George Bush and Chairman Mikhail Gorbachev and a question-and-answer session with reporters at Malta, Dec. 3, 1989, *Weekly Compilation of Presidential Documents,* Dec. 11, 1989, vol. 25, 1869–71.

I [President George Bush] first approached Chairman [Mikhail] Gorbachev about an informal meeting of this kind after my trip to Europe last July. Amazing changes that I witnessed in Poland and in Hungary—hopeful changes—led me to believe that it was time to sit down with Chairman Gorbachev face to face to see what he and I could do to seize the opportunities before us to move this relationship forward. He agreed with that concept of a meeting, and so, we got rapid agreement. And I think that the extraordinary developments in Europe since the time that the meeting was proposed only reinforce the importance of our getting together. . . .

For 40 years, the Western alliance has stood together in the cause of freedom. And now, with reform underway in the Soviet Union, we stand at the threshold of a brand new era of U.S.-Soviet relations. And it is within our grasp to contribute, each in our own way, to overcoming the division of Europe and ending the military confrontation there. We've got to do more to ameliorate the violence and suffering that afflicts so many regions in the world and to remove common threats to our future: the deterioration of the environment; the spread of nuclear and chemical weapons, ballistic missile technology; the narcotics trade. And our discussions here will give greater impetus to make real progress in these areas. . . .

The Chairman. Ladies and gentlemen, comrades, there are many symbolic things about this meeting, and one of them—it has never been in the history that the leaders of our two countries hold a joint press conference. This is also an important symbol. I share the view voiced by President Bush that we are satisfied, in general, with the results of the meeting. . . .

We not only discussed problems and explained our positions. I think that both sides had many elements which, if they are taken into account in our future activities—activities of both governments—then we can count on progress. This concerns the subject of the reduction of strategic offensive arms by 50 percent, and we have an optimistic assessment of the possibility to move even next year to the conclusion of the Vienna treaty. We both are in favor, and this is our position—naturally, we can be responsible only for our position—we are in favor of signing this document at the summit meeting. . . .

Q. Chairman Gorbachev, President Bush called on you to end the Cold War once and for all. Do you think that has been done now?

The Chairman. In the first place, I assured the President of the United States that the Soviet Union would never start hot war against the United States of America, and we would like our relations to develop in such a way that they would open greater possibilities for cooperation. Naturally, the President and I had a wide discussion—rather, we sought the answer to the question where we stand now. We stated, both of us, that the world leaves one epoch of cold war and enters another epoch. This is just the beginning. We're just at the very beginning of our long road to a longlasting peaceful period.

Document 19

Treaty on Conventional Armed Forces in Europe, Nov. 19, 1990, *Weekly Compilation of Presidential Documents: 1990*, 1868–72.

DECLARATION OF THE STATES PARTIES TO THE TREATY ON CONVENTIONAL ARMED FORCES IN EUROPE WITH RESPECT TO PERSONNEL STRENGTH

In connection with the signature of the Treaty on Conventional Armed Forces in Europe of November 19, 1990, and with a view to the follow-on negotiations referred to in Article XVIII of that Treaty, the States Parties to that Treaty declare that, for the period of these negotiations, they will not increase the total peacetime authorized personnel strength of their conventional armed forces pursuant to the Mandate in the area of application.

DECLARATION OF THE STATES PARTIES TO THE TREATY ON CONVENTIONAL ARMED FORCES IN EUROPE WITH RESPECT TO LAND-BASED NAVAL AIRCRAFT

To promote the implementation of the Treaty on Conventional Armed Forces in Europe, the States Parties to the Treaty undertake the following political commitments outside the framework of the Treaty.

1. No one State will have in the area of application of the treaty more than 400 permanently land-based combat naval aircraft. It is understood that this commitment applies to combat aircraft armed and equipped to engage surface or air targets and excludes types designed as maritime patrol aircraft.

2. The aggregate number of such permanently land-based combat naval aircraft held by either of the two groups of States defined under the terms of the Treaty will not exceed 430.

3. No one State will hold in its naval forces within the area of application any permanently land-based attack helicopters.

4. The limitations provided for in this Declaration will apply beginning 40 months after entry into force of the Treaty on Conventional Armed Forces in Europe.

5. This Declaration will become effective as of entry into force of the Treaty on Conventional Armed Forces in Europe.

WHITE HOUSE FACT SHEET

Today the 22 members of NATO and the Warsaw Pact signed a landmark agreement limiting conventional armed forces in Europe (CFE). The CFE treaty will establish parity in major conventional armaments between East and West in Europe from the Atlantic to the Urals. The treaty will limit the size of the Soviet forces to about one third of the total armaments permitted to all the countries in Europe. The treaty includes an unprecedented monitoring regime, including detailed information exchange, on-site inspection, challenge inspection, and monitoring of destruction.

East-West Limits

The treaty sets equal ceilings from the Atlantic to the Urals on key armaments essential for conducting surprise attack and initiating large-scale offensive operations. Neither side may have more than:

20,000 tanks
20,000 artillery pieces
30,000 armored combat vehicles (ACV's)
6,800 combat aircraft
2,000 attack helicopters.

To further limit the readiness of armed forces, the treaty sets equal ceilings on equipment that may be with active units. Other ground equipment must be in designated permanent storage sites. The limits for equipment each side may have in active units are:

16,500 tanks
17,000 artillery pieces
27,300 armored combat vehicles (ACV's).

In connection with the CFE treaty, the six members of the Warsaw Pact signed a treaty in Budapest on November 3, 1990, which divides the Warsaw Pact allocation by country. The members of NATO have consulted through NATO mechanisms and have agreed on national entitlements. These national entitlements may be adjusted.

Country Ceilings

The treaty limits the proportion of armaments that can be held by any one country in Europe to about one third of the total for all countries in Europe—the "sufficiency" rule. This provision constrains the size of Soviet forces more than any other in the treaty. These limits are:

13,300 tanks
13,700 artillery pieces
20,000 armored combat vehicles (ACV's)
5,150 combat aircraft
1,500 attack helicopters.

Regional Arrangements

In addition to limits on the number of armaments in each category on each side, the treaty also includes regional limits to prevent destabilizing force concentrations of ground equipment.

Destruction

Equipment reduced to meet the ceilings must be destroyed or, in a limited number of cases, have its military capability destroyed, allowing the chassis to be used for nonmilitary purposes. After the treaty enters into force, there will be a 4-month baseline inspection period. After the 4-month baseline period, 25 percent of the destruction must be complete by the end of 1 year, 60 percent by the end of 2 years, and all destruction required by the treaty must be complete by the end of 3 years. Parties have 5 years to convert limited amounts of equipment.

Large amounts of equipment will be destroyed to meet the obligations of the CFE treaty. The Soviet Union alone will be obliged to destroy thousands of weapons, much more equipment than will be reduced by all the NATO countries combined. NATO will meet its destruction obligations by destroying its oldest equipment. In a process called "cascading," NATO members with newer equipment, including the U.S., have agreed to transfer some of this equipment to allies with older equipment. Cascading will not reduce NATO's destruction obligation. Under the cascading system, no U.S. equipment must be destroyed to meet CFE ceilings. Some 2,000 pieces of U.S. equipment will be transferred to our NATO allies.

Verification

The treaty includes unprecedented provisions for detailed information exchanges, on-site inspections, challenge inspections, and on-site monitoring of destruction. At the initiative of the U.S., NATO has established a system to cooperate in monitoring the treaty. Parties have an unlimited right to monitor the process of destruction.

The CFE treaty is of unlimited duration and will enter into force 10 days after all parties have ratified the agreement. . . .

Text of the Joint Declaration of Twenty-Two States

November 19, 1990

The Heads of State or Government of Belgium, Bulgaria, Canada, the Czech and Slovak Federal Republic, Denmark, France, Germany, Greece, Hungary, Iceland, Italy, Luxembourg, the Netherlands, Norway, Poland, Portugal, Romania, Spain, Turkey, the Union of Soviet Socialist Republics, the United Kingdom and the United States of America

—greatly welcoming the historic changes in Europe,
—gratified by the growing implementation throughout Europe of a common commitment to pluralist democracy, the rule of law and human rights, which are essential to lasting security on the continent,
—affirming the end of the era of division and confrontation which has lasted for more than four decades, the improvement in relations among their countries and the contribution this makes to the security of all,
—confident that the signature of the Treaty on Conventional Armed Forces in Europe represents a major contribution to the common objective of increased security and stability in Europe, and
—convinced that these developments must form part of a continuing process of co-operation in building the structures of a more united continent,

Issue the following Declaration:

1. The signatories solemnly declare that, in the new era of European relations which is beginning, they are no longer adversaries, will build new partnerships and extend to each other the hand of friendship.

2. They recall their obligations under the Charter of the United Nations and reaffirm all of their commitments under the Helsinki Final Act. They stress that all of the ten Helsinki Principles are of primary significance and that, accordingly, they will be equally and unreservedly applied, each of them being interpreted taking into account the others. In that context, they affirm their obligation and commitment to refrain from the threat or use of force against the territorial integrity or the political independence of any State, from seeking to change existing borders by threat or use of force, and from acting in any other manner inconsistent with the principles and purposes of those documents. None of their weapons will ever be used except in self-defense or otherwise in accordance with the Charter of the United Nations.

3. They recognize that security is indivisible and that the security of each of their countries is inextricably linked to the security of all the States participating in the Conference on Security and Co-operation in Europe [CSCE].

4. They undertake to maintain only such military capabilities as are

necessary to prevent war and provide for effective defense. They will bear in mind the relationship between military capabilities and doctrines.

5. They reaffirm that every State has the right to be or not to be a party to a treaty of alliance.

6. They note with approval the intensification of political and military contacts among them to promote mutual understanding and confidence. They welcome in this context the positive responses made to recent proposals for new regular diplomatic liaison.

7. They declare their determination to contribute actively to conventional, nuclear and chemical arms control and disarmament agreements which enhance security and stability for all. In particular, they call for the early entry into force of the Treaty on Conventional Armed Forces in Europe and commit themselves to continue the process of strengthening peace in Europe through conventional arms control within the framework of the CSCE. They welcome the prospect of new negotiations between the United States and the Soviet Union on the reduction of their short-range nuclear forces.

8. They welcome the contribution that confidence- and security-building measures have made to lessening tensions and fully support the further development of such measures. They reaffirm the importance of the "Open Skies" initiative and their determination to bring the negotiations to a successful conclusion as soon as possible.

9. They pledge to work together with the other CSCE participating States to strengthen the CSCE process so that it can make an even greater contribution to security and stability in Europe. They recognize in particular the need to enhance political consultations among CSCE participants and to develop other CSCE mechanisms. They are convinced that the Treaty on Conventional Armed Forces in Europe and agreement on a substantial new set of CSBMs [Confidence and Security Building Measures], together with new patterns of co-operation in the framework of the CSCE, will lead to increased security and thus to enduring peace and stability in Europe.

10. They believe that the preceding points reflect the deep longing of their people for close co-operation and mutual understanding and declare that they will work steadily for the further development of their relations in accordance with the present Declaration as well as with the principles set forth in the Helsinki Final Act.

The original of this Declaration of which the English, French, German, Italian, Russian and Spanish texts are equally authentic will be transmitted to the Government of France which will retain it in its archives. The Government of France is requested to transmit the text of the Declaration to the Secretary-General of the United Nations, with a view to its circulation to all the members of the organization as an official document of the United Nations, indicating that it is not eligible for registration under Article 102 of the Charter of the United Nations. Each of the signatory States will receive from the Government of France a true copy of this Declaration.

CHAPTER 13

U.S. Relations with the Middle East: 1960s to the Present

Bruce R. Kuniholm

The two dominant issues confronting U.S. policymakers in the Middle East during the past thirty years have been the containment of the Soviet Union and the Arab-Israeli-Palestinian problem. The problem of containment must be seen within the historical context of Anglo-Russian rivalry in the region, a rivalry that was waged from the Balkans to Afghanistan. With the decline of the British Empire after World War II, the United States gradually assumed Britain's historic role of containing the Soviet Union.

By the 1960s, the British had withdrawn from the eastern Mediterranean (Greece, Turkey, Palestine, and Suez), and the United States had promulgated "doctrines" (the Truman and Eisenhower doctrines) that committed it to maintaining the balance of power in the Near East. On November 29, 1967, the last British troops left Aden (now part of the Republic of Yemen), and within a month Prime Minister Harold Wilson announced a similar withdrawal from "east of Suez" before the end of 1971. (doc. 1)

The Nixon administration, burdened by the war in Vietnam, was deeply concerned by Britain's impending withdrawal and shortly after taking office initiated a major review of U.S. policy in the Persian Gulf. The focus of the review was the question of how the "Nixon Doctrine," first enunciated by President Richard M. Nixon during informal remarks in Guam in July 1969, could best be applied to the region. As more clearly articulated in November 1969 (doc. 2), the Nixon Doctrine specified that the United States would furnish military and economic assistance to nations whose freedom was threatened but would expect those nations to assume primary responsibility for their own defense. The result of the policy review was the president's endorsement in November 1970 of the "twin-pillar" policy. Its rationale was that the United States had strategic interests in Iran (which American officials recognized as the region's predominant power) and Saudi Arabia. Because exclusive support for either would alienate the other, it was better to support both.

The twin-pillar policy was affected by several factors. Because Iran was willing to fill the vacuum left by the British and to pay for the necessary equipment out of its own revenues, President Nixon in May 1972 acquiesced in the desire of the shah, Mohammad Reza Shah Pahlavi, to obtain advanced American aircraft and insisted upon elimination of review procedures regarding what military equipment Iran could acquire. Controversy over whether this U.S. commitment was open-ended began after the policy (only partially revealed in doc. 3) was called into question by Secretary of Defense James Schlesinger in August 1975 and continued in the aftermath of the 1979 Iranian revolution, when critics cited it as one of the revolution's causes. Former Secretary of State Henry Kissinger argued that the commitment (never made public) was not open-ended and that arms sales to Iran were needed to maintain the balance of power. In retrospect, however, it seems clear that expenditures on high-technology military equipment were excessive in relation to international need. The exposed profile of many technical and advisory personnel necessary to make sophisticated equipment operational was a fundamental part of the shah's burgeoning domestic problems.

One event that facilitated the shah's massive purchases of U.S. weapons was the October 1973 Arab-Israeli (Yom Kippur) war. In the early 1970s, the region's oil-producing states were acquiring increased control over their oil resources. The most important benchmark of their success was the Arab embargo on oil shipments to the United States and the Netherlands that began during the 1973 war. Although the shah did not use Iranian oil to exert political pressure on the United States, he took advantage of increased oil production and a quadrupling of oil prices to increase expenditures on arms. Whereas the value of arms agreements between 1950 and 1972 amounted to slightly over $1.6 billion, in the next four years they totaled over $11.6 billion. The shah's massive arms expenditures, coupled with Iran's lack of a developed infrastructure and its shortage of trained manpower, magnified the opportunities for waste, corruption, and inefficiency. Fluctuations in the international oil market, meanwhile, wreaked havoc with Iran's overheated economy and contributed to the progressive breakdown of the economic and social system, which lacked any meaningful structures for political participation.

The twin-pillar framework served as the basis for U.S. policy in the Persian Gulf until 1979, when the Iranian revolution and the Soviet invasion of Afghanistan forced the United States to reexamine its policies. If there is a consensus among scholars about the causes of the Iranian revolution, it is that support for Ayatollah Ruhollah Khomeini derived less from what he stood for than from what he opposed: the Pahlavi regime, the monarchy itself, Western cultural domination, and foreign control (epitomized in Iranian eyes by the CIA's overthrow of Prime Minister Muhammad Musaddiq in 1953—see chap. 9). Khomeini's opposition to the Status of Forces Agreement of 1964 between the United States and Iran, for example, focused on its allowing the United States exclusive criminal jurisdiction over all American personnel in Iran. He was exiled because of his opposition and never forgave the United States for its role in the episode. Whatever its causes, the Iranian revolution undermined the twin-pillar policy that had been followed with little change by Presidents Gerald R. Ford and Jimmy Carter and raised serious questions about the central premise on U.S. policy—that regional states should be primarily responsible for their own defense.

In this context, the Carter administration developed for the region a security framework that essentially included an increased naval presence, an improved capability to introduce rapidly deployed forces, and access to military facilities in the area (as well as coordination with NATO allies) in order to support a broadened contingency capability. The Iranian seizure of American hostages in November 1979, followed by the aborted attempt to rescue them in April 1980, exposed the limitations on U.S. capacity to project power in the region.

The Soviet invasion of Afghanistan in December 1979, meanwhile, underscored the limitations on America's capabilities and revolutionized the geopolitical picture in the region. The Soviets apparently sought to prevent the certain collapse of a Marxist regime in Kabul and to replace a recalcitrant leader with one who was more responsive to Moscow's bidding. In so doing, they were concerned about their own security interests, the effects of a failure to take action on their own Muslim population, and the international implications of perceived Soviet weakness. Even though the invasion may have been motivated by defensive concerns, however, it also presented offensive possibilities for incursions into neighboring areas and made more urgent for the United States the development of a strategic framework that had been under discussion since the fall of the shah. That framework was fleshed out after President Carter explained its rationale in his State of the Union Message of January 21, 1980 (doc. 4), and his State of the Union Address of January 23, 1980 (doc. 5), a paragraph of which became known as the "Carter Doctrine."

The Carter Doctrine served notice to the Soviets that the "Persian Gulf region" was of vital importance to the United States; in a departure from the Nixon Doctrine, the United States clearly assumed ultimate responsibility for regional defense. Less clear was the area encompassed by the "Persian Gulf region." Pakistan, for example, sought but received no clarification as to whether it was included. The president's lack of precision, however, was not ill-considered. It was advisable to be wary of undertaking a commitment that could not be met. That the region was vital to the West and that regional insecurity required some kind of American commitment was unquestionable. Until the security framework was broadened, the Carter Doctrine served as a useful deterrent.

The Carter Doctrine defined a U.S. stake in the Persian Gulf region. In the Reagan administration, a focus on terrorism—the Soviet Union was perceived as one of the main sources—went hand in hand with Secretary of

State Alexander Haig's desire to "establish a consensus in the strategic-regional sense among the states of the area, stretching from Pakistan in the east to Egypt in the west, including Turkey, Israel, and other threatened states." (doc. 6) Despite more ambitious goals and a change in rhetoric ("strategic consensus," a term inaccurately drawn from Haig's testimony, for a time replaced "security framework" until it was recognized that there was no regional consensus on strategy), the Reagan administration essentially continued and consolidated the security framework initiated by its predecessors. Saudi Arabia now emerged as the new cornerstone of U.S. policy in the gulf and became the focus of the Reagan "corollary" to the Carter Doctrine (that is, the United States would not permit Saudi Arabia "to be an Iran"). During President Ronald Reagan's tenure, airstrips in the region were enlarged, facilities overbuilt, and matériel positioned in selected locations. The United States also secured access to bases and logistical support systems in Oman, Somalia, Kenya, and Egypt.

The Reagan administration, like the Carter administration, also sought to shore up Pakistan and Turkey and to ensure the channeling of covert assistance through Pakistan to Afghanistan. Concerns about nuclear proliferation, which had generated the Symington (1976) and Glenn (1977) amendments to the Foreign Assistance Act of 1961 (docs. 7 and 8), were temporarily put aside as strategic considerations made the region the most important to the United States outside of Europe. Indeed, Pakistan, Turkey, Israel, and Egypt became the four largest recipients of U.S. assistance. In Pakistan, President Mohammad Zia ul-Haq, who had rejected the Carter administration's offer of $400 million as "peanuts," subsequently accepted the Reagan administration's $3.2 billion assistance program. The White House hoped that the threat of the program's cancellation would impede a Pakistani decision to conduct a so-called peaceful nuclear explosion.

A U.S.-Turkey Defense and Economic Cooperation Agreement (DECA), signed in March 1980, somewhat assuaged Turkish bitterness over previous U.S. policies on the Cyprus question, which involved the clash of two ethnic groups divided by language, religion, and a history of hostility. The Greek Cypriots (roughly 80 percent of the population) wanted Cyprus to be a Hellenistic state and to dominate the island via a strong federal government. The Turkish Cypriots, the minority, sought to protect their own interests. The chief causes of Turkish acrimony were a letter from President Lyndon B. Johnson to Prime Minister Ismet Inonu in June 1964 (doc. 9) that prevented Turkish intervention on behalf of its minority on Cyprus during the crisis of 1963–64 and the congressional embargo on transfers of military equipment to Turkey (doc. 10) in reaction to its intervention in Cyprus during another crisis a decade afterward. In July 1974 Turkey had occupied the island to protect the Turkish minority from the so-called Hellenic Republic of Cyprus that was led by an international terrorist, installed by a coup, backed by the military dictatorship in Athens, and bent on union with Greece. A second Turkish intervention in August precipitated the U.S.

embargo. The Turks argued that their intervention was necessary to consolidate vulnerable positions, but the Greeks accused the Turks of trying to expand their base.

In reaction to the embargo, the Turks suspended U.S. operations at military installations in Turkey and made explicit what had been implicit until then: access to facilities in Turkey was directly related to U.S. decisions on military assistance. The embargo was eventually lifted on September 26, 1978. The importance of these military facilities for monitoring Soviet strategic nuclear activities, brought home by the loss of important monitoring stations in Iran following the fall of the shah in January 1979, was underscored by a supplemental agreement to the DECA in 1980. U.S.-Turkish relations were not impeded by the November 15, 1983, proclamation of the Turkish Republic of Northern Cyprus, which UN Security Council Resolution 541 called on all states not to recognize. (doc. 11) They were threatened, however, by a proposed congressional resolution that called for a day of remembrance for the alleged ''genocide'' of Armenians by Ottoman Turks in 1915. The resolution was narrowly defeated in early 1990, which helped preserve the U.S.-Turkish alliance, a valuable asset during the gulf war that began later that year.

Meanwhile, U.S. assistance to Afghanistan and Afghanistan's decentralized tribal system combined to thwart the Soviet occupation. Benefiting from the more pragmatic policies of a new Soviet leader, Mikhail Gorbachev, the Afghan resistance effected Soviet withdrawal. Like President Carter earlier, Gorbachev recognized the limits on his capacity to project power into the region. After six years of negotiations, Afghanistan and Pakistan signed the Geneva Accords (doc. 12) on April 14, 1988, with the United States and the Soviet Union as guarantors. Following Soviet withdrawal from Afghanistan in February 1989, differing interpretations of the Geneva Accords led the United States and the Soviet Union to exchange accusations of bad faith in the UN Security Council. But as the perception abated that each constituted a threat to the other's interests in the Middle East, the war in Afghanistan (which had cost over a million lives) continued among the Afghans. Five million Afghan refugees in Pakistan and Iran awaited its end.

During the Afghan war, Iran and Iraq fought another war that lasted almost as long and was almost as costly. The war began on September 22, 1980, in part because of the threat posed to Iraq by Khomeini's revolutionary ideology; Iraqi President Saddam Hussein's regional ambitions and belief in Iran's vulnerability; and opposing interpretations of the Algiers Agreement of March 1975. (doc. 13) Hussein was also bitter that past weakness, combined with his need in 1975 to terminate Iranian assistance to Kurdish rebels (mostly Sunni Muslims) in northern Iraq, had forced him to abandon Iraq's claim to full sovereignty over the Shatt al-Arab waterway (sanctioned by treaty in 1937 but disavowed by the shah in 1970) and to agree at Algiers that the boundary between Iran and Iraq should be the median line of the deepest navigational channel.

The Iran-Iraq war, which cost as many as a million lives, involved the use of ballistic missiles and poison gas and caused damage to over 400 ships, a loss equal to half the total tonnage sunk in World War II. Early attempts to mediate the war (when Iraq was winning) were to no avail; Iran saw Security Council Resolution 479 (doc. 14) as pro-Iraqi because it did not link a cease-fire to a withdrawal of forces to recognized boundaries.

Those attempting to mediate the war found it virtually impossible to be neutral. To support freedom of the seas or a cease-fire at sea favored Iran, because either measure kept Iran's economy going and allowed Iran (which had carried the war into Iraqi territory by 1982) to continue the war. To protect Kuwaiti tankers as nonbelligerents favored the Iraqi war effort. To call for a general cease-fire, as did Security Council Resolution 598 (doc. 15), also favored Iraq—Iran would be unable to deliver the final blow to Iraq and would go to the peace table short of achieving its aims. From the U.S. government's point of view, it was not advantageous for either side to win; despite the contradictory example of the Iran-*contra* fiasco, in which the United States sent covert arms shipments to Iran, U.S. policy required that Iraq contain Iran. As a result, the United States sought mandatory enforcement measures against the side not willing to accept a cease-fire, negotiations, and withdrawal to international borders. Ultimately, the economic and psychological costs of the war, coupled with Iraq's effective resistance and a U.S.-Soviet rapprochement, led the ailing Khomeini to accept on July 18, 1988, a cease-fire based on Security Council Resolution 598—a step that he characterized as ''more deadly for me than taking poison,'' but a step that ended one of the postwar world's bloodiest wars.

Approximately two years later, on August 2, 1990, Iraqi forces under Saddam Hussein invaded and occupied Kuwait. Hussein had long been extraordinarily ambitious and had aspired to be the leader of the Arab world, which had in part motivated his disastrous invasion of Iran ten years before. The eight-year war had caused him to incur a $70 billion debt; he now needed money to rebuild his economy and subsidize the large army and police state that ensured his continuation in power. He felt that other Arab countries were ungrateful for his role in containing revolutionary Iran, and he wanted to cancel his debt to the Kuwaitis (who angered him by overproducing their OPEC (Organization of Petroleum Exporting Countries) quotas, thus forcing oil prices down). He also saw the end of the Cold War as the end of any Soviet restraints on his ambitions and indeed the legitimization of them, because there was no one left to restrain what he saw as an Israeli-American alliance.

Hussein apparently had other objectives as well. In all probability, after incorporating Kuwait (and doubling his 10 percent share of the world's oil reserves), he hoped to intimidate, if not invade, Saudi Arabia, and thereby control over half of the world's crude oil reserves. This would have given him the capacity to determine the international price of oil; to undercut attempts to seek alternative sources of energy by making massive investments periodically cost-ineffective; to disrupt the international economy; to become a dominant regional power; and to continue playing on the alleged threat of Zionism and imperialism to justify the use of his expanding arsenal. His ultimate aim, as evidenced by his public speeches, was to become the leader of the Arab world. As such he would have posed a serious threat to every country in the region that opposed him and, ultimately, to the United States.

Hussein, meanwhile, apparently felt that the United States would not react immediately and in force, given its performance in Iran in 1979–80, in Lebanon in 1983–84, and its initial reluctance—changed only by Kuwaiti willingness to look to the Soviets as an alternative—to put Kuwaiti tankers under U.S. flags in 1986–87. That the United States had tilted toward Iraq during the Iran-Iraq war (which Hussein had started but which he then appeared to be losing) may have encouraged Hussein's cynicism and led him to believe that the international community would do little to oppose him.

The UN Security Council, prodded by U.S. initiatives, responded to the Iraqi attack by adopting a series of resolutions, the first of which, Resolution 660 (doc. 16), condemned the invasion and demanded Iraq's immediate and unconditional withdrawal from Kuwait. Subsequent resolutions called for an embargo against Iraq, rejected the validity of Iraq's claims, and called upon member states to enforce the embargo. On November 29, 1990, in a meeting attended by the foreign ministers of all the permanent members of the Security Council, the Security Council approved Resolution 678 (doc. 17), which authorized "all necessary means" to uphold and implement Resolution 660 and subsequent relevant resolutions unless Iraq withdrew from Kuwait by January 15, 1991.

The United States responded to Iraqi aggression by deploying military forces to Saudi Arabia. The most concrete reason was that the Persian Gulf contains over half of the world's trillion barrels of oil reserves. The possession of oil resources has extremely important international implications, and to treat oil as a commodity that one might or might not choose to buy is to trivialize what was at stake in the gulf—a trivialization most vividly exemplified by those who opposed U.S. involvement with the slogan "no blood for oil." If Hussein had been allowed to occupy Kuwait and intimidate Saudi Arabia, he would have controlled their oil resources. In the past ten years Hussein had spent an estimated $50 billion on armaments. He had acquired chemical and biological weapons (as well as systems that could deliver them); he had attempted to build nuclear weapons; and he had shown a willingness to use his weapons, in some cases on his own people.

The United States had made clear commitments to defend its vital interests in the region starting with the Carter Doctrine in 1980. U.S. officials believed that if they refused to honor their commitments in a region where their vital interests were at stake (one of many factors that differentiates the gulf crisis from the war in Vietnam), serious questions would have been raised about the trustworthiness of the United States as an ally. The world was entering a new, post-Cold War era in which the traditional balance of power in the region could no longer be relied upon to stabilize crises once they developed. Indeed, it is probable that if the Soviets had not had serious internal problems at this time and had still been a world power, Iraq would never have invaded Kuwait. The future of a new international order, the sanctity of which was being tested in the face of Hussein's unilateral use of force, was believed to be hanging in the balance, despite skepticism about the feasibility of that new international order. The combination of principle, commitment, vital interest, and capability—the United States had spent the ten years since the Carter Doctrine gearing up for such contingencies—suggested that if the United States and the international community did not respond to this situation, it was not clear when they would ever respond to any contingency, and what destabilizing behavior they would invite.

Once Hussein had been deterred from intimidating or attacking Saudi Arabia (by UN resolutions as well as by the deployment of U.S. and coalition forces to the region), the developing international coalition led by the United States confronted the problem of getting Iraq to withdraw from Kuwait. The question then was whether—and if so, when—military action would be necessary to force Iraq's withdrawal. Following passage of UN Security Council Resolution 678, President George Bush, on January 8, 1991, asked Congress for a resolution supporting the UN resolution. Four days later, after a vigorous and thoughtful debate, a joint congressional resolution (doc. 18) authorized the president, in accordance with Security Council Resolution 678, to use military force to implement earlier relevant resolutions. On January 16, after Secretary of State James Baker had failed to persuade the Iraqis that they must withdraw from Kuwait without condition or delay, and after Iraq had failed to meet the deadline set by Resolution 678, the United States, in conjunction with a number of the members of the 28-country alliance, launched "Operation Desert Storm" with an air attack on military targets in Iraq and occupied Kuwait.

On February 23 President Bush authorized the use of all forces available to eject the Iraqi army from Kuwait. By midnight on February 27–28, 100 hours after the start of ground operations and six weeks after the war had begun, Kuwait had been liberated, combat operations were suspended, and a provisional cease-fire began to take hold. For the allied coalition, casualties were light, numbering slightly over 300 dead. Iraqi casualties are difficult to estimate but may have numbered as many as a 100,000 dead. On April 3, 1991, Security Council Resolution 687 (doc. 19) set the terms of the cease-fire with regard to boundaries, the destruction of weapons, compensation by Iraq for war damage, and the lifting of economic sanctions. It also initiated a process that led to the creation of the UN Iraq-Kuwait Observation Mission. On April 10 Iraq formally accepted Resolution 687 and the provisional cease-fire became official.

But problems persisted, for in the meantime, a Kurdish rebellion in the north and a Shiite rebellion in the south of Iraq were crushed by Hussein's remaining forces, causing as many as two million refugees to flee to the Iranian and Turkish borders. Following Security Council Resolution 688 (doc. 20), which condemned Iraq's repression of its civilian population and which appealed for humanitarian relief efforts, the United States, again in conjunction with a number of coalition forces, launched an enormous relief effort on April 5 to assist the refugees. By the end of June, a terrible refugee situation had improved somewhat, and allied forces pursuing relief efforts in the safe havens of northern Iraq were hoping to turn over some of their protection and relief activities to the United Nations. Saddam Hussein, however, was still in power, negotiating with the Kurds once more on their status within Iraq. The embargo, meanwhile, was still in effect, and the allied coalition was strongly critical of Iraq's failure to comply with the conditions of the cease-fire.

As the postwar crisis continued, U.S. officials in the gulf continued to explore security arrangements, acknowledging the desirability of economic development in the region and emphasizing the necessity of a regional balance of power undergirded by a credible deterrent. They focused in particular on mechanisms for preventing the acquisition of excessive conventional forces and controlling weapons of mass destruction. Concerns that had generated the Symington and Glenn amendments were now expanded: India and Israel, of course, already possessed nuclear weapons. Pakistan now had the capacity to build them, and Iraq's nuclear ambitions were still being uncovered. In conjunction with the devastation wrought by the war in the gulf and the proliferation of poison gas and ballistic missiles throughout the Middle East and Southwest Asia, these expanded concerns underscored the need for arms control in the region, for the settlement of affairs between states on both regional and international levels, and for security arrangements that would keep the peace.

* * * *

We can now turn to the Arab-Israeli-Palestinian problem by focusing first on the Arab-Israeli war of 1967, which, like the 1948 and 1956 wars, had its roots in Israel's search for security and the Palestinians' drive for a homeland and self-determination. UN Security Council Resolution 242 (doc. 21), which was carefully worked out in the aftermath of the 1967 war, has become an important, if ambiguous, reference point for subsequent peace initiatives. The most problematic issues, from an Israeli point of view, have been "the inadmissibility of the acquisition of territory by war" (which Prime Minister Menachem Begin subsequently told President Carter he could not agree to under any circumstances) and whether "withdrawal of Israeli armed forces from territories" meant all or just some territories.

Most problematic for the Palestinians has been the reference to them simply as "the refugee problem," which constitutes a denial of their identity dating back to the Balfour Declaration of 1917 that referred to them as a "non-Jewish" community even though they constituted approximately 90 percent of the population. Also problematic has been their refusal until recently to accept Israel's right to exist. The fundamental notion undergirding Resolution 242 is that occupied territory should be given back and that (unlike Israel's withdrawal from the Sinai after the 1956 war with Egypt) it should be accompanied by the assurance of peace: territory, in effect, should be exchanged for peace.

The 1967 war had a profound effect on the Middle East. Israel's decisive victory allowed it to occupy the Golan Heights (previously part of Syria); the West Bank, including East Jerusalem (previously part of Jordan); the Gaza Strip and the Sinai Peninsula (previously part of Egypt). To some observers, Egyptian President Gamal Abdel Nasser's humiliating defeat signaled the end of Pan-Arabism; the Palestinians, many of whom once again became refugees, began to rely on themselves to solve their own problems. The Palestine Liberation Organization (PLO), founded in May 1964 under the leadership of a pro-Nasser orator who had threatened to throw the Jews into the sea, was now taken over by the guerrilla organization al-Fatah and its leader, Yasir Arafat. The revised Palestinian National Charter (doc. 22), adopted by the Palestine National Council in 1968, endorsed armed struggle to liberate and exercise total sovereignty over "Palestine" (that is, Israel *and* the occupied territories). The UN partition of Palestine in 1947 and the establishment of the state of Israel, the charter asserted, were illegal.

UN Security Council Resolution 338 (doc. 23), which was passed during the October 1973 war, again called for the implementation of Security Council Resolution 242. The war was followed by Secretary of State Henry Kissinger's step-by-step diplomacy that was motivated in part by a desire to defuse a situation that could escalate into a great-power conflict and also by an interest in terminating the oil embargo. Disengagement agreements were achieved between Israel and Egypt (on January 18, 1974) and between Israel and Syria (on May 31, 1974). The Palestinians were ignored, but the Arab states met at Rabat, Morocco, and on October 29, 1974, endorsed the PLO's role as "the sole legitimate representative of the Palestinian people." (doc. 24)

Kissinger proceeded to negotiate a second Israeli-Egyptian disengagement agreement (often referred to as "Sinai II") that was signed on September 1, 1975. A memorandum of agreement between Israel and the United States (doc. 25) that was part of Sinai II stipulated the conditions under which the United States could recognize and negotiate with the PLO. The memorandum did not, however, deter a trial balloon on the Palestinian problem. In November 1975, Kissinger approved a statement by Deputy Assistant Secretary of State Harold Saunders declaring the Palestine problem to be the "heart" of the Arab-Israeli conflict. But when confronted by hostile pro-Israeli reaction, Kissinger dismissed the statement reportedly cleared by President Ford as an "academic and theoretical exercise."

When Jimmy Carter became president, he discarded the step-by-step approach in favor of a more comprehensive one that addressed both the Palestinian question and his commitment to human rights. Preempted by Egyptian President Anwar el-Sadat's dramatic decision to go to Jerusalem and address the Israeli Knesset on November 20, 1977, Carter now focused on an agreement between Egypt and Israel. Lengthy negotiations resulted in the Camp David Accords (doc. 26) of September 17, 1978. The accords consisted of a set of procedures for resolving the Palestinian problem and an outline of the principles for a peace treaty between Egypt and Israel. Carter apparently believed that the ambiguous formulation of "autonomy" for the Palestinians would somehow allow for a solution that fulfilled what he saw as the legitimate objectives of both Palestinians and Israelis.

Prime Minister Begin's goals (docs. 27 and 28) appear to have been both different and more limited: a separate peace with Egypt (in which the Sinai would be traded for peace) and, along with rejection of a Palestinian state, a free hand for Israel in the rest of the occupied territories (the Golan Heights, Gaza Strip, and West Bank, which he referred to as Judea and Samaria). From a Palestinian perspective, "full autonomy" was a euphemism for Israeli control. From the Israeli government's perspective, full autonomy meant a limited form of "sovereignty" that was to be exercised by the "inhabitants" of that land over themselves—not over the land itself. Begin subsequently reserved the right to assert Israel's claim of sovereignty to all of the West Bank in negotiations on its final status.

As a result of these differing perspectives, the set of procedures for resolving the Palestinian problem was stillborn. Linkage between the two frameworks of the Camp David agreements, which Sadat had sought, was never effected. What was achieved was a separate peace between Egypt and Israel, which was signed on March 26, 1979 (doc. 29), and implemented over the next three years (when the Sinai was returned to Egypt). If the peace treaty gave Israel greater security in the region and decreased the likelihood of not only an Arab-Israeli war, but a U.S.-Soviet confrontation as well, the Palestinian problem remained unresolved. The PLO presence in Lebanon, the result of decades of displacement and its relocation after being crushed by Jordan's King Hussein in 1970, now became the object of Israeli Defense Minister Ariel Sharon's attention. His determination to crush the PLO in Lebanon, gain a freer hand with Palestinians on the West Bank, drive the Syrians out of Lebanon, and ensure Christian Maronite supremacy there all led to Israel's invasion of Lebanon in June 1982.

After the United States had helped to mediate the Israeli-Palestinian conflict and evacuate the PLO, President Reagan in September 1982 proposed still another plan for resolving the Palestinian problem. (doc. 30) The United States would not support Israeli annexation of the West Bank and Gaza, nor would it support the creation of a Palestinian state in those territories. Expressing the belief that peace must be based on Security Council

Resolution 242's formula of territory for peace, Reagan proposed a compromise between Israeli and Palestinian desires: self-government by the Palestinians in association with Jordan, with the extent of Israeli withdrawal determined by the quality of peace offered in return.

This so-called Jordan option was never a success. The peace process was overshadowed by the continuing civil war in Lebanon, where the Reagan administration's pro-Maronite policies generated a negative reaction (including the bombing of a U.S. Marine barracks in Beirut) that forced the United States to redeploy its limited military commitment. The effort was also impeded by domestic politics in Israel, where differences between the Labor and Likud parties did not augur well for any peace initiatives.

The Jordan option was effectively undermined by the Palestinian uprising, or *intifada*, which began in the West Bank and Gaza in December 1987, and by King Hussein's withdrawal of all claims to and responsibility for the West Bank, which he turned over to the Palestinians in July 1988. (doc. 31) Together these developments focused attention on the Palestinians themselves and their call for a Palestinian state in the occupied territories.

On November 15, 1988, in a speech before the Palestine National Council (PNC) in Algiers, PLO Chairman Arafat proclaimed the establishment of a Palestinian state (doc. 32), based on the 1947 UN General Assembly Resolution 181, which had partitioned Palestine into two states. The acceptance of a two-state solution in effect abrogated a number of elements in the Palestinian National Charter that had been objectionable to the Israelis and rooted the legitimacy of the Palestinian state in a UN resolution that also served as the basis for the legitimacy of Israel. The "Political Communiqué" of the PNC (doc. 33), adopted two days later, called for an international peace conference, convened on the basis of Security Council Resolutions 242 (which meant implicitly recognizing the existence of Israel within its pre-1967 borders) and 338.

Both the Palestinian declaration of independence and the Political Communiqué were adopted by a vote of 253 to 46, with 10 abstentions. Those who voted against the two documents nonetheless accepted the majority verdict. In December 1988, Arafat satisfied U.S. conditions specified in Sinai II (to which had been added the rejection of terrorism) for direct talks between the PLO and U.S. representatives, and talks began in Tunis later in the month. In April 1989, as the *intifada* continued, Arafat was unanimously elected by the PLO Executive Committee as the first president of the Palestinian state until democratic elections could take place.

In Israel, a coalition government, led by Prime Minister Yitzhak Shamir and prodded by the United States, proposed on May 14, 1989, a four-point plan (doc. 34) that included a call for elections in the occupied territories. The idea was to choose Palestinian leaders who would negotiate a plan for limited self-rule and participate in negotiations aimed at a final peace settlement.

Soon afterward, Secretary of State Baker, in an address to the

American-Israel Public Affairs Committee (doc. 35), called on Israel to forswear annexation, to stop settlement activity, and to "lay aside, once and for all, the unrealistic vision of a greater Israel." At the same time, he called on Palestinians to practice constructive diplomacy. Throughout the rest of 1989, Shamir's plan served as a basis for discussions among the United States, Egypt, and Israel. Despite attempts by Egyptian President Hosni Mubarak to advance Israel's election proposal with his own ten-point plan (doc. 36), there was little progress. In October, Baker presented five "suggested" points (doc. 37) in a futile effort to open a dialogue between Israel and a Palestinian delegation. Israel, which rejected Mubarak's plan, "accepted" Baker's points, but with conditions (e.g., the PLO must be excluded from the process, and talks would be limited to details of Israel's election proposal) that were tantamount to rejection. These conditions were unacceptable to the secretary of state even before the Israelis had formally adopted them and, as a result, were rejected.

Shamir's foot-dragging on his own plan led many, even in Israel, to believe that his plan was a smokescreen intended to preclude Israel's having to confront two fundamental questions: Would Israelis allow the Palestinians to choose their own representatives? If negotiations ever took place, would the Likud party be willing to trade territory for peace? Eventually, in March 1990, the Israeli coalition government broke up over the inability of the Labor and Likud parties to agree on Baker's plan for Israeli-Palestinian talks. The subsequent impasse in forming a government raised serious doubt about Israel's capacity to address fundamental differences between Labor and Likud without parliamentary reform.

The following May of 1990, the Israelis foiled a Palestinian guerrilla attack on Israel. When Arafat failed to condemn the attack or discipline those who were responsible for it, President Bush in June suspended the eighteen-month U.S.-PLO dialogue. In the same month, Shamir forged a new government that was considered to be the most conservative in Israeli history. As a result, no progress was made in the peace talks. In August 1990, after Iraq invaded Kuwait, Palestinian support for Saddam Hussein, explained (if not excused) by frustration over the failure to make any progress on the peace process, further complicated attempts to address the problem. Many in Israel who had been supportive of accommodation with the Palestinians developed serious misgivings about the possibility of a settlement. As the *intifada* ended its third year, over 700 Palestinians and over 50 Israelis had been killed. Subsequent Iraqi SCUD missile attacks on Israel in 1991, which were cheered by Palestinians, further divided Arabs and Jews.

In the aftermath of the gulf crisis, Arafat's wartime support for Saddam Hussein seriously compromised the dialogue that the Bush administration hoped to effect between the Palestinians and Israelis and led to a search for other interlocutors. Jordan's King Hussein initially may have been snubbed for his position on the gulf crisis, but if his reputation suffered in the West, the legitimacy of his rule was enhanced within his own country as well as among the Palestinians. He may yet serve a useful role as an intermediary. The United States, meanwhile, attempted to foster an Israeli-Palestinian dialogue, but concentrated primarily on state-to-state relations, in particular on a rapprochement between Israel and Syria. This "two-track" approach (docs. 38 and 39) focused primarily on procedural questions and avoided substantive issues.

The Israeli government preferred to avoid substantive questions, such as Israel's commitment to exchange territory for peace, because Prime Minister Shamir had no intention of doing so—particularly not before negotiations had begun. The Israelis wanted the Arab states first to forswear their state of belligerency against Israel and to renounce the boycott of Israel; Israelis also sought protection against premature pressure on them (hence their sensitivity about procedural questions) until the Arab states had demonstrated convincingly that they were committed to peace. Israelis wanted this demonstration to take place not only in the context of face-to-face negotiations but also in stages that could be implemented over time so as to ensure that they were not trading valuable assets for rhetoric.

Syria, on the other hand, wanted a commitment by Israel to exchange territory for peace. Without such a commitment, and a mechanism such as an ongoing international conference to push negotiations along, the Syrians envisaged being drawn into protracted negotiations where they would be stonewalled by the Israelis. The Syrians were concerned that such negotiations would lead nowhere and that, in the process, the status quo would be legitimized.

In this context, the United States appeared to be unwilling to risk pushing the peace process forward beyond a certain point and thus take a stand on some of the substantive issues in question. Although the administration recognized that U.S. interests in the Persian Gulf would be facilitated by progress toward an Arab-Israeli peace, the costs of President Bush's personal investment in the peace process (which would be necessary to make it move forward) appeared to be too great in view of the intractability of the problem and the small likelihood of success. As a result, the administration emphasized procedure—a Middle East peace conference co-sponsored by the United States and the Soviet Union. As of mid-October 1991, the talks were set to take place later that month in Madrid.

The Arab-Israeli-Palestinian problem, meanwhile, promises to be exacerbated by the massive influx of Soviet immigrants into Israel (200,000 arrived in 1990 and possibly as many as 400,000 were expected to arrive in each of the following two years) as well as by Israel's aggressive settlement policies and the continuing plight of the Palestinians in the occupied territories. Israel's housing needs will lead it to request $10 billion in loan guarantees from the United States, and the Palestinians will have to turn to others for assistance. Both of their needs will provide opportunities to structure incentives and clarify choices, but leadership will be required.

As the Cold War seemingly draws to an end, U.S. recognition of limited Soviet capacities to project power along the Northern Tier of the Middle East has diminished the importance of containing Soviet influence in the region. As the Soviet Union focuses on its internal problems and the need for stability on its borders, U.S. concern for the problem of containment has given way to a recognition that common interests dictate a more constructive attitude toward nuclear proliferation, arms control, and regional conflicts (such as that between India and Pakistan over Kashmir, or Iran and Iraq over a host of issues).

Not least among the regional conflicts that could threaten stability in the region is the continuing Arab-Israeli-Palestinian problem. The implications of a rapprochement between the United States and the Soviet Union for a peaceful settlement of the problem are positive in the sense that the two countries are the chief suppliers of weaponry to Israel and its main adversaries (Syria and Iraq). Whether growing cooperation along the Northern Tier can extend to this divisive conflict, however, with its complicated local, regional, and international components, remains to be seen.

Document 1

United Kingdom, House of Commons Debates, Jan. 16, 1968, vol. 756, columns 1577–84.

The Prime Minister (Mr. Harold Wilson): With permission, Mr. Speaker, I should like to make a statement.

1. On 18th December I informed the House that the Government were engaged in a major review of every field of public expenditure as one of the measures necessary to achieve a progressive and massive shift of resources from home consumption, public and private, to the requirements of exports, import replacement and productive investment.

2. This review has now been completed. Our purpose in this review is to make devaluation work, because until we do, until we are earning, year in and year out, a substantial surplus on our overseas payments, we are unable internally or externally to do all the things which, as a nation, we would like to do. But what this means for the immediate future is to ensure that we cut down our demands and our ambitions at home and abroad within the limits of what we can currently earn. At home, it means cutting back on excessive demands, both as individuals and as a community, and abroad it means reassessing our rôle in the world and realistically limiting our commitments and outgoings to our true capacities. On this basis, provided that our recovery is soundly based and lasting, we can go forward. The review we have undertaken, covering as it does our ambitions and expenditure at home, and our commitments and deployment abroad, is an essential step towards making these principles a reality. . . .

11. I begin with defence expenditure, the whole of which has been reviewed against the background of our commitments and alliances. Our decisions have been based on two main principles. First, the House will recognise that it is not only in our own interests but in those of our friends and allies for this

country to strengthen its economic base quickly and decisively. There is no military strength whether for Britain or for our alliances except on the basis of economic strength; and it is on this basis that we best ensure the security of this country. We therefore intend to make to the alliances of which we are members a contribution related to our economic capability while recognising that our security lies fundamentally in Europe and must be based on the North Atlantic Alliance. Second, reductions in capability, whether in terms of manpower or equipment, must follow and be based on a review of the commitments the Services are required to undertake. Defence must be related to the requirements of foreign policy, but it must not be asked in the name of foreign policy to undertake commitments beyond its capability. Major foreign policy decisions, therefore, are a prior requirement of economies in defence expenditure; and in taking these decisions we have to come to terms with our rôle in the world. It is not only at home that, these past years, we have been living beyond our means. Given the right decisions, above all given the full assertion of our economic strength, our real influence and power for peace will be strengthened by realistic priorities.

12. We have accordingly decided to accelerate the withdrawal of our forces from their stations in the Far East which was announced in the Supplementary Statement on Defence Policy of July 1967 (Cmnd. 3357) and to withdraw them by the end of 1971. We have also decided to withdraw our forces from the Persian Gulf by the same date. The broad effect is that, apart from our remaining Dependencies and certain other necessary exceptions, we shall by that date not be maintaining military bases outside Europe and the Mediterranean.

13. Again, by that date, we shall have withdrawn our forces from Malaysia and Singapore. We have told both Governments that we do not thereafter plan to retain a special military capability for use in the area. But we have assured them both, and our other Commonwealth partners and allies concerned, that we shall retain a general capability based in Europe—including the United Kingdom—which can be deployed overseas as, in our judgment, circumstances demand, including support for United Nations operations. . . .

14. We shall make an early reduction in the number of aircraft based in Cyprus while maintaining our membership of C.E.N.T.O. [Central Treaty Organization].

15. On the Gulf, we have indicated to the Governments concerned that our basic interest in the prosperity and security of the area remains; and, as I have said, the capability we shall be maintaining here will be available for deployment wherever, in our judgment, this is right having regard to the forces available.

16. As the House already knows, my right hon. Friend the Foreign Secretary has visited Washington to discuss our intentions with the United States Administration; and my right hon. Friend the Commonwealth Secretary has paid special visits to the four Commonwealth countries concerned with Far East defences so as to discuss with their Prime Ministers the intended changes in our political commitments and consequent military dispositions and the consequences flowing from them. My right hon. Friend the Minister of State, Foreign Office, has paid a special visit to the States of the Gulf for a similar purpose. Other Governments and Organisations concerned have already been made fully aware of our decisions. These decisions were taken in the knowledge, and in the light, of the views of our Commonwealth partners and of our allies directly concerned.

17. We recognise the deep feelings and anxieties of our allies and Commonwealth partners. We recognise, too, that these changes involve risks, but, in the circumstances, we believe they are risks that must be accepted. We are determined that our commitments, and the capacities of our forces to undertake them, should match and balance each other.

18. These decisions will entail major changes in the rôle, size and shape of the forces, in the nature and scale of the equipment which they will require, and in the supporting facilities which are necessary. Time will be needed to work out the precise implications: these will be embodied in a White Paper to be published and, if the House so wishes, debated later in the year. Nevertheless, I can now give some specific illustrations of the effects of our decisions in advance of the further detailed work. . . .

23. *Support facilities.* The more rapid withdrawal of our forces from outside Europe and the changes we intend to make in their rôle and equipment will impose a massive task on those responsible for providing the most efficient and economical logistic support for the three Services. Very substantial savings in base facilities staff overseas will follow as a consequence of withdrawal. The rundown in the forces will be increasingly reflected in reduced support facilities, such as training establishments in this country, but it is too early yet to indicate the extent of the total reduction of the United Kingdom base as a whole. In spite of the extra planning load placed upon it, we shall energetically continue the process of cutting the size of the Ministry of Defence.

Document 2

President Richard M. Nixon's address to the nation on the war in Vietnam, Nov. 3, 1969, *Public Papers of the Presidents of the United States* (hereafter referred to as PPP): *Richard M. Nixon, 1969,* Washington, D.C.: Government Printing Office, 1971, 905–6.

Now let me turn . . . to a more encouraging report on another front.

At the time we launched our search for peace I recognized we might not succeed in bringing an end to the war through negotiation. I, therefore, put into effect another plan to bring peace—a plan which will bring the war to an end regardless of what happens on the negotiating front.

It is in line with a major shift in U.S. foreign policy which I described in my press conference at Guam on July 25. Let me briefly explain what has been described as the Nixon Doctrine—a policy which not only will help end the war in Vietnam, but which is an essential element of our program to prevent future Vietnams.

We Americans are a do-it-yourself people. We are an impatient people. Instead of teaching someone else to do a job, we like to do it ourselves. And this trait has been carried over into our foreign policy.

In Korea and again in Vietnam, the United States furnished most of the money, most of the arms, and most of the men to help the people of those countries defend their freedom against Communist aggression.

Before any American troops were committed to Vietnam, a leader of another Asian country expressed this opinion to me when I was traveling in Asia as a private citizen. He said: "When you are trying to assist another nation defend its freedom, U.S. policy should be to help them fight the war but not to fight the war for them."

Well, in accordance with this wise counsel, I laid down in Guam three principles as guidelines for future American policy toward Asia:

—First, the United States will keep all of its treaty commitments.

—Second, we shall provide a shield if a nuclear power threatens the freedom of a nation allied with us or of a nation whose survival we consider vital to our security.

—Third, in cases involving other types of aggression, we shall furnish military and economic assistance when requested in accordance with our treaty commitments. But we shall look to the nation directly threatened to assume the primary responsibility of providing the manpower for its defense.

After I announced this policy, I found that the leaders of the Philippines, Thailand, Vietnam, South Korea, and other nations which might be threatened by Communist aggression, welcomed this new direction in American foreign policy.

The defense of freedom is everybody's business—not just America's business. And it is particularly the responsibility of the people whose freedom is threatened. In the previous administration, we Americanized the war in Vietnam. In this administration, we are Vietnamizing the search for peace.

The policy of the previous administration not only resulted in our assuming the primary responsibility for fighting the war, but even more significantly did not adequately stress the goal of strengthening the South Vietnamese so that they could defend themselves when we left.

Document 3

Joint communiqué following discussions in Teheran between President Richard M. Nixon and the shah of Iran, May 31, 1972, *PPP: Richard M. Nixon, 1972,* 1974, 651–52.

At the invitation of His Imperial Majesty the Shahanshah Arya Mehr and Her Imperial Majesty Shahbanou of Iran, the President of the United States of America and Mrs. Richard Nixon paid an official visit to Iran from May 30 to May 31, 1972. . . .

During his visit the President held discussions with His Imperial Majesty the Shahanshah in a warm and cordial atmosphere, reflecting the close and friendly relations that exist between the two countries.

The President and His Imperial Majesty discussed recent developments on the international scene. The President told His Imperial Majesty of his visits to Moscow and Peking and of his efforts to reduce East-West tensions and restore peace and stability to Southeast Asia. . . .

The President and His Imperial Majesty also discussed developments in the Middle East. They were gratified that a cease-fire continues to be observed but expressed their concern over the serious situation existing in the Middle East and reaffirmed their support for a peaceful settlement in accordance with Security Council Resolution 242.

The President and His Imperial Majesty agreed that the security and stability of the Persian Gulf is of vital importance to the littoral States. Both were of the view that the littoral States bore the primary responsibility for the security of the Persian Gulf.

His Imperial Majesty reaffirmed Iran's

determination to bear its share of this responsibility.

The President and His Imperial Majesty also agreed that the economic development and welfare of the bordering States of the Persian Gulf are of importance to the stability of the region. Iran declared itself ready and willing to cooperate with its neighbors in fostering an atmosphere in which stability and progress can flourish. . . .

The President expressed his admiration for Iran's impressive record in the development of a strong economy and the successful implementation of His Imperial Majesty's "White Revolution." . . . The President reiterated the readiness of the United States to cooperate with Iran as appropriate in this extensive program and important enterprise. . . .

Both sides expressed deep satisfaction over the excellence of relations between their two countries and the expectation that they would continue in the future. His Imperial Majesty stressed once again Iran's determination to strengthen its defensive capability to ensure the nation's security. The President confirmed that the United States would, as in the past, continue to cooperate with Iran in strengthening its defenses.

Document 4

President Jimmy Carter's State of the Union Message to Congress, Jan. 21, 1980, *PPP: Jimmy Carter, 1980–1981*, 1981, 114, 164–72.

My State of the Union Address will be devoted to a discussion of the most important challenges facing our country as we enter the 1980's.

Over the coming year, those challenges will receive my highest priority and greatest efforts. However, there will also be many other significant areas which will receive my personal commitment, as well as that of my Administration, during the 2nd Session of the 96th Congress.

It is important that Congress, along with the public, be aware of these other vital areas of concern as they listen to my State of the Union Address. In that way, the context of the Address, and my Administration's full message for 1980, can best be understood.

For that reason, I am sending this State of the Union Message to the Congress today, several days before my State of the Union Address. . . .

Enhancing National Security—
American Military Strength

The maintenance of national security is my first concern, as it has been for every President before me. . . .

We must pay whatever price is required to remain the strongest nation in the world. That price has increased as the military power of our major adversary has grown and its readiness to use that power been made all too evident in Afghanistan.

The U.S.-Soviet Relationship

We are demonstrating to the Soviet Union across a broad front that it will pay a heavy price for its aggression in terms of our relationship. Throughout the last decades U.S.-Soviet relations have been a mixture of cooperation and competition. The Soviet attack on Afghanistan and the ruthless extermination of its government have highlighted in the starkest terms the darker side of their policies—going well beyond competition and the legitimate pursuit of national interest, and violating all norms of international law and practice.

This attempt to subjugate an independent, non-aligned Islamic people is a callous violation of international law and the United Nations Charter, two fundamentals of international order. Hence, it is also a dangerous threat to world peace. For the first time since World War II, the Soviets have sent combat forces into an area that was not previously under their control, into a non-aligned and sovereign state.

On January 4 I therefore announced a number of measures, including the reduction of grain sales and the curtailment of trade and technology transfer, designed to demonstrate our firm opposition to Soviet actions in Afghanistan and to underscore our belief that in the face of this blatant transgression of international law, it was impossible to conduct business as usual. I have also been in consultation with our allies and with countries in the region regarding additional multilateral measures that might be taken to register our disapproval and bolster security in Southwest Asia. I have been heartened by the support expressed for our position, and by the fact that such support has been tangible, as well as moral.

The destruction of the independence of Afghanistan government and the occupation by the Soviet Union has altered the strategic situation in that part of the world in a very ominous fashion. It has brought the Soviet Union within striking distance of the Indian Ocean and even the Persian Gulf.

It has eliminated a buffer between the Soviet Union and Pakistan and presented a new threat to Iran. These two countries are now far more vulnerable to Soviet political intimidation. If that intimidation were to prove effective, the Soviet Union might well control an area of vital strategic and economic significance to the survival of Western Europe, the Far East, and ultimately the United States.

It is clear that the entire subcontinent of Asia and specifically Pakistan is threatened. Therefore, I am asking Congress, as the first order of business, to pass an economic and military aid package designed to assist Pakistan defend itself. . . .

Rapid Deployment Forces

We are systematically enhancing our ability to respond rapidly to non-NATO [North Atlantic Treaty Organization] contingencies wherever required by our commitments or when our vital interests are threatened.

The rapid deployment forces we are assembling will be extraordinarily flexible: They could range in size from a few ships or air squadrons to formations as large as 100,000 men, together with their support. Our forces will be prepared for rapid deployment to any region of strategic significance.

Among the specific initiatives we are taking to help us respond to crises outside of Europe are:

—the development and production of a new fleet of large cargo aircraft with intercontinental range;

—The design and procurement of a force of Maritime Prepositioning Ships that will carry heavy equipment and supplies for three Marine Corps brigades. . . .

Naval Forces

Seapower is indispensable to our global position—in peace and also in war. Our shipbuilding program will sustain a 550-ship Navy in the 1990s and we will continue to build the most capable ships afloat.

The program I have proposed will assure the ability of our Navy to operate in high threat areas, to maintain control of the seas and protect vital lines of communication—both military and economic—and to provide the strong maritime component of our rapid deployment forces. This is essential for operations in remote areas of the world, where we cannot predict far in advance the precise location of trouble, or preposition equipment on land. . . .

Regional Policies

Every President for over three decades has recognized that America's interests are global and that we must pursue a global foreign policy.

Two world wars have made clear our stake in Western Europe and the North Atlantic area. We are also inextricably linked with the Far East—politically, economically, and militarily. In both of these, the United States has a permanent presence and security commitments which would be automatically triggered. We have become increasingly conscious of our growing interests in a third area—the Middle East and the Persian Gulf area. . . .

Middle East—Persian Gulf—South Asia

Events in Iran and Afghanistan have dramatized for us the critical importance for American security and prosperity of the area running from the Middle East through the Persian Gulf to South Asia. This region provides two-thirds of the world's oil exports, supplying most of the energy needs of our allies in Europe and Japan. It has been a scene of almost constant conflict between nations, and of serious international instability within many countries. And now one of its nations has been invaded by the Soviet Union.

We are dealing with these multiple challenges in a number of ways.

Middle East

First, it has been a key goal of my Administration since 1977 to promote an enduring resolution of the Arab-Israeli conflict—which is so essential to bringing stability and peace to the entire region. Following the Camp David Summit of August 1978, in March 1979, I helped bring about the signing of a peace treaty between Egypt and Israel—the first time in 30 years of Middle East conflict that peace had shined with such a bright and promising flame. At the historic signing ceremony at the White House, Prime Minister [Menachem] Begin and President [Anwar el-]Sadat repeated their Camp David pledge to work for full autonomy for the West Bank and Gaza.

Since then Egypt and Israel have been working to complete this part of the Camp David framework and to provide an opportunity for the Palestinian people to participate in determining their future. I strongly support these efforts, and have pledged that we will be a full partner in the autonomy negotiations. We will continue to work vigorously for a comprehensive peace in the Middle East, building on the unprecedented achievements at Camp David.

At the same time, I have reinforced America's commitment to Israel's security, and to the right of all nations in the area to live at peace with their neighbors, within secure and recognized frontiers.

Persian Gulf

In recent years as our own fuel imports have soared, the Persian Gulf has become vital to the United States as it has been to many of our friends and allies. Over the longer term, the world's dependence on Persian Gulf oil is likely to increase. The denial of these oil supplies—to us or to others—would threaten our security and provoke an economic crisis greater than that of the Great Depression 50 years ago, with a fundamental change in the way we live.

Twin threats to the flow of oil—from

regional instability and now potentially from the Soviet Union—require that we firmly defend our vital interests when threatened.

In the past year, we have begun to increase our capacity to project military power into the Persian Gulf region, and are engaged in explorations of increased use of military facilities in the area. We have increased our naval presence in the Indian Ocean. We have been working with countries in the region on shared security concerns. Our rapid deployment forces, as described earlier, could be used in support of friendly governments in the Gulf and Southwest Asian region, as well as in other areas.

South Asia

The overwhelming challenge in this region will be dealing with the new situation posed by Soviet aggression in Afghanistan. We must help the regional states develop a capability to withstand Soviet pressures in a strengthened framework for cooperation in the region. We want to cooperate with all the states of the region in this regard—with India and Pakistan, with Sri Lanka, Bangladesh and Nepal.

In this new situation, we are proposing to the Congress a military and economic assistance program to enable Pakistan to buttress its defenses. This is a matter of the most urgent concern, and I strongly urge the earliest possible approval by the House and Senate. We are also working closely with other friends of Pakistan to increase the resources available for Pakistan's development and security.

We are also pursuing the possibility of gaining access to military facilities in the region in time of trouble. We are prepared to work closely with our friends in the region, on a cooperative basis, to do whatever is required to ensure that aggressors would bear heavy costs so that further aggression is deterred.

A high priority for us in the region is to manage our nuclear concerns with India and Pakistan in ways that are compatible with our global and regional priorities. The changed security situation in South Asia arising from the Soviet invasion of Afghanistan calls for legislative action to allow renewed assistance to Pakistan. But this in no way diminishes our commitment to work to prevent nuclear weapons proliferation, in Pakistan or elsewhere.

Steady growth of our economic assistance is also essential if the countries of South Asia are to achieve growth and true stability.

Document 5

President Jimmy Carter's State of the Union Address before Congress, Jan. 23, 1980, *PPP: Jimmy Carter, 1980–1981*, 1981, 194–99.

Mr. President, Mr. Speaker, Members of the 96th Congress, fellow citizens:

This last few months has not been an easy time for any of us. As we meet tonight, it has never been more clear that the state of our Union depends on the state of the world. And tonight, as throughout our own generation, freedom and peace in the world depend on the state of our Union.

The 1980's have been born in turmoil, strife, and change. This is a time of challenge to our interests and our values and it's a time that tests our wisdom and our skills.

At this time in Iran, 50 Americans are

still held captive, innocent victims of terrorism and anarchy. Also at this moment, massive Soviet troops are attempting to subjugate the fiercely independent and deeply religious people of Afghanistan. These two acts—one of international terrorism and one of military aggression—present a serious challenge to the United States of America and indeed to all the nations of the world. Together, we will meet these threats to peace. . . .

Three basic developments have helped to shape our challenges: the steady growth and increased projection of Soviet military power beyond its own borders; the overwhelming dependence of the Western democracies on oil supplies from the Middle East; and the press of social and religious and economic and political change in the many nations of the developing world, exemplified by the revolution in Iran. . . .

In response to the abhorrent act in Iran, our nation has never been aroused and unified so greatly in peacetime. Our position is clear. The United States will not yield to blackmail.

We continue to pursue these specific goals: first, to protect the present and long-range interests of the United States; secondly, to preserve the lives of the American hostages and to secure, as quickly as possible, their safe release, if possible, to avoid bloodshed which might further endanger the lives of our fellow citizens; to enlist the help of other nations in condemning this act of violence, which is shocking and violates the moral and the legal standards of a civilized world; and also to convince and to persuade the Iranian leaders that the real danger to their nation lies in the north, in the Soviet Union and from the Soviet troops now in Afghanistan, and that the unwarranted Iranian quarrel with the United States hampers their response to this far greater danger to them.

If the American hostages are harmed, a severe price will be paid. We will never rest until every one of the American hostages are released.

But now we face a broader and more fundamental challenge in this region because of the recent military action of the Soviet Union. . . .

. . . The Soviet Union has taken a radical and an aggressive new step. It's using its great military power against a relatively defenseless nation. The implications of the Soviet invasion of Afghanistan could pose the most serious threat to the peace since the Second World War. . . .

While this invasion continues, we and the other nations of the world cannot conduct business as usual with the Soviet Union. That's why the United States has imposed stiff economic penalties on the Soviet Union. . . .

The Soviet Union is going to have to answer some basic questions: Will it help promote a more stable international environment in which its own legitimate, peaceful concerns can be pursued? Or will it continue to expand its military power far beyond its genuine security needs, and use that power for colonial conquest? The Soviet Union must realize that its decision to use military force in Afghanistan will be costly to every political and economic relationship it values.

The region which is now threatened by Soviet troops in Afghanistan is of great strategic importance: It contains more than two-thirds of the world's exportable oil. The Soviet effort to dominate Afghanistan has brought Soviet military forces to within 300 miles of the Indian Ocean and close to the Straits of Hormuz, a waterway through which most of the world's oil must flow. The Soviet Union is now attempting to consolidate a strategic position, therefore, that poses a grave threat to the free movement of Middle East oil.

This situation demands careful thought, steady nerves, and resolute action, not only for this year but for many years to come. It demands collective efforts to meet this new threat to security in the Persian Gulf and in Southwest Asia. It demands the participation of all those who rely on oil from the Middle East and who are concerned with global peace and stability. And it demands consultation and close cooperation with countries in the area which might be threatened.

Meeting this challenge will take national will, diplomatic and political wisdom, economic sacrifice, and, of course, military capability. We must call on the best that is in us to preserve the security of this crucial region.

Let our position be absolutely clear: An attempt by any outside force to gain control of the Persian Gulf region will be regarded as an assault on the vital interests of the United States of America, and such an assault will be repelled by any means necessary, including military force.

. . . We are working with our allies to prevent conflict in the Middle East. The peace treaty between Egypt and Israel is a notable achievement which represents a strategic asset for America and which also enhances prospects for regional and world peace. We are now engaged in further negotiations to provide full autonomy for the people of the West Bank and Gaza, to resolve the Palestinian issue in all its aspects, and to preserve the peace and security of Israel. Let no one doubt our commitment to the security of Israel. In a few days we will observe an historic event when Israel makes another major withdrawal from the Sinai and when Ambassadors will be exchanged between Israel and Egypt. . . .

We've increased and strengthened our naval presence in the Indian Ocean, and we are now making arrangements for key naval and air facilities to be used by our forces in the region of northeast Africa and the Persian Gulf.

We've reconfirmed our 1959 agreement to help Pakistan preserve its independence and its integrity. The United States will take action consistent with our own laws to assist Pakistan in resisting any outside aggression. And I'm asking the Congress specifically to reaffirm this agreement. I'm also working, along with the leaders of other nations, to provide additional military and economic aid for Pakistan. That request will come to you in just a few days.

In the weeks ahead, we will further strengthen political and military ties with other nations in the region. We believe that there are no irreconcilable differences between us and any Islamic nation. We respect the faith of Islam, and we are ready to cooperate with all Moslem countries.

Finally, we are prepared to work with other countries in the region to share a cooperative security framework that respects differing values and political beliefs, yet which enhances the independence, security, and prosperity of all.

All these efforts combined emphasize our dedication to defend and preserve the vital interests of the region and of the nation which we represent and those of our allies—in Europe and the Pacific, and also in the parts of the world which have such great strategic importance to us, stretching especially through the Middle East and Southwest Asia. With your help, I will pursue these efforts with vigor and with determination. You and I will act as necessary to protect and to preserve our Nation's security. . . .

The crises in Iran and Afghanistan have dramatized a very important lesson: Our excessive dependence on foreign oil is a clear and present danger to our Nation's security. The need has never been more urgent. At long last, we must have a clear, comprehensive energy policy for the United States. . . .

The single biggest factor in the inflation rate last year, the increase in the inflation rate last year, was from one cause: the skyrocketing prices of OPEC [Organization of Petroleum Exporting Countries] oil. We must take whatever actions are necessary to reduce our dependence on foreign oil—and at the same time reduce inflation.

Document 6

Secretary of State Alexander Haig, testimony on Middle East issues, U.S. Congress, Senate, *Hearings Before the Committee on Foreign Relations*, 97th Cong., 1st sess., Mar. 19, 1981, 33–34.

Senator [Christopher] DODD. In your testimony this morning you were talking about our commitment to Israel and to Egypt and you said they will be receiving the lion's share of our security assistance. I wonder—regarding the issues of the Camp David summit, the peace process and the decision of this administration to sell Saudi Arabia enhanced equipment for the F-15's all come into the plan. Are we going to get anything back at all? There has been such reluctance—and that may be a mild word to use—on the part of the Saudis to embrace the peace process that it seems to me we perhaps are not being tough enough with some of our friends when it comes to lessening tensions and problems. I am sure you would not argue with the conclusion that I have reached, and which I think others have reached as well, that the Middle East certainly is highly volatile and the incursion of additional arms there at least can raise the possibility of additional tensions.

Are we going to be asking Saudi Arabia to take a different position with regard to the peace process?

Secretary HAIG. Senator, Saudi Arabia, in the broadest context of United States-Saudi relationships, has been a trusted ally and friend of this Nation. Events in the recent past—and I must tell you that we found the situation when we came into office in which there had been discussions with the Saudis on the subject of F-15 enhancement which had been rather extensive but, unfortunately, had been somewhat inconsistent. Our Saudi friends looked at Western failure and American failure to react perhaps sensitively to the Soviet incursions and the Cuban incursions in Africa, and especially in the horn.

We disappointed them in a number of ways in recent months and years. I don't think relationships between friends are best maintained by bargaining, but rather by a broad set of understandings in which you find convergence of policy as a result of mutual trust and overall demeanor of our relationship. That demeanor is not very good in Saudi Arabia today. I don't mean to suggest by this that there is a crisis stage, but I think there needs to be some improvement. Clearly, we are very conscious of your concerns and they will be dealt with I hope in a constructive way, but not in a way which suggests humiliation or that complicates the task that we seek.

That is a nonanswer to a very specific question.

Senator DODD. I am glad you made that point. I was about to myself.

The CHAIRMAN [Sen. Charles H. Percy] Thank you, Senator Dodd

Senator DODD. My time has expired. Thank you, Mr. Chairman.

The CHAIRMAN. Senator [Rudy] Boshwitz.

Senator BOSHWITZ. Mr. Secretary, let me pursue what [Sen.] Dodd has begun.

In your testimony you state:

In practical terms, this means that the air defense system we help a friendly state develop could one day serve as a prepositioned shield under which Western relief forces would move.

If I felt that there was some assurance that this indeed existed with respect to the F-15's, I think my attitude might be quite different.

Will we have any form of control? You used the term "prepositioned." Is this sale in any sense a prepositioning from the standpoint that in the event we feel our, or the free world's, position or strategic interests are threatened? In the event there is some disagreement with our friends, as you speak of them, the Saudis, would these F-15's be available to us until Western relief forces could move?

Secretary HAIG. I think it would be presumptuous of me to suggest that some arrangement of that kind was an inherent aspect of our provision, by sale, to a sovereign nation, a sovereign nation which clearly has reason to believe it is threatened in the context of what has occurred in Afghanistan, the difficulties to their east, in Iraq and Iran, the difficulties near their southern border in the two Yemen, the recent incursion by Southern Yemen into Northern Yemen, and the very threatening situation of a Marxist-Leninist Ethiopia to their west.

I just think this subject requires a clarity of thought. The situation has changed dramatically in that area in strategic terms, because of the very issues I just cited. I think it is in the American interest, in our interest to establish a consensus in the strategic-regional sense among the states of the area, stretching from Pakistan in the east to Egypt in the west, including Turkey, Israel, and the other threatened states. I think a climate that will effect such a strategic dialog only will occur by the reduction of the insecurities about which I spoke.

Second, I think the peace process, of such fundamental and vital importance to us all, in large measure is going to be a reflection of insecurities either by the negotiating parties themselves or those who influence those parties. I think this recommendation is a vitally important objective for all of the objectives I have outlined.

Document 7

Symington Amendment, Public Law 94-329, June 30, 1976, *U.S. Statutes at Large, 1976*, Washington, D.C.: Government Printing Office, vol. 90, part 1, 755–56.

NUCLEAR TRANSFERS

Sec. 305. Chapter 3 of part III of the Foreign Assistance Act of 1961 is amended by adding at the end thereof the following new section:

"Sec. 669. Nuclear Transfers.—(a) Except as provided in subsection (b), no funds authorized to be appropriated by this Act or the Arms Export Control Act may be used for the purpose of —

"(1) providing economic assistance;

"(2) providing military or security supporting assistance or grant military education and training; or

"(3) extending military credits or making guarantees; to any country which—

"(A) delivers nuclear reprocessing or enrichment equipment, materials, or technology to any other country; or

"(B) receives such equipment, materials or technology from any other country;

unless before such delivery—

"(i) the supplying country and receiving country have reached agreement to place all such equipment, materials, and technology, upon delivery, under multilateral auspices and management when available; and

"(ii) the recipient country has entered into an agreement with the International Atomic Energy Agency to place all such equipment, materials, technology, and all nuclear fuel and facilities in such country under the safeguards system of such Agency.

"(b) (1) Notwithstanding the provisions of subsection (a) of this section, the President may, by Executive order effective not less than 30 days following its date of promulgation, furnish assistance which would otherwise be prohibited under paragraph (1), (2), or (3) of such subsection if he determines and certifies in writing to the Speaker of the House of Representatives and the Committee on Foreign Relations of the Senate that—

"(A) the termination of such assistance would have a serious adverse effect on vital United States interests; and

"(B) he has received reliable assurances that the country in question will not acquire or develop nuclear weapons or assist other nations in doing so.

Such certification shall set forth the reasons supporting such determination in each particular case.

"(2) (A) The Congress may by joint resolution terminate or restrict assistance described in paragraphs (1) through (3) of subsection (a) with respect to a country to which the prohibition in such subsection applies or take any other action with respect to such assistance for such country as it deems appropriate.

"(B) Any such joint resolution with respect to a country shall, if introduced within 30 days after the transmittal of a certification under paragraph (1) with respect to such country, be considered in the Senate in accordance with the provisions of section 601(b) of the International Security Assistance and Arms Export Control Act of 1976."

Document 8

Glenn Amendment, Public Law 95-92, Aug. 4, 1977, *U.S. Statutes at Large, 1977*, Washington, D.C.: Government Printing Office, 1980, vol. 91, 620–21.

NUCLEAR ENRICHMENT
AND REPROCESSING TRANSFERS;
NUCLEAR DETONATIONS

Sec. 12. Chapter 3 of part III of the Foreign Assistance Act of 1961 is amended by striking out section 669 and inserting in lieu thereof the following new sections:

"Sec. 669. Nuclear Enrichment Transfers.—(a) Except as provided in subsection (b), no funds authorized to be appropriated by this Act or the Arms Export Control Act may be used for the purpose of providing economic assistance, providing military or security supporting assistance or grant military education and training, or extending military credits or making guarantees, to any country which, on or after the date of enactment of the International Security Assistance Act of 1977, delivers nuclear enrichment equipment, materials, or technology to any other country, or receives such equipment, materials, or technology from any other country, unless before such delivery—

"(1) the supplying country and

receiving country have reached agreement to place all such equipment, materials, or technology, upon delivery, under multilateral auspices and management when available; and

"(2) the recipient country has entered into an agreement with the International Atomic Energy Agency to place all such equipment, materials, technology, and all nuclear fuel and facilities in such country under the safeguards system of such Agency.

"(b)(1) Notwithstanding subsection (a) of this section, the President may furnish assistance which would otherwise be prohibited under such subsection if he determines and certifies in writing to the Speaker of the House of Representatives and the Committee on Foreign Relations of the Senate that-

"(A) the termination of such assistance would have a serious adverse effect on vital United States interests; and

"(B) he has received reliable assurances that the country in question will not acquire or develop nuclear weapons or assist other nations in doing so.

Such certification shall set forth the reasons supporting such determination in each particular case.

"(2) Any joint resolution which would terminate or restrict assistance described in subsection (a) with respect to a country to which the prohibition in such subsection applies shall, if introduced within thirty days after the transmittal of a certification under paragraph (1) of this subsection with respect to such country, be considered in the Senate in accordance with the provisions of section 601(b) of the International Security Assistance and Arms Export Control Act of 1976.

"Sec. 670. Nuclear Reprocessing Transfers and Nuclear Detonations.—(a) Except as provided in subsection (b), no funds authorized to be appropriated by this Act or the Arms Export Control Act may be used for the purpose of providing economic assistance, providing military or security supporting assistance or grant military education and training, or extending military credits or making guarantees, to any country which on or after the date of enactment of the International Security Assistance Act of 1977—

"(1) delivers nuclear reprocessing equipment, materials, or technology to any other country or receives such equipment, materials, or technology from any other country (except for the transfer of reprocessing technology associated with the investigation, under international evaluation programs in which the United States participates, of technologies which are alternatives to pure plutonium reprocessing); or

"(2) is not a nuclear-weapon state as defined in article IX (3) of the Treaty on the Non-Proliferation of Nuclear Weapons and which detonates a nuclear explosive device.

"(b)(1) Notwithstanding subsection (a) of this section, the President may furnish assistance which would otherwise be prohibited under such subsection if he determines and certifies in writing to the Speaker of the House of Representatives and the Committee on Foreign Relations of the Senate that the termination of such assistance would be seriously prejudicial to the achievement of United States nonproliferation objectives or otherwise jeopardize the common defense and security. The President shall transmit with such certification a statement setting forth the specific reasons therefor.

"(2) Any joint resolution which would terminate or restrict assistance described in subsection (a) with respect to a country to which the prohibition in such subsection applies shall, if introduced within thirty days after the transmittal of a certification under paragraph

(1) of this subsection with respect to such country, be considered in the Senate in accordance with the provisions of section 601(b) of the International Security Assistance and Arms Export Control Act of 1976.''

Document 9

President Lyndon B. Johnson to Turkey's Prime Minister Ismet Inonu, June 5, 1964, as released by the White House, Jan. 15, 1966, *The Middle East Journal,* Summer 1966, vol. 20, 386–88.

Dear Mr. Prime Minister:

I am gravely concerned by the information which I have had through Ambassador [Raymond A.] Hare from you and your Foreign Minister that the Turkish Government is contemplating a decision to intervene by military force to occupy a portion of Cyprus. I wish to emphasize, in the fullest friendship and frankness, that I do not consider that such a course of action by Turkey, fraught with such far-reaching consequences, is consistent with the commitment of your Government to consult fully in advance with us. Ambassador Hare has indicated that you have postponed your decision for a few hours in order to obtain my views. I put to you personally whether you really believe that it is appropriate for your Government, in effect, to present a unilateral decision of such consequence to an ally who has demonstrated such staunch support over the years as has the United States for Turkey. I must, therefore, first urge you to accept the responsibility for complete consultation with the United States before any such action is taken.

It is my impression that you believe that such intervention by Turkey is permissible under the provisions of the Treaty of Guarantee of 1960. I must call your attention, however, to our understanding that the proposed intervention by Turkey would be for the purpose of effecting a form of partition of the Island, a solution which is specifically excluded by the Treaty of Guarantee. Further, that Treaty requires consultation among the Guarantor Powers. It is the view of the United States that the possibilities of such consultation have by no means been exhausted in this situation and that, therefore, the reservation of the right to take unilateral action is not yet applicable.

I must call to your attention, also, Mr. Prime Minister, the obligations of NATO [North Atlantic Treaty Organization]. There can be no question in your mind that a Turkish intervention in Cyprus would lead to a military engagement between Turkish and Greek forces. Secretary of State [Dean] Rusk declared at the recent meeting of the Ministerial Council of NATO in The Hague that war between Turkey and Greece must be considered as ''literally unthinkable.'' Adhesion to NATO, in its very essence, means that NATO countries will not wage war on each other. Germany and France have buried centuries of animosity and hostility in becoming NATO allies; nothing less can be expected from Greece and Turkey. Furthermore, a military intervention in Cyprus by Turkey could lead to a direct involvement by the Soviet Union. I hope you will understand that your NATO allies have not had a chance to consider whether they have an obligation to protect Turkey against the Soviet Union if Turkey takes a step which results in Soviet intervention without the full consent and understanding of its NATO Allies. . . .

I wish also, Mr. Prime Minister, to call your attention to the bilateral agreement between the United States and Turkey in the field of military assistance. Under Article IV of the Agreement with Turkey of July 1947, your Government is required to obtain United States consent for the use of military assistance for purposes other than those for which such assistance was furnished. Your Government has on several occasions acknowledged to the United States that you fully understand this condition. I must tell you in all candor that the United States cannot agree to the use of any United States supplied military equipment for a Turkish intervention in Cyprus under present circumstances. . . .

You may consider that what I have said is much too severe and that we are disregardful of Turkish interests in the Cyprus situation. I should like to assure that this is not the case. . . . Your security and prosperity have been a deep concern of the American people and we have expressed that concern in the most practical terms. You and we have fought together to resist the ambitions of the Communist world revolution. . . . We have no intention of lending any support to any solution of Cyprus which endangers the Turkish Cypriot community. We have not been able to find a final solution because this is, admittedly, one of the most complex problems on earth. But I wish to assure you that we have been deeply concerned about the interests of Turkey and of the Turkish Cypriots and will remain so.

Finally, Mr. Prime Minister I must tell you that you have posed the gravest issues of war and peace. These are issues which go far beyond the bilateral relations between Turkey and the United States. They not only will certainly involve war between Turkey and Greece but could involve wider hostilities because of the unpredictable consequences which a unilateral intervention in Cyprus could produce. You have your responsibilities as Chief of the Government of Turkey; I also have mine as President of the United States. I must, therefore, inform you in the deepest friendship that unless I can have your assurance that you will not take such action without further and fullest consultation I cannot accept your injunction to Ambassador Hare of secrecy and must immediately ask for emergency meetings of the NATO Council and of the United Nations Security Council.

Document 10

Public Law 93-559, Dec. 30, 1974, *U.S. Statutes at Large, 1974*, Washington, D.C.: Government Printing Office, 1976, vol. 88, part 2, 1801–2.

SUSPENSION OF MILITARY ASSISTANCE TO TURKEY

Sec. 22. Section 620 of the Foreign Assistance Act of 1961 is amended by adding at the end thereof the following new subsection:

"(x) All military assistance, all sales of defense articles and services (whether for cash or by credit, guaranty, or any other means), and all licenses with respect to the transportation of arms, ammunitions, and implements of war (including technical data relating thereto) to the Government of Turkey, shall be suspended on the date of enactment of this subsection unless and until the President determines and certifies to the Congress that the Government of Turkey is in compliance with the Foreign Assistance Act of 1961, the Foreign Military Sales Act, and any agreement entered into under such Acts, and that substantial progress toward agreement has been made regarding military forces in Cyprus: *Provided*, That the President is authorized to suspend the provisions of this section and such Acts if he determines that such suspension will further negotiations for a peaceful solution of the Cyprus conflict. Any such suspension shall be effective only until February 5, 1975, and only if, during that time, Turkey shall observe the ceasefire and shall neither increase its forces on Cyprus nor transfer to Cyprus any United States supplied implements of war.''

Document 11

UN Security Council Resolution 541/83, Nov. 18, 1983, *Official Records: Resolutions and Decisions of the Security Council, 1983*, New York: United Nations, 1984, 330–31.

The Security Council,

Having heard *the statement of the Foreign Minister of the Government of the Republic of Cyprus,*

Concerned *at the declaration by the Turkish Cypriot authorities issued on 15 November 1983 which purports to create an independent state in northern Cyprus,*

Considering *that this declaration is incompatible with the 1960 Treaty concerning the establishment of the Republic of Cyprus and the 1960 Treaty of Guarantee,*

Considering *therefore that the attempt to create a 'Turkish Republic of Northern Cyprus' is invalid, and will contribute to a worsening of the situation in Cyprus,*

Reaffirming its resolutions 365 (1974) *and* 367 (1975),

Aware of the need *for a solution of the Cyprus problem based on the mission of good offices undertaken by the Secretary-General,*

Affirming *its continuing support for the United Nations Peace-Keeping Force in Cyprus,*

Taking note *of the Secretary-General's statement of 17 November 1983,*

1. **Deplores** *the declaration of the Turkish Cypriot authorities of the purported secession of part of the Republic of Cyprus,*

2. **Considers** *the declaration referred to above as legally invalid and calls for its withdrawal,*

3. **Calls for** *the urgent and effective implementation of its resolutions 365 (1974) and 367 (1975),*

4. **Requests** *the Secretary-General to pursue his mission of good offices in order to achieve the earliest possible progress towards a just and lasting settlement in Cyprus,*

5. **Calls upon** *the parties to cooperate fully with the Secretary-General in his mission of good offices,*

6. **Calls upon** *all states to respect the sovereignty, independence, territorial integrity and non-alignment of the Republic of Cyprus,*

7. **Calls upon** *all states not to recognise any Cypriot state other than the Republic of Cyprus,*

8. **Calls upon** *all states and the two communities in Cyprus to refrain from any action which might exacerbate the situation,*

9. **Requests** *the Secretary-General to keep the Security Council fully informed.*

Document 12

Agreement between Afghanistan and Pakistan, Apr. 14, 1988, *UN Chronicle: A Quarterly Magazine*, June 1988, vol. 25, 10–11.

Bilateral Agreement between the Republic of Afghanistan and the Islamic Republic of Pakistan on the Principles of Mutual Relations, in Particular Non-Interference and Non-Intervention

The Republic of Afghanistan and the Islamic Republic of Pakistan, hereinafter referred to as the High Contracting Parties,

Desiring to normalize relations and promote good-neighbourliness and co-operation as well as to strengthen international peace and security in the region,

Considering that full observance of the principle of non-interference and non-intervention in the internal and external affairs of States is of the greatest importance for the maintenance of international peace and security and for the fulfilment of the purposes and principles of the Charter of the United Nations. . . .

Have agreed as follows:

Article I Relations between the High Contracting Parties shall be conducted in strict compliance with the principle of non-interference and non-intervention by States in the affairs of other States.

Article II For the purpose of implementing the principle of non-interference and non-intervention each High Contracting Party undertakes to comply with the following obligations:

(1) to respect the sovereignty, political independence, territorial integrity, national unity, security and non-alignment of the other High Contracting Party, as well as the national identity and cultural heritage of its people; . . .

(3) to refrain from the threat or use of force in any form whatsoever so as not to violate the boundaries of each other, to disrupt the political, social or economic order of the other High Contracting Party, to overthrow or change the political system of the other High Contracting Party or its Government, or to cause tension between the High Contracting Parties;

(4) to ensure that its territory is not used in any manner which would violate the sovereignty, political independence, territorial integrity and national unity or disrupt the political, economic and social stability of the other High Contracting Party;

(5) to refrain from armed intervention, subversion, military occupation or any other form of intervention and interference, overt or covert, directed at the other High Contracting Party, or any act of military, political or economic interference in the internal affairs of the other High Contracting Party, including acts of reprisal involving the use of force;

(6) to refrain from any action or attempt in whatever form or under whatever pretext to destabilize or to undermine the stability of the other High Contracting Party or any of its institutions;

(7) to refrain from the promotion, encouragement or support, direct or indirect, of rebellious or secessionist activities against the other High Contracting Party, under any pretext whatsoever, or from any other action which seeks to disrupt the unity or to undermine or subvert the political order of the other High Contracting Party;

(8) to prevent within its territory the training, equipping, financing and recruitment of mercenaries from whatever

origin for the purpose of hostile activities against the other High Contracting Party, or the sending of such mercenaries into the territory of the other High Contracting Party and accordingly to deny facilities, including financing for the training, equipping and transit of such mercenaries;

(9) to refrain from making any agreements or arrangements with other States designed to intervene or interfere in the internal and external affairs of the other High Contracting Party;

(10) to abstain from any defamatory campaign, vilification or hostile propaganda for the purpose of intervening or interfering in the internal affairs of the other High Contracting Party;

(11) to prevent any assistance to or use of or tolerance of terrorist groups, saboteurs or subversive agents against the other High Contracting Party;

(12) to prevent within its territory the presence, harbouring, in camps and bases or otherwise, organizing, training, financing, equipping and arming of individuals and political, ethnic and any other groups for the purpose of creating subversion, disorder or unrest in the territory of the other High Contracting Party and accordingly also to prevent the use of mass media and the transportation of arms, ammunition and equipment by such individuals and groups;

(13) not to resort to or to allow any other action that could be considered as interference or intervention.

Article III The present Agreement shall enter into force on 15 May 1988. . . .

Done in five original copies at Geneva this fourteenth day of April 1988.

Declaration on International Guarantees

The Governments of the Union of Soviet Socialist Republics and of the United States of America,

Expressing support that the Republic of Afghanistan and the Islamic Republic of Pakistan have concluded a negotiated political settlement designed to normalize relations and promote good neighbourliness between the two countries as well as to strengthen international peace and security in the region;

Wishing in turn to contribute to the achievement of the objectives that the Republic of Afghanistan and the Islamic Republic of Pakistan have set themselves, and with a view to ensuring respect for their sovereignty, independence, territorial integrity and nonalignment;

Undertake to invariably refrain from any form of interference and intervention in the internal affairs of the Republic of Afghanistan and the Islamic Republic of Pakistan and to respect the commitments contained in the bilateral Agreement between the Republic of Afghanistan and the Islamic Republic of Pakistan on the principles of Mutual Relations, in particular on Non-Interference and Non-Intervention:

Urge all States to act likewise.

The present Declaration shall enter into force on 15 May 1988.

Done at Geneva, this fourteenth day of April 1988 in five original copies, each in the English and Russian languages, both texts being equally authentic.

Document 13

Communiqué issued by Iran and Iraq regarding talks on their disputes, Mar. 7, 1975, the *New York Times*, Mar. 8, 1975.

During the Algiers summit conference of member countries of OPEC [Organization of Petroleum Exporting Countries] and on President [Hauari] Boumediene's [of Algeria] initiative, H.M. Shah-in-Shah of Iran and H.E. Saddam Hussein, deputy chairman of the Revolutionary Command Council of Iraq met on two occasions and discussed at length relations between Iran and Iraq.

These conversations took place in President Boumediene's presence, were extremely frank and were characterized by a sincere desire on the part of the two parties to reach a permanent and lasting solution to all the problems existent between the two countries.

Permanent Demarcation

In application of the principles of territorial integrity inviolability of frontiers and noninterference in internal affairs, the high level contracting parties decided:

1. To proceed with a permanent demarcation of their land frontiers on the basis of the 1913 Constantinople protocol and the reports of the 1914 Commission for Delimitation of the Frontier.

2. To delimit their river frontiers according to the Thalweg Line [the median line of the navigational channel].

3. By doing this the two countries will re-establish reciprocal security and confidence along their common frontiers. They thus make an engagement to exercise a strict and effective control over these frontiers with a view to definitive cessation of all subversive infiltrations on both sides.

4. The two parties have decided to consider the above provisions as inseparable elements of a global ruling and, consequently, any infringement of one of the provisions is, plainly, incompatible with the spirit of the Algiers accord.

The two parties will remain in constant contact with President Boumediene, who will, if necessary, give Algeria's fraternal assistance in implementing the decisions taken.

The high-level parties have decided to re-establish traditional ties of good neighborliness and friendship, notably by eliminating all the negative factors in their relations, by constant exchange of points of view on questions of common interest and by promotion of mutual cooperation.

The two parties declare solemnly that the region must remain free of all external interference.

The Foreign Ministers of Iran and Iraq will meet with the Algerian Foreign Minister in Teheran on March 15, 1975, to determine working conditions of the mixed Iranian-Iraq commission created with the aim of putting into practice the decisions fixed above by common accord.

In conformity with the wishes of both parties, Algeria will be invited to all the meetings of the mixed Iranian-Iraqi commission.

The commission will draw up a calendar and working methods so as to meet, if necessary, alternately in Baghdad and in Teheran.

His Majesty the Shah-in-Shah accepted with pleasure the invitation extended to him in the name of His Excellency President Ahmed Hassan al-Bakr to make an official visit to Iraq. The date of that visit will be fixed by common accord.

Document 14

UN Security Council Resolution 479, Sept. 28, 1980, *Official Records: Resolutions and Decisions of the Security Council, 1980*, New York: United Nations, 1981, 23.

The Security Council,

Having begun consideration of the item entitled "The situation between Iran and Iraq",

Mindful that all Member States have undertaken, under the Charter of the United Nations, the obligation to settle their international disputes by peaceful means and in such a manner that international peace and security and justice are not endangered,

Mindful as well that all Member States are obliged to refrain in their international relations from the threat of or use of force against the territorial integrity or political independence of any State,

Recalling that under Article 24 of the Charter the Security Council has primary responsibility for the maintenance of international peace and security,

Deeply concerned about the developing situation between Iran and Iraq,

1. *Calls upon* Iran and Iraq to refrain immediately from any further use of force and to settle their dispute by peaceful means and in conformity with principles of justice and international law;

2. *Urges* them to accept any appropriate offer of mediation or conciliation or to resort to regional agencies or arrangements or other peaceful means of their own choice that would facilitate the fulfilment of their obligations under the Charter of the United Nations;

3. *Calls upon* all other States to exercise the utmost restraint and to refrain from any act which may lead to a further escalation and widening of the conflict;

4. *Supports* the efforts of the Secretary-General and the offer of his good offices for the resolution of this situation;

5. *Requests* the Secretary-General to report to the Security Council within forty-eight hours.

Document 15

UN Security Council Resolution 598, July 20, 1987, *Official Records: Resolutions and Decisions of the Security Council, 1987*, New York: United Nations, 1988, 5–6.

The Security Council,

Reaffirming its resolution 582 (1986),

Deeply concerned that, despite its calls for a cease-fire, the conflict between the Islamic Republic of Iran and Iraq continues unabated, with further heavy loss of human life and material destruction,

Deploring the initiation and continuation of the conflict,

Deploring also the bombing of purely civilian population centres, attacks on neutral shipping or civilian aircraft, the violation of international humanitarian law and other laws of armed conflict, and, in particular, the use of chemical weapons contrary to obligations under the 1925 Geneva Protocol,

Deeply concerned that further escalation and widening of the conflict may take place,

Deeply concerned to bring to an end all military actions between Iran and Iraq,

Convinced that a comprehensive, just, honourable and durable settlement should be achieved between Iran and Iraq,

Recalling the provisions of the Charter of the United Nations, and in particular the obligation of all Member States to settle their international disputes by peaceful means in such a manner that international peace and security and justice are not endangered,

Determining that there exists a breach of the peace as regards the conflict between Iran and Iraq,

Acting under Articles 39 and 40 of the Charter,

1. *Demands* that, as a first step towards a negotiated settlement, the Islamic Republic of Iran and Iraq observe an immediate cease-fire, discontinue all military actions on land, at sea and in the air, and withdraw all forces to the internationally recognized boundaries without delay;

2. *Requests* the Secretary-General to dispatch a team of United Nations observers to verify, confirm and supervise the cease-fire and withdrawal and further requests the Secretary-General to make the necessary arrangements in consultation with the Parties and to submit a report thereon to the Security Council;

3. *Urges* that prisoners-of-war be released and repatriated without delay after the cessation of active hostilities in accordance with the Third Geneva Convention of 12 August 1949;

4. *Calls upon* Iran and Iraq to cooperate with the Secretary-General in implementing this resolution and in mediation efforts to achieve a comprehensive, just and all honourable settlement, acceptable to both sides, of all outstanding issues, in accordance with the principles contained in the Charter of the United Nations;

5. *Calls upon* all other States to exercise the utmost restraint and to refrain from any act which may lead to further escalation and widening of the conflict, and thus to facilitate the implementation of the present resolution;

6. *Requests* the Secretary-General to explore, in consultation with Iran and Iraq, the question of entrusting an impartial body with inquiring into responsibility for the conflict and to report to the Council as soon as possible;

7. *Recognizes* the magnitude of the damage inflicted during the conflict and the need for reconstruction efforts, with appropriate international assistance, once the conflict is ended and, in this regard, requests the Secretary-General to assign a team of experts to study the question of reconstruction and to report to the Council;

8. *Further requests* the Secretary-General to examine, in consultation with Iran and Iraq and with other States of the region, measures to enhance the security and stability of the region;

9. *Requests* the Secretary-General to keep the Council informed on the implementation of this resolution;

10. *Decides* to meet again as necessary to consider further steps to ensure compliance with this resolution.

Document 16

UN Security Council Resolution 660, Aug. 2, 1990, *UN Security Council, General Distribution*, New York: United Nations, 1990, CRS-7.

The Security Council . . .

1. *Condemns* the Iraqi invasion of Kuwait;

2. *Demands* that Iraq withdraw immediately and unconditionally all its forces to the positions in which they were located on 1 August 1990;

3. *Calls upon* Iraq and Kuwait to begin immediately intensive negotiations for the resolution of their differences and supports all efforts in this regard, and especially those of the League of Arab States; . . . .

Document 17

UN Security Council Resolution 678, Nov. 29, 1990, *UN Security Council, General Distribution*, New York: United Nations, CRS-35.

The Security Council . . .

1. *Demands* that Iraq comply fully with resolution 660 (1990) and all subsequent relevant resolutions, and decides, while maintaining all its decisions, to allow Iraq one final opportunity, as a pause of goodwill, to do so;

2. *Authorizes* Member States cooperating with the Government of Kuwait, unless Iraq on or before 15 January 1991 fully implements, as set forth in paragraph 1 above, the foregoing resolutions, to use all necessary means to uphold and implement resolution 660 (1990) and all subsequent relevant resolutions and to restore international peace and security in the area;

3. *Requests* all States to provide appropriate support for the actions undertaken in pursuance of paragraph 2 of the present resolution; . . . .

Document 18

Joint Congressional Resolution, Jan. 12, 1991, U.S. Department of State Dispatch, Jan. 14, 1991, 15.

SEC. 2. AUTHORIZATION FOR USE OF UNITED STATES ARMED FORCES

(a) AUTHORIZATION—The President is authorized, subject to subsection (b) to use United States Armed Forces pursuant to United Nations Security Council Resolution 678 (1990) in order to achieve implementation of Security Council Resolutions 660, 661, 662, 664, 665, 666, 667, 669, 670, 674, and 677.

(b) REQUIREMENT FOR DETERMINATION THAT USE OF MILITARY FORCE IS NECESSARY.—Before exercising the authority granted in subsection (a), the President shall make available to the Speaker of the House of Representatives and the President pro tempore of the Senate his determination that—

(1) the United States has used all appropriate diplomatic and other peaceful means to obtain compliance by Iraq with the United Nations Security Council resolutions cited in subsection (a); and

(2) that those efforts have not been and would not be successful in obtaining such compliance.

(c) WAR POWER RESOLUTION REQUIREMENTS.—

(1) Specific Statutory Authorization.—Consistent with section 8(a1) of the War Powers Resolutions, the Congress declares that this section is intended to constitute specific statutory authorization within the meaning of section 5(b) of the War Powers Resolution.

(2) APPLICABILITY OF OTHER REQUIREMENTS.—Nothing in this resolution supersedes any requirements of the War Powers Resolution.

SEC. 3. REPORTS TO CONGRESS.

At least once every 60 days, the President shall submit to the Congress a summary on the status of efforts to obtain compliance by Iraq with the resolutions adopted by the United Nations Security Council in response to Iraq's aggression.

Vote: (H: 250-183, S: 52-47)

Document 19

UN Security Council Resolution 687, Apr. 3, 1991, U.S. Department of State Dispatch, Apr. 8, 1991, 234–35.

RESOLUTION 687:

• Affirms the 13 previous resolutions on the Gulf conflict.

International Boundary

• Declares the boundary between Iraq and Kuwait and the allocation of islands as that agreed by Iraq and Kuwait in 1963.

• Guarantees the inviolability of that boundary and asks Kuwait and Iraq, with the assistance of the Secretary General, to demarcate the 1963 boundary and report back within 1 month.

Observer Force

• Requests the Secretary General to submit a plan within 3 days for an observer force to monitor a demilitarized zone extending 10 km into Iraq and 5 km into Kuwait and to deploy it immediately after council approval.

Missile Systems and Weapons of Mass Destruction

• Requires Iraq to agree to the destruction or removal of all chemical and biological weapons and all ballistic missiles with a range of greater than 150 kilometers and to identify their locations within 15 days.

• Requests the Secretary General, in coordination with the coalition and the World Health Organization, to submit a plan to the council within 45 days designating a special commission which will inventory chemical and biological items and ballistic missile sites.

• Provides for a special commission, within 45 days following approval of the plan, to oversee destruction of missile systems and launchers and take possession of all chemical and biological weapons-related items/sites.

• Requires Iraq to submit a list of its nuclear weapons or nuclear weapons-usable material or related facilities to the Secretary General within 15 days and place all nuclear weapons-usable material under the exclusive control of the International Atomic Energy Agency for custody and removal.

• Requests the Secretary General to carry out immediate on-site inspection of Iraq's nuclear capabilities and develop a plan for their destruction within 45 days.

• Requires Iraq to declare that it will not acquire or develop chemical, biological, and nuclear weapons or ballistic missiles in the future. The special commission will develop a plan for on-going monitoring and verification of Iraqi compliance.

Compensation

• Reaffirms Iraqi liability for direct losses, including environmental damage, and creates a commission and fund to handle compensation.

• Directs the Secretary General to present a plan to the council within 30 days for administering the fund.

• Decides that a percentage of Iraqi oil revenues will go to the fund.

Sanctions

• Immediately lifts sanctions on food (with notification to the Sanctions Committee) and supplies for essential civilian needs (with Sanctions Committee approval) and provides for council review of remaining import sanctions every 60 days, taking account of Iraqi policies and practices.

• Indicates all sanctions on Iraqi exports will be lifted when Iraq agrees to the destruction of its weapons of mass destruction and missiles, provides their locations to the Special Commission, and agrees not to acquire or develop them in the future, and when the Security Council approves the Secretary General's plan for the compensation fund.

• Institutes an embargo on conventional armaments; weapons of mass destruction; missiles; licensing and technology transfer; personnel or materials for training, technical support, or maintenance. The council will review the embargo on conventional weapons periodically.

• Calls on states to institute controls to ensure compliance with the embargo.

Kuwait Property and Detainees

• Provides for return of Kuwaiti property and confirms Iraqi responsibility to repatriate and account for all Kuwaiti and third country nationals in coordination with the International Committee of the Red Cross.

Terrorism

• Requires a commitment from Iraq that it will not commit or support acts of terrorism or terrorist organizations.

Cease-fire

• Declares a cease-fire will go into effect upon formal Iraqi acceptance of the provisions of the resolution.

Document 20

UN Security Council Resolution 688, Apr. 5, 1991, U.S. Department of State Dispatch, Apr. 8, 1991, 233–34.

Resolution 688 (April 5, 1991)

The Security Council,

Mindful of its duties and its responsibilities under the Charter of the United Nations for the maintenance of international peace and security,

Recalling Article 2, paragraph 7, of the Charter of the United Nations,

Gravely concerned by the repression of the Iraqi civilian population in many parts of Iraq, including most recently in Kurdish populated areas which led to a massive flow of refugees towards and across international frontiers and to cross border incursions, which threaten international peace and security in the region,

Deeply disturbed by the magnitude of the human suffering involved,

Taking note of the letters sent by the representatives of Turkey and France to the United Nations dated 2 April 1991 and 4 April 1991, respectively (S/22435 and S/22442),

Taking note also of the letters sent by the Permanent Representative of the Islamic Republic of Iran to the United Nations dated 3 and 4 April 1991, respectively (S/22436 and S/22447),

Reaffirming the commitment of all Member States to the sovereignty, territorial integrity and political independence of Iraq and of all States in the area, . . .

1. *Condemns* the repression of the Iraqi civilian population in many parts of Iraq, including most recently in Kurdish populated areas, the consequences of which threaten international peace and security in the region;

2. *Demands* that Iraq, as a contribution to removing the threat to international peace and security in the region, immediately end this repression and expresses the hope in the same context that an open dialogue will take place to ensure that the human and political rights of all Iraqi citizens are respected;

3. *Insists* that Iraq allow immediate

access by international humanitarian organizations to all those in need of assistance in all parts of Iraq and to make available all necessary facilities for their operations;

4. *Requests* the Secretary-General to pursue his humanitarian efforts in Iraq and to report forthwith, if appropriate on the basis of a further mission to the region, on the plight of the Iraqi civilian population, and in particular the Kurdish population, suffering from the repression in all its forms inflicted by the Iraqi authorities;

5. *Requests* further the Secretary-General to use all the resources at his disposal, including those of the relevant United Nations agencies, to address urgently the critical needs of the refugees and displaced Iraqi population;

6. *Appeals* to all Member States and to all humanitarian organizations to contribute to these humanitarian relief efforts;

7. *Demands* that Iraq cooperate with the Secretary-General to these ends; . . . .

Document 21

UN Security Council Resolution 242, Nov. 22, 1967, U.S. Department of State Dispatch, New York: United Nations, 1968, 8–9.

The Security Council,

Expressing its continuing concern with the grave situation in the Middle East,

Emphasizing the inadmissibility of the acquisition of territory by war and the need to work for a just and lasting peace in which every state in the area can live in security,

Emphasizing further that all Member States in their acceptance of the Charter of the United Nations have undertaken a commitment to act in accordance with Article 2 of the Charter,

1. *Affirms* that the fulfillment of Charter principles requires the establishment of a just and lasting peace in the Middle East which should include the application of both the following principles;

(i) Withdrawal of Israel armed forces from territories occupied in the recent conflict;*

(ii) Termination of all claims or states of belligerency and respect for and acknowledgement of the sovereignty, territorial integrity and political independence of every State in the area and their right to live in peace within secure and recognized boundaries free from threats or acts of force;

2. *Affirms further* the necessity

(a) For guaranteeing freedom of navigation through international waterways in the area;

(b) For achieving a just settlement of the refugee problem;

(c) For guaranteeing the territorial inviolability and political independence of every State in the area, through measures including the establishment of demilitarized zones;

3. *Requests* the Secretary-General to designate a Special Representative to proceed to the Middle East to establish and maintain contacts with the States concerned in order to promote agreement and assist efforts to achieve a peaceful and accepted settlement in accordance with the provisions and principles in this resolution;

4. *Requests* the Secretary-General to report to the Security Council on the progress of the efforts of the Special Representative as soon as possible.

* The French version of section 1.(i), which is equally authoritative, states that Retrait des forces armées israéliennes des territoires occupés lors du récent conflit;

Document 22

Palestinian National Charter of 1968, in *Basic Political Documents of the Armed Palestinian Resistance Movement,* Leila S. Kadi, ed., Beirut: Palestine Liberation Organization Research Center, 1969, 137–42.

Article 1: Palestine is the homeland of the Arab Palestinian people; it is an indivisible part of the Arab homeland, and the Palestinian people are an integral part of the Arab nation.

Article 2: Palestine, with the boundaries it had during the British mandate, is an indivisible territorial unit.

Article 3: The Palestinian Arab people possess the legal right to their homeland and have the right to determine their destiny after achieving the liberation of their country in accordance with their wishes and entirely of their own accord and will.

Article 4: The Palestinian identity is a genuine, essential and inherent characteristic; it is transmitted from parents to children. The Zionist occupation and the dispersal of the Palestinian Arab people, through the disasters which befell them, do not make them lose their Palestinian identity and their membership of the Palestinian community, nor do they negate them.

Article 5: The Palestinians are those Arab nationals who, until 1947, normally resided in Palestine regardless of whether they were evicted from it or have stayed there. Anyone born, after that date, of a Palestinian father—whether inside Palestine or outside it—is also a Palestinian.

Article 6: The Jews who had normally resided in Palestine until the beginning of the Zionist invasion will be considered Palestinians. . . .

Article 9: Armed struggle is the only way to liberate Palestine. Thus it is the overall strategy, not merely a tactical phase. The Palestinian Arab people assert their absolute determination and firm resolution to continue their armed struggle and to work for an armed popular revolution for the liberation of their country and their return to it. They also assert their right to normal life in Palestine and to exercise their right to self-determination and sovereignty over it. . . .

Article 15: The liberation of Palestine, from an Arab viewpoint, is a national duty and it attempts to repel the Zionist and imperialist aggression against the Arab homeland, and aims at the elimination of Zionism in Palestine. . . .

Article 17: The liberation of Palestine, from a human point of view, will restore to the Palestinian individual his dignity, pride and freedom. Accordingly the Palestinian Arab people look forward to the support of all those who believe in the dignity of man and his freedom in the world. . . .

Article 19: The partition of Palestine in 1947 and the establishment of the state of Israel are entirely illegal, regardless of the passage of time, because they were contrary to the will of the Palestinian people and to their natural right in their homeland, and inconsistent with the principles embodied in the Charter of the United Nations, particularly the right to self-determination.

Article 20: The Balfour Declaration, the mandate for Palestine and everything that has been based upon them, are deemed null and void. Claims of historical or religious ties of Jews with Palestine are incompatible with the facts of history and the true conception of what constitutes statehood. Judaism, being a religion, is not an independent nationality. Nor do Jews constitute a single nation with an identity of its own; they are citizens of the states to which they belong.

Article 21: The Arab Palestinian

people, expressing themselves by the armed Palestinian revolution, reject all solutions which are substitutes for the total liberation of Palestine and reject all proposals aiming at the liquidation of the Palestinian problem, or its internationalization. . . .

Article 23: The demands of security and peace, as well as the demands of right and justice, require all states to consider Zionism an illegitimate movement, to outlaw its existence, and to ban its operations, in order that friendly relations among peoples may be preserved, and the loyalty of citizens to their respective homelands safeguarded. . . .

Article 33: This Charter shall not be amended save by (vote of) a majority of two-thirds of the total membership of the National Congress of the Palestine Liberation Organization (taken) at a special session convened for that purpose.

Document 23

UN Security Council Resolution 338, Oct. 22, 1973, *Official Records: Resolutions and Decisions of the Security Council, 1973*, New York: United Nations, 1974, 1189.

The Security Council

1. *Calls upon* all parties to the present fighting to cease all firing and terminate all military activity immediately, no later than 12 hours after the moment of the adoption of this decision, in the position they now occupy;

2. *Calls upon* the parties concerned to start immediately after the cease-fire the implementation of Security Council resolution 242 (1967) in all of its parts;

3. *Decides* that, immediately and concurrently with the cease-fire, negotiations start between the parties concerned under appropriate auspices aimed at establishing a just and durable peace in the Middle East.

Document 24

The Palestine Resolution of the Seventh Arab Summit Conference, Rabat, Morocco, Oct. 29, 1974, *Journal of Palestine Studies*, Winter 1975, vol. 4, 177–78.

The Seventh Arab Summit Conference after exhaustive and detailed discussions conducted by their Majesties, Excellencies, and Highnesses, the Kings, Presidents and Amirs on the Arab situation in general and the Palestine problem in particular, within their national and international frameworks; and after hearing the statements by His Majesty King Hussein, King of the Hashemite Kingdom of Jordan and His Excellency Brother Yasser Arafat, Chairman of the Palestine Liberation Organization, and after the statements of their Majesties and Excellencies the Kings and Presidents, in an atmosphere of candour and sincerity and full responsibility; and in view of the Arab leaders' appreciation of the joint national responsibility required of them at present for confronting aggression and performing duties of liberation, enjoined by the unity of the Arab cause and the unity of its struggle; and in view of the fact that all are aware of Zionist schemes still being made to eliminate the Palestinian existence and to obliterate the Palestinian national entity; and in view of the Arab leaders' belief in the necessity to frustrate these attempts and schemes and to counteract them by supporting and strengthening this Palestinian national entity, by providing all requirements to develop and increase its ability to ensure that the Palestinian people recover their rights in full; and by meeting responsibilities of close cooperation with its brothers within the framework of collective Arab commitment;

And in light of the victories achieved by Palestinian struggle in the confrontation with the Zionist enemy, at the Arab and international levels, at the United Nations, and of the obligation imposed thereby to continue joint Arab action to develop and increase the scope of these victories; and having received the views of all on all the above, and having succeeded in cooling the differences between brethren within the framework of consolidating Arab solidarity, the Seventh Arab Summit Conference resolves the following:

1. To affirm the right of the Palestinian people to self-determination and to return to their homeland;

2. To affirm the right of the Palestinian people to establish an independent national authority under the command of the Palestine Liberation Organization, the sole legitimate representative of the Palestinian people in any Palestinian territory that is liberated. This authority, once it is established, shall enjoy the support of the Arab states in all fields and at all levels;

3. To support the Palestine Liberation Organization in the exercise of its responsibility at the national and international levels within the framework of Arab commitment;

4. To call on the Hashemite Kingdom of Jordan, the Syrian Arab Republic, the Arab Republic of Egypt and the Palestine Liberation Organization to devise a formula for the regulation of relations between them in the light of these decisions so as to ensure their implementation;

5. That all the Arab states undertake to defend Palestinian national unity and not to interfere in the internal affairs of Palestinian action.

Document 25

Memorandum of agreement between the governments of Israel and the United States, Sept. 1, 1975, U.S. Congress, Senate, *Hearings before the Committee on Foreign Relations*, 94th Cong., 1st sess., Washington, D.C.: Government Printing Office, 1975, 252.

1. The Geneva Peace Conference will be reconvened at a time coordinated between the United States and Israel.

2. The United States will continue to adhere to its present policy with respect to the Palestine Liberation Organization, whereby it will not recognize or negotiate with the Palestine Liberation Organization so long as the Palestine Liberation Organization does not recognize Israel's right to exist and does not accept Security Council Resolutions 242 and 338. The United States Government will consult fully and seek to concert its position and strategy at the Geneva Peace Conference on this issue with the Government of Israel. Similarly, the United States will consult fully and seek to concert its position and strategy with Israel with regard to the participation of any other additional states. It is understood that the participation at a subsequent phase of the Conference of any possible additional state, group or organization will require the agreement of all the initial participants.

3. The United States will make every effort to ensure at the Conference that all the substantive negotiations will be on a bilateral basis.

4. The United States will oppose and, if necessary, vote against any initiative in the Security Council to alter adversely the terms of reference of the Geneva Peace Conference or to change Resolutions 242 and 338 in ways which are incompatible with their original purpose.

5. The United States will seek to ensure that the role of the cosponsors will be consistent with what was agreed in the Memorandum of Understanding between the United States Government and the Government of Israel of December 20, 1973.

6. The United States and Israel will concert action to assure that the Conference will be conducted in a manner consonant with the objectives of this document and with the declared purpose of the Conference, namely the advancement of a negotiated peace between Israel and each one of its neighbors.

Yigal Allon,
Deputy Prime Minister and
Minister of Foreign Affairs
(For the Government of Israel).
Henry A. Kissinger.
Secretary of State
(For the Government of the
United States).

Document 26

Camp David Accords, Sept. 17, 1978, U.S. Congress, House, *Hearing before the Subcommittee on Europe and the Middle East of the Committee on International Relations*, 95th Cong., 2d sess., Washington, D.C.: Government Printing Office, 1978, 450–56.

Framework

The parties are determined to reach a just, comprehensive, and durable settlement of the Middle East conflict through the conclusion of peace treaties based on Security Council Resolutions 242 and 338 in all their parts. Their purpose is to achieve peace and good neighborly relations. They recognize that, for peace to endure, it must involve all those who have been most deeply affected by the conflict. They therefore agree that this framework as appropriate is intended by them to constitute a basis for peace not only between Egypt and Israel, but also between Israel and each of its other neighbors which is prepared to negotiate peace with Israel on this basis. With that objective in mind, they have agreed to proceed as follows:

A. West Bank and Gaza

1. Egypt, Israel, Jordan and the representatives of the Palestinian people should participate in negotiations on the resolution of the Palestinian problem in all its aspects. To achieve that objective, negotiations relating to the West Bank and Gaza should proceed in three stages;

(a) Egypt and Israel agree that, in order to ensure a peaceful and orderly transfer of authority, and taking into account the security concerns of all the parties, there should be transitional arrangements for the West Bank and Gaza for a period not exceeding five years. In order to provide full autonomy to the inhabitants, under these arrangements the Israeli military government and its civilian administration will be withdrawn as soon as a self-governing authority has been freely elected by the inhabitants of these areas to replace the existing military government. To negotiate the details of a transitional arrangement, the Government of Jordan will be invited to join the negotiations on the basis of this framework. These new arrangements should give due consideration both to the principle of self-government by the inhabitants of these territories and to the legitimate security concerns of the parties involved.

(b) Egypt, Israel, and Jordan will agree on the modalities for establishing the elected self-governing authority in the West Bank and Gaza. The delegations of Egypt and Jordan may include Palestinians from the West Bank and Gaza or other Palestinians as mutually agreed. The parties will negotiate an agreement which will define the powers and responsibilities of the self-governing authority to be exercised in the West Bank and Gaza. A withdrawal of Israeli armed forces will take place and there will be a redeployment of the remaining Israeli forces into specified security locations. The agreement will also include arrangements for assuring internal and external security and public order. A strong local police force will be established, which may include Jordanian citizens. In addition, Israeli and Jordanian forces will participate in joint patrols and in the manning of control posts to assure the security of the borders.

(c) When the self-governing authority (administrative council) in the West Bank and Gaza is established and inaugurated, the transitional period of five years will begin. As soon as possible, but not later than the third year after the beginning of the transitional period, negotiations will take place to determine the final status of the West Bank and Gaza and its relationship with its neighbors, and to conclude a peace treaty between Israel and Jordan by the end of the transitional period. These negotiations will be conducted among Egypt, Israel, Jordan, and the elected representatives of the inhabitants of the West Bank and Gaza. Two separate but related committees will be convened, one committee, consisting of representatives of the four parties which will negotiate and agree on the final status of the West Bank and Gaza, and its relationship with its neighbors, and the second committee, consisting of representatives of Israel and representatives of Jordan to be joined by the elected representatives of the inhabitants of the West Bank and Gaza, to negotiate the peace treaty between Israel and Jordan, taking into account the agreement reached on the final status of the West Bank and Gaza. The negotiations shall be based on all the provisions and principles of UN Security Council Resolution 242. The negotiations will resolve, among other matters, the location of the boundaries and the nature of the security arrangements. The solution from the negotiations must also recognize the legitimate rights of the Palestinian people and their just requirements. In this way, the Palestinians will participate in the determination of their own future through:

(1) The negotiations among Egypt, Israel, Jordan and the representatives of the inhabitants of the West Bank and Gaza to agree on the final status of the West Bank and Gaza and other outstanding issues by the end of the transitional period.

(2) Submitting their agreement to a vote by the elected representatives of the inhabitants of the West Bank and Gaza.

(3) Providing for the elected representatives of the inhabitants of the West Bank and Gaza to decide how they shall govern themselves consistent with the provisions of their agreement.

(4) Participating as stated above in the work of the committee negotiating the peace treaty between Israel and Jordan.

2. All necessary measures will be taken and provisions made to assure the security of Israel and its neighbors during the transitional period and beyond. To assist in providing such security, a strong local police force will be constituted by the self-governing authority. It will be composed of inhabitants of the

West Bank and Gaza. The police will maintain continuing liaison on internal security matters with the designated Israeli, Jordanian, and Egyptian officers.

3. During the transitional period, representatives of Egypt, Israel, Jordan, and the self-governing authority will constitute a continuing committee to decide by agreement on the modalities of admission of persons displaced from the West Bank and Gaza in 1967, together with necessary measures to prevent disruption and disorder. Other matters of common concern may also be dealt with by this committee.

4. Egypt and Israel will work with each other and with other interested parties to establish agreed procedures for a prompt, just and permanent implementation of the resolution of the refugee problem.

B. Egypt-Israel

1. Egypt and Israel undertake not to resort to the threat or the use of force to settle disputes. Any disputes shall be settled by peaceful means in accordance with the provisions of Article 33 of the Charter of the United Nations.

2. In order to achieve peace between them, the parties agree to negotiate in good faith with a goal of concluding within three months from the signing of this Framework a peace treaty between them, while inviting the other parties to the conflict to proceed simultaneously to negotiate and conclude similar peace treaties with a view to achieving a comprehensive peace in the area. The Framework for the Conclusion of a Peace Treaty between Egypt and Israel will govern the peace negotiations between them. The parties will agree on the modalities and the timetable for the implementation of their obligations under the treaty.

C. Associated Principles

1. Egypt and Israel state that the principles and provisions described below should apply to peace treaties between Israel and each of its neighbors—Egypt, Jordan, Syria and Lebanon.

2. Signatories shall establish among themselves relationships normal to states at peace with one another. To this end, they should undertake to abide by all the provisions of the Charter of the United Nations. Steps to be taken in this respect include:

(a) full recognition;

(b) abolishing economic boycotts;

(c) guaranteeing that under their jurisdiction the citizens of the other parties shall enjoy the protection of the due process of law.

3. Signatories should explore possibilities for economic development in the context of final peace treaties, with the objective of contributing to the atmosphere of peace, cooperation and friendship which is their common goal.

4. Claims Commissions may be established for the mutual settlement of all financial claims.

5. The United States shall be invited to participate in the talks on matters related to the modalities of the implementation of the agreements and working out the timetable for the carrying out of the obligations of the parties.

6. The United Nations Security Council shall be requested to endorse the peace treaties and ensure that their provisions shall not be violated. The permanent members of the Security Council shall be requested to underwrite the peace treaties and ensure respect for their provisions. They shall also be requested to conform their policies and actions with the undertakings contained in this Framework.

For the Government of the Arab Republic of Egypt:

A. [Anwar el-]*Sadat*

For the Government of Israel:

M. [Menachem] *Begin*

Witnessed by:

Jimmy Carter,
Jimmy Carter, President of
The United States of America

FRAMEWORK FOR THE CONCLUSION OF A PEACE TREATY BETWEEN EGYPT AND ISRAEL

In order to achieve peace between them, Israel and Egypt agree to negotiate in good faith with a goal of concluding within three months of the signing of this framework a peace treaty between them.

It is agreed that:

The site of the negotiations will be under a United Nations flag at a location or locations to be mutually agreed.

All of the principles of UN Resolution 242 will apply in this resolution of the dispute between Israel and Egypt.

Unless otherwise mutually agreed, terms of the peace treaty will be implemented between two and three years after the peace treaty is signed.

The following matters are agreed between the parties:

(a) the full exercise of Egyptian sovereignty up to the internationally recognized border between Egypt and mandated Palestine;

(b) the withdrawal of Israeli armed forces from the Sinai;

(c) the use of airfields left by the Israelis near El Arish, Rafah, Ras en Naqb, and Sharm el Sheikh for civilian purposes only, including possible commercial use by all nations;

(d) the right of free passage by ships of Israel through the Gulf of Suez and the Suez Canal on the basis of the Constantinople Convention of 1888 applying to all nations; the Strait of Tiran and the Gulf of Aqaba are international waterways to be open to all nations for unimpeded and nonsuspendable freedom of navigation and overflight;

(e) the construction of a highway between the Sinai and Jordan near Elat with guaranteed free and peaceful passage by Egypt and Jordan; and

(f) the stationing of military forces listed below.

Stationing of Forces

A. No more than one division (mechanized or infantry) of Egyptian armed forces will be stationed within an area lying approximately 50 kilometers (km) east of the Gulf of Suez and the Suez Canal.

B. Only United Nations forces and civil police equipped with light weapons to perform normal police functions will be stationed within an area lying west of the international border and the Gulf of Aqaba, varying in width from 20 km to 40 km.

C. In the area within 3 km east of the international border there will be Israeli limited military forces not to exceed four infantry battalions and United Nations observers.

D. Border patrol units, not to exceed three battalions, will supplement the civil police in maintaining order in the area not included above.

The exact demarcation of the above areas will be as decided during the peace negotiations.

Early warning stations may exist to insure compliance with the terms of the agreement.

United Nations forces will be stationed: (a) in part of the area in the Sinai lying within about 20 km of the Mediterranean Sea and adjacent to the international border, and (b) in the Sharm el Sheikh area to ensure freedom of passage through the Strait of Tiran; and these forces will not be removed unless such removal is approved by the Security Council of the United Nations with a unanimous vote of the five permanent members.

After a peace treaty is signed, and after the interim withdrawal is complete, normal relations will be established between Egypt and Israel, including: full recognition, including diplomatic, economic and cultural relations; termination of economic boycotts and barriers to the free movement of goods and people; and mutual protection of citizens by the due process of law.

Interim Withdrawal

Between three months and nine months after the signing of the peace treaty, all Israeli forces will withdraw east of a line extending from a point east of El Arish to Ras Muhammad, the exact location of this line to be determined by mutual agreement.

For the Government of the Arab Republic of Egypt:
A. Sadat

For the Government of Israel:
M. Begin

Witnessed By:
Jimmy Carter
Jimmy Carter, President of the United States of America

Document 27

Platform of the Likud Coalition (from Israeli Prime Minister Menachem Begin's election platform), March 1977, in *The Israel-Arab Reader: A Documentary History of the Middle East Conflict*, Walter Laqueur and Barry Rubin, eds., New York: Penguin, 1984, 591–92.

The Right of the Jewish People to the Land of Israel (Eretz Israel)

a. The right of the Jewish people to the land of Israel is eternal and indisputable and is linked with the right to security and peace; therefore, Judaea and Samaria will not be handed to any foreign administration; between the sea and Jordan there will only be Israeli sovereignty.

b. A plan which relinquishes parts of western Eretz Israel, undermines our right to the country, unavoidably leads to the establishment of a ''Palestinian State,'' jeopardizes the security of the Jewish population, endangers the existence of the State of Israel, and frustrates any prospect of peace.

Genuine Peace—Our Central Objective

a. The Likud government will place its aspirations for peace at the top of its priorities and will spare no effort to promote peace. The Likud will act as a genuine partner at peace treaty negotiations with our neighbors, as is customary among the nations. The Likud government will attend the Geneva Conference. . . .

d. The Likud government's peace initiative will be positive. Directly or through a friendly state, Israel will invite her neighbors to hold direct negotiations, in order to sign peace agreements without pre-conditions on either side and without any solution formula invented by outsiders (''invented outside'').

At the negotiations each party will be free to make any proposals it deems fit.

Settlement

Settlement, both urban and rural, in all parts of the Land of Israel is the focal point of the Zionist effort to redeem the country, to maintain vital security areas and serves as a reservoir of strength and inspiration for the renewal of the pioneering spirit. The Likud government will call the younger generation in Israel and the dispersions to settle and help every group and individual in the task of inhabiting and cultivating the wasteland, while taking care not to dispossess anyone.

Arab Terror Organizations

The PLO is no national liberation organization but an organization of assassins, which the Arab countries use as a political and military tool, while also serving the interests of Soviet imperialism, to stir up the area. Its aim is to liquidate the State of Israel, set up an Arab country instead and make the Land of Israel part of the Arab world. The Likud government will strive to eliminate these murderous organizations in order to prevent them from carrying out their bloody deeds.

Document 28

Israeli government's Fundamental Policy Guidelines, from Israeli Prime Minister Menachem Begin Government's Second Coalition Agreement, Aug. 5, 1981, *Jerusalem Post*, Aug. 6, 1981, 9.

The right of the Jewish people to the land of Israel is an eternal right that cannot be called into question, which is intertwined with the right to security and peace.

The Government will continue to place its aspirations for peace at the head of its concerns, and no effort will be spared in order to further peace. The peace treaty between Israel and Egypt is a historic turning point in Israel's status in the Middle East.

The Government will continue to use all means to prevent war.

The Government will diligently observe the Camp David agreements.

The Government will work for the renewal of negotiations on the implementation of the agreement on full autonomy for the Arab residents of Judea, Samaria and the Gaza Strip.

The autonomy agreed upon at Camp David means neither sovereignty nor self-determination. The autonomy agreements set down at Camp David are guarantees that under no conditions will a Palestinian state emerge in the territory of western "Eretz Yisrael."

At the end of the transition period, set down in the Camp David agreements, Israel will raise its claim, and act to realize its right of sovereignty over Judea, Samaria and the Gaza Strip.

Settlement in the land of Israel is a right and an integral part of the nation's security. The Government will act to strengthen, expand and develop settlement. The Government will continue to honor the principle that Jewish settlement will not cause the eviction of any person from his land, his village or his city.

Equality of rights for all residents will continue to exist in the land of Israel, with no distinctions [on the basis] of religion, race, nationality, sex, or ethnic community.

Israel will not descend from the Golan Heights, nor will it remove any settlement established there. It is the Government that will decide on the appropriate timing for the imposition of Israeli law, jurisdiction and administration on the Golan Heights.

Document 29

Treaty of Peace Between the Arab Republic of Egypt and the State of Israel, Mar. 26, 1979, U.S. Department of State, *Selected Documents No. 11*, Washington, D.C.: Bureau of Public Affairs, April 1979, 1–3.

Article I

1. The state of war between the Parties will be terminated and peace will be established between them upon the exchange of instruments of ratification of this Treaty.

2. Israel will withdraw all its armed forces and civilians from the Sinai behind the international boundary between Egypt and mandated Palestine, . . . and Egypt will resume the exercise of its full sovereignty over the Sinai.

3. Upon completion of the interim withdrawal . . . , the Parties will establish normal and friendly relations, in accordance with Article III(3).

Article II

The permanent boundary between Egypt and Israel is the recognized international boundary between Egypt and the former mandated territory of Palestine, . . . without prejudice to the issue of the status of the Gaza Strip. The Parties recognize this boundary as inviolable. Each will respect the territorial integrity of the other, including their territorial waters and airspace.

Article III

1. The Parties will apply between them the provisions of the Charter of the United Nations and the principles of international law governing relations among states in times of peace. In particular:

a. They recognize and will respect each other's sovereignty, territorial integrity and political independence;

b. They recognize and will respect each other's right to live in peace within their secure and recognized boundaries;

c. They will refrain from the threat or use of force, directly or indirectly, against each other and will settle all disputes between them by peaceful means.

2. Each Party undertakes to ensure that acts or threats of belligerency, hostility, or violence do not originate from and are not committed from within its territory, or by any forces subject to its control or by any other forces stationed on its territory, against the population, citizens or property of the other Party. Each Party also undertakes to refrain from organizing, instigating, inciting, assisting or participating in acts or threats of belligerency, hostility, subversion or violence against the other Party, anywhere, and undertakes to ensure that perpetrators of such acts are brought to justice.

3. The Parties agree that the normal relationship established between them will include full recognition, diplomatic, economic and cultural relations, termination of economic boycotts and discriminatory barriers to the free movement of people and goods, and will guarantee the mutual enjoyment by citizens of the due process of law. . . .

Article IV

1. In order to provide maximum security for both Parties on the basis of reciprocity, agreed security arrangements will be established including limited force zones in Egyptian and Israeli territory, and United Nations forces and observers, . . . and other security arrangements the Parties may agree upon.

2. The Parties agree to the stationing of United Nations personnel in areas described. . . . The Parties agree not to

request withdrawal of the United Nations personnel and that these personnel will not be removed unless such removal is approved by the Security Council of the United Nations, with the affirmative vote of the five Permanent Members, unless the Parties otherwise agree.

3. A Joint Commission will be established to facilitate the implementation of the Treaty. . . .

4. The security arrangements provided for in paragraphs 1 and 2 of this Article may at the request of either party be reviewed and amended by mutual agreement of the Parties.

Article V

1. Ships of Israel, and cargoes destined for or coming from Israel, shall enjoy the right of free passage through the Suez Canal and its approaches through the Gulf of Suez and the Mediterranean Sea on the basis of the Constantinople Convention of 1888, applying to all nations. Israeli nationals, vessels and cargoes, as well as persons, vessels and cargoes destined for or coming from Israel, shall be accorded non-discriminatory treatment in all matters connected with usage of the canal.

2. The Parties consider the Strait of Tiran and the Gulf of Aqaba to be international waterways open to all nations for unimpeded and non-suspendable freedom of navigation and overflight. The Parties will respect each other's right to navigation and overflight for access to either country through the Strait of Tiran and the Gulf of Aqaba. . . .

Article VII

1. Disputes arising out of the application or interpretation of this Treaty shall be resolved by negotiations.

2. Any such disputes which cannot be settled by negotiations shall be resolved by conciliation or submitted to arbitration.

Article VIII

The Parties agree to establish a claims commission for the mutual settlement of all financial claims. . . .

Document 30

The Reagan Plan: President Ronald Reagan's speech, Sept. 1, 1982, "Talking Points" sent to Israeli Prime Minister Menachem Begin, the *New York Times*, Sept. 9, 1982.

These then are our general goals. What are the specific new American positions, and why are we taking them?

In the Camp David talks thus far, both Israel and Egypt have felt free to express openly their views as to what the outcome should be. Understandably, their views have differed on many points.

The United States has thus far sought to play the role of mediator. We have avoided public comment on the key issues. We have always recognized, and continue to recognize, that only the voluntary agreement of those parties most directly involved in the conflict can provide an enduring solution. But it has become evident to me that some clearer sense of America's position on the key issues is necessary to encourage wider support for the peace process.

First, as outlined in the Camp David accords, there must be a period of time during which the Palestinian inhabitants of the West Bank and Gaza will have full autonomy over their own affairs. Due consideration must be given to the principle of self-government by the inhabitants of the territories and to the legitimate security concerns of the parties involved.

The purpose of the five-year period of transition which would begin after free elections for a self-governing Palestinian authority is to prove to the Palestinians that they can run their own affairs, and that such Palestinian autonomy poses no threat to Israel's security.

The United States will not support the use of any additional land for the purpose of settlements during the transitional period. Indeed, the immediate adoption of a settlement freeze by Israel, more than any other action, could create the confidence needed for wider participation in these talks. Further settlement activity is in no way necessary for the security of Israel and only diminishes the confidence of the Arabs that a final outcome can be freely and fairly negotiated.

I want to make the American position well understood: The purpose of this transition period is the peaceful and orderly transfer of authority from Israel to the Palestinian inhabitants of the West Bank and Gaza. At the same time, such a transfer must not interfere with Israel's security requirements.

Beyond the transition period, as we look to the future of the West Bank and Gaza, it is clear to me that peace cannot be achieved by the formation of an independent Palestinian state in those territories. Nor is it achievable on the basis of Israeli sovereignty or permanent control over the West Bank and Gaza.

So the United States will not support the establishment of an independent Palestinian state in the West Bank and Gaza, and we will not support annexation or permanent control by Israel.

There is, however, another way to peace. The final status of these lands must, of course, be reached through the give-and-take of negotiations. But it is the firm view of the United States that self-government by the Palestinians of the West Bank and Gaza in association with Jordan offers the best chance for a durable, just and lasting peace.

We base our approach squarely on the principle that the Arab-Israeli conflict should be resolved through negotiations involving an exchange of territory for peace. This exchange is enshrined in United Nations Security Council Resolution 242 which is, in turn, incorporated in all its parts in the Camp David Agreements. U.N. Resolution 242 remains wholly valid as the foundation stone of America's Middle East peace effort.

It is the United States' position that—in return for peace—the withdrawal provision of Resolution 242 applies to all fronts, including the West Bank and Gaza.

When the border is negotiated between Jordan and Israel, our view on the extent to which Israel should be asked to give up territory will be heavily affected by the extent of true peace and normalization and the security arrangements offered in return.

Finally, we remain convinced that Jerusalem must remain undivided, but its final status should be decided through negotiations.

In the course of the negotiations to come, the United States will support positions that seem to us fair and reasonable compromises, and likely to promote a sound agreement. We will also put forward our own detailed proposals when we believe they can be helpful. And, make no mistake, the United States will oppose any proposal—from any party and at any point in the negotiating process—that threatens the security of Israel. America's commitment to the security of Israel is ironclad and, I might add, so is mine. . . .

["TALKING POINTS"]

General Principles

A. We will maintain our commitment to Camp David.

B. We will maintain our commitment to the conditions we require for recognition of and negotiation with the PLO.

C. We can offer guarantees on the position we will adopt in negotiations. We will not be able, however, to guarantee in advance the results of these negotiations.

Transitional Measures

A. Our position is that the objective of the transitional period is the peaceful and orderly transfer of authority from Israel to the Palestinian inhabitants.

B. We will support:

The decision of full autonomy as giving the Palestinian inhabitants real authority over themselves, the land and its resources, subject to fair safeguards on water.

Economic, commercial, social and cultural ties between the West Bank, Gaza and Jordan.

Participation by the Palestinian inhabitants of East Jerusalem in the election of the West Bank-Gaza authority.

Real settlement freeze.

Progressive Palestinian responsibility for internal security based on capability and performance.

C. We will oppose:

Dismantlement of the existing settlements.

Provisions which represent a legitimate threat to Israel's security, reasonably defined.

Isolation of the West Bank and Gaza from Israel.

Measures which accord either the Palestinians or the Israelis generally recognized sovereign rights with the exception of external security, which must remain in Israel's hands during the transitional period.

Final Status Issues

A. U.N.S.C. Resolution 242

It is our position that Resolution 242 applies to the West Bank and Gaza and requires Israeli withdrawal in return for peace. Negotiations must determine the borders. The U.S. position in these negotiations on the extent of the withdrawal will be significantly influenced by the extent and nature of the peace and security arrangements offered in return.

B. Israeli Sovereignty

It is our belief that the Palestinian problem cannot be resolved [through] Israeli sovereignty or control over the West Bank and Gaza. Accordingly, we will not support such a solution.

C. Palestinian State

The preference we will pursue in the final status negotiation is association of the West Bank and Gaza with Jordan. We will not support the formation of a Palestinian state in those negotiations. There is no foundation of political support in Israel or the United States for such a solution. The outcome, however, must be determined by negotiations.

D. Self-Determination

In the Middle East context the term self-determination has been identified exclusively with the formation of a Palestinian state. We will not support this definition of self-determination. We believe that the Palestinians must take the leading role in determining their own future and fully support the provision in Camp David providing for the elected representatives of the inhabitants of the West Bank and Gaza to decide how they shall govern themselves consistent with the provision of their agreement in the final status negotiations.

E. Jerusalem

We will fully support the position that the status of Jerusalem must be determined through negotiations.

F. Settlements

The status of Israeli settlements must be determined in the course of the final status negotiations. We will not support their continuation as extraterritorial outposts.

Additional Talking Points

1. Approach to [King] Hussein [of Jordan]

The President has approached Hussein to determine the extent to which he may be interested in participating.

King Hussein has received the same U.S. positions as you.

Hussein considers our proposals serious and gives them serious attention.

Hussein understands that Camp David is the only base that we will accept for negotiations.

We are also discussing these proposals with the Saudis.

2. Public Commitment

Whatever the support from these or other Arab States, this is what the President has concluded must be done.

The President is convinced his positions are fair and balanced and fully protective of Israel's security. Beyond that they offer the practical opportunity of eventually achieving the peace treaties Israel must have with its neighbors.

He will be making a speech announcing these positions, probably within a week.

3. Next Procedural Steps

Should the response to the President's proposal be positive, the U.S. would take immediate steps to relaunch the autonomy negotiations with the broadest possible participation as envisaged under the Camp David agreements.

We also contemplate an early visit by Secretary [of State George P.] Shultz in the area.

Should there not be a positive response, the President, as he has said in his letter to you, will nonetheless stand by his position with proper dedication.

Document 31

Jordan's King Hussein, speech on the West Bank, Amman, July 31, 1988, *Journal of Palestine Studies*, Autumn 1988, vol. 18, 279–83.

In the Name of God, the Compassionate, the Merciful, and peace be upon his faithful Arab Messenger.

Brother Citizens,

I send you my greetings, and I am pleased to address you in your cities and villages, in your camps and dwellings, in your institutions of learning, and in your places of work. I would like to address your hearts and your minds, in all parts of our beloved Jordanian land. This is all the more important at this juncture when we have initiated, after seeking God's assistance, and in light of a thorough and extensive study, a series of measures with the aim of enhancing the Palestinian national orientation, and highlighting the Palestinian identity. Our objective is the benefit of the Palestinian cause and the Arab-Palestinian people.

Our decision, as you know, comes after thirty-eight years of the unity of the two banks, and fourteen years after the Rabat summit resolution, designating the Palestine Liberation Organization (PLO) as the sole legitimate representative of the Palestinian people. It also comes six years after the Fez summit resolution that agreed unanimously on the establishment of an independent Palestinian state in the occupied West Bank and the Gaza Strip, as one of the bases, and results of the peaceful settlement.

We are certain that our decision to initiate these measures does not come as a surprise to you. Many among you have anticipated it, and some of you have been calling for it for some time. As for its contents, it has been, for everyone, a topic for discussion and consideration since the Rabat conference.

Nevertheless, some may wonder: why now? Why today, and not after the Rabat or Fez summits, for instance?

To answer this question, we need to recall certain facts that preceded the Rabat resolution. We also need to recall the factors that led to the debate, over the slogan-objective which the PLO raised, and worked to gain Arab and international support for: namely, the establishment of an independent Palestinian state. This meant, in addition to the PLO's ambition to embody the Palestinian identity on Palestinian national soil, the separation of the West Bank from the Hashemite Kingdom of Jordan.

I have reviewed the facts that preceded the Rabat resolution, as you recall, before the Arab leaders in the Algiers extraordinary summit last June. It may be important to recall that one of the main facts that I stated was the text of the Unity Resolution of the Two Banks, of April 1950. This resolution affirms, "the reservation of all Arab rights in Palestine and the defense of such rights by all legitimate means—without prejudice to the final settlement of the just cause of the Palestinian people, within the scope of the people's aspirations and of Arab cooperation and international justice."

Another of these facts was our proposal of 1972 outlining alternative forms for the relationship between Jordan and the occupied West Bank and Gaza Strip, after the latters' liberation. One of these alternatives was the maintenance of brotherly cooperation between the Hashemite Kingdom of Jordan and an independent Palestinian state, if the Palestinian people so preferred. This means, simply, that we have declared clearly our commitment to the Palestinian people's right to self-determination on their national soil, including their right to establish their independent Palestinian state, more than two years before the Rabat resolution, and we shall adhere to it until the Palestinian people realize their national goals completely, God willing.

The considerations leading to the search to identify the relationship between the West Bank and the Hashemite Kingdom of Jordan, against the background of the PLO's call for the establishment of an independent Palestinian state, are twofold:

I. The principle of Arab unity, this being a national objective to which all the Arab peoples aspire, and which they all seek to realize.

II. The political reality of the scope of benefit to the Palestinian struggle that accrues from maintaining the legal relationship between the two banks of the kingdom.

Our answer to the question, "Why now?" also derives from these two factors, and the background of the clear and constant Jordanian position on the Palestinian cause, as already outlined.

Regarding the principle of Arab unity, we believe that such unity between two or more Arab peoples is a right of choice for every Arab people. Based on that, we have responded to the wish of the representatives of the Palestinian people for unity with Jordan in 1950. Within this context, we respect the wish of the PLO, the sole, legitimate representative of the Palestinian people, to secede from us in an independent Palestinian state. We say this in all understanding. Nevertheless, Jordan will remain the proud bearer of the message of the great Arab revolt; faithful to its principles; believing in the common Arab destiny; and committed to joint Arab action.

Regarding the political factor, it has been our belief, since the Israeli aggression of June 1967, that our first priority should be to liberate the land and holy places from Israeli occupation.

Accordingly, as is well known, we have concentrated all our efforts during the twenty-one years since the occupation toward this goal. We had never imagined that the preservation of the legal and administrative links between the two banks could constitute an obstacle to the liberation of the occupied Palestinian land. Consequently, during the period before adopting these measures, we did not see a reason to do so, particularly since our position, which calls for, and supports, the Palestinian people's rights to self-determination, was clear beyond equivocation.

Lately, it has transpired that there is a general Palestinian and Arab orientation toward highlighting the Palestinian identity in a complete manner, in every effort or activity related to the Palestinian question and its developments. It has also become clear that there is a general conviction, that maintaining the legal and administrative links with the West Bank, and the ensuing Jordanian interaction with our Palestinian brothers under occupation, through Jordanian institutions in the occupied territories, contradicts this orientation. It is also viewed that these links hamper the Palestinian struggle to gain international support for the Palestinian cause, as the national cause of a people struggling against foreign occupation.

In view of this line of thought, which is certainly inspired by genuine Palestinian will, and Arab determination to support the Palestinian cause, it becomes our duty to be part of this direction, and to respond to its requirements. After all, we are a part of our nation, supportive of its causes, foremost among which is the Palestinian cause. Since there is a general conviction that the struggle to liberate the occupied Palestinian land could be enhanced by dismantling the legal and administrative links between the two banks, we have to fulfill our duty, and do what is required of us. At the Rabat summit of 1974 we responded to the Arab leaders' appeal to us to continue our interaction with the occupied West Bank through the Jordanian institutions, to support the steadfastness of our brothers there. Today we respond to the wish of the Palestine Liberation Organization, the sole, legitimate representative of the Palestinian people and to the Arab orientation to affirm the Palestinian identity in all its aspects. We pray God that this step be a substantive addition to the intensifying Palestinian struggle for freedom and independence.

Brother Citizens,

These are the reasons, considerations, and convictions that led us to respond to the wish of the PLO, and the general Arab direction consistent with it. We cannot continue in this state of suspension, which can neither serve Jordan nor the Palestinian cause. We had to leave the labyrinth of fears and doubts, toward clearer horizons where mutual trust, understanding, and cooperation can prevail, to the benefit of the Palestinian cause and Arab unity. This unity will remain a goal which all the Arab peoples cherish and seek to realize.

At the same time, it has to be understood in all clarity, and without any ambiguity or equivocation, that our measures regarding the West Bank, concern only the occupied Palestinian land and its people. They naturally do not relate in any way to the Jordanian citizens of Palestinian origin in the Hashemite Kingdom of Jordan. They all have the full rights of citizenship and all its obligations, the same as any other citizen irrespective of his origin. They are an integral part of the Jordanian state. They belong to it, they live on its land, and they participate in its life and all its activities. Jordan is not Palestine; and the independent Palestinian state will be established on the occupied Palestinian land after its liberation, God willing. There the Palestinian identity will be embodied, and there the Palestinian struggle shall come to fruition, as confirmed by the glorious uprising of the Palestinian people under occupation. . . .

. . . Jordan will not give up its commitment to take part in the peace process. We have contributed to the peace process until it reached the stage of a consensus to convene an international peace conference on the Middle East. The purpose of the conference would be to achieve a just and comprehensive peace settlement to the Arab Israeli conflict, and the settlement of the Palestinian problem in all its aspects.

Document 32

Palestine National Council's "Palestinian Declaration of Independence," Algiers, Nov. 15, 1988, *Journal of Palestine Studies*, Winter 1989, vol. 19, 213–16.

In the name of God, the Compassionate, the Merciful.

Palestine, the land of the three monotheistic faiths, is where the Palestinian Arab people was born, on which it grew, developed, and excelled. The Palestinian people was never separated from or diminished in its integral bonds with Palestine. Thus the Palestinian Arab people ensured for itself an everlasting union between itself, its land, and its history.

Resolute throughout that history, the Palestinian Arab people forged its national identity. . . .

Nourished by an unfolding series of civilizations and cultures, inspired by a heritage rich in variety and kind, the Palestinian Arab people added to its stature by consolidating a union between itself and its patrimonial land. The call went out from temple, church, and mosque to praise the Creator, to celebrate compassion, and peace was indeed the message of Palestine. . . .

When in the course of modern times a new order of values was declared with norms and values fair for all, it was the Palestinian Arab people that had been excluded from the destiny of all other peoples by a hostile array of local and foreign powers. . . .

And it was the Palestinian people, already wounded in its body, that was submitted to yet another type of occupation over which floated the falsehood that "Palestine was a land without people." This notion was foisted upon some in the world, whereas in Article 22 of the Covenant of the League of Nations (1919) and in the Treaty of Lausanne (1923), the community of nations had recognized that all the Arab territories, including Palestine, of the formerly Ottoman provinces were to have granted to them their freedom as provisionally independent nations.

Despite the historical injustice inflicted on the Palestinian Arab people resulting in their dispersion and depriving them of their right to self-determination, following upon UN General Assembly Resolution 181 (1947), which partitioned Palestine into two states, one Arab, one Jewish, yet it is this resolution that still provides those conditions of international legitimacy that ensure the right of the Palestinian Arab people to sovereignty and national independence.

By stages, the occupation of Palestine and parts of other Arab territories by Israeli forces, the willed dispossession and expulsion from their ancestral homes of the majority of Palestine's civilian inhabitants was achieved by organized terror; those Palestinians who remained, as a vestige subjugated in its homeland, were persecuted and forced to endure the destruction of their national life.

Thus were principles of international legitimacy violated. Thus were the Charter of the United Nations and its resolutions disfigured, for they had recognized the Palestinian Arab people's national rights, including the Right of Return, the Right to Independence, the Right to Sovereignty over territory and homeland.

In Palestine and on its perimeters, in exile distant and near, the Palestinian Arab people never faltered and never abandoned its conviction in its rights of return and independence. Occupation, massacres, and dispersion achieved no gain in the unabated Palestinian consciousness of self and political identity, as Palestinians went forward with their destiny, undeterred and unbowed. And from out of the long years of trial in evermounting struggle, the Palestinian political identity emerged further consolidated and confirmed. And the collective Palestinian national will forged itself in a political embodiment, the Palestine Liberation Organization, its sole, legitimate representative, recognized by the world community as a whole, as well as by related regional and international institutions. Standing on the very rock of conviction in the Palestinian people's inalienable rights, and on the ground of Arab national consensus, and of international legitimacy, the PLO led the campaigns of its great people, molded into unity and powerful resolve, one and indivisible in the triumphs, even as it suffered massacres and confinement within and without its home. And so Palestinian resistance was clarified and raised into the forefront of Arab and world awareness, as the struggle of the Palestinian Arab people achieved unique prominence among the world's liberation movements in the modern era.

The massive national uprising, the *intifadah*, now intensifying in cumulative scope and power on occupied Palestinian territories, as well as the unflinching resistance of the refugee camps outside the homeland, have elevated consciousness of the Palestinian truth and right into still higher realms of comprehension and actuality. Now at last the curtain has been dropped around a whole epoch of prevarication and negation. The Intifadah has set siege to the mind of official Israel, which has for too long relied exclusively upon myth and terror to deny Palestinian existence altogether. Because of the Intifadah and its revolutionary irreversible impulse, the history of Palestine has therefore arrived at a decisive juncture.

Whereas the Palestinian people reaffirms most definitely its inalienable rights in the land of its patrimony:

Now by virtue of natural, historical, and legal rights and the sacrifices of successive generations who gave of themselves in defense of the freedom and independence of their homeland;

In pursuance of resolutions adopted by Arab summit conferences and relying on the authority bestowed by international legitimacy as embodied in the resolutions of the United Nations Organization since 1947;

And in exercise by the Palestinian Arab people of its rights to self-determination, political independence, and sovereignty over its territory;

The Palestine National Council, in the name of God, and in the name of the Palestinian Arab people, hereby proclaims the establishment of the State of Palestine on our Palestinian territory with its capital Jerusalem (Al-Quds Ash-Sharif).

The State of Palestine is the state of Palestinians wherever they may be. The state is for them to enjoy in it their collective national and cultural identity, theirs to pursue in it a complete equality of rights. In it will be safeguarded their political and religious convictions and their human dignity by means of a parliamentary democratic system of governance, itself based on freedom of expression and the freedom to form parties. The rights of minorities will duly be respected by the majority, as minorities must abide by decisions of the majority. Governance will be based on principles of social justice, equality and nondiscrimination in public rights on grounds of race, religion, color, or sex under the aegis of a constitution which ensures the role of law and [an] independent judiciary. Thus shall these principles allow no departure from Palestine's age-old spiritual and civilizational heritage of tolerance and religious co-existence.

The State of Palestine is an Arab state, an integral and indivisible part of the Arab nation, at one with that nation in heritage and civilization, with it also in its aspiration for liberation, progress, democracy, and unity. The State of Palestine affirms its obligation to abide by the Charter of the League of Arab States, whereby the coordination of the Arab states with each other shall be strengthened. It calls upon Arab compatriots to consolidate and enhance the emergence in reality of our State, to mobilize potential, and to intensify efforts whose goal is to end Israeli occupation.

The State of Palestine proclaims its commitment to the principles and purposes of the United Nations, and to the Universal Declaration of Human Rights. It proclaims its commitment as well to the principles and policies of the Non-Aligned Movement.

It further announces itself to be a peace-loving state, in adherence to the principles of peaceful co-existence. It will join with all states and peoples in order to assure a permanent peace based upon justice and the respect of rights so that humanity's potential for well-being may be assured, an earnest competition for excellence be maintained, and in which confidence in the future will eliminate fear for those who are just and for whom justice is the only recourse.

In the context of its struggle for peace in the land of love and peace, the State of Palestine calls upon the United Nations to bear special responsibility for the Palestinian Arab people and its homeland. It calls upon all peace- and freedom-loving peoples and states to assist it in the attainment of its objectives, to provide it with security, to alleviate the tragedy of its people, and to help to terminate Israel's occupation of the Palestinian territories.

The State of Palestine herewith declares that it believes in the settlement of regional and international disputes by peaceful means, in accordance with the UN Charter and resolutions. Without prejudice to its natural right to defend its territorial integrity and independence, it therefore rejects the threat or use of force, violence, and terrorism against its territorial integrity, or political independence, as it also rejects their use against the territorial integrity of other states.

Therefore, on this day unlike all others, 15 November, 1988, as we stand at the threshold of a new dawn, in all honor and modesty we humbly bow to the sacred spirits of our fallen ones, Palestinian and Arab, by the purity of whose sacrifice for the homeland our sky has been illuminated and our land given life. Our hearts are lifted up and irradiated by the light emanating from the much blessed *intifadah,* from those who have endured and have fought the fight of the camps, of dispersion, of exile, from those who have borne the standard of freedom, our children, our aged, our youth, our prisoners, detainees, and wounded, all those whose ties to our sacred soil are confirmed in camp, village, and town. We render special tribute to that brave Palestinian woman, guardian of sustenance and life, keeper of our people's perennial flame.

To the souls of our sainted martyrs, to the whole of our Palestinian Arab people, to all free and honorable peoples everywhere, we pledge that our struggle shall be continued until the occupation ends, and the foundation of our sovereignty and independence shall be fortified accordingly.

Therefore, we call upon our great people to rally to the banner of Palestine, to cherish and defend it, so that it may forever be the symbol of our freedom and dignity in that homeland, which is a homeland for the free, now and always.

Document 33

Palestine National Council's Political Communiqué, Algiers, Nov. 15, 1988, *Journal of Palestine Studies,* Winter 1989, vol. 19, 219–23.

In accordance with the will of our masses in and outside of our homeland, and in fidelity to those of our people that have been martyred, wounded, or taken captive, the Palestine National Council resolves:

First: On The Escalation and Continuity of the Intifadah

A. To provide all the means and capabilities needed to escalate our people's *intifadah* in various ways and on various levels to guarantee its continuation and intensification.

B. To support the popular institutions and organizations in the occupied Palestinian territories.

C. To bolster and develop the popular committees and other specialized popular and trade union bodies, including the attack groups and the popular army, with a view to expanding their role and increasing their effectiveness.

D. To consolidate the national unity that emerged and developed during the *intifadah.*

E. To intensify efforts on the international level for the release of detainees, the return of those expelled, and the termination of the organized, official acts of repression and terrorism against our children, our women, our men, and our institutions.

F. To call on the United Nations to place the occupied Palestinian land under international supervision for the protection of our people and the termination of the Israeli occupation.

G. To call on the Palestinian people outside our homeland to intensify and increase their support, and to expand the family-assistance program.

H. To call on the Arab nation, its people, forces, institutions, and governments, to increase their political, material, and informational support for the *intifadah.*

I. To call on all free and honorable people worldwide to stand by our people, our revolution, our *intifadah* against the Israeli occupation, the repression, and the organized, fascist official terrorism to which occupation forces and the armed fanatic settlers are subjecting our people, our universities, our institutions, our national economy, and our Islamic and Christian holy places.

Second: In the Political Arena

Proceeding from the above, the Palestinian National Council, being responsible to the Palestinian people, their national rights and their desire for peace as expressed in the Declaration of Independence issued on 15 November 1988; and in response to the humanitarian quest for international entente, nuclear disarmament, and the settlement of regional conflict by peaceful means, affirms the determination of the Palestine Liberation Organization to arrive at a comprehensive settlement of the Arab-Israeli conflict and its core, which is the question of Palestine, within the framework of the United Nations Charter, the principles and provisions of international legality, the norms of international law, and the resolutions of the United Nations, the latest of which are Security Council resolutions 605, 607, and 608, and the resolutions of the Arab summits, in such a manner that safeguards the Palestinian Arab people's rights to return, to self-determination, and the establishment of their independent national state or their national soil, and that institutes arrangements for the security and peace of all states in the region.

Toward the achievement of this, the Palestine National Council affirms:

1. The necessity of convening the effective international conference on the issue of the Middle East and its core, the question of Palestine, under the auspices of the United Nations and with the participation of the permanent members of the Security Council and all parties to the conflict in the region including the Palestine Liberation Organization, the sole, legitimate representative of the Palestinian people, on an equal footing, and by considering that the international peace conference be convened on the basis of United Nations Security Council resolutions 242 and 338 and the attainment of the legitimate national rights of the Palestinian people, foremost among which is the right to self-determination and in accordance with the principles and provisions of the United Nations Charter concerning the right of peoples to self-determination, and by the inadmissibility of the acquisition of the territory of others by force or military conquest, and in accordance with the relevant United Nations resolutions on the question of Palestine.

2. The withdrawal of Israel from all the Palestinian and Arab territories it occupied in 1967, including Arab Jerusalem.

3. The annullment of all measures of annexation and appropriation and the removal of settlements established by Israel in the Palestinian and Arab territories since 1967.

4. Endeavoring to place the occupied Palestinian territories, including Arab Jerusalem, under the auspices of the United Nations for a limited period in order to protect our people and afford the appropriate atmosphere for the success of the proceeding of the international conference toward the attainment of a comprehensive political settlement and the attainment of peace and security for all on the basis of mutual acquiescence and consent, and to enable the Palestinian state to exercise its effective authority in these territories.

5. The settlement of the question of the Palestinian refugees in accordance with the relevant United Nations resolutions.

6. Guaranteeing the freedom of worship and religious practice for all faiths in the holy places in Palestine.

7. The Security Council is to formulate and guarantee arrangements for security and peace between all the states concerned in the region, including the Palestinian state.

The Palestine National Council affirms its previous resolutions concerning the distinctive relationship between the Jordanian and Palestinian peoples, and affirms that the future relationship between the two states of Palestine and Jordan should be on a confederal basis as a result the free and voluntary choice of the two fraternal peoples in order to strengthen the historical bonds and the vital interests they hold in common.

The National Council also renews its commitment to the United Nations resolutions that affirm the right of peoples to resist foreign occupation, colonialism, and racial discrimination, and their right to struggle for their independence, and reiterates its rejection of terrorism in all its forms, including state terrorism, affirming its commitment to previous resolutions in this respect and the resolution of the Arab summit in Algiers in 1988, and to UN resolutions 42/195 of 1987, and 40/61 of 1985, and that contained in the Cairo declaration of 1985 in this respect. . . .

The Council notes with considerable concern the growth of the Israeli forces of fascism and extremism and the escalation of their open calls for the implementation of their policy of annihilation and individual and mass expulsion of our people from their homeland, and calls for intensified efforts in all arenas to confront this fascist peril. The Council at the same time expresses its appreciation of the role and courage of the Israeli peace forces as they resist and expose the forces of fascism, racism, and aggression; support our people's struggle and their valiant *intifadah*; and back our people's right to self-determination and the establishment of an independent state. The Council confirms its past resolutions regarding the reinforcement and development of relations with these democratic forces.

The Palestine National Council also addresses itself to the American people, calling on them all to strive to put an end to the American policy that denies the Palestinian people's national rights, including their sacred right to self-determination, and urging them to work toward the adoption of policies that conform with the human rights charter and the international conventions and resolutions and serve the quest for peace in the Middle East and security for all its peoples, including the Palestinian people. . . .

In conclusion, the Palestine National Council affirms its complete confidence that the justice of the Palestinian cause and of the demands for which the Palestinian people are struggling will continue to draw increasing support from honorable and free people around the world; and also affirms its complete confidence in victory on the road to Jerusalem, the capital of our independent Palestinian state.

Document 34

Israeli Prime Minister Yitzhak Shamir's Four-Point Plan, Israeli government press release, May 14, 1989.

1. The Camp David Partners—Reconfirmation of the Commitment to Peace

Ten years ago, the peace treaty between Israel and Egypt was concluded on the basis of the Camp David Accords. When the accords were signed, it was expected that more Arab countries would shortly join the circle of peace. This expectation was not realized.

The strength of Israeli-Egyptian relations and the cooperation between the three partners to the accords have a decisive influence on the chances for Middle East peace, and the Israeli-Egyptian treaty is the cornerstone to the building of peace in the region.

Therefore, the prime minister has called on the three countries whose leaders affixed their signature to the Camp David Accords—the US, Egypt, and Israel—to renew, 10 years later, their commitment to the agreements and to peace.

2. The Arab Countries—From a State of War to a Process of Peace

The prime minister urged the US and

Egypt to call on the other Arab countries to desist from hostility toward Israel and to replace belligerency and boycott with negotiation and cooperation. Of all the Arab countries, only Egypt has recognized Israel and its right to exist. Many of these states actively participated in wars against Israel by direct involvement or indirect assistance. To this day, the Arab countries are partners in an economic boycott against Israel, refuse to recognize it, and refuse to establish diplomatic relations with it.

The solution to the Arab-Israeli conflict and the building of confidence leading to a permanent settlement require a change in the attitude of the Arab countries toward Israel. Israel, therefore, calls on these states to put an end to this historic anomaly and to join direct bilateral negotiations aimed at normalization and peace.

3. A Solution to the Refugee Problem—An International Effort

The prime minister has called for an international effort, led by the US and with the significant participation of Israel, to solve the problem of the Arab refugees. The refugee problem has been perpetuated by the leaders of the Arab countries, while Israel with its meagre resources is absorbing hundreds of thousands of Jewish refugees from Arab countries. Settling the refugees must not wait for a political process or come in its stead.

The matter must be viewed as a humanitarian problem and action must be taken to ease the human distress of the refugees and to ensure for their families appropriate living quarters and self-respect.

Some 300,000 people live in refugee camps in Judea, Samaria and the Gaza District. In the 1970s, Israel unilaterally undertook the rehabilitation of residents of refugee camps in Gaza and erected 10 neighborhoods in which 11,000 families reside. This operation was carried out in partnership with the residents despite PLO objections.

The time has now come to ensure appropriate infrastructure, living quarters and services for the rest of the residents of the camps who, at the same time, are victims of the conflict, hostages to it, and an element which perpetuates its continued existence.

Good will and an international effort to allocate the necessary resources will ensure a satisfactory solution to this humanitarian effort and will help improve the political climate in the region.

4. Free Elections in Judea, Samaria and Gaza on the Road to Negotiations

In order to bring about a process of political negotiations and in order to locate legitimate representatives of the Palestinian population, the prime minister proposes that free elections be held among the Arabs of Judea, Samaria and Gaza—elections that will be free of the intimidation and terror of the PLO.

These elections will permit the development of an authentic representation that is not self-appointed from the outside. This representation will be comprised of people who will be chosen by the population in free elections and who will express, in advance, their willingness to take part in the following diplomatic process.

The aim of the elections is to bring about the establishment of a delegation that will participate in negotiations on an interim settlement, in which a self-governing administration will be set up. The interim period will serve as an essential test of cooperation and coexistence. It will be followed by negotiations on the final settlement, in which Israel will be prepared to discuss any option which will be presented.

The US administration has expressed

its support for the idea, and following the prime minister's return, his proposals will be discussed here and the various questions surrounding the holding of elections will be examined. Contacts necessary for the implementation of the proposals will be maintained.

Document 35

Secretary of State James Baker, "Principles and Pragmatism: American Policy Toward the Arab-Israeli Conflict," address before American-Israel Public Affairs Committee (AIPAC), Washington, D.C., May 22, 1989, U.S. Department of State, *Bureau of Public Affairs*, May 1989, 2–3.

U.S. Views

. . . U.S. policies benefit from a long-standing commitment to sound principles, principles which have worked in practice to advance the peace process. Let me mention some of those principles for you.

First, the United States believes that the objective of the peace process is a comprehensive settlement achieved through negotiations based on UN Security Council Resolutions 242 and 338. In our view, these negotiations must involve territory for peace, security and recognition for Israel and all of the states of the region, and Palestinian political rights.

Second, for negotiations to succeed they must allow the parties to deal directly with each other, face to face. A properly structured international conference could be useful at an appropriate time, but only if it did not interfere with or in any way replace or be a substitute for direct talks between the parties.

Third, the issues involved in the negotiations are far too complex, and the emotions are far too deep, to move directly to a final settlement. Accordingly, some transitional period is needed, associated in time and sequence with negotiations on final status. Such a transition will allow the parties to take the measure of each other's performance, to encourage attitudes to change, and to demonstrate that peace and coexistence is desired.

Fourth, in advance of direct negotiations, neither the United States nor any other party, inside or outside, can or will dictate an outcome. That is why the United States does not support annexation or permanent Israeli control of the West Bank and Gaza, nor do we support the creation of an independent Palestinian state.

I would add here, that we do have an idea about the reasonable middle ground to which a settlement should be directed. That is, self-government for Palestinians in the West Bank and Gaza in a manner acceptable to Palestinians, Israel, and Jordan. Such a formula provides ample scope for Palestinians to achieve their full political rights. It also provides ample protection for Israel's security as well.

Prenegotiations

Following these principles, we face a pragmatic issue, the issue of how do we get negotiations underway. Unfortunately, the gap between the parties on key issues such as Palestinian representation and the shape of a final settlement remains very, very wide. Violence has soured the atmosphere, and so a quick move to negotiations is quite unlikely. And in the absence of either a minimum of good will or any movement to close the gap, a high-visibility American initiative, we think, has little basis on which to stand. . . .

We should not hide from ourselves the difficulties that face even these steps here at the very beginning. For many Israelis it will not be easy to enter a negotiating process whose successful outcome will in all probability involve territorial withdrawal and the emergence of a new political reality. For Palestinians such an outcome will mean an end to the illusion of control over all of Palestine, and it will mean full recognition of Israel as a neighbor and partner in trade and in human contact.

Challenges Ahead

We do not think there is a real constructive alternative to the process which I have outlined. Continuation of the status quo will lead to increasing violence and worsening prospects for peace. We think now is the time to move toward a serious negotiating process, to create the atmosphere for a renewed peace process.

Let the Arab world take concrete steps toward accommodation with Israel—not in place of the peace process, but as a catalyst for it. And so we would say: end the economic boycott; stop the challenges to Israel's standing in international organizations; repudiate the odious line that Zionism is racism.

For Israel, now is the time to lay aside, once and for all, the unrealistic vision of a greater Israel. Israeli interests in the West Bank and Gaza—security and otherwise—can be accommodated in a settlement based on Resolution 242. Forswear annexation. Stop settlement activity. Allow schools to reopen. Reach out to the Palestinians as neighbors who deserve political rights.

For Palestinians, now is the time to speak with one voice for peace. Renounce the policy of phases in all languages, not just those addressed to the West. Practice constructive diplomacy, not attempts to distort international organizations, such as the World Health Organization. Amend the covenant. Translate the dialogue of violence in the *intifada* into a dialogue of politics and diplomacy. Violence will not work. Reach out to Israelis and convince them of your peaceful intentions. You have the most to gain from doing so, and no one else can or *will* do it for you. Finally, understand that no one is going to "deliver" Israel for you.

For outside parties—in particular, the Soviet Union—now is the time to make "new thinking" a reality as it applies to the Middle East. I must say that Chairman [Mikhail] Gorbachev and Foreign Minister [Eduard] Shevardnadze told me in Moscow 10 days ago that Soviet policy is changing. New laws regarding emigration will soon be discussed by the Supreme Soviet. Jewish life in the Soviet Union is also looking better, with students beginning to study their heritage freely. Finally, the Soviet Union agreed with us last week that Prime Minister [Yitzhak] Shamir's election proposal was worthy of consideration.

These, of course, are all positive signs. But the Soviets must go further to demonstrate convincingly that they are serious about new thinking in the Arab-Israeli conflict. Let Moscow restore diplomatic ties with Israel, for example.

The Soviets should also help promote a serious peace process, not just empty slogans. And it is time for the Soviet Union, we think, to behave responsibly when it comes to arms and stop the supply of sophisticated weapons to countries like Libya. . . .

The policy I have described today reaffirms and renews that course. For our part, the United States will move ahead steadily and carefully, in a step-by-step approach designed to help the parties make the necessary decisions for peace.

Perhaps Judge Learned Hand expressed it best when he said, ". . . we shall have to be content with short steps; . . . but we shall have gone forward, if we bring to our task . . . patience, understanding, sympathy, forbearance, generosity, fortitude and above all an inflexible determination."

Document 36

Egyptian President Hosni Mubarak's "Ten Points," *Washington Post*, Sept. 24, 1989.

• The necessity for all citizens of the West Bank and Gaza Strip (including the residents of East Jerusalem) to participate in the elections, both in voting and as candidates. This allows for the participation of those under administrative detention, but excludes those convicted of crimes.

• Freedom to campaign before and during the elections.

• Acceptance of international supervision of the election process.

• Prior commitment of Israel's government to accept the results of the election.

• Israel's commitment that the elections will be part of the effort that will lead not only to an interim phase, but also to a final settlement, and that all efforts from beginning to end will be based on the principles of U.N. resolutions 242 and 338 and will ensure the security of all the states of the region, including Israel, and Palestinian political rights.

• Withdrawal of the Israeli army during the election process at least one kilometer outside the perimeters of the polling stations.

• Prohibition of Israelis from entering the West Bank and Gaza on election day, except those who work there and settlement residents.

• The preparatory period for elections should not exceed two months. Preparations shall be undertaken by a joint Israeli-Palestinian committee the United States and Egypt may assist in forming.

• A guarantee by the United States of all the above points and a prior declaration to that effect by Israel.

• A halt to further Jewish settlements.

Document 37

Secretary of State James Baker's proposed "Five Points" regarding Israeli-Palestinian talks, *Washington Post*, Dec. 7, 1989.

1. The United States understands that because Egypt and Israel have been working hard on the peace process, there is agreement that an Israeli delegation should conduct a dialogue with a Palestinian delegation in Cairo.

2. The United States understands that Egypt cannot substitute itself for the Palestinians and Egypt will consult with Palestinians on all aspects of that dialogue. Egypt will also consult with Israel and the United States.

3. The United States understands that Israel will attend the dialogue only after a satisfactory list of Palestinians has been worked out.

4. The United States understands that the government of Israel will come to the dialogue on the basis of the Israeli government's May 14 initiative. The United States further understands that Palestinians will come to the dialogue prepared to discuss elections and the negotiating process in accordance with Israel's initiative.

The U.S. understands, therefore, that

Palestinians would be free to raise issues that relate to their opinions on how to make elections and the negotiating process succeed.

5. In order to facilitate this process, the U.S. proposes that the foreign ministers of Israel, Egypt and the U.S. meet in Washington within two weeks.

Document 38

Secretary of State James Baker, news conference, "Two-Track Approach Toward Peace in the Middle East," Mar. 10, 1991, U.S. Department of State Dispatch, Mar. 18, 1991, 181.

I know you are interested in the peace process, so let me say a word or two about that, and then I'll try and respond to your questions. First of all, as you know, we have been trying to work a two-track approach. I've been exploring with our Arab coalition partners what steps they might be able to take to signal their commitment to peace and reconciliation with Israel. Before this trip began, we had communicated to Israel the general outlines of our two-track approach, and I am now going to have the opportunity, when we get to Israel, to talk in detail and specifically with their leadership about what steps they might be willing to consider. Let me say, I am not going to go into the specific steps now because we are still exploring that. We still have a long way to go. It is very, very early. We are trying to get a process going, and I would simply say that I have a sense that even though it is early, there is a greater willingness to be active on this issue in the aftermath of the Gulf crisis than there was before.

Q. Reading the statement tonight, both the Arab portion of it and the latter part, there doesn't appear to be anything here on the track of direct contacts with Israel, state to state. It all refers to the Palestinian issue, and I ask you—also, I should tell you that in the public statement of the ministers today, there was no indication of a willingness to go on that track. We have been told over and over again, this is a two-track process. Did you hear anything in private that would dissuade us from the view that the Arab foreign ministers and Gulf ministers were only talking about one track?

Secretary Baker. Well, we talked at length about two tracks, and I made it very clear, at a very early stage in what we hope will be a process, we have not as yet even arrived in Israel. We have not had detailed discussions with the Israeli government about what steps they might be willing to consider and so, therefore, I don't think it is surprising that you don't have Arab governments coming out and unilaterally making statements about steps that they would be willing to take in the absence of knowing a little bit more about what might develop as the process moves forward.

Q. You still are not really saying though whether the two-track approach is still alive and the second half of the question is in your statement: You say that the United States plans to signal peace and reconciliation to Israel. Is there any signal here beyond their traditional approach?

Secretary Baker. Well, you read the language. The wording you just read sounds to me like it's like a signal. In terms of whether it's still alive, let me simply say that it was only born very, very recently, so please don't declare it dead until it's actually dead. I happen to think that it's at least alive until we explore the concept and the possibilities with the leadership of Israel. Let me say that I think that the Arab governments with whom we talked generally about this today exhibited, as I have just indicated to you, a greater willingness to be active than they had in the past or than they did before the Gulf crisis was resolved, and I would interpret that to be a willingness to be active along both tracks, assuming it is a process that is embraced by others, including, most importantly, Israel.

Q. Did the Arab states with whom you met today give you specific concrete things they are willing to do assuming that there is reciprocity of some sort on the part of the Israelis?

Secretary Baker. We are not at that point. I did not ask them to commit themselves in the absence of knowing what might or might not be possible on the other side of the equation. What I asked them to do was to simply consider the possibility of participating in this process and developing, in due course, some specific steps that they would be willing to consider taking if there was a willingness expressed on the part of the government of Israel.

Document 39

Joint news conference by Secretary of State James Baker and Israeli Foreign Minister David Levy, Jerusalem, Mar. 11, 1991, U.S. Department of State Dispatch, Mar. 18, 1991, 182.

Q. Mr. Secretary, either in your talks tonight or in your meeting tomorrow with Prime Minister [Yitzhak] Shamir, have you or will you ask Israel to commit itself in principle to trading land for peace?

Secretary Baker. . . . I told the minister and his colleagues this evening that I think that there are great opportunities in the aftermath of the recently concluded war; that I think the time is now for us to try and seize the moment to try and take advantage of these opportunities; that I sensed during my 2 days in Riyadh the beginnings of perhaps a bit of a different attitude on the part of some countries; that we would like to pursue the possibilities of peace on a dual track—moving in parallel on the track of Arab state-Israeli relations and on the path of Israeli-Palestinian relations, dialogue, and so forth.

CHAPTER 14

The United States and Latin America since 1963

Lester D. Langley

The experience of the United States in Latin America in the aftermath of the Cuban missile crisis has been one of accomplishment and frustration. Essentially, the United States has sought twin goals: the preservation of its security interests, particularly in the Caribbean basin, and the sustenance of hemispheric economic development in accordance with Western political tradition. Latin America has largely rejected the Cuban socialist economic and political model, but it has adapted, rather than adopted, the U.S. capitalist example for its development. In the generation since President John F. Kennedy's death, Latin Americans have confronted the dual tasks of economic development and social policy with both civilian and military governments that range from left to right on the political spectrum. In the process, they have generally resisted U.S. intervention, particularly in the Dominican Republic in 1965, and have been critical of U.S. policies that reflect Washington's strategic concerns, such as those pursued in Central America in the 1980s. From the late 1960s, Latin America's leaders have sought greater economic independence from the United States while urging Washington to give more attention to trade inequities and debt.

On the surface, the issues dividing the United States and Latin America—and the common interests that unite them—would appear to be so unambiguous that political leaders on either side of the border should have little difficulty in articulating sensible policies or in reconciling disputes. Most Americans, for example, believe that the success of U.S. policy depends on either the willingness to use economic and/or military pressure to sustain strategic interests or, conversely, economic aid for governments that are striving to better the living conditions of their peoples. When *neither* pressure nor aid works, their reactions range from frustration and despair to indifference and, finally, acceptance of a military solution to a social and economic problem when U.S. strategic interests are at stake.

It can be argued—and U.S. policy in Central America since 1979 is often cited as an example—that Washington is so determined to preserve strategic interests and expand markets for American companies that it demands political subservience as the price of foreign aid. The argument is undeniable, but it cannot explain why policies work in one place but fail in another, why Latin American governments defy Washington's advice when it is in their interest to follow it, or why they can be indifferent to warnings about clear and present dangers to their survival. More fundamentally, it does not explain why Americans encounter both pro- and anti-American feelings in the same person in Latin America.

Every generalization about Latin America requires a qualification, but one is necessary to understand the dynamics of the inter-American relationship. Latin Americans make a distinction between the "United States" and "America." The United States is a political entity; America is a place. The United States, according to Latin American perceptions, has interests; America has principles. America says one thing; the United States does another (or vice versa). The United States made war on Fidel Castro's Cuba; America took Cuban refugees.

Throughout U.S. history, this duality has bequeathed a legacy. The Monroe Doctrine (enunciated in 1823 and reaffirmed in the aftermath of "Irangate," the Iran-*contra* affair, in 1987) had two faces: one reflected the strategic interests of the United States in the declaration of opposition to further European territorial expansion in the New World; the other expressed the aspirations of America for republican governments. In 1980, during the Mariel boatlift, President Jimmy Carter of America welcomed Cubans to freedom while President Jimmy Carter of the United States declared their entry a violation of its immigration laws. Thus the United States and America have bequeathed different hemispheres—the first crafted by governments, the other by their peoples.

The following documents illustrate the frustrations encountered by the United States in modern Latin America. More generally, they reveal the inevitable confusion over purpose that occurs when the United States strives to articulate and then carry out policies to safeguard its national interest. In the implementation of these policies, the United States violates the democratic promise of America: faith in individual liberty and self-determination for hemispheric peoples. In the first document, President Lyndon B. Johnson defends his decision to intervene in the Dominican Republic in 1965, which culminated in the dispatch of 20,000 troops (most of them American) to the island. (doc. 1) It is still widely believed among Latin Americans that Johnson's actions revived "gunboat diplomacy."

The Dominican affair occurred as the Alliance for Progress—the heralded social and economic program for Latin America that began in 1961, the first year of the Kennedy administration—was "losing its way." The alliance fell victim to the U.S. obsession with security interests, the shift toward a more pro-business foreign economic policy, the resurgence of Latin American militarism, and the distraction of Vietnam. Already, liberal congressmen expressed doubts about a foreign aid program that carried too few demands for participatory democracy or civilian government. At the same time, Latin Americans banded together to win greater influence in the Organization of American States (OAS), which was formed in 1948 to foster peace and cooperation among nations of the Western Hemisphere. Latin Americans called for alternative economic strategies to the Puerto Rican developmental model that Washington had implanted in the Alliance for Progress, an OAS program.

New York Governor Nelson Rockefeller's 1969 report on the quality of life in Latin America (doc. 2) seemed to validate cynical assessments of the alliance: despite heavy expenditures and impressive accomplishments, Latin America's poor were, in fact, poorer, and the threat of Communist insurgency was greater. Had the United States failed? Did it require a new approach to Latin America? Regrettably, too many Americans concurred with the first and acquiesced in the second. In the process they overlooked the quiet triumph of America in the 1960s, expressed most dramatically in a 1965 immigration law that allowed millions of Latin Americans, denied upward mobility in their own countries, to fulfill the alliance dream in a personal way by migrating to the United States. Although sixteen civilian governments fell to military coups in the first eight years of the alliance, Rockefeller pointed out that the modern Latin American officer, unlike his predecessor, often came from the lower classes. In other words, despite the U.S. view of military governments as bad, the military career offered upward social mobility, or, as Latin Americans viewed it, validated social democracy in terms of social status.

Such nuances befuddled Americans—and still do. Willing to concede that Latin America worked differently, they were willing to try new approaches. But they were loath to admit that often the determining forces in the outcome of policy lay beyond the effective reach of U.S. power. In the meantime, President Richard M. Nixon spoke of a "new dialogue" with Latin American governments that wanted "trade, not aid." But in Chile, the U.S. government tried to prevent socialist Salvador Allende's election to the presidency in 1970 and attempted to destabilize his government after he took office. (doc. 3) Allende joined Castro as the second socialist leader in the hemisphere. More ominously, Allende's Chile (unlike socialist Cuba) served as an example to Western Europe's socialists in an era when NATO (North Atlantic Treaty Organization) commanders were concerned about the peaceful triumph of socialism in their countries.

In 1973, however, the Chilean military overthrew Allende (he died in the fighting), and Chilean socialism quickly perished. The U.S. complicity in his downfall touched off two debates. The first occurred within the U.S. government (especially in Congress) and led to severe restrictions in the conduct of covert operations. A second debate centered on a call for new understanding and awareness of Latin America's dramatic changes and an "end to U.S. hegemony" in the hemisphere. In response, President Carter championed human rights in Latin America and signed new canal treaties with Panama. The latter prompted one of the great Senate debates between those who argued that the United States must do the "right" thing and those who said that it must preserve American "rights." (doc. 4)

In Nicaragua, a popular uprising led by Marxist Sandinista guerrillas in July 1979 toppled the dictatorship of Anastasio Somoza Debayle, whose family had been running the country since the U.S. Marines had left in 1934. A few months later, El Salvador's rightist military regime fell to a reformist military junta that called for civilian governance and land reform. By early 1980, that junta was in turn toppled, and the tiny nation was plunged into a civil war between Marxist guerrillas and the new and repressive military junta. In the beginning, the Carter administration tried to "guide" the Nicaraguan Sandinistas with promises of aid and called for reforms in El Salvador. Later, as evidence of Cuban involvement in El Salvador became more compelling, U.S. pressure increased with the presence of military advisers and military aid.

With the election of Ronald Reagan as president in 1980, U.S. policy shifted even farther to the right. Central America loomed quickly in the early 1980s as a "test case" for U.S. resolve in the East-West conflict. New tactics were required to confront the menace to U.S. security interests, but Central America was not to be "another Vietnam," as Reagan said. Instead, he opted for low-intensity warfare, which meant military aid for El Salvador and Honduras and a covert war against Nicaragua that used surrogate, anti-Sandinista rebels known as *contras*. At the same time, Reagan called for the Caribbean Basin Initiative (which included Central America) in an effort to demonstrate that the United States was responding to the social and economic needs of the region. In reality, the initiative offered too little; its real purpose was to channel funds to the Salvadoran government. The United States also supported José Napoleón Duarte, the Christian Democrat who, with the support of reform-seeking colonels, won the Salvadoran presidency in 1984.

Central America's crisis and U.S. involvement inspired another great either-or debate about U.S. policy in Latin America between those who called for protection of U.S. security interests and those who pressed the case for economic aid but insisted on political reforms from the recipients of that aid. (doc. 5) Congressional liberals, responding to widespread public concerns over the "*contra* war," moved in late 1982 to prohibit use of military funds for operations "in or against Nicaragua." But the House Intelligence Committee, chaired by Democrat Edward Boland, managed to derail this proposal with a substitute measure, the Boland Amendment (doc. 6), prohibiting use of classified funds to carry out paramilitary operations in Nicaragua. However, the measure permitted overt assistance to any Central American government (such as El Salvador) threatened by guerrillas receiving arms through Cuba or Nicaragua. After intense debate in the summer of 1983, the U.S. House of Representatives voted to end *contra* aid. In the following year, the Reagan administration managed to create a makeshift consensus in Congress and pursue the *contra* war. But in 1984, Congress again intruded with the so-called second Boland Amendment, a blanket prohibition of the use of funds by any U.S. government agency or entity involved in intelligence activities designed to support paramilitary operations against Nicaragua. Nonetheless, the Reagan administration argued that the Boland prohibition did not apply to the National Security Council (NSC). Oliver North, a Marine Corps lieutenant colonel assigned to the NSC, subsequently managed a secret network of arms procurement for the *contras*.

Ironically, each side in this debate argued that its approach better guaranteed U.S. security and more ably advanced the cause of democracy. As the decade ended, Central America's often contentious governments were thrashing out the details of a cease-fire initiative and thus were demonstrating that they, not the United States, held the key to regional peace. In the meantime, the revival of Latin American democracy, a process inspired largely from within the region and not from the United States, offered new hope for the hemisphere. The U.S. government then joined other Latin American democracies in condemning the continent's remaining dictators in Paraguay, Chile, and especially in Panama. Yet the U.S. role was negligible in the fall of Paraguayan strongman Alfredo Stroessner in 1989 and in the overwhelming Chilean vote to end military government in their country. Even in Panama, which was more vulnerable to U.S. power, Washington proved at first inept in trying to unseat the dictator, General Manuel Antonio Noriega, through diplomatic and economic sanctions. Embarrassed by Noriega's defiance as well as his drug-running activities, the George Bush administration chose military intervention in December 1989 to accomplish that task. The resort to "gunboat diplomacy" revived Latin American condemnations about U.S. imperialism, but Bush defended the Panamanian intervention as a defense of democracy. (doc. 7)

As the 1980s came to a close, many Latin Americans argued that the United States had to modernize its thinking about the region and exercise less concern about Latin American governments and more awareness of the long-run implications of hemispheric debt, as the economic problems of Mexico demonstrated. (doc. 8) Here, as in the common dilemmas over environmental deterioration and the drug trade, Washington became more amenable to the notion that the United States could not protect its interests with unilateral policies. In the economic arena, Secretary of the Treasury James Baker's plan for debt relief (which in reality rescheduled debts and required austerity measures as a condition for new loans) gave way in the late 1980s to Secretary of the Treasury Nicholas Brady's effort to scale down the debt without tremendous sacrifices. And finally, in groping for a solution to the pressing issue of environmental damage and the drug trade, there was solemn admission that the United States could not go it alone in the hemisphere.

The Panama affair revived an old debate—among both Latin Americans and Americans—about U.S. priorities in Latin America and, specifically, Washington's disposition to employ forceful measures to have its way with a weaker and more vulnerable hemispheric nation. Defenders of the Panama invasion (especially in the U.S. military and in Congress) argued that what happened in Panama was unique in light of Noriega's drug trafficking. The circumstances may have been so, but the choice of force as a solution to a putatively unique problem was certainly not unique. Even so, it seems unlikely that the United States can resolve its hemispheric security problems (which now incorporate the narcotics trade) by measures similar to those taken in Panama. First, Latin America is less vulnerable and certainly less disposed to tolerate such military incursions, despite American professions of acting on behalf of democracy. Latin Americans prefer democracy, but they also prefer governments resulting from their own choosing. Second, within the obvious constraints imposed by the global economy and the unappreciated economic burdens they must bear, Latin Americans are hesitantly charting their own economic agenda. Save for Cuba, they have rejected the Soviet model of development. But this does not imply their slavish acceptance of U.S. development strategies. Finally, despite the persistence of social inequities, the average Latin American coming of age in the 1990s has good reason to be more hopeful of the future than his or her counterpart of the 1960s.

One explanation for this optimism—what has been called a "bias for hope"—lies principally in the faith of this Latin American generation in its own ability to make a more democratic and a more just society. Another reason (one too little appreciated by those who attribute hemispheric change to the undeniable economic and military presence of the United States) rests with the sixteenth-century belief that the New World, including Latin America, would itself ultimately bring forth a new man.

Document 1

President Lyndon B. Johnson, address to the nation on the crisis in the Dominican Republic, May 2, 1965, U.S. Department of State, *Bulletin*, May 17, 1965, 744–47.

There are times in the affairs of nations when great principles are tested in an ordeal of conflict and danger. This is such a time for the American nations.

At stake are the lives of thousands, the liberty of a nation, and the principles and the values of all the American Republics.

That is why the hopes and the concern of this entire hemisphere are on this Sabbath Sunday focused on the Dominican Republic.

In the dark mist of conflict and violence, revolution and confusion, it is not easy to find clear and unclouded truths.

But certain things are clear. And they require equally clear action. . . .

Last week our observers warned of an approaching political storm in the Dominican Republic. I immediately asked our Ambassador [W. Tapley Bennett, Jr.] to return to Washington at once so that we might discuss the situation and might plan a course of conduct. But events soon outran our hopes for peace.

Saturday, April 24—8 days ago—while Ambassador Bennett was conferring with the highest officials of your Government, revolution erupted in the Dominican Republic. Elements of the military forces of that country overthrew their government. However, the rebels themselves were divided. Some wanted to restore former President Juan Bosch. Others opposed his restoration. President Bosch, elected after the fall of [Rafael] Trujillo and his assassination, had been driven from office by an earlier revolution in the Dominican Republic.

Those who opposed Mr. Bosch's return formed a military committee in an effort to control that country. The others took to the street, and they began to lead a revolt on behalf of President Bosch. Control and effective government dissolved in conflict and confusion.

Meanwhile the United States was making a constant effort to restore peace. From Saturday afternoon onward, our Embassy urged a cease-fire, and I and all the officials of the American Government worked with every weapon at our command to achieve it.

On Tuesday the situation of turmoil was presented to the Peace Committee of the Organization of the American States.

On Wednesday the entire Council of the Organization of American States received a full report from the Dominican Ambassador.

Meanwhile, all this time, from Saturday to Wednesday, the danger was mounting. Even though we were deeply saddened by bloodshed and violence in a close and friendly neighbor, we had no desire to interfere in the affairs of a sister Republic.

On Wednesday afternoon there was no longer any choice for the man who is your President. . . . I received a cable from our Ambassador, and he said that things were in danger; he had been informed the chief of police and governmental authorities could no longer protect us. . . .

The cable reported that Dominican law enforcement and military officials had informed our Embassy that the situation was completely out of control and that the police and the government could no longer give any guarantee concerning the safety of Americans or any foreign nationals.

Ambassador Bennett, who is one of our most experienced Foreign Service officers, went on in that cable to say that only an immediate landing of forces could safeguard and protect the lives of thousands of Americans and thousands of other citizens of some 30 other countries. Ambassador Bennett urged your President to order an immediate landing.

In this situation hesitation and vacillation could mean death for many of our people, as well as many of the citizens of other lands.

I thought that we could not and we did not hesitate. Our forces, American forces, were ordered in immediately to protect American lives. They have done that. They have attacked no one, and although some of our servicemen gave their lives, not a single American civilian or the civilian of any other nation, as a result of this protection, lost their lives.

There may be those in our own country who say that such action was good but we should have waited, or we should have delayed, or we should have consulted further, or we should have called a meeting. But from the very beginning, the United States, at my instructions, had worked for a cease-fire beginning the Saturday the revolution took place. The matter was before the OAS Peace Committee on Tuesday, at our suggestion. It was before the full Council on Wednesday, and when I made my announcement to the American people that evening, I announced then I was notifying the Council. . . .

The revolutionary movement took a tragic turn. Communist leaders, many of them trained in Cuba, seeing a chance to increase disorder, to gain a foothold, joined the revolution. . . .

. . . What began as a popular democratic revolution that was committed to democracy and social justice moved into the hands of a band of Communist conspirators. Many of the original leaders of the rebellion, the followers of President Bosch, took refuge in foreign embassies and they are there tonight.

The American nations cannot, must not, and will not permit the establishment of another Communist government in the Western Hemisphere.

Document 2

New York Governor Nelson Rockefeller's statement on The Rockefeller Report, Nov. 20, 1969, U.S. Congress, Senate, Committee on Foreign Relations, Subcommittee on Western Hemisphere Affairs, 91st Cong., 1st sess., *Rockefeller Report on Latin America: Hearings,* Washington, D.C.: Government Printing Office, 1970, 2–9.

We have the chance in this hemisphere to demonstrate that democracy and all it stands for can truly be a dynamic force, working for the well-being of all the people, throughout the hemisphere.

This is the great challenge to the United States and to the people of this country.

This is the essence of our report to the President—how to help improve the quality of life for all in this hemisphere.

To achieve this, we must face some very practical and difficult problems.

Fortunately, the opportunities far outweigh the problems, in my opinion—but these opportunities must not be missed. For our success in realizing these goals in this hemisphere could well be the determining factor as to our success as a nation as we travel through these turbulent times. . . .

Therefore, let's take a realistic look at the key issues we need to resolve in our Western Hemisphere relations:

1. Our basic concern is and must be the quality of life for all people in the Western Hemisphere.

This goal is paramount and we must not be diverted from it by selfish or special interest, by emotional whim or prejudice, or by individual quest for short-term political gains.

There is a tremendous job to be done—to overcome poverty and injustice.

But if we have the vision and the determination, the honesty and the realism to make this our goal and to set the right priorities, we can do it.

This must be a matter of national purpose and national commitment—in our own, long-term, self-interest as well as that of our neighbors.

Such a great noble undertaking, based on human concern, can give new meaning—a new sense of purpose and direction—to the lives of all the peoples of the hemisphere.

It could give us the kind of enthusiasm and dedication that we had as a nation and as a people in the early days of our country.

2. Secondly—and basic to achievement of this goal—is consultation and close cooperation among the governments of the hemisphere.

Only thus can we achieve unity and

progress while respecting the diversity of the widely different sovereign nations of this hemisphere. . . .

We cannot expect them to be made in our own image—particularly when such a high percentage of their people live under the deprived conditions that a remaining small percentage of our own people still have to face.

Therefore, let's stop prejudging our neighbors and feeling superior.

Let us recognize that they are struggling through very difficult times—through pressures and frustrations that may be far more difficult than any we have ever known.

Let us be understanding and work with them to achieve common goals for all our peoples, so they may enjoy the opportunities that so many of us have had the privilege to enjoy.

This means mutually beneficial cooperation in the economic and social fields.

It means helping to protect our freedom and security as nations.

It means helping to strengthen the forces of justice and individual dignity.

It means helping to preserve individual rights and the forces of democracy, for only in this way can we have effective economic and social progress and encourage the growth of democratic institutions. . . .

The United States can best achieve these objectives:

First, by recognizing the governments of the other American Republics as the formal and official contacts with the people of those countries and by working with them to improve the quality of the lives of their peoples in all aspects.

As was clearly set forth in article 35 of the 1948 Bogotá Conference, recognition of the government of another nation should not be considered as representing a moral judgment of that government or a moral endorsement of that government's internal policies.

On the contrary, recognition is a means, a channel for continuing our cooperation with the people of that country in our common interest. . . .

Second, the U.S. Government must organize itself internally to conduct its relations more effectively with the nations and the peoples of the Western Hemisphere.

With the present U.S. Government structure, Western Hemisphere policies can neither be soundly formulated nor effectively carried out.

The State Department controls less than half the decisions relating to the Western Hemisphere. Responsibility for policy and operations is scattered among many departments and agencies—for example, Treasury, Commerce, Agriculture, and Defense.

To cope with the diffusion of authority, there has grown up a complex and cumbersome system of interdepartmental committees within which there are interminable negotiations because no one member has the authority to make a final decision. . . .

Too often, agreement is reached on major subjects only by compromise in the lower echelons of government and often at the lowest common denominator of agreement.

To deal with this problem, I have made a series of recommendations in my report to the President.

These include proposals for the creation of a Secretary of Western Hemisphere Affairs.

A Western Hemisphere Policy Staff Director.

An Economic and Social Development Agency to supersede AID [Agency for International Development].

An Institute of Western Hemisphere Affairs as the principal operating corporation of the new development agency.

These and related proposals demand the highest priority, in my opinion.

For unless there is a major reorganization of the U.S. Government structure, with clear lines of responsibility and corresponding authority to make policy and direct operations in the Western Hemisphere, the effect of other recommendations would, at best, be marginal. . . .

The third point that I would like to stress here is that unless we drastically change our trade policies to allow the other American Republics a far greater share in the growth of our markets, we might as well forget any idea of Western Hemisphere unity or the goals of the Alliance for Progress. . . .

Fourth, the present debt and foreign exchange situation is becoming increasingly impossible for a growing percentage of the other Western Hemisphere nations. . . .

Fifth, there has been a lot of talk about terminating U.S. military cooperation with the other nations of the Western Hemisphere. In my opinion, this would be a serious disservice to our best national interests.

There probably aren't many here who remember that in 1940 the Nazis held the dominant position with the military throughout the other American republics—both in terms of training and equipment and—most important—in ideological influence.

There was deep concern in this country that if the war spread to this hemisphere, most of the military in the other American countries would be with our enemies—and that would have been a disaster. . . .

Since then the United States has worked to help these neighbors of ours in the training and basic equipment of their armed forces, as well as in their understanding of the concepts of democracy.

The importance of these relationships can only be fully understood in the light of the situation that existed in 1940, or in the light of the relationship that exists today between Cuba or Egypt, on the one hand, and the Soviet Union and the rest of the Communist world on the other hand.

In this context, it is my judgment that our interests can best be served by continuing the training programs upon request and, especially, by continuing the military aid program relating to equipment for internal security purposes.

As far as equipment for external security is concerned, I believe our best long-term national interest will be served by selling basic, essential needs through the military assistance program. If we do not, others are eager to do so, either the Western European or Eastern European nations.

The situation most dangerous to Western Hemisphere security would be to find ourselves faced with a mainland [Fidel] Castro equipped and supported by the Communist world.

Document 3

The United States and Chilean Socialism, 1970–73, U.S. Congress, Senate, Select Committee to Study Governmental Operations with Respect to Intelligence Activities, *Covert Action in Chile,* Washington, D.C.: Government Printing Office, 1975, 1–3, 12–13.

A. Overview: Covert Action in Chile

Covert United States involvement in Chile in the decade between 1963 and 1973 was extensive and continuous. The Central Intelligence Agency spent three million dollars in an effort to influence the outcome of the 1964 Chilean presidential elections. Eight million dollars was spent, covertly, in the three years between 1970 and the military coup in September 1973, with over three million dollars expended in fiscal year 1972 alone.

It is not easy to draw a neat box around what was "covert action." The range of clandestine activities undertaken by the CIA includes covert action, clandestine intelligence collection, liaison with local police and intelligence services, and counterintelligence. The distinctions among the types of activities are mirrored in organizational arrangements, both at Headquarters and in the field. Yet it is not always so easy to distinguish the effects of various activities. If the CIA provides financial support to a political party, this is called "covert action"; if the Agency develops a paid "asset" in that party for the purpose of information gathering, the project is "clandestine intelligence collection."

The goal of covert action is political impact. At the same time secret relationships developed for the clandestine collection of intelligence may also have political effects, even though no attempt is made by American officials to manipulate the relationship for short-run political gain. For example, in Chile between 1970 and 1973, CIA and American military attaché contacts with the Chilean military for the purpose of gathering intelligence enabled the United States to sustain communication with the group most likely to take power from President Salvador Allende.

What did covert CIA money buy in Chile? It financed activities covering a broad spectrum, from simple propaganda manipulation of the press to large-scale support for Chilean political parties, from public opinion polls to direct attempts to foment a military coup. The scope of "normal" activities of the CIA Station in Santiago included placement of Station-dictated material in the Chilean media through propaganda assets, direct support of publications, and efforts to oppose communist and left-wing influence in student, peasant and labor organizations.

In addition to these "routine" activities, the CIA Station in Santiago was several times called upon to undertake large, specific projects. When senior officials in Washington perceived special dangers, or opportunities, in Chile, special CIA projects were developed, often as part of a larger package of U.S. actions. For instance, the CIA spent over three million dollars in an election program in 1964.

Half a decade later, in 1970, the CIA engaged in another special effort, this time at the express request of President [Richard M.] Nixon and under the injunction not to inform the Departments of State or Defense or the Ambassador of the project. Nor was the 40 Committee [reviews proposed covert action] ever informed. The CIA attempted, directly, to foment a military coup in Chile. It passed three weapons to a group of Chilean officers who plotted a coup. Beginning with the kidnaping of Chilean Army Commander-in-Chief René Schneider. However, those guns were returned. The group which staged the abortive kidnap of Schneider, which resulted in his death, apparently was not the same as the group which received CIA weapons.

When the coup attempt failed and Allende was inaugurated President, the CIA was authorized by the 40 Committee to fund groups in opposition to Allende in Chile. The effort was massive. Eight million dollars was spent in the three years between the 1970 election and the military coup in September 1973. Money was furnished to media organizations, to opposition political parties and, in limited amounts, to private sector organizations.

Numerous allegations have been made about U.S. covert activities in Chile during 1970–73. Several of these are false; others are half-true. In most instances, the response to the allegation must be qualified:

> Was the United States *directly* involved, covertly, in the 1973 coup in Chile? The Committee has found no evidence that it was. However, the United States sought in 1970 to foment a military coup in Chile; after 1970 it adopted a policy both overt and covert, of opposition to Allende; and it remained in intelligence contact with the Chilean military, including officers who were participating in coup plotting.
>
> Did the U.S. provide covert support to striking truck-owners or other strikers during 1971–73? The 40 Committee did not approve any such support. However, the U.S. passed money to private sector groups which supported the strikers. And in at least one case, a small amount of CIA money was passed to the strikers by a private sector organization, contrary to CIA ground rules.
>
> Did the U.S. provide covert support to right-wing terrorist organizations during 1970–73? The CIA gave support in 1970 to one group whose tactics became more violent over time. Through 1971 that group received small sums of American money through third parties for specific purposes. And it is possible that money was passed to these groups on the extreme right from CIA-supported opposition political parties.

The pattern of United States covert action in Chile is striking but not unique. It arose in the context not only of American foreign policy, but also of covert U.S. involvement in other countries within and outside Latin America. The scale of CIA involvement in Chile was unusual but by no means unprecedented.

B. Issues

The Chilean case raises most of the issues connected with covert action as an instrument of American foreign policy. It consisted of long, frequently heavy involvement in Chilean politics: it involved the gamut of covert action methods, save only covert military operations; and it revealed a variety of different authorization procedures, with different implications for oversight and control. As one case of U.S. covert action, the judgments of past actions are framed not for their own sake; rather they are intended to serve as bases for formulating recommendations for the future.

The basic questions are easily stated:

(1) Why did the United States mount such an extensive covert action program in Chile? Why was that program continued and then expanded in the early 1970's?

(2) How was this major covert action program authorized and directed? What roles were played by the President, the 40 Committee, the CIA, the Ambassadors, and the Congress?

(3) Did U.S. policy-makers take into account the judgments of the intelligence analysts on Chile when they formulated and approved U.S. covert operations? Does the Chilean experience illustrate an inherent conflict between the role of the Director of Central Intelligence as a producer of intelligence and his role as manager of covert operations?

(4) Did the perceived threat in Chile justify the level of U.S. response? What was the effect of such large concentrated programs of covert political action in Chile? What were the effects, both abroad and at home, of the relationships which developed between the intelligence agencies and American based multinational corporations?

C. Historical Background to Recent United States-Chilean Relations

. . . In 1970, the U.S. government and several multinational corporations were linked in opposition to the candidacy and later the presidency of Salvador Allende. This CIA-multinational corporation connection can be divided into two phases. Phase I comprised actions taken by either the CIA or U.S.-based multinational companies at a time when it was official U.S. policy not to support, even covertly, any candidate or party in Chile. During this phase the Agency was, however, authorized to engage in a covert "spoiling" operation designed to defeat Salvador Allende. Phase II encompassed the relationship between intelligence agencies and multinational corporations after the September 1970 general election. During Phase II, the U.S. government opposed Allende and supported opposition elements. The Government sought the cooperation of multinational corporations in this effort.

A number of multinational corporations were apprehensive about the possibility that Allende would be elected President of Chile. Allende's public announcements indicated his intention, if elected, to nationalize basic industries and to bring under Chilean ownership service industries such as the national telephone company, which was at that time a subsidiary of ITT [International Telegraph and Telephone Corporation].

Document 4

Senate debate on the Panama Canal treaties, U.S. Congress, Senate, Committee on Foreign Relations, 96th Cong., 1st sess., *Senate Debate on the Panama Canal Treaties: A Compendium of Major Statements, Documents, Record Votes, and Relevant Events*, Washington, D.C.: Government Printing Office, 1979, 23–29, 109–11.

Senator Frank Church,
February 10, 1978

Will the treaties help promote military security for the canal? The best place to look for an answer, it seems to me, is to those who have the responsibility for defending it—the U.S. Armed Forces. According to the Chairman of the Joint Chiefs of Staff [General George Brown], the United States would "without question" have the right to act unilaterally to protect the canal against any international threat, including radical Panamanian rioters, for example. But again, the heart of it, the committee was told by General [Dennis] McAuliffe—who is directly responsible for the canal's defense—is that the treaties will create a "friendly environment around the canal in which to operate." We can conduct "our defense tasks better in a friendly rather than hostile environment," he said. And while sabotage can never be ruled out, the incentive can be taken away by giving the Panamanians a stake in the canal. . . .

. . . A natural tendency exists, after the Vietnam tragedy, to want an end to what some see as yielding and retreat by the United States. I see no point in debating here whether that perception is correct; my own judgment is that our foreign policy has been generally more realistic—and more humane—since our involvement in the Vietnam war ended. But whether that is true or not, the point must be made emphatically, that the treaties now before us do not represent a retreat. . . .

What are the disadvantages?

There are . . . arguments that have been made against the treaties. . . .

First, the familiar argument: We built it and paid for it. It is ours, and we should keep it. The answer is, I think, that we are keeping it, in the way that matters—the only way that matters. We are keeping it open and running, and that is what is important.

To argue about technical legal questions, such as who has "titular sovereignty," misses the point. It is use that counts. It is our right to protect the canal that counts. It is our right to go through first during emergencies that counts. And these rights are the ones guaranteed by the treaties.

We do not now possess "titular sovereignty" over the canal or the zone it occupies, under the current treaty, as the committee report makes clear. But even if we did, what good would it be if, in order to retain it, we had to jeopardize the canal's use?

So the answer, in short, is that the treaties do not give away our vital interests in the canal. They insure our ability to protect those interests. . . .

The . . . argument is that the treaties will be yet another retreat by the United States, a "withdrawal" in response to threats and coercion. There is the feeling that somehow things are not as they used to be, and that is so. The world has changed. It used to be that gunboat diplomacy would serve to enforce our will in the Caribbean and in Central America. . . .

The . . . argument . . . is made against the treaties that there is no guarantee that Panama will not nationalize the canal and demand that we leave immediately.

This is true. There is nothing to prevent them from doing that right now. Under the new treaties—which commit both the United States and Panama to protect and defend the canal's neutrality—the moral and legal case of the United States would be far stronger were such an eventuality to occur. If the treaties are ratified, General [Maxwell] Taylor testified, the "conflicts over the canal should cease to be a confrontation between an overbearing Uncle Sam, the Goliath of the affluent industrial world, and the tiny Panama, the David representing Latin America and the world's have-not community.". . .

Senator Paul Laxalt, April 18, 1978

Mr. President, this is, indeed, a historic occasion. As Senators, we will soon be called upon to decide a question that will go a long way toward determining the kind of people we are and the role we wish to play in the world. . . .

It is rare that this Senate comes to showdown votes on momentous questions with the outcome possibly hanging on a single vote. Any Senator thinking back historically, can easily think of votes such as that on the North Atlantic Treaty in 1949 which were important but not close. And, each of us has his own examples of cliffhangers of no particular moment. But, make no mistake about this one. Like the Versailles Treaty in 1919, the vote we are about to have on the Panama Canal Treaty is of immense import. . . .

In my judgment, a negative vote on the pending resolution of ratification could signal a similarly hopeful turn in our foreign policy. From our weak and vacillating current position, where we seem unable to determine where we are or where we wish to go, we are now afforded an opportunity to move in the direction of a mature, strong and self-confident posture which our people so clearly deserve.

In his campaign, President [Jimmy] Carter promised a government as good as the American people, but he has not yet delivered. Certainly, the Panama Canal Treaty fails to measure up. Our people know we cannot buy friends. Our people know that capitulation under threat of force simply merits graver threats. And, most importantly of all, our people know that in international affairs, while it is nice to be appreciated, it is even more important to be respected. And, this treaty in no way adds to the diminishing stock of respect in the world. . . .

Our people oppose this treaty. Although some effort was made in the debate on the Neutrality Treaty to argue that the American people had come around, that they had shifted from a position overwhelmingly in opposition to one slightly in favor, that effort was abandoned in the debate on the second treaty. This is because it has become clear that no such shift has occurred. Indeed, if the American people moved at all during the course of these debates, they have only grown more strongly opposed. . . .

. . . Our canal in Panama is a circumstance unique to world history. Dating virtually simultaneously from the birth of the Republic of Panama and conveying enormous benefits to the Panamanian people, it is in no sense a colonial possession. Unlike the Suez situation, where an ancient nation was dispossessed of its territory to create a canal, in Panama the canal and the neighboring nation came into being at the same time. . . .

Proponents argue that our relations with Latin America will be enhanced immeasurably should the Panama Canal Treaty be agreed to. As a Latin myself, I doubt it. Even more so than most peoples, we Latins respect firmness and are suspicious of vacillation and weakness. What is more, although Latin American leaders have to adhere publicly to a kind of antigringo solidarity on this issue, privately they have let it be known that they are concerned about an economic asset as valuable as the Panama Canal being left in the hands of the present Panamanian regime.

Document 5

Three statements on U.S. policy in Central America: Secretary of State George P. Shultz, Aug. 4, 1983, U.S. Congress, Senate, Committee on Foreign Relations, 98th Cong., 1st sess., *Central American Policy: Hearings*, Washington, D.C.: Government Printing Office, 1983, 2–7; *Report of the National Bipartisan Commission* [Kissinger Commission] *on Central America*, Washington, D.C.: The Commission, 1984, 1–6; Wayne Smith's statement on the Reagan administration's policy toward Nicaragua, U.S. Congress, Senate, Committee on Foreign Relations, 99th Cong., 2d sess., *U.S. Policy toward Nicaragua: Aid to Nicaraguan Resistance Proposal*, Washington, D.C.: Government Printing Office, 1986, 167–73.

[Preceding comments by Senator Claiborne Pell]

I know I am deeply concerned that the military exercises recently announced by the President will lead to the Americanization of the conflict in Central America. The American people and the Congress are really totally in the dark about the purpose, scope and danger to American forces of this significant projection of American military force.

Statements by the President at his July 26 [1983] press conference serve to confuse more than to clarify the issue of what we are doing in Central America. On the one hand, he appears to be playing hard ball with Nicaragua and Cuba by brandishing guns before their noses. On the other hand, he attempted to softsoap the American people by portraying these exercises as routine.

I believe, Mr. Secretary, that the administration cannot have it both ways. You cannot scare the Cubans and Nicaraguans and still expect to reassure the American people that the United States will not be drawn into another bloody conflict.

[1. Statement by Secretary of State George P. Shultz.]

I feel like I have been set up here by these opening comments. To me, the policy that we have is clear and consistent, and it is a multifaceted policy. It is a sophisticated policy, so you have an interplay among the parts of it. That means you have to emphasize one thing at one time and another thing at another, and that is the way a sophisticated policy is supposed to work. . . .

Our policy toward Central America today is just as the President set it forth to the Nation before the joint session of Congress on April 27, the speech to which you referred, Mr. Chairman, and with which you said you agreed. That night he identified our objectives as being to prevent a wider crisis and to bring about a lasting peace. And to achieve those ends, the President defined four activities to which we have committed ourselves:

Support for democracy, reform and human rights; support for economic development; support for dialog and negotiations among the countries of the region and within each country; and support for the security of the region's threatened nations as a shield for democratization, development, and diplomacy. . . .

First—and it belongs first—support for democracy, reform and human rights.

What we seek is a Central America more like Costa Rica than Cuba. We seek genuine democracy—not totalitarian charades but respect for human freedom and the rule of law—not repression but governments committed to the welfare of their own people. . . .

In 1981–82, we supported the transition to democracy in Honduras. Today defense of the constitutional democratic order in Honduras is a key objective.

In El Salvador, the Constituent Assembly elections a year ago last March were a stunning success, demonstrating that democracy can advance even in the face of guerrilla violence. . . .

What is happening in Central America will be further advanced by the President's Democracy Initiative. We have begun consultations—bipartisan, both at home and abroad—to build support for improved cooperation among political parties and other groups committed to democracy.

Second, economic development.

Between 1960 and 1979, the nations of Central America had high per capita growth rates. But rising expectations clashed with outmoded and unresponsive political institutions; then economic slowdown brought additional conflict and instability. In recent years, falling prices of export commodities, rising import prices, the rule or ruin strategy of the guerrillas in El Salvador, and the growing uncertainty caused by Nicaragua's policies have created an acute economic crisis, increasing the region's vulnerability to Communist strategies.

The United States has responded to these underlying economic problems with both generosity and imagination. Much of the $610 million in economic assistance budgeted for Central America this fiscal year is concentrated on stabilization efforts—to provide hard currency for essential imports to maintain production and employment. With the rest, the Agency for International Development is supporting about 120 individual development projects.

To take just one critical area—the agrarian reform in El Salvador—our assistance has helped that program to benefit more than 500,000 persons, or roughly 1 Salvadoran in every 10. Other AID projects are developing Costa Rica's northern zone, upgrading Honduras' forestry and livestock industries, and helping Guatemala's highland Indians. Regionwide, U.S. economic assistance is three times greater than our military aid.

Finally, we have worked hard with other nations and with you in the Congress to develop a new approach to assisting economic development—the Caribbean Basin Initiative [CBI]. The CBI provides 12 years of free trade guarantees and incentives for investment in Central America and the Caribbean. It will be a powerful, long-term instrument for development and the creation of new jobs. . . .

Third, dialog and negotiations.

Our diplomacy is designed to help develop political solutions to Central America's national and regional problems. In Nicaragua, the new Sandinista regime did not respond to U.S. efforts at "constructive engagement." We then sought to resolve our differences through dialog. And when bilateral approaches in 1981 and 1982 proved fruitless, we participated in the multilateral peace process launched last October in San Jose. From its beginning this year, we have supported the efforts of Colombia, Mexico, Panama, and Venezuela—the Contadora Group. That support continues today.

In El Salvador, we have consistently and systematically tried to facilitate reconciliation with those among the guerrillas and their associates who might prove willing to test their appeal in honest elections. We are now actively supporting the efforts of El Salvador's Peace Commission to open a dialog with the Democratic Revolutionary Front—the political arm of the guerrillas—to assure the safe participation of all parties in the democratic process. . . .

And fourth, military assistance and cooperation.

We seek a security shield, not as any kind of end in itself, but to provide the necessary protection, the necessary protection for the political, economic, and diplomatic goals I have just described.

The military components of the President's policy have been carefully calculated to do just that. Two kinds of activities are involved: activities to help others defend themselves, and activities to underline our own deterrent capability.

Military assistance is based on demonstrated needs in each country as measured against the threat to the country's security. The administration's requests for fiscal year 1984 are as follows: for Belize, $500,000 in grant aid and $100,000 in training; for Costa Rica, $2 million grant aid and $100,000 in training; for El Salvador, $55 million in grants, $1.3 million in training, and $30 million sales credits; for Guatemala, no grant aid, but $250,000 in training and $10 million in credit; and for Honduras, $40 million grant aid and $1 million in training. . . .

Nations as well as men and women need incentives to change their behavior. At least until recently, there has been no incentive for the Sandinistas, no incentive for the Salvadoran guerrillas, no incentive for Fidel Castro, and no incentive for the Soviets to believe that anything credible, anything difficult stood in the way of imposition of Communist rule by armed forces in El Salvador and in the rest of Central America. . . .

[2. National Bipartisan Commission on Central America (Kissinger Commission)]

For most people in the United States, Central America has long been what the entire New World was to Europeans of five centuries ago: *terra incognita*. Probably few of even the most educated could name all the countries of Central America and their capitals, much less recite much of their political and social backgrounds.

Most members of this Commission began with what we now see as an extremely limited understanding of the region, its needs and its importance. The more we learned, the more convinced we became that the crisis there is real, and acute; that the United States must act to meet it, and act boldly; that the stakes are large, for the United States, for the hemisphere, and, most poignantly, for the people of Central America.

In this report, we propose significant attention and help to a previously neglected area of the hemisphere. Some, who have not studied the area as we have, may think this disproportionate, dismissing it as the natural reaction of a commission created to deal with a single subject. We think any such judgment would be a grave mistake.

It is true that other parts of the world are troubled. Some of these, such as the Middle East, are genuinely in crisis. But the crisis in Central America makes a particularly urgent claim on the United States for several reasons.

First, Central America is our near neighbor. Because of this, it critically involves our own security interests. But more than that, what happens on our doorstep calls to our conscience. History, contiguity, consanguinity—all these tie us to the rest of the Western Hemisphere; they also tie us very particularly to the nations of Central America. When Franklin Roosevelt proclaimed what he called his "Good Neighbor Policy," that was more than a phrase. It was a concept that goes to the heart of civilized relationships not only among people but also among nations. When our neighbors are in trouble, we cannot close our eyes and still be true to ourselves.

Second, the crisis calls out to us because we *can* make a difference. Because the nations are small, because they are near, efforts that would be minor by the standards of other crises can have a large impact on this one.

Third, whatever the short-term costs of acting now, they are far less than the long-term costs of not acting now.

Fourth, a great power can choose what challenges to respond to, but it cannot choose where those challenges come—or when. Nor can it avoid the necessity of deliberate choice. Once challenged, a decision not to respond is fully as consequential as a decision to respond. We are challenged now in Central America. No agony of indecision will make that challenge go away. No wishing it were easier will make it easier.

Perhaps the United States should have paid more attention to Central America sooner. Perhaps, over the years, we should have intervened less or intervened more, or intervened differently. But all these are questions of what might have been. What confronts us now is a question of what might become. Whatever its roots in the past, the crisis in Central America exists urgently in the present, and its successful resolution is vital to the future. . . .

• First, the tortured history of Central America is such that neither the military nor the political nor the economic nor the social aspects of the crisis can be considered independently of the others. Unless rapid progress can be made on the political, economic and social fronts, peace on the military front will be elusive and would be fragile. But unless the externally-supported insurgencies are checked and the violence curbed, progress on those other fronts will be elusive and would be fragile.

• Second, the roots of the crisis are both indigenous and foreign. Discontents are real, and for much of the population conditions of life are miserable; just as Nicaragua was ripe for revolution, so the conditions that invite revolution are present elsewhere in the region as well. But these conditions have been exploited by hostile outside forces—specifically, by Cuba, backed by the Soviet Union and now operating through Nicaragua—which will turn any revolution they capture into a totalitarian state, threatening the region and robbing the people of their hopes for liberty.

• Third, indigenous reform, even indigenous revolution, is not a security threat to the United States. But the intrusion of aggressive outside powers exploiting local grievances to expand their own political influence and military control is a serious threat to the United States, and to the entire hemisphere.

• Fourth, we have a humanitarian interest in alleviating misery and helping the people of Central America meet their social and economic needs, and together with the other nations of the hemisphere we have a national interest in strengthening democratic institutions wherever in the hemisphere they are weak.

• Fifth, Central America needs help, both material and moral, governmental and nongovernmental. Both the commands of conscience and calculations of our own national interest require that we give that help.

• Sixth, ultimately, a solution of Central America's problems will depend on the Central Americans themselves. They need our help, but our help alone will not be enough. International reforms, outside assistance, bootstrap efforts, changed economic policies—all are necessary, and all must be coordinated. And other nations with the capacity to do so not only in this hemisphere, but in Europe and Asia, should join in the effort.

Seventh, the crisis will not wait. There is no time to lose.

[3. Wayne Smith (Retired Foreign Service Officer)]

I. *The failure of present policy.* Trying to either overthrow or pressure the Sandinistas by aiding the *contras* is not a new policy. It began in 1981. Five years later, it has produced nothing positive. Zero. On the contrary, it has made matters worse. To see just how totally it has failed, one need only list U.S. objectives and then see if present policy has advanced them:

1.) Objective—To reduce Soviet/Cuban influence and bring about the eventual withdrawal of all Soviet, Cuban, and other bloc military personnel.

Policy Result—The Sandinistas, as of 1981, were already sympathetic toward Moscow and Havana. Present policy has pushed them even further in that direction. Soviet/Cuban influence has increased as the Sandinistas, to defend themselves against the *contras*, the mining of their harbors, the bombing of targets inside Nicaragua, etc., have turned increasingly to Moscow and Havana for help. . . .

2.) Objective—To limit the size of the Sandinista military establishment and the nature of its armaments so that Nicaragua not be in a position to threaten its neighbors.

Policy Result—The Sandinista military apparatus is today larger and armed with more sophisticated weaponry than was the case five or even two years ago.

3.) Objective—To halt any support the Sandinistas may be giving to guerrilla movements in neighboring countries.

Policy Result—The Administration claims this problem continues unabated. Secretary of State [George P.] Shultz was here just the other day talking about Sandinista support not only for the guerrillas in El Salvador, but also for subversion in Colombia, Honduras, Costa Rica, the Dominican Republic, and several other countries. The Administration's evidence for all this is thin indeed, but again, the point is that the Administration itself, by making these claims, suggests that its policies have not solved the problem. . . .

While present policy has failed, it is instructive to note that during the period when the Sandinistas still thought the U.S. might be interested in a negotiated solution, they *did* accede to our demands in this regard. When our then

Ambassador in Managua, Larry Pezzullo, laid it on the line to the Sandinistas in December of 1980 and January 1981 that they had to cease arms shipments to the Salvadoran guerrillas or face the definitive termination of U.S. aid, the Sandinistas complied. . . .

4.) Objective—To encourage pluralism and respect for civil liberties.

Policy Result—Freedom of press, rights of opposition parties and civil liberties have all been reduced since 1931. Civil liberties have recently been suspended. In this respect also, our policy has been counterproductive. This should come as no surprise. A time-worn adage of politics is that one does not bring about internal liberalization by mounting an external threat. . . .

5.) Objective—To promote internal dialogue and national reconciliation.

Policy Result—In early 1981, various members of the Nicaraguan opposition, men such as Adolfo Calero, Alfonso Robelo and COSEP [Superior Council for Private Business] leaders Enrique Dreyfus and Ernesto Palazio, told Ambassador Pezzullo in Managua that it would be a mistake for the U.S. to cut off economic assistance and adopt a confrontational attitude toward the Sandinistas. . . .

In other words, the Administration's own policy was instrumental in halting the international dialogue in 1981. The Administration was not then interested; it wanted to organize the *contras* and pressure the Sandinistas instead. But now, five years later, the Administration says that the purpose of aiding the *contras* is to force the Sandinistas to negotiate with them. Now it demands the internal dialogue which it helped to break off in 1981. . . .

Better alternatives are available. Indeed, with imaginative, effective diplomacy, we could almost certainly achieve all our security objectives and accomplish far more to encourage pluralism, respect for civil liberties and national reconciliation. We could, through verifiable regional agreements, prohibit the establishment of any Soviet/Cuban bases, bring about the withdrawal of all Soviet/Cuban military personnel, place limits on the size of the Sandinista military establishment, and end any support the Sandinistas may still be giving guerrilla groups in other countries.

Document 6

Boland Amendment concerning U.S. military and paramilitary operations in Nicaragua, U.S. Congress, House, Committee on Foreign Affairs, 98th Cong., 1st sess., Washington, D.C.: Government Printing Office, 1983, 83–84.

"TITLE VIII—PROHIBITION ON COVERT ASSISTANCE FOR MILITARY OPERATIONS IN NICARAGUA; AUTHORIZATION OF OVERT INTERDICTION ASSISTANCE

"PROHIBITION ON COVERT ASSISTANCE FOR MILITARY OPERATIONS IN NICARAGUA

"Sec. 801. (a) None of the funds appropriated for fiscal year 1983 or 1984 for the Central Intelligence Agency or any other department, agency, or entity of the United States involved in intelligence activities may be obligated or expended for the purpose or which would have the effect of supporting, directly or indirectly, military or paramilitary operations in ~~or against~~ Nicaragua by any nation, group, organization, movement, or individual.[1] . . .

[1] The words "or against" appeared in the measure proposed in March 1983, but were deleted from this version.

"AUTHORIZATION OF OVERT INTERDICTION ASSISTANCE

"Sec. 802. (a) The Congress finds that—

"(1) in the absence of a state of declared war, the provision of military equipment to individuals, groups, organizations, or movements seeking to overthrow governments of countries in Central America violates international treaty obligations, including the Charter of the United Nations, the Charter of the Organization of American States, and the Rio Treaty of 1949; and

"(2) such activities by the Governments of Cuba and Nicaragua threaten the independence of El Salvador and threaten to destabilize the entire Central American region, and the Governments of Cuba and Nicaragua refuse to cease those activities.

"(b) The President is authorized to furnish assistance, on such terms and conditions as he may determine, to the government of any friendly country in Central America in order to provide such country with the ability to prevent use of its territory, or **to prevent to the extent permitted by international law** the use of international territory, for the transfer of military equipment from or through Cuba or Nicaragua **or any other country or agents of that country** to any individual, group, organization, or movement which the President determines seeks to overthrow the government of such friendly country or the government of any other country in Central America. Assistance under this section shall be provided openly, and shall not be provided in a manner which attempts to conceal United States involvement in the provision of such assistance.[2] . . .

[2]Phrases in boldface represent wording of Committee on Foreign Affairs.

Document 7

President George Bush's address to the nation on U.S. military action in Panama, Dec. 20, 1989, U.S. Department of State, *American Foreign Policy: Current Documents*, Washington, D.C.: Government Printing Office, 1990, 720–21.

My fellow citizens, last night I ordered U.S. military forces to Panama. No President takes such action lightly. This morning, I want to tell you what I did and why I did it.

For nearly 2 years, the United States, nations of Latin America and the Caribbean have worked together to resolve the crisis in Panama. The goals of the United States have been to safeguard the lives of Americans, to defend democracy in Panama, to combat drug trafficking, and to protect the integrity of the Panama Canal Treaty. Many attempts have been made to resolve this crisis through diplomacy and negotiations. All were rejected by the dictator of Panama, General Manuel Noriega, an indicted drug trafficker.

Last Friday, Noriega declared his military dictatorship to be in a state of war with the United States and publicly threatened the lives of Americans in Panama. The very next day, forces under his command shot and killed an unarmed American serviceman; wounded another; arrested and brutally beat a third American serviceman; and then brutally interrogated his wife, threatening her with sexual abuse. That was enough.

General Noriega's reckless threats and attacks upon Americans in Panama created an imminent danger to the 35,000

American citizens in Panama. As President, I have no higher obligation than to safeguard the lives of American citizens. And that is why I directed our Armed Forces to protect the lives of American citizens in Panama and to bring General Noriega to justice in the United States. I contacted the bipartisan leadership of Congress last night and informed them of this decision, and after taking this action, I also talked with leaders in Latin America, the Caribbean, and those of other U.S. allies.

At this moment, U.S. forces, including forces deployed from the United States last night, are engaged in action in Panama. The United States intends to withdraw the forces newly deployed to Panama as quickly as possible. Our forces have conducted themselves courageously and selflessly. And as Commander in Chief, I salute every one of them and thank them on behalf of our country.

Tragically, some Americans have lost their lives in defense of their fellow citizens, in defense of democracy. And my heart goes out to their families. We also regret the loss of innocent Panamanians.

The brave Panamanians elected by the people of Panama in the elections last May, President Guillermo Endara and Vice Presidents [Ricardo Arias] Calderon and [Guillermo] Ford, have assumed the rightful leadership of their country. You remember those horrible pictures of newly elected Vice President Ford, covered head to toe with blood, beaten mercilessly by so-called "dignity battalions." Well, the United States today recognizes the democratically elected government of President Endara. I will send our Ambassador back to Panama immediately.

Key military objectives have been achieved. Most organized resistance has been eliminated. But the operation is not over yet. General Noriega is in hiding. And, nevertheless, yesterday a dictator ruled Panama, and today constitutionally elected leaders govern.

I have today directed the Secretary of the Treasury and the Secretary of State to lift the economic sanctions with respect to the democratically elected government of Panama and, in cooperation with that government, to take steps to effect an orderly unblocking of Panamanian Government assets in the United States. I'm fully committed to implement the Panama Canal Treaties and turn over the Canal to Panama in the year 2000. The actions we have taken and the cooperation of a new, democratic government in Panama will permit us to honor these commitments. As soon as the new government recommends a qualified candidate, Panamanian, to be Administrator of the Canal, as called for in the treaties, I will submit this nominee to the Senate for expedited consideration.

I am committed to strengthening our relationship with the democratic nations in this hemisphere. I will continue to seek solutions to the problems of this region through dialog and multilateral diplomacy. I took this action only after reaching the conclusion that every other avenue was closed and the lives of American citizens were in grave danger. I hope that the people of Panama will put this dark chapter of dictatorship behind them and move forward together as citizens of a democratic Panama with this government that they themselves have elected.

The United States is eager to work with the Panamanian people in partnership and friendship to rebuild their economy. The Panamanian people want democracy, peace, and the chance for a better life in dignity and freedom. The people of the United States seek only to support them in pursuit of these noble goals. Thank you very much.

Document 8

Wayne Cornelius, political scientist, Latin American Debt and Its Impact: the Mexican Case, "The Redirection of Mexico's Political Economy," U.S. Congress, Senate, Committee on Foreign Relations, Subcommittee on International Economic Policy, Oceans, and Environment, 99th Cong., 1st sess., *U.S. Economic Growth and Third World Debt*, Washington, D.C.: Government Printing Office, 1986, 88–96, 105.

Three years ago, the government of Miguel de la Madrid embarked on a politically costly but financially necessary program of what it termed "economic realism." It combined short-term stabilization measures aimed at bringing down a 100% inflation rate and restoring confidence in the economy with an ambitious effort to promote long-term structural changes in the economy and in public finances, even at the price of slower growth in the short term.

Short-term stabilization was to be accomplished mainly through government belt-tightening and wage restraint enforced by the government-controlled labor unions. The prices of many goods and services produced by the public sector rose dramatically as the government tried to increase revenues, and the reduction of government subsidies to private producers caused similar increases in the price of food and other basic consumer goods.

Given the depletion of government revenues by December, 1982, and the conditions attached to Mexico's bail-out loan from the IMF [International Monetary Fund], there was no real alternative to a drastic austerity program. But De la Madrid seized upon the crisis as an opportunity to correct some of the country's basic structural problems; a highly inefficient and globally uncompetitive industrial plant, overcentralization of both public and private sector activities, proliferation of unprofitable state-owned enterprises, and an elaborate set of government subsidies, protectionist tariffs, and unrealistic exchange rate policies that were distorting the way in which resources in the economy were allocated. The De la Madrid group, joined by most leaders of the private sector, felt strongly that if a fundamental, qualitative change in national development strategy were not made, the problems that led to the financial crisis of 1976 and 1982 would inevitably reassert themselves, especially in the context of a world economy that was likely to hinder rather than facilitate Mexico's recovery.

Such a failure to provide effective, durable solutions to the country's problems would, in the De la Madrid administration's view, set the stage for a catastrophic breakdown of the political system. . . .

Controlling inflation thus became the new administration's top priority. Given that government spending was the principal contributor to the hyperinflation of the preceding *sexenio*, the fight against inflation precluded new, large-scale government programs and infrastructure projects. Under De la Madrid there would be no vast new rural development schemes, no massive job-creation programs, no spectacular public works in Mexico City. De la Madrid did pledge to protect as much as possible of the employment base by aiding financially distressed, debt-burdened private businesses (commercial credit to the private sector from the nationalized banks rose 17 percent during 1984 and continued strongly through the first two quarters of 1985). And the administration's substantial expenditures for health care, education, and social security have been aimed at maintaining as much as possible of the cushion of benefits that the government traditionally has offered to the more privileged segments of the working class (primarily unionized workers) and the middle class. Accordingly, the lion's share of cuts in government spending under De la Madrid have been in the capital investment budget rather than current expenditures.

The results of this program of short-term stabilization *cum* long-term restructuring have been a mixed bag. Annual inflation has been reduced from 100% to somewhere between 52–60%, but most of the reduction occurred during the first two years of the De la Madrid administration, and virtually no progress has been made on this front in recent months. . . .

Government spending has been significantly reduced, in real terms, and the deficit has been reduced by more than half since 1982, to about 7.2% of GDP [Gross Domestic Product]; but Mexico has not achieved its IMF target for deficit reduction (5.9% of GDP). De la Madrid has made real progress toward putting the public sector of the economy on sounder financial footing (including self-financing of expansion), bringing PEMEX (the state oil agency) under central control, and pruning back the public sector to eliminate non-essential and financially non-viable enterprises. He has ordered the merger, liquidation, or sale of 482 "non-strategic, low-priority" state enterprises, out of a total of 1,155 entities that formed part of the public sector at the end of 1982.

After negligible growth in 1982 and a disastrous contraction in 1983, the economy grew at 3.5% last year, and at least prior to the earthquakes of September, a similar performance was expected this year. Much of the new growth has been more capital-intensive, however, and the rate of job creation is still not sufficient to keep pace with the growth of the economically-active population, let alone help the more than 30% of the existing labor force who are either openly unemployed or underemployed. . . .

Left-nationalist critics condemn the administration for sacrificing socially necessary economic growth in an obsessive pursuit of lower inflation rates; for opening Mexico's economy too much to foreign investment and to foreign-made goods; for failing to bargain harder with the foreign banks and the IMF; for divesting too many state-owned enterprises to the private sector; and for trying to reduce government deficits mainly through spending cuts rather than increasing revenue through a crackdown on tax evasion by the wealthy, among other steps. . . .

De la Madrid's critics on the right—especially big businessmen—fault him not for the basic direction of his policies but rather for not going far enough: that is, by dismantling the state sector more rapidly, reducing the deficit through even more drastic cuts in spending, squeezing down inflation faster, and opening the economy even more to international market forces, e.g., by joining the GATT [General Agreement on Tariffs and Trade]. Conservatives see the De la Madrid administration as too willing to compromise its objectives for political reasons. . . .

Clearly, De la Madrid has not proven to be a miracle-worker. His policies have angered many of the government's traditional constituencies, and he has failed to develop a broad political consensus around his approach to the economic crisis. The policy debate within Mexico's ruling elite has become increasingly acrimonious and divisive. Tensions between the technocrats who set policy and the traditional career politicians who run the official party and its affiliated mass organizations have deepened. And the De la Madrid administration has failed to restore the confidence of most of the general public in the government's ability to manage the economy. Opinion polls taken just after De la

Madrid's most recent state-of-the-nation address showed that only 35% of those interviewed expressed confidence in the president's policies. The general public mood seems to be one of cynicism, skepticism about government initiatives, and hostility toward the political class, as well as a sense that their fate is being determined largely by external forces beyond their control (and, indeed beyond the government's control).

CHAPTER 15

U.S.-African Relations since 1960

Ralph F. de Bedts

The past three decades of African-American relations have been notable for the enormous turmoil characteristic of Third World anticolonial struggles. The situation in Africa has been particularly marked by the failure of the United States to understand these troubles, and by U.S. unwillingness to register strong disapproval of the white and racially segregated apartheid regime of South Africa.

In 1960, for example, the Congo finally broke free from nearly a century of Belgian exploitation. President Dwight D. Eisenhower sympathized with the Belgians but supported the United Nations attempt to bring about peace. Ralph Bunche, a black State Department official who had received the Nobel Peace Prize for his work in mediating the Arab-Israeli conflict, led the UN effort. When the new socialist prime minister, Patrice Lumumba, was refused aid by the United States to put down Katanga's attempts to secede, he accepted aid from the Soviets. Fearing a Communist takeover, Eisenhower approved a CIA plan to poison Lumumba. (doc. 1) The plan failed, but Lumumba was murdered by his rival and new American protégé, Colonel Joseph Mobutu.

In 1961 Eisenhower was succeeded by John F. Kennedy, who continued America's role in Africa. The youthful Kennedy admired movie hero John Wayne and the fictional spy James Bond. Kennedy likewise considered himself a man of action. To critics he seemed something of a romantic, with an unfortunate tendency to consider counterinsurgency as the answer to unrest throughout the Third World. Under Kennedy the CIA continued covert military aid to Mobutu. When leftist rebels seized European hostages, U.S. and Belgian troops intervened to rescue them. By 1965 the United States had become the dominant influence in the area, and the new Republic of Zaire (which contained most of the former Belgian Congo) became a base for covert U.S. aid to selected rebel forces in neighboring Angola. (doc. 2)

As a senator, Kennedy had remarked favorably on the course of the

Algerian struggle for independence from France, which did not endear him to the French. Before this bloody revolution in Arab northern Africa, a million Europeans had governed nine million Algerians (with the usual colonial history of injustices) since France's military conquest of the area in 1830. Even the declaration of Algeria as an integral part of the French Republic and not just a colony did not prevent serious inequalities of land ownership and justice, nor did it put a stop to the racism of the white colonial rulers. By Kennedy's second year in the White House, the revolution had come to an end after more than a million Muslims were killed and perhaps the same number of Europeans lost their homes. A small minority of Europeans could not govern—or conquer—nine million Algerians aroused to independence, even with the aid of dissident French army units. French President Charles de Gaulle, one of the few world statesmen who recognized the nationalist revolutionary spirit abroad in the Third World, convinced his country in 1962 that Algeria should be independent. The United States soon followed France in recognizing the new nation.

A notable event of the mid-1960s was Southern Rhodesia's Unilateral Declaration of Independence, by which a tiny white minority of the British colony, led by extremist Prime Minister Ian Smith, defied the British demand that black majority rule must precede independence. In what was largely a UN effort of sanctions and embargoes, the United States gingerly followed the lead of Great Britain in condemning Rhodesia's action. (doc. 3) In the United States, public sentiment favored the principle of majority rule in a situation where the white 5 percent of the population owned some 80 percent of the arable land, although ultraconservative organizations such as the Young Americans for Freedom and the John Birch Society supported the Ian Smith forces. After two years of waiting for international pressure to topple the Smith government, black liberation forces finally united. Years of fighting and many deaths later, the black sovereign state of Zimbabwe emerged in 1980 under its leader, Robert Mugabe.

The 1970s had meanwhile brought more anticolonial revolutions, including the culmination of long struggles for independence in Mozambique and Angola after centuries of Portuguese rule. Under President Richard M. Nixon and his national security adviser (and later secretary of state), Henry Kissinger, Africa was considered relatively unimportant. (doc. 4)

Kissinger was the chief influence behind the issuance in 1970 of the secret National Security Study Memo 39, which threw U.S. support behind the white governments of Portugal and South Africa (doc. 5)—an approach that was promptly and derisively labeled "the tar baby option." Dissenters correctly pointed out that the Portuguese could never overcome the strong nationalist revolutions in Mozambique and Angola.

Kissinger viewed the Third World as a battleground between U.S. and Soviet influence. The administration's stance demonstrated neither understanding nor regard for local and regional causes of anticolonial uprisings and revolutions, nor for the fact that nations finally achieving independence had no intention of binding themselves to a new mastery by either superpower. The Nixon administration emphasized instead that the "fomenting" of Third World revolutions was the result of Kremlin plots. Although the Soviets were just as keen as the United States to gain influence by means of equipment and advisers, as in the Congo and to a lesser extent in Angola, it is a highly questionable proposition to blame the Kremlin for revolutions that stemmed from centuries-old problems.

The revolution in Angola was in many ways representative of other African revolutions. This new nation on the southwestern coast of Africa was the product of fourteen years of struggle against Portuguese colonialism. The roots of the struggle go back five hundred years, when the Portuguese first invaded the land for the capture and sale of slaves. As late as the early twentieth century, the Portuguese had to put down several native rebellions. By the 1960s, several tribal groups were in an all-out war with their colonial masters—and with each other—especially MPLA (Popular Movement for the Liberation of Angola) under Dr. Agostinho Neto (later the first president of Angola) and UNITA (National Union for the Total Independence of Angola) under Jonas Savimbi. Portugal's costly colonial wars actually brought down 48 years of fascist rule at home under dictator Antonio Salazar, a change in government sparked by young army officers and supported by the Catholic church and the vast majority of the people. After the almost bloodless coup of 1974, the new government declared its former colonies of Guinea, Mozambique, and Angola independent in 1975.

There followed, however, years of intertribal civil war in Angola. Although this conflict could scarcely be seen as an East-West rivalry, policy planners in the Nixon and Ford administrations (doc. 6) perceived it as such because the triumphant MPLA received aid from the Soviets. (The MPLA also received aid from Canada and the Scandinavian countries.) The United States used the CIA (also during the Ronald Reagan and George Bush administrations) to furnish arms and funds to Savimbi's UNITA, the rival tribal group fighting the MPLA. (doc. 7)

When South African troops raided Angola in 1981 to destroy black guerrilla sanctuaries, Fidel Castro's government offered the use of Cuban troops. The Angolan government was amenable to outside aid and requested permission from the Organization of African Unity (OAU), which included all the nations on the continent of Africa, with the exception of South Africa. Unanimous permission was given to bring in foreign troops to help the outnumbered Angolan army defend itself. (doc. 8) Neither the U.S. government nor the mainstream media mentioned the approval of the African nations.

With the advent of the Jimmy Carter administration in 1977, Andrew Young became the U.S. ambassador to the United Nations. The highest ranking black man in the administration and a close friend of the president, Young in the 1960s had worked closely with Martin Luther King, Jr., and had shown himself to be both eloquent and skilled in negotiation. A staunch friend of the black African nations, Young had notable success in winning the cooperation of Nigeria, a large exporter of oil to the United States. Nigeria had previously refused to deal with Kissinger because of his anti-Angolan policy, but the country willingly cooperated with Young. Unfortunately, Young was pushed out in late 1979. He had held secret conversations with the PLO (Palestine Liberation Organization) observers in the UN, which was contrary to U.S. policy. Because Young had sharply condemned illegal Israeli arms shipments to South Africa, pro-Israeli lobbies used the occasion to force him out.

Young had been able to convince Carter that he should recognize the government of Angola, as America's NATO (North Atlantic Treaty Organization) allies had done. The presence of Cuban troops (their number had risen to 20,000) posed too much of a political liability for Carter's strife-torn administration, in which the hard-line national security adviser, Zbigniew Brzezinski, was frequently able to advance his policies over those of the more conciliatory secretary of state, Cyrus Vance.

Carter refused to adopt any measures against South Africa's apartheid government, other than those that were merely rhetorical. (doc. 9) He attempted to aid the government of Somalia in its feud with the Marxist regime in Ethiopia, but the Ethiopian government received a Soviet airlift of nearly 11,000 Cuban troops and 1,000 Soviet advisers. Although an invasion of Somalia did not take place, a long-term Soviet-Ethiopian alliance put a further strain on the superpower relationship. Thus, Carter's relations with Africa—and especially southern Africa—were largely fruitless.

Ronald Reagan capitalized on the assorted failures of the Carter administration's last two years in office to win the presidential election of 1980. To many observers, Reagan's record seemed intellectually barren, especially in foreign affairs. Indeed, his early appearances indicated mental laziness and frequent confusion. On one occasion, he inexplicably introduced Liberia's president, Samuel Doe, as "Chairman Moe." Reagan nonetheless was exceptionally able in getting his ideology accepted by an American public swayed by his TV charm and easy amiability.

The new administration dubbed its policy the "Reagan Doctrine." The essence of this policy was that the United States would intervene around the world "to nourish and defend freedom and democracy," and especially to "defy Soviet-supported aggression." "Freedom fighters" (meaning indigenous forces or mercenaries) and CIA covert aid, rather than large U.S. military forces, would carry the burden of displacing "pro-Soviet" regimes among the emerging nations.

The Reagan Doctrine contained various elements from the past. It emphasized the Wilsonian idea that American involvement would spread democracy worldwide. It also included the essence of Secretary of State Robert Lansing's 1915 memo to President Woodrow Wilson, which indicated that force must be used to "resist revolutions." And its implied threat to socialist regimes sounded to the Soviets like a recurrence of the John

Foster Dulles "rollback" policies of the 1950s. The Reagan Doctrine did not recognize a long history of the futility of such policies or their actual counterproductivity and renewed anti-Americanism abroad.

The Reagan administration's military plans also revealed a reinforced commitment to the role of the United States as world policeman. The goal of a 600-ship navy was announced. Unlike nuclear submarines, huge surface fleets would be of little use in a war with the Soviets; they were clearly destined for use in problems relating to Third World nations. Newly expanded and expensive varieties of rapid deployment forces were to be used in what the Pentagon called "low intensity conflicts" in the Third World.

In Africa, the Reagan administration was involved chiefly with Angola and South Africa. In the former, the CIA-supported guerrilla forces of Jonas Savimbi's UNITA (which was also supported strongly by South Africa) had no success in defeating combined Angolan and Cuban forces. Savimbi was brought to the United States, where he was promised financial support by numerous right-wing organizations—with President Reagan's blessing. (doc. 10) Although Reagan was successful in getting the repeal of the (Senator Dick) Clark Amendment of 1975, which had prohibited U.S. involvement in Angola, the business community erected barriers to further intervention. Despite its Marxist government, Angola welcomed Western investment and was the United States' largest trading partner in southern Africa. Additionally, its extensive oil facilities were owned and operated in conjunction with the Angolan government. Because Savimbi had threatened to drive out any foreign oil companies if he overthrew the Angolan government, a bizarre situation developed: Cuban troops defending American oil interests against the CIA-supported Savimbi.

Reagan refused to press for blanket sanctions against the white apartheid government of South Africa. He used as an excuse a heretofore unnoticed solicitude for the lot of the innocent black victims of such policies. (doc. 11) This stance ignored the wishes of black leaders and the African National Congress, which were, according to a *Times* of London poll, overwhelmingly in favor of international sanctions. Not only could living conditions for blacks scarcely be worse, but the leaders regarded sanctions as a definite sign of support for their cause. Reagan insisted that American corporations could ameliorate both living and working conditions for their black South African employees by raising wages and by training black workers for higher positions, a policy known as "constructive engagement."

The U.S. Navy also made a pitch for closer cooperation with South Africa for the purpose of installing naval bases. As justification, various articles in naval reviews cited the large number of oil tankers circling the Cape of Good Hope and the possibility of attack by Soviet vessels. These requests went unfulfilled, however, because critics blocked such a possibility by pointing out that the Soviets could far more readily attack oil supplies on their borders in the Persian Gulf and that in a naval war they would need all their forces in home waters rather than 3,000 miles away. Writer R.W. Johnson perhaps supplied the ultimate argument: "The whole idea of Russian submarines starving the West into submission by a strategy of protracted interdiction or blockage was . . . absurdly nineteenth century in its conception. The very first ship sinking would, after all, constitute a major act of war and the nuclear bombers and missiles would be in the air only a few minutes later."

The apartheid Afrikaner government, for its part, refused any move toward serious reform and dealt harshly with black protests. Under martial law, hundreds of blacks were killed and thousands of others were beaten and jailed for their protest marches and songs. Waves of revulsion swept the United States, where campus and stockholder demands forced many American firms to leave South Africa. The companies, pension funds, states, and municipalities were faced with boycotts and with demands that they divest themselves of stocks in companies with ties to South Africa. Reagan's policy of constructive engagement proved a failure, and in 1986 Congress voted tough economic sanctions over his veto.

As George Bush moved into the White House in 1989, efforts were under way by the United Nations to mediate an end to the guerrilla wars in Angola and Namibia. With Cuban help, Angola had defeated South African forces at Cuito Cuanavale (in southeastern Angola) in 1988, forcing a military retreat and helping to bring South Africa to the UN negotiations. According to final terms, Namibia, situated between South Africa and Angola and under the illegal occupation of the former for decades (doc. 12), would receive the opportunity to vote in its own independent government. As a quid pro quo, the Cuban forces in neighboring Angola would pull out in several stages. For the oppressed black majority of South Africa, meaningful reforms were far in the future, if at all. The specter of yet another revolution in Africa remains a possibility.

Document 1

"Alleged Assassination Plots Involving Foreign Leaders," an interim report of the Select Committee to Study Governmental Operations with Respect to Intelligence Activities, U.S. Congress, Senate, *United States Senate,* Washington, D.C.: Government Printing Office, 1975, 60–64.

It was greatly feared in Washington that Patrice Lumumba, the new leader of the native forces in the Congo, was far too attracted to Soviet military aid and far too amenable to a strong Soviet presence and influence.

A subcommittee of the National Security Council responsible for the planning of covert operations—the Special Group—met to discuss the problem. As the minutes of the meeting stated:

"The Group agreed that the action contemplated is very much in order. Mr. [Gordon] Gray [Special Assistant to the President for National Security Affairs] commented, however, that his associates had expressed extremely strong feelings on the necessity for very straightforward action in this situation, and he wondered whether the plans as outlined were sufficient to accomplish this.

It was finally agreed that planning for the Congo would not necessarily rule out 'consideration' of any particular kind of activity which might contribute to getting rid of Lumumba.''

[Gray told the Senate Intelligence Committee that his reference to his ''associates'' was a euphemism for the President, which was used to preserve ''plausible deniability'' . . .].

Richard Bissell, Deputy Director of the CIA, testified:

''The Agency had put a top priority, probably, on a range of different methods of getting rid of Lumumba in the sense of either destroying him physically, incapacitating him, or eliminat[ing] his political influence. When you use the language that no particular means were ruled out, that is obviously what it meant, and it meant that to everybody in the room. You didn't use language of that kind except to mean in effect, the Director is being told, get rid of the guy, and if you have to use extreme means up to and including assassination, go ahead.''

Document 2

Statement by U.S. Ambassador to the United Nations Adlai E. Stevenson on the Afro-Asian Resolution on Angola in the Security Council, Mar. 15, 1961, U.S. Department of State, *Bulletin*, Apr. 3, 1961, 497–98.

When he first raised the question of Angola in the Security Council, the distinguished representative of Liberia, Ambassador [George A.] Padmore, . . . emphasized several problems with which the UN must concern itself: the urgency in this era of rapid communication of acting with dispatch, the recognition of Angola's problem being part of the larger African scene, and the desirability of Portugal availing itself of UN cooperation and help in the development of its territories in Africa.

It was clear from his remarks that Ambassador Padmore was anticipating conditions which, if unchanged, might endanger the peace and security of Africa, if not the world. . . . We recognize full well that, while Angola and the conditions therein do not today endanger international peace and security, we believe they may, if not alleviated, lead to more disorders with many unfortunate and dangerous consequences.

. . . The U.S. would be remiss in its duties as a friend of Portugal if it failed to express honestly its conviction that step-by-step planning within Portuguese territories and its acceleration is now imperative for the successful political and economic and social advancement of all inhabitants under Portuguese administration—advancement, in brief, toward full self-determination.

Document 3

Secretary of State Dean Rusk, address before Department of State Post No. 68 of the American Legion, ''U.S. Outlines Interest In Southern Rhodesia,'' Washington, D.C., Dec. 16, 1966, *Washington Post*, Dec. 16, 1966, 44–45.

There has been some feeling in this country that the Southern Rhodesia rebellion, important as it is in its own right, is not of direct interest to the U.S. in view of our many other important world involvements.

Let me say flatly that nothing could be further from the truth.

We naturally have a stake in what is happening in Southern Rhodesia because of our traditional beliefs that government should be based on the consent of the governed and that all men are created equal.

. . . In addition to these historic beliefs, we have other vital U.S. interests at stake in Africa. We have, therefore, taken a hard-headed, realistic position against the continuance of the illegal Southern Rhodesian regime because we have an important self-interest in the likely consequences that may flow from the rash action of a white minority in Southern Rhodesia.

If the rebel regime in Southern Rhodesia successfully maintains control of four million black Africans by 220,000 whites without being brought down, a whole chain of critical consequences could be set in motion—all of which would affect the U.S. directly or indirectly.

These are some of those probable consequences:

This act of illegal rule by a selfish minority of 220,000 whites could jeopardize the rights, prestige, and good relations built up and enjoyed by some 1½ million other whites of European origin—a term that includes Americans—who live in areas of Africa other than Southern Rhodesia. It would put the white man in Africa in the same position, in effect, that we would be in this country if we had given Governors [Ross] Barnett and [George] Wallace complete freedom of action in Mississippi and Alabama to suppress Negro Americans and to flout the law of the land—except that in Southern Rhodesia it would be a small minority imposing its control over a large majority.

Document 4

President Richard M. Nixon's report to Congress on "United States Foreign Policy for the 1970's: Shaping a Durable Peace," *The White House,* Washington, D.C.: Government Printing Office, 1973, 795–97.

Our policy goals in Africa are unchanged: political stability, freedom from great power intervention, and a peaceful economic and social development.

. . . In the Portuguese territories we favor self-determination. We have clearly expressed this position in the UN and we continue to do so.

The U.S. continues to enforce—more strictly than many other countries—an embargo on sales of arms to all sides in Southern Africa and in the Portuguese territories. While we favor change, we do not regard violence as an acceptable form for human progress.

Document 5

Assistant Secretary for African Affairs David D. Newsome's statement to the Subcommittee on Africa of the House Committee on Foreign Affairs, Mar. 27, 1973, *U.S. House of Representatives, Committee on Foreign Affairs,* Washington, D.C.: Government Printing Office, 1973, 578–79.

The U.S. today has approximately $1 billion in investments in South Africa, represented by about 300 firms. Trade with South Africa amounted in 1972 to $597.1 million in exports; $324.7 million in imports.

To put the investment into perspective, this represents approximately 15% of the total foreign investment in South Africa. For the U.S., this represents 25% of our total investment on the African continent.

. . . The agencies of the U.S. Government responsible refrain from any promotion of either investment or trade of the type carried out in other countries. We counsel with prospective investors on the situation in South Africa to be sure they understand the economic as well as the political and social conditions in that country. We neither encourage nor discourage them. We extend neither guarantees nor insurance on investments nor any official financing. . . . We do not participate in special promotions, in trade missions, or trade fairs.

. . . As the subcommittee is aware, we adopt a much more restrictive policy with respect to Namibia, particularly because of our position that South Africa's presence in the territory is illegal since the termination of its mandate in 1966.

Document 6

Assistant Secretary for African Affairs David D. Newsome's address before The Royal Commonwealth Society, "The Realities of U.S.–African Relations," London, Mar. 14, 1973, U.S. Department of State, *Bulletin,* Apr. 16, 1973, 458–59.

Our policies toward Africa rest, to start with, on a clear definition of U.S. interests in Africa.

. . . As a major power, we desire effective diplomatic access to the governments of Africa, representing as they do almost one third of the membership of the UN. In full recognition of the sensitive nationalism of newly independent nations, we desire a fair opportunity for trade and investment.

. . . The question frequently is raised, particularly on this side of the Atlantic, of U.S. military intentions in Africa. We count this a lesser interest. We have two remaining military communication stations in Africa which we shall presumably need until technology makes them unnecessary. We recognize the importance to the Europeans of the Cape route; we do not, however, give this interest priority over other more direct concerns in Africa.

. . . We recognize that Africans do not wish to be pawns in a great-power conflict.

. . . In an African continent understandably sensitive on the issue of sovereignty, we Americans have had a special myth to overcome: the myth of manipulation. I hope that this is dead. I hope that we have been able to convince the African governments that we are not involved in any way in seeking to determine how they are governed or by whom.

Document 7

Newspaper article about CIA officer John Stockwell in Africa, *Washington Post*, Outlook section, Apr. 10, 1977.

In 1975 John Stockwell, a high-ranking CIA officer who had been raised in Zaire, spoke several African dialects, and had previous African assignments, was appointed head of the CIA Angolan Task Force. This was a newly formed covert paramilitary operation designed to "destabilize" the now independent government, as an outcome of Secretary of State [Henry] Kissinger's obsession with gaining influential footholds in the Third World before the Soviets were able to—this time in a country that was of little importance to either superpower. Kissinger had overruled his advisors' various options. His Assistant Secretary for African Affairs, Nathaniel Davis, had felt it necessary to resign after Kissinger rejected his recommendation for a diplomatic solution. The official argument for the intervention—a most likely one—was Angola's "strategic" location on the South Atlantic oil tanker route.

By 1977, Stockwell's disillusionment both with the CIA and with his African assignment became overwhelming, and he submitted an open letter of resignation to Admiral Stansfield Turner, head of the Central Intelligence Agency under President [Jimmy] Carter. In it he pointed out not only the dubious value of the Angolan operation, but also his irritation with the inexperience of the bureaucratic chain of command above him and the manipulation of funds by staff members for personal use.

". . . After Vietnam I received the assignment of Chief, Angolan Task Force. This was despite the fact that I and many other officers in the CIA and State Department thought the intervention irresponsible and ill-conceived, both in terms of the advancement of United States interests, and the moral question of contributing substantially to the escalation of an already bloody civil war, when there was no possibility that we would make a full commitment and ensure the victory of our allies.

"From a chess player's point of view the intervention was a blunder. In July 1975, the MPLA [Popular Movement for the Liberation of Angola] was clearly winning, already controlling 12 of the 15 provinces, and was thought by several responsible American officials and senators to be the best-qualified to run Angola; nor was it hostile to the United States. The CIA committed $31 million to opposing the MPLA victory, but six months later the MPLA had nevertheless decisively won, and 15,000 Cuban troops were entrenched in Angola with the full sympathy of much of the Third World, and the support of several influential African chiefs of state who previously had been critical of any extracontinental intervention in African affairs.

"At the same time the United States was solidly discredited, having been exposed for covert military intervention in African affairs, having allied itself with South Africa, and having lost."

Stockwell also made very clear objections to the morality of the tasks the CIA performed:

". . . A major point was made to me when I was recruited in 1964 that the CIA was high-minded and scrupulously kept itself clean of truly dirty skullduggery such as killings and coups, etc. At that exact time the CIA was making preparation for the assassination of certain Latin American politicians and covering its involvement in the assassination of Patrice Lumumba.

"Eventually we learned Lumumba was killed, not by our poisons, but beaten to death, apparently by men who were loyal to men who had Agency cryptonyms and received Agency salaries. In death he became an eternal martyr and by installing [Colonel Joseph] Mobutu in the Zairian presidency, we committed ourselves to the 'other side,' the losing side in Central and Southern Africa.

"We cast ourselves as the dull-witted Goliath, in a world of eager young Davids. I for one have applauded as Ambassador [Andrew] Young thrashed about trying to break us loose from this role and I keenly hope President Carter will continue to support him in some new thinking about Africa."

Document 8

"African Charter on Human and Peoples' Rights," adopted by the 18th Assembly of Heads of State and Government of the Organization of African Unity, Nairobi, Kenya, June 27, 1981, U.S. Congress, House, *Human Rights Documents*, Washington, D.C.: Government Printing Office, 1983, 155–56.

PREAMBLE

The African States, members of OAU [Organization of African Unity], parties to the present convention entitled, "African Charter on Human and Peoples' Rights," . . .

Considering the Charter of the OAU, which stipulates that "freedom, equality, justice and dignity are essential objectives for the achievement of the legitimate aspirations of the African peoples," . . .

Conscious of their duty to achieve the total liberation of the African peoples, some of which are still struggling for dignity and genuine independence, and undertaking to eliminate colonialism, neo-colonialism, apartheid, Zionism, and to dismantle aggressive foreign military bases and all forms of discrimination, particularly those based on race, ethnic group, color, sex, language, religion or political opinions;

Have agreed as follows:

Part I—Rights and Duties

Chapter I—Human and Peoples' Rights

Article I

The Member States of the OAU parties to the present Charter shall recognize the rights, duties, and freedoms enshrined in this Charter and shall undertake to adopt legislative or other measures to give effect to them. . . .

Document 9

Under Secretary for Political Affairs Philip C. Habib, "Southern Africa in the Global Context," statement before the Subcommittee on Africa of the House Committee on International Relations, Mar. 3, 1977, U.S. Department of State, *Bulletin*, Apr. 4, 1977, 318–19.

I particularly welcome the opportunity to appear before you at a time when the whole question of U.S. policy toward southern Africa is under urgent and comprehensive review within the Department of State and other concerned executive agencies.

. . . I can tell you that the general thrust of our policy review has been to find ways of strengthening the commitment of the U.S. to social justice and racial equality in southern Africa and of demonstrating that commitment in tangible and meaningful ways. . . . It is the

Administration's earnest hope that when the historical record is finally written, there will be no shadow of a doubt as to where the U.S. stood on one of the great moral and political issues of our time.

Perhaps the most concrete demonstration to date of that renewed sense of commitment is the Administration's unequivocal support for efforts to repeal the so-called [Senator Robert] Byrd Amendment, under which the U.S. has since 1971 imported raw materials from Southern Rhodesia in open violation of its international obligations as spelled out in the UN Charter. Secretary of State [Cyrus] Vance, testifying before the Senate Subcommittee on African Affairs February 10, stressed the importance which President [Jimmy] Carter personally attaches to the repeal of this measure.

. . . In constructing a policy to deal with the problems of that region, we must have a sure understanding of our own national interests and act accordingly. . . .

First, I believe that our foreign policy must be true to our ideals as a nation. President Carter has, on many occasions, stated clearly and forcefully his own personal commitment to human rights. That commitment requires our firm and clear opposition to racial and social injustice wherever it exists. A policy toward southern Africa that is not firmly grounded on this principle would be inconsistent with our national character and therefore would not command the support of the American people. . . .

Secondly, we believe firmly that the people of Africa hold the key to the solution of the African problems. . . . It is not for us, or for any other external power, to attempt to impose its own ideas and solutions. . . .

From the standpoint of our own economic and strategic interests, we maintain firmly that the U.S. has no reason to fear the necessary and inevitable achievement of racial equality and social justice in southern Africa. To hold any other view would be to refute the history of the past three decades and to deny the obvious fact that the U.S. has been able to establish cooperation and constructive relations with the newly emerging nations in Africa and elsewhere in the world. Indeed, it is only where progress toward social, racial, and political justice is delayed or frustrated that the U.S. has any cause for concern that conditions may arise that are inhospitable to our basic national interests. It is for this reason as well that we must remain fully committed to helping those who seek rapid, peaceful and orderly change in southern Africa.

Document 10

Assistant Secretary of State for African Affairs Chester A. Crocker, "The United States and Angola," statement before the Senate Committee on Foreign Relations, Feb. 18, 1986, U.S. Department of State, *Bulletin*, April 1986, 59–60.

Our objectives are clear: to restore and advance U.S. influence in this region; to expand our cooperative relations with the African States; and to deny to the Soviet Union the opportunity to use its influence to exacerbate already dangerous situations in Angola, South Africa, and other countries of the area.

. . . It took two years to engage Luanda and Pretoria in real negotiations. It took another year to begin to erode the mutual mistrust and build confidence in an American role. But with the Lusaka Accord of February,

1984, South Africa began the process of disengagement from their military positions in Angola in return for restraint by SWAPO [South West African People's Organization]. In November of the same year, the Angolans said they were ready to commit themselves to withdraw 20,000 Cuban troops over three years, starting with the beginnings of the implementation of UN Security Council Resolution No. 435, the internationally agreed plan for independence for Namibia.

. . . However, the negotiation process has always moved in fits and starts and has been characterized by mutual suspicion among parties to the conflict—South Africa; MPLA [Popular Movement for the Liberation of Angola]; UNITA [National Union for the Total Independence of Angola]; and SWAPO—and by continuing efforts, sometimes more intense than others, to pursue the military options.

. . . These negotiations, and the continuous warfare inside Angola and across its borders into Namibia, represent the backdrop against which the visit of Dr. Jonas Savimbi of UNITA occurred.

. . . We do support UNITA; it has sustained a long and brave fight against Soviet and Cuban political and military designs.

Document 11

President Ronald Reagan's remarks on the Executive Order on South Africa, Sept. 9, 1985, U.S. Department of State, *Bulletin*, October 1985, 1–2.

Our influence over South African society is limited. But we do have some influence, and the question is how to use it. . . . Our aim cannot be to punish South Africa with economic sanctions that would injure the very people we're trying to help.

. . . Before taking fateful steps, we must ponder the key question: Are we helping to change the system? Or are we punishing the blacks whom we seek to help?

American policy through several administrations has been to use our influence and our leverage against apartheid, not against innocent people who are victims of apartheid.

. . . Therefore, I am signing today an Executive Order that will put in place a set of measures designed and aimed against the machinery of apartheid without discriminating by punishing the people who are victims of that system—measures that disassociate the U.S. from apartheid but associate us positively with peaceful change. These steps include:

1. A ban on all computer exports to agencies involved in the enforcement of apartheid and to the security forces;
2. A prohibition on exports of nuclear goods or technology to South Africa, except as is required to implement nuclear proliferation safeguards of the International Atomic Energy Agency or those for humanitarian reasons to protect health and safety;
3. A ban on loans to the South African government, except certain loans which improve economic opportunities or education, housing, and health facilities that are open and accessible to South Africans of all races.

Document 12

Assistant Secretary for African Affairs Nathaniel Davis, statement before the Subcommittee on Africa of the Senate Committee on Foreign Relations, July 24, 1975, *U.S. Senate Committee on Foreign Relations,* Washington, D.C.: Government Printing Office, 1975, 270–71.

U.S. policy . . . is based upon our belief that the people of Namibia should be allowed to exercise freely their right of self-determination. Given our support for UN General Assembly Resolution 2145 of October 27, 1966, which terminated South Africa's League of Nations mandate over Namibia, and from the conclusions of the 1975 International Court of Justice advisory opinion re Namibia, which upheld the legality of Resolution 2145, we take the view that South Africa is illegally administering Namibia and should withdraw from the territory, which is properly the responsibility of the UN.

. . . Regarding the future of Namibia we hold the following views: a) All Namibia should within a short time be given the opportunity to express their views freely and under UN supervision on their political future and the constitutional structure of the territory; b) All Namibian political groups should be allowed to campaign for their views and to participate without hindrance in peaceful political activities in the course of self-determination; c) The territory should not be fragmented in accordance with apartheid policy contrary to the wishes of its people; and d) The future of Namibia should be determined by the freely expressed choice of its inhabitants.

CHAPTER 16

U.S. Relations with East Asia: 1960 to the Present

Nancy Bernkopf Tucker

Changes in America's relations with the countries of East Asia since 1960 have been striking. The United States and China have overcome profound hostility to enter the 1990s in a state of uneasy amity. Tokyo and Washington, although still close allies, face economic frictions that threaten three decades of collaboration. In Korea, Americans are not as welcome as they once were, and on the island of Taiwan (formerly Formosa), where democracy seems to be taking root, government leaders clearly understand the limits of American friendship and power. In Asia generally, the United States has been less assertive since President Richard M. Nixon's 1969 Nixon Doctrine and the end of the Vietnam War. Nevertheless, in the 1970s U.S. trade with Asia surpassed commerce with Europe for the first time. As the 1990s begin, the apparent end of the Cold War, the central factor in regional as well as global tensions for the past thirty years, poses new challenges for American policymakers.

When John F. Kennedy campaigned for the presidency in 1960 against Nixon, he bristled with righteous indignation over the foreign policy failures of the Dwight D. Eisenhower years that included two foolhardy crises over Quemoy and Matsu. Candidate Kennedy dismissed these islands offshore China as strategically indefensible and pledged himself only to protect Taiwan. (doc. 1) Part of the Camelot legend surrounding JFK suggests that he, as an alleged liberal, intended to improve relations with the Communist Chinese during his second term, when the politically powerful China Lobby (prominent Americans who staunchly supported the Chinese Nationalists) could be more easily ignored. He continued the Warsaw talks begun under Eisenhower and used that forum to avert a new Formosa Straits crisis in 1962.

But Kennedy seems to have taken instead a hard line on China. Contradicting previous presidents, he secretly guaranteed Chinese Nationalist leader Chiang Kai-shek that the United States would use its veto to keep the People's Republic of China out of the United Nations. He also coordinated covert infiltration operations with Taipei. Kennedy may even have proposed a joint Soviet-American military strike on Chinese research facilities out of fear that a Chinese atomic bomb was imminent.

Chinese rhetoric and behavior convinced many besides JFK to see the leaders in Beijing as fanatic and irresponsible. Attacks by China on Soviet Premier Nikita Khrushchev for backing down under American pressure during the Cuban missile crisis of 1962 strengthened the belligerent image of Communist party leader Mao Zedong, as did the Sino-Indian border war, which erupted in the midst of the missile crisis and seemed to confirm Chinese expansionist intentions.

Ironically, the Sino-Soviet split, which Harry S. Truman and even Eisenhower had hoped would make China more cooperative, actually alarmed officials in the 1960s. The Chinese appeared so much more unreasonable than the Soviet Union that without Soviet restraint, they looked capable of bringing on a nuclear war.

Nevertheless, in the fall of 1963, after Kennedy's death, Assistant Secretary of State Roger Hilsman delivered a speech in San Francisco that appeared to herald greater flexibility. In reality Hilsman offered little, since the major concession was a "two-Chinas" policy that both Beijing and Taipei had long rejected. (doc. 2) Hearings held by the Senate Foreign Relations Committee in 1966 went farther to indicate an interest by Congress and scholars in improved relations, even originating the slogan "containment without isolation." (doc. 3) But the timing was not auspicious. Political turmoil in China had begun to accelerate as the Socialist Education Campaign (1962–65) developed into the Great Proletarian Cultural Revolution (1966–76), which was an effort to sustain Mao's utopian vision and eliminate his political rivals. Preoccupied with the need to revive revolutionary zeal at home, China cut itself off from the outside world. In Beijing, Red Guards torched the British Embassy in 1967, doubtless making U.S. diplomats glad they had no burnable assets in the capital.

China's frenzy was alarming. During 1964 Beijing exploded its first atomic bomb and thereafter refused to participate in nonproliferation talks. Washington worried about increased Chinese involvement in Vietnam after Chinese Defense Minister Lin Biao's 1965 speech "Long Live the Victory of People's War" (doc. 4) and especially when the United States began bombing North Vietnam.

But a new era was just over the horizon. The Soviet invasion of Czechoslovakia and the "Brezhnev Doctrine" of 1968 (doc. 5) persuaded Mao and Premier Zhou Enlai to turn to the United States as a counterweight to Soviet troops massed along the Chinese frontier. Fortuitously, the new American president, Nixon, had been considering an improvement in relations with China that would allow him to win concessions from the Soviet Union, facilitate a Vietnam peace settlement, and score a foreign policy triumph with the domestic voting public. Progress was temporarily delayed by the 1970 American incursion into Cambodia and the 1971 foray into Laos, as well as by foot dragging by bureaucrats in both countries. But Nixon lowered restrictions on trade and travel and called Red China the People's Republic of China for the first time. When the Chinese responded to these advances with an invitation to a U.S. table tennis team to come to Beijing, the era of "Ping-Pong diplomacy" began.

A secret trip to Beijing by National Security Adviser Henry Kissinger in July 1971 made possible the February 1972 Nixon visit to China. In the interim, Washington acquiesced in China's admission to the United Nations and to Taiwan's expulsion. The Shanghai Communiqué emerging from the trip, although a landmark, was actually an agreement to disagree. The United States acknowledged that there was only one China and that Taiwan was a part of it but resisted demands to withdraw its forces until a peaceful resolution of the Taiwan issue could be reached. (doc. 6) In 1973 the United States and China facilitated ongoing political discussions by exchanging liaison representatives, and trade between the two countries reached $700 million. Nixon's opening of economic, cultural, and political contacts, however, was limited by the Watergate scandal, which required placating the Republican right by slowing down these advances. Throughout the subsequent Gerald R. Ford presidency there was little progress. By 1976 the Chinese too were preoccupied with the deaths of Zhou and Mao, the fall of the Gang of Four and their radical influence on the Chinese Cultural Revolution, and the upcoming return to power of the more moderate Deng Xiaoping.

President Jimmy Carter moved slowly on China, for he was diverted by the Panama Canal Treaty fight, his determination to get SALT II through Congress, and the dispute between his secretary of state, Cyrus Vance, who wanted parallel movement on Soviet and Chinese relations, and his national security adviser, Zbigniew Brzezinski, who hoped to use the China card against Moscow. Carter sided with Brzezinski, opting for normalization late in 1978. On the most difficult issue—arms sales to Taiwan—Washington insisted that it would continue to provide Taipei with defensive weaponry after a one-year moratorium during which the 1954 U.S.-Republic of China Mutual Defense Treaty would be abrogated. Deng proved willing to accept this undesirable American position because he wanted diplomatic relations in place before the planned Chinese invasion of Vietnam in 1979. (docs. 7, 8, and 9)

At the same time, Congress, angered by lack of consultation and worried about Taipei, passed the Taiwan Relations Act in February 1979, which ensured defensive arms sales and the establishment of unofficial liaison offices (the American Institute in Taiwan and the Coordination Council on North American Affairs). (doc. 10) Beijing's outrage at these developments was moderated by the Soviet invasion of Afghanistan, which also led to Sino-American discussions of military cooperation.

Tensions subsided only briefly, however, for with the presidential campaign and election of Ronald Reagan in 1980, relations between

Washington and Beijing entered their deepest slump since the Kennedy years. Reagan made clear that he opposed Nixon's Shanghai Communiqué and the Carter normalization and that he intended to reopen diplomatic relations with Taiwan. But in the end Reagan backed down, and on August 17, 1982, a new communiqué confirmed U.S. acceptance of the one-China formula and agreed that arms sales would not exceed in quality or quantity the 1978 levels and would gradually be reduced. (doc. 11)

From then on relations improved. Agreements for cultural, scientific, technological, naval, and even nuclear exchanges followed, and both trade and investment grew rapidly. Some 40,000 Chinese came to the United States to study, and every important university in China could boast of visiting scholars from the United States.

As the Chinese people were exposed to Western society and values, however, new problems arose. In addition to the influx of blue jeans, cosmetics, and discos, the leadership in Beijing became increasingly concerned about the popularity of ideas about democracy, freedom of the press, and human rights. Crackdowns—including the 1983 ''spiritual pollution campaign'' and the 1987 purge of party leader Hu Yaobang for allegedly supporting the demonstrators—invariably employed anti-American propaganda. In the spring of 1989 dissatisfaction again rose to the surface in what became massive demonstrations by students, workers, and party members in Tiananmen Square.

The signal embarrassment for the Chinese government came with the visit of Soviet leader Mikhail Gorbachev, to whom the students promptly appealed for support. Intended to be the capstone of Deng's career and of the Sino-Soviet normalization launched by Gorbachev in his July 1986 Vladivostok speech (doc. 12), the visit proved disastrous for China's leaders. While Gorbachev was in China, satellite TV sent pictures around the world of increasingly bitter antigovernment protests in Tiananmen Square. Students erected a ''goddess of democracy and freedom'' that bore a striking resemblance to the Statue of Liberty, and they mounted a hunger strike. But on June 4, government leaders sent in tanks and troops, killing hundreds, possibly thousands. The United States was blamed for provoking the demonstrations, particularly because one of China's leading dissidents, Fang Lizhi, took refuge in the U.S. Embassy. (doc. 13)

At year's end the turmoil had jeopardized Chinese-American relations. Secret efforts by President George Bush to keep lines of communication open and his veto of a bill to extend visas for Chinese students afraid of returning to China were perceived as kowtowing to the hard-line Chinese leadership. Beijing meanwhile suspended Fulbright Scholarship exchanges, threatened to stop sending students to the United States, and began efforts to restrict press coverage. As foreign correspondents and international lending organizations sought opportunities to renew financial and commercial contacts frozen in June, the Chinese government remained unwilling to relax restrictions. For Taiwan the contrast between repression on the mainland and growing democratic reform on the island promised significant future benefits. Liberalized political and diplomatic policies under Presidents Chiang Ching-kuo and Lee Teng-hui have begun to secure renewed international recognition and economic success. (U.S. aid was discontinued in 1965, and by 1989 Taiwan had become the thirteenth largest trading nation in the world, with $73.5 billion in foreign exchange reserves.) American trade and investment survived derecognition and the initial uncertainty about Taiwan's future. A well-financed Taiwan lobby operates in Washington, arms sales and scholarly exchanges continue (the Chiang Ching-kuo Foundation was inaugurated in 1989), and Taipei's human rights record, though still problematic, draws less critical comment in the United States.

* * * *

Although the alliance between the United States and Japan has remained strong throughout the postwar period, relations have nonetheless been strained from time to time. The 1960s began with a serious conflict over the U.S.-Japan Security Treaty of 1952. American military bases, although providing a vital defense force, also reminded the Japanese of defeat in World War II while occupying valuable farmland and threatening the involvement of Japan in Soviet-American conflicts. Moreover, the treaty allowed American troops to remain in Japan and nuclear weapons to be stockpiled on Japanese soil. In May 1960 violent protests against treaty renewal resulted in the cancellation of President Eisenhower's visit to Tokyo and, after the Diet approved the treaty, brought down the Nobosuke Kishi government. (doc. 14)

Americans were not as sensitive to Japanese concerns about U.S. bases and nuclear war as they might have been. Only in 1969 did President Nixon reach an accord in Washington with Prime Minister Sato Eisaku for return of Okinawa to Japan (finally accomplished in 1972). (doc. 15) Throughout the period afterward, however, the U.S. Navy provoked repeated protests by secretly bringing ships carrying nuclear missiles into Japanese waters. Confirmation of these violations by former Ambassador to Tokyo Edwin O. Reischauer caused a short-lived political storm in 1981.

In addition to the desire to curtail the visible American military presence, Japanese confidence in U.S. defense commitments also suffered. The Nixon Doctrine, articulated in July 1969, seemed to hand Japan unwelcome responsibilities as it suggested a pullback of American forces from Asia. (doc. 16; see also Nixon's Vietnam speech of Nov. 1969, chap. 13, doc. 2) More seriously, the so-called Nixon Shock dismayed Tokyo. On the one hand, this July 1971 announcement of a Sino-American rapprochement, without consultation or warning, undermined Japanese faith in the president. On the other hand, the Japanese had long urged improved relations with China and moved rapidly to establish diplomatic ties and cultivate trade.

conomics, not politics, has been central to the U.S.-Japanese relationship and the root of most bad feeling. In 1964, when Washington was still promoting Japan's recovery, economic concerns proved instrumental in securing Tokyo's membership in the Organization for Economic Cooperation and Development (OECD). The increased U.S. involvement in the Vietnam War meant burgeoning procurement purchases in Japan after 1965. The resulting threats to American jobs and wage standards had led the two governments to set up as early as 1961 the cabinet-level Joint U.S.-Japan Committee on Trade and Economic Affairs.

By the early 1970s, the Japanese economic miracle had made it a colossus in Asia: Japan was resented and feared by its neighbors, who worried about a re-creation of the Greater East Asia Co-Prosperity Sphere (Japan's claim during World War II of Asia for the Asians with Japan, Manchuria, and China at its center) in a new guise. Americans also complained increasingly about Japanese products flooding U.S. markets while Tokyo refused to liberalize trade and investment policies. The serious undervaluation of the yen, which Tokyo declined to rectify, finally convinced President Nixon to suspend convertibility of the dollar into gold and establish a 10 percent surcharge on imports in 1971. This second Nixon Shock further soured U.S.-Japanese relations, shattered the post-World War II international monetary system established at the Bretton Woods Conference in 1944, and in the end failed significantly to alter Japan's ability to sell its goods in the United States.

After minor adjustments, and an increase in the yen-dollar ratio, Japanese industry resumed its penetration of U.S. and Western European markets. Further efforts to curb Japan through "voluntary" quotas on items such as textiles and automobiles have continued as more Americans are buying Japanese products even while they engage in "Japan bashing." In 1986 the Maekawa Commission report to Prime Minister Nakasone Yasuhiro made clear that international harmony could only be regained by changes in Japanese consumption patterns and management practices to improve market access for foreigners. Little action followed, however, and U.S. complaints have continued. (doc. 17)

The third in the series of Nixon administration surprises for Japanese planners occurred in 1973. The president imposed a brief soybean embargo to protect American feed grain for livestock. Because Japan bought 98 percent of its soybean supplies from the United States, most of which fed humans rather than animals, the outcry by consumers as well as officials was bitter.

Such intertwining of the two economies was also evident in the 1976 Lockheed influence peddling scandal, which discredited powerful Liberal Democratic party leader Tanaka Kakuei. Witnesses in a U.S. Senate probe of multinational corporations testified that Lockheed had distributed $12.5 million in Japan. Tanaka was quickly convicted of taking bribes while he served as prime minister; he had tried to expedite purchases of aircraft from Lockheed by All Nippon Airways and the Japanese Self-Defense Force.

Tying economic and political frictions together has been the persistent demand from Washington that Japan increase its defense budget. Tokyo adamantly kept defense spending to less than 1 percent of its gross national product (GNP) until 1986, arguing that military growth was prohibited by the constitution, by public opinion, and by the nation's opposition to nuclear weaponry. In fact, Japan supports the seventh largest defense budget in the world because of its enormous GNP, although on a per capita basis the burden is far smaller than that of the American taxpayer. Further problems arose over procurement of FSX fighter planes. When Tokyo announced in 1987 its intention to build its own jet fighter, Washington pressed hard to have Japan purchase the expensive FSX from the United States. Compromise was reached in an agreement for coproduction signed in November 1988. But American opponents objected to Japan's acquisition of sophisticated technology that might subsequently be used to upgrade its domestic aviation industry and enter the market in competition with U.S. companies. Critics also feared leaks to the Communist bloc after the Reagan administration discovered that the Toshiba company had diverted technology to the Soviet Union that allowed it to build quieter submarines capable of eluding U.S. sonar surveillance. President Bush, however, decided to go ahead with the program.

Unwilling to decrease defense expenditures, Japan instead increased foreign aid funding, including support for Korea, Taiwan, and Indochinese refugees in the 1970s, and for the World Bank and the Asian Development Bank in the 1980s. In 1976 the "Fukuda Doctrine" made clear Tokyo's determination to assist the Association of Southeast Asian Nations and quickly led it to surpass the United States as the largest aid donor to Asia.

Japan has mounted other efforts to improve Japanese-American understanding, even while its heightening economic involvement in the United States continues to pose a threat. In 1979 it went along with American sanctions against the Soviet Union triggered by the Afghanistan invasion. Similarly, it cooperated with sanctions against Poland after the Communist government declared martial law to suppress the Solidarity trade union movement. To reach the American public more directly, Tokyo established the U.S.-Japan Foundation in 1981, thereby facilitating cultural and scholarly exchange. By the late 1980s, Japan's heavy investments in U.S. Treasury securities had become a critical factor in financing the American deficit. Moreover, with purchases of American businesses such as Columbia Pictures and New York's Rockefeller Center, Japan promised to become an increasingly influential arbiter of American tastes.

* * * *

In April 1960 the controversial tenure of Syngman Rhee as president of South Korea finally came to an end through public protest aided by

American pressure. The new regime abandoned Rhee's policy of marching north and accepted the idea, favored by the United States, of reunification through elections. Senator Mike Mansfield's suggestion that neutralization on the Austrian model might follow gave impetus to mass rallies considered Communist-inspired by the military, which carried out a May 16, 1961, coup d'etat under General Park Chung Hee.

Although domestic politics entered a prolonged authoritarian era, first under Park and after 1979 under subsequent coup leader, Chun Doo Hwan, Korea emerged as a rapidly developing economic power with impressive surges in per capita income, trade, and industry. The 1965 Republic of Korea-Japan treaty, fostered by the United States and bitterly opposed by many on both sides of the Tsushima Straits, encouraged Korea's economic expansion. As a result, trade frictions akin to those between the United States and Japan have also been a theme of Korean-American relations in recent years.

The key link between Washington and Seoul, of course, has been the continuing Korean War armistice with the ever-present possibility of renewed war against the Communist North Koreans. As in Japan, however, the presence of large numbers of American troops has proven controversial among the Korean people and financially burdensome to the United States. During the Vietnam War, Washington poured in funds, construction and service contracts, and military equipment to induce Seoul to contribute troops, creating what critics called a mercenary army as well as spurring an economic boom. Efforts to withdraw sizable U.S. contingents in the Nixon, Ford, and Carter years produced severe strains in bilateral relations. KCIA (Korean Central Intelligence Agency) efforts to prevent troop reductions through bribery of U.S. officials resulted in the destructive "Koreagate" episode. Finally, in 1979 Carter was forced to abandon his plans under the thin cover story of a previously underestimated North Korean army buildup. (doc. 18)

Another area of sensitivity between Washington and Seoul has been human rights. Efforts to prevent the execution of opposition leader Kim Dae Jung and secure his release from prison (which succeeded in 1983) did not, for many Koreans, absolve Americans of complicity in the 1980 Kwangju incident, when U.S. troops assisted Chun's forces in suppressing unexpectedly fierce anti-martial law demonstrations and South Korean newspapers claimed that the U.S. ambassador had approved the crackdown in advance. Reagan's decision to embrace Chun in 1981 seemed to reflect Washington's emphasis on security over political liberalization. More recently the democratically elected government of Roh Tae Woo has moved toward greater democracy as well as stability in South Korea. (doc. 19)

Relations between Washington and Pyongyang, the capital of North Korea, have been tense for most of the period under consideration. In 1968 North Korea seized an American spy ship, the USS *Pueblo*, and held its crew for eleven months. Coming almost at the same moment as trouble in

West Berlin and the Tet crisis in Vietnam, American leaders feared that it might be part of a coordinated Communist offensive. The 1972 shock of Sino-American rapprochement led North Korea to abandon its isolationism by becoming active in the "nonalignment movement" to the extent that, by the mid-1980s, the nation was enjoying diplomatic relations with some 110 countries. Pyongyang also began to invite prominent Americans to North Korea, including members of Congress. This more positive image was sullied by the apparent North Korean government-supported 1983 planting of a bomb in Rangoon, Burma, to assassinate South Korean President Chun Doo Hwan, which instead killed several cabinet officials. During 1987, nevertheless, Washington instructed American diplomats that they might henceforth engage in substantive conversations with North Koreans in informal settings.

The 1990s, then, herald a time of opportunities as well as dangers in East Asia. American relations with Taiwan and the Koreas may benefit from growing political flexibility in these Asian nations as well as decreased U.S. emphasis on security issues. The reduction of East-West tensions, however, suggests that difficulties between the United States and China can no longer be resolved by calling up images of strategic triangles, and that Japan will no longer cleave as willingly to the United States in an effort to fit under its nuclear umbrella. A new paradigm for American policy in the Pacific is needed.

Document 1

Senator John F. Kennedy, speech on Quemoy and Matsu, Oct. 12, 1960, James C. Thomson Papers, Box 14, Far East 1961–66, Folder: Chinese Communist Letters, Articles, Speeches, Commentary 1960, John F. Kennedy Library, Boston, Massachusetts.

I know something of what it means to be responsible for the lives of other men. And if there is one pledge to the American people which I would make above all others, it would be this:

Should I become your President, I will take whatever steps are necessary to defend our security and to maintain the cause of world freedom—but I will not risk American lives and a nuclear war by permitting any other nation to drag us into the wrong war at the wrong place at the wrong time through an unwise commitment that is unsound militarily, unnecessary to our security, and unsupported by our allies.

That is the pledge I make to you tonight—and that is the basic issue between Mr. [Richard M.] Nixon and myself concerning the islands of Quemoy and Matsu.

* * *

Communist artillery can pound (the islands) at will, at any time they please. Any time they want to create a crisis—any time they want to frighten world opinion by bringing us to the brink of war, or please world opinion by then halting bombardment—the Communists can decide whether to launch an attack on these islands—including a full-scale attack to take them over from the Chinese Nationalists.

Why should we keep this constant temptation beneath their very eyes? Why should we give them this convenient valve with which to turn on and off the pressure on our forces? Why should Mr. Nixon now want to draw our line of commitment to include these two little islands so vulnerable to Communist takeover?

It is not because these islands are essential to the defense of Formosa and the Pescadores. This nation is clearly pledged to that defense, and I want to make it clear that if I have anything to say about it, the next administration will stand by that pledge. For there our security is clearly involved. There our prestige is clearly at stake. There our commitment is precise.

But Quemoy and Matsu, according to the best military judgment expressed, are not of any strategic value. They are not essential to the defense of Formosa, some hundred miles away. They are not essential to any re-invasion of the mainland, if any—and they are not even defensible themselves against a full-scale invasion, except by attacking the mainland, and thus initiating all-out war.

It was General [Matthew] Ridgway who said it "would be an unwarranted and tragic mistake to go to war" over these islands "not useful" to our security.

It was General [J. Lawton] Collins and Admiral [Raymond A.] Spruance who said they were strategically worthless both for the defense of Formosa and the re-invasion of the mainland. It was John Foster Dulles and General Maxwell Taylor who indicated similar views. And it was President Dwight D. Eisenhower who said:

"Fundamentally anyone can see that the two islands as of themselves, as two pieces of territory, are not greatly vital to Formosa."

But Mr. Nixon disagrees with the views I have just quoted. The conclusions of our top military experts represent what he calls "woolly thinking." He regards his military judgment about the importance of these islands to Formosa and a "chain reaction" as superior to theirs.

He emphasizes, moreover, that "it is the principle involved"—not "these two little pieces of real estate. They are unimportant. It isn't the few people who live on them," he said, "they are not too important. It is the principle involved." . . .

Mr. Nixon is not interested in policies of caution in world affairs. He boasts that he is a "risk-taker" abroad and a conservative at home. But I am neither. And the American people had a sufficient glimpse of the kind of risks he would take in 1954 when he said "we must take the risk now of putting our boys in Indo-China on the side of the French if needed to avoid further Communist expansion there." If ever there was a war where we would have been engaged in a hopeless struggle, without allies, for an unpopular colonialist cause, it was in the 1954 war in Indo-China.

The only war that would make less sense would be a nuclear war over Quemoy and Matsu. The American people know this . . . [and] do not want a trigger happy President in the White House.

Document 2

Assistant Secretary of State Roger Hilsman, "United States Policy Toward Communist China," U.S. Department of State, *Bulletin,* Jan. 6, 1964, 12–17.

U.S. Does Not "Ignore" China

Let me begin by disposing of a myth. It is frequently charged that the United States Government is "ignoring" China and its 700 million people.

This is simply untrue. We do not ignore our ally, the Government of the Republic of China. We do not ignore the 12 million people in Taiwan. Nor, in fact, do we ignore the people on the mainland. We are very much aware of them, and we have a deep friendship for them. Nor, finally, do we ignore the Communist leadership which has established itself on the mainland. We meet with them from time to time, as at the periodic talks between our ambassadors in Warsaw. We should like to be less ignorant of them and for them to be less ignorant of us. To this end we have been striving for years to arrange an exchange of correspondents but we have been put off with the assertion that so long as the "principal issue"—which they define in terms of their absurd charge that we are "occupying" Taiwan—is unresolved, there can be no progress on "secondary issues."

If we have not persuaded the Chinese Communists to allow an exchange of correspondents and to lower the wall of secrecy with which they surround themselves, we have nevertheless spent considerable effort in trying to understand what manner of men the Chinese Communists are, what are their ambitions, and what are the problems which stand in their way. We have tried to be objective and to see to it that dislike of communism does not becloud our ability to see the facts. . . .

There is one other area in which questions have been raised about American policy and in which a clarification of this Government's position is timely. I refer to the apparent differences in the policies which we are adopting toward the Soviet Union and toward Communist China. We maintain a policy of nonrecognition and trade embargo of Communist China—at a time when we are willing to broaden contact with the Soviet Union.

The Soviet Union and Communist China do share the goal of communizing the world. But we see important differences in the thinking and tactics of the two. In the U.S.S.R. the Communists were developing a modern industrial society precisely when in China they were conducting a guerrilla war from rural bases. The Soviet leadership seems to have absorbed certain lessons from its more extended development—as to the values and priorities which one may safely pursue on a small planet and as to the price of miscalculating the nature of the outside world.

We believe that the policies which have proved their worth with Moscow are equally valid for our long-term relations with Peiping. But we also believe that our approach should be adapted to the differences in behavior between the two, as they relate to our own national objectives.

First and foremost, we fully honor our close and friendly ties with the people of the Republic of China on Taiwan and with their Government. We conceive of this relationship not as an historical accident but as a matter of basic principle. So long as Peiping insists on the destruction of this relationship as the *sine qua non* for any basic improvement in relations between ourselves and Communist China, there can be no prospect for such an improvement.

Our differing policies toward the

Soviet Union and Communist China derive, secondly, from their differing attitudes toward negotiations, as such, even in limited areas. Faced with the realities of the nuclear age, the Soviet Union appears to recognize that certain interests—notably survival—are shared by all mankind. Peiping, however, remains wedded to a fundamentalist form of communism which emphasizes violent revolution, even if it threatens the physical ruin of the civilized world. It refuses to admit that there are common interests which cross ideological lines.

Third, United States policy is influenced by Chinese communism's obsessive suspicion of the outside world, far exceeding even that of the Soviet Union. Whereas Moscow appears to have learned that free-world readiness to negotiate limited common interests is not a sign of weakness, Peiping regards any conciliatory gesture as evidence of weakness and an opportunity for exploitation.

Perhaps the best evidence of this paranoid view of the world came from Peiping's Foreign Minister Ch'en I, who declared, at the height of China's food crisis in 1962, that his government would never accept any aid from America because this would mean "handing our vast market over to America." Given the near-subsistence level of the society and the limited purchasing power of the government, this view of American intentions could only be conjured up by men possessed of an unremitting distrust of all external peoples and a naive sense of their own economic prospects.

Fourth are the differing circumstances and opportunities on the peripheries of the Soviet Union and Communist China. The Soviet Union and European members of its bloc border on long-established, relatively stable states defended by powerful, locally based—as well as more distant—deterrent and defensive forces. Communist China's neighbors, on the other hand, include newly established states struggling to maintain their independence, with very limited defense forces. There is a wider range of opportunities for aggression and subversion available to Peiping, which renders it even more important that in dealing with Peiping we not permit that regime to underestimate free-world firmness and determination.

Much speculation has turned around the question of possible commercial relations between private American firms and Communist China, especially in view of the declining trade between Communist China and its Soviet bloc partners. Peiping's own policies, however, seem crystal clear on this point. Peiping apparently wants none of it. As one of its trade officials recently declared, "We have a very clear attitude. We won't trade with the United States because the United States Government is hostile to us." The Chinese Communists follow Mao's [Mao Zedong] maxim that "politics and economics are inseparable." They made this clear in their unilateral rupture of contracts with Japanese firms in 1958 and their willingness to jeopardize major industrial projects as the price for carrying on their dispute with the Soviet Union in 1960.

In sum, while respecting the right of others to view the matter otherwise, we find important differences in the willingness and ability of the Soviet Union and Communist China, at the present stage of their respective development, to reach limited agreements which can bring some reduction of the terrible dangers and tensions of our present-day world. We believe that policies of strength and firmness, accompanied by a constant readiness to negotiate—policies long and effectively pursued with the Soviet Union—will best promote the changes which must take place on the China mainland before we can hope to achieve long-sought conditions of peace, security, and progress in this half of the globe.

President [Lyndon B.] Johnson said:

> We will be unceasing in the search for peace; resourceful in our pursuit of areas of agreement, even with those with whom we differ. . . . We must be prepared at one and the same time for both the confrontation of power and the limitation of power. We must be ready to defend the national interest and to negotiate the common interest.

We are confronted in Communist China with a regime which presently finds no ground of common interest with those whose ideals it does not share, which has used hatred as an engine of national policy. The United States is the central figure in their demonology and the target of a sustained fury of invective. After President [John F.] Kennedy's assassination, while other nations—Communist and free—shared our grief, the Chinese Communist Daily Worker published a cartoon of a man sprawled on the ground with the caption "Kennedy Bites the Dust." If this speaks for the Chinese Communist leadership, I am confident that it does not speak for most Chinese.

Americans—businessmen, missionaries, diplomats—have long felt a particularly close rapport with the Chinese. In World War II American pilots downed in Communist areas came out with moving accounts of Chinese helpfulness and friendliness. The Communists had not destroyed those attitudes then. I doubt they have succeeded in destroying them now.

We do not know what changes may occur in the attitudes of future Chinese leaders. But if I may paraphrase a classic canon of our past, we pursue today toward Communist China a policy of the open door: We are determined to keep the door open to the possibility of change and not to slam it shut against any developments which might advance our national good, serve the free world, and benefit the people of China. Patience is not unique to the Chinese. We too can maintain our positions without being provoked to unseemly action or despairing of what the future may hold. We will not sow the dragon's seed of hate which may bear bitter fruit in future generations of China's millions. But neither will we betray our interests and those of our allies to appease the ambitions of Communist China's leaders.

We hope that, confronted with firmness which will make foreign adventure unprofitable, and yet offered the prospect that the way back into the community of man is not closed to it, the Chinese Communist regime will eventually forsake its present venomous hatreds which spring from a rigid class view of society. We hope that they will rediscover the Chinese virtue of tolerance for a multitude of beliefs and faiths and that they will accept again a world of diversity in place of the gray monolith which seems to be communism's goal for human society.

On November 27th President Johnson said:

> The time has come for Americans of all races and creeds and political beliefs to understand and respect one another. Let us put an end to the teaching and the preaching of hate and evil and violence. Let us turn away from the fanatics of the far left and the far right. . . .

President Johnson was talking about America. But the words are valid for all mankind.

Document 3

Expert on China A. Doak Barnett, testimony, U.S. Congress, Senate, Committee on Foreign Relations, *U.S. Policy With Respect to Mainland China,* Washington, D.C.: Government Printing Office, 1966, 4–5.

U.S. POSTURE TOWARD COMMUNIST CHINA

I would like, right at the start, to state my own belief that there is a need for basic changes in the overall U.S. posture toward Communist China. For almost 17 years we have pursued a policy that might best be characterized as one aimed at containment and isolation of Communist China.

In my view, the element of containment—using this term in a very broad sense to include both military and nonmilitary measures to block threats posed by China to its neighbors—has been an essential part of our policy and has been, in some respects at least, fairly successful. Our power has played an important and necessary role in creating a counterbalance to Communist China's power in Asia, and we have contributed significantly to the task of gradually building stable non-Communist societies in areas that lie in China's shadow. But the U.S. attempt to isolate Communist China has been, in my opinion, unwise and, in a fundamental sense, unsuccessful, and it cannot, I believe, provide a basis for a sound, long-term policy that aims not only at containing and restraining Chinese power but also at reducing tensions, exerting a moderating influence on Peking, broadening the areas of non-Communist agreement on issues relating to China, and slowly involving Communist China in more normal patterns of international intercourse.

I strongly believe, therefore, that the time has come—even though the United States is now engaged in a bitter struggle in Vietnam—for our country to alter its posture toward Communist China and adopt a policy of containment but not isolation, a policy that would aim on the one hand at checking military or subversive threats and pressures emanating from Peking, but at the same time would aim at maximum contacts with and maximum involvement of the Chinese Communists in the international community.

Such a policy would involve continued commitments to help non-Communist regimes combat Communist subversion and insurrection, as in Vietnam, and continued pledges to defend areas on China's periphery, including Taiwan. But it would involve changes in many other aspects of our policies.

PROPOSALS FOR FUTURE U.S. POLICIES RE RED CHINA

While continuing to fulfill our pledge to defend Taiwan against attack, we should clearly and explicitly acknowledge the Chinese Communist regime as the de facto Government of the China mainland and state our desire to extend de jure recognition and exchange diplomatic representatives with Peking if and when it indicates that it would be prepared to reciprocate.

We should press in every way we can to encourage nonofficial contacts. We should, instead of embargoing all trade with the China mainland, restrict only trade in strategic items and encourage American businessmen to explore other opportunities for trade contacts. And within the United Nations we should work for the acceptance of some formula which would provide seats for both Communist China and Nationalist China. In taking these steps, we will have to do so in full recognition of the fact that Peking's initial reaction is almost certain to be negative and even hostile and that any changes in our posture will create some new problems. But we should take them, nevertheless, because initiatives on our part are clearly required if we are to work, however slowly, toward the long-term goal of a more stable, less-explosive situation in Asia and to explore the possibilities of trying to moderate Peking's policies.

Some people believe that a policy combining the differing elements I have suggested, that is, containment but also increased attempts to deal directly with Peking—would involve contradictory and inconsistent elements. I would argue that, on the contrary, in terms of our long-term aims the seemingly contradictory elements would in fact be complementary and mutually reinforcing.

Others argue that a change of posture such as the one I have suggested might be interpreted as a sign of weakness and irresolution on our part, and therefore be dangerous, particularly if taken while we are engaged in a major struggle against Communist insurrection in Vietnam. I would argue that our commitments and actions in Vietnam make it wholly clear, to both friend and foe, that we are not acting out of weakness and that while we search for areas of possible agreement and accommodation we will also continue in our determination to protect the interests of ourselves and our friends, to oppose violence as a means of political change, and to assist in the growth of viable, progressive, non-Communist regimes, in Asia, as elsewhere.

Document 4

People's Republic of China Defense Minister Lin Biao's speech, "Long Live the Victory of People's War," the *New York Times*, Sept. 4, 1965, 2.

In view of the fact that some people were afflicted with the fear of the imperialists and reactionaries, Comrade Mao Tse-tung put forward his famous thesis that "the imperialists and all reactionaries are paper tigers."

In appearance, the reactionaries are terrifying but in reality they are not so powerful. From a long-term point of view, it is not the reactionaries but the people who are really powerful. . . .

It must be emphasized that Comrade Mao Tse-tung's theory of the establishment of rural revolutionary base areas and the encirclement of cities from the countryside is of outstanding and universal practical importance for the present revolutionary struggles of all the oppressed nations and peoples, and particularly for the revolutionary struggles of the oppressed nations and peoples in Asia, Africa and Latin America against imperialism and its lackeys.

Many countries and peoples in Asia, Africa and Latin America are now being subjected to aggression and enslavement on a serious scale by the imperialists headed by the United States and their lackeys. The basic political and economic conditions in many of these countries have many similarities to those that prevailed in old China. As in China, the peasant question is extremely important in these regions. The peasants constitute the main force of the national-democratic revolution against the imperialists and their lackeys.

In committing aggression against these countries, the imperialists usually begin by seizing the big cities and the main lines of communication, but they are unable to bring the vast countryside completely under their control. The countryside, and the countryside alone, can provide the broad areas in which the revolutionaries can maneuver freely.

The countryside, and the countryside alone, can provide the revolutionary bases from which the revolutionaries can go forward to final victory. Precisely for this reason, Comrade Mao Tse-tung's theory of establishing revolutionary base areas in the rural districts and encircling the cities from the countryside is attracting more and more attention among the people in these regions.

Taking the entire globe, if North America and Western Europe can be called "the cities of the world," then Asia, Africa and Latin America constitute "the rural areas of the world." . . .

Today, the revolutionary base areas of the peoples of the world have grown to unprecedented proportions, their revolutionary movement is surging as never before. Imperialism is weaker than ever, and U.S. imperialism, the chieftain of world imperialism, is suffering one defeat after another.

We can say with ever greater confidence that the people's wars can be won and U.S. imperialism can be defeated in all countries.

The peoples of the world now have the lessons of the October Revolution, the anti-Fascist war, the Chinese people's war of resistance and war of liberation, the Korean people's war of resistance to U.S. aggression, the Vietnamese people's war of liberation and their war of resistance to U.S. aggression, and the people's revolutionary armed struggles in many other countries.

Provided each people studies these lessons well and creatively integrates them with the concrete practice of revolution in their own country, there is no doubt that the revolutionary peoples of the world will stage still more powerful and splendid dramas in the theater of people's war in their countries and that they will wipe off the earth once and for all the common enemy of all the peoples, U.S. imperialism, and its lackeys.

Peking Vows to Support Vietcong Until Victory

The struggle of the Vietnamese people against U.S. aggression and for national salvation is now the focus of the struggle of the people of the world against U.S. aggression.

The determination of the Chinese people to support and aid the Vietnamese people in their struggle against U.S. aggression and for national salvation is unshakable. No matter what U.S. imperialism may do to expand its war adventure, the Chinese people will do everything in their power to support the Vietnamese people until every single one of the U.S. aggressors is driven out of Vietnam.

The U.S. imperialists are now clamoring for another trial of strength with the Chinese people, for another large-scale ground war on the Asian mainland.

If they insist on following in the footsteps of the Japanese Fascists, well then, they may do so, if they please. The Chinese people definitely have ways of their own for coping with a U.S. imperialist war of aggression.

Our methods are no secret. The most important one is still mobilization of the people, reliance on the people, making every one a soldier and waging a people's war.

We want to tell the U.S. imperialists once again, that the vast ocean of several hundred million Chinese people in arms will be more than enough to submerge your few million aggressive troops.

If you dare to impose war on us we shall gain freedom of action. It will then not be up to you to decide how the war will be fought. We shall fight in the ways most advantageous to us to destroy the enemy and wherever the enemy can be most easily destroyed.

Since the Chinese people were able to destroy the Japanese aggressors 20 years ago, they are certainly still more capable of finishing off the U.S. aggressors today.

The naval and air superiority you boast about cannot intimidate the Chinese people and neither can the atom bomb you brandish at us.

Document 5

"The Brezhnev Doctrine," *Problems of Communism*, Nov./Dec. 1968, vol. 17, 25.

In connection with the events in Czechoslovakia, the question of the relationship and interconnection between the socialist countries' national interests and their internationalist obligations has assumed particular urgency and sharpness. The measures taken jointly by the Soviet Union and other socialist countries to defend the socialist gains of the Czechoslovak people are of enormous significance for strengthening the socialist commonwealth, which is the main achievement of the international working class.

At the same time it is impossible to ignore the allegations being heard in some places that the actions of the five socialist countries contradict the Marxist-Leninist principle of sovereignty and the right of the nations to self-determination.

Such arguments are untenable primarily because they are based on an abstract, non-class approach to the question of sovereignty and the right of nations to self-determination.

There is no doubt that the peoples of the socialist countries and the Communist parties have and must have freedom to determine their country's path of development. However, any decision of theirs must damage neither socialism in their own country, nor the fundamental interests of the other socialist countries, nor the world-wide workers' movement, which is waging a struggle for socialism. This means that every Communist party is responsible not only to its own people but also to all the socialist countries and to the entire Communist movement. Whoever forgets this is placing sole emphasis on the autonomy and independence of Communist parties, lapsing into one-sidedness, and shirking his internationalist obligations. . . .

Each Communist party is free to apply the principles of Marxism-Leninism and socialism in its own country, but it cannot deviate from these principles (if, of course, it remains a Communist party). In concrete terms this means primarily that no Communist party can fail to take into account in its activities such a decisive fact of our time as the struggle between the two antithetical social systems—capitalism and socialism. This struggle is an objective fact that does not depend on the will of people and is conditioned by the division of the world into the two antithetical social systems. . . .

It should be stressed that even if a socialist country seeks to take an "extrabloc" position, it in fact retains its national independence thanks precisely to the power of the socialist commonwealth—and primarily to its chief force, the Soviet Union, and the might of its armed forces. The weakening of any link in the world socialist system has a direct effect on all the socialist countries, which cannot be indifferent. Thus, the antisocialist forces in Czechoslovakia were in essence using talk about the right to self-determination to cover up demands for so-called neutrality and the CSSR's [Czechoslovak Soviet Socialist Republic] withdrawal from the socialist commonwealth. But implementation of such "self-determination," *i.e.*, Czechoslovakia's separation from the socialist commonwealth, would run counter to Czechoslovakia's fundamental interests and would harm the other socialist countries. Such "self-determination," as a result of which NATO troops might approach Soviet borders and the commonwealth of European socialist countries could be dismembered, in fact infringes on the vital interest of these countries' peoples, and fundamentally contradicts the right of these peoples to socialist self-determination. The Soviet Union and other socialist states, in fulfilling their internationalist duty to the fraternal peoples of Czechoslovakia and defending their own socialist gains, had to act and did act in resolute opposition to the antisocialist forces in Czechoslovakia. . . .

The assistance given to the working people of the CSSR by the other socialist countries, which prevented the export of counterrevolution from the outside, is in fact a struggle for the Czechoslovak Socialist Republic's sovereignty against those who would like to deprive it of this sovereignty by delivering the country to the imperialists.

Over a long period of time and with utmost restraint and patience, the fraternal Communist parties of the socialist countries took political measures to help the Czechoslovak people to halt the antisocialist forces' offensive in Czechoslovakia. And only after exhausting all such measures did they undertake to bring in armed forces.

The allied socialist countries' soldiers who are in Czechoslovakia are proving in deeds that they have no task other than to defend the socialist gains in that country. They are not interfering in the country's internal affairs, and they are waging a struggle not in words but in deeds for the principles of self-determination of Czechoslovakia's peoples, for their inalienable right to decide their destiny themselves after profound and careful consideration, without intimidation by counterrevolutionaries, without revisionist and nationalist demagoguery.

Those who speak of the "illegality" of the allied socialist countries' actions in Czechoslovakia forget that in a class society there is and can be no such thing as non-class law. Laws and the norms of law are subordinated to the laws of the class struggle and the laws of social development. These laws are clearly formulated in the documents jointly adopted by the Communist and Workers' parties.

The class approach to the matter cannot be discarded in the name of legalistic considerations. Whoever does so forfeits the only correct, class-oriented criterion for evaluating legal norms and begins to measure events with the yardsticks of bourgeois law. . . .

There is no doubt that the actions taken in Czechoslovakia by the five allied socialist countries in Czechoslovakia, actions aimed at defending the fundamental interests of the socialist commonwealth and primarily at defending Czechoslovakia's independence and sovereignty as a socialist state, will be increasingly supported by all who really value the interests of the present-day revolutionary movement, the peace and security of peoples, democracy and socialism.

—Excerpt from Sergei Kovalev's article in Pravda, *Sept. 26, 1968.*

Document 6

Joint communiqué issued at Shanghai, Feb. 27, 1972, U.S. Department of State, *Bulletin*, Mar. 20, 1972, 435–38.

President Richard Nixon of the United States of America visited the People's Republic of China at the invitation of Premier Chou En-lai of the People's Republic of China from February 21 to February 28, 1972. Accompanying the President were Mrs. Nixon, U.S. Secretary of State William Rogers, Assistant to the President Dr. Henry Kissinger, and other American officials.

President Nixon met with Chairman Mao Tse-tung of the Communist Party of China on February 21. The two leaders had a serious and frank exchange of views on Sino-U.S. relations and world affairs.

During the visit, extensive, earnest and frank discussions were held between President Nixon and Premier Chou En-lai on the normalization of relations between the United States of America and the People's Republic of China, as well as on other matters of interest to both sides. In addition, Secretary of State William Rogers and Foreign Minister Chi Peng-fei held talks in the same spirit.

President Nixon and his party visited Peking and viewed cultural, industrial and agricultural sites, and they also toured Hangchow and Shanghai where, continuing discussions with Chinese leaders, they viewed similar places of interest.

The leaders of the People's Republic of China and the United States of America found it beneficial to have this opportunity, after so many years without contact, to present candidly to one another their views on a variety of issues. They reviewed the international situation in which important changes and great upheavals are taking place and expounded their respective positions and attitudes.

The U.S. side stated: Peace in Asia and peace in the world requires efforts both to reduce immediate tensions and to eliminate the basic causes of conflict. The United States will work for a just and secure peace: just, because it fulfills the aspirations of peoples and nations for freedom and progress; secure, because it removes the danger of foreign aggression. The United States supports individual freedom and social progress for all the peoples of the world, free of outside pressure or intervention. The United States believes that the effort to reduce tensions is served by improving communication between countries that have different ideologies so as to lessen the risks of confrontation through accident, miscalculation or misunderstanding. Countries should treat each other with mutual respect and be willing to compete peacefully, letting performance be the ultimate judge. No country should claim infallibility and each country should be prepared to reexamine its own attitudes for the common good. The United States stressed that the peoples of Indochina should be allowed to determine their destiny without outside intervention; its constant primary objective has been a negotiated solution; the eight-point proposal put forward by the Republic of Vietnam and the United States on January 27, 1972 represents a basis for the attainment of that objective; in the absence of a negotiated settlement the United States envisages the ultimate withdrawal of all U.S. forces from the region consistent with the aim of self-determination for each country of Indochina. The United States will maintain its close ties with and support for the Republic of Korea; the United States will support efforts of the Republic of Korea to seek a relaxation of tension and increased communication in the Korean peninsula. The United States places the highest value on its friendly relations with Japan; it will continue to develop the existing close bonds. Consistent with the United Nations Security Council Resolution of December 21, 1971, the United States favors the continuation of the ceasefire between India and Pakistan and the withdrawal of all military forces to within their own territories and to their own sides of the ceasefire line in Jammu and Kashmir; the United States supports the right of the peoples of South Asia to shape their own future in peace, free of military threat, and without having the area become the subject of great power rivalry.

The Chinese side stated: Wherever there is oppression, there is resistance. Countries want independence, nations want liberation and the people want revolution—this has become the irresistible trend of history. All nations, big or small, should be equal; big nations should not bully the small and strong nations should not bully the weak. China will never be a superpower and it opposes hegemony and power politics of any kind. The Chinese side stated that it firmly supports the struggles of all the oppressed people and nations for freedom and liberation and that the people of all countries have the right to choose their social systems according to their own wishes and the right to safeguard the independence, sovereignty and territorial integrity of their own countries and oppose foreign aggression, interference, control and subversion. All foreign troops should be withdrawn to their own countries.

The Chinese side expressed its firm support to the peoples of Vietnam, Laos and Cambodia in their efforts for the attainment of their goal and its firm support to the seven-point proposal of the Provisional Revolutionary Government of the Republic of South Vietnam and the elaboration of February this year on the two key problems in the proposal, and to the Joint Declaration of the Summit Conference of the Indochinese Peoples. It firmly supports the eight-point program for the peaceful unification of Korea put forward by the Government of the Democratic People's Republic of Korea on April 12, 1971, and the stand for the abolition of the "U.N. Commission for the Unification and Rehabilitation of Korea." It firmly opposes the revival and outward expansion of Japanese militarism and firmly supports the Japanese people's desire to build an independent, democratic, peaceful and neutral Japan. It firmly maintains that India and Pakistan should, in accordance with the United Nations resolutions on the India-Pakistan question, immediately withdraw all their forces to their respective territories and to their own sides of the ceasefire line in Jammu and Kashmir and firmly supports the Pakistan Government and people in their struggle to preserve their independence and sovereignty and the people of Jammu and Kashmir in their struggle for the right of self-determination.

There are essential differences between China and the United States in their social systems and foreign policies. However, the two sides agreed that countries, regardless of their social systems, should conduct their relations on the principles of respect for the sovereignty and territorial integrity of all states, non-aggression against other states, non-interference in the internal affairs of other states, equality and mutual benefit, and peaceful coexistence. International disputes should be settled on this basis, without resorting to the use or threat of force. The United States and the People's Republic of China are prepared to apply these principles to their mutual relations.

With these principles of international relations in mind the two sides stated that:

—progress toward the normalization of relations between China and the United States is in the interests of all countries;

—both wish to reduce the danger of international military conflict;

—neither should seek hegemony in the Asia-Pacific region and each is opposed to efforts by any other country or group of countries to establish such hegemony; and

—neither is prepared to negotiate on behalf of any third party or to enter into agreements or understandings with the other directed at other states.

Both sides are of the view that it would be against the interests of the peoples of the world for any major country to collude with another against other countries, or for major countries to divide up the world into spheres of interest.

The two sides reviewed the long-standing serious disputes between China and the United States. The Chinese side reaffirmed its position: The Taiwan question is the crucial question obstructing the normalization of relations between China and the United States; the Government of the People's Republic of China is the sole legal government of China; Taiwan is a province of China which has long been returned to the motherland; the liberation of Taiwan is China's internal affair in which no other country has the right to interfere; and all U.S. forces and military installations must be withdrawn from Taiwan. The Chinese Government firmly opposes any activities which aim at the creation of "one China, one Taiwan," "one China, two governments," "two Chinas," and "independent Taiwan" or advocate that "the status of Taiwan remains to be determined."

The U.S. side declared: The United States acknowledges that all Chinese on either side of the Taiwan Strait maintain there is but one China and that Taiwan is a part of China. The United States Government does not challenge that position. It reaffirms its interest in a peaceful settlement of the Taiwan question by the Chinese themselves. With this prospect in mind, it affirms the ultimate objective of the withdrawal of all U.S. forces and military installations from Taiwan. In the meantime, it will progressively reduce its forces and military installations on Taiwan as the tension in the area diminishes.

The two sides agreed that it is desirable to broaden the understanding between the two peoples. To this end, they discussed specific areas in such fields as science, technology, culture, sports and journalism, in which people-to-people contacts and exchanges would be mutually beneficial. Each side undertakes to facilitate the further development of such contacts and exchanges.

Both sides view bilateral trade as another area from which mutual benefit can be derived, and agreed that economic relations based on equality and mutual benefit are in the interest of the peoples of the two countries. They agree to facilitate the progressive development of trade between their two countries.

The two sides agreed that they will stay in contact through various channels, including the sending of a senior U.S. representative to Peking from time to time for concrete consultations to further the normalization of relations between the two countries and continue to exchange views on issues of common interest.

The two sides expressed the hope that the gains achieved during this visit would open up new prospects for the relations between the two countries. They believe that the normalization of relations between the two countries is not only in the interest of the Chinese and American peoples but also contributes to the relaxation of tension in Asia and the world.

President Nixon, Mrs. Nixon and the American party expressed their appreciation for the gracious hospitality shown them by the Government and people of the People's Republic of China.

Document 7

Joint Communiqué on the Establishment of Diplomatic Relations Between the United States of America and the People's Republic of China, Dec. 15, 1978, U.S. Department of State, *Bulletin*, Jan. 1, 1979, 25.

The United States of America and the People's Republic of China have agreed to recognize each other and to establish diplomatic relations as of January 1, 1979.

The United States of America recognizes the Government of the People's Republic of China as the sole legal Government of China. Within this context, the people of the United States will maintain cultural, commercial, and other unofficial relations with the people of Taiwan.

The United States of America and the People's Republic of China reaffirm the principles agreed on by the two sides in the Shanghai Communiqué and emphasize once again that:

- Both wish to reduce the danger of international military conflict.
- Neither should seek hegemony in the Asia-Pacific region or in any other region of the world and each is opposed to efforts by any other country or group of countries to establish such hegemony.
- Neither is prepared to negotiate on behalf of any third party or to enter into agreements or understandings with the other directed at other states.
- The Government of the United States of America acknowledges the Chinese position that there is but one China and Taiwan is part of China.
- Both believe that normalization of Sino-American relations is not only in the interest of the Chinese and American peoples but also contributes to the cause of peace in Asia and the world.

The United States of America and the People's Republic of China will exchange Ambassadors and establish Embassies on March 1, 1979.

Document 8

U.S. statement on recognition of People's Republic of China, Dec. 15, 1978, U.S. Department of State, *Bulletin*, Jan. 1, 1979, 26.

As of January 1, 1979, the United States of America recognizes the People's Republic of China as the sole legal government of China. On the same date, the People's Republic of China accords similar recognition to the United States of America. The United States thereby establishes diplomatic relations with the People's Republic of China.

On that same date, January 1, 1979, the United States of America will notify Taiwan that it is terminating diplomatic relations and that the Mutual Defense Treaty between the United States and the Republic of China is being terminated in accordance with the provisions of the Treaty. The United States also states that it will be withdrawing its remaining military personnel from Taiwan within four months.

In the future, the American people and the people of Taiwan will maintain commercial, cultural, and other relations without official government representation and without diplomatic relations.

The Administration will seek adjustments to our laws and regulations to permit the maintenance of commercial, cultural, and other nongovernmental relationships in the new circumstances that will exist after normalization.

The United States is confident that the people of Taiwan face a peaceful and prosperous future. The United States continues to have an interest in the peaceful resolution of the Taiwan issue and expects that the Taiwan issue will be settled peacefully by the Chinese themselves.

The United States believes that the establishment of diplomatic relations with the People's Republic will contribute to the welfare of the American people, to the stability of Asia where the United States has major security and economic interest, and to the peace of the entire world.

Document 9

Statement of the People's Republic of China, Jan. 1, 1979, U.S. Department of State, Office of Chinese and Mongolian Affairs, Washington, D.C.

As of January 1, 1979, the People's Republic of China and the United States of America recognize each other and establish diplomatic relations, thereby ending the prolonged abnormal relationship between them. This is a historic event in Sino-U.S. relations.

As is known to all, the Government of the People's Republic of China is the sole legal government of China and Taiwan is a part of China. The question of Taiwan was the crucial issue obstructing the normalization of relations between China and the United States. It has now been resolved between the two countries in the spirit of the Shanghai Communiqué and through their joint efforts, thus enabling the normalization of relations so ardently desired by the people of the two countries. As for the way of bringing Taiwan back to the embrace of the motherland and reunifying the country, it is entirely China's internal affair.

At the invitation of the U.S. Government, Teng Hsiao-p'ing, Vice Premier of the State Council of the People's Republic of China, will pay an official visit to the United States in January 1979, with a view to further promoting the friendship between the two peoples and good relations between the two countries.

Document 10

Taiwan Relations Act (Public Law 96–8), Apr. 10, 1979, *Statutes at Large*, Washington, D.C.: Government Printing Office, 1981, vol. 93, 14–16.

An Act

To help maintain peace, security, and stability in the Western Pacific and to promote the foreign policy of the United States by authorizing the continuation of commercial, cultural, and other relations between the people of the United States and the people on Taiwan, and for other purposes.

Be it enacted by the Senate and House of Representatives of the United States of America in Congress assembled,

SHORT TITLE

Section 1. This Act may be cited as the "Taiwan Relations Act".

FINDINGS AND DECLARATION OF POLICY

Sec. 2 (a) The President having terminated governmental relations between the United States and the governing authorities on Taiwan recognized by the United States as the Republic of

China prior to January 1, 1979, the Congress finds that the enactment of this Act is necessary—

(1) to help maintain peace, security, and stability in the Western Pacific; and

(2) to promote the foreign policy of the United States by authorizing the continuation of commercial, cultural, and other relations between the people of the United States and the people on Taiwan.

(b) It is the policy of the United States—

(1) to preserve and promote extensive, close, and friendly commercial, cultural, and other relations between the people of the United States and the people on Taiwan, as well as the people on the China mainland and all other peoples of the Western Pacific area;

(2) to declare that peace and stability in the area are in the political, security, and economic interests of the United States, and are matters of international concern;

(3) to make clear that the United States decision to establish diplomatic relations with the People's Republic of China rests upon the expectation that the future of Taiwan will be determined by peaceful means;

(4) to consider any effort to determine the future of Taiwan by other than peaceful means, including by boycotts or embargoes, a threat to the peace and security of the Western Pacific area and of grave concern to the United States;

(5) to provide Taiwan with arms of a defensive character; and

(6) to maintain the capacity of the United States to resist any resort to force or other forms of coercion that would jeopardize the security, or the social or economic system, of the people on Taiwan.

(c) Nothing contained in this Act shall contravene the interest of the United States in human rights, especially with respect to the human rights of all the approximately eighteen million inhabitants of Taiwan. The preservation and enhancement of the human rights of all the people on Taiwan are hereby reaffirmed as objectives of the United States.

IMPLEMENTATION OF UNITED STATES POLICY WITH REGARD TO TAIWAN

Sec. 3. (a) In furtherance of the policy set forth in section 2 of this Act, the United States will make available to Taiwan such defense articles and defense services in such quantity as may be necessary to enable Taiwan to maintain a sufficient self-defense capability.

(b) The President and the Congress shall determine the nature and quantity of such defense articles and services based solely upon their judgment of the needs of Taiwan, in accordance with procedures established by law. Such determination of Taiwan's defense needs shall include review by United States military authorities in connection with recommendations to the President and the Congress.

(c) The President is directed to inform the Congress promptly of any threat to the security or the social or economic system of the people on Taiwan and any danger to the interests of the United States arising therefrom. The President and the Congress shall determine, in accordance with constitutional processes, appropriate action by the United States in response to any such danger.

APPLICATION OF LAWS; INTERNATIONAL AGREEMENTS

Sec. 4. (a) The absence of diplomatic relations or recognition shall not affect the application of the laws of the United States with respect to Taiwan, and the laws of the United States shall apply with respect to Taiwan in the manner that the laws of the United States applied with respect to Taiwan prior to January 1, 1979.

(b) The application of subsection (a) of this section shall include, but shall not be limited to, the following:

(1) Whenever the laws of the United States refer or relate to foreign countries, nations, states, governments, or similar entities, such terms shall include and such laws shall apply with respect to Taiwan.

(2) Whenever authorized by or pursuant to the laws of the United States to conduct or carry out programs, transactions, or other relations with respect to foreign countries, nations, states, governments, or similar entities, the President or any agency of the United States Government is authorized to conduct and carry out, in accordance with section 6 of this Act, such programs, transactions, and other relations with respect to Taiwan (including, but not limited to, the performance of services for the United States through contracts with commercial entities on Taiwan), in accordance with the applicable laws of the United States.

(3)(A) The absence of diplomatic relations and recognition with respect to Taiwan shall not abrogate, infringe, modify, deny, or otherwise affect in any way any rights or obligations (including but not limited to those involving contracts, debts, or property interests of any kind) under the laws of the United States heretofore or hereafter acquired by or with respect to Taiwan.

(B) For all purposes under the laws of the United States, including actions in any court in the United States, recognition of the People's Republic of China shall not affect in any way the ownership of or other rights or interests in properties, tangible and intangible, and other things of value, owned or held on or prior to December 31, 1978, or thereafter acquired or earned by the governing authorities on Taiwan.

(4) Whenever the application of the laws of the United States depends upon the law that is or was applicable on Taiwan or compliance therewith, the law applied by the people on Taiwan shall be considered the applicable law for that purpose.

(5) Nothing in this Act, nor the facts of the President's action in extending diplomatic recognition to the People's Republic of China, the absence of diplomatic relations between the people on Taiwan and the United States, or the lack of recognition by the United States, and attendant circumstances thereto, shall be construed in any administrative or judicial proceeding as a basis for any United States Government agency, commission, or department to make a finding of fact or determination of law, under the Atomic Energy Act of 1954 and the Nuclear Non-Proliferation Act of 1978, to deny an export license application or to revoke an existing export license for nuclear exports to Taiwan.

(6) For purposes of the Immigration and Nationality Act, Taiwan may be treated in the manner specified in the first sentence of section 202(b) of that Act.

(7) The capacity of Taiwan to sue and be sued in courts in the United States, in accordance with the laws of the United States, shall not be abrogated, infringed, modified, denied, or otherwise affected in any way by the absence of diplomatic relations or recognition.

(8) No requirement, whether expressed or implied, under the laws of the United States with respect to maintenance of diplomatic relations or recognition shall be applicable with respect to Taiwan.

(c) For all purposes, including actions in any court in the United

States, the Congress approves the continuation in force of all treaties and other international agreements, including multilateral conventions, entered into by the United States and the governing authorities on Taiwan recognized by the United States as the Republic of China prior to January 1, 1979, and in force between them on December 31, 1978, unless and until terminated in accordance with law.

(d) Nothing in this Act may be construed as a basis for supporting the exclusion or expulsion of Taiwan from continued membership in any international financial institution or any other international organization. . . .

Document 11

Joint communiqué issued by the governments of the United States and the People's Republic of China, Aug. 17, 1982, U.S. Department of State, *American Foreign Policy: Current Documents,* Washington, D.C.: Government Printing Office, 1983, 1038–39.

U.S. Arms Sales to Taiwan

1. In the Joint Communiqué on the Establishment of Diplomatic Relations on January 1, 1979, issued by the Government of the United States of America and the Government of the People's Republic of China, the United States of America recognized the Government of the People's Republic of China as the sole legal government of China, and it acknowledged the Chinese position that there is but one China, and Taiwan is part of China. Within that context, the two sides agreed that the people of the United States would continue to maintain cultural, commercial, and other unofficial relations with the people of Taiwan. On this basis, relations between the United States and China were normalized.

2. The question of United States arms sales to Taiwan was not settled in the course of negotiations between the two countries on establishing diplomatic relations. The two sides held differing positions, and the Chinese side stated that it would raise the issue again following normalization. Recognizing that this issue would seriously hamper the development of United States-China relations, they have held further discussions on it, during and since the meetings between President Ronald Reagan and Premier Zhao Ziyang and between Secretary of State Alexander M. Haig, Jr., and Vice Premier and Foreign Minister Huang Hua in October 1981.

3. Respect for each other's sovereignty and territorial integrity and noninterference in each other's internal affairs constitute the fundamental principles guiding United States-China relations. These principles were confirmed in the Shanghai Communiqué of February 28, 1972, and reaffirmed in the Joint Communiqué on the Establishment of Diplomatic Relations which came into effect on January 1, 1979. Both sides emphatically state that these principles continue to govern all aspects of their relations.

4. The Chinese Government reiterates that the question of Taiwan is China's internal affair. The Message to Compatriots in Taiwan issued by China on January 1, 1979, promulgated a fundamental policy of striving for peaceful reunification of the Motherland. The Nine-Point Proposal put forward by China on September 30, 1981, represented a further major effort under this fundamental policy to strive for a peaceful solution to the Taiwan question.

5. The United States Government attaches great importance to its relations

with China, and reiterates that it has no intention of infringing on Chinese sovereignty and territorial integrity, or interfering in China's internal affairs, or pursuing a policy of "Two Chinas" or "one China, one Taiwan." The United States Government understands and appreciates the Chinese policy of striving for a peaceful resolution of the Taiwan question as indicated in China's Message to Compatriots in Taiwan issued on January 1, 1979, and the Nine-Point Proposal put forward by China on September 30, 1981. The new situation which has emerged with regard to the Taiwan question also provides favorable conditions for the settlement of United States-China differences over the question of United States arms sales to Taiwan.

6. Having in mind the foregoing statements of both sides, the United States Government states that it does not seek to carry out a long-term policy of arms sales to Taiwan, that its arms sales to Taiwan will not exceed, either in qualitative or in quantitative terms, the level of those supplied in recent years since the establishment of diplomatic relations between the United States and China, and that it intends to reduce gradually its sales of arms to Taiwan, leading over a period of time to a final resolution. In so stating, the United States acknowledges China's consistent position regarding the thorough settlement of this issue.

7. In order to bring about, over a period of time, a final settlement of the question of United States arms sales to Taiwan, which is an issue rooted in history, the two governments will make every effort to adopt measures and create conditions conducive to the thorough settlement of this issue.

8. The development of United States-China relations is not only in the interests of the two peoples but also conducive to peace and stability in the world. The two sides are determined, on the principle of equality and mutual benefit, to strengthen their ties in the economic, cultural, educational, scientific, technological and other fields and make strong, joint efforts for the continued development of relations between the governments and peoples of the United States and China.

9. In order to bring about the healthy development of United States-China relations, maintain world peace and oppose aggression and expansion, the two governments reaffirm the principles agreed on by the two sides in the Shanghai Communiqué and the Joint Communiqué on the Establishment of Diplomatic Relations. The two sides will maintain contact and hold appropriate consultations on bilateral and international issues of common interest.

Document 12

Soviet Premier Mikhail Gorbachev, "International Affairs: Asia and the Pacific Region," July 1986, *Vital Speeches*, Sept. 15, 1986, vol. 52, 709–11.

A noticeable improvement occurred in our relations in recent years. I would like to reaffirm: The Soviet Union is prepared—at any time and at any level—to discuss with China questions of additional measures for creating an atmosphere of good-neighborliness. We hope that the border dividing (I would prefer to say linking) us will become a line of peace and friendship in the near future.

The Soviet people's attitude to the objective advanced by the Communist Party of China—to modernize the country and in the future build a socialist society worthy of a great people—is that of understanding and respect.

As far as it is possible to judge, we have similar priorities with China—those of accelerating social and economic development. Why not support each other, why not cooperate in implementing our plans wherever this will clearly benefit both sides? The better the relations, the more we shall be able to exchange our experience.

We note with satisfaction that a positive shift has become visible in economic ties. We are convinced that the historically established complementarity between the Soviet and the Chinese economies offers great opportunities for expanding these ties, in the border regions as well. Some of the major problems of cooperation are literally knocking at the door. For instance, we do not want the border river of Amur to be viewed as a "water obstacle." Let the basin of this mighty river unite the efforts of the Chinese and the Soviet peoples in using the rich resources available there to our mutual benefit and for building water management projects. An intergovernmental agreement on this account is being jointly worked out, and the official border could pass along the main shipping channel.

The Soviet Government is preparing a positive reply in respect to the issue of assistance in building a railroad to connect the Xinjiang Uygur Autonomous Region with Kazakhstan.

We suggested cooperation with the PRC [People's Republic of China] in space exploration, which could include the training of Chinese cosmonauts. There are great opportunities for mutually beneficial exchanges in the spheres of culture and education. We are prepared, and sincerely want all this.

On relations with Japan. There are emerging signs of a turn for the better here as well. It would be good if the turn did take place. The objective position of our two countries in the world demands profound cooperation on a sound, realistic basis, in a calm atmosphere free from the problems of the past. A beginning was made this year. The foreign ministers exchanged visits. On the agenda is an exchange of top-level visits.

Economic cooperation is of mutual interest. The point at issue is, first of all, our coastal regions, which already have business contacts with Japanese firms. It is possible to discuss the question of establishing joint enterprises in adjacent and nearby regions of the U.S.S.R. and Japan. Why not establish long-term cooperation in the investigation and comprehensive use of the ocean's resources? Why not link up the programs concerning the peaceful study and use of outer space? The Japanese, it seems, have a method of making relations more dynamic, called "economic diplomacy." Let it serve Soviet-Japanese cooperation this time.

In the Pacific region, the Soviet Union also shares a border with the United States. It is our next-door neighbor in the literal sense of the word, with only seven kilometers dividing us—the exact distance between the Soviet island of Big Diomede and the American island of Little Diomede.

We clearly realize that the U.S. is a great Pacific power, primarily because a considerable part of the country's population lives on the shores of this ocean. The western part of America, gravitating toward this area, is playing a growing part in the country's life and is showing dynamism. Besides, the United States undoubtedly has important, legitimate economic and political interests in the region.

No doubt, without the U.S., without its participation, it is impossible to resolve the problem of security and cooperation in the Pacific Ocean in a way that would satisfy all nations in the region. So far, regrettably, Washington has not shown interest in this; it is not even considering a serious talk on the subject of the Pacific. If this subject is taken up, it leads to the trodden path of the "Soviet threat" and to saber-rattling to corroborate the myth.

Our approach to relations with the U.S. is well known. We stand for peaceful, good-neighborly relations, for mutually beneficial cooperation which has, incidentally, considerable opportunities in the Far East and in the Pacific also. . . .

. . . Now let me talk about Southeast Asia and Kampuchea [former Cambodia]. The Khmer people sustained terrible losses. That country, its cities and villages came under American bombing raids more than once. With its suffering it has gained the right to choose friends and allies for itself. It is impermissible to try and draw it back into the tragic past, to decide the future of that state in distant capitals or even in the United Nations.

Here, like in other problems of Southeast Asia, much depends on the normalization of Sino-Vietnamese relations. It is a sovereign matter of the governments and the leadership of both countries. We can only express our interest in seeing the border between these socialist states again becoming a border of peace and good-neighborly relations, in seeing comradely dialogue resumed and the unnecessary suspicion and mistrust removed. It seems that the moment is good and that all of Asia needs that.

In our opinion, there are no insurmountable obstacles in the way of establishing mutually acceptable relations between the countries of Indochina and ASEAN [Association of Southeast Asian Nations]. Given goodwill and on the condition of nonintervention from outside, they could solve their problems which would benefit simultaneously the cause of security in Asia.

There is a possibility not only to lessen dangerous tensions in the Korean peninsula but also to start to move along the road of solving the national problem of the entire Korean people. As far as really Korean interests are concerned, there are no sensible reasons for evading the serious dialogue proposed by the Democratic People's Republic of Korea [DPRK].

Second, we stand for putting up a barrier in the way of the proliferation and buildup of nuclear weapons in Asia and the Pacific Ocean.

As is known, the U.S.S.R. pledged itself not to increase the number of medium-range nuclear missiles in the Asian part of the country.

The U.S.S.R. supports proclaiming the southern part of the Pacific a nuclear-free zone and urges all nuclear powers to guarantee its status in a unilateral or multi-lateral way.

The implementation of the proposal of the DPRK for the creation of a nuclear-free zone in the Korean peninsula would be a serious contribution. Well-deserved attention was aroused by the idea of creating such a zone in Southeast Asia.

Third, we propose starting talks on the reduction of the activity of fleets in the Pacific, above all nuclear-armed ships. Restriction of the rivalry in the sphere of antisubmarine weapons, specifically, the arrangement to curtail antisubmarine activity in certain zones of the Pacific would help strengthen stability. This could become a substantial confidence-building measure. In general, I would like to say that if the United States gave up military presence, say, in the Philippines, we would not leave this step unanswered.

We remain strongly in favor of resuming the talks on turning the Indian Ocean into a peace zone.

Fourth, the Soviet Union attaches much importance to the radical reduction of armed forces and conventional armaments in Asia to the limits of reasonable sufficiency. We realize that this problem should be tackled gradually, stage-by-stage, starting in one area, say, the Far East. In this context the U.S.S.R. is prepared to discuss with the PRC concrete steps aimed at proportionate lowering of the level of land forces.

Fifth, the Soviet Union holds that the time has long come to switch the discussion of confidence-building measures and the non-use of force in the region to a practical plan. A start could be made with the simpler measures, for instance, measures for the security of sea lanes in the Pacific, and for the prevention of international terrorism. . . .

And in conclusion, about Afghanistan. It was declared from the rostrum of the Twenty-seventh Congress of the CPSU [Communist Party of the Soviet Union] that we are ready to bring home the Soviet troops stationed in Afghanistan at the request of its government. As you know, the party now firmly adheres to the principle that words should be confirmed by deeds.

Having thoroughly assessed the situation that is shaping and having held consultations with the Government of the Democratic Republic of Afghanistan, the Soviet leadership has adopted a decision which I officially announce today: Six regiments will be brought home from Afghanistan before the end of 1986—one armored regiment, two motorized rifle regiments and three anti-aircraft artillery regiments—with their organic equipment and armaments. These units will be returned to the areas of their permanent deployment in the Soviet Union and in such a way that all those who take an interest in this could easily ascertain this. . . .

Comrades, this generation inherited many difficult, painful problems. In order to advance to their solution, it is necessary to get rid of the burden of the past, to seek new approaches, guiding oneself by the responsibility for the present and future.

The Soviet state calls on all Asian and Pacific nations to cooperate for the sake of peace and security. Everyone who is striving for these goals, who hopes for a better future for their peoples, will find us to be benevolent interlocutors and honest partners.

Mankind is living through a difficult, dramatic time. But it has a reserve of strength which allows it not simply to survive but also to learn to live in a new, civilized world, in other words, to live without the threat of war, in conditions of freedom, when the benefit of man and the maximum development of the possibilities of a personality will be the highest criterion. But this requires a persistent struggle against the common enemy—the threat of universal destruction.

Mobilization of the potential of common sense existing in the world, the partnership of reason, are now more important than ever to arrest the slide toward catastrophe. Our resolve to do our utmost for this remains unchanged. Everybody can be sure of this.

Document 13

President George Bush's news conference, June 8, 1989, the *New York Times*, June 9, 1989, A22.

Q. Mr. President, cutting off military sales to China does not seem to have made an impression on the rulers there, and they've become more repressive. What else are you going to do to express this nation's outrage, and do you have any other plans?

A. . . . I think the position we took, aiming not at the Chinese people, but at the military arrangements, was well received around the world and was followed by many countries. Right after we did that, many of the European countries followed suit. The events in China are such that we obviously deplore the violence and the loss of life, urge restoration of order, with recognition of the rights of the people. And I'm still hopeful that China will come together, respecting the urge for democracy on the part of the people. And what we will do in the future I will announce at appropriate times. But right now, we are engaged in diplomatic efforts, and other countries are doing the same thing. And let's hope that it does have an ameliorating effect on this situation.

Q. Mr. President, does your support of human rights and democracy extend to other places in the world—like South Africa, the West Bank—where they've been fighting a lot longer than in China—

A. Yes, it does.

Q. —against oppression?

A. It certainly does, concern is universal, and that's what I want the Chinese leaders to understand. You see, we've taken this action—I am one who lived in China, I understand the importance of the relationship with the Chinese people and with the Government, it is in the interests of the United States to have good relations. But because of what you—the question that you properly raised, we have to speak out in favor of human rights. And we aren't going to remake the world, but we should stand for something. And there's no question in the minds of these students that the United States is standing in their corner. . . .

Q. Mr. President, can the United States ever have normal relations with China as long as the hard-liners believed responsible for the massacre, such as Deng Xiaoping and Premier Li Peng remain in power? In other words, what will it take to get U.S.-Chinese relations back to normal?

A. It will take a recognition of the—of the rights of individuals, and respect for the rights of those who disagree. And you have cited two leaders, one of whom I might tell you that you mentioned, Deng Xiaoping, I'm not sure the American people know this: he was thrown out in a—by the Cultural Revolution crowd back in the late 60's. Came back in. In 1976 was put out again because he was seen as too forward-looking.

And all I'm saying from that experience is, let's not jump to conclusions as to how individual leaders in China feel when we aren't sure of that. But the broad question that you ask, we can't have totally normal relations unless there's a recognition that the—of the validity of the students' aspirations.

And I think that that will happen. We had a visit right here, upstairs in the White House, with Mr. Wan Li. I don't know whether he's in or out, but he said something to me that I think the American people would be interested in. He said the army loves the people. And then you've seen soldiers from the 27th Army coming in from outside of Beijing and clearly shooting people.

But I don't think—having said that, I don't think we ought to judge the whole People's Liberation Army of China by that terrible incident. And so let's—what I want to do is preserve this relationship as best I can, and I hope the conditions that lie ahead will permit me to preserve this relationship. . . .

Q. Mr. President, I'd like to return to China for a moment. You mention that your goal is to preserve our relationship with the Chinese Government. But what do you say to the American people who might wonder why we are not more forceful in being the world's leading advocate of democracy? And are we not living up to that responsibility in this situation?

A. Well, some have suggested, for example, to show our forcefulness that I bring the American Ambassador back. I disagree with that 180 degrees, and we've seen in the last few days a very good reason to have him there. In fact one of your colleagues, Richard Roth of CBS, was released partially because of the work of our embassy, of Jim Lilly, our very able Ambassador.

Some have suggested—well, you gotta go full sanctions on the economic side. I don't want to cut off grain, and we've just sold grain to the People's Republic of China. I think that would be counterproductive and would hurt the people.

What I do want to do is take whatever steps are most likely to demonstrate the concern that America feels. And I think I've done that, and I'll be looking for other ways to do it if we possibly can.

Dissident in Embassy

Q. Mr. President, Chinese dissident Fang Lizhi has taken refuge in the U.S. Embassy, apparently fearing for his own safety. The Chinese Government has called that a wanton interference in internal affairs and a violation of international law. What is your reaction to that? And will the United States grant Fang political asylum in the United States?

A. First, let me remind the audience here that we do not discuss asylum. It's almost like a public discussion of intelligence matters. But in terms of your question, we have acted in compliance with the international law as an extraordinary measure for humanitarian reasons. His personal safety was involved here, he felt. And then we try, historically, to work these things out in consultation with the sovereign state. So we are not violating international law, in the opinion of our attorneys. And it's awful hard—it is awful hard for the United States, when a man presents himself, a person who is a dissident, and says that his life is threatened—to turn him back. And that isn't one of the—one of the premises upon which the United States was founded. So we have a difference with them on that, you're right.

Document 14

Treaty of Mutual Cooperation and Security Between the United States of America and Japan, Jan. 19, 1960, *U.S. Treaties and Other International Agreements*, Washington, D.C.: Government Printing Office, 1961, vol. 11, 1634–35.

ARTICLE III

The Parties, individually and in cooperation with each other, by means of continuous and effective self-help and mutual aid will maintain and develop, subject to their constitutional provisions, their capacities to resist armed attack.

ARTICLE IV

The Parties will consult together from time to time regarding the implementation of this Treaty, and, at the request of either Party, whenever the security of Japan or international peace and security in the Far East is threatened.

ARTICLE V

Each Party recognizes that an armed attack against either Party in the territories under the administration of Japan would be dangerous to its own peace and safety and declares that it would act to meet the common danger in accordance with its constitutional provisions and processes.

Any such armed attack and all measures taken as a result thereof shall be immediately reported to the Security Council of the United Nations in accordance with the provisions of Article 51 of the Charter. Such measures shall be terminated when the Security Council has taken the measures necessary to restore and maintain international peace and security.

ARTICLE VI

For the purpose of contributing to the security of Japan and the maintenance of international peace and security in the Far East, the United States of America is granted the use by its land, air and naval forces of facilities and areas in Japan.

The use of these facilities and areas as well as the status of United States armed forces in Japan shall be governed by a separate agreement, replacing the Administrative Agreement under Article III of the Security Treaty between the United States of America and Japan, signed at Tokyo on February 28, 1952, as amended, and by such other arrangements as may be agreed upon.

ARTICLE VII

This Treaty does not affect and shall not be interpreted as affecting in any way the rights and obligations of the Parties under the Charter of the United Nations or the responsibility of the United Nations for the maintenance of international peace and security.

ARTICLE VIII

This Treaty shall be ratified by the United States of America and Japan in accordance with their respective constitutional processes and will enter into force on the date on which the instruments of ratification thereof have been exchanged by them in Tokyo.

ARTICLE IX

The Security Treaty between the United States of America and Japan signed at the city of San Francisco on September 8, 1951 shall expire upon the entering into force of this Treaty.

ARTICLE X

This Treaty shall remain in force until in the opinion of the Governments of the United States of America and Japan there shall have come into force such United Nations arrangements as will satisfactorily provide for the maintenance of international peace and security in the Japan area.

However, after the Treaty has been in force for ten years, either Party may give notice to the other Party of its intention to terminate the Treaty, in which case the Treaty shall terminate one year after such notice has been given.

In witness whereof the undersigned Plenipotentiaries have signed this Treaty.

Done in duplicate at Washington in the English and Japanese languages, both equally authentic, this 19th day of January, 1960.

FOR THE UNITED STATES OF AMERICA:

CHRISTIAN A. HERTER
DOUGLAS MACARTHUR 2nd
J GRAHAM PARSONS

FOR JAPAN:

NOBOSUKE KISHI
AIICHIRO FUJIYAMA
MITSUJIRO ISHII
TADASHI ADACHI
KOICHIRO ASAKAI

Document 15

President Richard M. Nixon and Prime Minister Sato Eisaku, joint communiqué, Nov. 21, 1969, *U.S. Foreign Policy, 1969–1970,* Washington, D.C.: Government Printing Office, 1971, 503–05.

1. President Nixon and Prime Minister Sato met in Washington on November 19, 20 and 21, 1969, to exchange views on the present international situation and on other matters of mutual interest to the United States and Japan.

2. The President and the Prime Minister recognized that both the United States and Japan have greatly benefited from their close association in a variety of fields, and they declared that guided by their common principles of democracy and liberty, the two countries would maintain and strengthen their fruitful cooperation in the continuing search for world peace and prosperity and in particular for the relaxation of international tensions. The President expressed his and his government's deep interest in Asia and stated his belief that the United States and Japan should cooperate in contributing to the peace and prosperity of the region. The Prime Minister states that Japan would make further active contributions to the peace and prosperity of Asia.

3. The President and the Prime Minister exchanged frank views on the current international situation, with particular attention to developments in the Far East. The President, while emphasizing that the countries in the area were expected to make their own efforts for the stability of the area, gave assurance that the United States would continue to contribute to the maintenance of international peace and security in the Far East by honoring its defense treaty obligations in the area. The Prime Minister, appreciating the determination of the United States, stressed that it was important for the peace and security of the Far East that the United States should be in a position to carry out fully its obligations referred to by the President. He further expressed his recognition that, in light of the present situation, the presence of United States forces in the Far East constituted a mainstay for the stability of the area.

4. The President and the Prime Minister specifically noted the continuing tension over the Korean peninsula. The Prime Minister deeply appreciated the peacekeeping efforts of the United Nations in the area and stated that the security of the Republic of Korea was essential to Japan's own security. The President and the Prime Minister shared the hope that Communist China would adopt a more cooperative and constructive attitude in its external relations. The President referred to the treaty obligations of his country to the Republic of China which the United States would uphold. The Prime Minister said that the maintenance of peace and security in the Taiwan area was also a most important factor for the security of Japan. The President described the earnest efforts made by the United States for a peaceful and just settlement of the Viet-Nam problem. The President and the Prime Minister expressed the strong hope that the war in Viet-Nam would be concluded before return of the administrative rights over Okinawa to Japan. In this connection they agreed that, should peace in Viet-Nam not have been realized by the time reversion of Okinawa is scheduled to take place, the two governments would fully consult with each other in the light of the situation at that time so that reversion would be accomplished without affecting the United States efforts to assure the South Vietnamese people the opportunity to determine their own political future without

outside interference. The Prime Minister stated that Japan was exploring what role she could play in bringing about stability in the Indochina area.

5. In light of the current situation and the prospects in the Far East, the President and the Prime Minister agreed that they highly valued the role played by the Treaty of Mutual Cooperation and Security in maintaining the peace and security of the Far East including Japan, and they affirmed the intention of the two governments firmly to maintain the Treaty on the basis of mutual trust and common evaluation of the international situation. They further agreed that the two governments should maintain close contact with each other on matters affecting the peace and security of the Far East including Japan, and on the implementation of the Treaty of Mutual Cooperation and Security.

6. The Prime Minister emphasized his view that the time had come to respond to the strong desire of the people of Japan, of both the mainland and Okinawa, to have the administrative rights over Okinawa returned to Japan on the basis of the friendly relations between the United States and Japan and thereby to restore Okinawa to its normal status. The President expressed appreciation of the Prime Minister's view. The President and the Prime Minister also recognized the vital role played by United States forces in Okinawa in the present situation in the Far East. As a result of their discussion it was agreed that the mutual security interests of the United States and Japan could be accommodated within arrangements for the return of the administrative rights over Okinawa to Japan. They therefore agreed that the two governments would immediately enter into consultations regarding specific arrangements for accomplishing the early reversion of Okinawa without detriment to the security of the Far East including Japan. They further agreed to expedite the consultations with a view to accomplishing the reversion during 1972 subject to the conclusion of these specific arrangements with the necessary legislative support. In this connection, the Prime Minister made clear the intention of his government, following reversion, to assume gradually the responsibility for the immediate defense of Okinawa as part of Japan's defense efforts for her own territories. The President and the Prime Minister agreed also that the United States would retain under the terms of the Treaty of Mutual Cooperation and Security such military facilities and areas in Okinawa as required in the mutual security of both countries.

7. The President and the Prime Minister agreed that, upon return of the administrative rights, the Treaty of Mutual Cooperation and Security and its related arrangements would apply to Okinawa without modification thereof. In this connection, the Prime Minister affirmed the recognition of his government that the security of Japan could not be adequately maintained without international peace and security in the Far East and, therefore, the security of countries in the Far East was a matter of serious concern for Japan. The Prime Minister was of the view that, in the light of such recognition on the part of the Japanese Government, the return of the administrative rights over Okinawa in the manner agreed above should not hinder the effective discharge of the international obligations assumed by the United States for the defense of countries in the Far East including Japan. The President replied that he shared the Prime Minister's view.

8. The Prime Minister described in detail the particular sentiment of the Japanese people against nuclear weapons and the policy of the Japanese Government reflecting such sentiment. The President expressed his deep

understanding and assured the Prime Minister that, without prejudice to the position of the United States Government with respect to the prior consultation system under the Treaty of Mutual Cooperation and Security, the reversion of Okinawa would be carried out in a manner consistent with the policy of the Japanese Government as described by the Prime Minister. . . .

11. The President and the Prime Minister expressed their conviction that a mutually satisfactory solution of the question of the return of the administrative rights over Okinawa to Japan, which is the last of the major issues between the two countries arising from the Second World War, would further strengthen United States-Japan relations which are based on friendship and mutual trust and would make a major contribution to the peace and security of the Far East.

12. In their discussion of economic matters, the President and the Prime Minister noted the marked growth in economic relations between the two countries. They also acknowledged that the leading positions which their countries occupy in the world economy impose important responsibilities on each for the maintenance and strengthening of the international trade and monetary system, especially in the light of the current large imbalances in trade and payments. In this regard, the President stressed his determination to bring inflation in the United States under control. He also reaffirmed the commitment of the United States to the principle of promoting freer trade. The Prime Minister indicated the intention of the Japanese Government to accelerate rapidly the reduction of Japan's trade and capital restrictions. Specifically, he stated the intention of the Japanese Government to remove Japan's residual import quota restrictions over a broad range of products by the end of 1971 and to make maximum efforts to accelerate the liberalization of the remaining items. He added that the Japanese Government intends to make periodic reviews of its liberalization program with a view to implementing trade liberalization at a more accelerated pace than hitherto. The President and the Prime Minister agreed that their respective actions would further solidify the foundation of overall U.S.-Japan relations.

13. The President and the Prime Minister agreed that attention to the economic needs of the developing countries was essential to the development of international peace and stability. The Prime Minister stated the intention of the Japanese Government to expand and improve its aid programs in Asia commensurate with the economic growth of Japan. The President welcomed this statement and confirmed that the United States would continue to contribute to the economic development of Asia. The President and Prime Minister recognized that there would be major requirements for the post-war rehabilitation of Viet-Nam and elsewhere in Southeast Asia. The Prime Minister stated the intention of the Japanese Government to make a substantial contribution to this end. . . .

Document 16

Nixon Doctrine, July 1969, *Public Papers of the Presidents of the United States: Richard M. Nixon*, Washington, D.C.: Government Printing Office, 1970, 546–49.

I think that one of the weaknesses in American foreign policy is that too often we react rather precipitately to events as they occur. We fail to have the perspective and the long-range view which is essential for a policy that will be viable.

As I see it, even though the war in Vietnam has been, as we all know, a terribly frustrating one, and, as a result of that frustration, even though there would be a tendency for many Americans to say, "After we are through with that, let's not become involved in Asia," I am convinced that the way to avoid becoming involved in another war in Asia is for the United States to continue to play a significant role.

I think the way that we could become involved would be to attempt withdrawal, because, whether we like it or not, geography makes us a Pacific power. And when we consider, for example, that Indonesia at its closest point is only 14 miles from the Philippines, when we consider that Guam, where we are presently standing, of course, is in the heart of Asia, when we consider the interests of the whole Pacific as they relate to Alaska and Hawaii, we can all realize this.

Also, as we look over the historical perspective, while World War II began in Europe, for the United States it began in the Pacific. It came from Asia. The Korean war came from Asia. The Vietnamese war came from Asia.

So, as we consider our past history, the United States involvement in war so often has been tied to our Pacific policy, or our lack of a Pacific policy, as the case might be.

As we look at Asia today, we see that the major world power which adopts a very aggressive attitude and a belligerent attitude in its foreign policy, Communist China, of course, is in Asia, and we find that the two minor world powers—minor, although they do have significant strength as we learned—that most greatly threaten the peace of the world, that adopt the most belligerent foreign policy, are in Asia, North Korea and, of course, North Vietnam.

When we consider those factors we, I think, realize that if we are thinking down the road, down the long road—not just 4 years, 5 years, but 10, 15 or 20—that if we are going to have peace in the world, that potentially the greatest threat to that peace will be in the Pacific.

I do not mean to suggest that the Mideast is not a potential threat to the peace of the world and that there are not problems in Latin America that concern us, or in Africa and, of course, over it all, we see the great potential conflict between the United States and the Soviet Union, the East-West conflict between the two super powers.

But as far as those other areas are concerned, the possibility of finding some kind of solution, I think, is potentially greater than it is in the Asia area.

Pursuing that line of reasoning a bit further then, I would like to put it in a more positive sense: When we look at the problems in Asia, the threat to peace that is presented by the growing power of Communist China, the belligerence of North Korea and North Vietnam, we should not let that obscure the great promise that is here.

As I have often said, the fastest rate of growth in the world is occurring in non-Communist Asia. Japan, in the last 10 years, has tripled its GNP [gross national product]; South Korea has doubled its

GNP; Taiwan has doubled its GNP; Thailand has doubled its GNP. The same is true of Singapore and of Malaysia. . . .

Questions

U.S. MILITARY RELATIONSHIPS IN ASIA

[4.] Q. Mr. President, sir, on the question of U.S. military relationships in Asia, if I may ask a hypothetical question: If a leader of one of the countries with which we have had close military relationships, either through SEATO [Southeast Asia Treaty Organization] or in Vietnam, should say, "Well, you are pulling out of Vietnam with your troops, we can read in the newspapers. How can we know that you will remain to play a significant role as you say you wish to do in security arrangements in Asia?" What kind of an approach can you take to that question?

THE PRESIDENT. I have already indicated that the answer to that question is not an easy one—not easy because we will be greatly tempted when that question is put to us to indicate that if any nation desires the assistance of the United States militarily in order to meet an internal or external threat, we will provide it.

However, I believe that the time has come when the United States, in our relations with all of our Asian friends, be quite emphatic on two points: One, that we will keep our treaty commitments, our treaty commitments, for example, with Thailand under SEATO; but, two, that as far as the problems of internal security are concerned, as far as the problems of military defense, except for the threat of a major power involving nuclear weapons, that the United States is going to encourage and has a right to expect that this problem will be increasingly handled by, and the responsibility for it be taken by, the Asian nations themselves.

I believe, incidentally, from my preliminary conversations with several Asian leaders over the past few months that they are going to be willing to undertake this responsibility. It will not be easy. But if the United States just continues down the road of responding to requests for assistance, of assuming the primary responsibility for defending these countries when they have internal problems or external problems, they are never going to take care of themselves.

I should add to that, too, that when we talk about collective security for Asia, I realize that at this time that looks like a weak reed. It actually is. But looking down the road—I am speaking now of 5 years from now, 10 years from now—I think collective security, insofar as it deals with internal threats to any of the countries, or insofar as it deals with a threat other than that posed by a nuclear power, I believe that this is an objective which. . .the United States should support.

Document 17

Secretary of Commerce Malcolm Baldrige, "Japan and Protectionism: No Words, Real Action," address to the Japan External Trade Organization, Japan Economic Foundation, and Japan Foreign Trade Council, Tokyo, Japan, July 29, 1986, *Vital Speeches*, Sept. 15, 1986, vol. 52, 712–13.

Good afternoon. I am pleased to have this opportunity to address this distinguished group. I have come to Japan for one reason: to personally express the gravity of the crisis our two countries face in our trading relationship. This was my message when I met with Prime Minister Nakasone [Yasuhiro] yesterday, this was my message to the members of the new cabinet whom I have also met, and this is my message this morning to you—Japan's business and government leaders.

We are about to see the serious problems between our two countries solved. But which solution it will be is still unknown. Will it be solved by those in our country who see the only solution as building walls around our borders equal to the walls around Japan's borders? Or will it be solved by Japan opening its markets?

We are on the edge of the first solution. Why? Because despite the adjustments in the exchange rates, the bilateral trade deficit will not be reduced this year. Instead, we expect Japan's surplus to exceed $55 billion this year, and some Japanese estimates are for higher surpluses yet in 1987.

The United States Congress is considering omnibus trade legislation which, if passed, will put a straitjacket around trade. It will take away from the President the flexibility he has to deal with trade problems. It will *force* reductions in the trade deficit with Japan. It will mandate strong actions to stop the flow of *your* imports into the United States. It will cut your ability to sell in our country. And the result will be disastrous for both sides.

Next week, the President [Ronald Reagan] will face the most serious challenge to his free trade policies. The Congress will consider overriding his veto of the textile bill, which limits textile imports to our country. I cannot stand here today and tell you honestly that we will be able to stave off that legislation, although I can say we are working with all our resources to do so, and I hope we can.

We are arriving close to the point in our trading relationship that has been coming for a long time—unilaterally stopping imports of Japanese goods. The reason we are at this point is that members of the United States Congress believe, as most of their constituents believe, that Japan is doing very little to resolve the problem besides talk. The talking has not produced results. In short, we cannot fight the fight for free trade with Japan and the rest of the world for six years without some help from the Japanese. My defense for the Japanese ever-growing surplus before Congress is wearing mighty thin.

This lack of results comes despite the courageous leadership Prime Minister Nakasone has shown on the huge trade problem. Under his guidance, Japanese tariffs have been reduced to among the lowest in the world. Many unfair standards and other technical barriers have been reduced. The Moss negotiations have opened up closed markets for foreign suppliers of telecommunications equipment, medical and pharmaceutical goods, forest products and electronics.

But nothing has happened to the volume of imports Japan will accept. On the contrary:

—Since 1980, Japanese imports from the world have actually fallen by 7 percent, from $140 billion to $130 billion. During the same period, Japan's exports rose by 35 percent.

—Even during the last year, 1985, when our trade talks reached a peak, Japanese imports declined by 5 percent.

—And even if oil imports were excluded, Japan's manufactured imports still declined by 1.1 percent at a time when their manufactured exports rose by 3.3 percent.

There is a Japanese expression—fugen jikko (foo-gen jee-koh)—"no words, real action." The world is looking to Japan—and especially to you, the industrialists and leaders of this country—to back up the Prime Minister's words with real action . . . not just with promises to take action. There are many, many examples where action should be taken.

One obvious one is seeing the Prime Minister's directive to create an "open door" in public works translated into real opportunity for foreign construction companies and equipment suppliers by truly competitive bidding—the same kind of bidding that Japanese construction companies enjoy in the United States.

His pledge to have restrictions only as the exception to the rule must be brought to action. We must uproot the barriers deeply buried in private business relationships and traditional practices. Believe me, I realize the difficulties involved, but the alternatives to continuing this seriously unfair practice are worse.

Another obvious example: you must resist the temptation to demand protection from imports because your industries are in the developing stage, or because they have excess capacity, or they are mature, or because the exchange rate has changed, or for fifty other reasons that are protectionistic. Dumping, predatory pricing, subsidizing—they are all essentially protectionist practices that are meant to influence trade balances.

And most important, you must take to heart the Prime Minister's appeal to increase imports as a national goal.

I would hope that in Japan a national consensus could develop for a vision on imports similar to the national vision on exports that Miti helped develop some years ago. Essentially, unless the Japanese industrialists, the Japanese bureaucracy and the Japanese people come to the conclusion that it is in their own self-interest to accept a significantly higher level of imports, the lowering of trade barriers themselves, whether tariff or non-tariff, will not help the dangerous trade problem Japan is facing.

But instead of following the Prime Minister's advice, so far we have seen the opposite in most Japanese trade actions.

—An $8 billion airport project—the symbol of Japan's growing trade links to the rest of the world—appears to be put off limits of foreign firms, according to some statements made in the recent past. I think this is being resolved. The Prime Minister and the Minister of Transportation have both assured me that the bidding will be accomplished on a fair and open basis with all firms. Regardless of nationality, all qualified firms will be given a fair opportunity to participate in the project.

—Despite the fact that supercomputers were invented in the United States, and despite the fact that the United States supercomputer cray is the standard by which the world builds supercomputers, we have yet to sell a single machine to a Japanese government bureau or to a Japanese university.

—Despite over three decades of space coordination between our two countries, the Japanese government still refuses to allow government entities to purchase foreign satellites.

—Although Japan has shouldered an increasing share of the overseas development burden, the second most powerful economy in the free world continues to use their aid program as a sales tool—requiring the poor countries of the world to buy not on the basis of most competitive bids, but on the basis of what Japanese industry wants to sell them.

—Whether it's soda ash or coal in a declining industry or supercomputers or satellites in a growth industry, we find the Japanese unwilling to take even our most competitive exports.

This is the Japan that many Americans and the rest of the world see. A Japan that has built itself into a world economic power, but a Japan not willing to take on the responsibilities that go with that power. A Japan afraid to open its borders to competitive goods. A Japan that finds ways to avoid imports even in the face of facts that demonstrate better products are available in many, many cases—enough to make a significant difference in the total volume of imports.

Japan has grown up, economically. Japan has grown so much that in September, you will assume your seat at the GATT [General Agreement on Tariffs and Trade] Ministerial Meeting as the second largest trading nation in the system—and, as the acknowledged beneficiary of that system. The Japanese people must decide if Japan will also continue being the major problem in the system.

Senator Bob Dole, the Senate Majority leader, said after a visit here, "There was a brief window of opportunity to make meaningful action to open Japanese markets and to address the concerns we raised. That window is about to be slammed shut. . . ."

And, Senator John Danforth, who used to be one of the freest traders in Congress, said here earlier this year, "No other nation contributes so little to the open trading system of the world in proportion to what it gains."

This is not just the United States' view. Just last week the European community agreed to send a message to the new Japanese government. It repeated its demand for market opening, structural change and expressing its concern over worsening trade figures . . . because of Japan's trade surplus.

This follows actions taken by Taiwan, which imposed restrictions on tenders for government procurement specifically prohibiting sourcing in Japan . . . because of Japan's trade surplus.

And this follows action by Korea, whose market diversification bans prohibit certain imports from Japan . . . because of Japan's trade surplus.

But it is very important to note that these actions have not been taken out of jealousy for Japan. They have been taken because the rest of the world does not enjoy the access to Japan's market that Japan enjoys in ours.

The central fact of this moment in Japanese history is this: Japan cannot continue to live with its trading partners on the basis of ever-increasing exports and slow or static imports. By almost any measure, Japan has great power in the world economy but has not taken the responsibility that comes with that power.

—For example, we all know the problems that the developing countries are having and the industrialized countries are trying to help them increase job opportunities. Yet as recently as 1984, the United States took 58 percent of the manufactured exports of the developing countries, Europe took 27 percent, while Japan only accepted 8 percent—proportionately about one seventh of what the United States did.

—Japan's imports of manufactured goods from all countries as a percent of GNP [gross national product] was 2.7 percent in 1985. The United States imports two and one half times as much proportionately and Germany over five times as much.

To export more, Japan must import more. Japan must do this—you, the members of this audience, must do this—not as a response to foreign pressure, not just out of loyalty to the Prime Minister, but as a matter of self interest and economic survival.

Yet importing more does not mean necessarily exporting less.

The Prime Minister's program to stimulate internal growth offers the opportunity to rely not only on exports for economic growth and stable employment, but on domestic growth. The result will be an increase in imports without sacrificing exports. The domestic benefit in lower consumer prices from a stronger yen should be passed through to the consumer. These lower prices could amount to over 13 trillion yen. This strong consumer benefit, along with the strong implementation of the Maekawa Plan, should boost domestic growth significantly.

There is one more point that I think about many times. Please consider this:

Each of our countries has had the best leadership possible for free trade in the last few years. Prime Minister Nakasone has provided courageous leadership trying to increase Japanese imports and open Japanese markets, and President Reagan has provided courageous leadership in keeping United States markets open in spite of a $150 billion trade deficit and an onslaught of protectionist pressures.

But, in spite of that strongest possible leadership, we have been unable to reduce our bilateral trade deficit. We have been unable to silence either Japanese protectionists—who clamor for the continued luxury of a protected home market—or American protectionists who continue to argue that the only way to build a level playing field is to raise trade barriers to your level.

Just think about this—if we can't get action that brings results during the remaining span of these two strong leaders, both courageous, both with the people behind them and both advocates of free trade, how can we look for anything better in the future when the problems will be worse? Gentlemen, you have to act now!

My Japanese friends—on the American side we will continue to fight protectionism, win or lose. On your side, you must take it into your hands to solve your share of the trade problem. I greatly fear if you don't, a solution will be forced on us that would harm both our countries—but Japan most of all. We have so much—so much—further to go, and time is running out.

Document 18

President Jimmy Carter, statement on U.S. troop withdrawals from Korea, July 20, 1979, U.S. Department of State, *Bulletin*, September 1979, 37.

Last February it was announced that withdrawals of U.S. ground combat forces from Korea would be held in abeyance pending the implications of recent political developments in the region. That reassessment has been completed, and these policy issues have been discussed with our key allies in Asia, with principal defense and foreign policy advisers, and leaders of the Congress. Circumstances require these further adjustments in the troop withdrawal plan.

- Withdrawals of combat elements of the 2d Division will remain in abeyance. The structure and function of the Combined Forces Command will continue as established last year.
- Between now and the end of 1980 some reductions of personnel in U.S. support units will continue. This will include one I-Hawk air defense battalion whose transfer to the R.O.K. [Republic of Korea] had been planned since 1976.
- The timing and pace of withdrawal beyond these will be reexamined in 1981. In that review the United States will pay special attention to the restoration of a satisfactory North-South military balance and evidence of tangible progress toward a reduction of tensions on the peninsula.

These decisions have been shaped by the following considerations.

- First, recent studies by the intelligence community have confirmed that the size of North Korea's ground forces, armor, firepower, and mobility are larger than previously estimated. Given the inherent economic strength of the Republic of Korea and with U.S. support, the existing imbalance in North-South military strength can be remedied. Holding further withdrawal of U.S. ground combat units in abeyance will help reinforce deterrence, avoid conveying misleading signals to the North, and provide additional time for the R.O.K. to put its ground defenses in order. For its part the Republic of Korea recognizes the need to augment its self-defense efforts, and President Park [Chung Hee] has stated that his government would expand defense spending significantly beyond previously planned levels and accord special urgency to improving its ground defenses.

• Second, during the recent visit to Seoul, President Park and President Carter jointly announced their desire to explore possibilities for reducing tensions in Korea with representatives of North Korea. Only through authoritative discussions between representatives of the North and South Korean Governments can a framework for peaceful coexistence between the North and South be established and progress toward eventual reunification of Korea be achieved. The United States is prepared to assist in that diplomatic effort. It is the judgment of the United States that further reductions of our combat elements in Korea should await credible indications that a satisfactory military balance has been restored and a reduction in tension is under way.

• Third, in recent months we have normalized relations with China and deepened defense cooperation with Japan. Concurrently we have witnessed the steady growth of Soviet military power in East Asia and the eruption of renewed conflict and new uncertainties in Southeast Asia. Under these circumstances, it is believed that these adjustments in our Korean withdrawal plan—together with the recent stabilization of our base agreement with the Philippines, initiation of defense planning discussions with Japan, and increased support for the security of ASEAN [Association of South East Asian Nations] countries—will serve wider U.S. strategic security interests by reassuring our principal allies of our steadiness and our resolve.

Over time we will continue to adjust the detailed features of our contribution to the security of the Republic of Korea to reflect growing R.O.K. economic and military strength and changes in the international situation. At present, however, these modifications in our withdrawal plans will best assure the maintenance of our security commitment, preserve an adequate deterrent, nurture the resumption of a serious North-South dialogue, and stabilize a favorable U.S. strategic position in East Asia.

Document 19

U.S. Department of State, "Republic of Korea," *Country Reports on Human Rights Practices for 1988*, Washington, D.C.: Government Printing Office, 1989, 842–46.

The South Korean Government describes the Republic of Korea (ROK) as a liberal democracy and, in fact, there were dramatic political changes in 1988. In February Roh Tae Woo became the first President directly elected by the people since 1971. At his inauguration, Roh proclaimed that his administration would be committed to democratic reform and political liberalization. In April National Assembly elections were held, and the opposition parties won control of the Assembly. The previous Chun Doo Hwan administration had come to power in a military coup in 1979 followed by an election held under strict martial law conditions and, many Koreans believe, maintained itself in power by strictly suppressing legitimate political dissent. As a result, the Chun regime suffered from a chronic lack of legitimacy in the eyes of most Koreans.

Determined to influence government policies, the current opposition-dominated Assembly played a much more independent role in domestic politics than had previous National Assemblies. In the fall, the Assembly held unprecedented televised hearings into alleged corruption and misdeeds of the former Chun Doo Hwan administration. Eventually, political pressure forced Chun to make a public apology on nationwide television, relinquish his wealth, and retire to the countryside. On November 26 President Roh asked the nation for leniency for Chun, promised to release political prisoners and restore their civil rights, compensate victims of past injustices, and amend the national security laws.

The security services have, for the first time in years, come under public criticism, and the opposition demanded that changes be made in their operations. However, in spite of some marginal changes—agents of the National Security Planning Agency (formerly the Korean CIA) were evicted from their offices in the National Assembly—the Korean security forces remain pervasive. Police are generally well trained and disciplined. While there are still credible reports of the excessive use of force by the police, they appear to be more restrained than in the past.

Korea's political evolution has been buoyed by its dynamic, expanding economy. In the first half of 1988, real gross national product growth registered almost 12 percent. Korea has become the 10th largest trading nation in the world. Labor disputes leading to negotiations have resulted in sizable wage increases over the last 2 years, with per capita income rising in 1988 to about $3,100 from $2,300 in 1986. Although rapid economic growth has eliminated abject poverty, it also has created a number of social dislocations, including a rapid rise in land prices and a severe shortage of housing in the big cities. The Government has recently begun to address some of the major social welfare issues.

Following up on progress made during the last half of 1987, the overall human rights situation continued to improve. The press enjoyed much greater freedom, and articles criticizing the Government appeared frequently. No major cases of torture or politically related killings came to light during the year. The major remaining human rights problem is political prisoners. The Roh Government has shown itself willing to release political prisoners in small groups. However, continued arrests resulted in a stable or slightly increased number of prisoners during much of the year. The Government carried out a major release of prisoners on December 21 and at the same time restored civil rights to a number of former political detainees. In spite of the growing spread of western-style, liberal democratic thought, Korean society still places great emphasis on the Confucian ideals of order and conformity. While the pace of positive political change is accelerating and the Roh Government's commitment to democratization seems firm, the evolution of South Korea's democracy is not yet complete.

RESPECT FOR HUMAN RIGHTS

Section 1 Respect for Integrity of the Person, Including Freedom from:

a. Political Killing

In contrast to 1987, when one student was tortured to death and one died from wounds suffered when he was hit in the head by shrapnel from a teargas grenade, there were no reported cases of politically related deaths in 1988. . . .

c. Torture and Other Cruel, Inhuman, or Degrading Treatment or Punishment

There were no reports of physical torture in 1988. During the summer a policeman convicted of sexually abusing a female detainee during a 1987 interrogation was sentenced to 5 years in prison. At times the Korean police still use excessive force, particularly when breaking up demonstrations. Police violence was particularly evident in mid-August when radical students attempted to organize a march to Panmunjom to meet with students from North Korea. However, students have been increasingly escalating the level of violence during their demonstrations, throwing Molotov cocktails and using various kinds of clubs. As a matter of policy, the police refrained from using tear gas on student demonstrators (except on one occasion) during the Olympics. Riot police do not carry firearms and rarely conduct baton charges.

Harsh treatment of prisoners still prevails. Many human rights activists report that political prisoners are sometimes deprived of sleep and that prison authorities frequently attempt to intimidate prisoners through severe psychological pressure.

Late in the year the Government announced a prison reform measure. If fully implemented, this reform would allow inmates greater access to books, newspapers, and television as well as allowing them to correspond with and receive visits from anyone they wish.

d. Arbitrary Arrest, Detention, or Exile

Although Koreans are freer to criticize the Government than in the past, Korea's sweeping National Security Law is still used against people who express views the Government considers dangerous. Arrests of students and dissidents under the security laws continued throughout 1988, although apparently in lesser numbers than in years past. Human rights activists put the number of new political arrests at about 400 for the period February through August. According to the Government, 211 ''security-related'' arrests were recorded during the first 6 months of the year, 48 fewer arrests than for the same period in 1987. This total number includes 46 arrests under the National Security Law, which was 40 fewer than for the same period last year.

Large numbers of students were detained during demonstrations in June and August calling for South/North student talks. Most of the detainees were quickly released, but a number of ''ringleaders'' were charged with various violations of the National Security Law. Although the Government tentatively began to increase access to materials originating from North Korea, a number of people were still arrested for spreading North Korean propaganda. Among them were the authors of articles on North Korea's Juche philosophy which appeared in various university newspapers in the fall. Some of the students arrested in these cases were freed without trial while others were tried and given suspended sentences. . . .

From the inauguration of the Sixth Republic in February through early October, the Government proclaimed a series of amnesties and paroles resulting in the release of over 400 prisoners. In the fall, human rights sources said that a like number of new arrests were made, and the number of political prisoners in Korea still hovered around the 500 to 600 mark.

On November 26, President Roh Tae Woo announced a major release of political prisoners. In early December, the Government freed a number of people under detention but not yet charged with politically related crimes. Then on December 21, the Government released 281 political prisoners, including such well-known dissidents as Chang Ki Pyo, Mun Pu Sik, and Kim Hyon Jang. The Government also restored civil rights to a number of former political detainees and called off police manhunts for those on the wanted list for political offenses.

Index